P9-BZQ-885

Tibet

the Bradt Travel Guide

Michael Buckley

edition
4

www.bradtguides.com

Bradt Travel Guides Ltd, UK
The Globe Pequot Press Inc, USA

SEP - - 2018

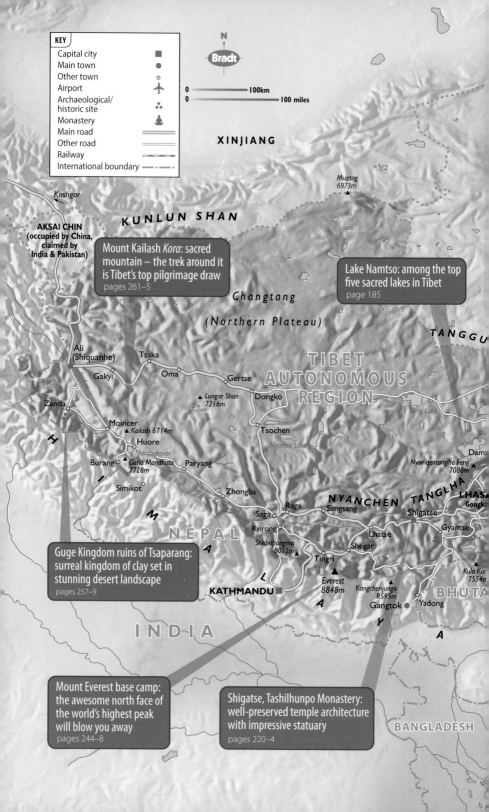

KEY
- Capital city ■
- Main town ●
- Other town ○
- Airport ✈
- Archaeological/ historic site
- Monastery
- Main road
- Other road
- Railway
- International boundary

N

Bradt

0   100km
0   100 miles

XINJIANG

Kashgar

Muztag 6973m

KUNLUN SHAN

AKSAI CHIN
(occupied by China, claimed by India & Pakistan)

Mount Kailash *Kora*: sacred mountain – the trek around it is Tibet's top pilgrimage draw
pages 261–5

Lake Namtso: among the top five sacred lakes in Tibet
page 185

Changtang

(Northern Plateau)

TANGGU

Ali (Shiquanhe)

Tsaka

TIBET AUTONOMOUS REGION

Gakyi

Oma

Gertse

Siling Lake

Zanda

Lungar Shan 7216m

Dongko

H

Moincer

Kailash 6714m

Tsochen

Damx

Huore

Manasarovar

Ngantse Lake

Nyainqentanglha Feng 7088m

Burang

Gurla Mandhata 7728m

Paryang

I

Simikot

Zhongba

NYANCHEN TANGLHA

LHAS

M

Yarlung Tsangpo

Saga

Raga

Sangsang

Shigatse

Gongka

NEPAL

A

Zhongba

Kyirong

Palku Tso

Lhatse

Gyantse

Guge Kingdom ruins of Tsaparang: surreal kingdom of clay set in stunning desert landscape
pages 257–9

Shishapangma 8012m

Shegar

Tingri

Kula Kar 7554m

KATHMANDU

L

A

Everest 8848m

Kangchenjunga 8595m

BHUTA

Y

Gangtok

Yadong

INDIA

A

Mount Everest base camp: the awesome north face of the world's highest peak will blow you away
pages 244–8

Shigatse, Tashilhunpo Monastery: well-preserved temple architecture with impressive statuary
pages 220–4

BANGLADESH

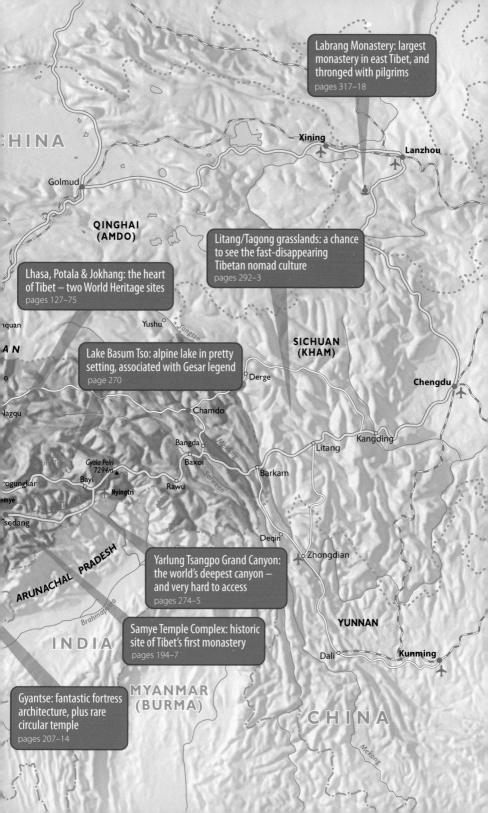

Labrang Monastery: largest monastery in east Tibet, and thronged with pilgrims
pages 317–18

Litang/Tagong grasslands: a chance to see the fast-disappearing Tibetan nomad culture
pages 292–3

Lhasa, Potala & Jokhang: the heart of Tibet – two World Heritage sites
pages 127–75

Lake Basum Tso: alpine lake in pretty setting, associated with Gesar legend
page 270

Yarlung Tsangpo Grand Canyon: the world's deepest canyon – and very hard to access
pages 274–5

Samye Temple Complex: historic site of Tibet's first monastery
pages 194–7

Gyantse: fantastic fortress architecture, plus rare circular temple
pages 207–14

CHINA

Golmud

QINGHAI (AMDO)

Xining

Lanzhou

Yushu

Yangtse

SICHUAN (KHAM)

Chengdu

Derge

nquan

AN

Nagqu

Chamdo

Bangda

Baxoi

Barkam

Litang

Kangding

Gyala Pelri 7294m

Bayi

Rawu

Mekong

Salween

ogungkar

Nyingtri

mye

sedang

Deqin

Zhongdian

ARUNACHAL PRADESH

Brahmaputra

INDIA

YUNNAN

Dali

Kunming

MYANMAR (BURMA)

CHINA

Mekong

Tibet
Don't
miss...

Asia's last nomads
Drop in for some
yak-butter tea
pages 22–4

Monks and monasteries
Witness timeless rituals
pages 26–9

Himalayan vistas, world-class trekking
Mount Everest, north face
(DP/S) pages 238-49

Tibet's fantastic fortress architecture
Gyantse Dzong
page 213

Pristine sacred lakes
Lake Yamdrok Tso
pages 205–6

Tibet in colour

above   Chinese tourists changing into Tibetan dress for a photo session at Potala Square page 166

below   Game changer: the train to Lhasa brings in large numbers of Chinese tourists and migrant workers pages 72–3

above   Rongbuk Gompa in the foreground,
           with the north face of Everest
           looming in the background
           pages 242–4

left   Mustard fields in valley in
           east Tibet (JJ)

below   Ruins of the mysterious
           10th-century Guge Kingdom,
           at Tsaparang pages 257–9

AUTHOR

Michael Buckley has travelled widely in Tibet, China, central Asia and the Himalaya, visiting many Tibetan enclaves. He is author of *Meltdown in Tibet*, a major work of investigative journalism about environmental issues in Tibet and beyond, along with a companion digital photobook *Tibet, Disrupted* (Apple iBooks). Buckley is also author of *Eccentric Explorers*, detailing the exploits of ten fearless adventurers to the Tibetan plateau, and of a travel narrative, *Travels in the Tibetan World*. For Bradt, he authored *Shangri-La: A Travel Guide to the Himalayan Dream*. In the course of numerous journeys to Tibet, Buckley has hitchhiked overland from Chengdu to Lhasa, trekked around Mount Kailash and mountain-biked from Lhasa to Kathmandu.

w **himmies.com** In support of this book is a special website with travellers' tales, dodgy advice and warped insights related to travel in the Tibetan world. Log on to find out more.

w **WildYakFilms.com** This website is companion to three short documentaries made by the author: *Meltdown in Tibet*, *From Nomad to Nobody* and *Plundering Tibet*. These short documentaries can be streamed from Vimeo for free.

AUTHOR'S STORY

There are things you take for granted in Tibet: magnificent snow caps, powerful gushing rivers, hearty nomads, yaks grazing the grasslands under vast open skies. I never imagined I would have to write the following line: that landscape is undergoing drastic change. The Himalayan snow caps are in meltdown mode, due to climate change – accelerated by a rain of black soot from massive coal-burning in both China and India. The mighty rivers of Tibet are being dammed by Chinese engineering consortiums to feed the mainland's desperate thirst for power. The grasslands of Tibet are being usurped by desert – due to climate change, and to the shortsighted Chinese policy of forcibly removing nomads from the grasslands and settling them in concrete hovels. Even yaks – the iconic creatures of Tibet – are vanishing from central Tibet.

When I first visited Tibet in the mid-1980s, none of this was apparent. This has all come to pass in a few short decades, unfolding right before my eyes. Accelerating the change was the 2006 arrival of the train to Lhasa, making possible a huge influx of Chinese settlers and tourists, and enabling exploitation of Tibet's resources on a large scale. Extensive mining in Tibet would not be possible without the train to export minerals. Nor would export of Tibet's groundwater in the form of bottled water. Nor would the construction of new mega-dams on Tibet's rivers be possible, as the train brings in materials and technology.

I believe it is the guidebook writer's duty to give the 'news' the way it is – the good, the bad and the ugly. Ugly refers to the harsh realities in today's Tibet. Tibetans live in a climate of fear: they have no say in preventing the reckless destruction of their sacred land. At the very least, a guidebook should give voice to those concerns. Despite these caveats, Tibet remains an extraordinary travel destination. If you delve into the pages of this book, you will find pockets of genuine Tibetan culture – places where the Tibetan pulse runs strong.

PUBLISHER'S FOREWORD   *Adrian Phillips*

The first Bradt travel guide was written in 1974 by George and Hilary Bradt on a river barge floating down the Amazon. Over the following years, Bradt earned a highly respected reputation as a ground-breaking publisher: its guidebooks were often the first to cover those destinations, and its authors were ahead of the game in promoting responsible travel. Now, over 40 years since the company was founded, Bradt has more than 200 books on its list, ranging from full-country and regional guides to wildlife titles and travel literature. And the pioneering spirit still burns strong. Whether focusing on countries overlooked by other publishers or areas a little more 'mainstream', Bradt seeks out those hidden corners and champions the road less travelled.

* * *

This has always been an important book for Bradt. Written by a recognised expert on Tibet, and used by Michael Palin during his *Himalaya* television series, it set the standard for sensitive coverage of this resilient country and its peace-loving culture. Visitors need this guide to help them understand and appreciate this unique place.

Fourth edition published July 2018
First published 2003
Bradt Travel Guides Ltd
IDC House, The Vale, Chalfont St Peter, Bucks SL9 9RZ, England
w bradtguides.com
Print edition published in the USA by The Globe Pequot Press Inc,
PO Box 480, Guilford, Connecticut 06437-0480

Text copyright © 2018 Michael Buckley
Maps copyright © 2018 Bradt Travel Guides Ltd; includes map data © OpenStreetMap contributors and Michael Buckley
Photographs copyright © 2018 Individual photographers (see below)
Project managers: Claire Strange and Carys Homer
Cover photo: Jørgen Johanson

ISBN: 978 1 78477 065 5 (print)
e-ISBN: 978 1 78477 524 7 (e-pub)
e-ISBN: 978 1 78477 425 7 (mobi)

British Library Cataloguing in Publication Data
A catalogue record for this book is available from the British Library

Photographs Photographs supplied by Michael Buckley unless otherwise stated. Jørgen Johanson (JJ); Chris Jones (CJ); Shutterstock.com: Dmitry Pichugin (DP/S), Vladimir Zhoga (VZ/S)
Front cover Tibetan monk (JJ)
Back cover Potala Palace; nomads on grasslands at Nangchen (Yushu) (JJ)
Title page Mt Jambeyang, Kham; Tibetan books in a library; Potala Palace with prayer flags
Maps David McCutcheon FBCart.S
Illustrations Carole Vincer

Typeset by Ian Spick, Bradt Travel Guides Ltd
Production managed by Jellyfish Print Solutions; printed in India
Digital conversion by www.dataworks.co.in

CONTRIBUTORS

Jamin 'Lobsang' York researched the eastern Tibet region for this fourth edition. He is the author of the popular Tibet travel website *The Land of Snows* (w *thelandofsnows. com*). He spent 15 years living full-time in Tibet and has travelled extensively, exploring nearly every area in the country. His company Himalaya Journey (w *himalayajourney.com*) arranges quality ethically responsible journeys in Tibet, Nepal and Bhutan.

Contributing writers to previous editions of this guidebook include **Bill Weir**, who revamped and expanded the Kham and Amdo sections, covering the best routes, many of which he experienced from the saddle of his trusty bicycle. **Bradley Rowe**, a past contributor to the Amdo section, has explored much of this vast region on foot. His photographs appear in publications under the name 'Stone Routes'.

WARNING

Your introduction to heavy-handed Chinese censorship may come early if you carry this guidebook openly in your bags. Meaning it could be confiscated. As a backup, you should seriously consider purchasing a digital version of this guidebook, stored on an iPad or tablet. A cat-and-mouse game is played out at baggage search points, such as on arrival in Tibet by air (yes, there is a baggage search at Lhasa airport) and at various military checkpoints along the highways and byways of Tibet. One traveller reported that he had his copy confiscated by a PLA officer at the Nepal–Tibet border – as it happens, a library copy that he had borrowed before leaving on the trip. The PLA officer was apparently not fond of some text in the guidebook about the PLA; when the traveller offered to rip out the offending pages, the officer laughed and told him he could pick up another copy somewhere along the line. Best to keep this book out of sight. Body searches are rare, so stash the book on your person somehow rather than in your bag.

Acknowledgements

INSPIRATION, INSIGHTS AND THANKS

Fellow travellers make a big difference to a project like this: on-the-road inspiration was provided by Gary McCue and Kathy Butler, Chris Jones, Pazu, Sonam, Gary, Terry and James Anstey, Kat, Rene and Kris, Thijsje, Johanna, Tess, Barbara, Kozo, Pema, Jorge, Markus, Keith, Tom, John Buchanan, Rocky Dang, Shelley Guardia, Doko, Marion Lahme, John Howarth, Vassilis, Dave Turner, Tony Williams, and all the other great people I met along the way. My gratitude to Roland Hardt for mapping input, to Pat and Baiba Morrow for mountaineering research, and to Tashi Gyal and Dickyi Dolkar for help with the Tibetan language section. Chung Tsering provided Tibetan script for the language section – a laborious task. Direct text contributions were provided by Jamin York, Bill Weir, Bradley Rowe, Matteo Pistono, John Ackerly, Geoff Flack and Brian Harris.

FEEDBACK REQUEST AND UPDATES WEBSITE

At Bradt Travel Guides we're aware that guidebooks start to go out of date on the day they're published – and that you, our readers, are out there in the field doing research of your own. You'll find out before us when a fine new family-run hotel opens or a favourite restaurant changes hands and goes downhill. So why not write and tell us about your experiences? Contact us on ☎ 01753 893444 or e info@bradtguides.com. We will forward emails to the author, who may post updates on the Bradt website at w bradtupdates.com/tibet. Alternatively you can add a review of the book to w bradtguides.com or Amazon.

MAPS On occasion, hotels or restaurants that are not listed in the guide (but which might serve as alternative options if required or serve as useful landmarks to aid navigation) are also included on the maps; these are marked with accommodation (🏠) or restaurant (✖) symbols.

Keys and symbols Maps include alphabetical keys covering the locations of those places to stay, eat or drink that are featured in the book. Note that regional maps may not show all hotels and restaurants in the area: other establishments may be located in towns shown on the map.

Grids and grid references Several maps use grid lines to allow easy location of sites. Map grid references are listed in square brackets after the name of the place or site of interest in the text, with page number followed by grid number, eg: [135 C3].

WEBSITES Although all third-party websites were working at the time of going to print, some may cease to function during this edition's lifetime. If a website doesn't work, you might want to check back at another time as they often function intermittently. Alternatively, you can let us know of any website issues by emailing info@bradtguides.com.

REVOLVING DOORS AND GATES The following symbol 🔒 indicates a destination that is accessible to domestic Chinese travellers but closed to foreigners at the time of writing. It might have been open to foreigners previously, and by the time you get there, it might be open again, so check the latest news.

ABBREVIATIONS

ATP	Alien Travel Permit, small cardboard folder
BOC	Bank of China
CCP	Chinese Communist Party
CITS	China International Travel Service, the official government travel agent
EBC	Everest base camp
HHDL	His Holiness the Dalai Lama
PAP	People's Armed Police (paramilitary group)
PLA	People's Liberation Army
PRC	People's Republic of China
PSB	Public Security Bureau (police)
TAC	Tibetan Autonomous County
TAP	Tibetan Autonomous Prefecture
TAR	Tibet Autonomous Region
TTB	Tibet Tourism Bureau
UNDP	United Nations Development Programme

Contents

LIST OF MAPS

Introduction

A visit to Tibet is a strange experience, with intense emotional highs and lows. It's weird because the real Tibet no longer exists. Since their military occupation in 1950, the Chinese have systematically dismantled the Tibetan social fabric, destroyed its great monasteries, persecuted its monks and nuns, forcibly resettled its nomads in housing ghettos, and wreaked devastating damage on Tibet's pristine environment. Any description of present-day Tibet and Tibetan culture must be framed in this context of iron-fisted Chinese occupation.

'Intense' is a word that applies to many aspects of Tibet. It applies to the amazing resilience of the Tibetan people in the face of extreme adversity. Their battle has been largely a pacifist one, of suffering and enduring – a game of ultimate patience and tolerance. 'Intense' captures the feel of the landscape. The intensity of colours at this elevation is extraordinary, with glacial-blue lakes, luminous-yellow fields of mustard, deep reds and browns of barren rock landscapes, and then, up on the horizon, looms an ethereal Himalayan snow cap, backed by piercing blue skies. The colours practically glow: when you show photographs of these landscapes to people who haven't been there, they question the unreal colours – what kind of filter did you use?

Travel in the Land of Snows is a guaranteed adventure, with the wildest, roughest road routes in High Asia. Here are the highest mountains and the highest trekking in the world – and the deepest gorges. Tibetan Buddhist monasteries blend into the landscape, becoming navigation landmarks; imposing fortress ruins cling to sheer hilltops; nomads herd yaks in snow-dusted pastures; pilgrims prostrate their way across the land to reach the sacred city of Lhasa. It is this combination of extraordinary landscape, extraordinary people and high adventure that makes Tibet so special.

There is only one drawback to visiting Tibet: you can easily become addicted to the place. It makes you reluctant to leave, and as you do, you're already plotting your return – a return not necessarily to Tibet itself, but to Tibetan culture. Sadly, real Tibetan culture is more likely to be found outside Tibet, in places where refugees continue their Buddhist practices, festivals and way of life in exile – in India, Nepal and Bhutan. A chapter in this book briefly introduces these places as well.

Travel to Tibet raises important ethical questions. One of the biggest is: should you go? Should you put money in Chinese coffers, thus indirectly subsidising Chinese military bills in Tibet? Most of the tourist business is in the hands of the Chinese, and some of the travel agencies are run by the military. This raises the thorny question of lending legitimacy to Chinese government operations by visiting, but more important for the Tibetans is the moral support they get from visitors. Your mere presence in Tibet provides a 'buffer zone' in an ugly situation between Chinese and Tibetans.

Tourists love monks. This is one of the great anomalies of tourism in Tibet: the monasteries are kept open and operating because of tourist demand to see them.

Apart from Himalayan landscapes, the main tourist 'attraction' in Tibet is its monks and monasteries, its Buddhist rituals and sutra-chanting. The Chinese really have no difficulty with this – they simply cash in on it. Apart from making a buck out of Buddhism, the Chinese have absolutely no interest in Tibet's rich culture, its religion or its language. If you go, you line the pockets of Chinese travel agents, hoteliers and airline agents, but if you stay away, you isolate the Tibetans.

The position of the Tibetan exile leadership is to encourage tourism. Addressing this ethical dilemma – to go or not to go – Nobel Peace Prize laureate the Dalai Lama responded to a question posed in Vancouver, Canada, in September 2006, about repression in Tibet: 'I think you must go [to Tibet] yourself, and spend some time, not only in towns but in the countryside. Go to the countryside, and with a translator, if possible one who speaks Tibetan, if not, then one who speaks Chinese. Go there. Study on the spot. Then I think you will get a real answer.' He knows that any Western visitor to Tibet will learn of conditions there and of the aspirations of Tibetans, will not fail to be moved by the experience, and will keep the Tibetan issue alive.

The Western tourist trade in Tibet represents a small fraction of the number of visitors going to China. By far the biggest group visiting Tibet is Chinese tourists, flocking to see this exotic corner of the Motherland. According to Chinese figures, over 20 million tourists visit Tibet annually – most of them domestic tourists from big cities like Shanghai, Beijing or Guangzhou. That number is highly exaggerated because the same tourists are counted several times in different locations like Lhasa, Shigatse or Everest. By the year 2020, China expects upwards of 35 million tourists a year to visit Tibet. This gives some idea of the invasive scale of Chinese tourism – the idea is to flood the place. Tourism is a mainstay of the economy in Tibet. Basically, whether you go to Tibet or not comes down to a personal choice, to be weighed by each traveller. If you can resolve the question of 'should you go?', the next thing to consider is 'can you go?' The Chinese are suspicious – with good reason – of the activities of independent travellers in Tibet, and have shepherded visitors into monitored, higher-paying group tours. Since major upheaval and large-scale protest across the entire Tibetan plateau in 2008, foreign visitors have only managed to gain access to Tibet on group tours. There are ways around this – particularly by visiting the eastern regions of Kham and Amdo, where such travel restrictions do not apply.

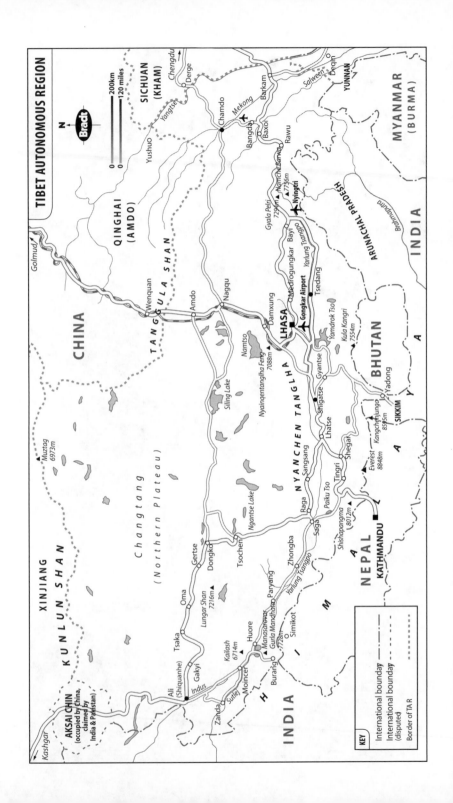

TIBET AUTONOMOUS REGION

KEY
International boundary
International boundary
(disputed)
Border of TAR

Part One

GENERAL INFORMATION

Location The landlocked region of the Tibetan plateau is the highest in Asia, with an average elevation of 4,600m; all major rivers in Asia are sourced in Tibet

Neighbouring countries India, Nepal, Bhutan, Burma – and China

Size/Area (km²): Ethnic Tibet: 2.3 million km²; Tibet Autonomous Region: 1.2 million km²

Climate Extreme, oscillating from freezing cold to searing heat; cool, high and dry

Status Nation under Communist occupation forces since Chinese invasion in 1950.

Population Ethnic Tibet: est. 6 million Tibetans and 7.5 million Han Chinese; Tibet Autonomous Region: 3 million Tibetans

Capital (and population) Lhasa, population estimated at 700,000 (Tibetan and Han Chinese)

Other main towns Shigatse, Gyantse, Tsedang, Bayi, Ali, Chamdo

Economy Agriculture (barley, wheat, millet and buckwheat) and animal husbandry; a key industry is craft production; major mineral reserves have been identified, including uranium. It is not known how much wealth is generated from mining in Tibet, but the figures could be very high. One official Chinese source cites the discovery of over 110 kinds of minerals in Tibet, conservatively estimated as being worth over US$120 billion. The real value could be ten times that amount. Mining will certainly become a significant part of economic exploitation of Tibet: most minerals are exported to mainland China.

GDP Accurate figures not known

Languages/Official language Tibetan; the official language is Mandarin

Religion Maoist-manipulated Tibetan Buddhism

Currency Chinese yuan renminbi (Y)

Exchange rate £1 = Y8.90; US$1 = Y6.28; €1 = Y7.77 (April, 2018)

Major airlines Air China (CA), China Southern Airlines (CZ), China Eastern Airlines (MU), Sichuan Airlines (3U) and Tibet Airlines (TV)

Principal airport Gongkar Airport, 60km from Lhasa

International telephone code +86 891 (Lhasa)

Time Tibet runs on Beijing time (GMT+8, PST+16)

Electrical voltage 220 volts, 50 hertz, with variety of plugs; erratic and unreliable

Weights and measures Standard metric

Flag Chinese flag – five yellow stars on blood-red background; the Tibetan snow lion flag is outlawed

National anthem Per Gyallu (outlawed in Tibet)

National sports Meditating (temples), horse racing (nomad summer festivals)

Public holidays Losar, Tibetan New Year – usually February; International Labour Day, 1–3 May; Chinese National Day, 1–3 October

1

Background Information

GEOGRAPHY

The defining element of Tibet is its extreme altitude – hovering above 4,000m. In this book, 'Tibet' refers to the entire Tibetan plateau region within the confines of the PRC. Altitude has shaped everything in Tibet – from its otherworldly landscape and majestic snow caps to its unique flora and fauna – and its special people and culture. Yaks, for instance, are superbly adapted to their high-altitude environment – and Tibetan nomad culture is entirely dependent upon them.

The Chinese and the Tibetans refer to different-sized areas when it comes to Tibet. The Tibetans refer to the much larger area of Ethnic Tibet, encompassing the entire Tibetan plateau, and including the northeastern and eastern areas of Kham and Amdo. Ethnic Tibet or Greater Tibet covers a quarter of China's total area: Ethnic Tibet is roughly 2.3 million km², which is almost double the size of what is now called 'Tibet' (Xizang Province) by the Chinese. In 1965, the Chinese created the Tibet Autonomous Region (TAR), having previously carved off much of Kham and Amdo and assimilated them into neighbouring Chinese provinces. Even so, the TAR is huge. With an area of 1.2 million km², the TAR is roughly the size of England, France, Germany and Austria put together, measuring 2,600km from west to east, and 1,300km from north to south.

Tibet within the People's Republic of China (PRC) straddles most of the geographical feature known as the Tibetan plateau. This is often referred to as 'the Third Pole', because outside of the Arctic and Antarctic regions, the Tibetan plateau holds the world's largest store of ice, snow and permafrost.

Superlatives abound when it comes to the subject of physical Tibet: the world's highest peaks and lakes – and the world's deepest gorges – are all located here. The landlocked region of Tibet borders India, Nepal, Bhutan, Burma – and China. Major rivers sourced on the Tibetan plateau are the Mekong, Yellow, Yangtse, Salween, Irrawaddy, Yarlung Tsangpo (source of the Brahmaputra), Indus, Sutlej and Karnali. On their wild journeys off the plateau, the rivers carve deep gorges. The tail ends of these rivers feed the world's largest deltas – prime rice-growing regions such as the Mekong Delta in Vietnam, the Irrawaddy Delta in Burma, and the Ganges-Brahmaputra Delta in Bangladesh.

In the south of Tibet, bordering Nepal, lie the 8,000m-plus Himalayan giants of Everest, Lhotse, Makalu and Cho Oyu. The world's 14th-highest peak, Shishapangma, lies wholly within Tibet. The Himalaya – Tibet's natural mountain border for centuries – have the world's highest snowline, and some 37,000 glaciers. To the north of Tibet are the Kunlun Mountains, while to the west are the Pamirs and the Karakoram Range.

Most of the Tibetan plateau is over 4,000m high. It was formed millions of years ago by a collision of the Indian and Asian continental plates. A glance at a satellite map will easily delineate this zone, and will show dramatic drop-offs

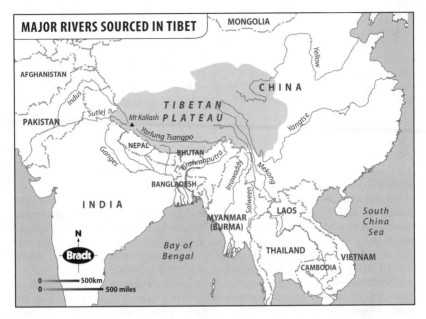

MAJOR RIVERS SOURCED IN TIBET

from the edge of the plateau to forested areas. The northern sector of Tibet is the forbidding Changtang, an immensely rocky and arid desert where nomads roam, eking out a tough living. To the northeast, in Amdo, the landscape turns to lush green, with rich grasslands irrigated by the Yellow River. In Kham, semi-monsoonal conditions and lower elevations result in copious forest cover – one of China's greatest sources of timber. The Yarlung Tsangpo River, running from the far west of Tibet to the east, is responsible for the rich pockets of farmland in central Tibet – it's considered the cradle of Tibetan civilisation, with historic Tibetan settlements along the riverbanks.

Tibet is landlocked: though many Tibetans have not seen the ocean, the pristine turquoise lakes of the plateau are vast – to the eye, the larger ones form their own inland sea. There has been little development at these lakes – Tibetans avoid eating fish, and they regard a number of the lakes as sacred places. The largest lakes are Manasarovar (west Tibet), Namtso (north), Yamdrok Tso (central Tibet) and Kokonor (Amdo).

Tibet's extreme altitude makes it a special place for hardy high-alpine flora, with secrets yet to be revealed. This rare flora attracted the attention of early 20th-century British plant hunters, who discovered the Himalayan blue poppy and many species of rhododendron. Of the world's estimated 900 rhododendron species, almost half are found on the Tibetan plateau, especially at lower elevations in the east and southeast. Over 2,000 species of medicinal plants have been documented by the Tibetans themselves. Herbal remedies lie at the core of Tibetan medicinal practices. For a brief introduction to Tibet's unusual wildlife, see pages 339–43.

CLIMATE

The climate of Tibet is cool and dry. With an average elevation of 4,500m, the weather in Tibet can best be described as extreme, oscillating from searing heat to freezing cold – sometimes in the course of a single day. It is possible to be simultaneously hot and cold, if a person's head is in the shade, but his or her legs are in the sun. Climatic conditions vary with elevation and exposure: there is little moisture in the atmosphere and intense UV rays can be problematic.

There is no best time to visit Tibet: the weather is unpredictable and, no matter which season, there are extreme conditions to deal with. Few travellers visit during the winter, however, because of treacherous road conditions, because access flights often close down for this period, and because Nepali hotel and restaurant managers head back to Kathmandu for the winter season.

SPRING March to May. Strong winds are possible and can whip up dust storms and sandstorms. However, this is one of the better trekking seasons, when conditions are not too hot.

SUMMER June to August. In this period are higher temperatures, which are conducive to staging festivals such as horse-racing fairs. Most of Tibet's rainfall occurs during July and August. In southern and eastern Tibet, the Himalaya form a barrier against the rain-bearing monsoons, so Tibet does not experience heavy monsoons like Nepal, Sikkim or Bhutan. However, in Tibet rainwater build-up combined with glacial meltwater can result in rampaging rivers and flooding in the autumn.

AUTUMN September to November. As a result of the aforementioned rampaging rivers, travel in autumn is prone to delays due to mudslides, flooding and bridges that have been swept away. Otherwise, it's not a bad time to travel, and it can be sunny.

WINTER December to early March. Severely cold conditions and snowfalls can shut down high passes to traffic. The Tibetans call the plateau Kangjong (Land of Snows), but the sun is quick to melt off snowfalls in the central Tibetan region. February and March are good festival months: Losar (Tibetan new year) falls in this period and during this time there are many nomads in Lhasa.

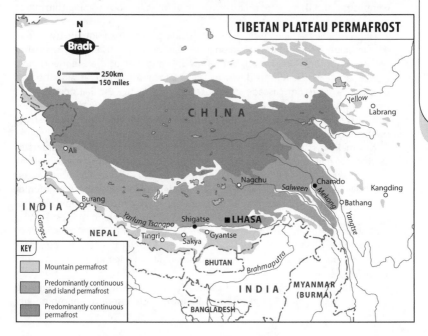

5

It seems incredible at the dawn of the 21st century that important new geographic discoveries are still being made. In 1998, and again in 2002, secrets of one of the world's last great uncharted rivers were finally revealed.

The river is the Yarlung Tsangpo. In the 1800s, the actual course of the river was unknown, and whether the Tsangpo (flowing from Tibet) and the Brahmaputra (flowing into India) were the same river, or two different rivers. The reason for the uncertainty lay in the river's dramatic course: for the first half of its 2,900km length, the Yarlung Tsangpo runs east through Tibet. Then it makes an abrupt hairpin turn and flows west into India – where it is called the Brahmaputra – and south again to its mouth in Bangladesh (where the river is known as the Jamuna).

This abrupt hairpin turn foxed geographers and adventurers for centuries, but equally mystifying was the river's dramatic drop: on its journey east, the Tsangpo roars into a 4,900m cleft between two mighty peaks – Namche Barwa (elevation 7,756m) and Gyala Pelri (7,294m). In a distance of around 240km, the Tsangpo plummets some 2,700m through what is now known as the Yarlung Tsangpo Grand Canyon, the world's deepest gorge. With a depth reaching over 5,300m near the Tibet–India border, this gorge is more than twice as deep as Arizona's Grand Canyon.

Geographers speculated that with such a precipitous drop, there had to be some huge waterfalls within the gorge, but because of its steep, forbidding walls, the site was considered inaccessible. In the 1880s, the British sent an Indian pundit by the name of Kintup into the area to determine if the Tsangpo and the Brahmaputra were indeed one and the same. His task was to launch 500 small, marked logs through the gorge to determine the course of the river. After a series of epic misadventures, Kintup completed mission impossible, launching all 500 logs (50 a day over a period of ten days), but his message back to headquarters went astray and there were no observers to witness the logs coming through at the other end.

Nobody believed Kintup's discoveries, including his claim of sighting a waterfall 45m in height. In forays to the region in 1911 and 1913, British officer Eric Bailey confirmed Kintup's exploration, but found only a 9m fall at the site mentioned. (Bailey later tracked Kintup down in Darjeeling and found that a scribe had confused a thin 45m cascade from a tributary with the 9m fall on the main river, and Kintup was illiterate: he could not read to check the account.) Bailey conclusively showed that the Tsangpo and Brahmaputra did form the same river, but he did not have the resources to fully explore the region.

Not making matters easier was the local custom of poisoning outsiders as sacrifices to evil spirits, but the British persevered. In 1924, British botanist Frank Kingdon-Ward spent 11 harrowing months surveying the gorge and discovered Rainbow Falls, which, observed from a considerable distance, he estimated at nine to 12m high. His reconnaissance was described in his 1926 book, *Riddle of the Tsangpo Gorges*. Ward discovered that the Tsangpo's precipitous descent was probably not due to one or two massive cascades, but rather was the result of a near-continuous succession of violent rapids. But still the secrets remained; Ward's reconnaissance reduced the unexplored part to one raging section about 15km long.

Even satellite imagery could not probe this section, as the gorge is deep and twisted, with overhanging vegetation. In 1987, a Chinese army photographer claimed to have photographed falls in the region while flying over the Upper Gorge in a military helicopter, but no accurate measurements of the height of the falls could be made from these pictures. In fact, the unexplored section was considered impenetrable until Nepal-based explorers Ian Baker and Ken Storm made persistent attempts in the 1990s. During a 1998 expedition they found a way through – and were able to get near to the falls – by following takin (goat-antelope) tracks. Using climbing ropes, Baker and Storm rappelled down the Tsangpo walls and got up close to Ward's Rainbow Falls, which they recalculated to be 22m high, double Kingdon-Ward's original estimate.

Then the team went where none had gone before: they continued their descent deeper into the canyon, and discovered a huge new waterfall, calculated at 32m high, which they christened Hidden Falls. That name probably won't appear on Chinese maps, however. Baker and Storm upstaged a Chinese scientific expedition in the same area at the same time: both teams claimed the prize discovery of the waterfall. Baker and Storm mounted an intense publicity campaign in the USA to reinforce their claim, and the Chinese responded by closing the Tsangpo Gorge region to foreigners for a significant period. Among rafters and kayakers, the Yarlung Tsangpo is regarded as the Everest of white water. The river claimed the lives of two kayakers attempting first descents: Yoshitaka Takei, who vanished in 1993, and Doug Gordon, who was lost in a massive rapid while on a *National Geographic*-sponsored expedition in 1998. After Gordon's death, white-water experts wrote the Tsangpo off as un-runnable.

In early February 2002, however, a team of explorers and kayakers from seven nations began a two-month expedition through the Upper Tsangpo Gorge. Their goal was twofold: to chart some of the unvisited parts of the gorge, and to complete its first white-water descent. The 80-man ground crew included Ken Storm, who had discovered Hidden Falls in 1998, and 68 Tibetan porters lugging 1,100kg of supplies.

Expedition leader Scott Lindgren, from California, had had his eyes on the gorge for more than a decade, after pioneering descents of other Himalayan rivers. He scouted the Tsangpo several times and concluded that the flow of water was suicidally high in the spring, but that late winter might work because of the lower flow.

Seven of the world's top kayakers launched into the wild water of the Upper Tsangpo Gorge – the most fearsome they had ever seen – and went where nobody had ever been before. They survived Class V+ rapids, thundering past boiling eddies, great vertical drops, massive lateral waves and huge boulders. Alternately paddling and portaging – and seal-launching from huge boulders – the team paddled about 90% of the Upper Gorge. Then the battered group started an epic winter portage over 3,600m Sechen La, to bypass the un-runnable Rainbow Falls and Hidden Falls. The expedition members and porters threaded their way up treacherous couloirs and steep snow-slopes, which must have looked a strange spectacle with kayaks in tow. Finally, they rejoined the river, but found that a flash flood had scoured the banks of the Tsangpo to near-vertical rock. At this point, Lindgren prudently decided to end the expedition. The team had covered 70 river kilometres – the first-ever descent of the Upper Tsangpo Gorge – and lived to tell the tale.

Back in the 13th century, explorer Marco Polo reported to incredulous Europeans that Chinese peasants burned a 'black rock' for heat. Today, more incredulous news: burning these black rocks is destroying the planet. Lumps of coal burned in households in China result in a tremendous output of CO_2 (not even taking industrial use of coal into account). That's China. On the other side of the Himalaya, a billion Indians are doing the same. And the emissions, known as black soot, are raining down on Himalayan peaks sited between the two heavily populated nations.

According to scientific studies, black soot deposition at some Himalayan glaciers has increased significantly over the last few decades. Shimmering white glaciers in theory reflect the sun's heat, while 'dirty' glaciers (caused by black soot depositions) will do the exact opposite: they will start absorbing the sun's rays, thereby accelerating glacial meltdown. Most soot in the region comes from diesel engines, coal-fired power plants and outdoor cooking stoves. Multiply the cooking stoves by several billion to get an idea of how much black soot may be floating around in the air.

This is not good news for Himalayan glaciers, which are melting rapidly due to climate-change factors. Tibet is the icebox of south Asia, with its myriad glaciers acting as major water-keeper for the entire region. With some 37,000 glaciers in Chinese-controlled Tibet alone, Lonnie Thompson, glaciologist at Ohio State University, calls the Himalayan region 'Asia's freshwater bank account'. It's an icebox where massive build-up of new snow and ice (deposits) has traditionally offset its annual run-off in rivers (withdrawals). But now the region is facing bankruptcy, because rapid withdrawals are depleting the account. Of the 680 glaciers currently monitored by Chinese scientists, 95% are shedding more ice than they are adding, particularly at the southern and eastern edges of the plateau. The glaciers are not simply retreating, they are losing mass from the surface down, says Thompson.

The first threat from glacial meltdown is GLOFs (Glacial Lake Outburst Floods). A GLOF is a large lake that is temporarily dammed by a glacier. If the 'dam' bursts, entire villages can be washed away in a deluge of mud and water. This has happened in both Tibet and Nepal. GLOFs pose serious threats in neighbouring Bhutan. Accelerated glacial meltdown in the Himalaya would lead initially to flooding from glacier-fed rivers. And much further down the road, it could lead to no water. If the glaciers vanish, the rivers would be reduced to a trickle. Monsoon rainwater alone is not enough to keep Himalayan rivers running at sufficient volume.

That's the snowline. Even more alarming is what is melting *under* the ground, in the ice below. The Tibetan plateau sits on the largest deposits of permafrost outside of the Arctic and Antarctic regions. Permafrost is found at various subsurface depths across the entire Tibetan plateau. Due to climate-change factors, the permafrost, frozen for millions of years, is gradually beginning to thaw. In the process of thawing, permafrost could release large amounts of carbon and methane, locked in ice crystals. In permafrost regions, methane hydrate is found trapped in layers between 150 and 2,000m deep. As a greenhouse gas, methane is thought to be over 20 times more potent than carbon dioxide in its ability to trap heat in the atmosphere. It is not known what effect the release of large amounts of methane into the atmosphere would have.

Though they had no sewage systems or concept of garbage disposal, in the realm of conservation the Tibetans were light years ahead of the West (at a time when the Tibetans were still in control of their environment). The Buddhist compassion for all life – human, other animal or insect – protected Tibet's wildlife, and in a sense made Tibet one great wildlife preserve. Because Tibet was isolated from the rest of the world for so long, it sheltered rare species: even in the 1990s, species thought long extinct were discovered in Tibet (a breed of small forest pony was found in Kham, and the Tibetan red deer was found in the Shannan district). Huge herds of wild gazelles, antelope, wild asses and yaks used to graze the grasslands of central Tibet. If animals were culled, the Tibetans took only what they needed, so impact on the wildlife was minimal.

In the 1940s, American adventurer Leonard Clark reported: 'Every few minutes we would spot a bear, a hunting wolf, herds of musk deer, *kiang* (wild ass), gazelles, big horned sheep, or foxes. This must be one of the last unspoiled big game paradises.' His words were in some ways prophetic: with the coming of the Chinese in the 1950s, everything changed rapidly. Chinese soldiers machine-gunned wildlife not only for food, but for export to China – and for sport. Some of Tibet's once-plentiful wildlife now faces extinction: in the last 40 years, large mammals have gone the way of the bison in North America. Apart from supplying China with meat, there is a demand for rare animals in Chinese restaurants and for Chinese traditional medicine. This has decimated numbers of the snow leopard, for instance.

Tibetan Buddhists have a profound sense of sacred landscape. Larger lakes and mountains were sacred and were left untouched, and mining was not practised. With its harsh environment, Tibet has a delicate ecological balance – one with which the Chinese are interfering. Such interference can have disastrous consequences, leading for example to increased desertification at Qinghai Lake, or destruction of an entire ecosystem. This may well be happening with the building of a hydro-electric project at Lake Yamdrok Tso – a highly controversial project that the Chinese have rushed, with uncertain results. Other large dams are under construction in Kham and dozens more are planned. The Chinese have made a priority of exploiting Tibet's untapped oil and mineral wealth. Oil fields in Amdo produce over a million tons of crude oil a year. In 2001, Chinese scientists announced the discovery of billions of tons of oil and gas in the remote Changtang region of northern Tibet.

The Dalai Lama once said that he could understand Chinese anger with Tibetan 'separatists', but what did they have against the trees? It is estimated that over 50% of Tibet's forests have been cut down since 1959 – mostly in eastern, northeastern and southeastern Tibet. If massive clear-cutting takes place on the slopes of the Tibetan plateau, there will be nothing to stop landslides and mudslides cascading down during monsoon season into neighbouring nations such as Burma and India. There could be unbridled erosion and flooding in these areas; the monsoon patterns themselves could be affected by changes in the ecological balance in Tibet. Severe flooding of the Yangtse in the late 1990s is, according to Chinese sources, directly attributable to deforestation at the edge of the Tibetan plateau. The situation became so critical that in 1998 Chinese authorities issued a ban on logging in the upper reaches of the Yangtse and Yellow rivers.

Apart from exploitation of natural resources comes the threat of pollution. Although Chinese officials have shied away from the topic, there is evidence that remote parts of Tibet have been used for the dumping of nuclear waste. China is intent on using Tibet as a missile-launching site, targeting Indian cities. There are a number of missile

Because Tibet has the highest terrain on the planet, it's easy to break world records. China seems bent on setting human rights violations in Tibet at record levels too. Here are some highs and lows.

HIGHS

Highest mountain Everest's 8,848m summit is shared by Nepal. Many records are associated with Everest: at the north face base camp is the world's highest monastery (Rongbuk, 4,950m) and the world's highest post office (5,150m).

Deepest gorge Yarlung Tsangpo Grand Canyon, east Tibet, is around 500km in length, and thought to have a maximum depth of over 5,300m. It is sited along the course of the world's highest major river, the Yarlung Tsangpo (average elevation 4,000m).

Highest airport Bangda, 4,334m, east Tibet; also has the world's longest runway at 5,500m in length. Eclipsing this will be a new airport at Nagqu, at 4,436m in elevation.

Highest railway station Tanggula Shan Station, 5,070m, on the Qinghai–Tibet border.

HIGH AND LOW

Golmud–Lhasa railway Completed in 2005, the line is simultaneously the world's highest and its most controversial, as it has unleashed a new invasion of Chinese immigrants into Tibet.

14th Dalai Lama The world's most popular spiritual figure, and most revered religious leader among Tibetans, is officially outlawed by Chinese authorities, who denounce him as a 'splittist'.

LOWS The darker side of life in the Middle Kingdom is hard to gauge because of secrecy and a complete lack of statistics, but here's how China ranks, with an eye on the situation in Tibet.

Executions China carries out by far the world's highest number of annual executions by any nation – in fact, more than the rest of the world combined.

Human rights A report released in 2011 by Freedom House ranked Tibet among the ten Worst of the Worst for human rights violations. Tibet was identified as a territory; the nation of China was not far behind in those rankings.

Press China is among the world's worst nations for tightest control over press, media and internet, in the company of repressive neighbours like Vietnam, Burma and North Korea.

bases and military airfields scattered around Tibet. Far more progressive is the Dalai Lama's vision. He calls for complete demilitarisation of the region of Tibet, to serve as a buffer between the nations of India and China. He envisages the transformation of Tibet into a sanctuary, a zone of peace – as it once used to be.

On paper, there have been attempts by Chinese officials to set up nature reserves, but in effect there is little protection or policing going on, and these are largely cosmetic. The reserve with the highest profile is Qomolangma Nature Preserve, in the Everest region, with a 34,000km² zone said to be under protection (although it is a mixed-use zone, with herders living within the boundaries). Under the guidance of renowned naturalist George Schaller, the mega Changtang Nature Reserve (around 247,000km²) was established in 1993, but poaching of Tibetan antelope proceeds at a brisk pace within its confines.

See also pages 339–43.

HISTORY AND POLITICS

To do justice to the subject, an account of history and politics in Tibet really requires a separate 800-page book. Even the modern era could easily provide enough content for a 500-page book. Two hefty tomes to consult are Melvyn Goldstein's *A History of Modern Tibet 1913–1951*, and Tsering Shakya's *The Dragon in the Land of Snows*, covering the period since 1947. The following is a very brief introduction, but one that should be read in combination with the section on *Tibetan Buddhism*, pages 26–36, because in Tibet you cannot separate religion from politics.

Tibetan recorded history dates back over 2,000 years. The emergence of Tibet as a geopolitical entity dates to the 7th century AD, when warrior-king Songtsen Gampo unified the clans of Tibet. At this time, Tibet was a great military power that expanded its boundaries south into India and east into China.

King Songtsen Gampo (c AD618–49) is regarded as a great religious king – he actively spread the teachings of Buddhism in regions under his control. The king had three Tibetan queens. As Tibet's power grew, neighbouring countries sought alliances through marriage: Princess Wencheng from China was sent to marry Songtsen Gampo, and Nepal sent a royal princess as a bride.

In the 8th century, King Trisong Detsen adopted Buddhism as the official religion of Tibet, bringing Buddhism into conflict with Tibet's ancient Bon shaman religion. Tibet waged war on China, occupying the Tang dynasty capital of Xian. In the 9th century, war broke out again between the Tibetans and the Chinese, with the Tibetans emerging victorious. At the centre of Lhasa, outside the Jokhang Temple, stands a stone obelisk that affirms in Tibetan and Chinese the terms of a peace treaty concluded between King Ralpachen and Chinese emperor Wangti in the year AD823. It is written in stone: 'Tibet and China shall abide by the frontiers of which they are now in occupation. All to the east is the country of Great China; and all to the west is, without question, the country of Great Tibet.'

In 826, Ralpachen was assassinated by his elder brother Langdarma who succeeded him and changed tack completely: he attempted to snuff out Buddhism under pressure from Bon priests. In 842, he was killed by a monk, and Tibet dissolved into chaotic factions. A hundred years later, Buddhism was introduced again in western Tibet, in the Guge Kingdom. By the 12th century, three Buddhist lineages or schools had emerged in Tibet: Nyingmapa, Kagyupa and Sakyapa. The fierce rivalry between them was not so much religious as political.

The snow-capped peaks and high deserts of the Tibetan plateau served as natural defences and increased Tibet's isolation. But in the 13th century, Tibet fell under

1

Mongol domination. The Mongol khans ruled an empire that stretched as far as Europe and encompassed all of China. The Mongols took a great interest in Tibetan Buddhism. In 1350, Tibet resumed its independent ways, but enjoyed a special patron–priest relationship with Mongolia over the next few centuries. Invited to educate the Mongols in spiritual matters, the Tibetans in turn accepted Mongolian guarantees to stave off would-be invaders.

It was the Mongolian leader Altan Khan who bestowed the title 'Dalai Lama' (Great Ocean, or Ocean of Wisdom) on Sonam Gyatso, the 16th-century leader of the Geluk or Yellow Hat sect. This reformist school had been established in the 14th century: Sonam Gyatso is regarded as the Third Dalai Lama (the title was conferred posthumously on his predecessors). The Geluk sect gradually assumed a dominant role in politics and from 1642 onwards they effectively ruled Tibet through their leader, the Fifth Dalai Lama. The 'Great Fifth' (Lobsang Gyatso) managed to reunify Tibet and extended his authority to the fringes of Tibetan territory. During his reign, Tibetan culture flourished – many monasteries were erected and the Potala was rebuilt. By this time, Tibet operated under one of the most unusual forms of government in the world: a theocracy, or a Buddhocracy (a system whereby the spiritual leader is also a king figure – sometimes referred to as 'god-king' – combining religious and political responsibilities). The system lasted over 300 years, up until the Chinese invasion in 1950.

By the 17th century, Mongol power was waning, and another set of invaders stormed the Great Wall to occupy China: the Manchus. By this time, Tibet had largely demilitarised – perhaps the first nation in history ever to do so. The national priorities lay in spiritual matters. The Manchus recognised Tibet as an independent nation under the authority of the Dalai Lama, and agreed to protect the peace of the demilitarised nation. Over the next three centuries, Tibet's fortunes fluctuated, with various incursions across its borders by the forces of Nepal and China. One of the stranger chapters in Tibetan history was an invasion in 1903 by the British colonial forces, intent on opening Tibet to trade and convinced that arch-rival Russia was influencing Tibet. After blasting their way through to Lhasa, the British stayed for two months. Failing to find anyone of real authority (the Dalai Lama had fled), the British concluded a useless treaty with some head lamas and then withdrew, leaving a telegraph line and a few trade links in place.

In 1911, with China weakened by civil war, the Tibetans seized the opportunity to formally announce Tibetan independence, expelling all Chinese from Tibetan soil. Between 1913 and 1950, Tibet asserted its independent status by controlling its own affairs, signing treaties with neighbouring nations, patrolling its own borders, bearing its own flag and issuing its own currency, passports and stamps. In this regard, it was ahead of its neighbours: India and China shook off the yoke of colonial rule only after World War II.

Curiously, the main Chinese claim to Tibet goes back to an era when China itself was occupied by a foreign power – the Mongols. If Tibet really were part of China, it's odd that the Chinese waited over a thousand years before staking their claim. A better explanation would be that the Tibetans successfully defended themselves against the Chinese for more than a thousand years. Over the last two thousand years, Tibet has nurtured a culture that is very different from that of China, with a separate language and literature, separate form of religion, separate economy and central government, and distinct forms of art and architecture. Out of this rare society – based on the tenets of Tibetan Buddhism – emerged a distinct 'Tibetan-ness'. It is this Tibetan-ness that forms the basis for their claim to independence. Pre-Chinese-occupied Tibet was not a paradise. It was a medieval society that was out of sync with the rest of the world, and which paid dearly for its isolationist policy and its failure to keep abreast of the times.

POST-1950 TIBET After their victory in the long-running civil war in 1949, the forces of Mao Zedong wasted little time in announcing their next target would be the 'return of Tibet to the embrace of the Motherland'. The Chinese invaded Tibet from the east in 1950. Their justification for invasion was to liberate the Tibetans from 'feudalism'. However, it is dubious whether this came to pass: Tibetan nobility and clergy were simply replaced with harsher Chinese masters.

Under a document called the 17-Point Agreement – dictated by the Chinese in 1951 – the 14th Dalai Lama would remain at the head of the Tibetan government, but China would be in charge of military matters and other key facets. The 17-Point Agreement quickly turned into a sham: monastic lands were confiscated, tribal lands were collectivised, and it soon became apparent that the Chinese idea of schooling was very different from the Tibetan idea. Tibetans had little empathy for the zeal of Maoism, and alongside the construction of hydro-electric stations, experimental farms and roads, armed resistance took place at various points (particularly in eastern Tibet) from 1954 to 1959. Concerned for his safety, those close to the Dalai Lama engineered his escape on horseback to India. In 1959, he crossed the border into northeast India and into exile. Behind him, Lhasa fell into chaotic fighting. Tens of thousands of Tibetans were killed in the subsequent uprising.

SAVING THE CHIRU

In March 2002, police in New Delhi intercepted two Kashmiri traders with 80 *shahtoosh* shawls. It takes the underwool of three antelope to make a single shahtoosh shawl, so that haul represented at least 240 dead Tibetan antelope. And on the international market, at US$5,000 a shawl (the average price for a fine one), the cache was worth US$400,000.

Renowned naturalist George Schaller has conducted extensive research on the chiru (Tibetan antelope) in their main habitat of Changtang in remote northern Tibet. Schaller says upwards of 20,000 chiru are poached each year for their underwool, from which shahtoosh shawls are made. This is pushing the chiru to the brink of extinction. The demand for shahtoosh shawls in the fashion centres of Western countries has boosted the trade. The wool of the chiru is the finest animal fibre in the world – finer than that of cashmere goats. This also makes it the most expensive fibre. Although the sale of shahtoosh shawls is supposedly banned around the world, they can be bought at haute couture boutiques, with clients paying up to US$20,000 for a single shawl.

The main centre for shahtoosh spinning is Kashmir, even though the trade was outlawed there in mid-2000. Kashmir is of course a renowned centre for spinning cashmere wool, also from Tibet. Poachers from Tibet trade chiru wool for tiger parts from India. The Kashmiris need the chiru wool, and the tiger parts are highly valued in Chinese traditional medicine. So here's a vicious circle involving two highly endangered species: poachers are using automatic weapons to gun down chiru so that Kashmiris can weave shahtoosh shawls to sell to high-fashion divas in the West. And Indian traders are poaching tigers, which the Kashmiris sell to the poachers in Tibet in exchange for chiru wool: the tiger parts are divided up for sale in Chinese traditional medicine potions which are mostly directed at boosting a flagging male libido.

Can Communism and Buddhism coexist? They are both rational, non-theistic (no belief in a superior god) and altruistic philosophies. So in theory they should be able to get along with each other. The problem is communist intolerance of Buddhism, not the reverse. In the early years after the Chinese invasion, the Dalai Lama claimed that he liked some of Mao Zedong's ideas, even going as far as saying he considered himself half-Marxist, half-Buddhist. And Buddhism had long been practised in China itself. But Mao Zedong told the Dalai Lama religion is poison.

One of the main reasons the Chinese claimed they set out to 'liberate' Tibet was to free it from 'feudalism', which, it transpired, meant not only Tibetan aristocrats but also the entire monastic system. The communists lumped Tibetan Buddhism in with the old 'feudal' ways of Tibet. The monks, claimed the Chinese, did nothing: they just sat around the monasteries and exploited the people, which prevented Tibet from modernising. The question remains: what would have happened if the Chinese had not invaded in 1950? The Dalai Lama – not old enough to rule at the time – was most certainly a progressive person who intended to introduce modern ways. He was – and is – fascinated by the West and by modern inventions.

Communist countries have historically replaced Buddhist teachings with communist ideology, weakening the power of the monasteries, eliminating the privileges of monks and discrediting the monastic leadership. Persecution of Buddhists in Russia and Mongolia nearly wiped them out. So what does the Chinese communist leadership do about a region that is overwhelmingly Tibetan Buddhist in faith? Well, they set up the Chinese Religious Affairs Bureau to oversee what is happening in the monasteries, to introduce Marxism into the curriculum and to demand allegiance to Beijing. During the Cultural Revolution, statuary at main altars in some Lhasa temples was replaced with portraits of Mao Zedong. Karl Marx believed religion to be the opiate of the masses, employed by repressive regimes to divert the attention of the people from their true enemies. In a true communist society, religion does not exist – it is replaced by loyalty to the Party. A modified version of this is that religious practices that do not harm political rule can be tolerated. In Tibet, however, monks and nuns often spearhead political protest.

In India, meanwhile, the Dalai Lama renounced the 17-Point Agreement and set up his government-in-exile.

Barely recovering from the vicious reprisals of 1959, Tibet was hurled headlong into the madness of the Cultural Revolution (1966–76), which hit Tibet harder than any other part of China.

Chinese officials would later blame destruction of monasteries on this period, when in fact many buildings were blown up or dismantled before the onset of the Cultural Revolution. With the flight of the Dalai Lama, the Chinese dissolved the remnants of the Tibetan government, and set up the Tibet Autonomous Region (1965), splitting the area of Ethnic Tibet in half. All forms of Tibetan customs and worship – public and private – were banned, including barter. Large numbers of Tibetans died in labour camps and prisons.

Since the 1960s, Chinese policy in Tibet has see-sawed – sometimes harsh and repressive, at other times loosening up. China's human rights record in Tibet,

On 18 May 2017, a Tibetan monk called Jamyang Losel set fire to himself near a prayer wheel in Chengtsa County, Qinghai Province, in northeast Tibet. The 29-year-old monk became the 150th person to self-immolate within Tibet since 2009. A grim milestone reached. Ten more Tibetans have self-immolated outside Tibet.

The first self-immolation within Tibet took place in Ngawa, eastern Tibet, in February 2009. While setting himself on fire, a monk from Kirti Gompa was shot several times by Chinese police. He was hauled away and never seen again.

The wave of Tibetan self-immolations since then has become the biggest such protest movement in modern history. In 2012 alone, there were 85 self-immolations inside Tibet. Over 150 Tibetans have died as a result of this extreme action. Although these protesters have been a diverse group from all walks of life and age groups, a high proportion of the self-immolators are monks and nuns.

Why are so many Tibetans self-immolating? According to activist Tsering Woeser, in her slim book *Tibet on Fire*, the reasons are often found with notes left behind – ranging from the trauma of forced resettlement, to lack of religious freedom, from the feeling of being helpless when opposing land grabs, to the futility of trying to stop mining companies from desecrating sacred mountains. Woeser's book has a unique cover designed by leading dissident Ai Wei Wei, with the names of Tibetan immolators embossed on the cover so that they can be read through touch. Woeser calls the self-immolations 'earth-shattering'. She writes: 'Self-immolation is the most hard-hitting thing that these isolated protesters can do while still respecting the principles of non-violence.'

Self-immolation has been branded a criminal activity by Chinese officials, who have arrested family members for being complicit. Self-immolators are labelled as 'terrorists' in Chinese media reports – if the immolation is indeed reported.

Military and paramilitary patrols in Lhasa have taken to carrying fire extinguishers on their backs – not to save lives, but to prevent pictures of the person on fire from being disseminated online. Such photos could damage China's image abroad. Chinese regulations criminalise self-immolation by punishing the immolators' next of kin, their monastic communities, and the towns where they set themselves alight. For instance, in Zoige County (Sichuan) regulations stipulate that farmland registered in the name of the immolator will be confiscated by the authorities. Large rewards are offered to those who provide information on people who may be planning to self-immolate, or information about those that have occurred. Dozens of friends, relatives and associates of self-immolators have been given jail sentences for their involvement, which may include offering religious rituals for the dead self-immolator.

meanwhile, has been appalling, constituting one of history's worst cases of cultural genocide.

In 1987 major rioting took place in Lhasa: this was followed by intermittent demonstrations that were brutally put down by Chinese troops. Martial law was imposed in 1989 and not lifted for over a year. Since 1996, it has been forbidden to own or display any image of the Dalai Lama in Tibet: this followed in the wake of a major falling-out over the choice of the 11th Panchen Lama (see pages 34–6). Little dialogue has taken place between the Chinese and the Tibetan government-in-exile over the issue of Tibet. China has tightened its grip on the region, ruling what is today the largest colony in the world.

The greatest uprising since 1959 took place in the spring of 2008. A protest that started in Lhasa, initiated by monks from Sera and Drepung, spread across the entire plateau, involving Tibetans from all walks of life – urban dwellers to nomads. A vicious crackdown ensued, with over a thousand Tibetans believed killed – and many more missing or imprisoned. Since 2009, over 150 Tibetans have self-immolated to protest against Chinese rule.

In mid-2016, Chinese authorities in Lhasa staged 'celebrations' to mark the 65th anniversary of the signing of the 17-Point Agreement for the 'peaceful liberation of Tibet'. Looking back on those 65 years, the Chinese see Tibet as a great success story – the socialist transformation for Tibetans from primitive feudalism to a much higher standard of living. From the Tibetan point of view, those 65 years have been a complete catastrophe, a sad story of pillage, rape, torture, dislocation and destruction – a deliberate attempt to obliterate their culture, their religion and their values.

ECONOMY AND RESOURCES

The traditional economy of Tibet is based on animal husbandry on rich pasturelands, with the raising of yaks, sheep and goats, as well as horses and mules. However, this is radically changing – and the grasslands themselves are disappearing. In exchange for yak meat, cheese and butter, Tibetan nomads used to barter for grains from farmers. That trade has now been severely disrupted due to large-scale forcible settlement of nomads in concrete ghettos. Tibetan farmers grow barley, wheat, millet and buckwheat. In larger towns, the main traditional industry is craft production – the making of carpets, Tibetan boots, *tankas* (wall hangings) and religious items.

Before the 1950s, industry in Lhasa was really only present in the form of a mint and an ammunition factory. Since then, light industry around Lhasa has ballooned to the point where pollution is a concern: industry includes power plants, machinery plants, printing shops, chemical factories, woollen textile plants,

THE FORBIDDEN FLAG

The Chinese flag shows five bright yellow stars on a deep red background. Red is the colour of revolution: the large yellow star is said to indicate the Party, while the four smaller stars represent the classes that uphold it – workers, peasants, soldiers and intellectuals. Interpretation of the star symbolism varies: another version has it that the big star is the Han majority, and the smaller stars indicate the key minorities – Tibetans, Uighurs, Mongols and Hui. The pre-1950 Tibetan flag shows two snow lions (white with turquoise manes and tails) upholding the three precious jewels of Buddhism, framed by a snow-covered mountain and a rising-sun motif with red and blue rays. This particular design was introduced by the 13th Dalai Lama in 1912, although various versions of the flag have existed for centuries. The flag is outlawed in Tibet: possessing one is cause for a lengthy jail sentence; displaying one in public has led to summary execution. Travellers should avoid carrying any artwork that shows the forbidden flag.

leather processing factories, grain processing factories, carpet factories, a concrete factory and a brewery.

A key factor in the Chinese 'development' of Tibet is finding or creating sources of energy. Hydro-electric projects are under way in parts of the plateau to tap the enormous power generated by rivers originating in Tibet. A number of these projects show little concern for the surrounding environment. The high altitude in Tibet results in intense solar radiation, which has successfully been utilised through solar panels and solar cookers. There is also great potential for harnessing geothermal energy and wind power.

Before 1950, Tibet was self-sufficient in food, with barley as the staple. In the 1960s and 1970s, the Chinese ordered wheat to be planted instead of barley, banned barter and formed communes – a disastrous policy that led to Tibet's first-ever famines. Now Beijing claims that it has to heavily subsidise the ailing economy in Tibet, but officials fail to mention several key factors, such as how much money is drained by propping up Chinese settlers and the military in Tibet. Estimates put the number of PLA (People's Liberation Army) troops in Tibet at between 200,000 and half a million. Long convoys of military trucks are a common sight, as are military garrisons, particularly in border areas. There are at least nine military airfields in Tibet, a number of radar stations and several missile bases. Tibet has become one of China's largest missile-launching bases, capable of targeting India and other areas near the Indian Ocean.

Although officially the Tibetan economy appears to be running at a loss, a factor not mentioned is how much of Tibet's natural wealth is being taken out. Since 1959, over half of Tibet's forests have been cut down. Tibet's mineral resources were largely untouched before 1950: the Chinese have identified reserves of gold, radium, titanium, lithium, iron, lead, bauxite and other minerals, including major deposits of uranium. For religious reasons, Tibetans did not mine – disturbing the earth was considered a bad omen. Today, it is rumoured that mining accounts for over 40% of Tibet's industrial output, with scores of mining sites opening up. Large deposits of oil and gas have been discovered in Tibet's northern Changtang region. In Qinghai, there are large deposits of shale gas and oil sands. Both require huge amounts of water to extract – water that can only be diverted from the rivers of Tibet. This raises the essential issue of what the Chinese are doing in Tibet in the first place. The answer is: they're doing what every colonial power has done throughout recorded history – they are exploiting the colony's resources. They are cutting down all the trees because China proper has run out of trees. And they have their eyes on Tibet's abundant fresh water resources because severe water shortages are looming in China proper.

VALLEYS OF THE DAMMED In the 21st century, as access to clean water dwindles and as population increases, nations will no longer be fighting over oil or other resources – they will be fighting over water. And the rivers of Tibet will be one of the flashpoints. Who owns a river? Does the country that controls the source of a river have the right to divert the water for its own purposes? Will neighbouring nations such as India and Vietnam stand idly by as they witness 'theft' of their rivers – the damming and diversion of Tibetan rivers by Chinese engineers?

China has an acute problem with water supply. Fresh water is becoming an increasingly rare commodity in the north of China, where agriculture depends on water to sustain food production. It is estimated that up to 70% of China's rivers are contaminated – to the point where the water is not drinkable, or even usable. China's new 'emperors' are not quite sure what to do about this, but if they want to avoid mobs of starving pitchfork-wielding peasants, they have to do something – and very soon. The regions of northern China are particularly hard up for water due to intensified desertification and increased industrial pollution. A dramatic example of water crisis surfaced in late 2005, when an explosion at a chemical plant near Harbin (northeast China) released 100 tonnes of cancer-causing benzene compounds into the Songhua River, from which the city draws its water supply. Three million Harbin residents were in a state of panic: they were without running water for almost a week until the toxins were cleaned up. The population of China's eastern region is heavily concentrated in large cities like Harbin.

The Chinese solution to the water problem appears to be a vast project to divert river waters from the south to the north. In this scheme are three diversion sectors: eastern, central and western. The western sector eyes the Tibetan plateau as a water-diversion target. Tibet is the principal watershed of Asia and the source of its ten major rivers: about 90% of run-off from Tibetan rivers flows downstream into China, India, Bangladesh, Nepal, Pakistan, Thailand, Burma, Laos, Cambodia and Vietnam.

In Tibet, a number of Chinese engineering projects are under way to harness hydropower. Several are in operation close to Lhasa. Lying 96km northeast of Lhasa is Zhikong Hydro-electric Power Station, with a dam 1.3km long. And 120km southwest of Lhasa is Yamzhog Yumco Pump Storage Power Station, a highly controversial project that has destroyed a sacred lake. The question here is: who are these dams for? In many Tibetan areas, houses are lucky if they have power for a few light bulbs; in fact, a number of Tibetan residences rely on solar dishes or solar panels as their main source. It would appear that the energy output from the dams close to Lhasa is intended to provide power for Chinese industrial concerns – and to new Chinese housing developments springing up on the fringes of Lhasa.

Dozens of major hydro-electric projects are planned for Tibetan rivers, with an eye on exporting the electricity to Chinese cities such as Chengdu, Xining and Lanzhou. With ultra-high-voltage lines now under installation, hydro-electric power from dams in Tibet can be exported all the way to eastern China. A cascade of five large dams is under way on the Tsangpo River, southeast of Lhasa, with 500MW Zangmu Dam operational since 2015. The most disturbing project on the drawing board is a blueprint for a mega-dam in eastern Tibet on the Tsangpo River, which could theoretically generate twice as much electricity as the Three Gorges Dam. The plan is to harness the enormous hydro potential at the Great Bend of the Tsangpo. There's one glitch with this plan: downriver on the Tsangpo, millions of people in India and Bangladesh are waiting for the water resources too – relying on the Brahmaputra River.

Currently, the main Chinese engineering focus is on the Kham area (southeastern Tibet), where fast-flowing rivers are concentrated. At the edge of the Tibetan plateau in upper Yunnan, more than 20 mega-dams are planned for the mighty Mekong within China. Six are already in operation. These dams are huge. Xiaowan Dam, towering to 292m in wall height (the height of a 90-storey building), is the largest arched dam in the world.

Opposition to China's actions is fierce from neighbouring countries, with both foreign NGOs and local environmentalists predicting environmental and social disaster. At stake is the livelihood of some 60 million people in the Mekong Basin – the majority being subsistence farmers and fishermen. The farmers are dependent on the river's rich sediment for riverside cultivation, and the people of these countries rely on the Mekong's abundant fish supply as staple food. The completion of eight dams in Yunnan could sound the death knell for the river.

MINING TIBET You may know more about the movie *Avatar* than you do about mining in Tibet, but the film offers uncanny parallels to the situation on the Roof of the World. Tibet is the largest colony in the world. Tibet is under military occupation by Chinese troops. Tibet is being ruthlessly exploited for its valuable minerals, against the wishes of the inhabitants, who deeply resent what is happening to their land. In *Avatar*, the action takes place some 150 years into the future on a distant moon called Pandora. Here, rapacious foreign CEOs and military figures seek a mineral of astronomical value called unobtanium. The only thing stopping them in this endeavour is the blue-skinned Na'vi, who refuse to allow mining on their land, which they regard as sacred. Tibetans for centuries did not permit any mining (except for gold) due to their belief that digging would scar the sacred surface of the earth. Today, many valuable minerals are being extracted in Tibet by Chinese and foreign companies. And one mineral alone would qualify for the status of 'unobtanium'. That is lithium. Lithium is used for making batteries for computers, mobile phones and many other gadgets, and lithium is a rare mineral, in very short global supply. Tibet is one of the prime sources: lithium is extracted from a handful of lakes in Tibet. In fact, you probably carry a tiny piece of Tibetan lithium around in the battery of your laptop, iPad, mobile phone or other device.

RAILWAY ON THE ROOFTOP A poster put out by China Mobile and China Construction Bank shows Lhasa as a futuristic land of high-rise buildings, telecom towers and flyover highways, with a train running through it all. There are just two Tibetan buildings depicted in the poster: Tibet Museum and the Potala Palace. This is Lhasa in the 21st century – a Chinese clone. The blueprint is to modernise, go high-rise, and bring in entrepreneurs to stimulate the market. The train in the poster has sleek aerodynamic lines like the Japanese Bullet Train or the French TGV.

And all this may yet come to pass, with the arrival of the Golmud–Lhasa railway line. It is the world's highest elevated track, eclipsing the Peruvian Central Railway of the Andes by several hundred metres. Chinese news sources wax lyrical about the engineering feat of building the railway, claiming it to be the fruit of growing national strength – and an achievement on a par with China's second manned space flight, 'which is arousing both pride and envy at home and abroad'. But for Tibetans in exile and activists abroad, the railway arouses only disgust and indignation: the project is highly controversial. The line got under way in 2001 and was completed in 2005 at a cost of over US$4.1 billion. In fact, over a four-year period, the railway racked up bills equivalent to double the entire budget spent in Tibet on education and health care since it was invaded by China in 1950. Obviously, the railway was not built for philanthropic purposes. Later, Beijing revealed that mining was a major factor in the decision to build the railway: that the income and benefits from mining would easily cover the cost of building it. Mining is not possible without the railway for shipping minerals.

The railway project took on a formidable engineering challenge, crossing bleak, frozen terrain through a region plagued with sandstorms in summer and blizzards in winter. European tunnelling engineers concluded that it was impossible to bore through the rock and ice of the Kunlun mountain range. But somehow Chinese engineers have pierced the Kunlun mountain barrier that has kept Tibet secluded for centuries – in the process creating the world's highest tunnel at 4,900m. The 1,140km line traverses the Kunlun mountain range, crossing more than 400 bridges, boring through 30km of tunnels, cresting two 5,000m passes, and running past more than 30 stations before reaching Lhasa.

American author Paul Theroux wrote in *Riding the Iron Rooster* that the reason Tibet remained un-Chinese for so long was because of the mountain barrier isolating it. 'The Kunlun Range is a guarantee that the railway will never get to Lhasa. That is probably a good thing. I thought I liked railways until I saw Tibet, and then I realised that I liked wilderness much more.'

The Kunlun 'guarantee' has been swept aside by Chinese engineering, and with that comes another threat: the railway is bound to disrupt Tibet's fragile ecosystem and impact on its rare wildlife. About 550km, or half of the line, is built over permafrost, which is unstable: any construction is bound to damage this environment. In the warmer summer months, the frozen ground can thaw during the day, which might cause railway track to buckle and sink. The Chinese claim to have made a technological breakthrough for dealing with this – by pumping cooling agents into the ground via underground pipes to ensure the earth remains frozen. The trains themselves require high-tech tinkering too, which is where foreign corporations come in. American company General Electric Transportation has a contract to supply locomotives. Two Canadian corporations, Bombardier and Power Corporation, supply special railway carriages, and another Canadian company, Nortel, supplies a digital wireless communications network for the railway. These companies have come under fire in the West for making possible a project that is bound to be detrimental to the survival of Tibetans, who face a massive influx of Chinese settlers arriving by train.

The railway is projected to move eight million tons of cargo annually, with at least 16 trains a day on the Golmud–Lhasa line (eight each way). The Golmud–Lhasa run takes 10–15 hours by train, knocking at least 10 hours off the best time by bus.

The Chinese claim that the TAR is the only part of China not connected by rail, and that a railway would accelerate economic and social development of Tibet. Those same two factors – viewed from a Tibetan perspective – amount to a nightmare. 'Economic development' could mean Chinese mining companies using the rail line as a way of extracting precious metals and other resources and freighting them back to China. 'Social development' could obliquely mean a new Chinese invasion – a massive influx of Chinese settlers, drawn by financial incentives and tax breaks. There are precedents here: you do not have to look any further than Golmud itself. Fifty years ago, Golmud was open steppe with nomad herders. After the railway reached town, immigrants from eastern China arrived in droves, leading to the present population of several hundred thousand and a sprawling town. A similar situation occurred, but much faster, in the remote northwest of China, in the Islamic centre of Kashgar, where the Chinese population increased by 30% in 2001 – the year after the railway to Kashgar was completed. Another major application of the railway reaching Tibet is strategic – with the line, it is easier to consolidate border defences.

Work is under way to extend the railway line west from Shigatse to Kathmandu, and east from Lhasa to Bayi. The long-range blueprint for Tibet calls for three more rail lines to reach Lhasa – from Lanzhou, Chengdu and Kunming.

PEOPLE

The main population groups are Tibetan and Han Chinese. The origins of the Tibetans as a race are sketchy: ethnologists place them in the Tibeto-Burman group. The earliest human habitation in Tibet can be traced back 4,700 years: it is believed that Tibetans migrated to the plateau in the late Neolithic Age. However, a recent find suggests that there was human presence in Tibet much earlier than that, as far back as the Ice Age. In 1995, researcher David Zhang Dian from Hong Kong

University found remnants of a stove and 19 handprints and footprints pressed into rock on a mountain slope 85km from Lhasa. He brought back rock samples and had them dated. The tests revealed they were from the Ice Age. And in 2002, at a location 120km north of Golmud, Chinese archaeologist Xu Xinguo found artefacts dating to the microlithic period (10,000–30,000 years ago).

On the Tibetan plateau, there are a number of ethnic Tibetan subgroups, differentiated by cultural, dress and linguistic variations. These groups include the Topa (far-west Tibet), the Khampa (east Tibet), the Golok (from the northeast), and a number of minority groups closely related to Tibetans, such as the Qiang (from upper Sichuan) and the Monba and Lhoba tribespeople (far southern Tibet, near the Bhutan border). In the Barkor in Lhasa, it's possible to see groups from very different regions who have arrived on pilgrimage to the sacred city. The groups are often identifiable by their dress. From Amdo come nomad women, with their braided hair done in 108 strands (a sacred number). The waist-length tresses must be redone at least once a week and smeared with yak butter. In former times, Tibetan women used to wear their wealth in the form of elaborate jewellery. This still holds true to some extent – you will see Amdo women with big chunks of turquoise or amber in their hair, or worn in bulky necklaces. From Golok come nomads who wear greasy sheepskin cloaks, yak-hide boots, and often sport felt bowler hats (a legacy of British invasion) or Stetson felt hats (made in eastern China). From eastern Tibet come the quick-tempered Khampas: the men have tassels of red or black yarn braided through their hair, and a dagger sheathed at the waist – not entirely decorative. Selling goods in the Barkor are also Nepali and Kashmiri traders, and Muslims from Xinjiang.

Any statistical data on Tibet – particularly on population – is dicey; facts and figures are fudged to suit whatever propaganda department is issuing them. Basically, the Chinese do not wish it to be known that they are flooding the region with Chinese settlers. Chinese figures from 2003 put the population of the TAR at 2.67 million, broken down into 93% Tibetan, 6% Han Chinese, and 1% 'ethnic minorities' such as Monba, Lhoba and Hui. But how can this breakdown possibly be accurate? A visual check on the streets of Lhasa – or Tsedang or Bayi – shows the Han Chinese are clearly in the majority in these places, and not the tiny minority indicated. Chinese figures do not take into account the number of roving (non-resident) Chinese businesspeople in Tibet, nor Chinese military stationed

ETHNIC TIBET

The map on page 22 shows the shifting political boundaries of Tibet, old and new. The wider area encompasses 'Ethnic Tibet' – the area recognised as Tibet by the British in the Simla Treaty of 1914 (which the Chinese did not ratify). Starting in the 1920s, the area bordering China to the east was slowly encroached upon. In the 1950s, the Amdo and Kham regions were carved up and incorporated into Chinese provinces, mostly as a collection of Tibetan Autonomous Prefectures (TAPs). In 1965, the Chinese administration created the Tibet Autonomous Region (TAR), reducing the area designated as 'Tibet' to half its former size. When the Chinese refer to 'Tibet', they mean Xizang or the TAR, which embraces the former Tibetan regions of Ü-Tsang and Ngari. When Tibetans talk about 'Tibet', however, they mean the much wider Ethnic Tibet region, embracing not only central and western Tibet, but also the former regions of Amdo and Kham.

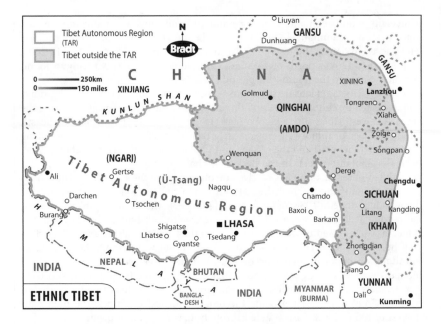

Tibet Autonomous Region (TAR)

Tibet outside the TAR

N

Bradt

0 ——— 250km
0 ——— 150 miles

CHINA

XINJIANG

KUNLUN SHAN

°Liuyan

GANSU

°Dunhuang

Golmud°

XINING •

Tongreno°

Lanzhou •

°Xiahe

QINGHAI

(AMDO)

Zoige°

Songpan°

GANSU

Tibet Autonomous Region

(NGARI)

°Gertse

•Ali

°Darchen

(Ü-Tsang)

°Tsochen

Nagqu°

Wenquan

Derge

•

Chamdo

°Baxoi

Barkam°

Litang°

Chengdu •

SICHUAN

Kangding

Burang°

Shigatse°

Lhatse°

Gyantse°

■**LHASA**

°Tsedang•

(KHAM)

Zhongdian°

INDIA

NEPAL

BHUTAN

Lijiang°

YUNNAN

ETHNIC TIBET

BANGLA-
DESH

INDIA

MYANMAR
(BURMA)

Dali°

Kunming •

there (estimated at 200,000–500,000 troops) – they would be registered in other provinces of China. It's possible, within the region of Ethnic Tibet, that the Chinese outnumber the Tibetans. The population of Ethnic Tibet could be 4.5–6 million, meaning more Tibetans live outside the TAR than in it. Within Tibet, nearly all Chinese live in urban areas, while about 80% of Tibetans live in rural areas, some continuing their nomadic ways.

LAST OF THE NOMADS Traditional occupations for Tibetans are farmer, merchant, trader or monk. But the lifestyle that really manifests the rugged spirit of Tibet is that of the hardy nomad, dependent on yaks and other animals to survive. Tibetans are among the last nomads in Asia – other pastoral nomads include the Mongols (now found mostly in Outer Mongolia) and the Turkic tribes of China's far northwest, such as the Kazaks. Tibetan nomads face a great battle to retain their way of life as the Chinese are suspicious of those on the move, and attempt to make them settle: as a result, the way of the nomad is fast disappearing. Chinese policy is attempting to put an end to Tibetan nomad culture. This started with large-scale fencing of traditional nomad grazing grounds with barbed wire in Amdo and Gansu – which has led to considerable acrimony over land and water rights, and exactly who has access to the richest grassland.

Early travellers to Tibet remarked on how cheery Tibetan nomads were in the face of one of the harshest environments in Asia – a high, treeless, windswept plateau. Maybe it's their ribald sense of humour that sustains them in sub-zero temperatures and howling gales. Whatever the case, the nomads are part of the romance of Tibet, with their yaks and yak-hair tents, their elaborate costumes and jewellery, and their raucous folk songs.

The *drokpas* are pastoral nomads, moving their tents in search of pasture for their animals. Livestock – yaks, goats, sheep and horses – are central to the livelihood of the nomads, and the basis of their culture. Their movements are seasonal, linked to weather conditions and availability of pasture. Pure nomadic life is becoming rare:

more often, nomadic groups move between designated areas with the change of the seasons. There are signs of 'modernisation': nomads wearing knock-off North Face jackets (not sheepskin), nomads riding motorcycles (not horses), and nomad women sporting two braids (not the traditional 108 braids). Solar panels sit on top of the yak-hair tent and power up lights at night.

True nomads are found in the grasslands of northern Tibet, and at the peripheral zones of Kham and Amdo. Hastening the demise of the nomads are occasional bitterly cold winters. The winter of 1997/8 was particularly savage, with a long snowfall and temperatures of −30°C to −40°C, which wiped out large herds of yaks and sheep. The death toll for nomads was unspecified, but it is certain that a number died.

Playing a key role in the survival of the nomads is the yak – a 'comical' creature best described as a cow with a skirt. The yak is the male animal: the female is called a *dri*, while a yak–cow hybrid is called a *dzo* (a very useful word to remember when you are playing Scrabble). Some insist that since only the females produce milk, the term 'yak butter' is incorrect. The fact is that most Westerners do not know what a 'dri' refers to, so the term 'yak' has been generalised to cover both male and female of the species for Westerners.

Wild yaks can weigh up to 1,000kg – double the size of domestic yaks. Due to their wild origins, yaks are superbly adapted to high-altitude living and cold conditions, and are sure-footed on mountain slopes. Tibetans use all parts of the yak. With a harsh climate and a lack of vegetables, meat eating is a necessity in Tibet. Yak meat is the principal meat eaten, preserved in dried or semi-dried form. The hair and hide of the yak are used for making thread, blankets, ropes, bags, clothing and boots. Yak milk, yoghurt, butter and cheese provide sustenance. Yak dung is collected and stacked – it is the main fuel source on the treeless plateau. Yaks are also used for riding (though they hate the idea), as a pack animal and in farm-work (for ploughing). Yak hide is even used to make ingenious small boats.

Nomads live in thick heavy tents woven from the hair of the yak. These tents can be dismantled piece by piece, rolled up, and loaded on to yaks or horses. Upon arrival at a new site, the tent is quickly reassembled. At the centre of the tent is usually a stove, fuelled by yak dung; one corner of the tent always has a little altar. To beat the cold, Tibetan nomads cocoon themselves in long sheepskin jackets – the top and sleeves can be shuffled off when temperatures rise. Much warmer than sheep wool is fox fur, often used in hats. Cashmere goats provide particularly fine wool, highly valued in the West. After several efforts to obtain breeding stock for cashmere (wrong animals, two of same sex), the British finally procured some cashmere goats and took them to the far north of Scotland, leaving them out in the freezing cold. However, it clearly wasn't cold enough – or windy enough – for the goats, who refused to grow their cashmere undercoat.

Tibetans are among the few people in Asia who thrive on dairy products – mostly yak and goat derivatives (milk, butter, yoghurt and cheese). The Mongols and the Kazaks eat similar fare. You might have trouble recognising these dairy products: yak butter floating in the tea, or tooth-breaking pieces of dried cheese, strung together like a necklace. Large amounts of tea are also consumed: three to five cups of tea are considered necessary for everyone in the morning, and some people might drink as many as 40 cups a day. Chinese brick tea was once considered so valuable it was a form of currency. Instead of milk, yak butter is used, and since sugar is hard to come by in Tibet, nomads just use salt (there are copious salt deposits found near lakes). Tea is made in a wooden churn, a long cylindrical object.

In 1979 and 1980, as part of ongoing negotiations with China, the Dalai Lama's government-in-exile sent three delegations from India to see Tibet first-hand. The news was not good. The Tibetans had suffered greatly under Chinese rule. One of the things that the delegates remarked upon was the silence of the grasslands – and the emptiness of the grasslands. Where teeming herds of wild animals roamed in the 1940s, there was nothing. The animals were slaughtered by the PLA and Chinese settlers for food and for sport. The wildlife vanished from the grasslands.

These days, the grasslands themselves are in danger of disappearing. Nomadic herders and their yaks are disappearing. And the grasslands themselves are undergoing degradation: they are slowly turning into desert.

For close on 4,000 years, Tibetan nomads have grazed their yak herds on these grasslands. The nomads are the real stewards of the grasslands: they have developed sophisticated knowledge of how to maintain the pastures, knowing that they must use them again. Defying all logic, Chinese officials have targeted Tibetan nomads for forced settlement. The Chinese view nomads as backward uneducated people, and the rationale behind Chinese policy is that nomads will have access to schools and medical assistance. But there appears to be a more sinister agenda. A large factor is the ability to control the nomads in fixed settlements. Nomads are viewed as unruly and too independent – beyond government control. And another reason is that nomads are sitting on rangeland where mining ventures want to move in, or in valleys where mega-dams are planned for construction. China makes no secret of its intention to settle all the nomads within a very short time frame. From 1995 to 2015, the objective was to transfer all of the nomads in housing settlements in remote areas, forcing them to sell or slaughter their yaks. Across the entire plateau, that involves at least two million Tibetan nomads. Tens of thousands of nomad families have been shifted to settlements that resemble concrete ghettos. Chinese policy previously

Often mixed with tea and rolled into balls is the great staple of the nomads – *tsampa*. This flour is usually made by roasting barley, but can also be made from corn, wheat, millet or oats. Tsampa is a tasteless flour, but highly sustaining – it is obtained through bartering, and held in cloth bags. It stores very well. Often eaten raw from the bag, tsampa can be consumed in cakes or soup. Another barley derivative is *chang*, a milky fermented beer that is brewed on special occasions and is frequently offered to guests. Chang can also be made from rice, wheat, corn, oats or millet. Since chang is home-brewed, the alcohol strength varies wildly.

LANGUAGE

Mandarin Chinese is the official language enforced in Tibet. Tibetan is spoken and written, but given a very low profile in schools and very little media exposure. The literacy rate among Tibetans is very low – thought to be less than 25%. Many have no access to proper education facilities. The Chinese practise linguistic colonialism: if a Tibetan wants to get ahead and reach the echelons of higher education, he or she must speak and write Mandarin Chinese. Very few Chinese living in Tibet speak any Tibetan or attempt to learn it.

The Tibetan language is part of the Tibeto-Burman language group, although the written form is distantly related to Sanskrit. The existence of many dialects makes targeted Mongolian nomads (Inner Mongolia) and Kazak nomads (Xinjiang) for settlement. Now, with those nomad cultures virtually erased, the attention has shifted to Tibetan nomads.

Chinese authorities cite climate-change factors to account for recent degradation of the grasslands, but in fact Chinese policy is largely to blame because of a widespread fencing policy. Previously, nomads were self-sufficient, getting everything they needed from their herds, and trading any surplus for grains from farmers. Now this barter system, which has been in place for thousands of years, has been disrupted. Chinese policy targets the nomads – and also targets their livestock. Yaks go to the slaughterhouse. One estimate claims that since the ludicrous policy of 'removing livestock to restore grasslands' was put in place, over 50% of herd animals have been removed from the TAR. Travelling in central Tibet today, yaks are noticeably missing. What you see more of is cows or yak–cow hybrids: these animals are more suited to village living. Yaks like to roam.

Nomads who are forcibly settled face serious problems with food supply and quality of living. They are totally dependent on state subsidies: they have no jobs, no money, no training. In their rush to settle the nomads, Chinese officials have made absolutely no provision for retraining nomads to adjust to semi-urban life. To lure nomads to settlements, Chinese officials make pledges to open schools and clinics, but these mostly turn out to be empty promises. Nomads cannot read or write Chinese (they cannot even write in Tibetan). Without those language skills, they have very little opportunity for training to get decent jobs. And they have no skills in farming. One of the very few avenues open for nomads to make real money is to collect exotic mushrooms and herbs from the highlands in the spring. From a model of sustainability (getting everything they need from their yaks and livestock), the nomads have been reduced to beggars in their own land.

it hard for Tibetans to communicate with each other. Lhasa dialect is the standard, but Lhasa court dialect is dying out. The script is more uniform throughout the Tibetan world, and although different writing styles are employed, they're more easily understood from one end of the Himalaya to the other than the spoken word. There's one catch here: the very high illiteracy rate.

The elegant Tibetan script consists of 30 consonants plus four vowels, and is easily rendered on computer in Macintosh and PC formats, though not much of this is in evidence in Lhasa, where virtually all computer access is in the much more complex Chinese characters.

Tibetan is the Latin of High Asia: it is hardly geared to the modern world. This ancient language lacks the vocabulary range for innovations such as 'email', 'mobile phone' or 'barcode'. Tibetan is flexible enough, though, that English or foreign words can be imported phonetically (which is the case for a lot of geographical terms) or Tibetans can try to make up new compound words. The Tibetan word for movie is *log-nyen*, meaning 'electric picture', the word for aeroplane is *namdru* ('ship of the sky') and in Amdo the word for bicycle is *sherta* ('iron horse'). But new vocabulary requires consensus among the scattered groups of Tibetans to gain wide acceptance, and thus to be widely understood. There could be one term used within Tibet (taken from Chinese) and a completely different one used in India (deriving from English or Hindi).

Scholars of Latin have achieved more success than Tibetans in agreeing on new vocabulary. They have used the internet to achieve this standardisation and to spread the word; societies in Europe regularly publish new Latin vocabulary. Nothing resembling this occurs in the Tibetan world, where computer access is rare or non-existent. See pages 344–57 for more about spoken Tibetan.

TIBETAN BUDDHISM

Tibetan Buddhism, practised by almost all Tibetans, is perhaps better described as 'showcase Buddhism' within the TAR, as it is rigidly controlled by the Chinese. Officially, the Chinese are atheistic, with the government and Motherland as the reigning deities. The spiritual and political leader of the Tibetans is the Dalai Lama, who is vilified by the Chinese as a 'separatist' and even as 'a major hindrance to the development of Tibetan Buddhism'.

Tibetan Buddhism has all the trappings of a religion – temples, abbots, monks, monasteries, sermons, holy texts – but is actually not a religion. With no belief in a superior god or supreme being, Buddhism does not qualify: in fact, it can be equated with agnosticism. (Note, however, that the terms 'religion' and 'religious' are used throughout this book for the sake of convenience.) Buddhism is non-dogmatic, encouraging practitioners to question – even challenge – authority, and to rely on evidence tested with their own senses. It suggests that the practitioner, not some external force, holds the answer to his or her own happiness, with the mind being both the obstacle and the key to understanding. Buddhism can thus be more accurately called a philosophy or a form of psychology. It is primarily a belief system based around respect for all living things and the concept of compassion, providing a code of ethics to live by. Tibetans are an extremely devout people – Tibetan Buddhism forms a significant part of their lives and their identity. Material gain is not high on the list of priorities for Tibetans: spiritual fulfilment is.

At the core of Buddhism is the concern with suffering, and how to overcome that suffering and achieve a full life. The higher goal of Buddhism is to attain enlightenment, which means to be fully awake to the reality of life, to have an understanding of suffering and how it may be overcome. The Buddha is the 'enlightened one' or 'he who is fully awake'.

Buddhism is fairly easy-going: it does not require (or expect) converts, or people to spread its message. Neither does it demand sole faith in Buddhism: you can be Jewish or Christian or atheist – or communist, for that matter. Except for monks, Buddhism does not require attendance at a fixed place of worship, nor does it have stringent rules or vows to follow.

There are a number of branches of Buddhism: the three major ones are Zen (mainly identified with Japan), Mahayana (identified with Tibet) and Theravada (identified with Thailand and Cambodia). Tibetan Buddhism is unique because it is a blend of Mahayana Buddhism (originally from India) and the ancient Tibetan shamanist cult of Bon, heavily associated with magic and sorcery.

In contrast to the stripped-down tenets of Zen, Tibetan Buddhism hosts a vast pantheon of animist spirits, protectors, tantric deities shown in blissful union with their consorts, and an array of bodhisattvas and Buddhas. Other icons are real figures – founders of the various sects and past Dalai Lamas (see pages 155–8 for more on Tibetan iconography).

There are few female deities in the Tibetan Buddhist pantheon; women have a low profile in the leadership of Tibetan Buddhist sects. This is a contentious area of

As a global spiritual icon, HH Dalai Lama has no peer. His closest rival, the Pope, commands a huge global audience, but he has an agenda to push. The Dalai Lama does not – he does not seek converts, and tells people to stay with their preferred religion. He offers general ethical advice. He commands a moral authority that China can only dream of. So Beijing relishes any opportunity to challenge that moral authority. Like exploiting a Tibetan ghost from the 17th century, known as Dorje Shugden.

Dorje Shugden is a Geluk protector spirit that gave the Fifth Dalai Lama considerable trouble. Somewhere in the 1990s, HH Dalai Lama declared Dorje Shugden a 'dark force' that was responsible for undermining the practice of the Geluk sect and for causing disharmony. He excommunicated the tantric spirit and set in motion plans to discourage worship of the guardian deity. But the deity has its followers, who objected. In particular, a rogue Tibetan monk called Kelsang Gyatso, who in 1991 established the British-based New Kadampa Tradition (NKT), a breakaway sect. Self-proclaimed leader Kelsang Gyatso was never ordained as a monk in the traditional system in Tibet, and his old school, Sera Monastery in Lhasa, went to the trouble of declaring his monk status invalid. Kelsang Gyatso's NKT is not taken seriously by any Tibetan Buddhist groups, nor other Buddhist groups for that matter. The NKT has been described as a radical cult with a bogus guru that bilks its followers.

This whole situation was seized upon by China as an opportunity to discredit HH Dalai Lama and to divide the Tibetan community in exile. When Western NKT folks dressed in Tibetan robes showed up to demonstrate against the Dalai Lama at his teaching venues, they were being flown around the world with expenses covered by CCP-fronted organisations. That's according to an investigative report by the news agency Reuters, released in December 2015, with this lengthy headline: 'China co-opts a Buddhist sect in global effort to smear Dalai Lama'. Meanwhile, back in Tibet, monasteries with Shugden-worship leanings found themselves well funded for restoration and expansion, and even funded for spreading the word, which must be a first for Tibetan Buddhism within Tibet. This is what could be termed 'Tibetan Buddhism with Chinese characteristics'.

Tibetan Buddhism, and one difficult for Western women to accept. Compared with men, women are considered to be a lower form of incarnation.

Most Tibetan Buddhists believe in reincarnation – on a higher plane, a person is reincarnated as a human, on a lower plane as an animal or an insect. But there is, in addition, belief in the concept of different realms after death. Similar to Christian beliefs in heaven and hell (which may have derived from Buddhism), there is belief in an earthly realm, a heavenly realm, a hell realm, and limbo zones such as the realm of hungry ghosts. For reincarnation, rebirth in the human world is far preferable to that of hell or hungry ghosts. Only high lamas are said to be able to direct a specific rebirth in their next incarnation. See pages 32–6 for more on reincarnation.

A related concept is karma. Tibetans believe that they may have inherited some bad karma from previous lives, a situation that must be corrected by doing good deeds in the present life. Many Buddhist practices hinge on accruing merit by doing good deeds. Merit can be accrued by making donations to temples; by assisting in the building or repair of temples, Buddha images or shrines; or by going on pilgrimages to sacred Buddhist sites. In their lifetime, many Tibetans want to undertake a pilgrimage to Lhasa and to Mount Kailash, among other holy places. Karma is cause and effect: good deeds have good effects, bad deeds have bad effects. By following the right path in this life, a person can accrue merit, with karmic carry-over to the next life. A tree drops a seed that becomes a tree – but this tree is not the same as the original one.

One of the ultimate forms of merit-making is to become a monk or a nun. In old Tibet, it was an honour for a family to be able to send a son to a monastery – this was seen as an opportunity to gain a proper education, since monasteries in old Tibet were the only schools. Tibetan culture is closely linked to Tibetan Buddhist beliefs – in former times most literature, music, dance and drama, painting, sculpture and architecture was inspired by those beliefs.

Since 1959, Tibetan Buddhism has been in a state of flux because traditions were severely disrupted by Chinese takeover, and lineage holders fled into exile. The Tibetans in exile say that real Tibetan Buddhism continues in freedom outside Tibet, but not inside Tibet. The Dalai Lama has attempted to draw the four main schools of Tibetan Buddhism together, the differences between them being more of a political nature than a religious one, but these attempts have seen little success.

The oldest school is the Nyingma sect, founded around the 7th century by Indian master Padmasambhava. The tradition is carried on through reincarnates of great teachers. The Sakya sect, founded in the 11th century, is not as prominent as the other three schools. At its head is the Sakya Trizin, who fled Tibet in 1959 and established his base in Dehra Dun, India. Sakya lineage holders are permitted to marry – the title is hereditary. Breaking with tradition, in 2017 the Sakya Trizin handed over his title to his son, Ratna Vajra Rinpoche, who became the 42nd Sakya Trizin and the plan from now on is for the leadership of the Sakya sect to be reviewed every three years.

The Kagyu sect also emerged in the 11th century; the lineage holder is the Karmapa. The 16th Karmapa fled Tibet in 1959 and founded Rumtek Monastery in Sikkim (a former kingdom in northeast India); on his death in 1981 a search was conducted for the 17th Karmapa. Eventually a boy from east Tibet, Ogyen Trinley Dorje, was installed at the traditional seat of Tsurphu Monastery near Lhasa in 1992. Ogyen Trinley Dorje escaped into exile in 2000 and now lives in India. Finally, the Geluk sect, founded in the 14th century by Tsongkhapa, is closely associated with the Dalai Lama. The lineage holder is the Ganden Tripa, who is elected every seven years in Dharamsala.

A number of new schools, subsects and offshoots have been founded in exile by various masters. Some very strange permutations have taken place in the West. Exiled Tibetan Kagyu lama Chogyam Trungpa (1939–87) established training centres and retreat communities where he promulgated his 'crazy wisdom' visionary approach. In 1970, he shocked his students in Scotland by marrying a young English woman and flying to North America, where he went on to establish a series of dharma centres under the banner of Shambhala International. Chogyam Trungpa was dubbed 'the cocktail lama' due to his scandalous predilection for women and wine, and his highly unconventional personality.

One thing that Tibetans in exile have attempted to do is cut down the amount of ritual involved in Tibetan Buddhist ceremonies, and to concentrate on the pure elements of Buddhism. In its 'purist form', Buddhism has gained wide appeal in the West. But how can the ancient faith of Tibetan Buddhism be in tune with the modern world? Buddhism appeals to the rational, scientific world because the Buddha did not insist that followers accept what he said: he told them to question everything, and test his words for their veracity. Attributed to the Buddha is this disclaimer: 'Like analysing gold through scorching, cutting and rubbing it, monks and scholars are to adopt my word not for the sake of respecting me, but upon analysing it well.'

That said, there remains a very unscientific facet to Tibetan Buddhism, verging on high superstition. One of the reasons that Tibet fell to the Chinese was that the clergy failed to modernise. In pre-1950 Tibet, modern advances and technology were seen as threats to spiritual life and traditional values. The clergy was highly suspicious of new gadgets and new-fangled ideas: in 1943, the Regent banned the use of motorcycles and the playing of football (football fever, which had gripped Lhasa, was seen as a powerful force that would undermine social stability).

There was – and still is – great faith among Tibetans in auspicious days and bad omens, which are interpreted by astrologers. Tibetan astrology or astronomy could hardly be called scientific: like medieval Western models, the mapping of the earth and the planets was firmly rooted in religious beliefs rather than scientific observation with telescopes. The Tibetan cosmos places Mount Meru, the abode of the gods, at the centre of the universe (it is identified as Mount Kailash on this earth). On the summit of Mount Meru is the celestial city of Sudarsana; above Meru float 25 more heavens of the gods, while under the mountain lie the hell realms. Mount Meru is surrounded by seven rings of golden mountains and seven oceans. At the outer edge of a flat circular disk, across the outer ocean from Meru, are a few spin-off worlds, such as the one we're on. This is identified as the continent of Jambudvipa, trapezoidal in shape, where inhabitants live for a century, and where the dharma flourishes. East of Meru lies the continent of Videha, which is white and half-moon shaped, with inhabitants whose faces resemble half-moons – they are said to be twice as tall as humans and live up to 500 years. Two other continents lie to the north and west – Uttarakuru, a square continent populated by square-jawed giants, and Godaniya, a circular continent populated by round-faced giants. Beyond all this are the paths of planets, with the mandalic (page 358) model enclosed by massive rings of fire.

Tibetan Buddhists have had to seriously reconsider their traditional cosmology model in the light of modern discoveries. Some Tibetans cling to the literal truth; others claim that Meru is merely symbolic. There is obviously no huge mountain at the navel of the world, there is no city on the top of that mountain, and there is no continent of lanky giants with half-moon faces to the east, either.

MONLAM AND SHOWCASE BUDDHISM To the casual tourist in Tibet, it may appear that Tibetan Buddhist culture flourishes and that freedom of religion is permitted. Monks chant in deep tones in dark assembly halls, butter lamps are lit in monastery courtyards by shiny-eyed pilgrims, and monastic festival days such as *tanka*-unfurling festivals are dutifully observed. But while monks and pilgrims appear to go through the ritual motions – turning prayer wheels, making offerings in temples, and prostrating – this may be all they are doing. These manifestations are largely cosmetic: the atheist Chinese tightly control what goes on through the Chinese Religious Affairs Bureau. This has led to a variety of 'showcase Buddhism' – purely ritualistic icing for tourists.

The crux of the problem for the Chinese is that monks and nuns are the ones who have spearheaded protests against Chinese presence in Tibet and demanded the right to freedom of worship, so a gathering of monks is something that the Chinese fear. Nowhere has this been more dramatically revealed than in the case of Monlam, a major festival resumed in 1986. Monlam Chenmo, the great Tibetan

1

prayer festival, coincides with lunar New Year celebrations, and takes place around February or March. Or used to. There have been no full Monlam celebrations since 1988, after a series of explosive events.

In 1986, for the first time in over 20 years, Monlam was revived in Lhasa at the request of the Chinese. Whether this was to be a spectacle for tourists, or to show the world that religious freedoms were being resumed, is not clear. Whatever the case, photography of the 1986 Monlam pops up in all kinds of Chinese sources – in photo books, in brochures bolstering the Chinese claim that there is complete religious freedom in Tibet, and even in video format on the Beijing-produced CD-ROM *Wonders of Tibet*. But the actual festival is no longer held with all monasteries participating.

In the 1950s, with monks coming from all over Tibet, Monlam became a focus for anti-Chinese protests. On 10 March 1959, at the tail-end of Monlam, the Lhasa Uprising took place, with monks taking up guns against the Chinese, so the end of Monlam is a particularly volatile time. In 1986, over a thousand monks from the different monasteries around Lhasa gathered for rites. Huge butter sculptures were displayed outside the Jokhang Temple at the heart of Lhasa, attracting crowds of up to 10,000 people from Lhasa and the valleys beyond.

Versions vary as to exactly what happened at the third Monlam to be staged. The last day of Monlam, 5 March 1988, turned into a riot (close on the heels of the pro-independence riots of October 1987). Apparently, when a procession was in progress around Barkor Bazaar in Lhasa, some monks chanted independence slogans. Stones were thrown at them, and they were warned to keep quiet by the Chinese. When the monks repeated the slogans, a Chinese policeman advanced, drawing his pistol. A Khampa tribesman from east Tibet stepped in to defend the monks, and was shot in the head at point-blank range. Infuriated, the monks paraded the dead man's body around the Barkor. At first the Chinese did not interfere, but by the third circuit of the Barkor, they were using batons and tear gas, then guns. Eighteen Tibetans died that day: hundreds of Chinese troops stormed the Jokhang Temple and beat a number of monks to death with iron bars; other monks were thrown off the rooftop. Some 800 Tibetans were arrested.

The following year, Monlam was boycotted by the monks. On 5 March 1989, the most severe rioting erupted – as many as a hundred Tibetans were killed, Chinese shops were burned, a state of martial law was declared, and all foreigners were ordered out of Lhasa. Martial law was not lifted in Lhasa for 13 months. By late 1991, the situation was back to normal, according to the Chinese. The place was once again open to tourism and it was business as usual, albeit with lots of permits, restrictions, checkpoints, and frequent chopping and changing of regulations.

In 1996, Chinese work teams occupied all of the monasteries and nunneries in Tibet as part of an extensive 're-education' campaign that involved signing of pledges by the monks and nuns to denounce the Dalai Lama and denounce the notion that Tibet might be a separate entity from China. Pictures, writings, audio recordings and videos of the revered Dalai Lama are banned in Tibet: those in possession of such items typically receive prison sentences. Since 1996, 'patriotic re-education' has been a staple for monastic studies, with monks required to study six books with titles like *Handbook on Crushing the Separatists* and *Handbook on Ethics for the Masses*. Testing is conducted on these handbooks.

Since 1959, the annual examination to award the Geshe degree (the highest rank in the Geluk school of Tibetan Buddhism) has fallen by the wayside. The Geshe examination is traditionally in the form of a rigorous question-and-answer debate, testing the applicant's knowledge to the fullest – the equivalent of a monastic PhD. The examination in Lhasa was suspended after 1959, was revived for three years from 1986 to 1988 (along with Monlam) and was suspended again following riots in Lhasa. After a hiatus of 16 years, the Geshe examination was revived in mid-2005, when six monks in their 70s were awarded the degree by the Beijing-based Buddhist Association of China, after taking the test at the Jokhang Temple in Lhasa. This will explain why there's a dearth of high-ranking clergy in Tibet: there's very little education going on, at least not of the monastic kind. The Tibetan government-in-exile, by contrast, has continued to offer the Geshe test every year. In 2005, Chinese authorities launched a campaign to blacklist not only the exiled Dalai Lama but also key religious figures close to him – banning those *rinpoches* (high lamas) from returning to their homeland, and forbidding any contact with them.

THE DALAI LAMA He's funny, he's charismatic and he has a deep, booming voice. He's a thorn in the side of the Chinese, who vigorously protested the award of the Nobel Peace Prize to him in 1989. He cracks jokes on the Larry King show. He's been a guest editor at French *Vogue*, and has written introductions to scores of books about Tibet. He's been featured on the covers of numerous magazines, and on billboard ads by Apple Computers as one of the great thinkers of the 20th century – in the same league as Einstein and Picasso (the Dalai Lama's picture, however, did not appear on billboards in Hong Kong).

Who is he? The title is synonymous with Tibet: the Dalai Lama is Tibet's greatest campaigner. Revered as the living incarnation of the bodhisattva of compassion, Tenzin Gyatso is the spiritual leader of all the Tibetan Buddhist sects. The Dalai Lama claims he is a simple monk ('a naughty Buddhist monk') but he's much more than that: his upper arm bears vaccination scars, revealing how well travelled he is. He is a fighter for Tibetan rights, the foremost proponent of world peace, and a tireless promoter of what he calls his real religion: kindness and compassion.

The Dalai Lama is an international icon, an inspiration to millions of Buddhists, and to millions of advocates of non-violence and right living. On a global basis, he has no equal (the Pope comes to mind, but the Pope is a proselytiser, seeking converts, while the Dalai Lama isn't). He cuts across barriers of race, religion and creed. All this is even more remarkable when you consider that the Dalai Lama's first language is not English, and that no government is willing to recognise him as a political leader – they accept him as a Nobel laureate or as leader of Tibetan Buddhism. The Dalai Lama has significantly raised awareness about Tibet, and the countries of Costa Rica, Poland and Norway have voiced support for Tibet in international forums.

The Dalai Lama's life has undergone fantastic twists and turns: the stuff that legends – and Hollywood movies – are made of. The Tibetan system of finding reincarnates, based on oracles and visions, dates back to the 15th century. Since lamas in the Geluk sect were celibate, a method of selecting the leader had to be arrived at. The resulting system of choosing a reincarnate worked beautifully, with no king's sons fighting each other for the throne, and no dispute over who would reign. It was, in addition, egalitarian, since the reincarnate could come from an impoverished nomad family. The 14th Dalai Lama was born in 1935 in a cowshed in Amdo Province, of a very poor family. At the age of two, he was identified by disguised lamas as the reincarnation of the 13th Dalai Lama, and hence the spiritual leader of four million Tibetans. His family were informed they would be moving to Lhasa. The boy was installed at the age of four upon the Lion Throne in Lhasa, and embarked upon a formidable course of monastic studies – training in Tibetan

1

Buddhist metaphysics that would continue for the next 18 years. His new home was the dark, thousand-room Potala Palace.

A month after the Chinese invaded Tibet in 1950, the Dalai Lama was rushed through an enthronement ceremony to give him his majority, and thus assume the leadership of Tibet in the face of Chinese aggression. He was just 15 at the time. At age 18, he was negotiating face to face with Mao Zedong and Zhou Enlai over the fate of Tibet. In 1959, at the age of 23, the Dalai Lama escaped from Lhasa – ironically disguised as a soldier – and fled into exile in India, losing his country and his people. He issued a statement condemning the Chinese. He was just a Tibetan refugee, and a humble monk – no passport, no country and no status.

The Dalai Lama still travels on a refugee's yellow identity certificate. If anyone had told him back in 1959 that he would still be in exile over 45 years later, he would not have believed it. Other Dalai Lamas had fled Tibet during political crises – to Mongolia and to India – but only for a period of a few years. Tibetans going into exile in 1959 all believed they would soon return, and have not tried to take out Indian citizenship because it would mean a loss of their Tibetan identity.

The Dalai Lama's idol is Mahatma Gandhi, from whom he learned the path of non-violence. But this path has produced no concrete results: the Dalai Lama is in a dilemma because nothing has come of his peaceful approaches in the last 45-odd years. The Chinese precondition for discussion about Tibet is that the Dalai Lama abandon any thought of independence. For a period, the Dalai Lama abandoned his position of asking for full independence and asked for autonomy within the PRC, a situation similar to that which existed in Tibet from 1950 to 1959. This is similar to the system guaranteed for 50 years in Hong Kong SAR (Special Administrative Region), whereby Hong Kong continues its free ways but cedes military power to the PRC. But even this did not bring the Chinese to the negotiating table, because the Chinese claim that Tibet already is autonomous and that what the Dalai Lama is really after is independence. What keeps the Dalai Lama going? 'A belief in the rights that we have,' he says. It is the Tibetan struggle in a nutshell.

After his dramatic escape in 1959, the Dalai Lama kept a low profile throughout the 1960s, engaging in personal retreats. In 1974, he took his first trip to the West. Since then he has globe-trotted at an astounding rate, spreading the message about Tibet and his ideas on world peace. The Dalai Lama's most endearing quality is what he calls a 'radical informality' – his uncanny skill at cutting to the heart of the matter, and being on the same wavelength as ordinary people. He is one of Tibet's most accomplished philosophers, trained in a traditional Tibetan system, and yet he comes across as a kind of jovial uncle. In March 2011, at the age of 75, the Dalai Lama announced his 'retirement', meaning that he would focus his attention on religious matters instead of acting as nominal head of the Tibetans in exile. In August 2011, Harvard-trained legal scholar Lobsang Sangay was sworn in as Prime Minister of the Tibetan government-in-exile, taking over political duties from the Dalai Lama.

REINCARNATES Tibetan Buddhism places great faith in master teachers, or *rinpoches*, and in the concept of reincarnation. With most of these rinpoches living in exile, that means the survival of Tibetan Buddhism lies outside Tibet. There are a number of obstacles to continuing the tradition of the masters: a major obstacle is how and where to find incarnates.

In Tibetan Buddhism, only a high lama is said to be able to redirect his soul into the body of another. The young reincarnate is known as a *tulku*, or living Buddha, and is usually found in a one- to three-year-old boy (if the search takes longer, the boy could be up to six or older). Most tulkus are officially instated at four or five years old. Finding the incarnation of a high lama upon his death is a complicated matter for the Tibetans – it involves the assessing of omens and portents, consulting the state oracle, performing divinations for clues, and perhaps visiting Tibet's sacred oracle lake, Lhamo Latso. Potential candidates are screened through extensive interviews; the final confirmation of a reincarnate is made by the Dalai Lama himself.

After the Dalai Lama's flight to India in 1959, the process of finding and verifying reincarnate lamas has become even more complicated because it must be determined if the incarnate has been born inside or outside Tibet. Most are now found outside Tibet: tulkus have been found among the Tibetan exile community in India and in Switzerland. If a tulku is discovered inside Tibet, it is difficult for the Dalai Lama's emissaries to carry out the selection process. This puzzles the Tibetan community in exile: where are the reincarnates to be found? And if one is discovered inside Tibet, what should be done about it? Can a reincarnate be a Westerner?

Asked about his own incarnation, the Dalai Lama has said that logically if he is in exile, his reincarnate can only be found in exile. But he has wavered on the question of whether the method of finding the Dalai Lama should be altered, and whether the Dalai Lama should be chosen democratically, like the Pope. In the case of the Geluk sect throne-holder, the process *has* been altered: the leader is elected in Dharamsala every seven years. The Dalai Lama has also taken the unusual step of saying in an interview that in future the Dalai Lama could be a woman (all 14 Dalai Lamas thus far have been men). Of course, that's only an idea, and one that would never stand a chance of getting off the ground with the Tibetan community in exile. The stories behind three controversial tulkus are briefly described here.

The Spanish lama Dharamsala, March 1987: a two-year-old boy, Osel Torres, is enthroned with much pomp and ceremony as the reincarnation of renowned teacher Lama Thubten Yeshe. Lama Yeshe was the founder of the Foundation for the Preservation of the Mahayana Tradition (FPMT), an international organisation with over 80 dharma centres worldwide. Osel ('Clear Light') was discovered through oracles and dreams by Lama Zopa Rinpoche, who took over directing the FPMT after the death of Lama Yeshe. Subjected to traditional tests, Osel passed with flying colours, and at the age of two was recognised by the Dalai Lama. The one major difference is that Osel is Western. Since globetrotting Lama Yeshe was one of the biggest transmitters of Tibetan Buddhism in the West, it was reasoned his reincarnate was Western also. Lama Osel is the son of Paco and María Torres, who were devoted followers of Lama Yeshe in Spain; the couple have five other children. Lama Osel went on to receive a formal Tibetan education at Sera Monastery in south India. Reincarnate lamas undergo severe training: without special qualities, most would collapse under the strain. The strain was greater on Osel as a Westerner – a celebrity lama scrutinised by the Western media. In Osel's case, his special monastic education did not quite do the trick: as an adult, he rebelled and reverted to being a normal citizen in Spain, saying he wanted to catch up on drinking, watching football, chasing women – and pursuing a career as a film-maker.

The politics of the Karmapa Officially the Chinese are atheist, and have ignored the selection of reincarnate lamas as 'feudal superstition'. This attitude, however, changed because the Chinese realised that these incarnates are very powerful, so it's become more a question of politics than religion. In 1992, the Chinese recognised an incarnate in the 17th Karmapa of the Kagyu sect, enthroned at Tsurphu Monastery and assisted by the Chinese Religious Affairs Bureau. This marked the first time since 1959 that the Chinese recognised an incarnate, although it appeared in this case that they wanted to direct the choice of the incarnate. The choice of the 17th Karmapa, a boy from eastern Tibet, caused a rift among Kagyu sect followers at Rumtek Monastery in Sikkim, where the 16th Karmapa lived in exile until his death. However, it appeared from the choice of the 17th Karmapa that it was possible for an incarnate to be found within Tibet and approved by both the Dalai Lama and the Chinese. This concurrence was short-lived: in early 1995, the Chinese and the Dalai Lama had a severe falling-out over the choice of the 11th Panchen Lama (see next section). See the *Tsurphu Monastery* section in *Chapter 5* to read more about the dramatic escape of the Karmapa and the case of several contenders for the throne.

The Tibetan monk known as His Holiness the 17th Gyalwang Karmapa, Ogyen Trinley Dorje, currently lives in Dharamsala, India, and is the Karmapa candidate recognised by the Dalai Lama.

Ogyen Trinley Dorje obtained refugee status in India in 2001. The most media-savvy of any title holder, he uses webcasting to reach out to his followers at dharma centres around the world (especially in the USA). He uses the tools of Facebook and Twitter; he owns a Nintendo Wii – and his favourite Western movie is *Kung Fu Panda*. One cool Karmapa – who got into a lot of hot water in 2011 when Indian police raided his monastery and found millions in cash, including a large amount of Chinese money. The Karmapa shrugged it off, saying it was donations. Among Tibet's high-profile lamas, Ogyen Trinley Dorje ranks close to the Dalai Lama, who acts as his spiritual teacher. The Gyalwang Karmapa is known for his innovations, such as facilitating the ordination of Tibetan nuns by allowing them to attain the highest Geshe degree, a privilege previously reserved exclusively for monks. He is also at the forefront of environmental protection and promoting green politics, and has set up a network among monasteries in India to promote environmental awareness.

The case of the missing lama In January 1989, when the tenth Panchen Lama died of a heart attack at Tashilhunpo Monastery in Shigatse, the Dalai Lama's government-in-exile started collecting names of potential candidates. In 1991, a divination was performed that determined the reincarnate had been born inside Tibet. Approaches to Beijing to co-operate in a search for the incarnate were rejected, but in 1993 a message was sent to India by Chatral Rinpoche, the head abbot of Tashilhunpo Monastery, explaining that the proper rituals were being carried out. The search by a committee from the monastery (sanctioned by the Chinese) had whittled down the number of candidates. A six-year-old boy from Nagqu (northern Tibet), named Gedhun Choekyi Nyima, looked the most promising.

Several divinations were performed in Dharamsala, India, in early 1995 to determine if the boy was the right candidate, and these proved positive. On this basis, in May 1995, the Dalai Lama declared the child the official 11th Panchen Lama. At this point, all the Chinese had to do was go along with the Dalai Lama's choice – the boy was, after all, one of their own sanctioned candidates. But Chinese officials were apparently infuriated that the choice of candidates had been 'leaked' to the Dalai Lama's government-in-exile.

This time, for the first time since taking over Tibet, the Chinese stepped in – in a big way. They condemned the Dalai Lama's choice, detained Chatral Rinpoche (the abbot responsible for the search), and took the six-year-old in question into custody – making him the world's youngest political prisoner. Neither the boy nor his parents have been seen in public since 1995, leading to fears for their safety.

In the meantime, Tashilhunpo Monastery split into pro-Dalai Lama and pro-Chinese factions – an estimated 50 Tibetans were detained following the fallout. In July 1995, the leading lamas at Tashilhunpo were sacked, and replaced with pro-Chinese head lamas. In November that year, 75 Tibetan Buddhist leaders were rushed to Beijing, lectured by President Jiang Zemin, told to reject the Dalai Lama's choice, and asked to prepare another list of candidates. The new candidate would be selected by drawing a ball from the Golden Urn – a lottery system from the 18th century, from an outdated Mongolian treaty.

In November 1995, another six-year-old boy from Nagqu, named Gyaltsen Norbu, was virtually hand-picked by the Chinese as the new Panchen Lama. Ten days later, a highly publicised enthronement ceremony took place. Security was tight, with hundreds of PLA troops deployed at Tashilhunpo Monastery. In January 1996, Gyaltsen Norbu was in Beijing, shown being greeted by President Jiang Zemin. The Chinese choice for Panchen Lama does not seem to spend much time in Shigatse – the reason given is safety concerns (ie: that he will be threatened by Tibetans).

The interference of atheist China in Tibetan Buddhist ritual is hard to fathom. Did it really matter to the Chinese which six-year-old boy from Nagqu was chosen? To the Tibetans it does – no Tibetan will accept a Panchen Lama who is not verified and sanctioned by the Dalai Lama. The only way the Tibetans will accept such a choice is under duress, and this is apparently the next step, as the Chinese force monks in major monasteries to swear that the Chinese choice is the only legitimate one, and to renounce the Dalai Lama. A deluge of Panchen Lama posters, pictures, books and videos spreads the word of the Chinese choice. As for the Dalai Lama's choice, black market pictures of the missing lama are sold in Lhasa, despite the risk of a jail sentence if found in possession of such a picture.

In the aftermath of these events, the abbot of Tashilhunpo Monastery, Chatral Rinpoche, was sentenced to six years in jail for 'leaking state secrets'. The head of the Tantric University at Tashilhunpo, Kachen Lobsang Choedrak, was detained; and the secretary of Tashilhunpo, Gyatrul Rinpoche, was fined and expelled for refusing to endorse the Chinese-chosen candidate. Chinese work teams moved into Tashilhunpo Monastery to force monks to pledge their loyalty to the Communist Party – those refusing to do so were expelled or imprisoned.

Conflicting reports have been given by the Chinese concerning the whereabouts of Gedhun Choekyi Nyima, the Dalai Lama's choice. Chinese officials have variously said the boy is living in Beijing, or in a town in the north of Tibet. In 1996, in the aftermath of the Panchen Lama run-in, an intense anti-Dalai Lama campaign was launched, with the removal of all Dalai Lama pictures, including those from the Potala. Monks were told to sign pledges denouncing the Dalai Lama and approving the Chinese choice of Panchen Lama.

Despite all this, attempts by Chinese authorities to give their appointed Panchen Lama, Gyaltsen Norbu, some religious credence among the Tibetans have gone seriously astray. In 1998, when officials sought to bring the Panchen Lama to Kumbum Monastery in Qinghai, the abbot of that monastery, Arjia Rinpoche, promptly fled China to seek asylum in the USA. The abbot later revealed that he did not want to be seen as a collaborator with the Chinese government.

In 2011, Chinese officials introduced new laws stipulating that Tibetan Buddhist monks must seek permission from the Chinese communist (atheist) regime for reincarnation. It is not clear how the metaphysics of that would work, but the laws are described by the Chinese Religious Affairs Bureau as an important move to 'institutionalise management of reincarnation'. Another law specifies that Buddhist monks outside of China are barred from being recognised as a reincarnation of the Dalai Lama. The Dalai Lama's choice for Panchen Lama has been missing for over 20 years.

MYTHOLOGY AND THE ARTS

Tibetan culture, isolated for thousands of years, developed along very different lines from that of neighbouring India or China. There are two streams to Tibetan culture: religious arts and folk arts – the sacred and the profane.

FOLK ARTS The folk arts of Tibet (the profane side) derive largely from the nomad herder culture, with hard drinking and partying at festival time, like the annual horse-racing festivals held all over the Ethnic Tibetan region. Rather like Wild West cowboy rodeos, these events are a mixture of horse races and other competitions, plus song-and-dance events. They are also a prime venue for matchmaking among the widely scattered nomad clans, so nomad women show up dressed in their finest clothing and jewellery. In exuberant foot-stomping dances, Tibetan boots become musical instruments all of their own, and with a simple horse-hair fiddle, nomad musicians can create strident music. High-pitched Tibetan 'yodelling', performed by women, is especially haunting and evocative of the vast grasslands. Often performed in a welcome ceremony is the yak dance. Two performers don a single yak-skin costume, with one performer up front, shaking the head and horns, and the other performer at the back, wagging the tail. The feisty yak may perform back-rolls, or it may charge – with horns forward – causing members of the audience to scatter in all directions. Similar in concept is the snow lion dance, again with two performers inside a single costume. Sometimes there may be male and female snow lion dancers, and a cub as well.

SACRED ARTS Tibetan culture is closely linked to Tibetan Buddhist beliefs – in former times most literature, music, dance and drama, painting, sculpture and architecture was inspired by those beliefs. The bulk of Tibetan literature is based on its Buddhism, as texts were printed with inked woodblocks at certain monasteries.

Two massive works of Buddhist literature are the Kanjur (Canon of Buddhist Law, 108 volumes) and the Tenjur (commentaries on the Kanjur, in 228 volumes). These are mostly translated from Sanskrit. An exception to religious literature is the epic of Gesar of Ling, the legendary 11th-century king who fought monsters, demons and even yak demons. This was a staple of Tibet's former wandering storytellers, who committed the long tale to memory. And they would have needed a prodigious memory because this thousand-year-old tale runs to millions of words. It is thought to be the longest verse saga ever written – even longer than Homer's *Odyssey*. If you can imagine a Tibetan *Lord of the Rings*, that might come close.

Unlike Theravadan Buddhist traditions, monks at Tibetan Buddhist monasteries are actively involved in the creation of artwork, using formulaic methods. Inspiration is the goal of the artwork – assisting the viewer with meditation and in attaining spiritual realisation – and thus the creation becomes far more important than the creator. As a result, most Tibetan art is anonymous. However, there are instances where great lamas and teachers also happen to be creators, like the lama-teacher-sculptor Zanabazar in Mongolia. Sculpture at monasteries is generally of bronze or copper with highlights in gold or gilt. Fine silver statuary is also found. Murals covering the entrance and interior walls of monasteries depict Buddhas and bodhisattvas, protector deities, and other themes. *Tankas* (wall hangings, either painted scrolls or appliquéd on cloth or silk) originated as objects of meditation and were formerly used for teaching purposes by travelling lamas (no longer seen within Tibet).

Other objects to assist with meditation are mandala murals and mandala *tankas* – the mandala is a mystic circle design or cosmogram. A unique Tibetan monastic art form is the creation of sand mandalas – circular sand paintings made by monks with coloured sand over a period of several weeks. Elaborate ceremonies take place at the monastery during and after completion of the sand mandala: it is then destroyed, to indicate the impermanence of all things.

Monasteries in Tibet used to stage an annual ceremony called Cham, with masked dances and accompanying longhorn music performed by the monks. In these rituals, the monks wore masks representing demons, spirits and mythical animals. Cham dance is still occasionally seen within Tibet, but the authorities are highly suspicious of any large gathering of Tibetans, so the chances of seeing a Cham dance in Tibet are rare (in fact, the chances of witnessing one are higher in other parts of the Tibetan world).

Because of their close link with Tibetan Buddhism, many of the Tibetan arts are proscribed or no longer practised in Tibet itself. That means you have to go to the exile community for the real culture. Tibet's cerebral sacred music is showcased in albums such as *Freedom Chants*, recorded in India by the exiled Gyuto Monks, who are also featured on the soundtracks for the movies *Kundun* and *Seven Years in Tibet*. These monks have mastered the Tibetan meditation technique of chanting with a deep three-note chord, which places such a strain on the vocal chords that the singer is in danger of becoming mute if he overdoes it. As the story goes, throat singing derives from the abbot of a monastery in Tibet who, some 600 years ago, saw a vision of Death. A strange noise came out of his chest and frightened Death away, and monks have been chanting like this ever since. To the untrained ear, it sounds like a human didgeridoo. The monks are able to chant three octaves in a single note because the area around their thorax is more relaxed than that of most mortals. This style of singing is eerily beautiful, and said to enhance meditation – though some find it most disturbing. The weird art of throat singing is also practised in some other Tibetan Buddhist realms such as Tuva and Mongolia, where a high-pitched whistle is added to the three-note dirge.

Oddly enough, Tibetan sacred music has found a place in New Age offerings. Firmly established with New Age musicians is a former monk, Nawang Kechog. Kechog has mastered a number of instruments including the bamboo flute, the Tibetan longhorn and the aboriginal didgeridoo: his albums include *Quiet Mind*, *Sounds of Peace* and *In a Distant Place* (page 364).

SAVING TIBETAN CULTURE

The ancient Tibetan culture developed along very different lines from others in High Asia. Saving this unique culture essentially comes down to the issue of religious freedom, because Tibet's cultural identity is tied in with its Buddhism, and the Chinese do not respect that religion. Ultimately, it's a question of human rights.

HUMAN RIGHTS On 10 December 1948 the United Nations adopted the Universal Declaration of Human Rights (UDHR). This document was principally crafted by Canadian law professor John Humphrey as the UN response to atrocities committed during World War II – ostensibly to ensure that horrors like the Jewish Holocaust would never happen again. In Tibet, they did happen again, within a scant ten years of that declaration. For more than 55 years, the UN has turned a blind eye to the devastation China has wreaked in Tibet, violating the majority of the 30 articles of the UDHR. In my view, the UN has no moral authority left; it has become a corrupt and bloated bureaucracy. True, in 1959, 1961 and 1965, resolutions were passed at the UN demanding that China respect the UDHR in

BLOWING IN THE WIND

Tibetan culture – ethnic stock, beliefs, customs, language, food – has little in common with Chinese culture. But possibly the best way to gauge a culture is not through its food or its customs, but through its mythology. Here, Tibetan culture truly comes into its own. On the roofs of Tibetan houses, atop nomad tents, on high passes, on sacred peaks, at holy lakes and on the upper ramparts of monasteries, you will always find prayer flags fluttering. There are a number of varieties of prayer flags, but the commonest are the five-coloured prayer flags, which are printed with Buddhist mantras. Depicted in the corners of each flag are the clawed supernatural animals of the four directions: garuda (wisdom), dragon (gentle power), tiger (confidence) and snow lion (fearless joy). A fifth mythical animal, appearing usually in the middle of the prayer flag, is the windhorse. Some of these mythical animals are found in other Asian cultures, but not the windhorse or the snow lion, which are uniquely Tibetan.

THE WINDHORSE The beautiful steed that brings good fortune, symbolised by the jewel on its back, is known as *lungta* in Tibetan. When prayer flags snap and flutter in the breeze, the windhorse printed on them is set in motion, carrying good fortune in all directions and galloping across the sky, spreading the teachings of Buddhism. The windhorse represents uplifting energy. Prayer flags are usually printed on cloth, using woodblocks. Some pilgrims cannot afford them, and resort to a modified inexpensive version – small squares of paper, embossed with windhorses. Pilgrims throw these in the air at sacred sites and shout '*Lha Gyalo!*' ('Victory to the gods!').

THE SNOW LION When the lion made the leap over the Himalaya from India, it became the residing deity of Tibet's snowy ranges, able to bound from snow peak to snow peak. This friendly doglike animal (*sengye* in Tibetan) is shown in temple frescoes with a white body and turquoise mane, or a blue body with vermilion mane and green eyes. The snow lion is a symbol of fearless joy – a mind free of doubt, clear and precise. The snow lion dance is performed at special events. Snow lions are part of the throne of Buddha, and are shown upholding the three precious jewels of Buddhism on the forbidden Tibetan flag. Snow lions appear on the crest and seal of the Dalai Lama; they also appear on Tibetan government seals of office, and on old banknotes and stamps.

There's a curious ideological battle involving snow lions, possibly because of their close association with the Dalai Lama and Tibetan nationalism. Snow lion statues stand guard at the gates of Norbulingka, the Dalai Lama's summer palace in Lhasa, but outside the front gates of the Potala stand statues of Chinese imperial lions, the same symbols of Chinese emperors found at the Forbidden City in Beijing. Chinese officials have even objected to a logo at a conference in Europe – the image in question was not the Tibetan flag, nor an image of the Dalai Lama, but simply a pair of snow lions.

Tibet, but there was no punch behind the resolutions. They were promulgated before 1970, the year that the PRC became one of the five permanent members of the UN Security Council, with full veto power. The UN Human Rights Council today includes voting members from such bastions of liberty as China, Cuba, Syria, Saudi Arabia, Sudan and Zambia, who do nothing but thwart its human-rights mandate.

Why Are We Silent? This is the title of a 60-second cinema ad about Tibet, marking the 50th anniversary of the UDHR in 1998. The clip features six film and rock stars reading extracts from the UDHR against a background of Tibetan imagery. In early 1998, members of the Tibetan Youth Congress staged a hunger strike in Delhi. Six hunger strikers, representing the six million people of Tibet, demanded that the UN resume its debate on the question of Tibet; that it appoint a Special Rapporteur to investigate the situation of human rights in Tibet; and that it appoint a Special Envoy to promote a peaceful settlement of the question of Tibet and initiate a UN-supervised plebiscite to ascertain the wishes of the Tibetan people. The lengthy strike was broken up by the Indian police.

China has one of the worst human rights violation records in the world. US Department of State reports on Tibet have slammed China for 'serious human rights abuses in Tibet' and for imposing 'intensified controls on fundamental freedoms'. Evidence for reports like this is drawn from interviews with credible Tibetan refugees, who tell of forced sterilisations and abortions, as well as arbitrary arrest, torture in prisons and cases of summary execution. Despite mounting evidence, China vigorously denies any transgressions, says that torture has been completely abolished, and claims that Tibetan people have gained real democracy and equality since 1959's 'democratic reforms'. Beijing blithely churns out glossy brochures in English that quote the UDHR to back up the Chinese claim that rights are better now than they were under the Dalai Lamas. This won't explain why Tibetan monks have been given long prison sentences for translating the UDHR into the Tibetan language.

What human rights do the Tibetans want? The basic ones: the right to freedom of speech, freedom of thought, and freedom to follow Tibetan Buddhist beliefs. The right to a proper education, the right to use the Tibetan language. The rights of the child. Even the most fundamental of human rights are denied to Tibetans. These include the rights to clean water, sufficient food, a home, health care, proper education, employment, protection from violence, equality of opportunity, and a say in their future. In Tibet, Chinese violations of the UDHR are so blatant that they have led scholar Robert Thurman to say that 'Tibetans are the baby seals of the human rights movement'. The Dalai Lama puts it this way: 'The Chinese are entitled to their happiness, but not at the expense of another nation or people.' He accuses the Chinese of pursuing a deliberate policy of cultural genocide in Tibet. By the government-in-exile count, over a million Tibetans have perished – directly or indirectly – at the hands of the Chinese since the 1950s.

POPULATION TRANSFER Before 1950, there were no Chinese settlers in the TAR. Accurate figures on current Chinese population in Tibet are hard to come by: Chinese figures do not include the sizeable military contingent. However, it is certain that China is providing incentives to bring settlers into Tibet – higher salaries, more benefits and tax breaks. In the provinces at the edge of the TAR, Han Chinese settlers outnumber the Tibetans. The Chinese do not integrate with the Tibetans, nor bother to learn the language. Not only are they starting to outnumber the Tibetans, they are reducing them to second-class citizens in their own land. For doing the same job, Chinese workers are usually paid a higher salary than Tibetans.

In Inner Mongolia, after 1949 when the communists took control, millions of Han Chinese flooded on to the steppes, thanks to government encouragement and incentives. The Mongols are now a minority in their own land – there are 20 million Han versus four million Mongolians. Mongol nomad livelihood has been severely disrupted by Han Chinese turning pasture into irrigated farmland. All this is in breach of the Geneva Conventions. A similar scenario appears to be under way in Tibet.

POLITICAL PRISONERS The number of political prisoners held in prisons in Tibet ranges from over a thousand (government-in-exile figure) to 50 (Chinese figure). The Chinese figure is skewed because Chinese officials maintain that prisoners in Tibet are common criminals, not political prisoners. If a prisoner is convicted for holding up a Tibetan flag, this is noted as 'prisoner trying to incite public disorder' so somehow it becomes a criminal offence, not a political one. Conditions in prison are poor, with beatings and torture routine. Across China, it is estimated that over 6,000 prisoners a year are executed (the exact number is not known, since figures are kept secret). For the year 2004, Amnesty International reports that 3,400 people were known to have been executed in China, a figure exponentially more than those executed in the rest of the world *combined*. By contrast, in 2004, there were 159 executed in Iran and 59 executed in the USA. Some prisoners in China are executed by lethal injection, but the majority are dispatched with a bullet to the back of the head: the bill for the bullet is often sent to the family of the executed as further humiliation. There is some evidence that body parts of executed prisoners are sold on the international market. Chinese spokespeople blithely deny that any of this ever takes place.

The world's youngest political prisoner is believed to be Gedhun Choekyi Nyima, the Dalai Lama's choice for 11th Panchen Lama. His whereabouts are unknown: he has not been seen in public since May 1995 (see pages 34–6).

In August 1995, Ngawang Choephel disappeared in Tibet. Choephel, a Fulbright scholar, was researching traditional music in Tibet and videotaping dance and song performances. It was not for another 14 months that his mother discovered that he was still alive, and in prison. He was charged with spying for the Tibetan government-in-exile and a sentence of 18 years was handed down. After a vigorous high-profile campaign by Western supporters, and after serving six years of his sentence, Ngawang Choephel was released on medical parole in January 2002, and flown back to the USA, where he applied for political asylum.

Ngawang Sangdrol is a nun who was 13 years old when she was first jailed for demonstrating for a free Tibet. After her release, she was forbidden to rejoin her nunnery. In 1992, she was arrested again for demonstrating and sentenced to three years in jail. In 1993, while in prison, Ngawang and 13 other nuns recorded Tibetan protest songs – the tape was smuggled out by a sympathiser and taken to the West. When they learned of this, the Chinese increased the nuns' sentences by a further six years. In 1996, Ngawang's sentence was increased by a further nine years. In a rare protest from the UN, in 1995 the Working Group on Arbitrary Detentions ruled the nun had been punished for exercising her rights to freedom of opinion. The group called on China to release her, in line with the principles of the UDHR – a call that was ignored by the Chinese. In 1998, as part of a campaign commemorating the 50th anniversary of the Universal Declaration, Ngawang Sangdrol was featured in a joint campaign by the Body Shop and Amnesty International, putting added pressure on the Chinese. In 2002, Ngawang was released from prison, and in 2003 she was permitted to fly to the USA for medical treatment. She was granted asylum in the USA shortly after, and is dedicated to working for the release of her fellow prisoners.

Religious freedom It is estimated that up to 70% of political prisoners in Tibet are monks and nuns. The reason they are imprisoned is a combination of their political attitudes and their fight for religious freedom. In the past, monks and nuns have spearheaded the Tibetan independence movement: their vows may empower them to act politically. Celibacy puts them in a better position to sacrifice their lives as opposed to those with families, and dying for Tibetan independence is a selfless act guaranteeing a human rebirth in the next life.

Since early 1996, Chinese officials have conducted a 'Strike Hard' campaign deliberately directed at monks and nuns. Chinese work teams have been dispatched to all monasteries and nunneries in Tibet for 'patriotic re-education' (an ongoing process). Dalai Lama pictures have been banned in all temples and public places, and Tibetan monks and nuns are required to sign a five-point agreement, pledging to oppose the idea of an independent Tibet, to denounce the Dalai Lama, to recognise the Chinese-appointed Panchen Lama, to oppose those advocating independence for Tibet, and to work for the unity of 'the Motherland'. According to China's own statements, the majority of Tibet's 46,000 monks and nuns in 1,700 monasteries and nunneries have come under the programme. As a result, in the first two years of the programme, it is estimated that 14 monks and nuns died, upwards of 300 were arrested, and over 3,000 were expelled from their monasteries or nunneries. In addition, seven monasteries and nunneries were completely closed down.

In June 2002, a tent encampment established in a remote valley near Serthar in Amdo (Sichuan Province) was broken up by Chinese officials with pickaxes, and thousands of residents were ordered to leave. The encampment at one point attracted up to 8,000 monks and nuns, of whom nearly a thousand were Chinese. They were drawn by the teachings of charismatic leader Khenpo Jigme Phuntsok, who started off Larung Gar encampment with a handful of students in the 1980s. At special teaching times, the numbers at Larung Gar swelled to over 15,000 participants – hence the Chinese nervousness that led to the break-up. Khenpo Jigme Phuntsok was held incommunicado for a year in Chengdu, and died in 2004 in a military hospital. In 2016, another assault was mounted on Larung Gar and nearby Yarchen Gar. Under the guise of 'renovation', hundreds of residences were bulldozed and the occupants were taken by bus out of the area and dispatched to their original towns.

In 2005, President Hu Jintao confided to President Bush (on an official visit to China) that China was 'continuously raising the level of human rights enjoyed by its people', but that such progress must reflect 'China's national conditions'. This gobbledegook was spoken by the same man who ruthlessly suppressed Tibetans and imposed martial law in the late 1980s (Hu Jintao was Party Secretary of the TAR from 1988 to 1992). If anything, repression of Tibetan Buddhism appears to be intensifying. In 2005, Chinese officials launched a campaign that blacklisted not only the Dalai Lama but also key religious figures in exile close to him, who maintain links to monasteries within Tibet.

HOLLYWOOD'S BRIEF ROMANCE WITH TIBET

In an interview in 2017, Richard Gere claimed that he had been dropped from Hollywood's A-list because of his long involvement with the Tibetan cause. By the 1990s, Gere was king of the box office, with a string of successful films to his name. His career stalled in the late 1990s: he says he has only been able to get roles with indie directors since. Today, with China being the second-largest market in the world for films, Hollywood has sold its soul to chase it. Films are vetted for content that might offend the Chinese and result in the film not being distributed there, scripts have been rewritten to cater to the

1

Chinese market, and Tibetan characters have been pulled from scripts of Marvel remakes. Disney has practically obliterated the word 'Tibet' from its films. That might have a lot to do with the opening of Disneyworlds in Shanghai and Hong Kong.

Hollywood has been tamed now, catering to Chinese whims, but this was not the spirit 20 years ago, when it was buzzing with romance for things Tibetan and when China did its level best to try to silence Hollywood's Tibetmania.

Gyantse, November 1987: a young British tourist, Kris Tait, is accosted by a Chinese soldier on a bicycle, who tries to tear off her T-shirt. She at first assumes he's trying to assault her, but when a Tibetan crowd gathers chanting 'Dalai Lama!' it occurs to her that the soldier is after the T-shirt, which appears to bear an image of the Dalai Lama printed on it. Actually, the T-shirt is embossed with the face of the late Phil Silvers, a cult figure from late night BBC reruns of the 1950s American television series, *Sergeant Bilko*. The woman manages to wrench free from the soldier, and flees to her guesthouse to change clothes. Tait, an avid Bilko fan, later says there is a resemblance between Silvers and the Dalai Lama – the same quizzical eyebrows, the same thick glasses. Hollywood's dust-up with the Chinese over the Dalai Lama has just begun.

Dissolve to 1997, when the sleeves are rolled up, and the big brawls begin, as Hollywood takes on China in earnest, with full-length movies about the Dalai Lama in the works. Disney's Touchstone Pictures is faced with the most momentous decision of its corporate career – sell Mickey Mouse in China, or humour director Martin Scorsese? Which goes? Whose wrath will be greater to face – that of surly Chinese officials, or of Scorsese without his morning coffee? Scorsese is filming a movie about the early life of the Dalai Lama, one that has raised the hackles of the Chinese, who threatened to halt work on the creation of a Disneyland near Shanghai. The clash of the titans has begun.

Flashback to 1937: Frank Capra's epic, *Lost Horizon*, is released by Columbia TriStar. Based on the book of the same name, the film is the first big-budget movie to use a Tibetan setting: a monastery high in the snow-capped mountains where the wisdom of the ages is preserved by wizened lamas. The film costs four times the amount of any Columbia TriStar film at the time, using a set considered the largest ever built in Hollywood. During World War II, Tibet remained neutral, a kind of Switzerland in High Asia (although the British Mission remained in Lhasa, without official diplomatic status). *Lost Horizon* was widely circulated among the armed forces during World War II – it bolstered the hope that there was a place during mankind's darkest days where the values of civilisation were preserved.

Sixty years later, Columbia TriStar released *Seven Years in Tibet*, quite a different version of Shangri-La – one man's vision of the last years before Tibet itself was engulfed in war and chaos.

Why the sudden Hollywood interest in Tibet after a 60-year silence on the subject? Why did the 1990s produce a rash of Tibet films? And why is Beijing upset about them? In part, Hollywood's interest in Tibet is attributable to the collapse of the USSR and the demise of the Cold War: China provides a new 'evil empire' to crusade against, in the vacuum left by the demise of Russia. China is the world's most populous nation, with expanding economic clout and a world-class nuclear arsenal. China is an up-and-coming superpower with a ruthless leadership: a change of Western attitude to China definitely occurred after the Tiananmen Square Massacre in 1989. Suddenly, what the Dalai Lama had been saying all along – that the Chinese were killing Tibetans – was blatantly demonstrated at Tiananmen when the Chinese opened fire on their own people. An indicator of this shift of evil empires was the plot of the 1997 James Bond film, *Tomorrow Never Dies*. No KGB here: the movie was originally slated to be about the handover of Hong Kong, but missed its timing so the script was changed to a stand-off between China and Britain, with the two teetering on the brink of war because of the ambitions of an out-of-control media megalomaniac (modelled on Rupert Murdoch).

In part, Hollywood's interest in Tibet is related to new-found interest in Buddhism in the USA, and to celebrity actors such as Richard Gere, Harrison Ford and Uma Thurman supporting the Tibetan cause. Tibet has become chic following the popularity of the Dalai Lama after his 1989 Nobel Peace Prize. The man has become Hollywood's favourite underdog – a non-violent rebel with a cause. The Dalai Lama has mingled with Cindy Crawford and Sharon Stone at Los Angeles parties. Perhaps this is not so unusual: he has been an avid fan of movies from an early age. In the late 1940s, he arranged for the building of a projection room in Lhasa to view films imported from India. In the early 1990s, he fine-tuned the script for *Kundun* (in readings with Melissa Mathison and Harrison Ford) and for *Seven Years in Tibet* (with Becky Johnston).

Another reason for Tibetmania is possibly that Tibet is the ultimate in exotic locations: there's renewed Hollywood interest in exotica following the phenomenal success of movies such as *The English Patient*. More likely, however, is that Tibet is hot simply because controversy fuels box-office hits – and there's no shortage of controversy when it comes to Tibet.

In the case of *Kundun* and *Seven Years in Tibet*, the controversy started before shooting began. Both movies set out to portray an idyllic pre-1950 Tibet, with a smiling, soft-spoken Dalai Lama at the helm – a Dalai Lama sworn to non-violence. The Chinese claim that pre-1950 Tibet was hell on earth – a medieval society where Tibetans had no freedom, and slaved away as serfs for the aristocracy. Both movies show the Chinese as brutal thugs. Sony, which owns Columbia TriStar, was threatened in China over *Seven Years in Tibet*, as was Disney, but no economic sanctions were applied. Both movie directors were blocked from filming in India, which was their first choice of location. One thing's for sure: films like *Kundun*, *Seven Years in Tibet* and *Red Corner* will never be shown in China. However, there's no reason why they can't be shown in Hong Kong, where technically the laws only empower authorities to check films for violence and sex. In fact, *Seven Years in Tibet* has been screened in Hong Kong despite stern criticism from Beijing. The movie brought Ngapoi Ngawang Jigme out on the attack in Hong Kong. He complained about the movie's portrayal of himself as a turncoat who betrayed the Tibetan Army and signed the 17-Point Agreement with China for its annexation of Tibet. It was poetic justice of a kind. Ngawang Jigme has rarely spoken to the press; he has lived in Beijing since 1967, where he and his clan hold high positions.

Seven Years in Tibet was also screened in Moscow, again despite Chinese Embassy objections. The Chinese vigorously protested a screening of the movie at a film festival in Japan (the film performed well in Japan, where Brad Pitt has a cult following – among teenage girls, anyway). Other Chinese objections were raised over *Kundun*, a movie that glorifies the Dalai Lama (and in one scene portrays China's great leader, Mao Zedong, as a crass, evil, chain-smoking buffoon). In May 1998, the Chinese Embassy demanded that the film *Windhorse* be removed from the Washington International Film Festival because it was meant to 'obviously smear China's policy toward Tibet'. The festival director invited Chinese Embassy officials to come to the screening of the movie and participate in an open dialogue about the film – they did not show up. The film went on to become the festival-goers' top choice.

Words are the only weapon that Tibetans have in the fight against Chinese repression of Tibetan culture and occupation of their land, and Tibetans have found words can have great impact when they are spoken on the big screen. In the USA and elsewhere, Tibetans have distributed leaflets and Tibet Action Kits outside screenings of the movies. China's problem with all of this is an issue of freedom of speech.

In a world where the international community has been spectacularly silent on the topic of Tibet, the films have pricked the Western conscience, and incurred the wrath of Chinese Embassy officials. China's greatest fear is that one of these Hollywood films will become a cult hit, with television reruns for the next 20 years – just like *Sergeant Bilko*.

TIBET ONLINE

For additional online content, articles, photos and more on Tibet, why not visit w bradtguides.com/tibet.

2

Practical Information

Travel to Tibet Autonomous Region (TAR) is rigidly controlled. You need a Tibet Tourism Bureau (TTB) permit before you can board a plane or train to Lhasa where most trips get started. The TTB permit can only be arranged through an agent who must detail your entire itinerary for your stay in Tibet before tickets in and out can be processed. You may also be required to show an onward air ticket out of China when applying for the permit, although you might be able to get out of this by saying you will go overland from Lhasa to Kathmandu. Given this rigid framework, you have to indulge in some large doses of logistics and think over your itinerary carefully. Whatever you do, work well in advance with your agent - preferably two or three months in advance – as permits for areas such as Kailash can take forever.

However, outside the TAR, in the Kham and Amdo regions to the east, none of this permit hokum applies: you can travel independently and play it by ear. Hopefully, the following pages can guide you through the complex paperwork, permits, logistics and options. If you come through all that at the other end, you arrive in Lhasa – a major achievement in itself.

WHEN TO VISIT

CLIMATE April to October is the best time. November is starting to get cold. December and January can be freezing, with heavy snow blocking high passes and poor driving conditions. February is Tibetan New Year and though cold it can be lively, if you can get in. April can be windy; there's a rainy season around July and August, when flooding can cut off roads and wash out bridges. Because Tibet is so large, climate conditions change from east to west and with the elevation. Because of these elements, Tibet is really only open to foreigners for seven months a year, from the start of April to the end of October. Read on to find out why March is likely to be closed.

TIMING, FESTIVALS AND SENSITIVE PERIODS Rules and regulations concerning travel in Tibet change as often as the weather does with El Niño, so the following sections may be out of date by the time you plan your visit. If so, make adjustments. There are several times of year when it is difficult or impossible to get into Lhasa. Winter is an obvious one – there are no flights from Kathmandu and fewer from Chengdu. The Chinese may be nervous if some military bigwig or political leader is visiting, and they might just shut the whole of Tibet down for a few weeks. Nothing is guaranteed in Tibet, and no guidebook written in stone. Allow for changing information.

The Tibetan calendar is filled with unofficial anniversaries, and security is tight at these times, with Chinese troops on alert ten days before and after the sensitive period. You may have trouble getting into Tibet or travelling around at these times.

The easiest travel months are April, June and August (however, June to August is the most heavily booked period for flights into Lhasa). Among the 'hot' times are:

Losar	Tibetan New Year, around February
5 March	Commemorating major protests in 1988–89
10 March	Anniversary of 1959 Lhasa uprising, and marks the start of the Tibetan spring – protests across the entire plateau in 2008
14 March	Commemorating riots of 2008 uprising
23 May	Marks the 1951 surrender to the Chinese with the 17-Point Agreement
6 July	Dalai Lama's birthday
27 September	Start of 1987 riots
1 October	1987 protest in which Tibetans were shot dead
10 December	International human-rights day, which sparked a protest in 1988

Tibetans sometimes gather at countryside locations to picnic and throw *tsampa* in the air to mark special occasions. In Lhasa, this practice has been banned by Chinese authorities.

Because the Chinese are nervous about large gatherings of Tibetans, traditional festivals are low profile – indeed, for a number of years, festivals were banned outright. If you get a chance to see something more formal, like a festival in the countryside, go! If you're lucky there might be a horse-racing festival in progress at Damxung (Damshung) or Gyantse, or a *tanka*-unfurling ceremony at one of the monasteries within reach of Lhasa. There used to be festivals at every full moon in Tibet, but many were abolished by the Chinese authorities. The festivals that survive are based on the lunar calendar, which is complex and unpredictable (usually only announced in February, at Losar or Tibetan New Year). Ask around when you arrive in Tibet to confirm if there are likely to be any festivals in progress.

HIGHLIGHTS

A key factor in route planning is addressing this question: what do you want to see? What piques your interest? It's a good idea to pinpoint places of high interest to determine where this takes you on an actual map. Photocopy maps from this guidebook, get a colour felt pen, circle destinations of high interest – and start joining the dots.

Highlights are subjective – they really depend on your interests. Some travellers see two or three monasteries and get 'templed out', while others seem to have an unlimited capacity for looking at monasteries. The key to visiting is to vary the sights – take in a temple or fort, go on a day hike or visit a hot spring. Sometimes you luck out and find these all in the same locale. The following is a shortlist of personal favourites, which is bound to be biased, of course. My bias is very simple: I favour things Tibetan – which may sound odd, but after you've been in Tibet a week or so, that comment will make perfect sense. Travellers come to Tibet looking for Tibet, not China. All too often what they get is a bull in a secondhand China shop. The main highlight of any visit to Tibet will be meeting the people. There are two guaranteed places you will see and meet lots of Tibetans: at festivals and at key pilgrimage sites. Tibetans have their own version of top sites, and these are sacred pilgrimage destinations such as Mount Kailash – the trip of a lifetime.

TOP PILGRIMAGE SITES You will find temple tripping much more enjoyable if you mingle with Tibetan pilgrims. Important pilgrimage sites are great for seeing people

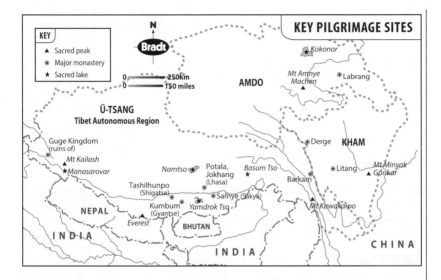

KEY
- ▲ Sacred peak
- ◉ Major monastery
- ★ Sacred lake

Ü-TSANG
Tibet Autonomous Region

AMDO

Kokonor

Mt Amnye Machen

Labrang

Guge Kingdom (ruins of)

Mt Kailash

Manasarovar

Namtso

Potala, Jokhang (Lhasa)

Basum Tso

Derge KHAM

Litang

Mt Minyak Gonkar

Tashilhunpo (Shigatse)

Barkam

Samye (Sakya)

Kumbum (Gyantse)

Yamdrok Tso

NEPAL

Everest

BHUTAN

Mt Kawakarpo

INDIA

INDIA

CHINA

from all parts of Tibet. And interacting with them. Shiny-eyed pilgrims turn out in throngs at the most sacred spots, including the Potala, Jokhang and Barkor (Lhasa); Tashilhunpo (Shigatse); Kailash (west Tibet); Kumbum; and Labrang (Amdo).

TIBETAN TOWN ARCHITECTURE Distinctive Tibetan style can be found in these places: the Tibetan Quarter, Potala, Norbulingka (Lhasa); Gyantse (Kumbum, fort, plus Pala Manor); Samye; and Xiahe (Labrang). It's becoming harder to find areas of pure Tibetan architecture due to encroachment by bland Chinese concrete-and-karaoke architecture.

BEST ATMOSPHERE Certain villages and small towns have a strong Tibetan ambience, with minimised Chinese influence, which means they are great places to stay longer and absorb. These places are more likely to be backwaters. In central Tibet, they include Tidrom hot springs, Samye and Gyantse. In west Tibet, the Kailash region is excellent. This is old Tibet – Tibet lost in time – where the Tibetan pulse runs strong.

BEST FORTS The majestic administrative centres of old Tibet. Most have been destroyed but these remain: Gyantse Dzong (used in the battle against British forces in 1904) and Yumbulagang (a rebuilt fortress-temple near Tsedang). The Potala in Lhasa is a prime example of fortress architecture. These castles in the sky are testament to the supreme stone-masonry skills of Tibetans.

TOP ACTIVE TEMPLES Chanting, rituals and monastic life (even monastic debating) can be experienced at the Jokhang (the most revered temple in Tibet), Sera and Drepung (Lhasa), Ganden, Samye Monastery (the oldest in Tibet), Tashilhunpo (Shigatse – magnificent statuary), Sakya (Mongolian fortress-style temple with grand chanting hall) and Labrang (entire monastic citadel in Xiahe, Gansu). Sera Monastery in Lhasa sees regular afternoon debating.

BEST HOT SPRINGS Tidrom Nunnery, Lhasa Prefecture – beautiful valley with Tibetan village and three enclosed hot springs for bathing.

Practical Information HIGHLIGHTS

2

49

BEST DAY HIKES Back of Sera Monastery in Lhasa; hike to Hepo Ri viewpoint in Samye; hikes around Sakya; hike to top of Shining Crystal Dzong ruins in Shegar.

TOP RUINS Guge Kingdom, in Zanda, west Tibet – though mostly destroyed, excellent murals can still be seen. Set in entrancing desert terrain riddled with caves.

MOUNTAINS, TOP TREKS Kailash, sacred mountain – three- to four-day pilgrim circuit in a stunning setting. Everest, north face – a three-day trek into the base camp (you can also drive there); from here the highest trek in the world (without crampons) leads to advanced base camp at over 6,400m. Closer to Lhasa, the five-day Ganden–Samye trek is popular.

YARLUNG TSANGPO GRAND CANYON Nothing comes close to this wonder of nature: it is more than double the depth of Arizona's Grand Canyon. Opening to Chinese tourism, but very difficult for foreign hikers or rafters to access. Closest approach is via Bayi and Linzhi in east Tibet.

SACRED LAKES Turquoise classics include Yamdrok Tso (with backdrop of peaks in Bhutan); Manasarovar (Kailash in background); Lake Namtso, with 7,000m peaks as backdrop; and Basum Tso, east Tibet. Pilgrims undertake *koras* (walking circuits) around sacred lakes. You can ride horses part-way along some circuits, such as Namtso and Manasarovar.

NOMADS AND GRASSLANDS Nomads are being rapidly settled across the Tibetan plateau, but pockets of pastoral nomadism survive. The best place to see traditional yak herding is the Kham region around Tagong and Litang, where you can make extended visits for several days, hiking or on horseback, and arrange homestays in traditional stone buildings.

ADVENTURE SPORTS Multiple-day camping trips can be organised from Lhasa – for rafting, kayaking, trekking or mountain bike forays. On your own, there are super trekking and mountain bike opportunities in Kham and Amdo.

GREAT ROAD TRIPS Lhasa to Kathmandu route; Lhasa to Chengdu or Kunming; Lanzhou via Labrang to Chengdu (Amdo); Kunming via Litang to Chengdu (Kham); Chengdu via Tagong to Xining; and the Karakoram Highway. These are among the greatest road trips in High Asia. Excellent for mountain biking too.

FESTIVALS These follow the lunar calendar, and timing is unpredictable as they're often not announced. If you get a chance, go – festivals offer great people encounters. Summer (June to August) sees horse-racing fairs in Gyantse and other locations. However, Nagqu and Yushu horse-racing festivals both take place in a stadium, not on the grasslands. Litang horse-racing festival is among the most spectacular. Monasteries occasionally stage *tanka*-unfurling ceremonies or annual Cham dances.

GIVE IT A MISS Avoid places where you see fake palm trees sprouting up. The worst town architecture prize goes to Tsedang, a complete Chinese town of the bathroom-tiling school of architecture, complemented by the odd fake palm. The town of Bayi in eastern Tibet is sprinkled with fake palm trees and mini-brothels. The most shocking experience in Lhasa is seeing Chinese high-rises – and fake palm trees on Yuthok Road.

TWO TIBETS Since large-scale protest by Tibetans erupted across the Tibetan plateau in the spring of 2008, access to the Tibet Autonomous Region (TAR) has been severely restricted by Chinese authorities. That situation may change, so best to check on current news about Tibet travel via websites (pages 366–9).

The rigid model for travel in the TAR is to present your whole itinerary up front to an agency, which will package airfare, vehicle and tour guide for central Tibet. The easiest place to arrange all this is Chengdu (Sichuan). You can arrange fixed itineraries for central Tibet from other gateway locations such as Zhongdian and Xining, again through agencies. Once in the TAR you can lose your minders for some of the time, and more of the time if you requested 'free days' built into your itinerary.

The rigid rules applied to travel in the TAR do not apply to the vast ethnic Tibetan areas outside the TAR, in Kham and Amdo, where you are relatively free to roam (except during times of unrest).

You are thus dealing with a case of two Tibets – central Tibet (TAR) is a very expensive option that requires you to present your whole itinerary up front so that permits can be acquired for closely monitored group touring. By contrast, to the far east, the regions of Kham and Amdo, outside the TAR, do not require permits (with a few exceptions) – and you are free to do what you please, at far lower cost – as long as your visa is valid.

Touring the 'two Tibets' requires a load of logistics. There are several important things to keep in mind when planning your itinerary in Tibet: the duration of your Chinese visa, how tight the permit situation is, the direction of travel, and allowing time to acclimatise to altitude. This is especially true if you want to attempt trekking in Tibet, such as trekking close to Everest, or tackling the *kora* at Mount Kailash. These treks require considerable physical stamina – and complex logistical support. Another parameter is just how deep your pockets are.

These factors go hand in hand. Getting permits within the Tibet Autonomous Region (TAR) is difficult and expensive, as you must travel with vehicle and guide in a group at all times. In practice, your 'group' can be just two people – or even just yourself. Outside the TAR, such restrictions do not apply: you are an independent traveller, and can use local transport.

The best advice that can be given here is to get the longest Chinese visa you can before you enter the Middle Kingdom (China). It should be possible to get a longer visa in Hong Kong, for instance. Some Chinese embassies and consulates dispense two-month visas: check online forums. Renewing your visa within China can be tricky – Chengdu has long been notorious for a slow and difficult extension process (try nearby Leshan instead).

A prime reason for keeping the 'two Tibets' strategy in mind is that periodically Chinese officials close the door to the TAR entirely, blocking it off for a month or so because of some sensitive anniversary. That means you would only be able to visit the Kham and Amdo regions, which lie outside the TAR. These regions have much to offer, and you could spend months exploring them.

Altitude strategy: it can take a week or longer to acclimatise to altitude, so best to go slow for the first week to adjust. Be active – take lots of walks – but avoid strenuous climbs as your body adjusts. See the *Health and safety* chapter, pages 109–23, for details. The higher you go, the more the acclimatisation time needed.

For all of these reasons, you have to think over your itinerary for the TAR very carefully, as once you have decided on a route and the timing, there may be little flexibility to alter it.

Practical Information TOURING STRATEGY

2

An American Tibetologist claims that one of the key factors for determining if a person is Tibetan is whether he or she eats *tsampa* (roasted barley flour) and actually enjoys it. Here's a shortlist of other criteria that would lead to the label 'very Tibetan'. When in Tibet, if you follow these customs, you'll be just like one of the family.

SIPPING YAK-BUTTER TEA Closely allied with *tsampa* because the *tsampa* is kneaded into balls with the addition of butter tea. Tibetan nomads drink up to 50 cups a day of yak-butter tea. You should attempt at least one cup if with Tibetans, but do not drain it – as the cup will instantly be refilled.

LIGHTING YAK-BUTTER LAMPS Required etiquette in temples, though vegetable oil is mostly used these days. Some offer the more expensive yak-butter lamps as special merit-making.

TURNING THE WHEELS Follow the pilgrims at temples and you will find giant prayer wheels in various styles. Good to keep the wheels turning.

WALKING THE *KORA* Tibetans find solidarity with foreigners walking a sacred circuit of a temple or sacred site. A great way to stretch your legs and get a workout to acclimatise.

TYING ON PRAYER FLAGS You can buy brightly coloured cloth prayer flags very cheaply in larger cities. Get a stack of them, and at the cairn that marks a high pass, tie some prayer flags on – and yell '*Lha Gyalo!*' at the top of your lungs. That's to appease the gods and ensure safe passage. Throwing handfuls of paper windhorse squares into the air also works well.

SHARING SACRED IMAGES Tibetans can spend ages poring over pictures of Mount Kailash or the Potala. If you have prints, the family shrine always needs new additions. The ultimate addition is HHDL images – very risky to be carrying. An image for personal use tends to be overlooked by officials.

CHASING WAYWARD YAKS Some yaks may diverge from the herd. Nomads have ways of keeping them in line. The main weapon is a woven yak-hair slingshot – wielded with astonishing accuracy to target a wayward yak by firing a small stone. Takes lots of practice to get it right, though.

SIDESTEPPING THE DOG Not just any dog – it's a Tibetan mastiff, thought to be the oldest guard dog in existence. This large lion-maned dog fearlessly defends nomad tents.

MINGLING WITH NOMADS In the summer, in July and August, nomads get together on the grasslands for a giant picnic with horses. Find out where these horse-racing festivals are and rub shoulders with hardy nomads.

HOW LONG DO I NEED? Ten to 20 days would be good. Six weeks would be better. Two months would be ideal if you plan on going trekking. You need time to adjust to the altitude, and you should build in extra time for delays due to breakdowns, road closures, overbooked flights and so on. The Western ethic of rushing around doesn't work well here.

TRIP DESIGN/ITINERARIES

Loop or linear? That is the essential question if planning a route that is a mix of the 'two Tibets'. The following are some sample itineraries, all starting from Chengdu, that can make the best use of your time in the region. There is a lot more detail about itineraries in specific regions in chapters devoted to those regions, such as the *Exploring Central Tibet* chapter, pages 179–200.

CHENGDU LOOPS These routes start and end in Chengdu (with a variation to start or end in Kunming). One strategy is to spend a few days in Chengdu with an agent,

---

🔒 REVOLVING DOORS AND GATES

Tibet travel regulations chop and change like the wind – so keep an ear to the ground and make allowances for modifying the following information. Or even abandoning it.

Since the events of 2008 (big protests in Lhasa and all over the Tibetan plateau), there has been a major clampdown on travel in Tibet for foreigners, and it shows no sign of letting up. Prior to 2008, many routes and regions were open, but there was a major shift after the protests.

The complete closure of Chamdo Prefecture to foreign travellers after 2008 has meant that the road routes through Kham and Amdo are not viable. However, there are signs that these routes may open again. Following the April 2015 mega-earthquake in Nepal, which also affected southern Tibet, the border crossing town of Zhangmu was heavily damaged. It was closed to foreigners, though it did pick up and see some local traffic at the border. Zhangmu has not been reopened to foreigners. Instead, in August 2017, a new border crossing at Kyirong was declared open to foreign travellers. So, a door closes down, and a window of opportunity opens up. Zhangmu and Nyalam are off the map for foreigners – they have become backwaters.

Meanwhile, in 2017, a much-expanded new airport terminal was christened at Nyingtri, to the east of Lhasa. With frequent flights to Chengdu and Chongqing, and lots more connecting flights projected, Nyingtri Airport has suddenly leaped into the front ranks of tourism in Tibet, with a five-star hotel popping up near the airport.

Now it's open, tomorrow it's not. It's closed for two years, then it reopens. Case in point: Larung Gar in west Sichuan was open for a while, but when Chinese officials started tearing down the residences of monks, nuns and devotees, the entire county of Serthar suddenly became off-limits and the welcome mat was pulled from under foreign feet. Foreigners are told they can drive through a region but cannot stop anywhere, or stay the night. But if you hand over lots of cash, maybe you can stop for a picnic, or even overnight. The discretion concerning which regions foreigners can access depends on which cadres are in power. If a cadre changes, then the doors and gates might suddenly be flung open. Before booking your trip, check for the latest exciting updates to the saga of revolving doors and gates.

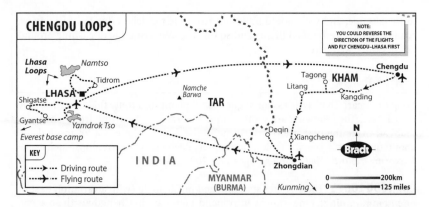

CHENGDU LOOPS

NOTE:
YOU COULD REVERSE THE
DIRECTION OF THE FLIGHTS
AND FLY CHENGDU–LHASA FIRST

Lhasa
Loops
Namtso
Tidrom
LHASA
Shigatse
Gyantse
Yamdrok Tso
Everest base camp

KEY
-----▶--- Driving route
-----✈--- Flying route

Namche
Barwa
TAR

INDIA

MYANMAR
(BURMA)

Kunming

Tagong KHAM
Litang
Kangding

Chengdu

Deqin
Xiangcheng

Zhongdian

N

Bradt

0 ━━━━━ 200km
0 ━━━━━ 125 miles

sorting out paperwork for Tibet, which will be forwarded to a related agency in Zhongdian. Then proceed from Chengdu by road to Tagong, Litang, Xiangcheng and Zhongdian. Pick up Tibet permits and tickets in Zhongdian via the contact from your Chengdu agency. Having spent time at altitude in Kham, you should be reasonably acclimatised and can hit the ground running when you fly into Lhasa, taking full advantage of the expensive sorties there. After flying Zhongdian–Lhasa, explore central Tibet for a week to ten days or more with driver and guide – either looping to Namtso or heading for Everest base camp, or both. Trek add-in: you could do the Ganden to Samye trek. Following the foray into central Tibet, return to Lhasa and fly back to Chengdu (or fly to Kunming).

Note that there is no direct flight from Chengdu to Zhongdian. On the first leg of this loop, you could fly Chengdu to Kunming and change planes for Kunming to Zhongdian, or go by road from either Chengdu or Kunming to Zhongdian. Paperwork for Tibet should still be done in Chengdu. Zhongdian–Lhasa flights are low frequency: be sure to book ahead from Chengdu.

Another Chengdu loop to consider: pick up paperwork in Chengdu, fly from Chengdu to Lhasa, and take it easy for the first few days to acclimatise. Then explore central Tibet towards Everest base camp for the next week or longer. Fly from Lhasa to Zhongdian. From here you can trek on your own where you please, hitting the towns of Xiangcheng, Litang and Tagong on the road to Chengdu. Or proceed by road from Zhongdian through Kham down to Kunming, and exit overland to Vietnam.

Another exit route to consider: leave Tibet by train from Lhasa to Xining, and weave your way south through Amdo and Kham *en route* to Chengdu.

LINEAR ROUTES: THE ROAD TO KATHMANDU A longer, linear route design: start in Chengdu, and arrange your group entry and itinerary for Tibet, but specify you will fly from Zhongdian to Lhasa (not from Chengdu to Lhasa). You can then proceed by road from Chengdu to Kham (no permits required), spend time there and acclimatise well to altitude, get on a plane from Zhongdian to Lhasa, tour central Tibet without having to worry about altitude adjustments, and exit by road through the Kyirong border to Kathmandu in Nepal. This trip would take at least three weeks.

Variation for central Tibet: drive from Lhasa to Namtso and on to Shigatse. Then go off-road to Everest base camp for a few days, with the option of trekking in the area.

For those who love epic overland journeys, try this route: start from Kunming and journey north the entire length of Kham and Amdo to Xining, then arrange a train ticket to Lhasa. With a prearranged small group, tour central Tibet and move

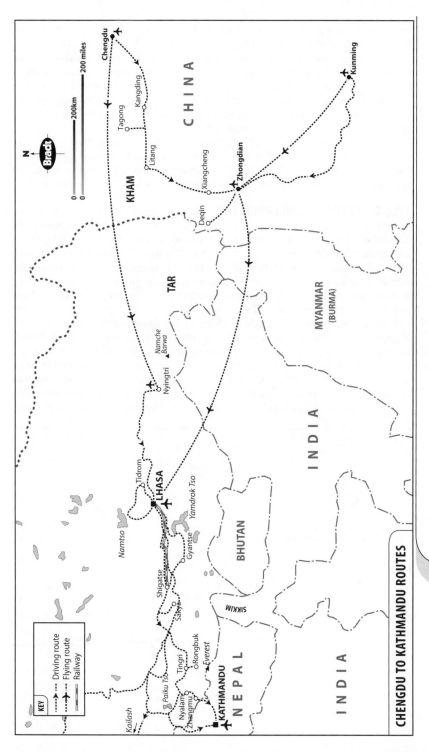

KEY
---- Driving route
--+-- Flying route
==== Railway

0 [====] 200km
0 [====] 200 miles

N

Bradt

CHINA

KHAM

TAR

Chengdu

Kangding

Tagong

Litang

Xiangcheng

Deqin

Zhongdian

Kunming

MYANMAR
(BURMA)

Namche
Barwa

Nyingtri

INDIA

Tidrom

LHASA

Namtso

Yamdrok Tso

Gyantse

Shigatse

BHUTAN

Sakya

SIKKIM

Paiku Tso

Tingri

Rongbuk

Everest

INDIA

Kailash

Nyalam

Zhangmu

KATHMANDU

NEPAL

on to Everest base camp and tackle the Kailash trek. Then drive past Lake Paiku Tso, head for the border town of Kyirong, and proceed to Kathmandu, Nepal.

Bad strategy: attempting that same trip in reverse. The reason is that you are entirely at the whims of the Chinese Embassy in Kathmandu when it comes to approval for Tibet – and these visa folks are sure to cancel a long Chinese visa you have previously acquired and replace it with a visa valid for the length of your fixed group-tour itinerary in Tibet, which might only be ten days. That's why the direction of travel is of great importance.

Coming from the other direction, from Tibet into Nepal, getting a Nepalese visa on arrival is a breeze. What will work, starting from Kathmandu, is a round-trip loop, flying Kathmandu to Lhasa and returning overland to Kathmandu. The agency in Kathmandu arranges the Chinese visa for the length of the tour.

TOUR COSTS AND POSSIBLE PROBLEMS Travel in Tibet is expensive. Getting there by air is expensive. Touring around in rented vehicles is expensive. Most foreigners travel the Tibet Autonomous Region in a rented vehicle with driver and guide – a combination that runs to more than US$240 a day, depending on the agency used, the itinerary and other factors. Three to five passengers can share the cost of a vehicle. A lower-cost arrangement is to travel in a larger group, say 12 people, using an arranged minibus. If you want lower-budget options, consider travel to Kham and Amdo, where group touring is not required.

Let's say you fly from Chengdu to Lhasa, spend three nights in Lhasa, drive to Namtso Lake (overnight), then drive to Shigatse (overnight), on to Sakya or Shegar (overnight), then Everest base camp (overnight), then head to the Nepal border. That's eight action-packed days and seven nights, with maybe one or two spent in the bathroom with altitude sickness. Such rapid trips are not recommended due to lack of time for acclimatisation, but for pricing purposes, this itinerary covers a lot of ground. You would be looking at about US$2,800 for the trip: split between four

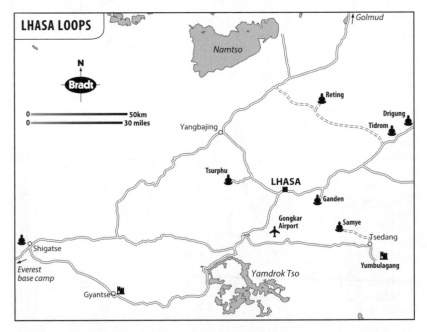

people that's around US$700 each, not including airfares and meals. If you have fewer than four passengers, expenses naturally go up: with two passengers, you could be looking at Tibet on a thousand dollars a week (each).

In a vehicle with four passengers, here's how it might break down. A tour guide at Y250 per day for eight days costs Y2,000 for the group, or Y500 a person. (For currency information see pages 78–81.) Permit price is around Y1,300 a person including express mail from Lhasa for permit delivery in Chengdu. Hotels in larger cities cost around Y300 for a double room; in smaller places, Y60 a bed. Total for entry fees for various monasteries along the route will be about Y650 per person. Add the entry fee at Everest base camp at Y180 a person plus Y400 fee for the vehicle to go there. Hire of a vehicle for the five-day tour (not used in Lhasa) is Y1,500 a day, including cost of driver and petrol. The return fee from the Nepal border (because the driver may come back empty) is an extra Y1,500. On top of this are the one-way Y1,700 airfare from Chengdu to Lhasa, and airport taxi pick-up for the group at Y200. Not included in the calculation are meals and drinks (probably around Y100–150 per person per day), extra charges levied at monasteries and sights for photography, and additional costs incurred for emergencies.

Negotiating for vehicle hire Because you are paying up front for hotels, tours with vehicle, driver and guide, here are some bargaining chips. The best idea here is not to pay everything up front. Leave a deposit (say 20–50%), with the rest to be handed over in Lhasa after you arrive there and have met your guide and driver and have looked over the vehicle. Think about what would happen if the trip gets cancelled (either by you or the agency) or if you fall sick during the trip and must leave early. What happens if your vehicle breaks down and cannot be fixed? What happens if the road is blocked by landslides? What are the provisions for a full or partial refund? It would be good to get some kind of written contract covering these items. Another thing to bargain: you do not need a vehicle for every day in Lhasa. Build in some time for walking around the old quarter by yourself, and thus no need to pay for a vehicle for those days.

It's important to be flexible with vehicle arrangements: you can't push your driver if a bridge is down, and you won't get much out of a driver if you back him into a corner. On a contract, put down a rate for extra days. If a delay is caused by the driver or vehicle breakdown, then the agency covers the cost; if the delay is due to illness of a passenger, the group covers the cost; if the delay is due to bad weather or road conditions, you can divide the cost between the agency and the group.

Some questions to be raised. What are you paying for exactly? Are your hotels included or not? What standard of hotel? Who pays for the accommodation and food for driver and guide? Who pays entry fees to the temples and other sites? One difference will be the hotel standard: you can save money by using budget hotels in Lhasa but you will lose on clean bathrooms.

In a number of cases, it appears that agencies subcontract. In Lhasa, I wanted to visit the office of the tour agency contracted from Chengdu, but it turned out there was no bricks-and-mortar office. The contact in Lhasa worked from his apartment and put together a driver with a guide at the last minute for the trip. When asked for a receipt, the contact produced a letterhead bearing the logo of a company that I had never heard of.

You need to go over everything to clarify so there are no misunderstandings or shoddy arrangements. Get copies of all itineraries and paperwork. Insist on a Tibetan driver and Tibetan guide only. Insist on a vehicle in good shape. The road to Kathmandu is well maintained, and so is the road to Everest base camp. Most agencies use Hyundai or Buick small vans that seat seven or eight passengers. But if you intend to go somewhere on a dirt track, such as Kharta (Everest east base camp), then you will need a 4x4. Insist on no smoking in the vehicle, and insist that mobile phones be turned off inside the vehicle. The driver may attempt to use a mobile phone while driving down a huge switchback, which could prove fatal. The guide may blabber on the mobile phone to his friends in Lhasa for the entire trip unless you pull the plug.

And a very important point: tell your agency that you are running the timing, not the guide or the driver. Some guides will take charge and try to control the itinerary. There is some flexibility here. What lies on the road between towns like Lhasa and Gyantse can be truly spectacular, and worth lots of stops for photography. The guide may try to rush you through that landscape because both driver and guide have seen it all many times before. The easiest way to deal with this is to tell the driver and guide that you are all very keen photographers and expect to be stopping in many spots for photo-ops.

You may have absolutely no problem with your vehicle – just a few loose kidneys at the end of the ride. But some travellers tell horror stories about vehicles that break down (or disintegrate) in transit, drivers who refuse to follow the itinerary, belligerent guides – the nightmare goes on. A last thought on travelling: make sure you get along with the others in your group, as you'll be seeing a lot of them. If you spend 20 days on the road to Kailash, you'll want congenial company. Compatibility is a very important consideration for long road trips like this.

LOSING YOUR SHADOW If you can afford it, arrange 'free days' to be built into your itinerary, with no destination or sights specified. This will give you more flexibility and allow you the freedom to explore on your own. On paper, the reason for these 'free days' would be to allow time for acclimatisation. For example, you could build in two or three extra 'free days' for Lhasa. These extra days need not be consecutive – they can be scattered. On the free days, you will not need a vehicle and driver, so that will bring the cost down. However, in theory you still need a guide shadowing you.

Here's how this might work: if you arrive fully acclimatised from, say, Kham you could step off the plane in Lhasa, lose the guide on one of your free days, rent a mountain bike, and ride all over town – on your own. Follow-up strategy: how to wear your guide out. A shocked guide, upon discovering that I rented a mountain bike in Lhasa, insisted that he had to accompany me. So I arranged for him to get a mountain bike too, and we rode out to Drepung Monastery, which is a steep climb on a bike. He was knackered by the time he got there, and I suggested that he take the rest of the day off – which he did, allowing me to carry on with my own agenda. However, I probably could not have gotten into Drepung on my own: Drepung is one of the renegade monasteries where the PSB keeps a very close eye on the monks and screens all visitors.

You might enjoy the company of your guide, in which case there is no need to follow these suggestions. Your guide may be very knowledgeable and know all the right places to go, and be great to talk with. Or your guide might just be there on duty, looking blank and bored, following you around like a shadow.

It's very useful to have a mobile phone to contact your guide when needed in situations where you might run into trouble (he speaks on your phone for you), and also to liaise with guide and driver about when you want to depart. As a foreigner, you are expected to have a guide at all times while in Tibet, but there's nothing stipulating how long the guide is meant to be with you each day. It could be 6 hours, or it could be 2 hours. You decide. If you want to strike out on your own to explore, the important thing to do is to get copies (colour photocopies are best) of any permits or documents that the guide normally keeps. Those documents enable you to fob off curious officials if questioned as they provide you with a layer of legitimacy.

TOUR OPERATORS

INTERNATIONAL GROUP-TOUR OPERATORS The majority of travellers to Tibet are on group tours. The Chinese would prefer that all foreigners travel this way. Why? Because tours are easy to monitor and because they get a sanitised version of Tibet. Participants are carefully insulated from the Tibetans, and chaperoned by Chinese guides with a totally warped sense of history (and no sense of culture). Group-tour operators take care of all the logistical problems – permits, transport, food and so on – but in the process you may lose out on other dimensions. Group tours to Tibet are quite costly – even the ones organised out of Kathmandu rack up the bills. How high the bills go depend on style – some operators seek out the best hotels and food in each location. They will even arrange comfortable tents for sites considered lacking in hotels of a decent standard (ie: clients will not like what they see at the outhouse). An example of this is Tidrom hot springs in central Tibet: fabulous location, but disgusting toilets at the humble guesthouses there, so high-end groups camp out in a valley close by.

On the plus side, group-tour operators seem to magically transcend all the permit obstacles, and offer a guaranteed timetable. They can mount trips and treks that individuals drool over – the vanguard of what's possible. Groups cross the border from Kailash into Nepal or India; they trek into the Karta Valley east of Everest; they engage Bactrian camels to trek into K2 base camp north of Ali; they cross the Nepalese border into Tibet with their own Western truck and driver. Some European outfits have been permitted to use their own truck and driver on the route from Kathmandu to Lhasa and onwards into Qinghai and Gansu: one of these is Dragoman (w *dragoman.com*). Expeditions liaising with Tibet Mountaineering Association (TMA) or Tibet International Sports Travel (TIST) have arranged a number of firsts – taking on trekking peaks, white-water rafting, mountain biking, hot-air ballooning and paragliding in Tibet. Commercial rafting companies have made test runs along some sections of the Yarlung Tsangpo Gorges and claim there is potential for guided trips. Because of the specialised nature of these trips, a group may be assembled from clients from different continents through outfit liaison.

For business reasons, many operators play the game of not offending Chinese sensibilities. However, some operators have Buddhist links and provide a tour leader who is a Western cultural expert well versed in the history and culture of Tibet. Funding generated from these high-paying tours may not benefit the Tibetans – if considering an operator, enquire whether your driver and guide will be Tibetan. If you are embarking on a trekking or mountaineering type of tour, enquire about equipment and safety conditions for porters, as the tour company is responsible for their well-being. Outfits that combine innovative trips with small groups and an ethical approach would be the most desirable.

International adventure-touring operators such as Exodus (UK), Geographic Expeditions (USA), Wilderness Travel (USA) and Intrepid Travel (Australia) can easily be located online. Your trip hinges on the knowledge and skills of the guide. Enquire about the staff: will you get a Tibetan driver and Tibetan guide, or will you be escorted by a Chinese guide who doesn't speak a word of Tibetan?

TOUR OPERATORS ON THE GROUND The listing here is for a handful of agencies that are on the ground in Tibet. They are Tibetan-managed, use Tibetan drivers and guides, and offer imaginative choices such as photography journeys, wildlife tours or Tibetan homestays.

Tibet EcoTravel w tibetecotravel.com. This outfit is a collective of 18 tour operators spread across the plateau, from Lhasa to Shangri-La & back again. Lots of great ideas can be gleaned from surveying the website. Once you find a suitable operator, you can contact them directly from the information provided. The agencies are mostly Tibetan-run & operated, & adhere to the concepts of ecotourism & responsible touring. See ad, page 46.

Himalaya Journey ☏+1 253 289 9166 (USA); ☏+44 20 3239 2917 (UK); ☏+61 2 8003 5630 (Australia); ☏+977 980 300 1060 (Nepal); e info@himalayajourney.com; w himalayajourney.com. Arranges trips in Tibet, Nepal, Ladakh & Bhutan. Owner & lead guide is Jamin 'Lobsang' York, who has decades of experience with travel in Tibet & the Tibetan world. See ad, page 45.

Explore Tibet 4–5 Hse, Namsel No 3, Doudi Rd, Lhasa; ☏0891 830 5152; ☏+124 0778 0765 (USA); e sales@ExploreTibet.com; ⓢ ExploreTibetTour; w ExploreTibet.com. Explore Tibet is a Tibetan-owned operator. The general manager is Sonam, based in Lhasa. This

outfit is involved in supporting some community projects.

Tibet Highland Tours m 1390 898 5060; w tibethighlandtours.com. One of the longest-operating companies in Lhasa, Tibet Highland Tours specialises in all areas of the TAR, including the eastern regions of Lhoka & Nyingtri.

Kham Voyage m 1838 218 6668; w khamvoyage.com/en/. Based in Chengdu (Sichuan), this Tibetan-owned company is headed by Nyima Tashi from the Kham region. He arranges unique photography & cultural journeys that usually involve homestays or monastery stays.

Mystic Tibet Tours m 1820 971 5464; w mystictibettours.com. Based in Xining (Qinghai). Tibetan owner Gonkho serves as the lead guide for this company, which specialises in treks & cultural journeys in the more remote mountains of Amdo & Kham.

Gesar Tour m 1390 976 9192; w gesartour.com. The only international travel agency based in Yushu (Qinghai). It organises wildlife tours, photography journeys & cultural tours all over Yushu & Ganzi prefectures.

SMALL-GROUP TOURING If you organise your own small group of three or four, you can liaise with agents in Chengdu or Xining and set up customised itineraries. This should be less expensive than going with a larger foreign operator. More time-consuming (and not guaranteed to work) is to find other like-minded travellers in these places and team up for an overland run from Lhasa to Kathmandu, sharing the costs. Agencies in Chengdu or Xining may be able to place you on one of their standard fixed-departure itineraries for a route like that but because more people are involved (could be ten on a bus), you will lose flexibility and will have fewer choices. You can also liaise directly with a travel agent in Lhasa to arrange your tour: see the shortlist of travel agents in the *Lhasa* chapter, page 133. This would probably mean using Lhasa as your starting point.

NON-GROUP TOURING The only freedom you will have as an independent traveller is in the Kham and Amdo regions, outside the TAR. Here, solo travel is fine, and it is considerably cheaper than group touring in the TAR. You can try a mixed approach – join a group for touring the TAR, then revert to independent travel in Kham and Amdo. Make sure your Chinese visa covers all bases.

RED TAPE

This may sound odd, but the best place to get a long Chinese **visa** is within China – in Hong Kong. Hong Kong, since the handover, operates as a Special Administrative

Region (SAR), with the Chinese Embassy simply altering its name to PRC Visa Issuing Office. The office is located in the China Resources Building in Wanchai – you can approach this office yourself, but travellers usually go through agents for convenience. In short order, in Hong Kong, you can pick up a one-month visa (can be processed next day, HK$350/US$45). Multiple-entry visas are possible, valid for one month each entry. Some travellers, especially Americans, may only be granted a one-month visa. A three-month visa for HK$350/US$45 was previously available but now seems elusive. The Chinese Embassy insists on receiving passport photos taken with a light blue background: the travel agency can arrange this.

There are certain things with which you should be careful when applying for a visa. Do not mention Tibet or Xinjiang as destinations. Travellers have had their visa application knocked back solely for doing this, and been told they need special permission to travel to those places. Safer destinations to mention are Beijing and Shanghai. Reason for visit: tourism. Your job: do not put reporter, journalist, writer, photographer, missionary, diplomat or politician, as your visa will not be processed. These people require special permission to travel in places like Tibet – this involves a complex procedure that may not succeed. Travel agents in Hong Kong will advise you how to fill in the application.

Visas have a coding on them: the L visa (*luyo*) designates a regular tourist; the F visa (*fangwen*) is a longer 'business' visa, also issued to cultural exchange students – this visa can raise eyebrows if you stray into Tibet; the Z visa is issued to those working in China. A visa issued in Hong Kong may start running immediately (from the date of issue), which means you'll lose a week or so just getting to Tibet. Visas from other embassies usually start from the date of entry into China, and will give you a two- or three-month leeway to get there.

According to the Chinese, Tibet is an integral part of China. When you apply for the visa, however, do not mention you want to go to Tibet. While a Chinese visa is good for Tibet, authorities there may not extend your initial visa in Lhasa without fulfilling demands like joining a tour. Therefore get the longest visa you can – two months, three months – at the point of origin. Not all Chinese embassies abroad are created equal. Some will grant you three months, others two months maximum, and still others only one month.

Embassies closer to China are the most liberal in issuing longer visas, it seems. Hong Kong is good (three-month visa or longer is possible); Hanoi is not bad (two months possible); Islamabad offers a two-month visa; the Delhi embassy may provide a two-month visa if prodded (but otherwise will only issue one month); the Bangkok embassy normally issues visas of only one month. You might try your home country to see if you can wangle a three-month visa. Explain that China is a big place and you need a long time to see it all. Visa extensions are dodgy within Tibet, but may be possible in big cities in China.

Applying for a Chinese visa in Kathmandu is troublesome, because the Chinese Embassy there is in the habit of only issuing visas for the length of a tour to Tibet booked through an agent in Kathmandu. You cannot apply to the embassy as an individual: you can only approach them through a travel agent. If you already have a Chinese visa issued elsewhere and apply for a short Tibet tour in Kathmandu, the embassy in Kathmandu is likely to cancel it and reissue another visa valid for the length of the tour. If you do not want this to happen, argue the case that you want to fly on from Lhasa to Beijing after their tour and need the extra visa time.

CHINESE EMBASSIES AND CONSULATES Chinese embassies and consulates abroad are approachable for longer visas. Enquire whether the visa starts running immediately. Chinese embassies and consulates are found throughout Europe, Africa, the Middle East, Central Asia, Asia/Indian subcontinent, Australasia/Oceania and North America.

There are Chinese embassies/consulates in Cambodia (Phnom Penh); India (Delhi, Mumbai); Indonesia (Jakarta); Japan (Tokyo, Osaka, Fukuoka, Sapporo, Nagasaki); Laos (Vientiane); Malaysia (Kuala Lumpur); Mongolia (Ulaanbaatar); Myanmar (Yangon, Mandalay); Nepal (Kathmandu); Pakistan (Islamabad, Karachi); Singapore; Thailand (Bangkok, Songkhla, Chiang Mai); and Vietnam (Hanoi, Saigon).

For a complete listing of Chinese embassies and consulates, with full address data including fax and email addresses, consult the website of the Ministry of Foreign Affairs of the PRC (w *fmprc.gov.cn/eng*). Click on 'The Ministry' link in the top bar for addresses for relevant embassy websites – these provide information on visa requirements and even downloadable visa application forms.

Within Asia, visa validity varies considerably. You may be able to wrangle a two-month visa in Hanoi or Ulaanbaatar, but only one month (maximum) might be given in Bangkok. Islamabad may hand out two months, but New Delhi only one month. Some visas allow up to three months to get there; others may start running immediately.

FOREIGN EMBASSIES AND CONSULATES There are no foreign embassies or consulates in Tibet to provide assistance if you get in to trouble; the best advice is to get right out of Tibet as fast as you can – fly to Kathmandu or Chengdu. There is a US Consulate in Chengdu, but that would be of dubious assistance if you are an American in Lhasa.

CUSTOMS AND SEARCHES Official Chinese sources specify that you cannot bring into China any material (CDs, DVDs, films, tapes, etc) that is 'detrimental to the political, economic, emotional or moral interests of China'. That's a very wide net. Does that include Lady Gaga and Britney Spears videos? Even if you are on a domestic flight from Chengdu to Gongkar, you may have your bags searched (body searches are rare). Customs and checkpoint searches in Tibet are of the hit-and-miss variety. Some are waved through, others get the third degree. If a suspicious item is found in a vehicle, all the baggage may be searched. Your baggage may be searched on entry to Tibet, while in Tibet, and on exit. Military checkpoints on the Kathmandu to Lhasa route are on the lookout for material readily purchased in Kathmandu, such as Dalai Lama pictures or tapes. Some foreigners have been hauled off at a military checkpoint and questioned about books in their possession – one of these was an autobiography by the Dalai Lama. On exit, Chinese customs may be looking for 'antiques', which means anything Tibetan that is older than 1959. One passenger had a souvenir prayer wheel dismantled at Lhasa Airport upon exiting, to see if any messages from Tibetans were being carried in it. In case that makes you feel really paranoid, I hasten to add this was highly irregular.

ALIEN HEALTH DECLARATION You may be required to fill in a Passenger Health Declaration when flying into China or Tibet. It starts out: 'Any Alien suffering from AIDS, venereal disease, leprosy, psychiatric disorder or open pulmonary tuberculosis is not allowed to enter the territory' and goes on to solemnly ask you to declare if you are carrying any biological products, blood products, or old clothes. Your health certificate may be asked for, but probably won't be. Other things you are not allowed to bring in: poisons of all kinds, opium, and foodstuffs from epidemic zones.

The map on page 64 shows major access points into Tibet, as follows (clockwise from Chengdu):

From Chengdu, Sichuan Main air gateway to Lhasa, with daily flights, and other flights to Nyingtri, Shigatse, Yushu and Ngari. Within Sichuan, flights to Daocheng, Jiuzhaigou, and Kangding. Rail route from Chengdu via Xining to Lhasa. Rough overland route to Lhasa, but may be closed. Frequent flights to Beijing/Shanghai, Hong Kong/Shenzhen/Guangzhou, and Hanoi/Bangkok/Singapore.

From Chongqing Direct flights to Lhasa, also to Nyingtri. Direct flights to Hong Kong and Macao.

From Zhongdian, Yunnan Low-frequency flights to Lhasa and Kunming. The Zhongdian–Lhasa flights are staggered in winter months. Rough overland route from Zhongdian to Lhasa may not be open.

From Kunming, Yunnan Several flights a week via Zhongdian to Lhasa. Rough overland route to Lhasa, but may not be open to foreigners. Bus route to Hanoi, Vietnam. Frequent flights to Bangkok, Chiang Mai, Hong Kong. Less frequent to Hanoi, Singapore, Vientiane, Phnom Penh and Rangoon.

From Gangtok, Sikkim Overland road route linking Gangktok (Sikkim) up to Gyantse and Lhasa, opened in 2006 after Beijing finally relinquished its territorial claims to Sikkim. Not much sign of foreigners using this route. The border crossing is at 4,500m Nathu La pass. This is mainly used by locals for cross-border trade.

From Kathmandu, Nepal Direct flight to Lhasa. Or spectacular overland route to Lhasa via Kyirong border crossing. Flights are suspended for the winter months (November–March inclusive). Frequent flights from Kathmandu to Hong Kong, Bangkok, India and Europe.

From Kashgar, Xinjiang Rough overland route via Ali to Lhasa by sleeper bus is most likely off-limits. Rail, road and frequent flights to Urumqi. Spectacular Karakoram Highway route to Islamabad in Pakistan.

From Golmud, Qinghai Rail connection to Lhasa started in 2006, roughly paralleling the road route. The Golmud–Lhasa run is the main overland route into Tibet.

From Xining, Qinghai Direct flights to Lhasa. Also flights to Yushu. Rail connection via Golmud to Lhasa.

From Yushu, Qinghai Direct flights to Lhasa, and also to Xining. Overland route to Lhasa.

Many travellers choose to enter Tibet from one point, such as Chengdu, and exit from another, such as Kathmandu, giving the opportunity to travel more widely in the region.

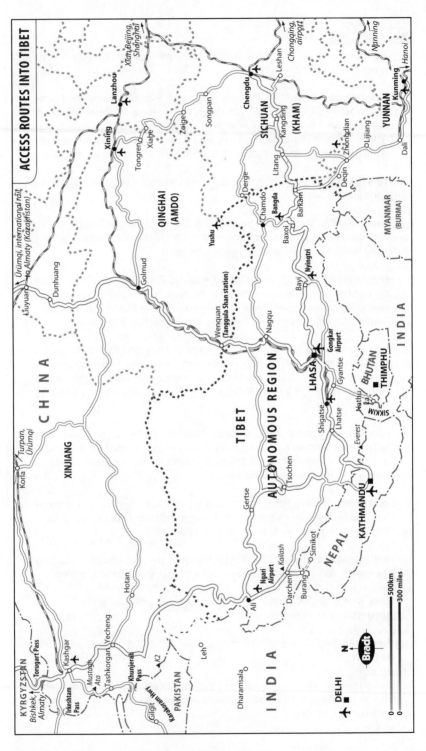

ACCESS ROUTES INTO TIBET

Ürümqi, international rail to Almaty (Kazakhstan)

Xian,Beijing, Shanghai

Chongqing, airport

Nanning

Hanoi

Lanzhou

Leshan

Chengdu

SICHUAN

YUNNAN

Kunming

Xining

Tongren

Xiahe

Zoige

Songpan

Kangding

Zhongdian

Lijiang

Dali

Zoige

(KHAM)

Litang

Deqin

Derge

QINGHAI
(AMDO)

Chamdo

Bangda

Barkam

Baxoi

Golmud

Yushu

MYANMAR
(BURMA)

Dunhuang

Liuyuan

Wenquan
(Tanggula Shan station)

Nyingtri

Bayi

Nagqu

CHINA

Korla

Turpan,
Ürümqi

Lhasa

LHASA

Gongkar
Airport

Gyantse

BHUTAN

THIMPHU

INDIA

XINJIANG

TIBET

AUTONOMOUS REGION

Shigatse

Lhatse

Nathu
La

SIKKIM

Hotan

Tsochen

Everest

Gertse

NEPAL

KATHMANDU

KYRGYZSTAN

Bishkek,
Almaty

Torugart Pass

Kashgar

Yecheng

Tashkorgan

Mustagh
Ata

Khunjerab
Pass

Simikot

Darchen

Burang

Irkeshtam
Pass

Ali

Ngari
Airport

Kailash

Leh

K2

Karakoram Hwy

Gilgit

PAKISTAN

Dharamsala

INDIA

DELHI

N

Bradt

0   500km
0   300 miles

64

Getting into Tibet is a two-, three- or four-part operation. First you need to cue up arrangements well in advance with an agent for the TAR itinerary. Then you have to make it to a staging-point such as Bangkok, Hong Kong, Kathmandu or Chengdu. Then you wrangle with more paperwork and ticketing, run the gauntlet of Chinese officialdom into China, and strike for Lhasa. Think of this exercise as 'hitting the roof' – an oblique reference to the way you will feel when you deal with Chinese officials. It's also what will probably happen to you when you ride in a rental vehicle in Tibet.

ROUTE STRATEGIES Direction of travel becomes very important in Tibet. Getting in from Kathmandu to Lhasa is a killer (problems with permits and altitude), but exiting from Lhasa to Kathmandu is a piece of cake. Because Nepal to Tibet is an international arrival, it leads to many more visa and red-tape complications. Travellers obsessed with getting to Tibet go to great lengths: having found their route stymied in Kathmandu, some travellers have flown all the way back to Hong Kong and *back* to Chengdu, and then *back* to Lhasa! (There's also a direct Kathmandu–Chengdu flight, but it is very expensive). If you look at the map, you can see why that rerouting costs a small fortune as opposed to a direct Kathmandu–Lhasa flight. Occasionally Chengdu is blocked too – possibly because of some Chinese official visiting Tibet – and travellers have proceeded all the way up to Golmud by land, and then overland to Lhasa.

More than in most places, you need to think about your route to and from Tibet because of visa complications. There's only one consulate in Lhasa – the Nepalese (you actually don't need a Nepalese visa as you can pick it up on arrival). That's fine, but what about going overland to Kashgar, via Xining, and then exiting on the Karakoram Highway into Pakistan? The nearest place for a Pakistan visa is Beijing. The overland travel situation is much easier in Kunming, which has consulates for Vietnam, Laos, Burma and Thailand. Visa acupuncture points for Asia include Kathmandu, Hong Kong, Bangkok, Hanoi, Singapore, Beijing, Islamabad and Delhi. Some visas are readily available upon arrival by land or air: these include the Nepalese visa, Thai visa, and Hong Kong entry visa.

TTB monopoly Since 2000, the Chinese-government-operated TTB (Tibet Tourism Bureau) has created a monopoly for hire cars in Tibet. The main agent dealing with the 'Tibet permit' in places such as Chengdu, Kunming, Shanghai and other points is likely to be the TTB-affiliated office. So TTBS is Tibet Tourism Bureau of Shanghai (w *tibet-tour.com*). There are also TTB offices in Hong Kong and Kathmandu. The TTB monopoly intensified after 2008 demonstrations by Tibetans across the plateau, effectively clamping down on all individual travel in the TAR.

Staging points The first stepping stone for many is to get to Hong Kong Special Administrative Region (SAR), Bangkok or Kathmandu. More information on these can be found in the sections following.

Hong Kong SAR No visa is required of most Westerners for stays of a month or longer in Hong Kong SAR. Supposedly, the economic, social and legal status quo will stay in place for 50 years from the handover to China on 1 July 1997. However, this promise fell apart after just five years when dissident Harry Wu was arrested at Hong Kong Airport, held for half a day and deported. Falun Gong members have

Practical Information   GETTING THERE AND AWAY

2

65

been refused entry at the airport also. There is pressure from Chinese authorities on the media and certain taboos are in place, amounting to self-censorship of sorts. Taboo topics include the Falun Gong, insulting senior Communist Party leaders, advocating independence for Taiwan or Tibet (or Hong Kong), and being off the mark about the Tiananmen Square Massacre. The *South China Morning Post*, once among the most opinionated newspapers in Asia, laid off most of its foreign staff and replaced them with mainland stooges as reporters and editors.

All that said, there's a wide range of books available in stores, with material on Tibet freely available, but for how much longer is not known.

In 2015, five colleagues from a publishing house called Mighty Current were abducted either in mainland China or elsewhere (one in Thailand). Mighty Current specialised in scurrilous novels about the sex lives of top Chinese leaders, which obviously got them mighty annoyed. One publisher later appeared on Chinese TV, tearfully confessing to a crime he supposedly committed ten years previously. Another was dispatched back to Hong Kong to retrieve a list of all his client readers, but he decided to stay and tell all about his abduction. Bookstores around Hong Kong yanked the contentious titles off their shelves, along with a lot of other titles critical of Chinese politics. The litmus test for a bookstore that hasn't yanked titles is to enquire innocently if they have any books about Falun Gong organ harvesting, or the Tiananmen Square Massacre. Hong Kong is a good place to stock up on cash US dollars, medicines or whatever else you are short of.

Chinese visas are easy to get in Hong Kong SAR, and can usually be obtained within a few days. There is a direct charter flight from Hong Kong via Chengdu to Lhasa once a week, but this is only for groups and is quite expensive. You can achieve a similar routing, but at far reduced prices, by pre-booking an air ticket from either Shenzhen or Guangzhou to Chengdu. You proceed overland from Hong Kong to Shenzhen or Guangzhou and transfer to the airport the same day. The more scenic option is the ferry to Shenzhen, which connects with an airport shuttle bus.

A recommended agent is:

Phoenix Services Agency Room 1404, 14th
Floor, Austin Tower, 22–26 Austin Av, Kowloon;
☏852 2722 7378; e info@phoenixtrvl.com

Bangkok, Thailand No visa is normally required for most Westerners arriving in Thailand for a stay of one month. Bangkok is the major hub of southeast Asia, and an excellent place to go shopping – or visa shopping. ATM machines abound, and it's easy to turn US travellers' cheques into cash US dollars at banks, on low commission, normally around 1%. To get around town, you would be wise to keep to the Skytrain, underground Metro, or the Chao Praya express boats – everything else crawls. There are good bookstores in Bangkok: the two largest English-language book chains in Thailand are Asia Books and Bookazine. The Kinokuniya chain runs two mega-bookstores (the largest in the city) – one located on Siam Paragon Store's third floor (Siam Skytrain) and the other in The EmQuartier (Phrom Phong Skytrain).

Agents can arrange visas and ticketing onwards from Bangkok, with direct flights to Chengdu or Kunming. One stumbling block from Bangkok is that the Chinese Embassy there will only issue a 30-day visa. Khao San Road has a large cluster of travel agents – make sure the phone is plugged into the wall. A reliable agent in the Silom area is:

STA Travel Wall Street Tower, 14th Floor, Room
1406, 33 Surawong Rd; ✆ 02 360 262; e help@
statravel.co.th; w statravel.co.th

Hanoi, Vietnam You need a visa in advance to gain entry to Vietnam. Two-month Chinese visas may be possible to wrangle in Hanoi within a few days. Getting from Hanoi overland to Kunming in Yunnan is cheaper than flying. Hanoi is a very pleasant city, with lakes, cafés, bicycle rentals and streetside beer stalls (the beer is cheaper than bottled water). You can obtain cash US dollars from the Vietcombank for a small commission charge (changing from US dollar travellers' cheques). From Hanoi, you can take a train to the Chinese border, then transfer for a stunning bus ride on the Chinese side to Kunming, twisting through mountainous terrain. From Kunming, you could board a plane direct to Lhasa if your paperwork is in order, or continue by rail to Chengdu and arrange a package to Lhasa from there. An alternative is to fly from Hanoi direct to Kunming. A reliable agent in Hanoi is:

New Indochina Travel 60 Tran Vu St, Truc Bach
Lake; ✆ 844 715 0343; e new-indochina@fpt.vn.
This agent is the STA representative for Vietnam.

Direct air routes Flights into Lhasa are usually on Boeing 737s or 757s, Airbus A340s or A320s, operated by regional carriers Tibet Airlines (TV), Air China (CA), China Southern Airlines (CZ), China Eastern Airlines (MU) and Sichuan Airlines (3U). All five carriers fly from Chengdu to Lhasa. You may still see some CAAC signs around the place, and it may pop up in the inflight magazines. CAAC stands for Civil Aviation Administration of China, which was the state monopoly until it was broken up into regional carriers, with Beijing-based Air China taking a large slice of the pie. Starting up in 2011, Tibet Airlines is a regional division of Air China that is based at Gongkar, the main airport near Lhasa. China Southern Airlines is based in Guangzhou, while China Eastern Airlines is based in Shanghai. Hopefully, the different carriers will induce some competition, because Lhasa flights remain overpriced.

Chengdu (pages 69–70) is the main domestic gateway to Tibet, with the best connections and options, and numerous daily flights – sometimes ten a day or more. Flights from other destinations may be less frequent, with fewer carriers. There are other flights coming into Lhasa from Chongqing, Xian, Zhongdian, Kunming and Kathmandu.

Approximate durations on flights to Lhasa are: from Kathmandu, 1 hour 10 minutes; from Chengdu, 1 hour 45 minutes; from Xian, 2 hours 30 minutes. No sign of any Tibetan pilots yet – call back in another 25 years or so – but there may be some Tibetan stewardesses on the planes; they wear striped Tibetan trim on their aprons. This is progress. Inflight films may introduce you to the wonderful world of Tibet, but you would do a lot better looking out the window; the remote and savage snowy ranges between Chengdu and Lhasa are the stuff that dreams are made of.

You will not be allowed to purchase an air ticket to Lhasa from any destination unless you have the right paperwork, meaning you have to go through an agent in those places.

Gongkar Airport Pilots landing at Gongkar – which serves Lhasa – must be trained in aerial manoeuvres at 3,700m. Due to air currents, most flights in or out of Tibet are often scheduled for the morning, as the wind can pick up in the

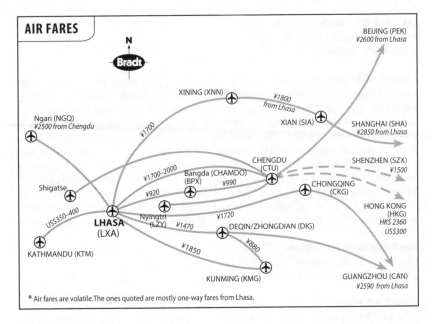

* Air fares are volatile. The ones quoted are mostly one-way fares from Lhasa.

afternoon. On arrival at Gongkar your baggage may be searched, even if you are on a domestic flight. Gongkar Airport is about 75km from Lhasa and takes an hour by road on the Galashan Tunnel route. This 2,447m-long tunnel bores right through a mountain and is connected to long bridges at both ends. The Galashan Tunnel route shaved half an hour off the previous Gongkar–Lhasa route, which went via the 3,788m-long Tsangpo Bridge located just west of Galashan. A taxi from Gongkar Airport into Lhasa varies from Y130 to Y200. There is lodging and food in the town of Gongkar, an easy walk from the airport. For information on departing Tibet by air, see page 130.

Other plateau airports While there are a number of military airfields in Tibet, there are only a handful of civilian ones. Nyingtri Airport (elevation 2,955m, located close to Bayi, east Tibet) has a tricky landing, with planes having to approach along a winding valley. This is the second-largest civilian airport in Tibet, and takes the pressure off Lhasa, with many Chengdu–Nyingtri flights daily, and connections direct to Chongqing. There are more links upcoming for flights to Beijing, Xian, Kunming, Guangzhou and Shenzhen.

For leapfrogging from the TAR into Tibetan areas outside the TAR, there is a flight from Lhasa to Yushu (Qinghai), with further connections from Yushu to Xining or Chengdu. In Kham, a large airport at Zhongdian (3,275m) in Diqing Tibetan Autonomous Prefecture (upper Yunnan) started operating in 2000. The airport is officially named Diqing Shangri-La Airport: this lies in Yunnan, outside the TAR, so no permits are required to fly into this place from Lhasa. You can also fly from Zhongdian to Lhasa on a package deal similar to those offered in Kunming (from where the flight originates).

Ngari airfield, 30km from Ali (west Tibet) has limited domestic flights to Lhasa. Bangda Airport, located about 100km south of Chamdo, is probably off-limits to foreign travellers. It ranks as one of the highest airports in the world, at 4,334m. It takes an hour to fly from Lhasa to Bangda. There is another flight from Bangda to Chengdu. Confusingly, Bangda is also called Bamda, Pomda and Changdu (so there's a Changdu–Chengdu flight). In northern TAR at Nagqu is an airfield that eclipses Bangda's record by 100m. Nagqu Airport, at 4,436m, opened in 2015, but it's not so useful since the train runs from Lhasa to Nagqu.

Some sample airfares (one-way): Kunming–Lhasa Y1,850; Zhongdian–Lhasa Y1,470; Beijing–Lhasa Y2,600; Shanghai–Lhasa Y2,850; Xining–Lhasa Y1,200; Chengdu–Lhasa Y1,800; Kathmandu–Lhasa Y2,540.

Chengdu gateway Chengdu, in southwest China, is the main air gateway to Lhasa, with year-round flights and sometimes more than ten flights a day. The flight into Lhasa crosses the snow caps of eastern Tibet, with great 757 wingtip vistas. Flight time is 1 hour 45 minutes. This is the most reliable way to reach Tibet. Chengdu has frequent onward connections to destinations such as Beijing, Shenzhen, Guangzhou and Hong Kong SAR; international connections from Chengdu can be made to Bangkok, Singapore and elsewhere. Chengdu has a handful of consulates, including those of Thailand, Singapore, South Korea, USA, France and Germany.

Renewal of your Chinese visa in Chengdu can take a week. Agents recommend a trip to see the Big Buddha at Leshan, where your visa may be extended overnight.

Because it mounts the most regular flights into Tibet, Chengdu is a magnet for individual travellers, who can be packaged into set-group itineraries by local agents. The coding on the air ticket is CTU–LXA (Chengdu–Lhasa). Peak months, with heavy bookings, are July and August. Apart from the Chengdu–Lhasa route, there are less frequent Chengdu–Lhasa–Ngari flights, and Chengdu–Shigatse and Chengdu–Nyingtri departures. You can connect to many parts of China via Chengdu. Chengdu Airport is located 12km from downtown Chengdu.

Chengdu agents Travellers can form their own small group of say two or three and approach agents in Chengdu to set up a customised itinerary. This will take time to get off the ground, so start it rolling and then go and visit the pandas and the Leshan Buddha. Permits and air tickets must be arranged: the paperwork is sent to the TTB and must come back after approval. The minimum turnaround time is two working days, and it could take longer. If you plan to go to Kailash, for instance, permits will take four days to obtain. You can work ahead via email to set up paperwork so that it proceeds faster: the agent will probably ask for a deposit. To save time, some agents can book you on a train to Lhasa without a permit, and send the paperwork to the guide, waiting for you in Lhasa. In that case, you will need a letter of agreement from the agent explaining all this in Chinese. Work well in advance for planning all this: go to the agent websites to get the latest information. Another strategy is to start the paperwork in Chengdu, then leave by road for Zhongdian, and pick up your permit and air ticket there (forwarded by the same agent).

Some travel agents to contact:

Kham Voyage m 1838 218 6668; w khamvoyage.com/en. Based in Chengdu, this Tibetan-owned company is headed by Nyima

Tashi from the Kham region. He arranges unique photography & cultural journeys that usually involve homestays or monastery stays.

Other travel agents can be sourced in hotels, such as:

Lazybones Hostel (40 rooms) Yangshi Jie, north of the Mao statue; ☎ 028 653

77889; e chengduhostel@hotmail.com; w chengduhostels.sxl.cn/home. This hostel has dorms & dbls & is well run. Décor uses parodies of Mao-era posters & other avant-garde artwork. Run by the same folks is Mix Hostel, 23 Ren Jia Wan; ☎028 832 22271; e mixhostel@hotmail.com. Both hostels can set up Tibet touring, but they go through bigger fish to cue it up.

Hello Chengdu Youth Hostel (170 rooms) 211 North Section 4, First Ring Rd; ☎028 819 79337. Formerly known as Sim's Cozy Garden Hostel, this cavernous enterprise promises to get you anything you want in the way of travel wishes, including local panda tours, Tibet permits, onward flights, etc.

Permits to enter Tibet all pass through TTB Chengdu, located in Room 1418, 14th floor of Tibet Hotel, at 10 Renmin Bei Lu. You cannot get a permit directly through them – you must go through an agent. Tibet Hotel has both an airline office and a travel agent within: the latter is called Sichuan Everbright (☎*028 831 98329*).

Kunming gateway The flight from Kunming to Lhasa via Zhongdian goes several times a week. A one-way air ticket costs Y1,850. For bookings, the best plan is to stay at the Camellia Hotel (*Chahua Binguan; 96 East Dongfeng Rd;* ☎*0871 6516 8818; dorms Y30, dbls from Y100–300*). The Chamabar, located in the Camellia Hotel compound, is a good place to chat with travellers (and on the internet too). Kunming is connected by overland route from Hanoi in Vietnam (pick up a Chinese visa in Hanoi), and you can go overland from Luang Namtha in Laos to Kunming (pick up a Chinese visa in Vientiane – could be a multi-month visa).

Kunming agent The main agent for Tibet travel (overland or by air) is Mr Chen (*Room 3115, No 3 Bldg, Camellia Hotel;* ☎*0871 318 8114*).

Zhongdian gateway Several outfits in Zhongdian can arrange travel to Tibet but, because of less competition, these agents are pricier than those in Chengdu. You would be better off arranging a tour from Chengdu, and picking up paperwork in Zhongdian (such as air ticket and Tibet permit). Flights from Zhongdian to Lhasa are low frequency, so it is essential to book ahead in peak months. The air ticket to Lhasa is Y1,470 one-way. Going overland from Zhongdian to Lhasa is a very expensive 4x4 trip, costing around US$3,500 for the journey. At the time of research, this route was closed, but was rumoured to be reopening. See the section on Zhongdian, page 286, for accommodation details.

Zhongdian agents Khampa Caravan, at the centre of Zhongdian (☎*0887 828 8648; e info@khampacaravan.com; w khampacaravan.com*) offers package tours and overland tours to Lhasa for a hefty tariff. Also try the TTB-affiliated office (*Room 2206, Shangbala Hotel;* ☎*0887 822 9028*).

Xining Gateway Since the Lhasa line opened, Xining has stepped up to the plate as a viable staging-point for Tibet – going by train, of course. There are flights to Lhasa, but these are irregular (Xining is a stop on the flight from Shanghai to Lhasa). See pages 310–11 for more about Xining accommodation.

Xining agents There are several agents that deal with the Tibet trade, including:

Mystic Tibet Tours m 1820 971 5464; w mystictibettours.com. Tibetan owner Gonkho serves as the lead guide for this company, which specialises in treks & cultural journeys in the more remote mountains of Amdo & Kham.

Snow Lion Tours Suite 408, Xiadu Dajie St; ☎0971 816 3350; e info@snowliontours.com; w snowliontours.com). They also have an office in Lhasa.

Tibetan Connections 18th floor, #5 Guoji Cungong Yu; \0189 9720 0974; e info@ tibetanconnections.com; w tibetanconnections. com.

Other Chinese gateways The flight from Beijing stops in Chengdu, then continues to Lhasa. Frequency may vary from once a week to daily; in any case, the Chengdu–Lhasa leg is daily. Less frequent flights go to Lhasa from Guangzhou via Chongqing (rumoured to be once or twice weekly), or to Lhasa from Shanghai via Xian and Xining (two or three times a week). There are several snags involved with these flights. The first is that they are very expensive – Beijing to Lhasa is Y2,520 and Shanghai is even more expensive. Listing of a flight on a timetable does not guarantee that the plane will actually depart. Chinese planes may only fly when seat space is sufficiently filled: if not, the plane could be cancelled or delayed.

Kathmandu gateway The only international flight into Lhasa is from Kathmandu, Nepal. A group of five may be required for ticket reservations. Flights should be booked two to four weeks in advance through a travel agent. The flight costs Y2,540 one-way (US$390). To go from Kathmandu to Lhasa you need a full package price with an organised tour, including air ticket, hire vehicle, Tibet permit, accommodation, the whole shebang – probably with a minimum of eight days. It would cost at least US$800 per person for an all-inclusive week in Tibet, round trip to Kathmandu, in a group.

In Kathmandu, it seems that everyone can offer a tour to Tibet, but beware. Most of these companies operate as subcontractors and may cancel tours at the last minute due to lack of clients. They have a tendency to tell you what you want to hear: that expenses are all included (when they are not), that you can leave after the tour in Lhasa and carry on by yourself (unlikely), and that you can get a visa extension in Lhasa (highly unlikely). Make sure you know what services you are paying for, and are getting the itinerary you desire.

On these tours, there is most likely going to be a group visa – a single piece of paper covering all the people involved, and this is not stamped in your passport. That means you will be forced to stay with the group to exit China because you have no other paperwork. There's one loophole: some agents can book you on an eight-day tour from Kathmandu overland to Lhasa, and then allow you to wander off on your own in Lhasa for a few more 'rest' days.

Agents in Kathmandu do not like it if you have a Chinese visa already stamped in your passport (obtained elsewhere) as this spells trouble. The Chinese Embassy in Kathmandu is prone to cancelling a visa issued elsewhere and replacing it with a group visa valid for the length of the tour you've booked. There's a (tiny) chance you can salvage the situation by leaning on the agent and impressing upon the Chinese Embassy that the visa should remain unchanged because you will be travelling onwards from Lhasa to the heart of the great Motherland (Beijing) and other parts of mainland China after the Tibet portion of the trip, and China being a very large country, this will all take time. There are no guarantees this strategy will work – in fact, the chances are not good. Other embassy games: normal visa processing fee is US$58, taking seven working days. For US citizens, it's US$144 for that visa. But for a group application for travel to Tibet, you will need to get a 'fast-track' visa that takes three days to obtain, and costs US$80 for most nationalities (or US$180 for US nationals). A one-day turnaround is again more expensive.

Despite the visa handicaps in Kathmandu, there are excellent agents who can set you up with great itineraries, and do it right. You could, for instance, cue up an entire trip to Kailash, starting with a flight to Lhasa, acclimatisation and touring in central

Tibet, and hire vehicle to Lhatse, meet a Nepalese crew of Sherpas in a truck there, continue to Kailash (camping out), complete the *kora*, then exit back to Nepal by road.

No Nepalese aircraft fly the Tibet route – it's all on Air China, so again the ticketing problems come up (you can't buy the ticket yourself). Kathmandu to Lhasa flights operate two or three times weekly in season (the flight is closed down for the winter months – November to March inclusive). Peak months, with heavy bookings, are July and August. The flight lasts 70 minutes, and goes straight over the Himalaya – the pilot uses Everest as a navigation landmark when turning. If you fly from Lhasa to Kathmandu, due to time zone differences you will arrive before you left – which is neither here nor there but a handy piece of trivia to know.

Kathmandu agents You can find information about Kathmandu agents, with address, email and website listings, at w kotan.org (go to the side panel for Tibetan Cultural Region Directory, then click on Nepal). Scores of travel agents handle trips to Tibet, particularly those around the Thamel district of Kathmandu. Some recommended agents are:

Eco Trek 320 Tridevi Marg, Thamel; ✆9771 442 4112; e info@ecotrek.com.np; w ecotrek.com.np. Covers overland tours as well as trips to Kailash.

Royal Mountain Travel Lal Durbar Marg; ✆9771 444 4376; e info@royalmt.com.np; w royalmt.com.np. See ad, page 108.

The railway Track for the Lhasa–Golmud (western China) line was completed in October 2005, with passenger services starting in 2006. The railway line closely parallels the road route, meaning that any sizeable town along the way is now a railway station. Along the line, there are 11 stations with permanent staff, 18 stations without staff, and five to ten scenic observation stops. The train can move at speeds of 100–160km/h, covering the 1,140km distance in half the time the bus takes, and in much more comfort. The railway carriages have a system of oxygen enrichment, which means feeding in oxygen as higher elevations are reached; there are individual oxygen tubes for passengers who are blue in the face. A great hardship for Chinese passengers is that smoking is forbidden at altitude, because of the potentially explosive combination of oxygen-enriched air and cigarette lighters.

Despite these precautions, when you are issued a ticket, you may need to sign a slip of paper that testifies that you are aware of the risks of altitude and swear you can adapt to elevations above 3,000m. Other conditions specify that passengers with 'diabetes out of control' or 'abnormal heart beats above 100 times a minute' will not be permitted to board. Nor will 'highly dangerous pregnant women'.

The highest station along the route is Tanggula Shan, which at 5,070m is actually the highest in the world. From Golmud and Xining, the railway system across China is accessible to Beijing, Shanghai, Chengdu or Guangzhou. The 4,000km rail journey from Beijing to Lhasa can be accomplished in a mere 47 hours by express train, with only six stops along the way – effectively ending Tibet's legendary isolation.

Pricing on the Lhasa line varies, factoring in agent surcharges, the type of sleeper acquired, and the season. In high season (June to September) prices spike because of heavy bookings, meaning agents have to pay touts to acquire sleepers. Some sample prices: Xining–Lhasa Y523 hard sleeper, Y810 soft sleeper (26 hours); Chengdu–Lhasa Y845 hard sleeper, Y1,100 soft sleeper (45 hours).

Much more lavish is an Orient Express style of rail travel being marketed by GW Travel in the UK and by RailPartners in North America. Their ultra-luxury carriages have bathrooms, television, gourmet meals and butler service, and a price tag to match.

Another railway route possible is west from Lhasa to Shigatse, a line that opened in late 2014. The 250km trip takes around 3 hours. Under construction at the time of writing is a line going east from Lhasa to Bayi.

Road routes into Tibet
There are two major road routes into Lhasa – one from Golmud and one from Kathmandu. China uses the metric system, and there are kilometre marker stones along all major routes, so you can track your progress. You can also use these marker stones to figure out turn-offs. In Tibet, there are usually road maintenance stations every 10km, just like in imperial Rome.

Roads in Tibet are designed with military and air force in mind. The 45-km drive from Shigatse Peace Airport into town is along a 25m-wide road, which can be used by armoured vehicles – or as a runway by lighter planes. The same is true of the highway built from Lhasa to Nyingtri airport. More Chinese are migrating to Tibet to build infrastructure – railways, roads, bridges, towns; according to official sources, highways across Tibet reached 80,000km in extent in 2016–an increase of nearly 19,000km since 2011.

Golmud route The 1,130km journey from Golmud to Lhasa is an overnight epic that qualifies for the most boring bus ride in Asia. Most skip it and take the train instead. Golmud (3,200m) is a bland town of 90,000. The mostly paved road traverses high terrain, passing the world's highest inhabited place (Wenquan, at 5,100m, established by the Chinese in 1955), and shortly after crossing Tangu La (5,180m). If you've left Lhasa and reached Golmud overland, you might want to look into continuing overland from Xining via Labrang to Chengdu – a great run through Tibetan areas. For more details, see pages 316–20.

Kathmandu route By contrast, the Kathmandu to Lhasa route cuts through diverse altitude zones and draws you past an enthralling Himalayan landscape. However, this route is better tackled as an exit, for reasons of permits, choices and altitude: see pages 201–35 for details. The first problem you will have is getting a Chinese visa. Unless you book a tour from Kathmandu, the Chinese Embassy will not issue a visa. The majority of travellers entering Tibet overland from Kathmandu do so on an eight-day tour; some negotiate a stay of a few more days in Lhasa on their own. A package includes land transport to Lhasa, hotels *en route*, and flight back from Lhasa.

Longer overland routes There are various epic routes into Lhasa that traverse the plateau and you get to see half of Tibet along the way. However, the following two road routes were closed at the time of research, though slated to reopen. **Chengdu to Lhasa** overland takes about 10–15 days without stops, and crosses some 15 high passes. Past Kangding at Xinduqiao, the route diverges, a northern branch going through Derge and Chamdo, and a southern route passing through Litang and Barkam. Both routes join up again near Bangda, and the road continues past Namche Barwa, the highest peak in eastern Tibet, at 7,756m. For a very long time, geographers speculated that there had to be a huge waterfall in the area close to Namche Barwa because the Yarlung Tsangpo dropped radically as it transformed into India's Brahmaputra River. There's no big waterfall, but the river stages a dramatic U-turn around Namche Barwa, cutting through the deepest gorge in the world.

Towns along the Chengdu to Lhasa route are mostly truck stops. Officials and truck-stop inns don't see a lot of foreigners, and problems can surface. One group that stopped at Bayi, was fined heavily for staying overnight at a non-PSB-approved hotel (PSB wanted them to stay at a very expensive approved hotel). Chengdu to

Lhasa is 2,400km via Chamdo (north route) and 2,080km via Litang (south route). Some details for these routes are given in the *East Tibet, Kham and Amdo* chapter.

Coming up **from Kunming** is a stunning route that travels through the scenic towns of Dali, Lijiang and Zhongdian before joining the route to Lhasa near Barkam. Kunming to Barkam is 1,200km, and it's another 1,100km from Barkam to Lhasa. Kunming is a good staging-point. If you're into long overland trips, you can reach Kunming from either the Lao Cai border (connecting to Hanoi by road) or the Ban Boten border (connecting through Laos to Thailand). Going the other way, there is a Lao consulate in Kunming and also a Vietnamese consulate, to enable land crossings into those countries. For Thailand, you can get a visa on arrival at any airport or land border crossing.

The wildest route of all into Lhasa is the 3,100km journey **from Kashgar** in the far west of Xinjiang province, southward through Yecheng and Mazar to Ali, and then on to Lhasa. The route traverses passes over 5,000m. That looks like a long stretch, but actually it can be covered in 12 days: one high-end hotel in Lhasa announced a trip using 800cc BMW motorcycles that took in Everest and Kailash along the way. The only problem was the price tag: Y44,000 for each person based on three riders. The old silk route trading town of Kashgar looks like it's a long way from anywhere, but actually it's only a few days down the Karakoram Highway from Kashgar to Islamabad in Pakistan. This is one of the greatest mountain road trips in High Asia, crossing the 4,700m Khunjerab pass. Another way of reaching Kashgar is from Bishkek (Kyrgyzstan) over the Torugart pass.

The Jules Verne challenge By stringing together some of these routes, you can develop a journey on a grand scale, clocking up over 10,000km by road. In 1992, the London-based adventure tour operator Voyages Jules Verne sponsored a car rally commemorating a historic 1907 race from Paris to Peking. The 1992 rally cars left London headed for Saigon, by way of Moscow, Tashkent, Kashgar, Yarkand, Shigatse, Lhasa, Xining, Chengdu, Nanning and Hanoi. Taking a cue from this, you can set up your own Jules Verne challenge. You can overland from Saigon up through Hanoi, continuing by road to Kunming and Chengdu, then go by road or air to Lhasa, continue by road to Kathmandu, and carry on overland all the way to Istanbul. A silk route variation would be to take the same trail to Lhasa, and head north to Golmud and Dunhuang, perhaps fly from Urumqi to Kashgar (or take a train), zip down the Karakoram Highway into Pakistan, and then travel overland to Istanbul. There's an international rail crossing from Urumqi to Almaty, connecting all the way to Moscow.

Routes restricted to high-end groups High-paying group tours walk to the Kojinath border crossing in western Tibet, trekking in for five days from Simikot (Nepal), and are then picked up by 4x4 to take them on to Burang, and up to Kailash. A similar trek up the Indian side, crossing at Lipu Lek pass, is sanctioned for high-paying group tours.

Opened in 2006 after a closure of more than 40 years is Nathu La pass, 4,500m, on the Sikkim–Tibet border. Currently, this route is restricted to locals crossing for trading purposes. If it were to open fully, this route would make it possible to travel from Gyantse (Tibet) to Gangtok (Sikkim). This was the main gateway for British access to Tibet by horse in the early 20th century, coming up from Kalimpong and Darjeeling. On the Tibetan side, the road passes viewpoints looking across at Kangchenjunga, the third-highest peak in the world. The mountain can be seen easily from Darjeeling and Gangtok in India.

Good heavy ammunition boots are the best for men, and stout ankle boots for women, and both may, if desired, be hobnailed. A pair of comfortable slippers are a great relief after the day's march is done, and should not be forgotten. Woollen socks and stockings are the best, and should be thick. To avoid chafing, boric powder should be dusted inside them before putting them on, and the toes and heels rubbed on the outside with soap. In the event of blisters developing, they should be pricked with a sterilised needle, Germolene applied, and a lint and cotton wool pad placed over them to protect them from further chafing while marching.

This paragraph comes from *Touring in Sikkim in Tibet*, a slim guidebook written in 1930 by David Macdonald, former British Trade Agent in Gyantse. He makes travel sound painful; in the 1930s, travellers rode or marched into Tibet with pack animals and an entourage of porters, carrying 30kg tents, a portable bath, hurricane lanterns, stove and so on. One porter was assigned to carry the tiffin basket, which contained crockery, cutlery and provisions for lunch. Times have changed – those 1930s travellers would be amazed at the strong, lightweight camping gear and clothing on the market now, with the wonders of Gore-tex and Velcro.

Even so, on a trip to Tibet, you may end up with a lot of gear. What to take? Pepper spray for the dogs? A shovel for the propaganda? A shortwave radio to get your news fix? A GPS device to find out where you are? All kinds of equipment spring to mind, but can you carry it? A good idea, before you set out, is to assemble all your gear, shoulder it, and walk a dozen blocks – or better yet, hike up the nearest mountain. Carrying luggage at altitude is much harder work than at sea level: the emphasis in your gear should be on strong, lightweight stuff that performs multiple functions. And you should remember that the gear you take is not the final weight: you may purchase souvenirs or books *en route*, not to mention food and drink, all of which will add to the burden, so you have to figure out where the weight lies, and how to reduce it without compromising on essentials such as medical supplies.

High on my list, in the clothing/footwear category, would be a good pair of hiking shoes with ankle support – lightweight, strong and well broken-in. You rely on your feet a lot in Tibet. The next priority would be a strong flashlight that has a long battery life (and a supply of spare batteries). Due to erratic or non-existent electrical supply in Tibet, you constantly need a flashlight – for illuminating dark frescoes in monasteries, for finding your way around at night, for visiting the outhouse at night, etc. Clothing for dealing with extremes of heat, cold and wind is essential. Rain and dampness are not so much of a problem, as Tibet is high and extremely dry. Dust is a big problem, though. Pure cotton clothing is of dubious value in the mountains because it takes too long to dry – if you sweat, the sweat stays, and you can freeze as a result. Quick-dry synthetics are preferable, such as nylon/polyester mixes with the feel of cotton, or else cotton/polyester mixes. Silk items favoured by skiers are ideal for insulating because they're lightweight and durable. You can find silk items made in China on sale in Lhasa, along with lots of cheap outdoor clothing of reasonable quality. A thick-pile fleece and a windproof jacket (Gore-tex is good) should provide protection against biting wind and cold. For more on clothing, sunglasses and protection from the elements, see pages 109–23, which has a rundown of essential medical supplies.

If you plan to get off the track in Tibet, you need a good sleeping bag, preferably rated to –10°C or even –20°C. These are bulky, but you'll find a Chinese quilt is much more bulky – though these are supplied in most guesthouses, off the track they may not be, and you can't afford to freeze or lose sleep. If a guesthouse is already warm enough, you can use a sleeping bag to cushion the bed. A sleeping bag with a down fill is recommended because it's compact, lightweight and insulates well – get one rated to sub-zero temperatures. You can buy cheap Chinese-made sleeping bags in Lhasa for under US$50. A compact Therm-a-Rest (ultra-light air mattress) is also a good idea in case you end up sleeping on the floor of a teahouse. You can buy a very lightweight one that packs up small. Keeping you off the ground with a layer of air will take care of cold temperatures as well as offering a comfortable night's sleep.

In the gadget line, an altimeter may be helpful – make sure it goes to 6,000m. Some wristwatches have in-built altimeters, so the question is not what time, but how high.

The selection of camping and outdoor equipment has vastly improved in Lhasa, with a string of specialised stores along Beijing Road and Tengyeling Road. You could arrive in Lhasa in a pair of shorts and a T-shirt and be fully outfitted for camping and outdoor clothing within a few days, and at low prices compared with similar items in the West. One of the top Chinese brands is Ozark, makers of tents and other camping equipment. Discarded expedition gear may also be on sale in Lhasa.

If you are planning to go cycling or do a lot of trekking, you might want to think about importing your own freeze-dried food and other supplies. Concentrate on food that can be 'cooked' by adding hot water to the package and letting it sit for a few minutes. This way you can use the vacuum flasks of hot water supplied in most hotels. While you can buy a stove in Lhasa, it might be an unwieldy kerosene one. If you want to be sure of a light, compact stove that operates off any fuel source, bring it with you. The rot-gut Chinese liquor sold in various parts of Tibet can power a stove.

What you bring really depends on what kind of trip you're planning. If travelling in a rental vehicle, consider that luggage space in the back is minimal if sharing with three other passengers. Obviously if you want to go trekking, you will need to be fairly self-sufficient gear-wise. You may find that your backpack or main duffle bag is out of reach, buried under other baggage. Thus you need to keep a daypack with essential items such as camera and so on with you; some daypacks have an external mesh holder for a water bottle. Within easy reach also should be the food supplies if you stop for lunch: some travellers purchase a cheap vinyl bag in Lhasa to hold food supplies and things such as candles, separating this from the main baggage. If staying longer in Tibet, you can use Lhasa as a base, so you could leave a duffle bag in guesthouse storage while off gallivanting around. Cargo duffles have lockable zippers on them to deter prying fingers.

While on the subject of locks and security, think about bringing your own small, sturdy padlock for hotel rooms. A number of rooms use a door-clasp secured with a padlock, but they will only supply one key. That's not convenient if you are sharing with three other people, as you would have to leave the key at front reception, and the reception person may be hard to find. A better idea is to carry your own padlock with four keys (you can have extra keys cut in the marketplace if needed). Or use a combination lock.

Bring all photography supplies with you. To rephrase that: bring a lot more digital storage cards than you think you'll need. If you're passing through, Hong Kong and Bangkok are good places to make prints. See the section on pages 90–1 for more details on filming in Tibet.

Electrical supply in Tibet is 220 volts, 50 hertz, with a variety of plugs; wall sockets mostly accept two flat-prong American plugs or two round-pin European plugs. Bring an adaptor. Supply is erratic, intermittent or unreliable, with possible blackouts. It's best to bring good battery backup, such as a power bank, for any electronic devices, and use the power supply from that to recharge your other batteries. A surge protector is a good idea. Some multi-plug units have a surge protector built in and so do electrical adaptors.

A couple of other notes on gear: if you don't have it, maybe your fellow travellers do. Message boards at the budget hotels in Lhasa carry ads from Chinese backpackers selling sleeping bags, camping gear, medicines – or even left-over oxygen. Travellers can become fixated with their stuff and spend hours in needless aggravation over what to take. Get that part over quickly and shift your attention to more important matters like plotting your route, reading up on the areas you plan to visit, reading up on Tibetan culture and learning some Tibetan language (buy a phrasebook). Knowledge is the most important thing to carry with you.

And while on that subject, a note about gifts: those inflight magazines and news magazines that you might discard elsewhere would be greatly appreciated within Tibet: they make ideal gifts because it is impossible to obtain foreign magazines in Lhasa.

MAPS Research all map material before you go to Tibet, and bring it with you. Within Tibet, if you have good Wi-Fi or mobile data access, you can check Google Earth mapping for locations or directions, but don't count on it being accurate. Google Earth maps use odd Chinese spellings for place names. An app that works without satellite is Maps.me (you need to download the Tibet module online first, and best to do this outside of China).

Within Tibet, the only maps available are Chinese-produced. The best place to find maps of Tibet is in Kathmandu, where you can even find pirated editions of maps that are long out of print in Europe, such as Stanfords' *South-Central Tibet: Lhasa to Kathmandu Route Map.*

Handy map collections can be found in several books. A highly ambitious project is *Mapping the Tibetan World* (page 364), a book that collates over 280 maps, with fine detail seen nowhere else, including trekking maps. Victor Chan's *Tibet Handbook*, though somewhat unwieldy (it has been christened 'Vic the Brick'), contains a collated set of *US Department of Defense Aerial Survey Maps*. These provide selected coverage of Tibet's topography – very useful for trekkers – but they are old, and while the geographical features are fine, the size and location of towns may have changed.

For sheet maps, Hungarian cartographic company GiziMap publishes several fine maps that cover the Tibetan plateau in detail. Canadian cartographic company ITMB (w itmb.com) publishes a map of Tibet with similar area coverage, as well as maps of neighbouring nations such as Bhutan. German cartography of Tibet includes Berndtson and Berndtson's *Tibet*; the RV Verlag/GeoCenter map *Tibet, Nepal and Bhutan*; and Himalayan maps in the Nelles series.

A series by Swiss-based Gecko Maps (w geckomaps.com) features *East Tibet* (road map), *Himalaya-Tibet* (road map), *Kailash* (trek map, plus a panoramic map), *Everest* (panoramic map), *Nepal* and *Kathmandu*. In the same series is the *Lhasa Map*, a superb theme map focusing on Lhasa's historic buildings (meaning traditional Tibetan architecture): this map is an offshoot of the book *The Lhasa Atlas*. Promoted as being waterproof and tear-resistant is a laminated double-sided map of *Tibet* by TerraQuest, including side maps of areas such as Everest. Since this map was published in 2013, some configurations such as road details have changed.

Tibetans themselves never really needed maps, nor bothered to create them, except in artistic renditions. So Tibetan-created maps of Tibet are a recent phenomenon, and an attempt to fight back on the cartographic front. From the Amnye Machen Institute in Dharamsala comes the highly detailed map *Lhasa City* (issued 1995), with a separate gazetteer in English and Tibetan. The map lists 590 locations, including sites such as educational institutions, prisons and PLA bases, which are of no interest to the casual tourist. That aside, the map provides an excellent overview of Lhasa, with contour lines useful for hiking sorties. Published in 1998 by Amnye Machen is *Tibet and Adjacent Areas under Chinese Communist Occupation*, with some focus on ethnic groups of the plateau.

Surely the strangest map guide ever produced is *On This Spot: Lhasa*, issued by ICT Washington, 2001. This unconventional map is backed up by a wealth of detail on Lhasa's rapidly changing face and its tragic human rights situation; it tells you what happens behind the scenes in the capital and includes some subversive photos. The map was released as part of an International Campaign for Tibet (ICT) initiative to educate travellers about China's occupation of Tibet, and to redress the balance in guidebooks on Tibet, which often omit information on the human rights situation. The map can be ordered through ICT's website (w *savetibet.org*). Also available from ICT is a double-sided map titled *The Eastern Regions of Tibet*, which gives details on Kham and Amdo, with a lot of historical annotations.

Within Tibet/China The only maps available within Tibet and the PRC are the Chinese-produced ones. This is probably because of 'cartographic correctness' – Chinese maps show all of Arunachal Pradesh lying in Chinese territory, much to the chagrin of India.

On sale in Lhasa are the following maps: *China Tibet Tour Map*, a foldout map of Tibet (published by the Mapping Bureau of the TAR, 1993), *Lhasa Tourist Map* (Chengdu Cartographic Publishing House, 2004) and *Tourist Map of Tibet*, with one side featuring Tibet, and the other side devoted to Lhasa (Xian Map Press, 2010). Significantly, there are few Tibetan-language maps for sale. The best map of China is a joint-venture effort between the Cartographic Publishing House of China and Liber Kartor AB, Sweden (1995): it's a large wall map, but you could slice off the Tibet part to make it easy to carry.

Maps are very cheap in China, but the maps published in English are weak in detail, while the maps published in Chinese are more complete (a kind of reverse censorship – the Chinese need to find their way around their own colony but they don't want foreigners to access the material). For the traveller, maps with Chinese and English on them are best, so you can point to the characters for your destination when talking to Chinese drivers.

The basic problem with maps of Tibet is that the Chinese have all the data, but treat it as a military secret – it's only partially revealed in Chinese-produced maps. On Western maps, there are conflicting names for destinations depending on whether the Tibetan name, the Chinese name or the old English name is referred to, and which transliteration system is used. Everest, for example (English name), is known as Chomolungma in Tibetan, and transliterated as Qomolangma in Pinyin Chinese. Maps of Tibet are an ideological battleground. Tibetan exile maps show Tibet covering the entire Tibetan plateau, while Chinese maps show the much-reduced area of the Tibet Autonomous Region, created in 1965 (Xizang Province). Street names in Lhasa may be referred to by a Tibetan name (such as Dekyi Shar Lam) or a Chinese name (Beijing Road). There are ongoing battles between cartography departments in China and neighbouring countries. Chinese maps continue to show Tibet extending into Arunachal Pradesh. Indian customs officials scrutinise books for any maps with these inflated borders, and handstamp over them this message: 'Borders neither authentic nor correct.'

MONEY AND PRICING

Two forms of readily exchangeable money are **travellers' cheques** and **US cash**. It's wise to carry some of both. Credit cards are of limited use in China and Tibet, and are only usable at major hotels in Lhasa (Lhasa Hotel takes them). Cash advances on a credit card are possible in Lhasa at the Bank of China (BOC). Changing travellers' cheques or US cash is not a problem within Tibet or China. The whole idea is that you spend lots of money, otherwise Tibet wouldn't be open, so you can find Bank of China branches in Lhasa, Shigatse, Tsedang, Ali and other large Chinese towns. If not, major hotels can change travellers' cheques. The two most widely recognised travellers' cheques are American Express and Thomas Cook. Although cash and travellers' cheques in different currencies are accepted by the Bank of China, in places like hotels or on the street, US dollars are more easily negotiated. If you're short on cash US dollars, you can convert US travellers' cheques into US cash at Bank of China branches for a little over 1% commission (so a US$500 cheque would net you around US$494 in US cash). There's a very small black market in US dollars, so if banks are closed, you can always change in a shop or maybe at a hotel reception desk.

Chinese currency is renminbi yuan (Y or RMB, people's money): it comes in denominations of 1, 2, 5, 10, 20, 50 and 100 yuan paper bills, and small change in the form of 100 fen to the yuan. The older 10-yuan bill shows Tibet – well, the north face of Everest – and one variety of the 50-yuan bill shows the Potala. Exchange rates hover at around Y6.3 (renminbi) to the US dollar (with travellers' cheques, a small commission is deducted by the Bank of China; rates should be uniform across the country). The rate is slightly lower for cash. Other relevant exchange rates are: Nepal, about 104 rupees for US$1 (there's a black market in US cash, with higher rates for bigger bills); and Hong Kong SAR: HK$7.8 for US$1.

Within Asia, you can use ATM machines to access your home bank account using your usual bank card with a four-digit PIN number. ATM machines are common in Hong Kong, Bangkok and Singapore, and can also be found in Kathmandu and a number of large Chinese cities (look for Bank of China ATM machines). ATM machines are not common in Tibet, but are available in Lhasa and Shigatse, where BOC branches dispense cash. You can also find them in Kham, in places such as Zhongdian and Litang.

DUAL-PRICING SYSTEM
Pricing in this book is quoted in either US dollars (US$10, for example) or Chinese yuan (Y20, for example) – and sometimes in Hong Kong dollars (HK$40, for instance). Because pricing fluctuates and is often negotiable, variations may occur. Pricing is not a problem for restaurants and hotels in Tibet – you get used to the expected prices fairly quickly. Prices are negotiable because of the Chinese dual-pricing system (one country, two systems). The highest expenses in Tibet are for long-distance transportation – ie: flights to and from Lhasa – and the cost of hiring a vehicle.

PAYING THROUGH THE NOSE
If you are from Europe, Australia or North America and have a beak-like nose, you are known as *da bizi* (big-nose) by the Chinese, or *waiguoren* (outland person) or *yangguizi* (foreign devil – derogatory). This is a kind of separate ethnic group – in the Chinese system, Tibetans are barbarians, and foreigners are aliens. The bigger the nose, the more you pay through it. Although in theory there is no dual-pricing system in China, in practice you can pay two, three, ten or a hundred times more for certain services. When you buy a Y100 (US$15) ticket to go and see the Potala, you are paying at least ten times the going price that a Chinese or Tibetan person pays. Negotiating prices depends on what you look like, how desperate you look, and how long you're willing to argue. You can bargain for student price for some items (such as the Potala entry ticket, and even bus tickets), but this argument may only be accepted if you're a student in

2

China, with valid ID. Chinese who live overseas (called overseas Chinese) are often charged a rate that is above the Chinese price, but lower than the Western price. Usually, the seller deduces they are overseas Chinese (or from Hong Kong) from their clothing or cameras. Westerners of Asian ethnic background who speak good Chinese can confuse Chinese sellers as they can't rank them in the pricing system.

BUDGETING

HOTELS AND GUESTHOUSES These can be easily sized up – they fall into budget/low-end, mid-range or group-tour (high-end) categories. In some places, such as Lhasa and Shigatse, there are five-star hotels. Rooms in five-star hotels in Lhasa start around US$150 and up. High-end (group-tour) hotels charge US$65 and up per room – the tariff can go to US$200 and up for suites in Lhasa. Mid-range hotels charge US$20–65 for the room (whether occupied by one person, two or three). Low-end guesthouses charge around US$10 per bed in two-bed, three-bed or larger rooms.

RESTAURANTS The cost of food is not really a big issue in Tibet, as food, if it is available, will be available at inexpensive teahouses or restaurants, costing around US$5 or less for a meal. Restaurants in deluxe Lhasa hotels could charge US$5–15 per dish. Above US$15 is expensive for Tibet. Occasionally, Chinese-run places might try to gouge Western customers by serving up something that looks like a banquet. Be wary of places that pile on extra dishes – ones that you never ordered – or lay on extras such as face towels and bowls of peanuts, as these will appear on the bill.

PERMITS AND ENTRY FEES Entry fees for monasteries and tourist attractions (forts, palaces, etc) are usually around US$5 per person, with the asking price for major monasteries hovering around US$10 (the Potala Palace charges US$30). Posted photo and video permission fees are high: US$23 for taking still photos at Tashilhunpo Monastery and US$275 for videoing.

Across the plateau, there are annoying entry fees to natural attractions, such as the Kailash circuit. Officials will chase you down and haul your vehicle over to inspect tickets – and if you do not have the right tickets, you will be charged on the spot. Permission and entry fees to get to Everest base camp chalk up a significant bill. Permit fees to visit certain parts of Tibet can be high, but usually one piece of paper is issued, so all names of passport holders can go on it to minimise costs. Alien Travel Permits (ATPs) cost only a dollar (for the group) but a military permit can be US$10 a person. Cultural Bureau permits for Zanda and Tsaparang can run to US$50 or so. The 'permission' to buy a plane ticket into Tibet can run to US$80 a person.

TIPPING Tipping is not customary in Tibet or China. There is no tipping in hotels, restaurants or taxis. Increasingly, however, those who are savvy in the tourist trade involving Westerners are looking for tips. You may want to tip the driver and guide at the end of a sortie. As with all tips, the amount offered should be contingent on doing a good job – and you should indicate this early into the trip as a way to leverage higher standards. Clothing (such as a down jacket) and equipment that is no longer needed would make good gifts. In Nepal, some trek operators work on a fixed amount, collecting in advance say US$3 a day from each client for the duration of a trek, then divvying up the pot at the end of the trip between the *sirdar*

THE BRIGHT FUTURE OF TOURISM

When not busy imprisoning monks or forcing them to renounce the Dalai Lama, Chinese authorities are preoccupied with building Tibet's bright socialist future. On the horizon are plans for more and bigger cities, improved roads, and an expansion of tourist facilities. Among Chinese tourists, Tibet is seen as an exotic corner of the Chinese realm. Miss Tibet contests have been staged in Lhasa, and fashion magazine crews from Beijing have arrived to shoot models on location (we're talking about cameras here). So you see a picture of a Beijing model posing in semi-ethnic gear outside the Potala, or posing next to pilgrims outside the Jokhang.

What's next? Well, the Chinese haven't really yet begun to tap Tibet's tourist potential. There's a lot of scope for mountaineering, trekking, horseriding tours, mountain biking, rafting, kayaking and other adventure sports. Golf in Tibet, anyone? Hilton Linzhi Resort near Nyingtri hosts Tibet's first highland golf grounds. In eastern Tibet lies Yarlung Tsangpo Grand Canyon – by far the deepest in the world, and barely touched by tourism. White-water rafting has been launched on the rivers of central Tibet, while the eastern region of Kham has hosted activities like cliff-jumping (paragliding). Less well advertised are hunting trips organised to parts of Qinghai Province whereby Western hunters are allowed (for large sums of money) to shoot rare wildlife such as Argali bighorn sheep as trophies. Car and motorcycle rallies across the rooftop of the world have been staged. Also on the board are plans for the creation of tourist theme locations, such as a therapeutic hot spring centre for health care, or a fisherman's island where tourists can learn about yak-hide boats (and cruise around in them).

(leader), the cook and the porters. That removes the tipping guesswork headache for the trekkers, and puts it back in the hands of the agency.

TRANSPORTATION Bicycle hire is about US$5 a day in Lhasa. Taxis are a few dollars to get across town. Local long-distance buses are cheap, even if you pay double as a foreigner. Hiring a Toyota Landcruiser or similar vehicle with driver and guide runs to about US$230 a day, depending on the agency, the itinerary and other factors. This rate includes the driver, the guide, the vehicle and the fuel, but nothing else. The formula is based largely on kilometres covered on the trip (fuel consumption), terrain (wear and tear on vehicle), rest days, and so on. The guide fee of US$25–40 a day is usually included with the cost of the vehicle.

GETTING AROUND

All roads lead to Lhasa. Sooner or later, you will end up there. Getting around the towns in Tibet presents little problem: they are mostly small enough to walk around. Larger cities like Lhasa, Shigatse and Tsedang have public buses plying the streets, and fleets of Volkswagen taxis roving around (you can also hire these by the day or half-day). Another taxi-like option is using the motorised three-wheelers and foot-powered trishaws as transport. Renting a bicycle is another excellent way of getting around, if you can find one (easy in Lhasa). In Shigatse, you can take a walking-tractor – a tractor with handlebars controlling the engine up front, and a carriage at the back – across town for a small tariff.

2

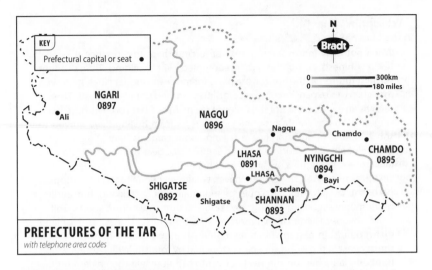

PREFECTURES OF THE TAR
with telephone area codes

PERMITS AND PREFECTURES Within Tibet you are classed as an alien, and you require an Alien Travel Permit (ATP). Various annoying pieces of paper with fancy chops (Chinese signature markers) and seals dog your movements into and around Tibet – this is not like mainland China where you can virtually travel without restriction. Apart from ATPs, other permits are issued: TTB, military, Foreign Affairs, Cultural Bureau permits. Foreigners are usually never shown these documents, nor allowed to keep them – they're classed as secret. The guide will keep the permits (you could try to get a photocopy). To get an overview of the complicated situation for permits, consult the map (see above) showing prefectures of the TAR with area codes. The TAR is divided into seven prefectures, each with its prefectural capital or seat, and each with its own telephone area code. Permits are normally only issued in the prefectural capital, although permits for any destination can be issued in Lhasa through agents. Key destinations of interest are found in the following prefectures.

Lhasa Prefecture Includes the key monasteries of Tsurphu, Drigung and Ganden, as well as Namtso Lake.

Shigatse Prefecture Gyantse and Everest base camp both fall in Shigatse Prefecture, as does Sakya.

Shannan Prefecture The prefectural capital is Tsedang. Other areas covered include Gongkar Airport, Samye, Yambulagang and Samding Monastery.

Ngari Prefecture Ali is the prefectural capital. Key sites include Mount Kailash and the Guge Kingdom.

BY RENTAL VEHICLE AND GUIDE The Chinese insist that the only way you (as a foreigner) can get around Tibet is in a hired vehicle (usually a Toyota Landcruiser or similar means of transport, such as a Hyundai van, Buick van, Toyota van or Mitsubishi Pajero) with a driver and guide. This works out to about US$230 a day which, split between four paying passengers, is less damaging. Most of the operators are connected to Chinese channels – routes may be monopolised by TTB-connected vehicles.

Vehicle hire is the greatest expense you'll incur in Tibet. Many vehicles operate on the Lhasa to Kyirong run (to the Nepalese border). You can possibly find them in Shigatse (but don't count on it). Most make use of Lhasa as the home base. One peculiar phenomenon you will have to deal with in Tibet is called 'hitting the roof'. This is when the vehicle (which has no seat belts) hits a rut and launches those in the back seat straight into the roof. It hurts! To soften the impact, think about wearing a wool hat or something similar. The idea of padded interiors has not caught on yet.

BY TAXI Taxis are intended to be a mode for getting around larger towns like Lhasa, Shigatse or Tsedang. However, they also commute from Gongkar Airport into Lhasa, a distance of around 75km, so think about this: they're much cheaper than hiring your own transport. Taxis are viable if the road is paved and in good condition: you can also hire a taxi by the half-day or full day and use it as your touring vehicle, which makes sense if three or four travellers get together to share the rental.

ON YOUR OWN You need considerable stamina, perseverance and devious ingenuity to mount your own trips in Tibet and break away from the vehicle and guide syndrome. In the pre-2008 days of Tibet travel, when permits were lax, travellers hitchhiked on trucks and took local buses, or proceeded on foot. Crazy dreamers have found ingenious ways of getting around inside Tibet. Back in the early days of independent travel in Tibet, in the 1980s, two Americans transported their kayaks up to Lake Manasarovar and started paddling the Yarlung Tsangpo – they made it part of the way. A young Englishman managed to bluff his way through the Nepal–Tibet border with a motorcycle, and he was out by the Great Wall by the time the authorities caught up with him. Others have rented (or bought) yaks or donkeys to carry their gear, and headed off on long hikes, and have indulged in camping and horse racing combination forays.

If you have money coming out your ears, of course, you can arrange to realise any dream you want through official channels. All the paperwork and aggravation might take some of the joy out of it, though. I've met several trios of motorcyclists from Europe who've been all over Tibet and Xinjiang on their imported bikes. They would not, however, divulge the cost of the entourage of vehicles accompanying them (with national guide, local guide, translators, medic, etc). A high-end hotel in Lhasa quoted a price tag of Y12,000 for each motorcyclist on a five-day sortie to Everest base camp (based on three riders, with BMW 800cc motorcycle supplied).

KAYAKING AND RAFTING Consult the website w windhorsetibet.com (click on 'River Journeys') for details about white-water rafting and kayaking in Tibet. This outfit handles everything from first-time rafters to first descents. Wind Horse Adventure also handles multi-day camping trips with horseriding, and adventure sports such as mountaineering, customised for small groups. See also w griffonexpeditions.com.

ACCOMMODATION

Except in larger towns like Lhasa and Shigatse, be prepared for very low standards of food and lodging. It's best to bring your own supplies as backup: bring a Therm-a-Rest (ultra-light air mattress) and a good sleeping bag to soften the beds and to stay warm, and bring packets of soup, or whatever, to compensate for the lack of restaurants. As an official guide and driver are required for all travel in Tibet these days, the tour operator that arranges your itinerary will book you into hotels that suit the budget quoted, usually ranging from 2-star to 4-star hotels. However,

ACCOMMODATION PRICE CODES

Based on a double room per night

Luxury	$$$$	Y950+	US$145+
Mid-range	$$$	Y460 to Y950	US$70–145
Budget	$$	Y130 to Y460	US$20–70
Shoestring	$	Y130 or less	US$20 or less

pre-departure, you should check on some of these hotels online to ensure that they are up to scratch – particularly in Lhasa – and that the operator is not trying to cut corners.

HOTELS AND GUESTHOUSES Low-end guesthouses, teahouse inns and truck-stop places generally offer a bed and not much else. These usually work out at US$2–5 a bed, in dormitory-type accommodation with perhaps four beds to a room. If there's a dirt floor, a lumpy bed and a tap in the yard, you've hit rock bottom. Bedbugs can be a problem in low-end hotels.

A notch up are Chinese concrete-blockhouse hotels, usually with several storeys, and possibly some internal plumbing. These places charge about US$10–25 for the room, no matter if your party is single, double or triple, so you can reduce costs by sharing. The more creature comforts you get, the higher the tariff. If you get your very own bathroom, with your own plumbing, rates are even higher. Because of shoddy workmanship, it often turns out that half of these gadgets fail to function, and yet you are paying for them being in the room. Some foreigners have successfully bargained down the price of a room due to absence of electricity to power devices such as the television. In this range are hotels designed for visiting Chinese, some of which may be off-limits to Westerners.

At the high end are group-tour hotels, with rooms from US$30–80 and up (if you have three people sharing a room, this may still only be US$20 a bed). These definitely have plumbing – and even hot water – and rooms with real light bulbs, and possibly even television reception. Even so, the prices for the rooms are often inflated, and discounts are frequently offered to tour operators. The hotel lobby often features a dining hall, souvenir shop, bar and so on. It may even have a foreign exchange counter and a small business section able to handle faxes and IDD calls. Even if you don't stay in a high-end hotel, you can wander in and shop or use the services there: naturally, the tariff will be higher than normal. There are hotels of this standard in Lhasa, and several in Shigatse, Gyantse and Tsedang. These high-end hotels may have cheap dormitories tucked away, so it's worth enquiring.

At the time of writing, homestays were not possible for foreigners visiting the TAR, but can be arranged outside the TAR in the regions of Kham and Amdo. Check the lists at these two websites: w plateauhomestays.org and w www.gaoyuanzhijia. com. About a third of the entries on these websites are homestays and eco-resorts.

Plumbing notes Although mid-range hotels in places like Lhasa and Shigatse provide hot showers, and solar-heated showers are popping up in places like Sakya, in more remote regions this could be a rarity. Off the track, you may be dependent on hot water from the large Chinese vacuum flasks at hotels, which is boiled up by solar cookers on the rooftop or with a furnace. Hotels do not automatically provide vacuum flasks. You may have to ask – or wheedle or cajole – to get one. By using a bucket or washbasin, you can manage basic ablutions. The hot water flasks can also be used for making soup or tea, and if you let it cool overnight, the water can be carried in your own bottle as drinking water. Tibetan and Chinese toilets are of the bomb-bay door design (squat and hope). They're usually filthy. In high-end hotels, there are Western sit-down models. When Shigatse Hotel started operation, fancy imported plumbing was brought in. An overweight woman on a group tour sat on one of these brand-new pieces of porcelain and the sit-down unit broke away from its mooring. The woman was not injured, but she was furious – she threatened to sue the manager over the poorly installed equipment. The hotel manager promptly confiscated the passports for the group and said that they would not be returned unless he was compensated for the full value of the imported plumbing that had been destroyed. Confronted with this, the group's tour leader decided to pay up.

✘ EATING AND DRINKING

Tibet is not noted for its culinary arts. China, however, is – ergo, find a Chinese-run restaurant if you want more variety. There's lots of variety in Lhasa – Tibetan, Chinese, Indian, Nepalese and Western cuisines are all available. On the streets you can find fresh fruit and vegetables in abundance, and fresh bread and tangy yoghurt. You can even get good fresh cheese imported from Nepal. Yak cheese is excellent, but only when made with Swiss or Norwegian technology (as it is in Bhutan, Nepal and in parts of northern India). There are some small cheese-making concerns in Lhasa that employ European technology, but more commonly what you'll find on sale are small pieces of rock-hard yak cheese, strung together like a necklace. These are almost impossible to eat, and are treated like sweets by the nomads, who suck on the pieces all day.

Tibetans are more inclined to run teahouses with low carpeted tables, which serve tea and *momos* (meat dumplings) and perhaps the odd potato. They offer lots of atmosphere, but not a whole lot of food. Lhasa is fine for food and so is Shigatse, but once out in the countryside, it's pretty much just noodles. In the wilder areas, it's *tsampa* (roasted barley flour) all the way. *Tsampa* is boring but quite sustaining, and you can mix it with soup or noodles (some connoisseurs add powdered milk or other substances to this Tibetan goulash). Not many travellers take to *tsampa*, though more take to army-ration biscuits. Chinese packaged goods are not much more appetising. Olive-green army cans with stewed mandarins or pork or something equally disgusting are resold on the black market. When travelling in Tibet, you should always bring along some food as a backup, for the times when you're stuck. You can load up in Lhasa on packaged soup and so on. Some bring in freeze-dried food from the West.

Bottled mineral water is available in Lhasa, Shigatse and larger towns in Tibet, where brands include Tibet Magic Water and Potala Palace Mineral Water. Cheaper than bottled water is Chinese beer. Since beer goes through a fermenting process, it's safe to drink, but this is not advisable at altitude until you've acclimatised (beer should not be drunk if you have the runs, either). Available Chinese brands include Huanghe (Yellow River), Lhasa Beer, Snow Beer and Pabst Blue Ribbon.

RESTAURANT PRICE CODES

Based on a main course meal, not including drinks

Expensive	$$$	Y100+	US$15+
Mid-range	$$	Y35 to Y100	US$5 to US$15
Inexpensive	$	Y35 or less	US$5 or less

On a bicycle you have the freedom to go at your own pace and enjoy unobstructed views of Tibet's spectacular scenery. It's easy to stop and meet people, admire the views, or grab that great photo opportunity. Maps and guidebooks, supplemented by recent internet postings, will help you plan the trip of your dreams. A search on the internet will turn up interesting travelogues of cycling in Tibet.

The rewards of cycling in Tibet come with challenges of sustained high-altitude travel, changeable weather, and toughest of all – permit uncertainties. In the past, the Chinese government's attitude towards foreign cyclists has ranged from very easy-going to intolerant. The whole region may close if major anti-government protests have taken place recently or are expected to take place. Don't let this worry you: Tibet has wonderfully adventurous cycling. Just have Plan B ready in case you don't get in or through. Tibetan areas outside the TAR are well worth visiting – you'll find the same culture and scenery without the permit restrictions in northwestern Yunnan, western Sichuan, southwestern Gansu and southern Qinghai provinces.

Several routes stand out for cyclists. The classic Lhasa to Kathmandu route runs through the heart of Tibet, passing famous monastery towns and fantastic Himalayan panoramas; a side road goes all the way to Everest base camp with an amazing view of the north side of the world's highest mountain. Nearing Nepal, you can experience a jaw-dropping 4,500m descent off the plateau from Tong La pass right down into subtropical valleys.

The ride across eastern Tibet between Yunnan or Sichuan provinces and Lhasa has ups and downs like no other place on earth, as you repeatedly descend into deep valleys of the Mekong, Yangtse and other great rivers, then climb high passes. Western Tibet is the toughest of all with vast distances, few places for supplies and long stretches of unpaved road. Only the most determined cyclists have pedalled all the way from Kashgar in China's extreme west via Mount Kailash and on to Lhasa. On longer hauls like this, you might want to consider a hybrid trip: cycle for part of the distance, then put the cycle on top of a vehicle for the remainder.

The Chinese have put great effort into improving the main roads in recent years, so cycling has become easier and less dusty. Food and accommodation have also improved with more places springing up. Camping and cooking gear are more a matter of personal choice than necessities on the main routes, though it's worth carrying a tent, pad and warm sleeping bag for emergencies, or if venturing into western Tibet or other remote lands. Cyclists have loaded up with as much as 50 days of supplies and disappeared into remote uninhabited regions to commune with the mountains.

The current mood of Chinese officials will affect what sort of trip you can do. If they are lenient you may be able to come and go as you please with just a regular Chinese visa. Border areas near India are very sensitive, and you can expect to be turned back if you get close. When officials follow strict regulations, your only option may be to go on a tour, which you can arrange through approved travel agencies. A tour will involve a guide, driver and vehicle as well as the permit. This is expensive, of course, but the more cyclists in your group the lower the cost per person. It might be possible to arrange a cycling guide without the costly car, so ask around to see if this is possible. If you're in a group and have the funds, it's worth thinking about arranging a tour even if not required for the added convenience of carrying gear and a safety backup. It's possible to have a cook come along, so you can camp and relax at the end of the day and wait to be served dinner. If tours are required and you have a low budget, consider that northern Tibet is the cheapest trip followed by Lhasa–Kathmandu, eastern Tibet, and the very long haul across western Tibet.

If you enter Tibet from Nepal, your only option may be on a tour with a group visa; any Chinese visa that you had beforehand will be cancelled. Getting the group visa changed later on to an individual visa to travel onwards through China may not be possible. If you wish to travel extensively in both China and Tibet, your best bet will be to enter China first on an individual visa, then go to Tibet and on to Nepal. And, of course, never mention 'Tibet' or 'bicycle' on your visa application.

Your own bicycle will probably be the best bet if you are comfortable with it and have the panniers and touring gear already sorted out. The other option is to buy a bicycle in Lhasa, Chengdu, Kunming, Hong Kong, or other large city in China. American mountain bikes made in Shenzhen (such as Diamondbacks) are sold around China, but these may take time to track down as they are mainly for export. You can also find Taiwanese-made mountain bikes (such as Giant brand) even in Lhasa. Panniers and accessories are available, too. Costs for bicycles and accessories tend to be lower than in more developed countries, but don't count on the same standards that you may be accustomed to at home. Long-legged cyclists may find seatposts too short and frames too small. One tall European tried to use a local mountain bike in Lhasa with a handlebar for a seatpost, but the arrangement never worked well. Avoid the cheapie Chinese-made mountain bikes, as brakes may fail and pedals break off. For shorter trips in the Lhasa area, you can rent your steed (page 131). Many young Chinese cyclists hit the road from Sichuan Province and ride on to Lhasa (or tackle sections of this route), and they often sell their mountain bikes in Lhasa, which explains the high-quality rentals available and why bicycle accessories are on sale here. The right accessories can be the hardest things to find – such as good bicycle water bottles. Cyclists revel in wearing a wristwatch that tells not only the time but the altitude – or having a handlebar cycle computer that does the same.

Opportunistic theft is a problem in the cities and something to be aware of in the countryside. Be sure to lock the bicycle and park it in an area where it looks like it's being watched. Bus and train stations are places where you need to be extra careful. At night, you can usually take the bicycle into your guesthouse or hotel.

The Chinese tend to be very helpful with taking bicycles on flights or the train. Either way, it's best to box the bicycle; bicycle shops sell boxes and enterprising Chinese were selling bicycle boxes on the sidewalk in Lhasa across from the Kirey Hotel, so ask around. Chinese airlines usually charge for overweight, but not for oversize. Trains charge a fixed fee: weight and size are not usually a factor. Your bicycle may go on a different train from you and must be checked at a separate parcel office. This is best done a day or two ahead of time.

Cyclists are a peculiar breed: talk revolves around headwinds, gradients, water quality and, in Tibet, animals. There are two animals to watch out for: yaks and dogs. Yaks are not a problem – they will bolt at the approach of a bike (mistaking it for a rival species?) but may upset the yak herder when they thunder off. Dogs, on the other hand, may come straight for you, fangs bared. The best strategy here is to pick up a stone, or at least pretend to do so. Dogs know what stones can do, as most Tibetans are crack shots. For more about dealing with dogs and cycling logistics, see box, pages 302–3.

2

TIBETAN FUSION Tibet is not famous for its cuisine. As anyone who has attempted to choke down a few cups of yak-butter tea can tell you, this drink is an acquired taste. And yet, paradoxically, yak-butter tea contains all the ingredients needed to counter altitude. It has a high fat content to counter the cold, and it has salt to restore hydration. It is healthy, but it could take a long time to get used to that rancid yak butter floating around.

Here's the thing: your taste buds don't work as well at altitude. The air is cold and very dry – and when the air lacks humidity, your nasal passages, mouth and throat lose their moisture, impairing your sense of smell and taste. At extreme altitude, everything tastes terrible – or else appears to be lacking in taste. Your perception of salt can drop by as much as 30%, while sugar perception dulls by up to 20%. But not all food turns out the same way. Some tastes actually improve at altitude. Airlines have discovered that flying along in a cabin pressurised to 2,000 metres, passengers develop a sudden craving for tomato juice – because it actually tastes better in the air than on the ground. Something to do with greater acidity. Certain red wine vintages do well at altitude, while others do not.

In 2017, Hong Kong-based Cathay Pacific introduced Betsy Beer, touted as the world's first hand-crafted beer designed to be enjoyed while cruising above the clouds at 11,000m. Heavens to Betsy! Among the ingredients is Dragon-Eye fruit, known for its aromatic properties, New Territories-sourced honey, and Fuggle, a hop that is a mainstay of British craft ales.

The most memorable dish I have ever eaten in Tibet was a plate of golden mushrooms that appeared in a humble restaurant in the middle of nowhere, was lightly cooked in sauce, and tasted fabulous. After that, I sought out these wild mushrooms in markets to buy, and would take them into a restaurant kitchen to have cooked up. There is tasty Tibetan food out there – especially when liberally interpreted by others, in India, or in the West. Here are some Tibetan fusion ideas.

Yak pizza On travels in Tibet, you will inevitably come across yak burgers (a matter of time before someone opens a chain called YakDonald's), yak sizzler (yak steak sizzling on a wooden platter), braised yak ribs, and yak-meat *momos*. In Tawang (India) you may be served yak-meat stew flavoured with spices and stinky fermented yak cheese that is aged several months or years. But here's another combination to consider: yak pizza. Want some yak cheese with that? Or olives? It opens up a whole realm of possibilities. When it comes to yak fusion, China has never been short on ideas for medicinal variations said to cure various ailments – cooking up yak tongue, braised yak hooves (don't ask), and yak-penis soup (definitely don't ask).

Yak cheese, European-style Cheese addicts will be ecstatic to learn that Swiss-style yak cheese is made in Langtang, Nepal. Huge barrel cheeses are said to be connected to a Swiss NGO aid programme. This nutty-tasting cheese finds its way to Kathmandu and Lhasa and is highly nutritious, being rich in protein because yaks eat a much wider range of herbs and grasses than cows do. Also, up Langtang way is a small operation run by François, who heads up Himalayan French Cheese. He produces a small yak cheese in the foothills and is working on making yak feta. He also thinks yak blue is going to work. That's right – a stinky blue yak cheese.

Vodka butter-chicken *momos* When *momos*, the dumplings that are Tibet's original fast food, crossed over the Himalayas to India, some weird things happened. Chefs in Delhi and Mumbai began experimenting, catering to fussy palates, and branched out with paneer *momos*, Mongolian *momos*, Afghani *momos*, Punjabi *momos*, and Mexican-style *momos*. Pineapple **momos** are popular in Mumbai. So are shitake *momos*. Taking the *momo* to dizzy new heights, a Delhi restaurant came up with a recipe for vodka butter-chicken *momos*. Vodka is kneaded into the dough and added to the filling of butter chicken. And in Mumbai, a chef has come up with a *momo* burger, which sees several *momos* placed between buns, slathered with red sauce, coriander sauce and mayonnaise.

Tsampa super-soup *Tsampa*, the roasted barley-flour staple of Tibet, is highly nutritious but tastes very bland. Some might say it tastes awful. Solution: add it to *thukpa* (Tibetan soup) to thicken the soup. While on Himalayan expeditions decades ago, Patagonia founder Yvon Chouinard discovered his sherpas relied totally on *tsampa* while on expeditions, turning their noses up at his donations of freeze-dried food. The sherpas would rehydrate their *tsampa* with boiling water, spices and yak butter to make a basic soup. Years later, Chouinard experimented and came up with some tasty variations on *tsampa*, by adding powdered soup, salmon jerky, parmesan and olive oil to the mix. This is sold by Patagonia Provisions as a kind of freeze-dried food. Or just bring your own parmesan and cans of olives into Tibet, and the *tsampa* might just work.

SHOPPING

Facilities inside Tibet are poor compared with those in neighbouring regions. Most of the infrastructure, buying and selling are concentrated in Lhasa, so you can glean more about shopping from the *Lhasa* chapter, pages 145–8, and the section on *Shigatse*, page 218. You can ship purchases (even very heavy ones) out of Lhasa without problem through China Post, the main post office. Carpet companies in Lhasa will arrange the shipping for you direct from their showroom.

ENTERTAINMENT

Unless you like karaoke bars, or parlours showing ear-splitting kung fu videos, nightlife is mostly limited to restaurants. There are some restaurant venues where Tibetan dance is staged (page 145). Tibetans frequent Nangma clubs in Lhasa, which stage singing and dancing shows – and beer drinking. For the performing arts, the best bet is to time your trip with a festival, such as the Yoghurt Festival in Lhasa or the horse-racing fair in Namtso.

PHOTOGRAPHY

Tibet is highly inspirational for photography, and you will find yourself clicking through lots of pictures. So when shooting **digital**, bring as many solid-state cards (CF, SD or micro-SD) as you can. This is due to potential problems at altitude: you could have a problem with a backup device that uses a hard drive. Manufacturers are reluctant to mention this, but many devices that employ hard drives are not guaranteed to work above 3,000m, because they spin on a cushion of air – and the air pressure is different at altitude, leading to possible crashes. You might have absolutely no problem – or you might end up losing all your photos stored on a hard drive. The solution to this is to use solid-state or flash-based memory. Try to get an external hard drive that is solid-state. There are laptops on the market that use solid-state drives (no moving parts). Apple's iPad uses flash memory. Digital pictures can be backed up to a 256GB USB memory stick, or burned to DVD as a backup at internet cafés in Lhasa. You can make prints from digital cameras at these places too, often within a few hours. Prints would make great gifts for Tibetan friends.

Film is sold in Lhasa, but the variety is limited and the quality is dubious: it's best to bring your entire supply in yourself (there is no limit to the amount of film that can be brought in). The light in outdoor situations in Tibet is so intense that you can make wonderful use of fine-grain slide film. You will probably want a polarising filter to reduce glare. Another situation commonly encountered is exactly the opposite: a dim interior where you need high-speed film, as flash may be forbidden.

Special photography hazards in Tibet include yak butter, fine dust and frozen batteries. In freezing conditions, remove batteries and keep them in a shirt pocket, worn on your body overnight (near your body is not close enough). Fine dust is a particular hazard for digital cameras in Tibet. Some manufacturers sell 'rugged' cameras which are supposed to be sealed against dust and moisture; other manufacturers claim to have an automatic dust removal system. Avoid changing lenses outdoors to prevent dust entering the camera. Even if you keep the same lens on the camera, dust can find its way down the barrel of the lens, leaving dust spots on the sensor. As for yak butter: there is a lot of the stuff in Tibetan temples, and it may find its way on to your lens. Oily stuff on the lens is not good news. For this reason, be wary of handing over your camera to pilgrims, who may stick a yak-butter fingerprint right on the lens.

To bring in professional video or motion-picture equipment, special clearance is required, meaning you probably won't get it without a ton of paperwork and grovelling. There is no restriction, however, on bringing hand-held **camcorders** and

amateur video equipment – plenty of Chinese visitors to Tibet bring such gadgets. The equipment is not the problem, it's how and when you use it. A policeman might overlook it if you are in a closed or sensitive region, but making a record that can later be aired in public is a very different case. Taboo subjects include the Chinese military (especially on patrol in Lhasa, or on manoeuvres and at highway checkpoints) and strategic locations such as bridges or the airport. Tibetans do not appreciate camera flashes in temples, nor photography of sky burial rituals (which is particularly sensitive). Some foreigners have had their film confiscated, and even their camera equipment. At a checkpoint on the Kathmandu–Lhasa road, a bored passenger stood aside and photographed a luggage search in progress. An army officer promptly seized his camera, and it was only after considerable argument that the camera was returned, minus the offending film.

MEDIA AND COMMUNICATIONS

China's one-party state controls all forms of media, making independent reporting impossible. All local news media are closely monitored. In Tibet, foreign news media are not permitted entry unless reporters are considered pro-China and will toe the party line. The TTB produces a glossy magazine on Tibet called *Tibet Tour* (printed in Shenzhen), but this is mostly in Chinese. Slick colour brochures on human rights and other 'hot topics' are distributed to major hotels in Chengdu and Lhasa.

PRINTED MATTER Anything printed outside China – like this guidebook – may be scrutinised (and seized) by Chinese customs and at Chinese road checkpoints. However, non-political books such as Gary McCue's *Trekking Tibet* have been spotted for sale at the Lhasa Hotel, along with *Tintin in Tibet* (which has been translated into 27 languages, including the Tibetan language itself). 'Printed matter' extends to messages on T-shirts: these have caused Westerners some trouble, although Tintin T-shirts are acceptable, and sold in Lhasa.

Photocopying A corollary to the above is that you may have to photocopy the relevant pages of books from other travellers. That's easy to do, as there are a number of places with good quality photocopy machines in Lhasa. Outside of Lhasa, you might try high-end hotels, as they often have a business centre for guests with photocopy, fax and internet facilities.

RADIO Tibet Radio is the official Chinese station in Lhasa, which is about all you'd want to say about it. If you bring a shortwave radio, you can pick up the BBC World Service (the Dalai Lama's favourite station – he's addicted) which broadcasts in English.

Voice of America (VOA) and Radio Free Asia (RFA) are operated by the USA: both broadcast in Tibetan. RFA started in late 1996 and reaches Thailand, Indochina, Indonesia and China – it espouses a free press to authoritarian governments. Apart from a Mandarin segment, there's an RFA Tibetan service. The Chinese don't seem to like either broadcast: in mid-1998, three RFA journalists who were due to accompany Clinton on his visit to China had their visas revoked. The head of the Tibet section in Washington was Ngapo Jigme, one of 12 sons and daughters of Tibet's greatest turncoat, Ngapo Ngawang Jigme, who died in Beijing in 2009. Ngapo Jigme defected from Tibet in 1985 and worked for the RFA Tibetan service in Washington for 16 years before he was suddenly fired without any reason.

Because Tibet is at such high altitude, there's excellent reception. However, around Lhasa, authorities jam signals by broadcasting on the same frequencies.

Broadcasting in Tibetan is Voice of Tibet (VOT), a station run by Tibetan journalists stationed in India and other countries (the target area is Tibet and neighbouring countries: VOT cannot be heard outside this range, but can be picked up on the website w vot.org).

TELEVISION Lhasa has two television broadcasting stations: Xizang TV, which is parked near the Potala, and Lhasa TV, to the eastern fringe of town. Other stations or transmitters are located in Shigatse, Tsedang and Gyantse. A couple of channels broadcast in Tibetan, others in Chinese – these programmes run the boring socialist gamut from pig farming in central China to ear-splitting Sichuan opera performances and revolutionary ballet performed by PLA soldiers. Beijing's CCTV (China Central TV) broadcasts on four or five channels, with CCTV-9 broadcasting mostly in English or with English subtitling on the programmes.

Because of the elevation, satellite television reception is excellent on the Tibetan plateau, but dishes must be licensed and are carefully monitored. In Lhasa, the mid-range and high-end hotels may be able to pick up VTV, a kind of Indian MTV. On larger satellite dishes – notably the one at Lhasa Hotel – is CNN. Of course, the average Tibetan gets nowhere near a satellite receiver, but occasionally things work for the better. In 1996, stunned Tibetan staff at a Lhasa hotel gathered to watch a broadcast of *Larry King Live* where one of the guests was the Dalai Lama.

Hong Kong-based StarTV programming may also be available on satellite, including the Star Movie Channel (English movies), Star Sports and a Chinese movie channel, but not BBC News. In 1994, Rupert Murdoch, chairman of News Corporation (which owns StarTV), removed BBC News from his satellite services to China to calm tense relations with Chinese officials who complained about a BBC profile of Mao Zedong and objected to coverage of Chinese dissidents. Although Murdoch has styled himself as a foe of totalitarianism and a champion of individual liberty and free speech, in the PRC's case he decided to brush all that under the carpet because he has extensive holdings in China and ambitious plans to expand them. In 1997, the BBC came under further fire from the PRC because it aired a programme on the disappearance of the 11th Panchen Lama.

More missing news: in October 2001, AOL Time Warner signed a deal with the Chinese government to expand its Mandarin-language cable channel China Entertainment Television (CETV) into Guangdong Province, southern China. AOL Time Warner acquired CETV from a Singapore entrepreneur who said his successful formula for reaching the Chinese market was 'no sex, no violence – and no news'. CETV shows dramas, game shows and situation comedies from Taiwan and Hong Kong. The no-news part sounds quite bizarre for a company best known for CNN. Meanwhile, Time Warner Cable has agreed to distribute Beijing's CCTV-9 in the USA, and that station carries Chinese news.

STAYING IN TOUCH May your mail be opened, may your phone calls be monitored, may your text messages be scanned, may your email be scrambled. This is not an ancient curse – it's a reality in today's Tibet, policed by the paranoid Chinese.

Skype calls may work from within Tibet, but do not count on this. The same goes for Facebook Messenger (Facebook is blocked in China). Or just use a VPN to get around the blocks.

The mailing system in Tibet is quite efficient – letters can get from Lhasa to Europe or North America within a few weeks. Poste restante exists at the main post office in Lhasa, or you can have letters mailed care of specific hotels (a better option).

Sending faxes is expensive, but still cheaper than repeating complex details over the phone (when you will still be charged even if you get an answering machine at the other end). Fax is often employed by travel agents within Tibet to make bookings at hotels where the staff never answer the phone.

Once out of Lhasa or Shigatse, communication becomes more difficult. If planning to send postcards, buy all the stamps in Lhasa, because you may only find small-value stamps in other places, and they will cover the entire postcard. Bring your own posting materials if out of Lhasa. Although places are remote, if there's an army base around, there are probably communication towers and satellite dishes to serve the military. That means IDD phones, sometimes even in remote corners of Tibet.

Telephone If you bring your own mobile phone, you can purchase a SIM card in Lhasa from a China Mobile outlet. Due to odd territorial restrictions, it is probably better to buy this SIM in Lhasa rather than elsewhere, although a SIM card purchased in Chengdu works. Be aware that in addition to heavily filtering the internet and scanning email, Beijing has issued regulations to Chinese mobile phone companies requiring them to police and filter SMS text messages. This directive followed widespread text messaging in the winter of 2003 that exposed the government's cover-up of the SARS outbreak.

You can use IDD phones to call direct from Lhasa through major hotels or at the main post office. Most China-wide and international destinations can be reached direct. Prepaid cards are much cheaper than hotel calls – around Y4 a minute for international calls (global reach) versus Y12–15 a minute for calls placed through a hotel system. There are two kinds of card: the IC yellow phonecard, and the IP hotel phonecard. The IC yellow phonecard can be purchased with values such as Y50 or Y100. You will see yellow phones on the street; they can also be found in some hotel lobbies.

Phone area codes are designated by prefecture, which is very useful for figuring out whose jurisdiction you are in for permits. The area codes are Lhasa Prefecture

THE TWILIGHT ZONE

Feeling out of sync? Having trouble figuring out what time of day it is in Lhasa? You wouldn't be the only one. All China runs on Beijing time, due to the communist craze for centralised planning, although it should strictly have five or six time zones from east to west. Even though Lhasa is thousands of kilometres to the southwest of Beijing and should be on the same time zone as Nepal (which is 2¼ hours behind Beijing time), it runs on Beijing's clock. If you fly from Lhasa to Kathmandu, that means you actually arrive before you left! So everything is out of sync in Lhasa. Sunday is the non-working day; Saturday might be a half-day. From Monday to Saturday, Chinese business hours for banks and other offices are (in summer) 09.00 to 12.30, then *xiuxi* (siesta – some offices have beds in the back rooms), and then 15.00 to 18.30. When they say 09.00, it's actually more like 07.00 in real time. Tibetans run on Tibetan time, which is like stepping back a few centuries. It's timeless: get up when the sun comes up, and go home when the sun goes down. Beijing time is Greenwich Mean Time +8 hours, or Pacific Standard Time +16 hours.

0891, Shigatse 0892, Shannan 0893, Nyingchi 0894, Chamdo 0895, Nagqu 0896 and Ali Prefecture 0897. If dialling from outside the country, drop the 0 in this prefix. Let's say the local seven-digit number in Lhasa is 633 3446. If you are in Lhasa, you would dial the number as is. If you are in Shigatse trying to reach Lhasa, you would dial 0891 633 3446. If you are in Canada, trying to reach Lhasa, you would dial 011 86 891 633 3446. The 011 sequence gets you out of Canada, 86 is country code for China, 891 is area code for Lhasa (you drop the 0 prefix from 0891 for this dial-up), followed by the local number. Lhasa phone numbers are seven digits, but mobile phones are usually 11 digits (with 1390 often being the first four). That means if you are trying to reach a mobile phone in Lhasa from outside the country, you would have to dial around 20 digits.

Other areas of Tibet may have erratic five-digit numbers – or no phones at all. Some other area codes for Chinese cities are Xining 0971, Zhongdian 0887, Kunming 0871 and Chengdu 028.

Email and internet What the fax machine was to the dissidents of the 1980s ('seek truth from fax'), the anarchic internet is to those of the new era. Surfers in Beijing can be fined if caught using the wrong websites – the crime is 'splitting the Motherland'. Cybercafés are located in most of the popular tourist sites and cities of China, and in other parts of Asia (Kathmandu, Hong Kong, Bangkok, Kuala Lumpur, etc).

The rules of engagement for use of the net in China are that many sites are 'sensitive'. However, you are not told which ones. It's possible that the laws that apply to locals do not apply to foreigners. If foreigners are used to looking at their favourite newspaper and suddenly find it blocked, they might get upset. The net is your lifeline for news and information: consult pages 366–9 for useful sites.

Email is monitored, though with the sheer volume of web-based mail, it is hard to fathom how this could possibly work. Proof of monitoring is that some foreigners have discovered their email accounts entirely shut down – because of recent email discussion about the Falun Gong. There is good email access in Lhasa, Shigatse and Gyantse, and some email access in key towns like Golmud or Nagqu. Elsewhere in Tibet, net access may be limited or non-existent.

Your email may go through unmonitored, or it may be monitored by keywords. Words such as 'Dalai Lama', 'Tibet', 'Taiwan' and 'Tiananmen Square' are bound to raise a few red flags – probably ones with yellow stars on them. If you put all those into a single sentence and add the words 'freedom', 'independence' and 'democracy', don't be surprised if your Yahoo! account suddenly starts acting funny – and vanishes from the screen. To get around restrictions, some travellers have resorted to high-tech methods that leave no trace on computers used in cybercafés.

Customising your smartphone or tablet for Tibet A customised smartphone or tablet – or both – can be very useful as a travel tool in Tibet, but you need to consider some limitations. A smartphone with a dead battery is just a piece of metal. A smartphone with a fully charged battery allows you to take full advantage of an array of tools, from using the on-board camera for panoramic photos to finding out what altitude you're experiencing.

The greatest limitation for these devices is the power, which in the case of a smartphone may only be a day, and maybe two days for a tablet. Consider all the bizarre wall plugs you will encounter in Tibet, and how to get around that with adaptors. And think about plugs high up on the wall somewhere, requiring an extension cord. Think about cold nights in Tibet, which will quickly drain your lithium batteries unless you have a way of keeping your devices warm (put in sleeping bag!). On the plus side, Tibet gets incredibly strong sun in the daytime, so you can power up your batteries from a portable solar charger such as Powertraveller's Solarmonkey Adventurer (which can also be powered from an electric source). Think about how to keep devices going from a portable lithium power bank with, say, three or four USB connector outlets and with power up to 30,000mAh output. A tablet requires more power to charge up – so ensure that the power bank has several 2.1V inputs. A power bank could keep your devices up and running for three days. You can also use the power bank as a hub while plugged into the wall. Another power source is the cigarette lighter in your hired vehicle – if you have the right connector for that.

Reading your device's screen may prove extremely difficult under direct high-altitude sun conditions in Tibet. The glare could make it impossible to view. You should test that out in advance and come up with a hooded solution.

Do not depend on cloud or internet links – both may be sadly lacking in Tibet. You need apps that are fully downloaded and which run without an internet connection. Ditto for books – download them all, as there will be no cloud reading. Another option is to make sure to purchase lots of data with your cell phone package, as this will increase the chances of internet reception, and you can use your cell phone as a hot spot to tether it to your tablet.

Virtual private network (VPN) Popular sites such as Facebook, Instagram and YouTube are blocked in China, and email systems like Gmail, Hotmail and Yahoo may also be blocked. If you do plan to use the internet a VPN is vital to work around blocked sites, of which there are many in Tibet. The VPN shifts you over to another country when you log in, thus getting around the Great Firewall. Since VPN usage can slow down your internet reception, you need to gauge the speed of the VPN.

The top three VPNs for Asia are Astrill, VyprVPN and ExpressVPN. These have free levels and paid-for levels. All VPNs are forbidden in China – ExpressVPN and others have been removed from Apple's App Store offerings for the iPhone inside China, along with apps for Skype, the *New York Times* and others. But there's nothing to stop you installing the VPN on an iPhone if done outside of China. For Android users, Google's Play Store is simply not available in China. A site called w greatfire.org offers FreeBrowser, a free VPN for use in China – and also monitors what is getting past the Great Firewall. To check if a website is blocked, go to the site w greatfirewallofchina.org and enter the relevant URL. A quick test reveals that Facebook and YouTube are blocked.

Monitoring of communication For communication, WhatsApp may or may not work because it is owned by Facebook. The Chinese-owned WeChat works very well – it is the most popular app among Chinese mobile users. But here's the downside: all data generated on WeChat is sent back to Chinese officials to monitor. If you use a banned keyword (such as 'Tiananmen', 'Taiwan' or 'Tibet'), your original message may never get through – it will be automatically blocked. WeChat users have been put behind bars for messages sent. In fact, it appears that all Chinese tech companies have an agreement that requires them to send user data to Chinese officials to monitor.

The Skype app was removed from Chinese smartphones in late 2017 – it may or may not work. If these apps do work, be careful what you say. Someone may be listening in. Tibetans routinely use code words when talking about subjects that are likely to land them in trouble with Chinese authorities.

Before you store data of any sort on your phone, make sure it is encrypted with a strong password so that a customs person cannot crack it. Downloaded books may be very sensitive in Tibet. Some suggestions for useful apps for travel in Tibet include the following. Once you get started, no doubt you will discover lots more apps, some paid-for, some free.

Language apps These are priceless – check for Tibetan language (preferably with audio) and Mandarin. You might also consider a Nepali language app. Some apps also bear written phrases that you can point to (assuming that person can read, which may not be the case in Tibet).

Navigation apps Very useful for navigation are apps for compass and altimeter. Some apps combine the two. For mapping, the best out there is Google Earth, but unfortunately this app is somewhat skewed in China, meaning it has been deliberately thrown off-kilter in the terms of accuracy by the Chinese themselves, who use a non-standard system when it comes to GPS positioning. This is known as GPS shift. If you set out with your trusty cell phone in hand and expect to navigate down the streets of Lhasa to a specific landmark, you might find yourself 100–600 metres off-target when using Apple's maps. Chinese geographic regulations demand that GPS functions must either be disabled on hand-held devices or they must be made to display the off-target readings (which Apple has kindly acquiesced to supplying). In fact, making maps or storing map data without official permission is highly illegal in China – and some foreigners have been apprehended and fined for engaging in said activity. Since 2002, geographic information about the PRC has been declared a matter of national security, so that private surveying and mapping activities are illegal in mainland China.

This has strange side effects for someone intending to use a light drone for photography, because drones use GPS positioning for pinpoint accuracy. For DJI drones (made in China), there is a special setting just for China that must be activated so that the drone does not end up in a distant river when attempting to land using GPS readings, apparently. Again, drone photography can be considered to be aerial reconnaissance, and your Chinese-made drone is likely to relay your footage back to a monitoring agency.

China has developed its own satellite navigation system called BeiDou, enabling it to end its dependence on America's GPS or Europe's Galileo. BeiDou is connected by around 30 satellites, narrowing its accuracy to below 10m (as compared with GPS, which can pinpoint to a metre or less).

All this mapping data filters down (meaning carefully screened) to Baidu Maps (w *map.baidu.com*), which is used on millions of smartphones in China. Using Baidu Maps is one way of determining direction within China – but, being Chinese software, it will invariably send all your data, location and activity back to Chinese monitoring agencies, which may not be a good idea. Apps such as Google Earth depend on cell phone towers and high-speed connections. If using your cell phone data, that could work in say Lhasa, but in more remote areas, forget that idea. A navigation app that does not depend on a net/cell phone connection is Maps.me. You must download the desired region – such as the Tibetan region – on to your cell phone or tablet beforehand.

Other apps More useful apps: a flashlight app is invaluable. And you'll be surprised how much you become interested in weather conditions – and how little information is available about the weather in Tibet. So install several good weather apps to keep track – though these will depend on a net connection or mobile connection. And now for the smog forecast: an app called AirVisual will terrify you with daily PM2.5 readings for places like Kathmandu, Beijing or Delhi – if you hit the red zone, time to put a mask on.

You can store downloaded books via Apple iBooks or Amazon Kindle – this guidebook as a backup, for instance, and a medical pocket book. Using the same platforms you can store PDFs, such as the Medex free handbook *Travel at High Altitude* (w *altitude.org/altitude_handbook.php*). Storing PDF manuals for cameras and other devices being carried saves on weight, and the PDF is easier to search. A few weeks' worth of music downloaded to your devices will help pass the time when stuck in airports.

CULTURAL ETIQUETTE

Tibetans are a spontaneous lot – they have no trouble breaking the ice. They'll probably examine your camera, fondle your luggage or shake you down for Dalai Lama pictures. Or give you a big grin. Tibetans have a great sense of humour, they're self-reliant, amazingly hardy, and have none of the shyness or coolness that the Chinese bring to bear on foreigners. They are usually direct, open and honest in their dealings. Tibetan women have a fairly high status, although they still do heavier work than the men. Outside of Lhasa, few Tibetans speak English: those who do are likely to have been educated in India. Put a Tibetan phrasebook to good use: any attempt at speaking the language is greatly appreciated. There are other ways to communicate: gestures such as thumbs up work well, as does singing in any language. If you're patient enough, it's only a matter of time before you are invited in for tea – or something stronger. Any kind of pictures you have are a great way of communicating. That extends to picture books on Tibet – these are engrossing to your host.

Interactions with Tibetans are not always as pleasant. Unfortunately, for a lengthy period Tibet has been open mostly to group tours, which are in the habit of handing out pens and candy to Tibetan kids: these same urchins may expect similar gifts from you, and will get antsy if nothing is forthcoming. On a more serious note, when interacting with Tibetans, you have a responsibility. When it comes to an overheard political discussion, not a lot will happen to you, a foreigner – at worst, you'll be booted out of Tibet. For the Tibetan, however, it could mean interrogation and jail. An Italian tourist interviewed a monk on video about Tibetan independence, and then took the videotape to a Chinese Embassy back in Italy to protest the treatment of Tibetans. The monk in the video was traced and received a 14-year jail sentence. Avoid putting Tibetans at risk – if a Tibetan talks to you about something politically sensitive, make sure to keep your interaction private and guard their identity. There are Tibetan informants as well as Chinese ones. Common sense will serve you well in most situations, but keep in mind just how serious Chinese authorities are towards punishing Tibetans who speak their mind, or express their support for any notion of independence.

There are several online sources related to ethical travel in Tibet.

You can view or download the International Campaign for Tibet's online guide, *Interpreting Tibet: A Political Guide to Traveling in Tibet*. This is available as a PDF download at: w tibetpolicy.eu/wp-content/uploads/TibetanChinaTravelGuide.pdf. For further up-to-date information and advice, contact the International Campaign for Tibet (*1825 Jefferson Pl NW, Washington, DC 20036, USA;* w *savetibet.org*) or ICT Europe (*Keizersgracht 302, 1016EX Amsterdam, Netherlands*). The following section has been adapted from a set of ethical guidelines published by the International Campaign for Tibet.

RESPECTING CUSTOMS Tibetans are extremely religious people and appreciate foreigners respecting a few simple customs; always walk clockwise around Buddhist religious sites and within monasteries or nunneries. Take hats off, do not smoke and do not touch figures or use flash photography inside monasteries or nunneries unless it has been cleared with the monks or nuns. Do not jump queues of pilgrims within monasteries nor interrupt ceremonies. Try to be an unobtrusive visitor but feel free to show interest and ask questions. It is also important not to touch the heads of or point your feet towards monks or nuns, and be careful with physical contact with them. Dress appropriately when going to any religious site – remember, it is a holy place.

Sky burial Do not encroach on Tibetan burial rituals (known as sky or celestial burials). This unique system of disposing of the remains of the dead is a sacred and private affair – it is not proper for visitors to Tibet to intrude into a family's last rites. Some Tibetans believe photographs can steal their soul. At any rate, taking pictures of people can be rude and intrusive. Put yourself in their place.

SUPPORT RELIGIOUS FREEDOM Entry fees at large monasteries will go to a committee controlled by the Chinese Communist Party, and will not necessarily be used for religious purposes. Donations left on altars may benefit monks and nuns, or donations can be made directly to individual monks and nuns, or given in kind. Clothing, food, film or books are much appreciated, but don't give your dirty cast-offs. Donations to smaller, out-of-the-way monasteries will be used properly, according to traditional Tibetan custom, since they are not as tightly regulated by Chinese authorities. Items such as candles, prayer flags, a bag of *tsampa* or some tea are always appreciated at remote monasteries. A wonderful way to spend some time with monastic people is to share your food. Walk the Barkor at sunrise with the Tibetans. It's a peaceful experience and allows you to be with the Tibetan people in a way that shows your support for their religious freedom.

BUY FROM TIBETANS If you want to support the Tibetan people, culture and economy, buy from Tibetan shops and stalls. A large influx of Chinese immigrants in Lhasa and other Tibetan cities is now taking over the economy and putting Tibetans out of work. The Dalai Lama has called this influx possibly the greatest threat to the survival of Tibetan culture. This general rule also applies to Tibetan restaurants and tea stalls. Eat Tibetan food rather than Chinese imported foodstuffs. Inflation is also a very real problem in Tibet. You contribute to this by paying exorbitant prices to vendors, which can increase prices Tibetans must pay for goods. Don't be cheap, on the other hand. If you find a piece of finely woven cloth or a carving you like, pay a fair price for the amount of work entailed. Bargaining is a part of Tibetan life – unfortunately, being ripped off by tourists is also becoming a part of their life.

DO NOT BUY ANTIQUES Most of Tibet's artistic treasures have already been destroyed or plundered by Chinese troops. Please leave antiques in Tibet. This goes for all family heirlooms as well as religious items. Since it is difficult to tell what is antique and what is not, a good rule of thumb to follow is that if someone tries to sell you something secretly, don't buy it. Stick to public stores and stalls. Families are often forced to sell their treasured items to put food on the table. Be creative and find other ways of helping Tibetans without taking away their culture.

ECOTOURISM Help protect Tibet's wildlife – do not buy products made from wild animals, especially from endangered species (ie: skins of the snow leopard and tiger, horns of Tibetan antelope, paws of the Himalayan brown bear, or any medicinal products made from animals). If you see these items, take photographs and notify the World Wide Fund for Nature (WWF) or the International Campaign for Tibet. This holds true for cities in Tibet, as well as Nepal, China, Hong Kong or anywhere else you come across them.

Leave only footprints The Himalayan ecosystem is a fragile one. If you go trekking use kerosene, even where wood is available. Trash should be buried 30m (100ft) from a water source, paper burned, and cans and bottles packed up and taken to a hotel or large town. Do not leave this up to your guide as environmental awareness is often low, especially among the Chinese. Plan ahead and bring food that has little packaging. Bring your own water bottle that can be filled up from vacuum flasks, as the quantity of discarded plastic mineral water bottles is frightening enough. Travel light and don't demand five-course meals. Bring your own food as villages rarely have surplus. If you want to bring presents for locals along the way, think carefully. Don't bring plastic baubles or contribute to begging by handing out a lot of freebies. It is much more appropriate to share time and a cup of tea with people, or play a game of jacks with the children. Tibet is becoming littered with human waste and toilet paper, so bury excrement and burn toilet paper. Be careful where you hike as erosion and damage to fragile plants are increasingly becoming a threat to the environmental health of the plateau and mountains.

INTERACTING Try to use knowledgeable Tibetan guides. All travel companies must work through a travel operator in Lhasa. It is important to select a company that works with a Lhasa-based operator, run and staffed by Tibetans as opposed to Chinese. To quote one experienced guide, 'When you go to France, you don't want a German tour guide; when you go to Tibet you don't want a Chinese one.' Moreover, using Tibetan-staffed companies promotes Tibetan culture and employs Tibetans. Check and see if one of the Tibetan-run agencies is operating at the time of your visit to Tibet.

If you are on a tour with an official Chinese government guide, do not expect accurate answers to historical, religious or political questions. Educate yourself before you leave. Read books about the history of Tibet and its people. John Avedon's *In Exile from the Land of Snows* is a classic and the Dalai Lama's autobiography *Freedom in Exile* is very informative (page 363). Reading some Chinese propaganda before you leave may help you to recognise false statements encountered in Tibet.

Breaking away Almost everyone who visits Tibet says that the best part was their interaction with Tibetans. In small groups, wander the streets, follow the hillside paths or get outside of the town and visit a village. Revisit a monastery without the group or spend time at a tea stall in the market. Photographs of your family and neighbourhood or Tibetan communities and celebrations abroad are great conversation pieces – don't worry about the language barrier. Tibetans would much rather have you attempt their own language rather than speak Chinese. Be mindful of approaching Tibetans in front of Chinese, particularly soldiers. Depending on current Chinese restrictions, Tibetans can be openly criticised or interrogated for associations with foreigners. Always be careful around dogs; they are numerous in most parts of Tibet and are trained to protect their territory.

Being critical Don't be frightened by dire warnings that the Chinese will lock you in jail and throw away the key for your support of the Tibetans. You should, however, be careful, and never endanger the Tibetans. Let the Chinese know when you disapprove of actions such as the use of monasteries for grain storage, the malevolence shown by police in and around religious sites, and unfair hiring and school enrolment practices. You can do a lot for the Tibetans and their cause, and will most probably want to after you come to know these wonderful people.

DEALING WITH OFFICIALDOM

There are a lot of unwritten laws in Tibet. You will probably be told you cannot ride a bicycle in Lhasa (not true) and that you cannot go into the Jokhang by yourself (not true). Or that your camera or film will be confiscated if you take pictures of Chinese military at checkpoints (a good chance this could happen). There are rare occasions when rules are written down. The following Public Security Bureau (PSB) notice appeared on the walls of budget hotels in Lhasa sometime back. Curiously, there is no mention of 'Tibet' or 'Tibetans' – the latter are referred to either as 'Chinese citizens' or 'Minority Nationality'.

> NOTICE: Ladies and Gentlemen: Welcome to Lhasa. So you may have safe and enjoyable travels, we would like you to be aware of the following government regulations.

> 1 Foreigners travelling to China must abide by Chinese law and must not endanger the national security of China, harm its public interests, disturb the public order, or engage in any other activities incompatible with tourist status.

> 2 If Chinese citizens are holding a rally or demonstration, it is strictly forbidden for foreigners to participate, follow along with, take pictures, or video film any of these activities. Foreigners are not permitted to interfere in Chinese internal affairs.

> 3 Foreigners are forbidden to distribute any propaganda material and join in any religious activity.

> 4 In accordance with regulations, foreign tourists must go through all registration formality and stay only at a designated hotel. Without prior permission, it is forbidden to travel in unopened areas, to operate individual business or privately take up an occupation.

> 5 It is forbidden to visit or photo the sky burial site according to the local government's regulations for the minority nationality's habits and customs. The tourist who breaks this regulation will be punished strictly.

BEING WATCHED Without being too paranoid about things, you should be aware that if you appear to be any kind of activist or have any connections to the Tibetan government-in-exile, your actions may be watched. You may be followed, your interaction with Tibetans noted, and your room may even be bugged. Sounds unreal? It has happened. In one case, in Beijing, a person speaking on the phone in French was asked by a Chinese wire-tapper to switch to English because he couldn't follow the conversation! In Lhasa, in 1996, a traveller wrote a political comment about Tibet in a book (for complaints) at the counter of the Bank of China. The PSB promptly tracked him down, exacted a confession, cancelled his visa and gave him

DALAI LAMA PICTURES

Since 1996 the trade in Dalai Lama pictures has been banned, and there have been several incidents of tourists being detained, interrogated and searched after they were seen giving pictures to Tibetans. Of course, the gifts most appreciated by Tibetans are photographs and postcards of the Dalai Lama and books by or about him. However, if a Chinese guide or the police see you giving them to a Tibetan, both of you could get into serious trouble. Possession of Dalai Lama images, audio tapes and video has resulted in stiff jail sentences for Tibetans.

There's nothing to stop you talking about the Dalai Lama, however – if you have seen the Dalai Lama on television or have read a newspaper story about him, tell the Tibetans about it and assure them of his good health. Tibetans like to have a Dalai Lama picture to place on their home altar if they can (under current conditions in Kham, east Tibet, images of the Dalai Lama are permitted for display). However, that's not the only picture they put there. They'd be quite happy to place a picture of the Potala Palace or the Jokhang Temple or sacred Mount Kailash there as well. Pilgrims would be very happy to receive these pictures, and they're all street legal.

an exit visa – meaning he had three days to fly out of Lhasa, back to Kathmandu. The Chinese are not good sports when it comes to criticism.

ENCOUNTERS WITH THE PSB There's no particular reason to be worried when dealing with police, army or other officials. If you are formally arrested, your embassy must usually be notified within four days. You have the right to speak to a consular officer and can demand that a call be placed to your embassy. Incidents involving foreigners in Tibet have ranged from warnings to hotel interrogations, to confinement to a hotel for four days (Dalai Lama tapes found in baggage in Shigatse after police were tipped off), to deportation. Three tourists watching demonstrations in Lhasa in 1994 had their passports confiscated. There have also been reports of Westerners being given a mild dusting-up – kicked or punched – when dealing with security officials.

In the Chinese system, if you are arrested, you are automatically guilty of something. Do not assume that innocence in a Western situation would mean you're in the clear in China. Chinese logic is different. Cast aside any notions of justice, put aside ideas of politeness and gentility and respect. There is no innocent here: you're either guilty and you admit it – and you'll get off lightly – or you're guilty and you deny it, in which case you'll be heavily fined, deported at your expense or otherwise punished. The arresting person would lose face if you were entirely innocent. You must leave a way out for the arresting officer – the usual method is making a written confession. There is nothing binding about these confessions – they're not legal documents. You can promise to the hilt on a confession, and then go out and break those promises the next day.

Under no circumstances should you let someone else write that confession for you (especially in Chinese!) to be signed. Insist that you write it yourself. Irksome though confessions may sound, they are really meaningless pieces of paper. Phrases that please are 'my ancestors would be ashamed of me', or 'I will never even think of doing this again'. In the early days of Tibet travel, a British backpacker was busy writing his confession about being in a closed area when

2

China is the only country in the world to enshrine in law the concept of a 'web political criminal'. In 2000, the State Council barred nine types of content from websites, bulletin boards and chat rooms – including anything that might 'harm the state' or 'disturb social order'. Other countries have jailed bloggers for criticising the government, but no country has gone after cyber-dissidents with as much zeal as China. In April 2005, 11 years after its initial connection to the World Wide Web, China launched the US$800 million Golden Shield Project – an automatic digital system of policing the internet, in effect denying Chinese people the right to free information. The Golden Shield's objective is to monitor every thought and action of those Chinese people who use the internet. Internet 'gateways' in China mainly monitor and filter political information. Technical functions include blocking foreign websites, filtering content and key words on web pages, monitoring email and internet cafés, hijacking PCs, sending out viruses, and enabling connections between Chinese policing systems. There is a lot to keep the Golden Shield busy. China is terrified of social media networks after watching events unfold in the revolutionary 'Arab Spring' of 2011. Facebook, YouTube and Twitter are routinely blocked and countless websites have been shut down.

The development of this technology has only been possible through the software, guidance and input of Western companies. Among those deeply involved are Yahoo, Microsoft, Nortel, Cisco and Sun Microsystems – and Apple and Google. Well, Google was involved, until it ran into problems with officials in Beijing. Google started out in China by omitting banned websites from its search results in China, completely blocking the BBC, for instance (the Chinese can neither watch nor read Chinese-language BBC broadcasts on the web, though the English versions may come through). Comically, in its effort to bend over backwards to please China, Google infuriated others: the Taiwanese foreign ministry discovered that the mapping software Google Earth called Taiwan 'a province of China'. When Google found out that its servers had been hacked from within China in an attempt to access information about Chinese dissidents, the company decided to pull out of Beijing and move its base to Hong Kong.

China's first web criminal, Lin Haiyin, was imprisoned for subversive actions in 2000. Since then, over a hundred cyber-dissidents have been caught in the 'web'. In September 2005, Zheng Yichun was sentenced to seven years for posting an essay to an overseas Chinese-language website, voicing the opinion that China's one-party system is 'the root of all evil'. He posted the essay to dajiyuan.com, which is popular with Chinese intellectuals overseas – and blacklisted in China, which means that nobody in China can access it anyway. In April 2005, journalist Shi Tao was imprisoned for ten years for the crime of 'revealing state secrets'. Shi Tao posted to a US website a list of topics that Chinese newspapers are forbidden to cover, including the anniversary of the 1989 Tiananmen Square Massacre. The Paris-based organisation Reporters Without Borders claimed that Yahoo's Hong Kong unit helped Chinese authorities to link Shi Tao to a US-based website, which led to his conviction. In response, Yahoo officials said they had no choice but to abide by the 'laws, regulations and customs' of the country where it does business. Reporters Without Borders accused Yahoo of helping Chinese authorities in at least two other conviction cases. In May 2011, members of the Falun Gong in America filed a lawsuit in California against Cisco, claiming that the company helped China customise its Golden Shield Project to trace dissidents in China – in particular, Falun Gong members.

Powerful corporations like Yahoo and Microsoft are kowtowing to a sign over the gateway to the Middle Kingdom that reads: 'Abandon company ethics, all ye who enter here.' Microsoft has aided Chinese censors in removing words such as 'freedom', 'democracy', 'human rights', 'Tibet', and 'Dalai Lama' from the net in China, and with software packages that prevent bloggers and others from using these and other politically sensitive words on their websites. This censorship, it appears, extends to Microsoft software such as the Chinese version of Encarta. And while Bill Gates toadies up to Chinese leaders, praising them for their 'brand new form of capitalism', there's an inherent conflict of interest with Western values – the values of democracy and freedom, privacy and integrity.

Canadian communications giant Nortel has worked for a number of years with the Chinese government to develop surveillance technology for use on Chinese citizens. This would seem to be at rather large odds with Nortel's privacy statement for the internet, which swears it will not sell, rent or share personal data with any other organisation or third party. The company's blurb on ethical business practices cites integrity as its cornerstone: 'We strive to do the right thing for individuals, organisations and society in general.' And yet Nortel is supplying a digital communications network for the Golmud–Lhasa railway line, which the Dalai Lama has denounced as a major part of China's plans for 'cultural genocide' in Tibet.

In November 2005, a group of social investment funds from Western countries called for internet firms to refrain from supporting repressive human rights practices in China and other nations. The group of 25 investment funds (based in the USA, Canada, Switzerland and Australia) sent out a letter to firms ranging from Yahoo to Cisco warning of the risks involved in 'collaborating to suppress freedom of opinion and expression'. The investment fund group sending the letter included Ethical Funds of Canada, Fondation Ethos of Switzerland and Conscious Investors of Australia. They maintain that companies can – and should – retain integrity while doing business.

Are powerful companies responsible – and accountable – for ethical abuses? When it comes to cases of pollution, such as accidental oil spills, definitely yes – there are laws in place, and severe penalties for offenders in many nations. In the case of internet filtering and surveillance, in early 2006 the US Congress began to address concerns that US-based internet companies are assisting the Chinese government in silencing dissidents. Under consideration is legislation for a Global Online Freedom Act to ensure global access to information on the net. But when it comes to the question of assisting genocidal regimes, it seems that governments are willing to turn a blind eye. Consider the case of New York-based IBM, conducting highly profitable business with Nazi Germany in the 1930s. There were no computers then, but there was a precursor: the IBM punch-card machine. In co-operation with Nazi authorities, IBM, working through European subsidiaries, customised punch-card machines for the sole purpose of persecuting the Jews. After World War II finished, IBM rushed to destroy evidence of its links to Nazi Germany, managed to evade any hint of responsibility for wartime reparations, and evaded any accusation of complicity in war crimes – in genocide, in fact. Investigative journalist Edwin Black details what IBM did in his remarkable book *IBM and the Holocaust*, published in 2001 (the book is supported by a website: w ibmandtheholocaust.com).

Engaged Buddhism refers to Buddhists who are seeking ways to practically apply insights from their meditation practice and spiritual teachings to social, political, environmental and economic suffering and injustice. While the roots of Engaged Buddhism may be found in the teachings and actions of the Buddha himself, and other great teachers of the past, Engaged Buddhism can also be understood principally as a movement that began in the late 19th century as a response to Western colonialism in Asia. It is best known through its political movements, such as the struggles by the Tibetan, Burmese and Vietnamese Buddhists for self-determination, democracy and peace.

Engaged Buddhism is not simply being a Buddhist and involved in politics and social justice. Rather, Engaged Buddhists critically and creatively apply the Buddha's teachings to transform themselves and their societies. Thich Nhat Hanh of Vietnam, Ajan Maha Ghosanand of Cambodia, The Dalai Lama of Tibet, and Ajan Sulak Sivaraksa of Thailand are modern-day leaders who embody Engaged Buddhist principles and have guided organisations such as the Buddhist Peace Fellowship, the International Network of Engaged Buddhists, and the Zen Peacemakers.

When I first went to Tibet in the late 1990s, I was on a pilgrimage and did not intend to involve myself with politics in general, or practise Engaged Buddhism. The road map for my pilgrimage was the far-ranging travels across Tibet by a 19th-century mystic known as Tertön Sogyal. I meditated among hermits in remote sanctuaries and slept in caves where Tertön Sogyal had experienced spiritual visions. On foot, on horseback and in dilapidated buses, I crossed the same snow-covered passes that he had used to travel from eastern Tibet to Lhasa. I was searching out the living masters and yogis who uphold Tertön Sogyal's spiritual lineage and could tell me the oral history of his life and teachings.

But my pilgrimage took an unexpected turn. The more time I spent in Tibet delving into the 19th-century teachings of Tertön Sogyal, the more often I met Tibetans who wanted to tell me their stories of present-day frustration and suffering in what they see as Chinese occupation of their country. And the Tibetans spoke of their never-ending hope that one day the exiled Dalai Lama would return to Tibet. Travelling as a Buddhist pilgrim, I gained the trust of Tibetans. Political prisoners who had experienced abuse and torture in Chinese prisons showed me scars. Monks and nuns who had been kicked out of their monasteries gave me their expulsion notices from the local security bureau. I was taken to meet a Buddhist leader who had been scalded with boiling water and then jailed for five years for publicly praying to the Dalai Lama.

Tibetans not only told me their stories, but early into my pilgrimage they asked me to spirit such first-hand accounts of human rights abuses out of Tibet and into

the arresting officer noticed that he'd extended his own visa – the highest level of naughtiness conceivable. Unperturbed, the traveller continued writing his confession: 'In addition to the above, I must humbly confess that I have extended my own visa, for which ...'

Close encounters are usually of the PSB kind, ie: over travel permits. As long as your papers are in order, there's nothing to worry about: if you get off the track, the legality of your travels is sometimes at the whim of the particular PSB official you are dealing with, at which point a small 'fine' may be levied, going directly into the hands of Western governments and advocacy groups. I became a courier of often graphic accounts of torture and abuse. This required evading China's vast security network of plainclothes security agents, undercover cops in monks' robes, and sophisticated cyber police. I began photographing Chinese secret prisons where Tibetan monks and nuns are incarcerated for their Buddhist beliefs. The decade-long journey in Tertön Sogyal's footsteps became a different kind of pilgrimage – one that became the dual narrative of the book *In the Shadow of the Buddha: Secret Journey, Sacred Histories, and Spiritual Discovery in Tibet.*

While I do not claim to have benefited anyone from my human rights work, I can say that I have tried to apply what the Buddha and my teachers have taught me about acting for the benefit of others. This is how I entered the path of Engaged Buddhism. I have given voice to what I have witnessed. I know in politics, ultimately, there are no winners, for every politician will die and every government will eventually fall – the real question is not if a political system will survive, but when will it fail. Because everything is impermanent, including politicians and their governments, we have a responsibility to effect change that will bring about the conditions *right now* for others to find contentment and happiness. For me this is Engaged Buddhism.

Like many others who have been profoundly affected by Tibet's unique wisdom culture, I cannot let the world forget about Tibet. China wants governments and people around the world to forget about Tibet, to turn their backs on monks, nuns, musicians and bloggers who languish in prison for their religious beliefs and their peaceful expression of political views. It is the responsibility of those who have the freedom to travel, to write and express our opinions, to talk to our governments – and to not only bear witness but act to change injustice. This is why I documented China's human rights abuses in Tibet and why I wrote *In the Shadow of the Buddha*. I do not expect everyone to take up the Tibet issue. That is not my reason for writing. Rather, it is my hope that wherever we find ourselves in the world, we never lose hope and faith and a sense of responsibility to those who are suffering in our family, in our community or in other countries.

I believe progressing on our spiritual path means doing what each of us needs to do for ourselves to bring about true and lasting contentment, beyond suffering. And accomplishing the path of social engagement means creating the conditions for others to find that same lasting satisfaction. These are the commitments I've learned from my venerable teachers, and ones that I continue to take with me.

Matteo Pistono is the author of In the Shadow of the Buddha *(for more details, see* w *matteopistono.com). He is founder of Nekorpa, a foundation working to protect sacred pilgrimage sites around the world.*

his pocket. These fines are negotiable: if he asks for US$100, wait until it drops to US$20 or US$10. Packets of foreign-brand cigarettes go down well with the Beijing Boys. Sometimes the crime is just too 'serious' and the PSB won't back off. Two Germans who were caught collecting high-altitude bug specimens were fined over US$300 by the PSB for their illicit activities. PSB officers have amusing English-language phrasebooks for dealing with foreigners in situations like this ('Please sign your interrogation' – things like that). The military – mostly teenaged recruits – do not seem particularly concerned about foreigners, except at checkpoints.

There are estimated to be 45 million blind people worldwide: 90% of these people live in non-affluent countries. Remarkably, 80% of this blindness is either preventable or curable.

In the Tibet Autonomous Region alone, there are probably over 30,000 blind people. In the Tibetan-populated regions of neighbouring provinces, there could be a further 30,000 blind people. That makes a total of perhaps 60,000 blind Tibetans. With cataract surgery, over half of these people could see again. The main cause of cataract blindness is simply the ageing process; however, in Tibet the incidence is believed to be increased due to poor nutrition and to a greater exposure to ultraviolet light. At 4,500m there is less atmosphere to filter out its harmful effects.

The Seva Foundation in the USA and its sister organisation Seva Canada are among the few NGOs working in Tibet to address the problem of reversible blindness. Seva has worked with the Tibet Development Fund, centred in Lhasa, for over seven years to help Tibetans develop eye-care services in each of the main hospitals in Tibet, by building a regional eye-care programme to reduce this immense backlog of cataract surgeries.

Although more than 40 doctors work in various eye clinics in Tibet, few have medical degrees and none are fully qualified ophthalmologists. Eye-care services in the region are very limited; the eye doctors are poorly trained, equipment is inadequate and outdated, and complication rates have been very high. Seva's Tibetan Sight Programme attempts to address these urgent needs. Seva has developed training programmes for surgical teams from each of the 12 principal hospitals in Tibet, to teach staff safe cataract surgery techniques and other eye-care skills. Seva has also supported eye camps in Tibet, providing up to 500 cataract surgeries each to supplement the limited eye-care services available. Now, the Tibetan doctors Seva has trained are conducting their own eye camps each year.

When Seva first started working in Tibet a decade ago, one of its first major goals was to find and train local medical doctors in modern cataract surgery. Among the early trainees was a team of doctors from Menzikhang, the hospital of traditional Tibetan medicine in Lhasa. Actually, Seva did not plan to work within the traditional medical model, but the Menzikhang had the space to conduct eye camps and its traditional doctors were very keen to learn modern ophthalmology. Tibetan medicine is a complex system of medical practice, inseparable from its spiritual foundation in Tibetan Buddhism. The Tibetan medical tradition has historically included a form of surgical treatment for cataract. Thus, Seva was not challenging any major conceptual assumptions of Tibetan medicine. Several years later Seva also learned that Tibetan medicine includes the recognition of different eye diseases and several treatments for these conditions.

TRAVELLING POSITIVELY

For many living in the Himalaya, life is far from paradise. How is your karma-meter? Gold, silver or bronze? Giving doesn't have to mean money. It could mean lending your expertise in education, medical care, or assistance with computer operations. Scanning the following websites will give you ideas on voluntourism, including requests for doctors, nurses and physiotherapists, and teaching English to new arrivals from Tibet. Teaching can cover a much

Now, after years of training and participating in many co-operative eye camps, there is an effective local cataract surgery team. But despite having excellent surgical techniques, these doctors don't understand many of the basic tenets of Western medical ophthalmology. There are inherent dilemmas and very practical risks that arise when modern ophthalmology is incorporated into traditional medical practices without this new way of medical thinking to act as a bridge. Providing this theoretical bridge without undermining the very important traditional medical system is one of the many challenges Seva encounters in Tibet.

Another instructive example of the conundrums created by modern ophthalmology's meeting with traditional belief is when an elderly Tibetan refuses to have this free, 15-minute, sight-restoring cataract surgery because their blindness is understood to be their karma or spiritual destiny. It is very important to respect such deeply held religious belief.

Seva continues to work with Menzikhang because it is clearly committed to serving the poorest people in Tibet and this hospital is the most trusted by the local people. In order to develop a comprehensive blindness prevention programme, Seva is still exploring the best way to add preventative care and medical treatments for other diseases to its existing programme of cataract surgery.

Seva does seek skilled volunteers for Tibet. Ophthalmologists, optometrists and ophthalmic assistants who can make a long-term commitment are especially welcome. Non-clinical volunteers including computer and health education specialists are also sought.

The rewards? Here's what ophthalmic surgeon Dr Pratt-Johnson says of his volunteer work in Nepal, India and Bangladesh:

You soon get the feeling that you are doing so little and yet it means so incredibly much to our partners and particularly to the patients, who express their overwhelming gratitude in a mixture of gestures, tears and happy smiles. You try and wish you could do more. You return with an afterglow that warms your heart and soul. This psychologically resets the equilibrium of one's life, fulfilment and joy. We ophthalmic surgeons need to be conscious of having skills that place us in a privileged position, coming close to performing miracles – restoring sight to the blind. Share it with as many as you can. Giving through volunteering is such an adventure and a lot of fun.

For more information about Seva's work in Tibet and other parts of the world you can contact the following offices in the USA and Canada:

Seva Foundation 786 Fifth St, Berkeley, CA 94710; 510 845 7382; e admin@seva.org; w seva.org
Seva Canada Suite 100 – 2000 West 12th Av, Vancouver, BC, V6J 2G2; 604 713 6622; e service@seva.ca; w seva.ca

wider range: at monastic schools, students are keen to learn English, arithmetic, science, computer skills, gardening, leadership skills, accounting, health care and other subjects. Here are some opportunities for working with Tibetans, both in Tibet and in exile:

jamyang.org/pages/volunteer.php This San Diego-based organisation welcomes volunteers at its educational programmes for Buddhist girls & women in the Indian Himalayas, including Zanskar, Spiti & Kinnaur. Many skills are needed, including help with planting trees & gardens.

rokpa.org/en/home.html British-based worldwide charity Rokpa was founded in 1980, with a variety of projects in Tibet & Nepal – from eye-care to education.

tibetanvillageproject.org Go on a trip & help at the same time, with projects in villages in the Kham region. Click on the 'Ecotourism' tab.

tras.ca The Trans-Himalayan Aid Society, established in 1962, has projects in Tibet, Nepal & northern India to assist in building schools & medical centres. The NGO depends on volunteers.

workaway.info This is a general volunteer site, connecting hosts to volunteers, online & worldwide. You can get great ideas from this website. Then focus on the Himalayan regions, with volunteer opportunities in Nepal, India, Mongolia & other regions.

3

Health and Safety

in consultation with Dr Felicity Nicholson

The material in this chapter is not intended to scare you away from visiting Tibet. Rather, it is intended to make you aware of the dangers involved if you happen to get really sick, to encourage you to travel with at least one friend as a backup in case things go wrong, and to urge you to obtain comprehensive evacuation insurance before setting off.

The following medical issues may venture into uncharted territory, especially concerning **altitude sickness**. It offers a broad outline and does not cover matters in great detail. Draw your own conclusions – and then consult other sources and experts for more thorough answers. Information on altitude sickness is hard to come by because it's not a common problem in the West. There are some books on the subject, but these tend to get out of date as knowledge evolves. For general health concerns, the Center for Disease Control and Prevention, based in Atlanta, Georgia, maintains a website (w *cdc.gov/travel*) with the latest information on prevention guidelines and strategies. See also the shortlist of websites in *Appendix 4* under *Health*, page 367. Note that CDC advice may not agree with UK advice. We would suggest using w travelhealthpro.org.uk.

BEFORE YOU GO

Some important facts to know before you go: Tibetan and Chinese hygiene standards are very poor, and Chinese medical facilities within Tibet are extremely limited. Some conclusions to draw: you may have to be your own doctor in Tibet, you have to be willing to help fellow travellers in dire situations, and you have to be prepared to evacuate if the need arises.

Prior to departure, go and visit your local health unit or travel clinic (page 110) and get an armful of relevant shots. You would be wise to be up to date with **tetanus**, **polio** and **diphtheria** (all ten-yearly), **typhoid** and **hepatitis A** (Havrix Monodose or Avaxim). You would also be wise to consider **rabies** vaccine for even short trips as there is a shortage of treatment if you have not had pre-exposure vaccine before an incident. For longer trips (four weeks or longer) consider **hepatitis B**. Both rabies and hepatitis B involve three doses of vaccine, which can take up to two months to give depending on the age of the traveller.

Travellers going to western Tibet should consider vaccinating against tick-borne encephalitis. Two doses of vaccine are ideally given at least a month apart but can be given at a two-week interval if time is short. The third dose is given 5–12 months later if you are at continued risk. Talk to your doctor and arm yourself with drugs – Azithromycin or Ciprofloxacin (antibiotics for diarrhoea or respiratory problems), Tinidazole (for giardia or amoebic dysentery) and Diamox (to prevent altitude sickness). Assemble a good medical kit (page 111). Check out where your embassies lie in China and in the neighbouring region – note down the addresses

Deep vein thrombosis (DVT) is a concern where long-haul immobility is involved, as in long air flights, lengthy bus rides, car jaunts that last for days, and riding Chinese railways for several days to get closer to Tibet (or indeed into Tibet). Prolonged immobility may cause blood clots to form in the legs. Although most clots are reabsorbed without the passenger ever becoming aware of the problem, some clots may break off and travel through the blood vessels to the lungs, causing life-threatening complications.

People at the highest risk and who should seek medical advice before they go are:

- People with heart disease
- People with cancer
- People with clotting disorders
- People who have had recent surgery, especially on the legs
- Women on the pill or other oestrogen therapy
- Pregnant women

The main symptoms of travel-related DVT are swelling or pain of the foot, ankle or calf, usually on just one side. A blood clot moving to the lungs can cause chest pain and difficulty in breathing. To prevent DVT on aeroplanes or trains, the solution is simple: stay mobile. Walk up and down the aisles, do exercises to contract leg muscles, and drink lots of fluids (but not alcohol). For long-haul bus or rental-vehicle trips, you will just have to find a way to do similar things – creative yoga on the bus, or getting out of the vehicle periodically to stretch. For more information about travel-related DVT, go to the website w travelhealth.co.uk and run a search for the topic.

and contact numbers. Bring a health certificate to China (it may be checked). Find out your blood group and record it on that document. If you haven't had time to get all or any of your vaccinations/medicines before you leave home then the **CIWEC Hospital and Travel Medicine Center** in Kathmandu is an excellent place to go. It is run by Western doctors and is located near the British Council (w *ciwec-clinic. com;* ☎*+977 1 442 4111*).

TRAVEL CLINICS AND HEALTH INFORMATION A full list of current travel clinic websites worldwide is available on w istm.org. For other journey preparation information, consult w travelhealthpro.org.uk (UK) or w cdc.gov/travel (USA). Information about various medications may be found on w netdoctor.co.uk/travel. All advice found online should be used in conjunction with expert advice received prior to or during travel.

EVACUATION INSURANCE You are strongly advised to carry comprehensive air evacuation insurance for a trip to Tibet. Hopefully, you won't have to use it. Your best strategy if you fall really sick in Tibet is to get right out of Tibet – and China – as fast as you can, and make a beeline for somewhere with better hospitals, such as Singapore. Use regular scheduled flights to get out of Tibet if possible. If the plane looks full, insist that a regular passenger gets bumped off the flight for the emergency patient.

Evacuation by chartered flight can cost a fortune. Check your travel insurance to ensure that it covers emergency evacuation costs and, more specifically, if it will cover evacuation by crews like SOS/AEA, which has clinics in Beijing with expat doctors and imported medicines. Better yet, take out direct insurance with SOS/AEA (check their website w internationalsos.com for addresses and contact numbers, and see the section on evacuation on page 121).

HIMALAYAN MEDICAL KIT Failing adequate health care in Tibet, you really need to be your own doctor. There are Chinese pharmacies in Lhasa, but medication may bear Chinese instructions and may not be familiar to Western eyes. Kathmandu and Hong Kong are quite well stocked with Western drugs and will issue medication without prescription. You can easily find drugs like Diamox in Kathmandu (check expiry dates). While you can't be a travelling drugstore, you'll need a larger than usual medical kit in Tibet. If travelling with a friend or a small group, divide up a medical kit to share the weight. Camping stores in the West sell pre-packaged medical kits that you can customise to your needs. Items such as antiseptic cream and Band-Aids (plasters) are hard to find in Lhasa. Take along a Swiss Army knife with scissors and tweezers. You'll need your own water bottle and purifying tablets (or filter).

A medical kit may contain a ready-made package – sealed and labelled – with sterile needles and syringes. It is highly recommended you carry these in case blood samples or injections are required. Make sure that you obtain a certificate signed by a doctor stating that they are for your own personal use for medical situations. Take along any prescription drugs you need, as well as backups of things you are dependent upon, such as glasses. Your chances of finding contact lens solution in Shigatse are zero: dust can be a major problem for contact lenses in Tibet (take along regular glasses as a backup). Glasses or no glasses, dust can cause eye irritation – you might want to pack soothing eye drops.

Read the following sections for ideas on arming yourself for the rigours of Tibet – you will need medications such as cough lozenges, codeine-based medicines and decongestants (for colds); moisturisers, lip balm, sunglasses, sunscreen and other balms will help combat the effects of sun, wind and altitude. Recommended drugs for Tibet include: Diamox to help acclimatise, Azithromycin or Ciprofloxacin for diarrhoea associated with blood or mucus and/or a fever, Tinidazole for giardia and amoebic dysentery and a phial of chlorine dioxide tablets for purifying water.

Medical knowledge Travellers may buy a medical kit but overlook the importance of the medical knowledge required to go with it. The best way to fill this gap is to download a PDF or app with comprehensive medical information on to your tablet or smartphone. You can download a free PDF for the excellent handbook *Travel at High Altitude* at w altitude.org/altitude_handbook.php. You can buy and download a pocket guide such as *First Aid and Wilderness Medicine* (Cicerone, 2013). You can also buy a pocket-sized booklet – there are several on the market. Notable are two booklets by the same author, Dr Stephen Bezruchka, both published by The Mountaineers Books in 2005: *The Pocket Doctor: A Passport to Healthy Travel*, and the more specialised *Altitude Illness: Prevention and Treatment*. If you're leaving Tibet and returning directly home, you should consider selling or donating your precious cache of medicines and other supplies to incoming travellers. Drugs like Diamox have an expiry period and will be of little use to you in the West anyway.

THE BUDDY SYSTEM When you go diving, you use the buddy system. You watch out for your friend underwater, which is an alien environment and a potentially

3

dangerous one. You could draw close parallels in Tibet: high altitude is an alien environment. If someone gets altitude sickness, he or she becomes confused and disorientated, and cannot make the right decisions. Someone else has to take those decisions. Back yourself up in Tibet with at least one buddy. And be prepared to watch out for others in a group if someone falls sick.

COMMON HEALTH AND SAFETY PROBLEMS IN TIBET

RUNNING ON EMPTY To keep your system ticking over properly, you need good nutrition and high fluid intake. And that's hard to achieve outside Lhasa. So carry vitamin pills, freeze-dried soups and extra food supplies (such as dried fruit) to supplement the meagre local offerings. You should think in terms of what can be 'cooked' with the hot water supplied in vacuum flasks in hotels and truck stops: check the cooking times on soup packets (ideally, only a few minutes in hot water). Packets of soup are the best item here – soup is easily prepared and gives the illusion of a hot meal. Tsampa, the Tibetan food staple, is sustaining but tasteless – it can be mixed in with soup to make it more palatable. You can get run down without proper nutrition intake: this makes you more susceptible to coming down with other ailments.

FLUID INTAKE Two essentials concerning water: making sure the water is safe to drink; and drinking enough of it. Even though Tibet is high and the water looks crystal-clear, it could be contaminated by herders and livestock on higher ground. It's best to always filter water or boil it. Staying hydrated is essential in Tibet to combat dryness and the effects of altitude. Even if you have to overload your system, keep drinking your quota of water – about three to four litres a day. If you get a case of the runs, you'll lose a lot of body fluids, so you need to keep drinking water to stay hydrated. You can buy bottled water in Lhasa and larger towns in Tibet – make sure the seal is intact. The water supplied in Chinese vacuum flasks in hotels is usually reliable since it has been boiled at high temperature. You have to wait for this to cool down, or else drink it in tea. You should take along your own water purifying devices – chlorine dioxide tablets can be purchased cheaply in the West. Chlorine-treated water tastes unpleasant but you can buy another tablet that removes that taste. Or take Gatorade flavouring crystals with you to neutralise the taste. These and other electrolyte powders (such as Electrolade) are sodium and potassium, which will help restore body fluid balance (one of the main ingredients in sweat is sodium). However, chlorine dioxide will not work if there is any particulate matter in the water. Using the Aquapure water filter (mechanical) will remove all viruses, protozoans and bacteria and will filter out particulate matter, too. One bottle will filter 350 litres of water, enough to drink 3 litres a day for 3 months.

HYGIENE HAZARDS Washing and cleaning activities are a low priority with Tibetans: explanations range from lack of hot water to layering themselves with dirt to protect the skin from sun. Both Tibetan and Chinese hygiene standards fall far short of those of western Europe. You have to be careful about the handling of food and water – do not accept the cold face towels offered in restaurants. Stick to well-cooked hot food in restaurants (noodles are fine). Boil it, peel it – or forget it. Some travellers prefer to use their own eating utensils, such as an aluminium mug and spoon (soup can be served in the mug).

Although hot showers are readily available in Lhasa, Shigatse and Gyantse, in the rest of Tibet you may not be so lucky. Solar hot showers are on the rise, and there are the occasional hot springs to soak in, but that's about it: the rivers and lakes are pretty cold. Out of Lhasa, you have to rely on the vacuum flask of hot water supplied to your room (or ask for it). The flask is a source of hot water for tea, or for making soup – and can also be used for bathing. A metal basin is often supplied in the room (sometimes with a special wooden stand to hold it), so you can pour water in and wash yourself in stages (hair one day, and so on). Another technique is to soak a thin towel (preferably your own) and apply it Japanese-style, as in a sushi restaurant. Thin, spongy Western sport towels are ideal for this as you can wring them out to dry quickly.

DIARRHOEA Because of low hygiene standards, it is eminently possible that you will get a case of the runs. Usually, this is not a problem – just stick to a simple diet with liquid backup: water, clear soups and unsweetened juices. Do not drink beer or milk, and avoid spicy or fatty foods as they can aggravate your condition. The problem should pass within a day or two. In Kathmandu, you can buy packets of rehydration salts – a mixture of glucose and salt. If these are unavailable, you can make your own by adding two or three teaspoons of salt and a similar amount of sugar to a litre bottle of purified water. Packets of electrolyte rehydration powders (sodium/potassium crystals) are efficacious. If problems persist, it may be a case of bacterial diarrhoea – refer to the section on *Intestinal bugs* (page 115).

THE ELEMENTS Sunburn, windburn, chapped lips, lobster-face and red-eye are definite hazards in Tibet due to the (at times) ferocious effects of the sun, wind and cold. Once you get cracked lips or chapped hands, you'll find these take a long time to heal and can be very bothersome. Moisturisers are the answer: bring along hand- and face-cream moisturisers (though these can also be purchased in Lhasa). You need a good sunblock cream and lip balm. A hat of some kind – preferably covering the ears and neck – is essential, as are high-quality sunglasses or glacier glasses that block UV rays (ideal are dark polarising lenses). The use of certain drugs such as the antibiotic Tetracycline can render a person more sun-sensitised, and result in bad sunburn. One of the greatest hazards in Tibet is dust. It can get into your eyes, so contact lenses are not a great idea – dust can be very irritating if it gets under them. A silk scarf or bandana, wrapped around your nose, throat and mouth (bandito style) will generally filter the dust out of your breathing apparatus in extreme conditions, and the same scarf can be used round your neck to keep you warm in a sudden change of temperature.

ACUTE EXPOSURE It can get *very* cold overnight in Tibet. Silk articles, favoured by Western skiers, are especially useful for countering the cold – they're light and pack easily (balaclavas, long johns, T-shirts, scarves, gloves). Wool and polypropylene clothing also insulates well. A woollen *tuke* or similar headgear will go a long way towards countering the cold. A dangerous condition, caused by rapid heat loss, is hypothermia: this is brought about by physical exhaustion when cold and wet. Symptoms include uncontrolled shivering. Shelter is the most important thing here: strip off wet clothing and replace with dry. In severe cases, the person should be stripped and placed in a sleeping bag with another person to share body heat. Do not rub affected limbs.

Frostbite is the most extreme result of rapid body-heat loss. It affects the tips of the extremities first – toes, fingers and nose. In these areas the blood freezes, preventing circulation as ice crystals expand in the cells. Again, it is essential to find shelter, and immerse the affected part in lukewarm water if available. Surface frostbite can be thawed with another person's body heat – do not rub the affected

3

part. Snow blindness results when bright sun reflected off snow (or ice or water surfaces) burns the cornea of the eye. The eyes feel like there is grit in them, appear bloodshot, and eyelids may puff up and swell shut. The condition is alarming but temporary – rest and soothe the eyes with cold compresses or eye drops, and the problem should clear up in a few days. Wearing glacier glasses with total UV block is the way to prevent this condition.

COUGHS, COLDS AND SORE THROATS Respiratory ailments are quite common in Tibet, and can turn very nasty when combined with the effects of extreme dryness and altitude. Take care. These are not your normal colds – they can be persistent and debilitating. Virulent (mutating) strains of flu, originating in China, can be knockouts. The best way to avoid this syndrome is to make sure you don't undergo drastic changes of body temperature. Make sure that you have clothing that you can layer on or off, to cope with the extremes of heat and cold – sometimes occurring on the same day in Tibet. This also applies to sleeping arrangements – there's not much heating in hotels in Tibet. Bring your own medicines for coughs, colds and sore throats. Some stronger drugs (codeine compounds) can be multi-purpose – for headaches, pains, coughs or colds.

TUBERCULOSIS The 'white plague' is threatening to make the comeback of the 21st century. Vaccines, antibiotics and improved hygiene nearly erased TB from industrialised nations; however, the disease now appears to be resistant to most of the drugs previously used to treat it. Tuberculosis thrives in crowded and dirty living conditions where both ventilation and the people are poor. Tuberculosis certainly is a problem in Tibet, Nepal and India: the airborne bacteria are transmitted through coughing, sneezing or spitting by people in an infectious stage of TB. Conditions can be very smoky in Tibetan teahouses – with a fire burning away in the middle, and no ventilation. Catching TB is a matter of repeated exposure to the bacteria over a period of time.

AVIAN FLU Sporadic lethal outbreaks of avian influenza A (H5N1) have been reported in China and other Asian countries since 2003, and in April 2017, cases with H7N9 were reported in Tibet. These outbreaks have occurred among wild birds and bats; among domestic chickens, ducks, quail and pigs; and more alarmingly, among humans. Avian flu is spread through saliva, nasal secretions and faeces from infected birds. Most cases of avian flu infection in humans have resulted from contact with infected birds or contaminated surfaces. There have now been reports from the World Health Organization that avian flu can also be caught through eating under-cooked infected poultry or possibly eggs. Ensure that all food is well cooked and if in doubt don't eat it. This is less likely to happen in Tibet as poultry is not a staple on the plateau (though there was a minor outbreak of bird flu among chickens at a farm close to Lhasa in mid-2005). However, Tibet does have lots of wild birds – and wild birds are known to play a role in spreading the virus.

SARS Severe Acute Respiratory Syndrome (SARS) was first detected in Hong Kong in November 2002. The illness spread to more than two dozen countries worldwide with devastating results, before being brought under control. Symptoms include high fever, headache and body aches. Mild respiratory problems are present at the outset, later developing into a dry cough and pneumonia. To prevent the spread of SARS in Asia, devices appeared at major airports with the capability of scanning incoming passengers for high forehead temperature. In 2003, Tibet was closed to travellers for most of the high season because of SARS outbreaks in China. However, there have been no further reported cases since 2003.

INTESTINAL BUGS AND WORMS If diarrhoea is persistent, with blood or mucus in the stool, this indicates a more serious illness such as amoebic or bacillary dysentery. In this case, you need a stool test to identify the culprit – merely guessing and indulging in 'drug cocktails' may be detrimental. Facilities to identify bugs like this are not available in Lhasa; the nearest place is the Western-run CIWEC clinic in Kathmandu (page 110). From Chengdu, the closest reliable medical testing facilities are found in Bangkok, Singapore and Hong Kong. For bacillary dysentery (recognised by blood or mucus in the stools, which may be accompanied by a fever), the best treatment is to take Azithromycin. Other antibiotic drugs include Ciprofloxacin and Norfloxacin. More of a problem is giardia, caused by a microscopic parasite that can elude some water filters (iodine kills it). Giardia-like symptoms include stomach cramps, sulphurous burps or gas, and persistent diarrhoea. You can treat it with Tinidazole (another drug is Metronidazole, also known as Flagyl, though this may not be as good, has to be taken for longer and has more side effects).

Various types of intestinal worms are also prevalent in Nepal – the larvae are often present in unwashed vegetables or under-cooked meat. Intestinal worms are awful to contemplate, but not of great concern since drugs like Mebendazole are highly effective in killing them. Stool tests can detect the culprits.

HIGH-ALTITUDE MOSQUITOES It used to be that mosquitoes could not overcome an altitude barrier of around 2,500m and could not survive the bitter cold at higher elevations. But since 2009, mosquitoes have somehow found their way into Lhasa city for the first time in recorded history. This bizarre phenomenon can be attributed to a number of factors: climate change (hotter summers in Lhasa), the railway to Lhasa (mosquitoes hitching a ride), and immigration (Han Chinese entering Tibet). Whatever the cause, the mosquitoes have broken the altitude barrier, setting up in Lhasa at 3,650m. Thus far, it appears that these mosquitoes may cause swelling to sensitive people, but do not appear to be transmitters of diseases such as malaria, though this could change.

HEPATITIS Hepatitis is a viral infection of the liver, primarily spread through contaminated food and water (hepatitis A) or dirty needles and body fluids, including sexual transmission (hepatitis B). Since both types are prevalent in Nepal and Tibet and prevention is better than cure, obtain vaccinations prior to travel. At the very least, have one shot of hepatitis A vaccine. This will last for a year when a booster dose can be given to extend coverage for at least 25 years. Protection for hepatitis B (eg: Engerix B) consists of three shots over a minimum of 21 days (for those aged 16 or over). You can now do both at once (again three shots over 21 days) by using Twinrix. For those under 16, the minimum time for hepatitis B or the junior Twinrix is over two months, so allow plenty of time before travel. You would also be wise to have typhoid vaccine.

RABIES Tibet is considered to be a high-risk rabies country. Rabies can be contracted through a bite, a scratch or simply saliva on skin from any mammal, although dogs are the most likely culprits. They can be infectious several days before showing symptoms, so an animal can look perfectly healthy. Thoroughly wash any contaminated skin with soap and water for a good 10–15 minutes. Rinse any mucous membranes with the cleanest water you can find. If you have not had the pre-exposure course of rabies vaccine before travelling, then you will need to start a post-exposure course as soon as possible. This comprises five days of vaccine given over a month. In addition, if you have been bitten and possibly scratched, then you need more rapid protection. This is given in the form of rabies immunoglobulin (RIG) – ideally human, but horse RIG will do. This is very hard to come by in Tibet and will almost certainly mean you will have to evacuate. If you have had the pre-exposure course (three doses of vaccine over about a month) then the post-exposure treatment is reduced to just needing two doses of vaccine three days apart. This makes the situation much easier to manage and may avoid the need to evacuate. Remember, rabies is nearly 100% fatal and is a horrible way to die.

TICK-BORNE ENCEPHALITIS Tick-borne encephalitis (TBE) is a potentially fatal viral infection transmitted by the bite of infected ticks. Less commonly, cases of TBE can occur following ingestion of unpasteurised milk products. The ticks that carry the disease are more common in early spring and late autumn, and cases have been reported in the western province of Tibet.

Travellers are at increased risk during outdoor activities such as hiking in vegetated areas, when the ticks can fall from overhanging leaves and branches.

Vaccination against tick-borne encephalitis is available in the UK (Ticovac and Ticovac Junior below the age of 16) and comprises a series of two injections that can be done one to three months apart. If time is short and urgent immunisation is required, then the vaccine can be given two weeks apart. A third dose should be given from five to 12 months to complete the primary course.

Ticks should ideally be removed as soon as possible, as leaving ticks on the body increases the chance of infection. They should be removed with special tick tweezers that can be bought in good travel shops. Failing that, you can use your finger nails by grasping the tick as close to your body as possible and pulling steadily and firmly away at right angles to your skin. The tick will then come away complete, as long as you do not jerk or twist. If possible, douse the wound with alcohol (any spirit will do) or iodine. Irritants (eg: Olbas oil) or lit cigarettes are to be discouraged since they can cause the ticks to regurgitate and therefore increase the risk of disease. It is best to get a travelling companion to check you for ticks, and if you are travelling with small children, remember to check their heads, particularly behind the ears. An area of spreading redness around the bite site – or a rash or fever coming on a few days or more after the bite – should stimulate a trip to the doctor.

ALTITUDE SICKNESS When Sherpas say climbing is in their blood, they may mean it literally. Sherpas have a physiology adapted to the high-altitude environment – their blood has a higher red-cell count and their lung capacity is larger. Ability to adapt to altitude is thought to be in your genes. That may mean you either have the high-altitude genes or you don't. If you do, you can adapt quickly; if you don't, it will take longer – or so the theory goes. At higher altitudes, air pressure is lower and the air is thinner. Although it contains the same percentage of oxygen as it does at sea level, there's less oxygen delivered in each lungful of air. So you have to breathe harder, and your body adapts over time by increasing the number of red blood cells enabling more oxygen to be carried through the system.

Altitude sickness is something of a mystery. It does not appear to depend on being in shape: athletes have come down with it, and it may occur suddenly in subjects who have not experienced it before. Altitude sickness can occur at elevations above

2,000m, and about 50% of people will experience some symptoms at 3,500m. The higher you go the more pronounced the symptoms could become. So adjustment is required at each 400m of elevation gain after that.

Terrain above 5,000m (common enough in Tibet) is a harsh, alien environment – above 6,000m is a zone where humans were never meant to go. Like diving at depth, going to high altitudes requires special adjustments. To adapt, you have to be in tune with your body. You need to travel with someone who can monitor your condition – and back you up (get you out) if something should go wrong. Consider this: if you were to be transported in a hot-air balloon and dropped on the summit of Everest, without oxygen you would collapse within 10 minutes, and die within an hour. However, a handful of climbers have summitted Everest without oxygen: by attaining a degree of acclimatisation, they have been able to achieve this. A similar analogy could be drawn with flying in from Chengdu, which is barely above sea level, to Lhasa, at 3,650m. That's a 3,500m gain in an hour or so. You need to rest and recover.

The study of altitude sickness is still evolving. Recent studies suggest that altitude sickness may be due to leaky membranes – which are more permeable as you go up in elevation. It was unknown if a person could survive above 7,500m without oxygen until 1978, when Messner and Habeler summitted Everest. Actually, a hundred years earlier, in 1875, French balloonist Tissandier reached 8,000m after a 3-hour ascent and lost consciousness: the balloon descended and Tissandier survived but his two companions died. Messner was told he would come back from Everest a raving madman, or, at the very least, a brain-damaged automaton if he attempted the peak without oxygen. Messner got his timing right, got to the top, and went on to bag all the 8,000m peaks without oxygen. Climbers like Messner, however, will admit to impaired functions at higher elevations – and to strange encounters. Messner recalls talking to his ice axe, talking to his feet, talking to an imaginary companion and having hallucinations.

Altitude strategy It is essential to take it easy for the first three or four days after arriving at altitude; most acclimatisation takes place within the first ten days (it can take two or three months to fully acclimatise). When reaching altitude, most travellers experience discomfort – headaches, fatigue, nausea, vomiting, lack of appetite, swelling or tingling of the hands or feet, difficulty sleeping. This condition is usually mild and short-lived. Headaches can be treated with paracetamol or ibuprofen: if a headache persists, or intensifies – or if the person wakes up with a headache – this is a sign of real altitude sickness. The critical question is how to distinguish between mild altitude sickness and more serious cases. You don't acclimatise by sitting around doing nothing – get some simple exercise such as walking, and drink lots of water. Do not drink alcohol, as it contributes to dehydration. Smoking, of course, will be a major problem at altitude.

Never underestimate altitude – it can be a killer. Go slow, be careful, experiment before you go higher. The climber's maxim is 'walk high, sleep low' – climbers may trek higher during the day, but retire to lower levels to sleep. The maximum rate of ascent when trekking should be about 400m a day. If you're acclimatised to Lhasa (3,650m) you really need to undergo a second acclimatisation phase to handle a visit to Lake Namtso (at 4,650m). On a brighter note, once you've acclimatised to a particular altitude, the altered blood chemistry should stay with you for about ten days. So if you acclimatise to the 5,000m level and then go down to 3,500m, you should be able to go back up to 5,000m again without ill effects, provided you do so within ten days.

This text comes with a few caveats. Mainly, that there are a lot of unknowns when it comes to altitude sickness. What works for one person may not work for another. The only guaranteed cure for altitude sickness is immediate descent to lower elevations and administration of oxygen to the patient. Drugs can reduce symptoms of altitude sickness, but may also mask symptoms: the taking of these drugs should never be used to avoid descent or to enable further ascent.

HERBAL DRUGS Dr Stephen Bezruchka, in his book *Altitude Illness: Prevention and Treatment* (Mountaineers Books, 2005), says:

> The herb, Ginkgo biloba, 80mg to 120mg twice a day, beginning five days before ascent and continued a day at altitude, appears to prevent AMS. It interferes with platelet activity in the blood, so its safety for those taking other drugs that have such effects is unknown. It also improves blood circulation to the hands in the cold. Its role at altitude remains to be clarified, but it has few side effects and should be considered.

Chinese visitors to Tibet use a variety of traditional herbal medicines to counter the effect of altitude, but what is in these remedies is often not specified. The fruits of the Chinese wolfberry are thought to be efficacious for altitude problems, but the plant that shows up most frequently in herbal remedies is the Tibetan Radix rhodiolae plant, which grows on the plateau at elevations of 3,500 to 5,000m. Also known as 'plateau ginseng', this plant, according to Chinese sources, is efficacious for relieving high blood pressure, high blood fat, diabetes, senility and 'internet addiction'. In any case, it appears to improve blood flow, which is good at altitude. Rhodiola concoctions are sold in Lhasa in capsules, as a liquid in glass phials and

ACUTE MOUNTAIN SICKNESS Acute mountain sickness (AMS) is a general term for a whole raft of altitude-related maladies. Symptoms of AMS include gastro-intestinal turmoil (loss of appetite, nausea, vomiting), extreme fatigue or weakness, dizziness or light-headedness, and difficulty breathing or sleeping.

A case of severe AMS may result in high-altitude pulmonary oedema (HAPE), when a small amount of fluid that appears in the lungs at altitude is not absorbed normally. Instead, it accumulates, obstructing the flow of oxygen and drowning the victim in his or her own fluids. Symptoms include rapid respiratory rate and rapid pulse, cough, crackles or wheezing in one or both lungs, frothy or bloodstained sputum, and severe shortness of breath. Another serious complication is high-altitude cerebral oedema (HACE), where the fluid problem is in the brain. A person with HACE is disoriented, has an unsteady gait and trouble using the hands, is irritable, suffers from drowsiness and nightmares, and may suffer hallucinations. Memory, judgement and perception are impaired.

To counter HAPE and HACE, mountaineering expeditions sometimes tote a Gamow bag, which weighs about 8kg. It is a body-enclosing bag that can be hand-pumped to replicate atmospheric pressure at much lower levels. Recent studies suggest that a 1-hour treatment corresponds to a descent of 1,500m: this leads to short-term improvements, but nothing lasting. Some group-tour operators carry a tank of oxygen to deal with cases – but that tank may only hold 30 minutes of oxygen (drivers sometimes carry oxygen). Drugs like Diamox are also used to counter the effects of altitude (see box, above). The best solution, however, in all cases, is simply in various teas. Cans of rhodiola drink (on sale in Lhasa) list rhodiola, honey, water and citric acid as ingredients. Another drink available around Lhasa is a kind of high-altitude tea. Similar to *maté de coca* (the Andean remedy, from coca leaves), this tea is said to relieve headaches, insomnia, nausea and dizziness brought about by altitude. The tea is called *Gaoyuanan* and is made in Tibet. You can buy a box of sachets in Lhasa at several of the hotels or at Dunya Restaurant (which serves it as 'altitude relax tea').

DIAMOX Diamox (acetazolamide) is a diuretic that can help the rate of acclimatisation and may be recommended for individuals who are flying in to Lhasa and don't have time to acclimatise. It may also improve the quality of sleep at altitude. Since it's a diuretic, it leads to increased urination and to dehydration, so you need to keep drinking more if you use it. Other side effects include a tingling sensation in the lips and fingertips, and the medication may give a strange taste to carbonated drinks. There is now good evidence that if it suits you it is worth taking as it reduces the chance of getting altitude sickness. Do a trial at sea level for two days at least two weeks before travel. Take a 125mg tablet in the morning and again at 16.00. If you get side effects then it is probably best to avoid using it as a prophylactic medicine. People who are allergic to sulphur drugs may not be suitable to take Diamox. If it suits you then start taking the tablets one to two days before reaching 3,500m and continue to maximum altitude and for two to three days after if you are continuing to be at altitude. If a person comes down with Acute Mountain Sickness (AMS), then the first thing to do is to descend at least 500m. If treatment with Diamox is considered necessary, then the dosage can be increased to 250mg every 6 hours.

to transport the patient to a lower elevation as fast as possible (if this means moving in the middle of the night, do so). Unfortunately, on the Tibetan plateau, descent to lower elevation is not always feasible. In serious cases, the focus is often evacuation by road to Kathmandu, or by air to either Kathmandu or Chengdu.

ACCIDENTS AND RECKLESS DRIVING By far the biggest potential threat for travellers in Tibet is possible injury caused by vehicle collisions or road accidents. It's unknown how many foreigners have perished in Tibet due to driving accidents, but there have certainly been cases of trucks and rental vehicles being totalled, and foreigners killed. There are no safety devices along precipitous mountain roads in Tibet and few warning signs. Your fate rests with your driver's road skills.

Drivers range from excellent to downright dangerous. Assess the state of your driver and his judgement calls – if he's going too fast or taking unnecessary risks, tell him. Some macho drivers seem to make a sport out of overtaking everything in sight – on blind corners or perilous cliff edges. If the driver makes a dangerous move, signal for him to pull over and stop, and explain that there is no rush to reach the destination (you don't mind arriving half an hour later), and therefore there is no need to overtake all the time. Get the driver used to the idea of going slower so you can take in the scenery and make photo stops. A tired driver is definitely a hazard: if the driver looks sleepy, keep him awake – or rearrange the itinerary so you stay in the nearest hotel, where he can rest up. Danger increases exponentially with driving at night. Visibility is much reduced, and drivers may choose not to

3

turn on their headlights, preferring to navigate in total darkness, which is deadly.

You are bound to experience some pretty close calls in Tibet. One 4x4 hit a flock of sheep – resulting in a smashed front windshield. The passengers were all right, but the incensed shepherd had to be compensated, and the group continued, albeit a bit frozen with the windshield missing. In another situation, our driver played 'chicken' with a military convoy, doing daredevil overtakes on mountain roads with sheer drop-offs. After overtaking all the trucks, the driver called for a pit stop – at which time all the army trucks overtook us again.

You most likely don't want to even think about this, but you have to consider what would happen if there was an accident. The biggest problem could be loss of blood. It's not known to what degree hospitals in China or Tibet screen their blood – tainted blood carries all kinds of viruses, including hepatitis and HIV. Then there's the question of whether your blood type will even be stocked. Blood Type O is rare. The Chinese neither have nor store Rh-negative blood for transfusions: you'd have to be evacuated to the nearest Rh-negative country.

DOGS Tibetans are fond of dogs: these hounds perform guard duties in many villages around Tibet. Dogs are believed to be reincarnates of renegade monks who didn't quite make the grade, and hence are accepted at monasteries. Some are in good shape; others are mangy and flea-bitten. Sometimes dogs operate in packs around monasteries, in which case they can be benign (lazing around, or curled up in corners) or they can be extremely dangerous. Travellers have been attacked and dragged to the ground in some places, and then rescued by monks. This can lead to lacerations requiring stitches – not a pleasant thought. Since the market for selling Tibetan mastiffs crashed in China, a number of these dogs have been abandoned by both masters and sellers. That has become a problem in places like Yushu (northern Tibet), once a major breeding centre.

If a bite from a dog punctures the skin, it can lead to a far greater problem: rabies. See the *Rabies* section, pages 115–16.

CHINESE MEDICAL FACILITIES

Chinese hospitals are of a very low standard in China generally, and completely primitive in Tibet, when compared with Western medical facilities. It could be said that should you fall ill, rather than stay in a hospital you would do a lot better by taking a good hotel room. I have personally seen, in Tibetan clinics, rusting antiquated equipment, and filthy wards and operating theatres. There's a shortage of sterile equipment and supplies; the most basic facilities for diagnosis and treatment are generally absent; doctors and nurses are poorly trained. Surgical gloves may be washed and re-used – and the same with syringes. A disturbing trend in some hospitals in Tibet is to subject the patient to a cardiogram, an X-ray and a glucose drip – regardless of what illness is presented – and then charge for these services. Other hospitals are prone to giving the patient lots of antibiotics.

In Lhasa, the best facilities are at the Military Hospital, but this place is not usually accessible to tourists. The People's Hospital has an emergency centre, but no mechanism for dealing with seriously injured people. An Italian NGO has been supplying equipment and training at the People's Hospital. Costs for foreigners staying at the People's Hospital in Lhasa can be very high, and payment may be expected in Chinese cash (travellers' cheques will probably not be accepted, and nor will credit cards).

The nearest places in China for good medical attention are Chengdu (a hospital can run to US$120 a day for foreigners), Hong Kong (even more expensive) and major cities such as Beijing and Shanghai. Elsewhere in Asia, any place that has a lot of foreign embassies is good for clinics and hospitals with Western standards, often staffed by Western doctors. The best are found in Singapore, Nepal (the CIWEC Clinic, see page 110) and Bangkok. See also *Medical* in Lhasa, pages 148–9. This is why having good medical insurance is so important.

MEDEVAC CREWS

International SOS is a medevac organisation which comes under the umbrella of parent company Asia Emergency Assistance (AEA) and has its head office in Singapore (*331 North Bridge Rd, #17-00 Odeon Towers;* +65 6338 2311; w *internationalsos.com*). They are the world's leading specialists in medical evacuation and travel security, being involved in evacuations in the aftermath of the tsunami at Fukushima, and various terrorist incidents occurring across Asia. International SOS will evacuate to Singapore, Bangkok or Hong Kong if possible; there are branch offices in Beijing, Shanghai and Guangzhou in the PRC. Check their website for full contact details and for information about their Assistance App, which offers medical and travel guides to members. International SOS Assistance Centres in the following locations are all open 24 hours: Singapore (+65 6338 7800), Bangkok (+66 2 205 7866) and Hong Kong (+852 2528 9900). AEA has been able to fly a Lear jet from Hong Kong into Lhasa for an evacuation, but the procedure is extremely complicated and costly.

RISKY SITUATIONS AND EVACUATION

The best advice that can be offered in risky medical situations in Tibet is this: when in doubt, evacuate. Get on a scheduled flight to Kathmandu or Chengdu (an alternative is to take a 4x4 down to Nepal, but this could take three days or more). If the patient can be brought to Gongkar airport without too much trauma, then you can organise the evacuation yourself. When sufficiently pressured, airline authorities will bump passengers off a regular flight to Chengdu or Kathmandu to create space for an emergency case, so the idea is to get to Gongkar airport as fast as possible.

Although helicopter evacuation is employed for injured trekkers in Nepal, it is simply not an option in Tibet. Although the Chinese military have Sikorsky and Boeing CH-47 high-altitude choppers, these are strictly for military applications and under no circumstances will be diverted for civilian use. The elevation limit for conventional helicopters is around 6,000m (although a French helicopter pilot landed on the summit of Everest in May 2005).

If it's a case of altitude sickness, it's essential to get oxygen for the patient as fast as possible. Lhasa Hotel has oxygen 'pillows' (pillows with nasal tubes attached); you can also buy oxygen in a sort of aerosol can (or larger tank) in Lhasa itself at a commercial outlet just west of the Potala.

The above evacuation advice is offered because (a) medical facilities in Tibet are very basic and (b) there is no system of helicopter rescue in Tibet. Travellers have died in the past after not being evacuated, so these risks should be taken very seriously.

SAFETY AND SECURITY

As with any Third World travel situation, you need to keep your wits about you in Tibet. Theft of luggage is uncommon on the plateau, but it does happen. Ditto with rented bicycles – lock yours in a secure, highly visible location. Luggage has even gone missing from some budget hotel storage rooms in Lhasa; to reduce the risk of this happening, identify your baggage with your passport number prominently displayed on an attached label. Keep an eye on your bags when on the move. Pilfering of personal items is known to be a risk when trekking in some areas, particularly the Everest region.

Because of the heavy Chinese military presence in Tibet, armed robbery or similar crimes are extremely rare, though in old Tibet banditry certainly existed in more remote areas. A greater threat to life and limb is on 4x4 sorties and through resulting confrontations that may develop on these trips. Apart from the major health hazard it presents, high altitude is known to befuddle the brain, making you irritable and unable to focus when making decisions or when judgement is required. And there are important decisions that need to be made: for example, to size up quickly those on whom your life depends. That means that, if a rental vehicle or taxi driver refuses to slow down and keeps overtaking recklessly, you may have to bail out.

Confrontations between drivers, guides and passengers over changes of itinerary or other problems can turn ugly. Incidents have involved both Tibetan and Chinese driving crews. In the Everest region, when a driver and his guide (both Tibetan) refused to drive beyond Rongbuk Gompa for the extra dozen kilometres to Everest base camp, a passenger swore at the guide. The guide picked up a rock and hurled it at the passenger. The rock missed, but the passenger was in a state of shock that he would even attempt such a thing. Disagreements between passengers themselves can also turn nasty. Other arguments may erupt over permits and permission with Chinese authorities, who are not noted for their politeness. In all of these situations, mediation skills are called for: stay cool, be patient, be polite yet insistent, and keep your temper to yourself.

WOMEN TRAVELLERS

Although Tibetan Buddhism promotes a code of respect, there have been cases of harassment of Western women by Tibetan men, especially on crowded buses and when hitching rides in trucks. Tibetan women dress modestly, with little flesh exposed, and that may be the key here: a Western woman wearing shorts and a revealing top may send out the wrong message, and is bound to attract the wrong kind of attention. For these reasons, travelling solo in Tibet is not advisable for a woman. However, a woman who speaks enough Tibetan – and who dresses modestly – should not have a problem. Chinese men and Chinese military appear to have little interest in sexual advances to Western women, perhaps due to the phenomenon of numerous Chinese prostitutes plying their trade at karaoke bars in the larger towns of Tibet.

TRAVELLING WITH A DISABILITY

Until the 1990s, there was only one elevator in the whole of Tibet, at what was then known as the Holiday Inn in Lhasa. Tibetans used to sneak into the hotel to experience this wonder of the Western world. That will give some idea of the problems facing disabled travellers: Tibet can be a very rough ride. If hotels lack elevators, think about monasteries – none of them have anything remotely resembling an elevator. And monasteries and fortresses are often built on hilltops, with steep access.

Still, if a blind climber can overcome the obstacles and make it to the top of Everest, then nothing is impossible. Erik Weihenmayer made it to the summit in 2001 from the Nepalese side. In 2004, he came to Tibet to visit his friends Sabriye

Tenberken and Paul Kronenberg, the co-founders of Braille Without Borders (w *braillewithoutborders.org*), a project in Lhasa to help blind Tibetans. Erik inspired blind teenagers at this school to climb on Rongbuk Glacier at the north side of Everest. A documentary called *Blindsight* was released in 2006, describing these encounters. The best advice for disabled travellers is to ensure that you are going with a travel agent knowledgeable about potential problems and hazards, and who can provide the logistical support and help needed. Navyo Nepal (w *navyonepal. com*) is a Kathmandu-based operator with experience in organising tours for disabled travellers in Nepal and Tibet.

TRAVELLING WITH CHILDREN

Tibet presents challenges for travel with young children, as the dryness and altitude can make them irritable. Then again, as so few foreigners come to Tibet with children, this is of great fascination to local Tibetans, who fawn over the kids. Be aware that medical facilities are sub-standard in Tibet, so you will need to second-guess on the medical front and arrive well prepared for any contingencies. It's hard to say what would make Tibet entertaining for kids. Monasteries, probably not. But kids love yaks – they are new creatures to marvel at. Going to see the yak dance at a place like Shangri-La Bar in Lhasa will be a definite hit.

To set up connections with Tibetan culture, buy some picture books for kids. Available in Delhi or Kathmandu is a ten-page book titled *I am a Yak*, which introduces nomad culture. Others in this series published in India include *How the Yak got his Long Hair*, *A Snowlion's Lesson* and *The Three Silver Coins*. In the West, Tibetan folklore and Buddhist animal tales are available in books for young readers. And the classic story about the yeti is found in Hergé's comicbook, *Tintin in Tibet*.

LGBT TRAVELLERS

There are no particular taboos or caveats for gay and lesbian travellers visiting Tibetan regions. Buddhism is an easy-going religion, and highly tolerant. In a country (China) where men (or women) often stroll hand in hand as a show of friendship, gay travellers should not raise any eyebrows. Some tour agents market gay and lesbian tours to Tibet, or have done so in the past. These include Out Adventures (w *out-adventures.com*) and Hanns Ebensten Travel (w *hetravel.com*).

Part Two

THE GUIDE

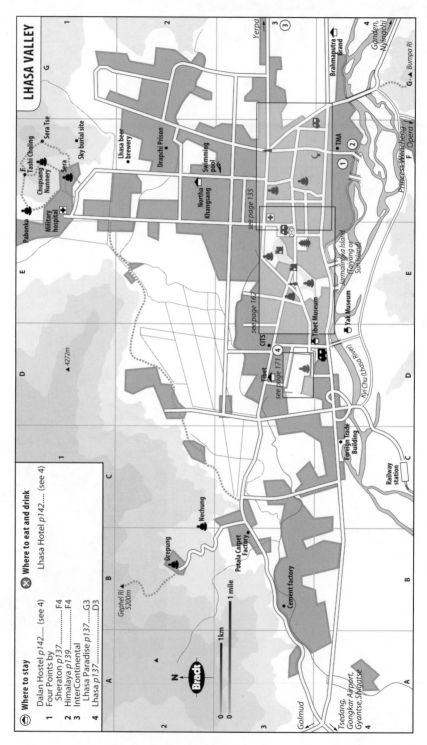

LHASA VALLEY

Where to stay

1 Dalan Hostel p142.... (see 4)
   Four Points by
   Sheraton p137..............F4
2 Himalaya p139..............F4
3 InterContinental
   Lhasa Paradise p137......G3
4 Lhasa p137...................D3

Where to eat and drink

Lhasa Hotel p142.... (see 4)

Gephel Ri
5200m

Golmud

Tsedang,
Gongkar Airport,
Gyantse, Shigatse

Drepung

Nechung

Potala Carpet
Factory

Cement factory

Foreign Trade
Building

Railway
station

Tibet

CITS

see page 171

see page 162

Tibet Museum

Yak Museum

see page 135

Northa
Khangsang

Swimming
pool

Drapchi Prison

Lhasa beer
brewery

Pabonka

Military
hospital

Chupsang
Nunnery

Sera

Sera Tse

Tashi Choling

Sky burial site

4272m

Kyi Chu (Lhasa River)

Jarmalingka Island
(Haiyang or
Sun Island)

Princess Wencheng

TMA

F Opera

Brahmaputra
Grand

Ganden,
Nyingchi

Bumpa Ri

Yerpa

4

Lhasa

Telephone code 0891

SECRETS OF THE CITY

The name Lhasa is thought to derive from the Tibetan words *lha* (sacred) and *sa* (earth). In the late 19th and early 20th centuries, Lhasa was the most reclusive city on the face of the planet – a sacred place that was as difficult a goal as Mecca to reach. Even the greatest Western explorers of the era – Nikolai Prejavalsky, Sven Hedin – failed to make it.

Now this shroud of secrecy has been ripped away, to reveal … a humdrum Chinese town. Lhasa is one large Chinatown now, with rows and rows of faceless Chinese apartment blocks and government buildings. 'It's just another Chinese city with a few Tibetans thrown in for colour,' says a Tibetan-born American visitor. The most disturbing aspect of Lhasa is not only the overwhelming Chinese presence: it is the Tibetan absence. The Tibetans are a minority in their own capital. The population of Lhasa is estimated at more than 700,000. A hefty number are migrant workers from provinces like Sichuan, working in markets, restaurants and as taxi drivers. It is not known whether estimated Lhasa population figures include or exclude the sizeable Chinese military, police and paramilitary presence that rings the city, living in special bases.

If you are disappointed with Lhasa, or feel cheated of the mystique you had expected, you won't be the first. The eccentric English traveller Thomas Manning tried to forge a route through to Peking, and by chance reached Lhasa in 1812, disguised as a Chinese physician. He found the Potala extraordinary, and the rest of the place a dump. Here's his description of Old Lhasa, one of the first 'snapshots' of the Potala ever recorded by a Westerner:

> The road here, as it winds past the palace, is royally broad; it is level and free from stones, and combined with the view of the lofty towering palace, which forms a majestic mountain of a building, has a magnificent effect. The roads about the palace swarmed with monks; its nooks and angles with beggars lounging and basking in the sun … As a whole [the Potala] seemed perfect enough; but I could not comprehend its plan in detail … If the palace exceeded my expectations, the town as far fell short of them. There is nothing striking, nothing pleasing in its appearance. The habitations are begrimed with smut and dirt; the avenues are full of dogs …

Manning not only managed to get to Lhasa, he also gained an unprecedented audience with the seven-year-old Dalai Lama (IX), which he recorded as a moving experience. Almost a century later, in 1904, the invading English under Francis Younghusband found their triumphal march into Lhasa impeded by piles of refuse, stagnant pools of water, open sewers, and various rabid animals foraging for putrid scraps of food. They did, however, note that the gleaming gold roofs of the Jokhang and other temples restored the balance in favour of the majestic.

Lhasa was never a big city. There was no census taken in the Lhasa of 1949 or earlier, but the population was estimated at 30,000. There were an additional 7,000 monks at Sera Monastery and 9,000 monks at Drepung. This brought the figure to around 45,000, and probably double that number would be in Lhasa during festivals. Lhasa's design was based not so much on practical as sacred aspects. In the 7th century, King Songtsen Gampo moved his capital from the Yarlung Valley to the site of Lhasa. Later, as the residence of the Dalai Lamas, Lhasa became the religious centre of Tibet, and the seat of government. Lhasa was (and is) dominated by the Potala Palace, the winter residence of the Dalai Lama, with his summer palace, the Norbulingka, below. Within the front, walled section of the Potala was the entire Tibetan government administration, where the nobles lived. These buildings have now largely disappeared. Across town, separated by meadows, was the Jokhang Temple with a market and artisan section. A third edifice was the Palace of the Regent – the man who ruled in times when the Dalai Lama was not of age.

Old Lhasa disappeared with the Chinese invasion of Tibet in 1950 and with the flight of the Dalai Lama to India in 1959. Transformation was swift: few of those Tibetans who fled in 1959 would have recognised Lhasa in 1964, when pro-Chinese writer Israel Epstein said:

> Lhasa is becoming a beautiful modern city. Not long ago, the Potala, the temples and a few mansions stood amid hovels and cesspools of medieval squalor. Now there are miles of well lit, asphalted streets and underground drains ... Electricity is supplied to 90 per cent of all homes for illumination and often for cooking (ex-serfs and slaves get it free). A working people's Cultural Palace and a hall seating twelve hundred is used for meetings, plays and films; there are also two other film theatres. A State Emporium built this year, the biggest of many new shops and stores, sells everything from needles and thread to sewing machines, bicycles and transistor radios ...

Picture this process accelerated over the next 40-odd years, and you get an idea of what's occurred in Lhasa. A Tibetan resident commented that Lhasa had changed more since the 1990s than it had over the previous few hundred years. The urban area of Lhasa has rapidly expanded, with many new Chinese-built apartment buildings and offices. By Chinese figures, the number of vehicles in Lhasa has risen dramatically, but few parking facilities have been built to keep pace with this. Meanwhile, more than 40 auto retailers have set up shop in Lhasa, notching up brisk sales of private cars and SUVs. In northern Lhasa, an industrial fringe has cropped up, with a concrete factory and a brewery. And the coming of the railway to Lhasa is bound to accelerate Chinese construction and development – and pollution. Condominium developments have sprouted around Lhasa in readiness for a real estate boom generated by the arrival of the railway.

While technological change is a positive thing, the fact is that in Lhasa these changes have not been in the interest of the Tibetans – they're for the Chinese. The Tibetans 'still preferred independence to electricity, and freedom to sewers', as French explorer and writer Michel Peissel put it. The Chinese settlers demand electricity and street lighting, Chinese soldiers need roads, and Chinese officials need cultural palaces, and girlie bars and karaoke salons with their glitter and neon. Rows of barbershops near the Potala do a brisk business late at night. Why? Because they are fronts for prostitution – one of Lhasa's dirty secrets. Holy city or whorehouse? For Tibetan pilgrims, Lhasa remains the Holy City, but to even the casual visitor, the Chinese layering of scores of bars and karaoke salons is glaring. And that's not to mention the heavy Chinese military and paramilitary presence, with army bases ringing the city, and a network of prisons. The end result is that Lhasa has become increasingly sinicised. You see it in small details, such as the statuary around the city – pairs of Chinese lions outside the entrance to the Potala, a Chinese dragon sculpture in the fountain in Potala Square, a concrete statue of Chinese mountaineers atop Everest, Chinese flags flying at strategic points, and glowing Chinese neon signs at night.

Since the arrival of the railway in 2006, followed by mass tourism Chinese style, Lhasa has turned into a kind of theme park – what you might call 'Tibet Disney' or 'the Disneyland of Snows'. Parts of the capital have Tibetan trimmings and appear Tibetan, but in fact are not. There are quasi-Tibetan-style buildings. Chinese department store staff may dress Tibetan style.

Patrolling this 'theme park' is a massive security force, one that is heavily armed. PLA troops in camouflage fatigues occupy bunkers on the main streets of Lhasa. Small groups of PLA with machine guns patrol the back alleys. Other teams, dressed in black with SWAT shoulder patches, keep an eye on pilgrims near the Jokhang. Sitting on rooftops under Coca-Cola umbrellas are soldiers with high-powered guns, scanning the Barkor below with binoculars.

In 2012, construction started on a real theme park on the outskirts of Lhasa, showcasing a pop-up version of the Tibetan Quarter and the Potala Palace as a gigantic backdrop for a musical extravaganza about Chinese Princess Wencheng (see box, pages 146–7). Performances started in 2015. Costing millions of dollars to stage, with a cast

LHASA GOES HIGH-RISE

When you picture Lhasa, you may not conjure up a metropolis of high-rises and soaring telecom towers, but this is the way Lhasa is going: upward. Previously, the only building that approached a skyscraper was the Potala, which gets most of its height from the hill it sits on. It is still the tallest place in town, but only because of the hill. Back in 1990, the tallest structure in the Lhasa Valley was a wing of the Holiday Inn, reaching a height of seven floors, with a lift – the only one in Tibet at the time and an object of great curiosity among Tibetans. But now there are lots of lifts in Lhasa, and they ride much higher. The Tibet Foreign Trade and Economic Co-operation Building, to the west side of Lhasa near the Kyi Chu River, takes the skyscraper prize with 17 floors, shimmering with a green-tinted glass façade. Other tall glass façades belong to the China Telecom building (ten floors) and the Tibet International Grand Hotel (11 floors). On the Sera Road is a 13-storey block – the ominous City Police HQ. These soaring steel and glass towers do not exactly blend in with existing Tibetan architecture: glass was rarely employed in pre-1950 Tibet (it had to be brought in overland from India) and Tibetan traditional buildings were rarely built higher than four floors. There is still lots of scope for new architectural monstrosities in Lhasa as Chinese architects continue to experiment with slapping mock-Tibetan façades on to Chinese structures, or mixing the two styles – resulting in spectacular clashes.

Very few new buildings in Lhasa have been constructed with Tibetan architectural flair: one instance is the Tibet Museum. Another is Lhasa Railway Station, which does not go high-rise, but extends horizontally. The Chinese architects claim this structure is based on traditional Tibetan elements, with an inward-sloping façade. It does, at least, have an element of fortress architecture, with little glass showing on the exterior.

of over 600 performers, this musical is about the princess's marriage to Tibetan King Songtsen Gampo – acting in what is essentially an elaborate Chinese propaganda spiel.

To make Lhasa more attractive to coastal entrepreneurs (who, according to the Chinese, 'go to Tibet to offer their expertise to help develop the local economy') some anomalies have popped up. Chinese office blocks are going up around the town; for the first time in its long history, Lhasa is seeing traffic jams, caused by the importation of taxis. Chinese taxi drivers can earn up to five times as much in Lhasa as they can in other cities; other incentives for Chinese immigrants include preferential tax and loan policies. Keeping track of investments is the Tibet Stocks Business Centre, which has a satellite feed listing prices on China's stock exchanges in Shenzhen and Shanghai. Keeping Chinese residents comfortable requires improved communications, so Lhasa is hooked up to China's main mobile phone networks. Satellite reception is provided in Lhasa by Xizang TV and by LBTV. There is, however, a blackout on foreign media and connections: there are no foreign news agencies in Lhasa, there is virtually no foreign television reception, foreign radio signals are jammed, and only a handful of carefully screened foreign NGOs are allowed to operate within Tibet.

GETTING THERE AND AWAY

Getting to Lhasa is practically synonymous with getting to Tibet, since Lhasa is the main transport hub: all flights and overland travel are routed through the capital. Consult the route descriptions on pages 65–74 for details on the intricacies of long-distance travel to Tibet (Lhasa) by road, rail or air.

Lhasa **railway station** [126 C4] lies 4km to the southwest of town, on the south bank of the Kyi Chu. For reasons of tight security, taxis are not permitted to draw up next to the station entrance: you must walk a fair distance from the taxi pick-up point. A taxi into town is around Y40. The station is a strange piece of architecture – a mock-Tibetan structure with inward-sloping façade. Two major bridges close to Lhasa were constructed to link with the railway. There's a white triple-arched railway bridge with a 929m span several kilometres to the west of Lhasa. And close to the Foreign Trade Building downtown is a motor vehicle bridge spanning the Kyi Chu to provide access to downtown Lhasa from the railway station. For domestic trips, the railway is useful for trains to Shigatse or Nagqu.

For locals, the long-distance **bus station** [126 D4] in Lhasa is located to the southwest side of town, near the Tibet Museum.

Lhasa is the hub for **plane arrivals and departures** to Tibet. Ticketing to and from Kathmandu, Beijing, Shanghai, Chengdu, Zhongdian, Yushu, Xining, Xiahe or Ngari should be booked well ahead, especially around peak holiday periods like National Day. Carriers flying into Lhasa include China Eastern, Air China, Sichuan Airlines and Tibet Airlines. Tibet Airlines, headquartered in Lhasa, started operating in 2011 with a flight from Lhasa to Ngari, far-west Tibet. The airline has expanded its fleet and its routes since then, even inaugurating an international flight from Chengdu to Samui, Thailand. Other international flights are on the drawing board.

Taxis charge around Y130 for the run from Lhasa to Gongkar Airport. Nyingtri Airport (page 68) is an alternate flight entry point for central Tibet, with direct flights from both Chengdu and Chongqing.

GETTING AROUND

Lhasa is a small town. It's easy to navigate by prominent landmarks such as the Potala or the TV tower atop Chakpori Hill. Key roundabouts can be readily identified by statuary – Golden Yak statues, Mountaineers-on-Everest statue. You could call them the 'Golden Yak roundabout' or the 'Mountaineers-on-Everest roundabout'. The 13-storey City Police HQ, a glass-and-steel block with two small towers at the top, is a key landmark at the northern side of town.

Old Tibetan street names have been changed to Chinese ones, or names that are easier for Chinese speakers to pronounce. Thus the name Yuthok Lam becomes Yutuo Lu, Lingkor Lam becomes Linkuo Lu, and Dekyi Lam becomes Deji Lu. Ramoche Lam is Xiaozhaosi Lu in Chinese, and Beijing Shar Lam is Beijing Dong Lu.

Being mostly Chinese, taxi drivers respond best to Mandarin versions. So you should quickly learn the Chinese compass points. Beijing Road (Beijing Lu) crosses the entire city and changes name along its length, starting with Beijing Donglu (East Road), morphing into Beijing Zhonglu (Middle Road) and then Beijing Xilu (West Road). Other roads may be designated as being North (Beilu) or South (Nanlu). Thus, Sera Beilu is Sera North Road.

BY TAXI Foot-powered bicycle-taxis rove the streets – they seat two passengers. Regular Volkswagen cabs (imported from east China) cruise the streets and are easy to flag down. They don't have meters – you usually pay a flat rate of Y10 for any distance, but if your destination is a long way out, it may be Y15. You can also hire taxis by the hour, or by the half-day or full day for touring, which makes sense if you have three or four people.

BY BICYCLE You may be informed by your guide and others that cycling is not possible for foreign travellers, or that cycling is only possible in Lhasa if accompanied at all times by a guide, also on a bicycle. This is a load of crock. There are no written rules saying foreigners cannot use a bicycle. If you have free time in Lhasa (free meaning downtime with no guide), try to get your hands on a bicycle. Nobody will stop you careening around the streets. Cycling is an excellent way of getting around – since the town is mostly flat, you can go a long way, even on a gearless Chinese roadster. Flat is easy, but if you tackle any inclines, you need to be well acclimatised, as the altitude can be a knockout.

Young Chinese travellers who cycle in from as far away as Sichuan often end up selling their bikes in Lhasa, which means there are good quality mountain bikes around, possibly available as rentals. The best mountain bikes are Taiwanese imports with front suspension. Take the alley next to Dunya Restaurant (page 143) to find a place called HDF Youth Hostel. You might find bikes there.

Lhasa has a public rental system for bicycles, as in European cities, with bikes stationed at various points. However, you will need to get past the ID rigmarole to use this.

BY PRIVATE VEHICLE HIRE These days, with roads paved to Mount Kailash, the most common vehicles used for tourism are seven- or eight-seat Hyundai minivans or similar. You may see copies of the Toyota Landcruiser, like the Beijing-built version of the Jeep Cherokee. For some dirt-road destinations, you may need a 4x4 vehicle like the Toyota Landcruiser or Mitsubishi Pajero. The Toyota Landcruiser 4500 is a good choice if you can afford it as it has double-capacity fuel tanks, giving it a range of perhaps 700km without refuelling. It comes with an array of fog lights and other extras, and rides higher off the ground. However, the Landcruiser 4500 normally only seats four passengers (meaning three passengers plus guide), while the older Landcruiser seats five passengers (four passengers plus guide). This is because of front-seat configuration, which is bucket seat for the Landcruiser 4500 (driver and

Lhasa has nowhere near the number of adventure tour outfits that operate out of Kathmandu, but things are starting to pick up: some adventure tour operators from Nepal have shifted their focus and their expertise to Tibet.

Most adventure tour operators (such as those for mountain biking) make arrangements with clients long before they get to Tibet. However, if you have built 'free days' into your itinerary for Lhasa, it is possible to arrange small-group adventure touring on the spot. Two options that spring to mind are bicycling around Lhasa, or combination jeep-biking. If you want to mount your own day trips by bike, head east on the road to Ganden: there is far less traffic in this direction. See page 131 for ideas on where to cycle around Lhasa.

In a group of four or more, you can join exhilarating rafting trips out of Lhasa, either as day trips or multiple-day camping sorties (see box, page 181).

one passenger in front). In the older Landcruiser you can squeeze a driver and two passengers in the front seat (although this is not entirely comfortable because of the gear sticks). If you can afford it, go with three paying passengers and guide (this is what group tours regularly do). If you all have a lot of gear, the baggage weight alone will limit the vehicle to three passengers. If you have say seven people, you could hire two Landcruisers, sharing one guide.

Landcruisers and other 4x4s cost about Y1,500 (US$230) a day, depending on the route, the distance, the itinerary and so on. Pricing may be based on kilometres covered: calculate on about Y5 per kilometre. If you go into Everest there's a lot of wear and tear on the vehicle, which operators don't like, so the price will rise for that itinerary. If you're making a one-way run to the Nepal border, the agency expects a return subsidy to cover cost of fuel (even though the driver may pick up new passengers).

It is worth inspecting your vehicle before heading out of Lhasa. Get the driver to take you for a short spin to Drepung or Sera. Are the tyres bald? Do the seats have any springs left in them? What about mirrors – does your vehicle have any? These are basic things that can – and should – be remedied before you set off on a cross-Tibet saga. If you are going to pay through the nose for vehicle hire, make sure the vehicle is in decent shape, or demand another one. Same with the guide: if he or she mumbles incoherently in broken English, ask to have him or her changed. A guide has to speak adequate English – that is part of the job description.

BY BUS AND MINIBUS Although a local minibus system exists, most travellers don't bother with it because they will invariably have a rented vehicle at their disposal. However, if you have some free time on your itinerary, you could look into taking a bus or minibus from Beijing Road out to, say, Drepung Monastery or Sera Monastery. Locals take minibuses all over Tibet – to places like Shigatse, Samye, Tsedang or Nagqu. There are crack-of-dawn pilgrim bus departures from the west side of Barkor Square, heading for Ganden, and less frequently to Tsurphu or Drigung. Chinese backpackers use these services. For Gongkar Airport, there are airline bus departures several times daily from the airline ticket office, located just north of Tibet Post Hotel. Lhasa's main bus and minibus station is located near the Norbulingka Palace and has a large board listing places all over the map. At the time of going to press, every foreigner visiting Tibet is required to travel only with a vehicle and guide. However, if you have free (rest) days in Lhasa and you do not want to pay for the vehicle, then you could take a local bus to Sera or Drepung monasteries, perhaps with the guide in tow, or even no guide. We have included the information above because restrictions may loosen, as they have in the past.

TOUR AGENCIES

There are a number of agencies in Lhasa that handle travel with small or large groups that have made all arrangements before entering Tibet or China. Some agents have offices in the hotels. The trade is heavily controlled by the TTB and Chinese official management. Here are some recommended agencies:

Explore Tibet 4–5 Hse, Namsel No 3, Doudi Rd, Lhasa; ✆830 5152; ✆+124 0778 0765 (USA); e sales@ExploreTibet.com; w ExploreTibet.com. Explore Tibet is a Tibetan-owned agency that is highly recommended.

Tibet Highland Tours m 1390 898 5060; w tibethighlandtours.com. One of the longest-operating companies in Lhasa, Tibet Highland Tours specialises in all areas of the TAR, including the eastern regions of Lhoka & Nyingtri.

Tibet Wind Horse Adventure Sera North Rd No 8; ✆683 3009; e info@windhorsetibet.com; w windhorsetibet.com. Specialises in high-end, customised tours & innovative trekking, bicycling, mountaineering, camping & rafting trips.

Spinn Café and Tours [140 B1] 135 Beijing Donglu in a back alley; m 1365 952 3997; e info@

cafespinn.com; w cafespinn.com. This is a travel meet-up point: great for information exchange. Arranges some budget touring to places like Everest base camp & gives sound advice on website. Serves Vietnamese coffee, pizza, Hong Kong noodles, cocktails & cold beer.

Shangri-La Tours [135 C2] Ohdan Hotel; ✆656 3009; e info@shangrilatours.com; w shangrilatours.com. Small operation, but small in Tibet is actually better. This agency is very attentive to detail & goes the extra distance. It is Tibetan-managed, with Tibetan guides.

Shigatse Travels [140 B1] Yak Hotel compound, 100 Beijing Donglu; ✆633 0489; e info@ shigatsetravels.com; w shigatsetravels.com. With lots of experience in Tibet, this agency has links to a sister agency in Nepal.

The agencies operating out of the ground floor of Lhasa Hotel are higher priced and CITS-linked; across the street is the head office of China International Travel Service (CITS), with TTC (Tibet Tourist Corporation), Tibet Adventure Travel and Tibet/China Travel Service all coming under the CITS wing. Handling sports aficionados is TIST (Tibet International Sports Travel), operating from the grounds of the Himalaya Hotel. Close by is the TMA (Tibet Mountaineering Association), which deals with mountaineers. Golden Bridge Travel Service is run by the PLA, and Asian Dragon Travel is run by the dreaded People's Armed Police. The catch is that agencies linked to the military or CITS can arrange permits more easily than others.

PERMITS AND PAPERWORK

Start early on the origami mastery in Lhasa: to expedite permits and paperwork, and for saving time at hotel check-in, obtain photocopies of your initial passport page plus Chinese visa page, showing entry stamp – all collated on to a single sheet of paper (possibly back to back). You can hand this photocopy over to a hotel desk, for instance, where they will spend ages copying down all the details by hand. Also procure copies of any paperwork that your guide is holding, such as Tibet Tourism Bureau (TTB) permit, Alien Travel Permits (ATPs) and so on, on the pretext that if the guide loses these items or cannot find them, you would have backup copies.

What permits does your guide hold? Well, definitely a TTB permit, plus ATP for towns *en route*. Most rental vehicles with foreign passengers carry a TTB sticker on the front window that says 'China Tibet Tour'. For more remote locations in far west or far east Tibet, extra permits are required – military permit (for restricted areas and getting past military checkpoints), Foreign Affairs Permit, and Cultural Bureau Permit (for visiting sites of special architectural or cultural interest such as the Guge Kingdom). These can take time to obtain in Lhasa.

NEPALESE CONSULATE The only consulate in Lhasa is the Royal Nepal Consulate-General [map, page 171] (☎ *683 0609, 681 5744*). The visa-issuing section is located near the road at the north side of the Norbulingka (*10.00–noon Mon–Fri*). You can pick up a 30-day Nepalese visa within a day for US$30 or Y240, or a 60-day visa for US$100, about Y800. Double-entry or multiple-entry visas can also be obtained (price will double or triple), and there may be a half-price visa valid for 15 days. It's not really necessary to obtain a Nepalese visa as you can get the same visa for the same price on arrival in Nepal by air or by road. However, some like the cachet of the exotic visa issued in Lhasa.

WHERE TO STAY

The following hotels and guesthouses are arranged by location and pricing. Location means a lot in Lhasa – the closer you are to the Barkor area, the better, because that's where all the Tibetan action is and where you can stroll around at will. There are other factors to consider. How is the plumbing? What time does the front door close at night? Is there secure storage if you leave bags behind for a week or more? Apart from location and price, there's one very important factor to consider: who runs the place? More kudos to you if you stick with Tibetan management.

As for Chinese management: well, they may not want you in their hotel at all. Apartheid is a standard Chinese practice, segregating Chinese tourists from foreign tourists. A number of hotels are restricted to Chinese only, and PSB would rather keep foreigners isolated in a select number of hotels where they can keep an eye on them. Out near the Mountaineers-on-Everest roundabout, the Plateau Hotel seems to cater exclusively to a Chinese clientele. The same is true of Gold Grain Hotel, which is a bland 50-room block on Yuthok Road, with prices in the mid-range. Close by this is Ying Binguan, which is exclusively reserved for visiting Chinese officials. Catering to well-heeled Chinese clientele is the modern Tibet Royal Hotel, with a big disco-karaoke complex, on the southern section of the Lingkor. Out on 'Karaoke Row' (west of the Golden Yak roundabout) are some glitzy Chinese places with names like Hotel Dream Paris. And scattered around Lhasa are hotels that deal mostly with Chinese group tours, such as the Century Grand Hotel or the Snow Mountain Grand Hotel. The hotels specialising in Chinese clientele are not detailed in the following selection, because they are boring, away from the centre, and the staff mostly do not speak anything other than Chinese. However, such hotels may appear on the various maps of Lhasa in this chapter because they serve as navigation landmarks. It is easier to establish your location from identifying a large hotel than it is to try to decode the jumble of street names.

Pricing notes: many hotels in Lhasa charge the same for single, twin (two beds) or double rooms (either one large bed, or two beds). Others offer discounted rates for singles, but the interpretation of 'single' seems to vary. Some hotels charge more for single rooms because 'single' means one large bed, and there may be a balcony or additional features in this room. Some hotels include all service charges in the price; others include breakfast as well – and even, in high-end hotels, free oxygen! In mid-range and high-end hotels, a service charge of 10% may well be added to bills. These hotels claim to accept a wide range of credit cards: American Express,

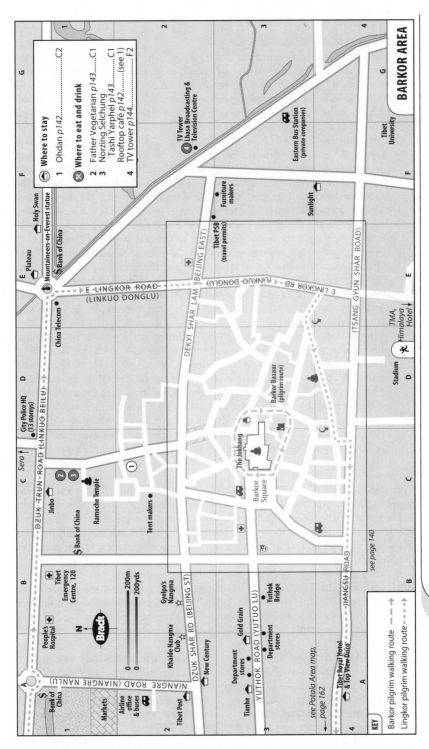

BARKOR AREA

Where to stay
1 Ohdan *p142* C2

Where to eat and drink
2 Father Vegetarian *p143* C1
3 Norzing Selchung C1
   Tashi Yarphel *p143* C1
   Rooftop café *p142* .... (see 1)
4 TV tower *p144* F2

People's Hospital

Tibet Emergency Centre, 120

City Police HQ (13 storeys)

Bank of China

China Telecom

Plateau

Mountaineers-on-Everest statue

Holy Swan

Bank of China

E LINGKOR ROAD (LINKUO DONGLU)

E LINGKOR ROAD (LINKUO DONGLU)

DZUK TRUN ROAD (LINKUO BEILU)

Jimbo

Bank of China

Ramoche Temple

Tent makers

DEKYI SHAR LAM (BEIJING EAST)

Tibet PSB (travel permits)

Furniture makers

Sunlight

TV Tower

Lhasa Broadcasting & Television Centre

Eastern Bus Station (private companies)

The Jokhang

Barkor Bazaar (pilgrim route)

Barkor Square

E LINGKOR RD (LINKUO DONGLU)

E LINGKOR RD

(TSANG GYUN SHAR ROAD)

Stadium

TMA; Himalaya Hotel

Tibet University

N

Sera

Gyelpo's Nangma

Khaide Nangma Club

New Century

0   200m
0   200yds

DZUK SHAR RD (BEIJING ST)

NIANGRE ROAD (NIANGRE NANLU)

Bank of China

Markets

Airline office & buses

Tibet Post

Tianhe

Department stores

Department stores

Gold Grain

YUTHOK ROAD (YUTUO LU)

Yuthok Bridge

JHANGSU ROAD

Tibet Royal Hotel & Top View Disco

see Potala Area map, page 162

see page 140

Bradt

KEY
Barkor pilgrim walking route ‑ ‑ ‑ →
Lingkor pilgrim walking route ‑ ‑ ‑ →

Lhasa WHERE TO STAY

4

135

It's late afternoon on the rooftop of the Jokhang, and a Chinese woman with her hair braided Tibetan style (with small chunks of turquoise in it) is on her mobile phone, chatting with relatives in Shanghai. The monks are doing a roaring trade selling drinks and lucky charms to a cluster of Chinese tourists, all happily snapping pictures of each other. Among them are some 'military tourists' – in uniform, off duty and carrying cameras with big lenses.

These are well-heeled Chinese tourists; a trip to Tibet is not cheap. Some wear their wealth: one tourist I met came armed not only with a video camera but with two digital still cameras – he downloaded the images to his laptop and then sent them off to friends from a cybercafé in Lhasa. Tibet is a 'cool' place to go among the wealthy. In 1997, statistics say 260,000 Chinese visitors came to Tibet; by 2005, the number had quadrupled, with over a million Chinese tourists visiting Tibet that year. By 2010, the figure had reached over six million Chinese tourists annually, which is more than the entire population of Tibetans living in ethnic Tibet. By 2016, the figure skyrocketed to an incredible 23 million Chinese tourists annually, although apparently that figure counts the same tourists multiple times, visiting different parts of Tibet such as Shigatse or Namtso, so the real number could be under half (or even a third) of that statistic. The wave of Western backpackers that washed through Lhasa in the 1980s and 1990s has now been replaced by a wave of Chinese backpackers.

The Chinese tourist phenomenon in Tibet means that you will inevitably mix with sometimes unwieldy numbers of them at key sites, such as the Jokhang. Interactions are interesting here – not a single Chinese tourist I came across would venture an opinion on the Dalai Lama or Buddhism in Tibet. Of course, to broach such topics with Chinese settlers, hard-nosed administrators or the military living in Tibet is impossible, but you'd think that a Chinese tourist might be willing to talk.

An obligatory stop for Chinese visitors is Potala Square, where they dress up in Tibetan cloaks and fox-fur hats to have their photos taken with the Potala in the background. Dress-up charades in fact abound in Lhasa: Chinese women

---

Visa, Diners, MasterCard, Dragon, JCB, Great Wall and Peony. The high season for travel to Tibet is April to October: prices may fluctuate seasonally, dipping lower in the shoulder (between high and low seasons) and low seasons. Travellers have bargained lower rates than those posted on the reception boards, especially for stays of a week or longer. Rates can plummet in winter months, along with temperatures (and no heating).

HIGH-END HOTELS Lhasa's top hotels charge Y950 a room and sometimes more, and are mainly Chinese-run, although the best hotels involve joint-venture operations with foreign hotel consortiums who have the experience with running luxury enclaves smoothly.

🏠 **Shangri-La Hotel Lhasa** [162 A3] (262 rooms, 17 suites) 19 Norbulingka Rd; `655 8888; e slls@shangri-la.com; w shangri-la.com. Starting in the 1970s, the Malaysia-based Kuok family appropriated James Hilton's Shangri-La utopia as the branding device for their string of luxury hotels, making them billionaires in the process. The Shangri-La Lhasa is 5-star with all the bells & whistles – limo service, butler service, sat TV in rooms, 4 restaurants, Horizon Club Lounge, gym, indoor swimming pool, medical clinic & signature Chi Spa. **$$$$**

posing as Tibetan women (wearing Tibetan-style long dresses) have been sighted working in department stores, selling tickets at key attractions, and as receptionists in some hotels.

Despite communist leadership vilification of the Dalai Lama, trendy Chinese can shop for Tibetan jewellery at boutiques in Shanghai, or buy an astonishing variety of Tibetan products (made by state-run companies) such as ginseng-berry juice or Tibetan barley wine (Shangelila label). And though China is officially atheist, Buddhism is resurfacing, with some high-profile figures openly practising the religion. You will find, at some pilgrimage sites around Tibet, Chinese participating in rituals like tying on prayer flags, burning juniper and chanting 'Om Mani Padme Hum' (see the entry 'mantra' in the glossary).

That's exactly what Chinese chanteuse Dadawa did on a track of her 1995 album, *Sister Drum*. Dadawa achieved the remarkable feat of infuriating both Tibetans and Chinese simultaneously with this album. Dadawa (Moon) is her adopted Tibetan name: her real name is Zhu Zheqin. On the album she croons songs like 'Sky Burial' and 'The Sixth Dalai Lama's Love Song'. In the cover art, she appears dressed in monastic robes, but her hair is not shaven (it is hidden under a monastic hood) and she is wearing jewellery, which neither monks nor nuns do in Tibet. In London, Tibetans gathered outside the office of her record label to protest exploitation of Tibetan culture. But in Tibet itself, reticence turned to jubilation when Tibetans discovered that in the background track of her top hit was the voice of a woman praising the Dalai Lama in Tibetan! Dadawa had to recall her album and have it re-edited, and her videos are still banned in Tibet. In 2002, a Tibetan monk attending a Dadawa concert in Beijing expected to hear a twisted version of his culture. However, he said he was pleasantly surprised to hear Dadawa accompanied by Tibetan musicians, who were allowed liberties not extended to their brethren in Tibet itself. Dadawa's albums are partly responsible for the phenomenon of Tibet Chic, which draws legions of Chinese tourists to visit Tibet.

🏠 **InterContinental Lhasa Paradise** [126 G3] (1,300 rooms & suites) 1 Jiangsu Rd, Chengguan District, on the eastern outskirts of Lhasa; ☏656 9999; w intercontinental.com. The InterContinental is a bizarre mix of architectural styles. It consists of a huge lobby area covered by a glass pyramid-shaped structure: inside is a Tibetan-style village which functions as a hub for restaurants, bars & spa. Radiating out from this are four large wings, each housing up to 400 rooms, decorated European-style. The idea of paradise in Lhasa has raised hackles with the Free Tibet Campaign in the UK, which has targeted InterContinental Hotels Group with protests over running a hotel in a place with such a repressive human rights record. **$$$$**

🏠 **St Regis Lhasa Resort** [140 F4] (156 rooms, 26 villas, 23 suites) 22 Jiangsu Rd; ☏680 8888; e reservation.lhasa@stregis.com; w stregis.

com/lhasaresort. Run by US-based Starwood Hotels Group, this sprawling 5-star hotel occupies a large corner on the south side of Lhasa & started operation in 2010. Constructed with Tibetan features in both architecture & décor. The hotel is dubbed a 'Resort' because of its gold-tiled swimming pool that is part of the Iridium luxury spa, along with 6 treatment suites, a yoga studio & meditation garden. On the ultimate Lhasa pampering list, the St Regis offers butler service, plasma TV sets & in-room Wi-Fi. **$$$$**

🏠 **Four Points by Sheraton** [126 F4] (103 rooms & suites) On a side road off Jiangsu Lu; ☏634 8888; w fourpoints.com/lhasa. Part of the Starwood Hotels Group, this place opened in 2006. **$$$$**

🏠 **Lhasa Hotel** [126 D3] (468 rooms & suites) 1 Minzu Lu; ☏683 2221; e sales@lhasahotel.

com.cn; w lhasahotel.com.cn. Has a swimming pool – but nobody seems to use it, because it's poorly maintained (or simply because there may be no water in it). Even if it is a luxury hotel, Lhasa Hotel has its problems. Built in 1985, it is falling apart in places, with water-damaged walls. Lhasa Hotel still has a sign up saying 'Former Holiday Inn Lhasa', but does not explain the background (see box, below). The hotel boasts 3 tower wings, each with a lift (the 1st to arrive in Tibet). The hotel has the full gamut of services, including telecom & business centre, currency exchange counter & several gift shops. There's a fitness centre with sauna & jacuzzi. Restaurants include the Tibetan-style Himalaya (styled like a Tibetan teahouse), Chinese-style Kailash & the Western-style Hard Yak Café. The banquet hall can seat 600. For the price of a drink you can drop in & watch CNN & other programmes on sat TV by going to tiny Chang's Bar, on the ground floor. **$$$$**

BOUTIQUE HOTELS Sited in Lhasa's **old quarter**, the following places are boutique hotels imbued with heritage history. Old Tibetan courtyard housing has been

THE FORMER HOLIDAY INN

In late 1997 it was announced that the Holiday Inn management group would not renew its contract for running the branch in Lhasa – the only luxury hotel in Tibet at the time. No reason was given, and the international giant continues to run its numerous other branches around China. Victory was claimed by various campaign groups in the West, particularly the Free Tibet Campaign in England, which launched a boycott of Holiday Inn operations and those of its British parent company, Bass PLC (brewers of Bass beer), in 1993. In 1997, Students for a Free Tibet and 50 other Tibet support groups joined the campaign.

In its heyday, the Holiday Inn Lhasa was run in partnership with the Chinese government and was the largest foreign currency earner in Lhasa – catering to well-heeled group tours. The original hotel was completed by the Chinese in 1986: the Holiday Inn corporation modernised the building and renamed it. A trusted brand name like Holiday Inn brought a certain amount of prestige, a veneer of respectability, and a seal of approval for Chinese operations in Tibet. There were even Miss Tibet contests conducted in 1992 to attract tourism during the slack winter months. You had to wonder how long it would take McDonald's, Pizza Hut and the rest of the multi-national gang to get there in the wake of Holiday Inn.

After the Holiday Inn management left, the building reverted to its original name, Lhasa Hotel, but the sign out front and the hotel brochures still bear the legend: 'The Former Holiday Inn Lhasa'. A hilarious account of life at the former Holiday Inn is given in Alec Le Sueur's book, *Running a Hotel on the Roof of the World*. Although Tibetans work at the hotel, there is no Tibetan presence in the management – profits only benefit the Chinese. Top-ranking Chinese military like to stay here, and it appears that the staff are in cahoots with security forces.

Foreign protesters have now moved on to targeting other Western luxury hotel groups operating in Lhasa, such as InterContinental. Another enterprise sparking protests is the beer company Pabst. Pabst Blue Ribbon operates a Sino-American joint venture: in 2001, its Chinese partner strung up a large banner in Lhasa congratulating the Chinese on the 50th anniversary of the takeover of Tibet. There is one other beer joint venture in Lhasa: Carlsberg has shares in Lhasa Beer company.

lovingly restored to turn structures into mini-hotels with Tibetan décor – and loads of character. Some are former residences of nobles or important dignitaries in old Lhasa. All are small – and expensive, hitting the high-end and medium ranges. They are listed here more as sights. While wandering Barkor back alleys, you might want to take a peek to see what the traditional architecture looked like. And you may be able to access an interior courtyard or rooftop restaurant.

🏠 **Yabshi Phunkhang** [140 B1] (21 rooms) 68 Beijing Donglu; ☎632 8885. This heritage building underwent a 4-year restoration. The hotel is constructed in a complex that long ago was built for the parents of the 11th Dalai Lama. Large rooms, great courtyards. May not cater to foreign guests. **$$$$**

🏠 **House of Shambhala** [140 D1] (9 rooms) 7 Jiri Erxiang; ☎632 6533. Stylish boutique hotel down a quiet back alley. Has a great rooftop terrace. The hotel is the pet project of Laurence Brahm, a former New York lawyer who lives in Beijing & who is obsessed with finding Shambhala. Nearby, also run by the owner, is Shambhala

Spa. An offshoot of the hotel, called **Shambhala Palace**, also in the old quarter, offers 17 rooms. **$$$**

🏠 **Lingtsang** [140 B3] (9 rooms) South of Barkor Sq; ☎689 9991; e lingtsanghotel@163. com. A boutique hotel in what was once the residence of a tutor of the Dalai Lama. On the roof is a restaurant with views of the Jokhang. **$$$**

🏠 **Trichang Labrang** [140 C4] 11 Luguwu Xiang; ☎630 9555. Former residence of Trichang Rinpoche, previous tutor to the 14th Dalai Lama. Great courtyard garden with a good restaurant called Lhasa Namaste. **$$$**

MID-RANGE HOTELS Tariff is Y460–Y950 for a double in these hotels, rated three-star by Chinese tourism authorities. You can easily tell classier hotels by lifts in the lobby, oxygen piped into rooms (or supplied through a machine), and saunas. Although they may have some token Tibetan interior design, the following mid-range hotels are Chinese-run (except for the Dhood Gu and Kyichu, which are Nepalese-run). Most offer rooms with hot water, colour television, IDD phone, air conditioning and other comforts. Lobby facilities include business centre, fitness centre, travel agent, gift shops and so on. A peculiar item on the tariffs is the 'o'clock room': this is a room that is rented by the hour for Y100–200, probably for short-time flings. Even the high-end Tibet Hotel has them.

🏠 **Kyichu** [140 A1] (aka Kechu or Kecho) (around 50 rooms) 149 Beijing Donglu; ☎633 1541; e lhasakyichuhotel@gmail.com; w lhasakyichuhotel.com. This Nepali-managed hotel hosts small 5-storey wings enclosing a garden. Very clean, highly recommended. Excellent restaurant & gift shop. **$$$**

🏠 **Shangbala** [140 B2] (70+ rooms) 1 Tengyeling Rd; ☎632 3888. Chinese blockhouse with some Tibetan trimmings, used by tour groups. Strange atmosphere. **$$$**

🏠 **Dhood Gu** [140 C1] (67 rooms) Near Tromsikhang market; ☎632 2555; e dhoodgu@ yahoo.cn. A 5-storey Tibetan-style hotel. The rooftop has fine views of the Potala. **$$$**

🏠 **Xiongbala** [140 C4] (83 rooms & suites) 28 Jiangsu Lu, South Lingkor; ☎633 8888. Comfortable place with adequate rooms: some upper-floor rooms have Potala views. Mixed reviews from foreign guests due to spotty service & haphazard management style. **$$$**

🏠 **Himalaya Hotel** [126 F4] (130+ rooms) 6 Lingkor Donglu; ☎632 2293; e himalayahotel@ tist.net. Rooms with bath, arrayed in several wings, the main one being a high-rise building. Sports-related groups often lodge out this way because TIST (Tibet International Sports Travel) & the TMA (Tibet Mountaineering Association) have offices in the vicinity. There are possible traditional dance performances taking place at night here. **$$$**

BUDGET HOTELS Budget here denotes pricing for double rooms. But within the same hotels could well be shoestring prices, as a number of hotels in Lhasa

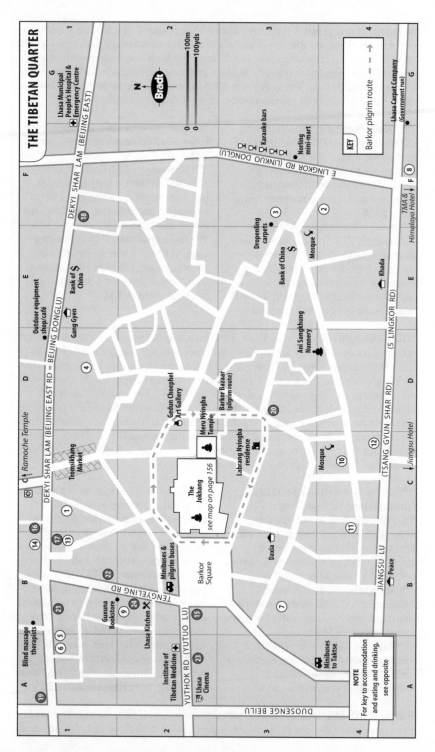

◉ **Where to stay**

1	Dhood Gu *p139*.........................C1	6 Kyichu *p139*............A1	10 Tibet Gorkha *p142*................C4
2	Flora *p141*.................................F4	7 Lingtsang *p139*......B3	11 Trichang Labrang *p139*.......C4
3	Heritage *p141*...........................F3	8 St Regis Lhasa	12 Xiongbala *p139*....................C4
4	House of Shambhala *p139*.....D1	Resort *p137*..........F4	13 Yabshi Phunkhang *p139*.....B1
5	Kailash *p141*.............................A1	9 Shangbala *p139*....B2	14 Yak *p141*..............................B1

⊗ **Where to eat and drink**

Ani Sangkhung Nunnery
Teahouse (see Ani
Sangkhung
Nunnery) *p144*..............D4
15 Burger King *p143*............ B2
16 Dunya *p143*.......................C1
17 Ganglamedo *p145*..........B1
18 Holiland Bakery *p142*.....F1
19 KFC *p143*............................A1

Khang Dolgar *p143*.......(see 21)
Lhasa Namaste *p143*....(see 11)
20 Makye Ame *p143*....................D3
Namaste (see Lhasa
Cinema) *p143*......................A2
Norling *p143*......................(see 6)
Rooftop Café *p144*............(see 1)
21 Spinn Café *p145*.....................B1
Summit Café *p144*..........(see 9)

Teahouse (see the
Jokhang) *p144*...............C2
Teahouse *p144*......(see 14)
22 Tibetan Family
Kitchen *p143*.................B1
23 Tibet Kunphan
Vegetarian *p143*..........A2
24 Woeser Zedroe *p143*.....B2

offer accommodation from dormitory up to deluxe double rooms. Though few backpackers manage to get into Lhasa independently these days, there are many young Chinese backpackers on the loose – and lots of low-end hotels that cater to them. The tariff in this group is Y20–50 for a dorm bed, Y80–200 for a double room and Y200–400 for a double with bath. The hotels listed in the Barkor and Sera Road areas are mostly Tibetan-managed or Nepalese-managed, which is why they are placed up front. Those in the Lingkor area are likely to be Chinese-run.

A British traveller who stayed at a mid-range hotel (included with an arrival tour by mistake) says that his Y500 room at the Shangbala Hotel was equivalent to a Y50 room at the Yak Hotel (but with no bathroom included at the Yak for this price). For a double with bath, much better value is to stay at the Yak for around Y260, or at the Flora Hotel for Y180. The Tibetan-run Flora Hotel operates on a similar formula – offering a range of accommodation, and an on-site shop, email and internet access, restaurant and travel agent. These hotels have hot showers, laundry facilities and will store baggage while you're off on a trip. Some hotels offer a few services for free, such as free laundry or free internet. In the low-end to mid-range price category, Nepalese-managed hotels are a good choice because they favour Tibetan staff and Tibetan-style décor.

Barkor area

🏠 **Yak** [140 B1] (130 rooms) 100 Beijing Donglu; ✆632 3496; e lhasayak_hotel@hotmail. com. This is one of the best-known hotels in Lhasa, & a prominent landmark. The owner of the hotel, Dorje Tashi, was one of Tibet's wealthiest businessmen. He was a millionaire & a member of the Communist Party. Apparently, he donated some of his wealth to help exiled Tibetan groups – at least that is thought to be the charge against him. He vanished off the map in 2008. In mid-2010 he was put on trial in secret & sentenced to life in prison. At the time he was in his mid-30s. Not much has been heard about him since. The Yak Hotel is a large, efficient operation with central courtyard. The quiet main section is removed from the road. Excellent rooftop teahouse with

expansive views. Rooms range from dorm to deluxe & include buffet b/fast at the Dunya Restaurant next door (page 143). **$$**

🏠 **Flora** [140 F4] Off east Barkor on Hobaling Rd, near the mosque; ✆632 4491; e florahtl@ hotmail.com. This hotel is well run, with a small courtyard garden café & internet section. The main building has 20 rooms. Excellent value. **$$**

🏠 **Kailash** [140 A1] 143 Beijing Donglu; ✆632 2220. Group-tour hotel with some Tibetan-style standard rooms & some attempt at Tibetan décor, with Tibetan staff, although it's Chinese-run. **$$**

🏠 **Heritage Hotel** [140 F3] (21 rooms) Inside the courtyard of Dropenling craft centre; ✆691 1333. Stylish place with rooms featuring wooden floors & Tibetan wall hangings. **$$**

Ohdan [135 C2] (25 rooms) Near Ramoche Temple; ☎634 4999; e ohdan_guesthouse@ yahoo.com. Large 4-storey building with restaurant-bar on the ground floor & a 5th-floor rooftop café with great views. The ground-floor Tibetan-style restaurant stages special movie nights, *momo*-making classes & other events. **$$**

Tibet Gorkha Hotel [140 C4] (around 40 rooms) 45 Jiangsu Lu, South Lingkor Rd; ☎627 2222; e tibetgorkhahotel@yahoo.com. This splendid hotel lies on an alley off the main road near the south Lingkor circuit. It is built around several enclosed gardens, with the back castle-like structure originally being the old Nepalese (Gorkha) consulate. The hotel is Nepalese-managed & has a restaurant facing an interior courtyard garden – a pleasant place to hang out & have a drink, even if you are not staying at the hotel. Tibetan tent teahouse on the roof. 25 rooms are standard dbls. **$$**

Dalan Hostel 172 Beijing Zhonglu, opposite the northern gate of Lhasa Hotel [126 D3]; ☎672 5172. This is one of the handful of hostels with dormitories that has a licence to accept foreigners in Lhasa. Dorm beds here start around Y28 to Y38, depending on the season. **$**

✖ WHERE TO EAT AND DRINK

Lhasa is well supplied with food: you can even buy fresh bananas (from Central America), peaches and mangoes from street vendors. You can throw together your own food in Lhasa: there are places where you can find fresh-baked flatbreads, delicious yak curd (yoghurt) and bananas – start putting these things together and you'll have a great breakfast. It's fun to wander the streets around the Barkor to get your daily yoghurt.

There are two bakery chains in Lhasa: Bread Talk and Holiland. The latter is preferable, as the bread seems to have a more authentic taste. Holiland is located on Beijing Donglu.

A number of restaurants listed here double as suppliers of food for trekkers and those on guided trips. In the self-catering line, department stores around Lhasa stock a good range of fruit juices, dried fruit, almonds, nuts and Dove chocolate. Mini-marts do well, too: Norling mini-mart [140 F3], a Tibetan-run place on East Lingkor Road near the Flora Hotel, stocks supplies such as trekkers' muesli from Nepal, mango Frooti drink, peanut butter from India, sunblock and so on.

Watch out for dirty restaurant kitchens – diarrhoea and food poisoning are the threats here. Many travellers in Lhasa have stomach problems or coughs, colds and flu. Stomach problems are probably traceable to water that's not properly boiled, or to uncooked vegetables. On Tengyeling Road, to the north of Barkor Square, are several Muslim noodle houses with hearty fare at low prices: these bear green banners with the Muslim crescent moon on them. Opposite Sheng Shia Hotel, west of the Potala, is a string of hotpot places where food is cooked at the table. Watch out for heavy Chinese food or greasy food. Peking duck, for instance, is very rich – and hard on your system when not fully acclimatised.

If you are feeling really acclimatised, you can wash down dinner with some wine (alcohol will go to your head very quickly at altitude). Avoid the cheap Chinese champagne on the shelves – this is only good for bathing in. The bottle to purchase is Dynasty white wine, which is made in Tianjin as part of a French joint-venture enterprise. Another good brand is Great Wall red.

With some exceptions, the prime restaurant area tends to be around the Barkor. Consult the maps in this chapter for approximate locations, but be aware that in the labyrinthine back alleys, finding the restaurant listed may well prove a challenge. Nothing like getting lost in Lhasa to build up an appetite.

✖ **Lhasa Hotel** [126 D3] (pages 137–8) Has several overpriced restaurants, including the Hard Yak Café (serving yak burgers) & an ice cream café (with good gelato). The Himalaya restaurant at

Lhasa Hotel serves a range of food from Indian to German, plus Tibetan dishes such as yak tartare, or minced yak with Tibetan spices. Traditional Tibetan music groups sometimes perform at the restaurant. $$$

✖ **Norling Restaurant** [140 A1] Inside Kyichu Hotel (page 139). Overlooking a courtyard garden, this upmarket restaurant serves great Indian, Nepalese & Western fare with wonderful atmosphere, though it's a tad pricey. You can dine at outdoor tables in the courtyard garden – a pleasant retreat from the trenches & pillboxes on Beijing St outside. $$$

✖ **Lhasa Namaste Restaurant** [140 C4] In the garden courtyard of boutique hotel Trichang Labrang (page 139). Tasty curries & yak sizzlers, plus yak burgers. $$$

✖ **Woeser Zedroe** [140 B2] Close to the Jokhang. Great Tibetan atmosphere & excellent *momos*, especially the yak meat & cheese varieties. $$

✖ **Tibetan Family Kitchen** [140 B1] This place serves homemade Tibetan recipes (yak meat in tomato sauce) & the chef hosts cooking classes to teach you how to make your own authentic *momos* & Amdo-style noodles. $$

✖ **Tibet Kunphan Vegetarian** [140 A2] Downtown on Yuthok Lam. This Buddhist place serves a range of all-veg dishes, including buffet lunch. No alcohol served. $$

✖ **Norzing Selchung Tashi Yarphel** [135 C1] Specialises in Amdo fare, & has great views of the street below, taking in the pilgrims visiting Ramoche Temple next door. $$

✖ **Makye Ame** [140 D3] Back of the Barkor. This 2nd-floor restaurant has a laid-back atmosphere, & big bay windows overlooking the Barkor, where you can watch the Tibetan pilgrim world turn & turn. The restaurant is Tibetan-run & serves an eclectic menu from *thukpa* (noodle soup) to pizza. You can also visit for drinks alone – go up to the tented rooftop section for even better views of the Barkor. Makye Ame also rents out books if you leave a deposit. The restaurant has branches in Beijing & Kunming. Behind Makye Ame is a lot of history. Makye Ame is thought to be the name of a beautiful woman that the 6th Dalai Lama pursued while in disguise. He wrote a famous poem about her. The original tavern on this site was said to be the trysting place – & was thus allowed the honour of having its exterior painted in royal yellow. $$

✖ **Dunya** [140 C1] Next door to Yak Hotel; ☎ 633 3374. Dunya has cornered the market in safe eating: the place is run by Europeans & is very clean & spacious, with wooden tables, candles at night & a great ambience. It features a mixed menu, including Tibetan, Italian & Indonesian. On the menu is 'yak sizzler', which is yak steak, French fries & vegetables served in a hot skillet – so hot that it sizzles. For those looking for a cheese fix, Dunya sells tasty Nepali-made yak cheese by the half-kilo. $$

✖ **KFC** [140 A1] Shenli Shidai shopping mall, Beijing Zhonglu. The first American fast-food brand to find its way to Lhasa, & the Dalai Lama hates the idea. In 2012, he sent a letter to KFC on behalf of PETA, asking them not to set up shop in Lhasa because of the corporation's support for cruelty & mass slaughter of chickens. But KFC ignored the advice & the Lhasa franchise opened its doors in 2016. The 500m² interior décor is emblazoned with paintings of Lhasa's landmarks, such as the Potala Palace. The franchise targets mainly Chinese tourists as its fare is on the expensive side (frozen chickens need to be imported into Lhasa). $$

✖ **Burger King** [140 B2] Near Barkor Sq. Hot on the heels of KFC is Burger King, another scion of the American fast-food gang. $$

✖ **Namaste** [140 A2] Above Lhasa Cinema, near the intersection of Yuthok Rd & Duosenge North Rd. Among the most popular Nepali restaurants for local Tibetans. Serves burgers, chicken tikka & tandoori. $$

✖ **Khang Dolgar** Very close to Spinn Café [140 B1]. Popular with local Tibetans, due to its Tibetan noodles with chilli paste. Has a speciality called *chu-ru* – a mix of black fungus, *tsampa* & yak meat. Yum! $

✖ **Father Vegetarian** [135 C1] Cheap & homey, but with limited English interpretation. Tibetan-style fried mushrooms recommended. $

TEAHOUSES AND ROOFTOP CAFÉS There are pleasant teahouses in Lhasa where you can soak up the views as well as the drinks. One of these is **Lukhang teahouse** [162 F1] in the northeast corner of Lukhang Park – it offers a great view of the back of the Potala and is a peaceful place. The teahouse serves 'eight treasures tea' and there are often fresh flowers on the tables from the adjacent nursery. Another viewpoint on the Potala is from the front, at a **Chinese pavilion** with restaurant and teahouse [162 F3], overlooking a lake to the Potala's south side. There's a Tibetan-style **teahouse** inside the Red Palace [162 E1] of the Potala itself.

Ranking as surely the most unusual teahouse in Lhasa is **Ani Sangkhung Nunnery Teahouse** [140 D3], located in the old quarter. The teahouse is found in the courtyard of Lhasa's most active nunnery – active meaning political – and is, of course, run by nuns. The customers are mostly Chinese backpackers drinking dissident tea – which can taste bitter.

On the rooftop of the **Jokhang** [140 C2] is a tented teahouse run by the monks, although only in the summer months, and mainly for Chinese tourists. In the courtyard of Shangbala Hotel, and very close to the Jokhang, is **Summit Café** [140 B2], with arguably the best espresso coffee and smoothies in town, plus free Wi-Fi to boot.

Around the back of the Barkor, **Makye Ame Restaurant's** [140 D3] rooftop on the third floor has great views over the parade of pilgrims. From various hotel rooftops, you can also get good views of Lhasa, and see paper kites launched from other rooftops. These include the fifth-floor teahouse at **Yak Hotel** [140 B1], the fifth-floor rooftop café at **Ohdan Hotel** [135 C2] and the rooftop of the **Dhood Gu Hotel** [140 C1].

The ultimate for views may be the **TV tower restaurant** [135 F2], way up at the top of the TV tower in eastern Lhasa. This is a revolving restaurant where the Chinese have actually got the direction right for a change – it revolves clockwise. Revolving is hit and miss, as is the food. But you'd go for the views (assuming the place is open and accessible).

ENTERTAINMENT AND NIGHTLIFE

Lhasa's handful of hotels and restaurants are nightlife and entertainment venues by default: they are gathering points for information exchange. Source and sauce:

OVER THE GREAT FIREWALL

The Dalai Lama's image has been banned in Tibet since a major fallout over the choice of Panchen Lama in 1996. Even more incriminating are tapes or books by him or about him, or movies about him. Even the Potala Palace is bereft of his portrait – the last big portrait was taken down around 1997. The image you might see in monasteries (possibly) is of a younger Dalai Lama with Mao Zedong in Beijing in the 1950s, as this seems to be politically correct. Otherwise, the Dalai Lama is commonly denounced as a 'revolutionary splittist' or 'a wolf in monk's garb'.

But the irrepressible Dalai Lama is easy to find on the internet. You can bring him up at any time – he's on so many sites, they can't all be blocked. He pops up on the cover of all his books, for starters. In a cybercafé in Lhasa, I was hunting for information on the Karmapa (who is not yet blacklisted by the Chinese), when a magazine cover popped up. It was an issue of *Time Asia*, with a cover story on political repression in Tibet. And featured on the cover were two monks in burgundy robes – the Karmapa and the Dalai Lama. *Time Asia* itself is firewalled in China, but somehow this cover arrived by a different route, past the firewall. Amazed Tibetans crowded round the screen to witness this, probably the first time they'd seen a photograph of the two high lamas together. But the cybercafé operator, fearful of having his licence revoked – or fearful of starting a riot – asked me to switch sites.

other travellers provide the latest information, and you digest it over a steaming bowl of noodles. **Spinn Café** [140 B1] and **Dunya Restaurant** [140 C1] function as traveller cafés. This is how travellers mostly pass their nights. Chinese nightlife consists of crooning, carousing and chasing Sichuan women around in karaoke bars or places like **Top View Disco** [135 A4] (some Westerners venture in here, too). Tibetan nightlife consists of crowding into tiny video salons where sound distortion and flasks of *chang* are the big things.

DINNER-DANCE SHOWS AND NANGMA CLUBS Some hotels stage dinner-dance performances – a mix of traditional dance and music, with the highlight being the exuberant yak dance, performed by two Tibetans hidden inside a yak skin. It is traditionally performed as a welcome dance. The 'yak' rolls on the floor, flicks its tail around, and charges into the audience.

Scattered around Lhasa are more than 30 Nangma nightclubs, which get under way from 23.00 onwards and host a range of live singers and dancers, and a dance floor up front. These places are the closest you'll get to Tibetan nightlife, and are great fun. Tibetan singers are garlanded with *katas* during performances – some end up with so many scarves they have trouble moving around. One of the better-known Nangma clubs is **Khaide** [135 A2], located on Beijing Road. Close by is **Gyelpo's Nangma** [135 B2], named after a famous dancer on Tibet TV.

BARS Popular with foreigners is the upstairs bar at **Dunya Restaurant** [140 C1], next to the Yak Hotel. You can't miss the Heineken sign out the front (the bar was set up by a Dutchman). Opposite the Yak Hotel is **Ganglamedo** [140 B1], a trendy Chinese-run restaurant and bar: the food is bland, but this is a good place to quaff Lhasa Beer or Snow Beer, and stays open late. There are a number of small bars catering to upscale Chinese visitors: some have imaginative décor.

SHOPPING

If you can't find it in Lhasa, you probably won't find it anywhere in Tibet, except possibly in Shigatse. Whether outfitting for a trip or shopping for Tibetan artefacts, Lhasa has the biggest selection, though it has nothing on Kathmandu.

CAMPING AND OUTDOOR GEAR Camping and outdoor supplies in Lhasa are very good: you could arrive in Lhasa with nothing and be fully kitted out within a few days. There are numerous outdoor equipment shops around Lhasa, particularly along Beijing Road and Tengyeling Road. These vary from small shops to cavernous stores, selling a range of top Chinese brands like Ozark. A few of the larger stores are located to the west of Lhasa, such as **Wilderness Outside Camp Store** near the Golden Yak roundabout [162 C2].

Chinese-made equipment is cheap compared with what it would cost in the West. Sleeping bags can be purchased for under US$50. North Face jackets and gillets go for low prices: these could be copies, or could be factory off-runs. Other brands on sale include Mountain Hardwear and Columbia. Some places stock high-quality imported gear, including stoves and useful gadgets. Others sell gear recycled from mountaineering expeditions – and may rent this equipment, too. Department stores sell formless but functional clothing, and there's PLA surplus gear for sale on the streets. If you are looking for a good sleeping bag, you should check the noticeboards at places like the Yak hotel, as Chinese backpackers will advertise there.

The Princess Wencheng Opera is a full-blown opera that is staged for tourists (mainly Chinese) on a regular basis at night. It is essentially Chinese propaganda, packaged as a musical extravaganza. That said, there is not a lot happening in Lhasa at night, so it makes an interesting expedition.

ADVANCE INFORMATION: allow lots of time, at least an hour, to get to the opera venue, sited on a hilltop south of Tibet Museum, across the Lhasa River [126 F4]. There is often a large traffic jam of tour buses and minivans as patrons pour in for the evening extravaganza. Vehicles must park well below the venue: the next part of the journey is to mount 400 steps. This is definitely not something to tackle if you are new in Lhasa as mastering stairs at this altitude takes some acclimatisation. One Western visitor reported that earlier in the day he and his wife had visited the Potala (which also requires climbing steep steps) and that going to the Wencheng Opera the same evening pretty much knocked his wife out – she had to go to hospital next morning for oxygen treatment.

The performance is open air, meaning you must be prepared to deal with potential cold conditions and possibly even rain. The organisers thoughtfully rent out winter jackets to keep audience members warm under the stars, and even hand out disposable ponchos if it starts to drizzle. Another caveat to consider is the high cost. Tickets start at around Y350 a person. If you include a waiting taxi or hired transport, costs escalate. The opera is 90 minutes long, divided into five acts, and starts after sunset, around 21.30.

The subject of the multimillion-dollar opera is Chinese Princess Wencheng Gongzhu's romantic marriage to Tibetan King Songtsen Gampo in the 7th century AD. She undertook a long journey from Beijing in around AD640 to marry the king. The original version of this opera was commissioned by Zhou Enlai in the wake of the 1959 Lhasa uprising – the idea being to emphasise Wencheng as a symbol of the long-lasting 'friendship' between China and Tibet. In other words, the opera is an elaborate propaganda piece to justify China's claims over Tibet. The commissioned work subsequently became the subject of TV soap operas, books,

FRESH/PACKAGED FOOD If you're going on a long trip – for instance, to Kailash – stock up on as much food as you can in Lhasa (the only other place to get supplies is Shigatse). For fresh food, go to **Tromsikhang** [140 C1], the Tibetan market to the north of the Jokhang. This has the biggest selection (for items like potatoes, dried fruit and so on). Department stores downtown are a source of packaged goods, such as teabags, chocolate and biscuits. **Lhasa Department Store** [162 F3] has a good stock in its mini-mart. There is a Tibetan-run Norling **mini-mart** on East Lingkor Road [140 F3] with a good stock of Nepalese-imported items such as muesli and peanut butter.

TIBETAN ARTEFACTS The main array of souvenir shops lines **Barkor Bazaar** [140 D3], but watch out for Chinese clones. Some souvenirs are obviously not Tibetan at all: a few brass Buddha statues are from Thailand; others come from Kathmandu. Much the same stock is sold at gift shops in major hotels at more inflated prices, at souvenir kiosks at the Potala entrance, and at the Norbulingka. Watch out for fake turquoise and other stones if buying jewellery. The dilemma faced by purchasers who do not know what they are looking at is best exemplified by the trade in *dzi*

DVDs – and the current mammoth opera, which was first staged in Beijing in 2013, and later transported to Lhasa, opening in 2015.

Princess Wencheng is credited by Chinese sources with bringing all sorts of miraculous benefits to Tibet – variously embracing highland barley, medical knowledge and even Buddhism (the main statue in the Jokhang is said to be a replica of a statue brought by Wencheng). Here's where the narrative goes haywire – King Songtsen Gampo, it is claimed, built the Potala Palace as a tribute to his Chinese love. In fact, the Potala was not completed until a thousand years later. Although parts of the original structure date from the 7th century AD, the White Palace was not completed until 1653, and the Red Palace another 40 years later.

The Tibetan version of the royal romance is very different: King Songtsen Gampo had at least four wives (some say six consorts), of which two were foreign. The Tibetan queens wield significant power in the Tibetan narrative, while the foreign queens play a minor role. Vassal states like Nepal and China offer 'peace marriages' to placate the marauding Tibetans and stop them raiding their borderlands.

Princess Wencheng may not even have existed – she could be fictional. Tibetan writer Woeser says the Princess Wencheng Opera is 'a vast project that rewrites history and wipes out the memory and culture of an entire people. They can brainwash people and make money at the same time.'

But on to the show. The opera is a vast spectacle taking place on a ground the size of a football pitch. There is seating for 3,000 in an amphitheatre. The extravaganza plays out under the stars, employing over 700 actors and 100 live animals (horses, sheep and yaks). It makes use of lavish costumes, giant props, theatrical lighting and side-projection screens with subtitles in Mandarin, Tibetan and English. The extravaganza is essentially a song-and-dance musical (with some dialogue). Numbers are sung in three languages. Clever lighting illuminates Lhasa's real mountains in the background. At one point, in a winter scene, it snows on the audience. At the end of the show, a giant set that replicates the Potala Palace and the Tibetan Quarter pops up. The show attests to great Chinese skill in creating a theme park for Lhasa. Which is what the real Lhasa has essentially become.

stones. These are agate talismans with 'eyes' that involve human crafting in the process. If a *dzi* stone is an ancient heirloom, passed down for generations, it could be worth millions of yuan. If it is a brand-new import from Taiwan, it might be worth Y10. Even experts flounder when it comes to telling the difference between valuable *dzi* stones and worthless ones.

A similar dilemma surrounds the label '100% Pashmina'. If it is real pashmina (the finest-grade underwool of the cashmere goat), it would be expensive. More likely to be sold is a mix with regular cashmere or sheep wool, or even synthetics. If you can get a small piece of the fabric and burn it with a cigarette lighter, it should at least smell like hair burning if it purports to be from a cashmere goat. If it smells like paper when burned, it is not pashmina, it is a synthetic mix. Some places try to pass off yak wool as something special. In fact, yak hair is too coarse to be up against the skin (it will irritate your skin), and is best left to blankets and carpets rather than sweaters or scarves. Some places mix yak wool and sheep wool to make scarves and other clothing items.

You might want to get to the source of items crafted in Lhasa, as the **factories** are a sight in themselves. There are several Tibetan **tent-making workshops** in the city – the easiest to find is in an alley near the Yak Hotel [140 B1]. Among other items, this place sells fine cotton door-hangings with Tibetan lucky symbols hand-embroidered on them. At the eastern side of the Barkor (located down alleys north of the mosque; follow signs) is **Dropenling** [140 F3], run by a non-profit UNDP-backed artisan enterprise and designed to bolster Tibetan handicrafts in the face of rampant Nepalese and Chinese imports. On sale are *tankas*, weavings, silverware, woodcarvings, saddle carpets and other handcrafted items. You can watch craftsmen at work, which makes it well worth a visit.

There are several **carpet factories** in town, including one to the southeast side of Lhasa and another out near Drepung. **Potala Carpet Factory** [126 B3], 300m past the turn-off for Drepung, welcomes visitors – you can see women weaving and singing here as they work on complex patterns. There is an exhibition and retail room on the premises. Check out the various designs: a Tibetan dragon has four claws, the Chinese imperial dragon has five.

Other places selling Tibetan carpets are **Snow Leopard Carpet Industries** (with a tiny showroom at 2 Danjielin Lu; also sells yak-wool blankets) and **Lhasa Carpet Company** [135 E4], a showroom near St Regis Lhasa Resort.

BOOKS AND MAPS You might dredge up the odd map, poster or Tibetan music cassette from the **Xinhua Bookstore** at the west end of Yuthok Road [162 F3]; otherwise, pickings are slim. There's also a Xinhua Bookstore branch out near Lhasa Hotel. Prices for maps and books can be absurdly low if produced by the Chinese government. Maps in Chinese characters are easy to find; maps in English are more difficult and not nearly as detailed. *Lhasa Tourist Map*, produced by Chengdu Cartographic Publishing House, is a sheet map dated 2004 and selling for Y16. This large, double-sided map carries an impressive wealth of detail and a selection of mini-guide material. However, it is missing some newer details such as the bridge leading over the Kyi Chu River close to the railway station. For those details you would have to hunt down the more recent *Tourist Map of Tibet*, published in 2010 by Xian Map Press: one side of this sheet map features Lhasa, and the other side shows the TAR.

The souvenir shops at **Lhasa Hotel** [126 D3] and **Tibet Hotel** [140 C4] are good for books, though more expensive. **Guxuna bookstore** [140 B1] on Tengyeling Road has an array of books, but mainly in Chinese. **Souvenir kiosks** at key sights around town also sell books and postcards. Rule of thumb: when you see something you really want, bargain and buy it – you might not see it again. Other Chinese bookstores are scattered around; there's one at the east side of Barkor Bazaar.

OTHER PRACTICALITIES

BANKING The main branch of the Bank of China [162 D2] is located just northeast of the Golden Yak roundabout. It provides full services, including credit card advances (although commissions can be high) and ATM machines. The BOC is open 09.00–18.30 Monday to Friday (in winter, 09.30–18.30); 10.00–17.00 Saturdays; and possibly open Sundays. There are sub-branches in a few other locations. Major hotels such as Lhasa Hotel [126 D3] have their own exchange counter, but the rate is not as good. ATMs for the BOC in Lhasa dispense a maximum Y2,000 per card per day, while those for the Agricultural Bank offer a maximum of Y1,000 per day.

MEDICAL You're best off moving to a comfortable hotel in the event of a medical problem. High-end hotels usually supply oxygen pillows and may have a doctor

Need a blast of oxygen? A high-altitude cocktail? Lhasa Hotel was reputed to have rooms where oxygen was piped in, but this system no longer seems to function because guests kept going out and leaving the oxygen on. If guests have trouble with the altitude, they are usually given an oxygen pillow to make sleeping smoother. There is nothing more scary than sleeping at altitude and waking up in the middle of the night completely out of breath, heart pounding, gulping for air, with a throat like the Sahara. This is where the oxygen pillow comes to the fore – it is a pillow of oxygen with nasal tubes attached. The pillows are also taken along on vehicle trips from Lhasa Hotel in case a guest is feeling under the weather. Drivers may also keep a tank of oxygen in the vehicle, rather like a fire extinguisher unit. Oxygen does not solve the acclimatisation problem, but it does provide temporary respite.

Several outfits in Lhasa sell oxygen devices, manufactured as far afield as Xiamen. These range from small scuba-like tanks to aerosol spray cans for those who need a blast of fresh air. You can rent the scuba tanks for a dollar or so a day (with a large deposit). The capacity is 30 minutes of oxygen. At top-end hotels guests can use a card system to hook up to a larger oxygen-dispensing device.

on call. Hospitals in Lhasa cost a fortune for foreigners to stay in, and the medical attention is dubious anyway. Lhasa's finest is the Military Hospital at the north end of town [126 F1], but that's not for foreigners. The People's Hospital [140 G1] is basic, although one unit is supported by an Italian NGO project for equipment and training and there's an X-ray unit there. The Emergency Centre (\ *120 or 632 2200*) at this hospital has a small ambulance. This is the best option for foreigners in trouble.

BLIND MASSAGE THERAPY Massage therapists in a programme set up by Braille Without Borders run a small, efficient massage operation, located on the second floor of a building opposite the Kailash Hotel [140 B1]. Unfortunately, like the handful of other initiatives linked with foreign NGOs in Lhasa, the fate of this facility is unclear, as red tape obstacles have been raised by Chinese officialdom. In August 2017, the NGO's agreement with the local government counterpart expired, and no handover agreement was decided on. For news about this facility, consult the NGO website (w *braillewithoutborders.org*).

If it is operating, a relaxing 1-hour acupressure massage here costs Y80; appointments can be booked by phone (\ *632 0870*). The brochures claim massage will ease altitude problems and jet lag and relieve headaches – by increasing blood circulation, of course. And brochures suggest you might need to recover from 'travel-related back and neck pain' – probably an oblique reference to the rigours of 4x4 travel. The massage therapists are all blind. If you want to learn more about the remarkable training of blind people in Lhasa, you can visit Braille Without Borders, found down a back alley just west of Peace Hotel [140 B4] (enquire about exact visiting hours, as the facility is only open for tours several times a week). The training facility was set up in 1998 by Sabriye Tenberken, a blind German woman who worked out the first-ever system for rendering the Tibetan language into Braille. Again, this facility may or may not be operating, as its status was in limbo at the time of research.

Spa treatments are on offer at Lhasa's high-end hotels. But the most curious treatments can be found at Chi Spa, within the Shangri-La Lhasa Hotel (page 136). This is a signature spa which is replicated at other Shangri-La hotels around the globe. It features not Thai-style massage, nor Swedish, but a mix of Tibetan and Chinese, in keeping with the idea of the mythical Shangri-La utopia which combined Tibetan and Chinese elements. The concept of Chi Spa is as much for males as females: males feel at ease with the monkish décor. In fact, this signature spa has hit on a great concept – a monkish spa for jet-lagged urban warriors in cities such as Beijing.

The décor attempts to replicate the atmosphere of a Tibetan monastery, complete with dark, lofty halls, lit by candles. For mood music, there's a Tibetan-monkish dirge of chanting in the background. The creators claim that the spa is derived from ancient Tibetan and Chinese healing methods, but the finger points in quite a different direction: New Age. Brochures burble on about 'finding your inner Shangri-La', 'finding beauty within yourself' and 'finding harmony in our ancient rituals'. The spa starts out with the eerie sound of Tibetan singing bowls, which are a fabrication concocted by hippies in Nepal in the 1970s, and proceeds with a *tsampa* rub. *Tsampa*, the Tibetan staple food, is mixed with herbs, and used as a kind of sandpaper for exfoliating.

This is followed by a hot stone treatment with Tibetan lucky symbols and sacred mantras inscribed on stones, which are heated in oil. The masseuse runs the stones along the length of the body, wielding one in either hand, sometimes applying deep pressure, and other times leaving them on parts of the body to supposedly improve the flow of energy. When hot stones are paired up with New Age music, you can only be left suspicious as to the origins.

After being thoroughly massaged, pummelled, scrubbed, rubbed with *tsampa*, healed with hot stones, detoxified and exfoliated, you emerge glowing from the spa, and are provided with a luxurious cashmere gown, sit down to sip herbal tea from a jade teacup and listen to more singing bowls. Is it a gimmick? Yes, but a curious one – the spa mystique repackaged in Himalayan myth and New Age hokum.

COMMUNICATIONS AND MEDIA The Potala **post office** [162 F2], the main branch for telecommunications, lies near the Potala on Beijing Road. The sending of regular mail and parcels takes place here; bring along your own packing materials as few are supplied (for larger items, you might have to open your package for customs inspection). Some hotels deliver mail to the post office.

Part of the China Post complex on this block is a large store devoted to Chinese magazines – everything from car magazines to fashion periodicals – to keep the settlers happy. The news is all from China, and thus all screened. In English, there are only stray copies of *China Daily* floating around, and even those are hard to come by. There is a media blackout in Tibet: you cannot find any foreign magazines at all. So you have to resort to internet news sites, a number of which are blocked. And despite the great advances the Chinese say they have made in Tibet, not a single Tibetan newspaper is on sale in the shops of Lhasa. There is a pathetic rag the size of a newsletter called *Tibet Daily*, but that is rehashed propaganda, and is only sold by roving vendors.

Fax and phone There's a long-distance calling office next door to the main post office [162 F2] (calls are most likely routed through Beijing); the same office will allow you to send faxes. Faxes can also be sent from some hotel business centres, but that will be more expensive. International phone calls can be placed through hotels, even at the budget hotels. To keep costs reasonable, use prepaid calling cards, which can be bought for fixed amounts such as Y50 or Y100. These come in two main varieties. A prepaid IC card can be activated by dialling a number sequence, either on a hotel phone or at one of the tiny telecom shops found around Lhasa. A prepaid IP card (China Telecom is best) can be used with a yellow phone, with booths found on the street, and sometimes also in hotel lobbies. The country code (China) is 86; the Lhasa area code is 0891 (for calls within China) or 891 (for incoming international calls). Another possibility is net phoning via services such as Skype.

Mobile phones If staying longer in Tibet and China, set yourself up with a SIM card for a mobile phone from China Mobile [162 C2] (office near China Post). Their SIM card can be installed on the spot: you can switch to English-language menu, and you can top up the talk time with prepaid cards of Y50–500. The network includes SMS text messaging, which can be sent in English, Chinese characters, even Tibetan script. Mobile phone and SMS coverage reaches across China, but does not extend to Hong Kong SAR. The reason for this is simple: the press in Hong Kong is much freer than in China proper, and text messaging is a method of relaying news. You should be aware that Chinese mobile phone companies may police and filter text messages – do not write anything risqué on SMS. Mobile phone and SMS reception across Tibet can be erratic as it depends on whether there is a telecom tower within range. But these reception towers can pop up in remote places – such as Rongbuk Gompa, near Everest base camp.

Email and internet Net access is available through hotel Wi-Fi (often in-room) and through cybercafés. Connection speeds vary – connection is sometimes good, sometimes slow and sometimes non-existent (come back later). Internet use is cheap – mostly under Y5 an hour. A number of hotels in Lhasa host their own small internet cafés. The ones at the Kyichu [140 A1] and Yak [140 B1] hotels are good. Upper-end hotels have internet access through Wi-Fi and business centres. Cybercafés are sprinkled around town: these are closely monitored by 'internet police'. The café owners may give you the third degree on ID before you are allowed to surf. For email, it's difficult to see how such a large volume of messages could be scrutinised, but monitoring is done by flagging keywords such as 'Tibet', 'independence' or 'democracy'. Chinese authorities are extremely sensitive about what you can access on the net (for websites, see pages 366–9). Taboo sites are those concerned with human rights, Tibetan exile groups, Taiwan; the list goes on. That means sites could be blocked or firewalled, but it's surprising what you can still pick up in Lhasa. If you do get through to sensitive sites, it could mean trouble for the cybercafé owner. However, there is no official list of what is forbidden and what is allowed. In theory, though, there is filtering software in place at cybercafés that will block certain sites: if sensitive material is not filtered, the café could be closed down. It is dubious whether foreigners are subject to these regulations – the logic being that foreigners are accustomed to viewing such sites.

Satellite television High-end hotels may have sat TV reception: some can pick up VTV (India) or StarTV (Hong Kong). Access to these stations is strictly controlled: even if the hotel has a satellite dish, this does not guarantee it has permission to

KHAMPA MONA LISA

Mona Lisa's enigmatic smile undergoes a twist in Lhasa. You may see her painted with Khampa-style dress and turquoise jewellery studded in her hair. This is definitely not traditional. The painting is part of an effort to break away from traditional Tibetan art forms, which in the past focused exclusively on religion. Khampa Mona Lisa is definitely a very different take on iconography. Several paintings of her have been spotted – some created by Tibetan artists, some by Chinese artists.

Located at the northeast corner of the Barkor is a three-floor gallery displaying modern works by members of Gedun Choephel Artists' Guild. The guild is Lhasa's only centre of modern Tibetan art, although the painting of modern themes has generated a cottage industry among Han Chinese artists resident in Lhasa, vying for the tourist market. These artists paint the Van Gogh-style wares and other high-kitsch art seen hanging on café and hotel-lobby walls in Lhasa, and on sale to Western and Chinese tourists in small shops.

For centuries, Tibetan artists painted only formulaic *tanka* art for monasteries: Gedun Choephel Artists' Guild was started up in 2003 with the aim of expressing Tibetan themes in modern styles, ranging from realism to surrealism. There are more than 20 artists in the group. Gade, an artist in his 30s, attempts to bridge the old world of Tibet with the modern globalised world: he paints Buddha images that include references to Hollywood movies, sentences in English and Russian, even short SMS messages.

The group takes its name from Gedun Choephel, a Tibetan intellectual and accomplished artist from Amdo who headed south to India in the 1930s to visit important pilgrimage sites. The chain-smoking Choephel had formidable powers of concentration – he could debate with the best of them, even when totally inebriated. Apparently, Choephel could cause monastic debating opponents to freeze into shocked silence. His unorthodox views upset many people in high places, including the British colonial rulers of India, the aristocrats and the ruling clergy in Tibet. After 13 years in India and Sri Lanka, Choephel decided to return to Lhasa in the mid-1940s to write the definitive history of independent Tibet. He was promptly thrown into a dank dungeon in Lhasa on trumped-up charges. In 1949, when communist invasion of Tibet seemed imminent, a general amnesty for prisoners was declared in Lhasa. Choephel emerged from jail in emaciated condition, dressed in rags, a shadow of his former self. Tibet's foremost intellectual died in 1951 at the age of 46, but his legend lives on, inspiring many young Tibetans.

receive certain channels (for which a decoder is needed). In places like Shangri-La Hotel or Lhasa Hotel, owners seem to have the best contacts for permission, with CNN broadcasts from Beijing available in guest rooms: there may be places within high-end hotels where non-guests can watch TV (for instance, at Chang's Bar in Lhasa Hotel). The larger the dish, the greater the reception: satellite receivers require special permission to operate within China, and the foreign programmes are not intended for local eyes. Xizang TV (XZTV) and Lhasa TV (Lhasa Broadcasting and Television Centre) are the local stations. Tibetans mostly watch XZTV. CCTV-9 from Beijing broadcasts news daily in English (all programmes on this station are broadcast either in English or else Chinese with English subtitles, as this is Beijing's pan-Asian voice). CCTV channels 1 to 12 are broadcast from Beijing; there are about 30 more regional channels that are picked up in Lhasa.

PHOTOGRAPHY Internet cafés found within hotels can burn DVDs from your camera cards, and offer printing services on photo-quality paper. Printed photos would make fine gifts for Tibetan friends. Print film is sold in Lhasa, but quality may be suspect.

WHAT TO SEE AND DO

ORIENTING YOURSELF To get a better idea of the layout of Lhasa, there are a number of places that offer expansive views. The Jokhang rooftop has stunning vistas, and the rooftops of hotels such as the Yak and Ohdan offer views over the Barkor and beyond.

Traditionally, Tibetan pilgrims approaching the holy city embarked on four sacred circuits: the inner circuit of the Jokhang Temple (called the Nangkor), the 20-minute outer circuit of the same temple (around the Barkor), a 25-minute circuit of the Potala Palace (called the Tsekor), and a 90-minute circuit around Lhasa itself (called the Lingkor). The first three are eminently possible, but the Lingkor is no longer easy to follow – it has been disrupted by modern Chinese buildings. The description of sights that follows is based on clockwise circuits of the Nangkor, Barkor, Tsekor and Lingkor – that is, starting at the Jokhang Temple, and spiralling outwards around Lhasa.

There is one very good reason why you should follow these ancient walking routes: the pilgrims, with their fervent devotional practices, are in fact the main 'sight' of Lhasa, if it can be phrased that way – and their interaction with sacred sites is what makes these places so special. Many visiting Lhasa are disappointed by what they see – a large Chinese city, essentially. The Potala is a museum, and it's easy to feel that tightly controlled temples are more interested in ensuring that you have paid the exorbitant entrance fee than helping you understand the faith that is at the heart of Tibetan society. To get a glimpse of a more spiritual Tibet, try the Jokhang early in the morning and queue with the pilgrims (be prepared for the crush when the doors open!) or pace the Barkor *kora* at dusk (several times). If you have more time, be sure to hike to the sacred sites and *koras* at the outskirts of Lhasa – at Bumpa Ri [126 G4], and at Pabonka (above Sera) [126 F1], for instance. The pilgrim pulse fares better on the edges of Lhasa at the former great monastic citadels of Sera and Drepung.

You have to read between the lines in Lhasa when it comes to the sacred and the secret. There's been so much upheaval in the Holy City that half the time you don't know if what you're looking at is sacred or not – whether the statuary at the Jokhang is real or not, whether the West Gate is original or reconstructed. From the real to the unreal, from the sublime to the ridiculous: one minute you're admiring the stunning structure of the Potala – and the next minute, you're examining a fake palm tree, wondering how on earth that ended up on the streets of Lhasa.

ENTRY PROTOCOL AND FEES Despite what agencies and guides tell you, it is possible to access key sites in Lhasa by yourself – but have lots of paperwork handy, such as passport (for Potala and Jokhang) and copy of TTB permit. The charge to enter the Potala is Y200 a person in high season, and Y100 a person in the November–April off-season, and it's Y85 to go into the Jokhang. The Norbulingka charges Y60. Sera has a Y50 entry fee, and so does Drepung. Sera and Drepung may be difficult to get into

4

if you show up without a guide because they each have a large police station building situated near the entrance, snooping on all visitors. Entry fees at other sites around Lhasa generally range from Y20 to Y60. It all starts to add up. Hefty extra fees are levied for taking still pictures inside top attractions (a charge of Y30–150 is common). The charge for taking video is astronomical (around Y850–1,800 per video camera).

BARKOR AREA There are two areas left in Lhasa where the Tibetan pulse can still be felt: at the Potala (a faint museum pulse) and Barkor Bazaar (throbbing pilgrim pulse). Other than that you're looking at Chinatown. It seems absurd to put it this way, but you really have to visit the 'Tibetan Quarter' – the quarter around the Jokhang Temple and the Barkor – to catch any Tibetans in action. Sadly, this quarter only comprises a small fraction of Lhasa's land area.

The Jokhang [140 C2] The Jokhang or Tsug Lakhang (central cathedral) is Tibet's most sacred temple – the heart of Tibet – with streams of pilgrims coursing through. The temple was built in the 7th century by King Songtsen Gampo when he moved his capital to Lhasa. Apart from his three Tibetan wives, the powerful Songtsen Gampo had two wives offered by neighbouring nations – Nepalese queen Tritsun and Chinese Princess Wencheng. The Jokhang was originally designed by Nepalese craftsmen to house a Buddha image brought by the Nepalese queen. Upon Songtsen Gampo's death, Princess Wencheng switched the statue she had brought (the Jowo Sakyamuni) from the Ramoche Temple to the Jokhang, apparently to hide it from Chinese troops. That's why one part of the Jokhang (Chapel 13) is called the 'Chapel where the Jowo was hidden'. In time, the Jowo Sakyamuni statue became the chief object of veneration. The Jokhang was enlarged and embellished by subsequent rulers and Dalai Lamas. Although the building is as old as Lhasa, much of the statuary is quite new. During the Cultural Revolution, the temple was used as a military barracks and a slaughterhouse; later it was used as a hotel for Chinese officials. Much of the statuary was lost, destroyed or damaged, so it has been replaced with newer copies of the originals.

In 2000, the Jokhang was inscribed on the UNESCO World Heritage list as an addition to the Potala Palace. Initially, this was greeted as good news, as it implied protection of the buildings in the immediate vicinity. However, ancient buildings around the Barkor have since been knocked down and replaced with Chinese copies, on the dubious grounds of superior plumbing and facilities. Then in early 2018, disaster struck: on the second day of Losar, a huge fire broke out in the rooftop area of the Jokhang, causing considerable damage from fire and water.

Outside the Jokhang Fronting the Jokhang are flagstones where Tibetans gather to prostrate before the temple. A bit further back are two small walled enclosures with obelisks inside. One enclosure shelters two stone obelisks with an edict in Chinese about curing smallpox – the edict, from 1794, is largely illegible because Tibetans gouged pieces out of it, supposing that the stone itself had curative properties. The second enclosure, with a tall thin obelisk, bears a bilingual inscription about a peace treaty between Tibetan king Ralpachen and Chinese emperor Wangti, concluded in AD823, delineating the borders between the nations of China and Tibet. The brick enclosures around the obelisks were put up when Barkor Square was created in 1985.

Access In the morning, until 11.00, you can enter the Jokhang directly through the front doors; otherwise, entry and exit may be via a side-door courtyard. An entry fee of Y85 is charged: for that you get a tacky ticket with a 3D image of the

Jokhang embedded. It may not mean much to you, but hang on to that ticket – it makes a super gift for Tibetans in remote regions. It's best to visit the Jokhang in the mornings, from 09.00 to noon. Parts of the Jokhang may be closed on Sundays. Entering the inner sanctum of the ground-floor chapels may be difficult for Tibetan pilgrims. As a tourist, you are privileged to be allowed in. Photography is allowed in certain parts of the Jokhang – if in doubt, ask first. Second-floor chapels may be closed off and only accessible to monks residing at the Jokhang. You should respect this limitation. It should be all right to access the rooftop, however, and you might be able to visit the rooftop at times when the ground-floor chapels are closed.

The rooftop You can take a staircase near the ticket booth at the front straight up to the golden rooftop of the Jokhang, with excellent views over Lhasa rooftops and the Potala in the distance. In the summer months there is a tented teahouse up on the Jokhang rooftop, run by the monks. Visiting the rooftop seems to be a privilege reserved for tourists – both Western and Chinese – as you don't see Tibetan pilgrims up here. The monks at the teahouse do a roaring trade with Chinese tour groups, selling Jokhang talismans and postcards, as well as T-shirts, books, souvenirs and drinks. Chinese tourists excitedly chatter on their mobile phones to callers across China (they even talk on mobile phones when visiting the shrines in the Jokhang – including the Jowo shrine). Although it can, at times, turn into a Chinese photo-taking zoo, the rooftop is a bright, peaceful spot – a refreshing place after the dark, smoky chapels of the Jokhang interior. There are beautiful ornaments hanging from the eaves of the gilded sloping roofs, some in the shape of dragons, others in the shape of mythical birds.

Ground-floor icons Walking through the dark corridors and chapels of the Jokhang, you enter another world. Dim light is provided by a galaxy of butter lamps; the air is thick with the odour of yak butter and incense; echoing through the halls is the sound of murmuring from throngs of Tibetan pilgrims. If your timing is right, the inner sanctum may reverberate with the sound of deep, hypnotic chanting by monks at prayer. About a hundred monks live at the Jokhang, residing on the upper levels.

Some of the chapels in the Jokhang have been destroyed and reconstructed, and statuary has been defaced, replaced, restored and shifted around, so the plan on page 156 may not match exactly with what is on the ground. Chapels may close and reopen, depending on reconstruction. With this jumble of old and new, it is also debatable which statuary is original and which is copied.

The world you enter seems quite complex and confusing, with no point of reference, no rhyme or reason. However, that may be a matter of familiarising yourself with the icons of Tibetan Buddhism which, admittedly, are bewildering in their scope and number. If you want to explore Tibetan temple iconography, the Jokhang has the lot – a virtual Who's Who of the Tibetan Buddhist pantheon. Using the plan of the Jokhang in this section, you can identify which images are Avalokitesvara, Sakyamuni, King Songtsen Gampo and so on. The same icons pop up in many other temples in Tibet, and are referred to in other parts of this book. Only some of the ground-floor chapels are described here: the emphasis is on the icons.

Unlike most temples, the Jokhang is not identified with a particular sect. Leaders and teachers from the different sects are shown in statuary and murals. **Tsongkhapa** (Chapel 1) is the founder of the Geluk (Yellow Hat) sect. There's a finer image of him in Chapel 6, wearing a monk's robes and a pointed yellow cap; he lived from 1357 to 1419. Between Chapel 3 and Chapel 4 is a statue of the great poet-saint **Milarepa** (1040–1123), with his hand cocked to one ear so that he can better hear the music of the spheres and the voice of teachings. The sage appears with skin of a

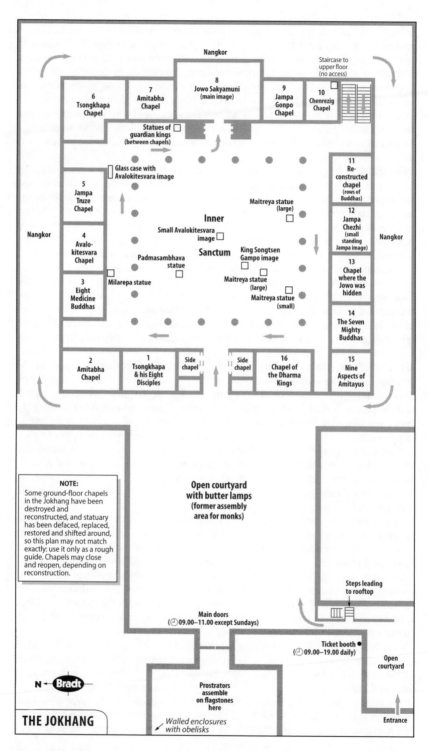

Nangkor

8
Jowo Sakyamuni
(main image)

Staircase to
upper floor
(no access)

6
Tsongkhapa
Chapel

7
Amitabha
Chapel

9
Jampa
Gonpo
Chapel

10
Chenrezig
Chapel

Statues of
guardian kings
(between chapels)

Glass case with
Avalokitesvara image

11
Re-
constructed
chapel
(rows of
Buddhas)

5
Jampa
Truze
Chapel

Inner

Maitreya statue
(large)

12
Jampa
Chezhi
(small
standing
Jampa image)

4
Avalo-
kitesvara
Chapel

Small Avalokitesvara
image

Sanctum

King Songtsen
Gampo image

13
Chapel
where the
Jowo was
hidden

Nangkor

Padmasambhava
statue

Nangkor

3
Eight
Medicine
Buddhas

Milarepa statue

Maitreya statue
(large)

Maitreya statue
(small)

14
The Seven
Mighty
Buddhas

2
Amitabha
Chapel

1
Tsongkhapa
& his Eight
Disciples

Side
chapel

Side
chapel

16
Chapel of
the Dharma
Kings

15
Nine
Aspects of
Amitayus

NOTE:
Some ground-floor chapels
in the Jokhang have been
destroyed and
reconstructed, and statuary
has been defaced, replaced,
restored and shifted around,
so this plan may not match
exactly: use it only as a rough
guide. Chapels may close
and reopen, depending on
reconstruction.

**Open courtyard
with butter lamps**
(former assembly
area for monks)

Steps leading
to rooftop

Main doors
(🕘 09.00–11.00 except Sundays)

Ticket booth ●
(🕘 09.00–19.00 daily)

Open
courtyard

N ◄ Bradt

Prostrators
assemble
on flagstones
here

Entrance

Walled enclosures
with obelisks

THE JOKHANG

greenish hue – a case of nettle anaemia (he dined solely on nettle soup for a number of years). Milarepa was a founding member of the Kagyu sect. Another historical figure seen in chapels and in larger statues at the inner sanctum is **Padmasambhava**, the 8th-century tantric Indian master who is credited with establishing Buddhism in Tibet. He is the founder of the Nyingma sect, and is shown with a stern expression and a curled moustache, wearing a folded red hat.

In the Tibetan pantheon are many Buddhas and bodhisattvas. A bodhisattva is a being on the way to becoming a Buddha, but one who has decided to delay the pursuit of nirvana and devote himself or herself to the welfare of others. The Dalai Lama is thought to be an emanation of **Avalokitesvara**, the bodhisattva of compassion (Chenrezig in Tibetan). Often shown in a standing statue, Avalokitesvara has 11 heads (one of which is wrathful) and multiple arms, and may be encircled by a thousand hands. The many heads are said to have burst from the original head as a result of contemplating the suffering of living beings.

The figure of Avalokitesvara is found in several parts of the ground floor – in Chapel 4, outside Chapel 5 in a glass case, in Chapel 10, and right at the centre of the inner sanctum. The image in Chapel 4 has a long story behind it: some parts of the statue are original, some are copies. The image was commissioned by Songtsen Gampo in the 7th century. During the Cultural Revolution, this image and others were tossed into the streets. Tibetans managed to salvage a wrathful and a peaceful aspect of the faces of Avalokitesvara, and the images were smuggled out via Nepal to India. The faces were eventually made into a new image of Avalokitesvara at the Tsug Lakhang in Dharamsala.

Tara (Drolma in Tibetan) is said to be the spiritual consort of Avalokitesvara, and possesses more than 20 forms. **White Tara** is identified with Princess Wencheng and the fertile aspect of compassion, while **Green Tara** is identified with Queen Tritsun and the motherly aspect of compassion. Green Tara is the patron female saint of Tibet; she sits with her right leg extended slightly, resting on a lotus blossom. Tara sits cross-legged upon a lotus flower. She is easily recognised by the eyes depicted in the palms of her hands: she is believed to have sprung from a tear of compassion falling from the eye of Avalokitesvara. While there is little statuary of Tara in the ground-floor chapels, her image appears in a number of murals. A Tara fresco is shown on a wall recessed at the back of Chapel 16.

Tibetans believe that the historical Buddha (Sakyamuni) is the Buddha of the present era, but only one of the many Buddhas to appear in the past, present and future. The Buddha is 'he who is fully awake' – an enlightened being. **Amitabha**, appearing in Chapel 2, is the Buddha of Infinite Light (Opame in Tibetan) – usually depicted in a red colour, with hands clasping an alms bowl. The Panchen Lama is thought to be an incarnation of Amitabha. A row of eight **Medicine Buddhas** is shown in Chapel 3 – these are the Buddhas of healing, and caring for the sick. **Jampa** is the Buddha of the Future, also known as Champa or the Maitreya Buddha. This Buddha is not usually shown cross-legged, but seated conventionally on a throne. The Jampa statue shown in Chapel 5 is a copy of one brought to Tibet from Nepal by Queen Tritsun. In Chapel 9 is an image of Jampa (brought in from Drepung to replace a destroyed image); this statue was once paraded around the Barkor at Monlam. In the inner sanctum are two Jampa images.

The centrepiece of the Jokhang is a 1.5m-high gilded statue of **Jowo Sakyamuni**, the Buddha of the Present, born in 543BC in Nepal. The image was supposedly brought to Tibet by Princess Wencheng, but this is disputed – disputed as to whether it is the original statue, and disputed as to whether Princess Wencheng even existed at all. The statue depicts the Sakyamuni Buddha at the age of 12:

features such as long earlobes and a cranial bump are special marks of the Buddha. The highly revered statue bears an elaborate headdress and is encrusted with jewels; pilgrims crowd in to make offerings, and to walk around the statue.

Revered as deities are the early religious kings of Tibet, who converted to Buddhism. Easily identified in the ground-floor chapels is **King Songtsen Gampo** (c AD608–50), the first of the great religious kings, considered to be a manifestation of Avalokitesvara. He wears a high orange or gold turban; his Chinese wife, **Princess Wencheng** is on the viewer's right; his Nepalese wife, **Queen Tritsun**, on the viewer's left. This is the arrangement for a group to the left of the Jowo Sakyamuni image. The three great religious kings of Tibet are found in the Chapel of the Dharma Kings (Chapel 16) – the central figure being Songtsen Gampo; to the viewer's right, **Trisong Detsen** (the second religious king, who ruled from AD755 to 797); and to the viewer's left, **Tri Ralpachen** (who ruled from AD815 to 838).

Entering or exiting the inner Jokhang sanctuary, you pass two **side chapels**. The one to the left (on the north side) contains a statue of Palden Lhamo, the main protective deity of the Jokhang, as well as of fierce guardian deities. To the right, on the south side, are three Naga deity statues, also with a protective role.

Barkor Bazaar [140 D3] Barkor Bazaar is a lively combination of marketplace, pilgrim circuit and ethnic melting pot. The 20-minute hexagonal circuit, running clockwise around the Jokhang and other structures, is always busy, especially at dawn and dusk. Join the pilgrims for a few circuits – it's good for exercise and for people-watching.

The Barkor has been remodelled to suit Chinese whims: it was completely repaved in 2003 with flatter stones (hence easier to drive over), and a series of Tiananmen-style lamp posts were put up around the circuit, matching those at Potala Square.

At the front of the Jokhang, just inside the temple, you can see some of the original stones. The flagstones are worn smooth, polished from many years of pilgrims performing prostrations. Two-metre-high conical incense burners billow clouds of smoke, and the smell of juniper fills the air. Vendors – mostly Chinese making a buck off Buddhism – sell *kata* scarves (page 358), prayer flags and prayer wheels to the pilgrims. Arriving on pilgrimage from far-flung regions, such as the Kham or Golok areas, pilgrims mutter mantras as they circumambulate. You might see nomad women from eastern Tibet, their long tresses smeared in yak butter; or an old woman leading her favourite sheep around the circuit; or a proud Khampa from eastern Tibet with tassels of red yarn braided through his hair, and a dagger on his belt (not entirely decorative); or a hardy prostrator with rubber apron and padded gloves flinging himself forward on the ground, completing the circuit on his stomach.

The Barkor is a magnet for beggars seeking alms, and for pilgrims seeking funds for their return home (and to support themselves in Lhasa in the meantime). More sophisticated are sutra chanters: for a small sum, they will recite from sacred texts. And finally, there is the bazaar itself – shops and businesses line the entire circuit. Competing with these are open-air stalls laden with souvenirs and household goods; and there are roving vendors with bags of Tibetan music cassettes or other items. Since 1987, Barkor Bazaar has assumed another role – as the focus of protesters who encircle the Barkor when demonstrating against the Chinese occupation of Tibet. This explains the presence of police and security personnel in the area, ready to intercept any demonstrators.

Barkor Square [140 B2] Officially, Barkor Square was completed in 1985 to mark the 20th year of the creation of the TAR. Unofficially, it was built to provide full military access to the troublesome Tibetan quarter and the maze of alleyways in the Barkor beyond. In the process, the Jokhang – previously hidden from view – has been exposed by a large plaza. There used to be a small square in front of the Jokhang – used as a marketplace – but nothing on the scale of the present plaza. This architectural approach might suit a grand European cathedral, but it is a travesty when applied to an intimate corner like the Jokhang.

Barkor Square is lined with shops and eateries, but it is also an elaborate parking lot for army trucks should trouble arise. A lot of older housing was ripped up and then replaced with mock-Tibetan shops, but these do not quite look the same. For one thing, the outer walls of these newer buildings are vertical, not bevelled as in old Lhasa. Old Lhasan housing is conservative in style, with an 'extraordinary biblical severity … preserving for us living architectural forms of ancient civilisations', as one writer noted. Typical housing consisted of flat-roofed two- or three-storey structures made of stone or sun-baked brick. Some buildings in the Barkor area date back to the 17th century and have withstood the test of time. Like the great masons of ancient Egypt or the Inca Empire, Tibetans used no nails or cement: they fitted large blocks of stone closely together and relied on gravity, which meant inward-sloping walls were constructed.

In the PRC, squares like this are used for mass shows of solidarity with the Party, but occasionally (as at Tiananmen Square in 1989) they can be used for mass demonstrations against the Party. In Barkor Square, if 20 or so Tibetans congregate, the police will break the gathering up, nervous of a repeat of the rioting that has taken place in the past.

Barkor back alleys The Barkor area was proposed as a UN World Heritage Site, but ironically it did not qualify because of too much destruction. However, in 2000, the Jokhang Temple was inscribed on the World Heritage list, so hopefully that will slow down Chinese dismantling of the area. The Chinese are systematically tearing down as much of the old quarter as possible on the grounds that the buildings are unstable: these same buildings are then replaced with newer ones of a similar design. The area around the Barkor used to be prime real estate, with residences of high-ranking nobles or lamas. Some of the better-preserved residences are at the southeast side of the Barkor: here you can find Labrang Nyingba, the former residence of aristocratic families [140 C3].

Despite destruction and reconstruction, the Barkor area is a real delight for strays and alley cats, with small markets and temples tucked away, and Tibetans playing billiards. You can explore on foot or bicycle. Around here, you step into a time warp, catching glimpses of what life must have been like centuries, or even a millennium, ago. Ramoche Temple, to the northern side of the Barkor [135 C1], is thought to date back to the 7th century – it is older than the Jokhang. The Ramoche is Lhasa's second-largest temple and is best viewed during prayer sessions (early morning or late afternoon) for real atmosphere. An entry fee (usually around Y20 or Y30) is charged; you might be allowed to access the rooftop, with good views of the area. The wide alley that leads to the Ramoche Temple is lined with curious shops, some merchants selling gold teeth, others gilded temple-top ornaments.

Waiting for you to discover them are a host of small temples and shrines tucked into the back alleys. Easy to find are two temples directly at the back of the Jokhang (east side), off the Barkor circuit. The larger of these is Meru Nyingba [140 C2], founded in the 17th century as the Lhasa residence of the state oracle. On the edge of the Barkor area, on the southeast side, is Ani Sangkhung [140 D3], one of the three nunneries in Lhasa. Upward of 80 nuns live at Ani Sangkhung, while a number

4

Lhasa has an air of mystery and intrigue still – but not quite the way you'd think. The big mysteries today are what all those Chinese buildings are, with the guards out front holding AK-47s or with pistols on their belts. The Chinese military have their own living quarters, exclusive markets, teahouses, restaurants, bars, discos and clubs tucked away, but you can walk into some of them. A lot of buildings are off-limits or Chinese-only or sensitive, and photography is frowned upon. Army bases are self-contained units with high walls – they usually have their own shops and facilities within, including their own video cinema.

To assist the paranoid Chinese in their endeavours to snoop on Tibetans is a nefarious network of informants – human listening posts – and video surveillance cameras. The video cameras are mounted around the Potala and Barkor areas, and at major intersections of the city. The cameras were initially sold by Western countries to China for use in monitoring traffic flow. Since Lhasa doesn't have a traffic flow problem, obviously they are being put to other uses here. The Chinese network of Tibetan informants includes plainclothes police, monks in robes, and beggars. One Tibetan described these people as 'Tibetans who do Chinese work'. In the Barkor area, a man in rags was seen begging one moment, and the next using a mobile phone to inform police of what was going on. The Chinese are convinced that demonstrations by the Tibetans could flare up at any moment. And then there is the threat of bombs. There have been sporadic reports of bomb blasts around Lhasa since the mid-1990s. The nature of the bombing is mysterious, and Chinese authorities have largely remained silent on the subject. The bombs do not appear designed to cause loss of life – rather, to drive home a message of protest.

In June 1995, police defused an explosive device at the Qinghai–Tibet Highway monument, an obelisk to the west of the city, opposite the bus station.

of nuns from this place are serving time in Drapchi Prison for demonstrating. The nunnery is difficult to find – keep asking for Ani Gompa. Also in this vicinity are several small mosques, combining Muslim and Tibetan architectural features.

Institute of Tibetan Medicine [140 A2] Tibetan medicine is an amalgam of herbal cures, astrology and Tibetan Buddhism. No surgery is used – for this, the patient would have to go to other practitioners. Diagnosis in Tibetan medicine is done mainly by reading the pulse (urine samples are also checked). By reading the pulse, a traditional physician determines which humour-flow (bile, wind or phlegm) has been blocked, or is excessive, and which herbal remedies to prescribe to set the system in harmony. Apart from the three main 'humours' there are over 20,000 'channels' operating through the body. Though this may sound like medieval alchemy, in fact there is strong evidence to suggest the herbal cures, developed over a millennium, have considerable effect.

Since the medical college on Chakpori Hill was razed in 1959, the institute is the only traditional medicine facility left in Lhasa. In its present form – a bland concrete building located just west off Barkor Square – the institute opened in 1977. It has in-patient, out-patient and pharmaceutical production sections, as well as an astro/medical teaching institute.

Put together a small group and you can arrange a short tour of the Institute (⊕ 09.00–12.30 Mon–Sat), which will include a visit to a second-floor museum, and the top-floor medical *tanka* room. Here hundreds of rare medical *tankas* are

The monument commemorates the completion of roads linking the TAR to the provinces of Qinghai and Sichuan. Authorities were nervous because the explosive device was discovered a few months before the 30th anniversary of the founding of the TAR, scheduled for September 1995. With 500 government officials and their families from all over China expected for the celebration, security was considerably tightened, and half a dozen checkpoints established on the Gongkar–Lhasa road. Two European tourists who took photographs of the obelisk a week later were detained and questioned for 2 hours, and had their film confiscated. In another 1995 incident, a tourist sent a fax from the Holiday Inn speculating about a bomb explosion: Chinese police intercepted the fax, arrested the tourist, detained him for 48 hours, and then deported him.

In May 1996, Chinese authorities admitted to three bomb blasts in Lhasa, blaming them on separatists. In December 1996, a bomb damaged the gatehouse of the Metropolitan District Government Offices. The blast was confirmed on Tibet Radio, which described the incident as 'yet another counter-revolutionary bombing staged by the Dalai clique in Lhasa City' and calling it 'an appalling act of terrorism'. A substantial reward was posted for information leading to the capture of the person or persons responsible

There are closed-circuit surveillance cameras mounted inside the Potala to eavesdrop on the caretaker monks there. Even though the Potala is Lhasa's major tourist attraction, and one of its most sacred sites, its last resident – the 14th Dalai Lama – is vilified by the Chinese. His picture is banned, along with that of the young 11th Panchen Lama (the one chosen by the Dalai Lama). So the whole trade in Dalai Lama and Panchen Lama pictures – once freely pursued in the Barkor – has simply gone underground.

stored – teaching devices showing which plants should be collected, anatomical charts with energy channels, and so on. You will be shown copies of the originals. In the same section are three statues of famous medical practitioners. In the middle is a white-bearded figure (Yutok Yonten Gonpo, 9th-century founder of Tibetan medical science), flanked on the left by the regent of the Fifth Dalai Lama (Desi Sanggye Gyatso, 17th-century founder of Chakpori medical college) and on the right by the most renowned physician of the 20th century (Khyenrab Norbu, physician to the 13th Dalai Lama).

POTALA AREA
The Lingkor The Lingkor is the outer pilgrim circuit of Lhasa, taking about 90 minutes to complete on foot (or half that time by bicycle). Hardy pilgrims with prayer wheels and pet dogs (or pet sheep) follow the route, perhaps breaking the journey for a spot of food shopping *en route*. Once they realise that you are joining them for the *kora*, you will get lots of reassuring grins and thumbs-up gestures. There is no finer way to get into the spirit of Lhasa – what's left of Lhasa, that is.

Tibetans still follow the full Lingkor circuit, though it has lost much of its sacred appeal on the eastern and southern sides, where small bars and karaoke salons have mushroomed. These places may be fronts for prostitution. Nudes or noodles? Probably a bit of both, washed down with beer. Prostitutes are flown in from Sichuan Province. Other fronts: barbershops west of the Potala, and certain restaurants with partitioned sections. How big is the trade? Very big. At the bridge to Jarmalingka

4

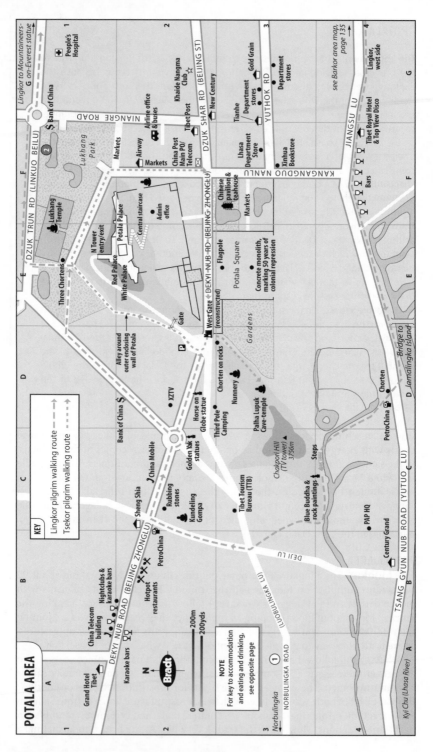

POTALA AREA

KEY
Lingkor pilgrim walking route — — —
Tsekor pilgrim walking route · · · · · ·

N

Bradt

0   200m
0   200yds

NOTE
For key to accommodation and eating and drinking, see opposite page

Lingkor to Mountaineers-
G on-Everest statue

People's Hospital

Khaide Nangma Club ☆

Bank of China $

DZUK TRUN RD (LINKUO BEILU)

NIANGRE ROAD

Airline office & buses

Airway

Tibet Post

China Post Main PO/ Telecom

New Century

DZUK SHAR RD (BEIJING ST)

Tianhe

Department stores

Gold Grain

YUTHOK RD

Department stores

Lukhang Park

Lukhang Temple

Markets

Markets

Lhasa Department Store

Xinhua Bookstore

KANGANGDUO NANLU

Three Chortens

N Tower entry/exit

Potala Palace

Central staircase

Admin office

Red Palace
White Palace

Gate

Chinese pavilion & teahouse

Markets

Flagpole

Potala Square

Concrete monolith, marking 50 years of colonial repression

Bridge to
D Jamdalingka Island

JIANGSU LU

Tibet Royal Hotel & Top View Disco

Lingkor, west side

Bars

Alley around outer enclosing wall of Potala

West Gate ← DEKYI-NUB RD (BEIJING ZHONGLU)
(reconstructed)

P

Gardens

Chorten on rocks

Nunnery

Palha Lupuk Cave-temple

Bank of China $

XZTV

Horse on Globe statue

Third Pole Camping

Chakpori Hill (TV tower) ▲ 3756m

Steps

Chorten

PetroChina

CHINA MOBILE

Golden Yak statues

Rubbing stones

Kundeling Gompa

Tibet Tourism Bureau (TTB)

Blue Buddha & rock paintings

PAP HQ

Century Grand

Sheng Shia

PetroChina

Hotpot restaurants

Nightclubs & karaoke bars

China Telecom building

Grand Hotel Tibet

Karaoke bars

DEKYI NUB ROAD (BEIJING ZHONGLU)

DEJI LU

TSANG GYUN NUB ROAD (YUTUO LU)

Norbulingka

NORBULINGKA ROAD

(LUOBULINGKA LU)

Kyi Chu (Lhasa River)

see Barkor area map, page 135

162

⊖ **Where to stay**
1 Shangri-La *p136*..........................A3

⊗ **Where to eat and drink**
2 Lukhang teahouse *p143*............F1
   Teahouse (see Chinese
      pavilion) *p144*.........................F3
   Teahouse
      (see Red Palace) *p144*............E2

Island, the news doesn't get any better. An old wooden bridge here used to lead to an undeveloped area where Tibetans would congregate under the trees for picnics. The bridge was torn down and replaced by a wider concrete one – to develop Jarmalingka. The island's greenery disappeared, and the area sprouted into a Chinese entertainment zone, with row-housing, nightclubs, hairdressers, brothels, karaoke bars, fairground, restaurants and hotels. The area is today known by various names – Kumalingka, Taiyang (Sun Island) and Zhonghe International City.

The Lingkor as a sacred circuit really gets under way at a cairn of stones with some prayer flags, just west of Jarmalingka Bridge. This marks the turn-off for a walking track that leads to the Blue Buddha. If you bicycle the route, there are steps near the Blue Buddha which require you to carry the bike. Otherwise, it's easy riding, with smooth, flat sections.

Blue Buddha [162 C3] The way up past the south base of Chakpori Hill is a staircase lined with prayer flags. Further on is an entire cliff face depicting religious figures, which have been carved in bas-relief and painted in bright colours. Some carvings date back over a thousand years, with countless additions over the centuries. The largest carving is the Blue Buddha, shown seated in a meditation pose. In this area, pilgrims pay their respects, and off to the side, carvers chip text into *mani* stones. If you follow the pilgrims, heading north, you'll reach another PetroChina station at Dekyi Nub Road. Just before reaching that junction, set back off the road lies Kundeling Gompa, a small active monastery that is little visited. On Dekyi Nub Road is a section with some well-worn rocks. These are special rubbing stones that pilgrims apply their knees or backs to. From here, pilgrims continue to the Golden Yak statues.

Golden Yak statues [162 C2] Two Golden Yak statues, which now sit in a park overlooking a major roundabout, were unveiled in May 1991 to celebrate the 40th anniversary of the 'peaceful liberation' of Tibet by Chinese troops. Tibetans have christened the incongruous statues 'Tenzin and Raidi', a reference to the two Tibetan deputy secretaries of the Communist Party in Tibet who are trotted out when the Chinese need to present a Tibetan face to the media. In the background at this site sits the modern office building housing Xizang TV (XZTV), the main radio and TV broadcasting unit in Lhasa. The operation is solar powered. The Golden Yak statues are something of a navigation landmark, referred to in this chapter as the Golden Yak roundabout.

Three Chortens [162 E1] From the Golden Yak roundabout, the Lingkor route heads northward, turning through a park where the route is lined with vendors – a chance to indulge in some food shopping. Proceeding onwards, you arrive at a busy junction with three *chortens* (shrines). All change at Three Chortens: you can diverge and complete the Tsekor (circuit of Potala Palace), or you can access entry to Lukhang Park, or you can carry on with the whole Lingkor route. Or combinations of these routes. From the three *chortens*, Lingkor pilgrims march north on a narrow walkway that is sectioned off from Lukhang Park by a wire fence. They stop to feed

Lhasa WHAT TO SEE AND DO

4

geese and fish in Lukhang Lake and give money to beggars, thereby gaining more merit. A bridge festooned with prayer flags is located near the main road: this spot offers fine views of the back of the Potala Palace. At the end of the bridge, there is a gateway that leads into Lukhang Park. The Lingkor route continues eastward but loses its lustre – and its purpose – among bland Chinese buildings.

The Tsekor The Tsekor is a *kora* (complete loop) of the outer enclosing walls of the Potala Palace. The following description proceeds clockwise from the West Gate, though you might want to start at Lukhang Park if coming off the Lingkor circuit.

West Gate [162 D2] As part of the 1995 'celebrations' of the 30th anniversary of the founding of the TAR, Lhasa's West Gate and two accompanying *chortens* were resurrected. Passing through the *chorten*-like West Gate was once the only way into the sacred city, and reaching it was the dream of many explorers. It was the gate that British troops marched through in 1904; the gate that Heinrich Harrer and Peter Aufschnaiter reached in rags in 1946, after two years of wandering. Now you see it, now you don't: the original West Gate was completely destroyed in the Cultural Revolution, and then completely rebuilt for the 1995 ceremonies. Tibetan pilgrims pose next to the 1995 version of the West Gate for photographs, but Tibetans say that the structure was not properly consecrated by monks, and in any case, there are no hidden treasures within the *chorten*-like structure that required consecration. Nevertheless, there is some fine artwork lining the interior of the West Gate, especially a mandalic mural on the inside ceiling.

From the West Gate, pilgrims proceed north along a narrow walkway lined on one side with an endless row of prayer wheels, and on the other side with an endless row of stalls – and vendors shouting their wares. This walkway follows the outer Potala Palace walls to the three *chortens* area. From here, you can carry on and complete the Tsekor circuit, or you can take a stroll through Lukhang Park and rejoin the Tsekor.

Lukhang Park [162 F1] The park at the back of the Potala was a site where the Tibetan aristocracy used to picnic or drink tea. It has since lost its noble atmosphere – it's down at the proletariat level now, renamed Jiefang (Victory) Park. However, you can still take tea here, and contemplate the excellent views of the Potala. There are three entrances to the park – one at the northwest side, one at the northeast and one at the south side. At the entrances, you pay a token fee (extra for a bicycle). Lukhang Park attracts picnickers, strollers and people relaxing, and it's great for cycling around. At the northeast corner is a teahouse with outdoor tables and umbrellas overlooking a small artificial lake, with the towers of the Potala looming above. A plant nursery is attached to the teahouse: potted plants and flowers make this a very pleasant place. You can park yourself over a cup of *ba bao cha* (eight treasures tea) – this is provided in a cup with a lid, and contains a big lump of rock sugar with dried berries and herbs, to which steaming hot water is added.

Lukhang Temple [162 E1] On an island in the middle of the lake is Lukhang Temple, a tiny three-storey chapel constructed in the form of a mandala. The building of the temple is attributed to the Sixth Dalai Lama, and it was used as a quiet retreat for arcane meditation practices by successive Dalai Lamas.

Lukhang Temple is one of those corners that provide an illusion of old Lhasa: it is sequestered in greenery, with only the back of the Potala visible, so you can get a feeling for what Tibet once was. There are a few monks currently in residence at Lukhang Temple. You can visit, but not all parts of the building are accessible. There are murals on each of the three storeys: the most interesting are those on the third floor, believed to date to the 18th century. You will need a flashlight to see these gems – they are protected by a wire shield, which doesn't make the viewing any easier. The murals show subjects that are rare to find in Tibetan temples today. Among them are depictions of Indian ascetics in yogic poses, and others striking blissful tantric poses. One wall shows the stages of human life, with detailed anatomical pictures acting as a kind of Tibetan medicine primer (in which system an imbalance of humours leads to sickness and dysfunction). Attached to this is a set of murals based on *The Tibetan Book of the Dead*.

THE MYSTERIOUS SIXTH

The Sixth Dalai Lama was Tsangyang Gyatso, whose name means 'Ocean of Melodious Songs'. He is thought to have lived from 1683 to 1706. He took over as Dalai Lama under very unusual circumstances. The Fifth Dalai Lama had died during the construction of the Potala but his death was concealed by the Regent for some 15 years to ensure completion of the work (the Fifth Dalai Lama was replaced by a double and was said to be engaged in long meditation retreats). The Sixth Dalai Lama took over as an adolescent, not an infant like his predecessors. He did not take any celibacy vows and was never fully ordained as a lama. He showed little interest in either his political or religious duty. His passions lay elsewhere. He was a prolific rake – no woman in Lhasa was said to be safe from his indulgences:

> I dwell apart in the Potala
> A God on earth am I
> But in the town the chief of rogues
> And boisterous revelry

Lukhang Temple has been variously described as the Sixth Dalai Lama's personal retreat, and as his favourite trysting place. He was said to sneak out of a back gate of the Potala to meet his lovers. Apart from his love of wine and women, he was renowned as a melodious singer of love songs, and writer of romantic lyrics:

> Drops of rain wash away
> The love songs written in
> Black and white
> But love, though unwritten,
> Remains long after, in the heart

Despite his behaviour, the Sixth was revered by the people, who came to the conclusion that the living Buddha had two bodies – one which stayed in the Potala and meditated, and the other that got rotten drunk and chased Lhasa women. The Sixth disappeared under mysterious circumstances at the age of 23. One account claims that he had a son by a special lover, and that high lamas – fearing the office of the Dalai Lama would become hereditary – drove the Sixth into exile and imprisoned his lover and their son. Another account claims he was murdered at Litang.

Potala Square [162 E3] Potala Square was created in 1995 in time to mark 'celebrations' for the 30th anniversary of the TAR. A large area of ramshackle Tibetan housing was razed to create the paving; the inhabitants were moved to concrete housing north of the Potala. The concept of a large square or plaza is alien to Tibetan town planning: this is a Chinese idea. The Tibetans would have no use for such a square because it allows the bitter winter wind to roar through. Potala Square has a lot in common with Beijing's Tiananmen Square, including the same chandelier-lamp fixtures with propaganda speakers attached. Tiananmen Square was Mao Zedong's creation, designed for military parades and mass solidarity parades, and meanwhile used for weekend amusement such as photography or kite flying.

This is exactly what Potala Square is used for: the military use it as one big parking lot; concerts for the military have been staged here; shows of force and parades by the PLA have taken place; and trade fairs with vendors promoting Chinese products have been conducted here. Potala Square is the premier Chinese photo-opportunity site. There is a slew of photo shops just to the west of the square, catering to Chinese tourism. A flagpole at the front of the square is a favourite place for Chinese tourists to have their photos taken. All Chinese dignitaries and military honchos arriving in Lhasa stop near the flagpole to have photographs or video taken with the Potala in the background.

In 2002, a 37m-high concrete monolith was constructed near the fountain to commemorate the 50th anniversary of the liberation of Tibet. This monstrosity, said to be an abstract rendition of Everest, is flanked by two concrete bunkers, intended as exhibition halls. The monument is reported to have cost US$1.7 million to build, prompting exiled Tibetans to call it a million-dollar insult. Directly in front of the monolith is a hidden musical fountain – for special events, waterworks spring up, synchronised with music from loudspeakers.

On a more positive note, in time for the 40th anniversary of the founding of the TAR in 2005, some shoddy Chinese shops were pulled down to the west side of Potala Square, and in their place a green belt with gardens was added. This green belt is a favoured spot for Tibetans to take photos.

Palha Lupuk Cave-temple [162 D3] As an extension of the Tsekor circuit, pilgrims diverge to visit Palha Lupuk, an extraordinary cave-temple set into the lower section of Chakpori Hill. You can reach it by a path leading from the West Gate; entry is Y20. The brown and ochre-coloured Palha Lupuk temple, with a dozen monks in residence, offers a superb viewpoint of the Potala, giving it a foreground of rocks and trees. Close by are two small caves – the larger one is lined with several rows of brightly painted bas-relief images, believed to date back as far as the 7th century (which qualifies them as the oldest in Lhasa). The central image here is Sakyamuni, while at the back is a small statue of Palden Lhamo, the protectress of Lhasa. The intimate scale of the temple and cave make Palha Lupuk very special – it offers perspectives that you will find nowhere else in Lhasa. There's a second (minor) cave with an image of Avalokitesvara in the vicinity; above Palha Lupuk to the right is a small active nunnery. Another hike to consider is up Chakpori Hill. This hill was once crowned by the fortresslike medical college of Lhasa – the institute, founded in the 15th century, was razed by shelling in the 1959 uprising. The hill is now crowned with a TV tower, which you may be able to climb partway for views of the Potala.

Potala Palace [162 E2] The Potala was inscribed on the UNESCO World Heritage list in 1994. The citation says: 'The Potala, winter palace of the Dalai Lama since the 7th century AD, symbolises Tibetan Buddhism and its central role in the traditional administration of Tibet.' Chinese authorities conducted a five-year multimillion-dollar restoration of the Potala, completing work in 1995. Why restore a palace that is the former abode of Public Enemy Number One? Because it's a major tourist attraction, of course – and one that generates millions of dollars in income annually. Unlike the Jokhang or the monasteries around Lhasa, the Potala is run by Chinese tourist authorities: the practice of Buddhism is essentially banned in the palace.

Once humming with spiritual activity, the Potala is now a lifeless museum, a haunted castle. A lot of the Chinese restoration was directed at the enclosing walls, which were damaged by Chinese shelling during the 1959 uprising. Adding considerably to the bill is the 'wiring' of the Potala. Electrical hook-ups have been enhanced and video surveillance cameras have been installed throughout. The cameras are to monitor the 60-odd caretakers at the Potala, who pad around in purple trench coats. On a more practical note, fire extinguishers and other devices have been installed (following a disastrous fire that broke out in 1984 due to a short circuit).

Below the Potala, within the enclosing walls, used to lie the Tibetan administrative quarter of Shol. Some buildings in this zone have been destroyed. One building has been turned into a hotel; the others are used as art galleries, souvenir shops, or occupied as residences. Before 1950, Shol quartered the offices of the Tibetan government, Tibetan Army officials, guard offices and a prison. Other sections of the Potala were used to house Namgyal Monastery, as well as a community of monks and a school for monk officials.

History and architecture The Potala is a 13-storey castle – rising over 117m high – built of rammed earth, wood and stone. Crowning a mass of solid rock, the mazelike structure contains over a thousand rooms, and is thought to house 10,000 shrines and 200,000 statues. The architecture at first appears to be regular, but is not – storeys are not continuous, and access to halls may be hidden behind pillars or shrines. The walls – varying in thickness between 2m and 5m – were strengthened against earthquakes by pouring in molten copper. No steel frame was used, and no nails were used in the woodwork. The Potala is a layered structure: successive Dalai Lamas worked on the project. Although original construction dates back to the 7th century, the White Palace was not completed until 1653, and the Red Palace not until 1694: at this time, the wheel had not been introduced to Tibet, so stones were lugged in on donkey-back, or on the backs of humans. Simple equipment was used to fashion this skyscraper – an achievement on a par with the building of the pyramids.

The skyscraper itself created a transport problem. The Potala had no plumbing, electricity or heating, so there was a constant stream of porters with water for tea, yak butter for the prayer lamps, and firewood for the fireplaces. The Dalai Lama was portered in and out of the palace in a palanquin; high lamas were piggybacked up to the entrance of the Potala by porters.

Access Opening hours for the Potala seem to chop and change, and vary with the season. You can follow the logic of the hours described here, but there could well be modifications. The Potala is supposed to be open to tourists 09.00–17.00 daily, including holidays. The best time to visit is mornings; the last tickets are sold around 15.00. In high season (July–August), there are long queues to get in. Tickets were previously limited to 1,600 visitors a day, but that figure was boosted to 2,300 after the July 2006 opening of the railway. After the daily maximum is reached, even Tibetan pilgrims (who pay Y2) are turned away. To discourage visitors, the palace is contemplating a steep increase in ticket admission prices. This would also be in the interests of preserving the architecture itself, which is at risk from heavy use by tourists. To avoid disappointments and queues, in peak season you should buy tickets ahead – buy them after 14.00 on the day prior to your visit.

Important note: to purchase tickets, you need to show proper ID such as a passport. From May to October, entry costs Y200 for big-noses; in the 'slack season' (November–April) the ticket price may be reduced to Y100. Photography of interiors at the Potala is not permitted, though you can shoot in exterior courtyards.

Due to heavy demand, with conga lines of tourists snaking through the Potala, a tactic of limiting your time in the palace has been adopted. Your guide will try to rush you through in 60–90 minutes, start to finish. For some folks, that's fine. Others like to go slower. The 1-hour stipulation, like many other rules in Tibet, is unwritten. Therefore, ask your guide to show you where it says you only get 1 hour to visit, and just ignore the pressure. The tide of humanity surging through may speed you along on certain stretches, particularly if you get caught in throngs of pilgrims. Fisticuffs have broken out at entrances to certain highly revered rooms as pilgrims and Chinese tourists jockey for the best vantage points.

The Potala is open to Tibetan pilgrims, who pay a token entry fee. It appears that the pilgrims are allowed entry on Monday, Wednesday and Friday mornings, but this could change. When there are lots of pilgrims, key shrines may become very crowded, with long queues. Here's a paradox: things are much more lively with Tibetan pilgrims around (you can observe what they are doing – muttering mantras, flinging *katas*, and spooning yak butter into lamps at shrines) but at the same time, it's more crowded and uncomfortable. The solution here is to visit the Potala several times: first to see the architecture and statuary, the second time to go and mingle with the Tibetan pilgrims.

Entry to the Potala is via the central staircase, which is taxing to negotiate at altitude – take it slowly here. Group tours may have permission to access easier ways of reaching the top of the Potala. Only a fraction of the Potala's thousand-odd rooms are accessible to the touring public: the contents of many are rumoured to have been destroyed or carted off. The rooms seem to open and close without rhyme or reason, so the following description may hit the mark – or it may not. You should be able to follow the overall logic. The way things are currently set up, you enter the palace by the central staircase. From there you mount staircases to the open rooftop area of the Potala, and then spiral downward to the bowels of the building, where you exit by the North Tower. This is actually a car ramp. Heading down from the North Tower at the back of the Potala, you get a view of north Lhasa that is not revealed from the rooftop: a sea of apartment blocks stretching towards Sera – the heavy Chinese concrete hand at work.

Inside the Potala The Potala is divided into the White Palace and the Red Palace. The White Palace was secular in nature (used for offices, a printing house and so on), while the Red Palace fulfilled a religious function (comprising the tombs of the Dalai Lamas, scores of chapels and shrines, and libraries of sacred texts). Most of the White Palace is inaccessible; you can see a fair number of rooms in the Red Palace.

The 14th Dalai Lama's quarters Huffing and puffing up staircases, you arrive at an open rooftop area of the Potala. Green-maned snow lions are the gargoyles here – pilgrims touch the mouths of the lions and ring attached bells. To the west side of the open area are the former living quarters of the 13th and 14th Dalai Lamas, attached to the White Palace. The only section accessible here takes you into the former reception hall, dominated by a large throne. On the wall nearby hangs a portrait painting of the 13th Dalai Lama, but a portrait of the 14th that used to hang alongside it has been removed. So ludicrous is the Chinese removal of 14th Dalai Lama images that in a lavishly illustrated Beijing hardcover about the Potala, he is only seen in one picture – shaking hands with Mao Zedong in 1954.

In the same reception hall, near the entrance, is a large mural of the legendary land of Shambhala. Beyond the hall lie the private quarters of the 14th Dalai Lama. You may or may not be allowed to see these, depending on the mood of caretakers. Try tagging along behind an official tour. At the 14th Dalai Lama's tearoom and meditation room, pilgrims leave *katas* and other offerings; beyond is His Holiness's bedroom, vacant since 1959.

The Red Palace Entering the Red Palace from the rooftop area, you spiral downward through four levels, eventually exiting at the North Tower. The upper levels of the Red Palace enclose an open skylight space, with chapels arrayed in a gallery-like rectangle around it. Interspersed through the many chapels and shrines of the Red Palace are the eight gold-plated stupas, each containing the salt-dried body of a past Dalai Lama – from the Fifth to the 13th, with the exception of the Sixth, who disappeared. Four of the reliquary stupas are on the upper level, and four are on the ground level.

Upper level The upper level provides access to chapels with the stupas of the Seventh, Eighth, Ninth and 13th Dalai Lamas. You may have difficulty getting permission to see the stupa of the 13th Dalai Lama, which is 14m high, made of gold, and fronted by a three-dimensional mandala said to contain 200,000 pearls. The tomb ranges over several storeys and is well lit. One wall bears fine murals of the 13th Dalai Lama surrounded by his ministers and tutors, as well as scenes from his life. Another highlight of the upper level is the former throne room of the Seventh Dalai Lama, which contains a beautiful silver image of 11-headed Avalokitesvara, the bodhisattva of compassion – this statue was commissioned by the 13th Dalai Lama.

Revered by Tibetan pilgrims as the most sacred part of the entire Potala is the **Avalokitesvara Chapel** (Phakpa Lakhang), on the northwest side of the upper level. The tiny chapel gets very crowded when there are lots of pilgrims. It is reached by a small triple staircase. The centre of pilgrim attention is a tiny gilded standing statue of Avalokitesvara, thought to have come from Nepal. Legend has it that the image was found miraculously embedded in a Nepalese sandalwood tree when its trunk split open. Flanking it are two other images derived from the same source, one of Avalokitesvara again, the other of Tara. To the right of this chapel is the massive funerary *chorten* of the Seventh Dalai Lama, rising to a height of 9m, and studded with precious stones. Next to that is the tomb of the Ninth Dalai Lama.

Mid-levels Downstairs, there is a Tibetan-style tearoom with a souvenir shop. On the same level is the Cultural Relics Museum, which charges Y10 entry and features a display of armour and instruments. There are two levels of galleries at the mid-levels, but rooms on the lower level are most likely to be closed (these contain murals depicting the construction of the Potala and major Tibetan monasteries). The highlight of the mid-levels is the **Kalachakra Chapel** (Dukhor Lakhang), which contains a stunning three-dimensional mandala of the palace of the Kalachakra deity. Made of copper and gold, it measures over 6m in diameter. To one side of the mandala is a life-sized statue of the multi-headed, multi-armed Kalachakra deity in union with his consort. On shelves nearby are the seven religious kings of Tibet and the 25 kings of the mythical realm of Shambhala.

Very popular with Tibetan pilgrims on this level is the oldest chamber in the Potala, the Chapel of the Dharma Kings, thought to have been the meditation chamber of King Songtsen Gampo. This cave-within-the-castle is approached by a ramp; the niches lining the cavern are filled with statuary of past kings, royal family members and ministers. The most highly regarded statue is that of Songtsen Gampo himself. You can expect a pilgrim traffic jam in this area and foreign group tours are likely to be ushered past the line-ups.

Ground level After negotiating several steep, dark flights of stairs, you come into a large assembly hall with columns – the Great Western Assembly Hall. This is the largest room in the Potala Palace, with dozens of pillars wrapped in raw silk. It contains the throne of the Seventh Dalai Lama; the walls are coated in murals and appliqué *tankas*.

There are four chapels open on this level. The first you come to is Lamrin Lakhang, dedicated to the ancient lineage masters of the Geluk school, particularly Tsongkhapa. The next chapel, Rigdzin Lakhang, is dedicated to the great Nyingma lineage holder, Padmasambhava, showing eight manifestations of the master; in the same line-up of statues here are seven other great Indian masters.

The next chapel, Dzamling Gyenchik, contains the astounding tomb of the Fifth Dalai Lama, which reaches a height of over 14m, and is said to contain 3,700kg of gold. It is studded with jewels and precious stones. In this line-up of tombs are eight more dedicated to Sakyamuni Buddha, commemorating the eight major events in his life. In the same chapel are the more modest stupas of the Tenth and 12th Dalai Lamas, who both perished as minors, failing to attain their majority. The Dalai Lamas from the Sixth through to the 12th all died young and under mysterious circumstances – possibly poisoned.

The last chapel on the ground level is Tungrab Lakhang, featuring a central double throne with two statues – a gold one of Sakyamuni and a silver one of the Fifth Dalai Lama. This chapel contains the tomb of the 11th Dalai Lama; three statues of the Buddha (past, present and future); and statues of the eight Medicine Buddhas.

You can exit Tungrab Lakhang by a dark hidden corridor at the back of the statues – this leads out of the rear of the Potala at the North Tower.

NORBULINGKA AREA
The Norbulingka [map, page 171] In contrast to the lofty, monumental Potala, the Norbulingka is a small-scale, down-to-earth summer palace. In former times, an elaborate procession would wind out of the Potala, escorting the Dalai Lama to the Norbulingka, his home for up to six months of the year. In better days, the walled summer palace exuded an idyllic atmosphere, with picnic pavilions and well-tended gardens, peacocks roaming the grounds, and Brahminy ducks flocking to the lakes. Norbulingka in fact means 'Jewelled Garden'. Visiting in the 1930s, members of a British delegation were astonished to find roses and petunias flourishing at 3,650m, as well as hollyhocks, marigolds, chrysanthemums, and rows of potted herbs or rare plants. In addition, there were apple, peach and apricot trees – though the fruits did not ripen in Lhasa – and stands of poplar trees and bamboo.

The Norbulingka was shelled during the 1959 uprising, and a number of buildings were destroyed. Following a long period of dereliction, in 2003 the gardens and grounds of the Norbulingka underwent extensive restoration, bringing back the greenery, the floral beds and the miniature lakes. The Norbulingka is mainly identified with the 13th and 14th Dalai Lamas, who commissioned most of

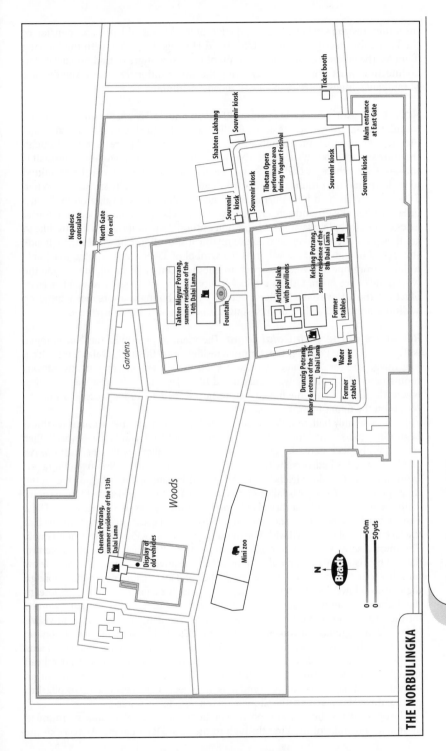

THE NORBULINGKA

Chensek Potrang, summer residence of the 13th Dalai Lama

Display of old vehicles

Woods

Mini zoo

N

Bract

0   50m
0   50yds

Chensek Potrang, summer residence of the 13th Dalai Lama

Gardens

Takten Migyur Potrang, summer residence of the 14th Dalai Lama

Fountain

Nepalese consulate

North Gate (no exit)

Shabten Lakhang

Souvenir kiosk

Souvenir kiosk

Souvenir kiosk

Tibetan Opera performance area during Yoghurt Festival

Drunzig Potrang, library & retreat of the 13th Dalai Lama

Water tower

Former stables

Artificial lake with pavilions

Kelsang Potrang, summer residence of the 8th Dalai Lama

Former stables

Souvenir kiosk

Souvenir kiosk

Ticket booth

Main entrance at East Gate

the structures you see here. In 2001, the Norbulingka was added as an extension of the Potala for inscription on the UN World Heritage list, along with the Jokhang Temple. The citation quoted preservation of the last vestiges of traditional Tibetan architecture: what is meant here is saving the last traditional structures in the face of rampant Chinese development and reconstruction in Lhasa.

Access The Norbulingka is open 09.30–12.30 and 15.30–18.30 (summer hours) Monday to Saturday. Tickets cost Y60. To get to the Norbulingka, you can walk, bicycle, take a taxi, or take a number 2 bus from the Barkor Square vicinity. Although there are several gateways at the Norbulingka, the only one open for entry and exit is the East Gate, where a ticket booth is located. If on a bicycle, you may be permitted to cycle around the grounds of the Norbulingka, which are quite spread out. When Tibetan opera is held here during the Yoghurt (Shoton) Festival, around August or September, the grounds are crowded with picnickers. Flanking the massive east gates of the Norbulingka are two snow lion statues, draped in *katas*. Tibetans like to get their photograph taken next to the mythical snow lion (the one to the left side shelters a lion cub). The snow lion is the symbol of Tibet – it is reputed to be able to jump from one snow-capped peak to another. Only a few buildings inside the Norbulingka are open. Others are locked up, used as storage, or as residences or offices by those involved with the upkeep of the Norbulingka. More recent building additions are kiosks selling drinks, souvenir books and Tibetan artefacts.

Residence of the 14th Dalai Lama The main attraction at the Norbulingka is Takten Migyur Potrang, the summer residence of the 14th Dalai Lama. It's a pilgrimage site for Tibetans, who leave *katas* and other offerings in the various rooms here. The building was constructed from 1954 to 1956, and was the place where the Dalai Lama meditated before he escaped to India. Access is only to rooms on the upper floor.

In the assembly hall, murals portray a detailed history of Tibet, from its mythical beginnings to its early kings to the discovery of the 14th Dalai Lama. Several other rooms can be seen here: the Dalai Lama's study chambers, with a beautiful *tanka* of Atisha; and his bedroom, with an Art Deco bed and a 1956 Phillips radio (a gift from India). A side door leads to a bathroom with state-of-the-art (for Tibet at the time) plumbing. You may be allowed to visit a small library and a meditation room.

In the reception hall is a carved golden throne which was used to carry the Dalai Lama when he went outside the Norbulingka for special occasions. One entire wall of the reception hall is covered with fine murals, painted in 1956 by artist Amdo Jampa. The murals show – with photo-like realism – the 14th Dalai Lama at the centre, flanked by his mother at the right, ministers and relatives at the left, secretary below him, his four tutors above him, various tribes of Tibet at lower right, and foreign dignitaries at lower left. Under all this is a row of mythical figures. Among the foreign dignitaries you can make out Hugh Richardson (hat and tie) who originally worked for the British and stayed on to represent the new Indian government. Also visible is an Indian dignitary, a Russian wearing medals, and a Mongolian ambassador. Unfortunately, most of the mural – especially the section showing the Dalai Lama – is likely to be roped off, and light reflections make it difficult to view. An overhead surveillance camera ensures that pilgrims get no closer. This is one of the rare images of the Dalai Lama still left in Lhasa and thus the object of great veneration by pilgrims passing through, an activity the Chinese do not wish to encourage.

The opposite wall bears a large portrait of the Great Fifth Dalai Lama, surrounded by smaller portraits of the First through to the 13th Dalai Lamas. As you exit the doorway, there's a round Shambhala fresco with a Kalachakra mandala. Harder to access are other sections of the building, including the dining room, and various meeting and reception rooms.

Retreats, vintage cars and a mini zoo Moving along through the grounds of the Norbulingka, of milder interest is **Kelsang Potrang**, the summer residence of the Eighth Dalai Lama, completed in the 18th century. This section may be closed; if it's open, you can view some fine *tankas* depicting White Tara. On the eastern wall in this area is a viewing pavilion that looks over the opera grounds. The Dalai Lamas would sit here to take in performances, which are still held during the Yoghurt Festival (in August or September). The festival derives its name from traditional offerings of yoghurt to monks at this time. To the west of this, in a separate compound (approached from the west wall), is **Drunzig Potrang**, constructed as the library and retreat of the 13th Dalai Lama. It has the atmosphere of a place of worship, with an assembly hall redolent of butter lamps. It contains a newer wooden statue of Avalokitesvara, and thousands of sacred texts. Nearby is an area with outdoor pavilions, probably used for picnics or drinking tea. Following substantial renovations, the ponds here have been revived, which has brought wild birds back – you might even spot some bar-headed geese.

There are several locations where horses were formerly stabled, though these are hard to pinpoint today. The back of each stable was decorated with bright frescoes of equestrian subjects, ranging from horse anatomy to legends of flying horses, and nearby was the Dalai Lama's garage.

The Dalai Lama's cars, however, have been shifted over to a display of vehicles at **Chensek Potrang**. A fair walk away, in the northwest corner of the grounds, **Chensek Potrang** is the summer residence of the 13th Dalai Lama. It was built in 1922, and is preserved much as it was in 1933, when the 13th Dalai Lama died. Only the assembly hall may be accessible.

Inside the Chensek Potrang Chapel is a fascinating display of vehicles, ranging from palanquins (covered litters for one person, moved on foot by bearers) to landaus (elaborate horse-drawn carriages with side lamps). There is even a bicycle and a tricycle (gifts from the British to the 13th and 14th Dalai Lamas). This is all the more fascinating when you consider that the wheel was not much used in pre-1950 Tibet, and the use of vehicles such as motorcycles was banned by the monastic powers.

In the courtyard here you might be able to make out the rusted remains of several cars that originally belonged to the 13th Dalai Lama and were inherited by the 14th Dalai Lama. The cars were gifts from British political officers, carried in pieces by yaks over the Himalaya from India and reassembled by an Indian chauffeur and mechanic. Two were 1920s Baby Austins (one with the number plate Tibet 1); the third was a 1931 orange Dodge. They were used for special occasions, and were the only cars in Tibet at the time, apart from an American Jeep. Their range was limited by a lack of roads and a lack of fuel, which had to be carried in from India. By the 1940s, they had fallen into disrepair, but the young 14th Dalai Lama managed to get them running again. He took a Baby Austin out for a spin at the Norbulingka – and promptly crashed into a tree. One of these cars was later adapted to power a generator for the 14th Dalai Lama's private cinema. Somewhere in the inner gardens of the Norbulingka there used to be a film theatre, constructed in 1949 for the Dalai Lama by Heinrich Harrer (there was another cine-projection room at the British Mission, run by radio operator Reginald Fox).

In the same vicinity, south of Chensek Potrang, is a derelict mini **zoo**, with some cages lying empty. In residence is a motley collection of bears, spotted deer,

4

rhesus monkeys, foxes, lynxes, Argali bighorn sheep, bar-headed geese and bearded vultures, none of whom look especially thrilled about living on bare concrete. Looking very out of place are some imported lions.

Tibet Museum [126 D4] Located in the same vicinity as Norbulingka Summer Palace is the largest structure built in Tibetan style in the last few decades, which is … a museum. Completed in 2000, the multimillion-dollar Tibet Museum encloses a vast exhibition space, spread over three floors. At the time of writing, this vast place was under renovation: the aim is to double its size, though it is difficult to fathom how much more propaganda can be stuffed in. The museum is long on ethnography and short (or warped) on history; short on religion, and very short on the Dalai Lamas. There is only one photograph of the 14th Dalai Lama on display – taken when he was a child – but in the caption for this picture, he is not identified as the 14th in the lineage. He is identified as the reincarnation of the 13th. The museum is liberally sprinkled with Chinese propaganda: the history section features such items as an original copy of the 17-Point Agreement signed in 1951, marking Tibet's takeover by the Chinese; and the Golden Urn, used by the Chinese to determine their choice of the 11th Panchen Lama in 1995.

Despite this slant, with its large collection of manuscripts, *tankas*, masks and costumes, the museum marks the passage of a great civilisation, with original, striking art and architecture. The ground floor focuses on prehistory and manuscripts and tankas; the middle floor is largely devoted to nomad culture; and the top floor concentrates on Tibet's flora and fauna. One small salon features rare tankas. Among these is a beautiful 15th-century masterpiece portraying White Tara in silk appliqué. In the same salon is a patchwork embroidery tanka of the deity Hevajra, with figures added in silk, satin and brocade: a slight 3D relief effect results from the use of cotton batting as stuffing.

The museum has a huge ground-floor gift shop, selling everything from books to *dzi* stones. Given out with tickets are audio-tour devices programmed with different languages – available in English, Chinese, Japanese and, yes, even in Tibetan. Entry tickets are Y30, or Y20 for students. The museum is open daily, 09.00–13.00 and 14.00–18.00. The museum has extraordinary security procedures at the entrance. It is like going through security at an airport, with large scanning devices and frisking of tourists. And as at airports, water bottles and cigarette lighters are confiscated; they cannot be taken inside the museum.

OTHER MUSEUMS
Brahmaputra Grand Private Museum [126 G4] In contrast to Tibet Museum, this bizarre collection is gutsy – and it's free. The collection is housed on the second floor of the Brahmaputra Grand Hotel, a long way east on Jiangsu Lu. This private museum consists of objets d'art collected by supermarket tycoon Zhang Xiaohong. The second-floor museum houses ethnographic displays, displays of Tibetan armour and opera masks, and displays of turquoise and amber jewellery. The Tibetan statuary is top-notch, but the black-and-white photos displayed are simply reproductions of historic ones taken by early foreign visitors to Lhasa.

Heritage housing Consult the *Boutique hotels* listing for locations of restored and renovated former residences of nobles and important dignitaries from pre-1950s Lhasa. Since these function as small hotels, you may or may not be able to gain access to the interior courtyards. Success is more likely if you purchase something at a café or restaurant within, such as at Trichang Labrang.

Yak Museum [126 D4] (*Liuwu New District, south of Tibet Museum, over a bridge across Lhasa River*) The world's first yak-themed museum opened its doors in Lhasa in late 2014. It covers 8,000m², with the primary mission of celebrating the 'spirit of yaks'. This is highly ironic when you consider that China has decimated both the wild yaks (gunned down by Chinese soldiers and settlers) and the domestic yaks of the plateau. Domesticated yaks provide milk, butter, cheese, dung for fuel, and wool for blankets, ropes and bags. Yak butter provides the oil for lamps at temples, and yak horns and skulls are carved and left at shrines. Yaks also provide transportation as beasts of burden over rugged snowbound terrain. However, since 1995, there has been a deliberate Chinese policy of snuffing out the yak-dependent nomad culture by forcibly removing nomads from their traditional grasslands and shifting them into concrete ghettos and selling their yaks to slaughterhouses to be turned into yak steak and yak jerky. So the museum fulfils a need to enshrine yaks while there are still some in existence on the plateau.

There are three exhibition halls: yaks in science and nature, yaks in humanity and history, and yaks in art and spirit. Museum exhibits include stuffed specimens, yak skeletons, yak heads, documents, audio and video materials related to nature and history, as well as artwork featuring yaks. The museum's mission is apparently to help tourists to better understand Tibetan culture and the importance of yaks to people living on the roof of the world. But of course, the displays are missing the vital information about massive enforced settlement of nomads by Chinese authorities and yaks going to slaughterhouses – the nomad culture has become a museum exhibit.

OUTSKIRTS OF LHASA

BIKING AND HIKING One of the saving graces of Lhasa is its clean air – far cleaner than in Kathmandu or other Asian cities. Compared with Chinese cities, traffic in Lhasa is light, and the place is ringed by mountains. The outskirts of Lhasa present great hiking and bicycling opportunities. You can combine those by hiring a mountain bike and setting off, later exploring on foot. Offering novel perspectives on Lhasa Valley are ridge-top viewpoints – at Bumpa Ri to the southeast side, above Sera to the north side and at Gephel Ri to the northwest side. The easiest one to tackle is Bumpa Ri. To get to the base of Bumpa Ri, you can bicycle out over Lhasa Bridge, which spans the Kyi Chu River. The bridge was built in 1965 – it is 530m long, and is guarded by sentries at both ends. Find a place to keep your bike and climb up towards prayer flags planted on top of Bumpa Ri. If you want something less strenuous, you can take on smaller hills in this area, also planted with prayer flags. For a return trip by bicycle, consider cycling west along the south bank of the Kyi Chu River – there's a dirt road here that leads to a long bridge spanning the river close to the railway station.

At the back of Sera Monastery are fine hiking trails linking shrines. You can take a bus or minivan service to either Sera or Drepung monastery, bicycle out, share a taxi, hitch a ride, or walk. If you have a mountain bike, day trips or overnight trips can be mounted – due east and northeast of Lhasa are the best directions to go, as there is less traffic.

Sera [126 F1] The three great Geluk monastic citadels close to Lhasa – Sera, Drepung and Ganden – developed a considerable rivalry in old Lhasa. They were all established in the early 15th century – Ganden in 1409, Drepung in 1416 and Sera in 1419. Sera's population hovered around 7,000 monks, eclipsed by the 9,000 at Drepung, while Ganden's quota was probably 5,000 monks.

Sera, 4km to the north of Lhasa, was at one time famous for its fighting monks, who spent years perfecting the martial arts. They were hired out as bodyguards to the wealthy, and even took on the Tibetan Army in 1947 during protests following the imprisonment of Reting Rinpoche. Once a year, the fighting monks of Sera used to race starkers along the Kyi Chu riverbank for several kilometres to toughen up. Sera means 'merciful hail' – the origin of the name is thought to derive from the fact that Sera was in constant competition with Drepung ('rice heap monastery') and that the 'hail' of Sera destroyed the 'rice' of Drepung. Today, only a few hundred monks remain at Sera, a shadow of its former self. You can wander around and view the interiors of the two main colleges – Sera Me and Sera Je – as well as the main assembly hall.

Monastic debating One of the biggest draws at Sera is Tibetan-style debating, which takes place in the afternoon, starting around 14.00 or 15.00. Weather permitting, the venue is an open courtyard to the north side, where monks gather on cushions under the shade of trees. They debate religious and philosophical questions in the peculiar Tibetan style of slapping the palm of the hand to make a point. All highly photogenic. Monastic debating is the method used for passing exams to obtain monastic degrees, though this system has lapsed under communist control.

Entry to Sera costs Y50. Near the entrance to Sera is a monastery restaurant that serves noodles, vegetables and bread at low prices. There's a pleasant outdoor section at the back, shaded by birch trees, where pilgrims gather.

Hiking behind Sera A bigger draw than the temple interiors is the hiking out this way. Behind Sera to the northeast, on a mountainside, is the hermitage of Tsongkhapa – a simple shrine. In the vicinity are striking rock carvings on boulders. A walking circuit around Sera takes about an hour to complete. If you are well acclimatised, there are more ambitious, longer, steeper hikes behind Sera that offer superb views. Dotted around the hill backing Sera are a number of caves, hermitages and sacred sites that are among the oldest in Lhasa. A circuit of sorts leads past Sera to Pabonka, a small temple with two dozen monks; from there you can carry on to Tashi Choling Hermitage, and climb a ridge to Chupsang Nunnery, which has 80 nuns in residence. This makes for a worthwhile but fairly strenuous day.

Sera to Drepung Instead of going back through downtown Lhasa to get from Sera to Drepung, you can take a more interesting shortcut by traversing a marshy area southwest of Sera. Some of the time there's a dirt road to follow, other times not. It's possible to bicycle most of the route, which leads past a rock quarry. Unless you have a mountain bike with gears, it's better not to attempt the steep route up from the base of the hill leading to Drepung. Leave the bike with a shop owner (with a token payment) and hitch a ride with whatever comes along (most likely a walking-tractor or number 3 bus).

Drepung [126 B2] If Sera used to be famous for its fighting monks, Drepung was famed for its scholars. Spectacularly sited – enclosed on three sides by boulder-strewn peaks – Drepung is an entire monastic town that once housed a community of some 9,000 monks, qualifying it as the largest in the world. There are perhaps 500 monks living here today, although their numbers are uncertain following a major re-education campaign in the late 1990s, where monks were forced to denounce the Dalai Lama. Drepung has been singled out as a priority for re-education because of its larger contingent of monks and because of its previous involvement in Lhasa demonstrations.

To the north of Lhasa is a kind of 'dead end', with Drapchi Prison, Lhasa Military Hospital and – to the northeast – a large flat-topped boulder, on top of which sky burials take place. Upon death, the body is thought to return to one of the elements – earth, air, fire, water or wood. Earth burial is rare in Tibet: the ground is hard to break up, and could be frozen in winter. Cremation (return to fire) is also rare because wood is a scarce commodity. A high lama might be cremated, and the ashes placed in a silver *chorten* in his monastery. Two other forms reserved for high lamas are wood burial (the body is placed in a hollow tree-trunk) and embalming (the body is preserved in a seated pose by an ancient Tibetan embalming technique). Water burial – whereby the body is eaten by fish – is reserved for small children and paupers.

In Tibet, the most common form of dispatching the dead is not under the ground, but the opposite – releasing the body to the air. This is sky burial. The body is taken to a site on a rock on a mountainside and hacked into pieces with machetes. The bones are pounded together with *tsampa*, and when the work is complete, a signal is given to waiting flocks of vultures – which know the timing well – to feast on the rock. This way, the body is thought to be taken closer to the heavens. Sky burial takes place all over Tibet, but is more common in Lhasa because of the larger resident population.

In the mid-1980s, travellers were allowed to sit near the rock where sky burial takes place. As long as they were respectful of the customs and did not take photos, they were tolerated by the Tibetans. However, a number of ugly incidents involving photography upset the Tibetans. In particular, one Westerner climbed up behind the rock, intending to sneak photographs of the site with a long lens. In the process, he scared off the vultures who sit on the ridge above the sky burial site, so they did not come down at the completion of rites – a very bad omen. Since the early 1990s, the site has been off-limits to tourists. However, you may be able to see the sky burial ceremony at other sites around the Tibetan plateau, such as Litang.

Tibetans are not the only people to dispatch the dead this way. The Parsi Zoroastrians in India, descended from Persians, follow a similar custom. However, the ancient Parsi religious custom is in danger of disappearing because the vultures that eat the bodies are headed for extinction in India, due to farmers' use of the drug Diclofenac on livestock. Ravens and kites have taken over some of the duties for dispatching the dead.

Drepung is 8km west of downtown Lhasa. You can bicycle out this way, or take a number 3 bus, which runs past the Potala and goes all the way up to the gates of Drepung. The monastery charges a Y55 entry fee. On the way in or out of Drepung, you might want to visit the Potala Carpet Factory [126 B3], which is about 300m west of the turn-off to Drepung. You can see women weaving and singing at the factory.

Like other large-scale monasteries, Drepung is divided into colleges with attached residences, rather like a campus where different disciplines are pursued. There are four major colleges – Ngakpa, Loseling, Gomang and Deyang. In previous times, all the monks at Drepung would gather on special occasions at the vast main assembly hall. Now the hall is little used. The hall is three storeys high: you can climb on to the flat rooftop for great views over Lhasa Valley (Drepung lies a few hundred metres above Lhasa). If you like climbing, there's a very strenuous hike behind Drepung to the top of Gephel Ri [126 B2]. The climb up and back would take a full day and you need to be very well acclimatised, as the top of Gephel Ri is 5,200m in altitude.

Nechung [126 C2] On the lower slopes of the hill leading up to Drepung is Nechung Monastery, a small temple that fulfilled an important function in old Lhasa. It was the seat of the state oracle, who was consulted by the Lhasa government when making important decisions. The monks who lived at Nechung were trained in the secret rituals that accompanied the trances of the oracle. When in a trance, the oracle was said to be possessed by the spirit Dorje Drakden – the oracle shook, trembled, barked, rolled his eyes and stuck out his tongue. Monk-attendants quickly strapped on the oracle's impossibly heavy headpiece and he would dance around. Questions were asked, cryptic answers were given. The state oracle's last cryptic answers in Tibet concerned whether the Dalai Lama should leave or not – the answer was interpreted as yes. The state oracle himself escaped to India with the exodus of exiles in 1959; he died in 1985, but his successor was found, and the tradition has been kept alive in Dharamsala, India.

In keeping with its unusual function, Nechung Monastery has some strange, striking and imaginative murals lining the walls of the inner courtyard and main chapel – paintings of flayed humans held from the rafters by serpents, figures with dangling eyeballs, disembodied heads and legs, wrathful deities with garlands of skulls, and other ghoulish artwork. It also features an array of mythical animals, such as murals of snakes and dragons coiled around support beams in the main hall. There's a statue of Dorje Drakden in the main assembly hall, as well as a photograph showing the Nechung Oracle in a trance. Adjoining chapels were once used by the various Dalai Lamas when they visited or conducted retreats here. Some 20 monks currently reside at Nechung.

5

Exploring Central Tibet

Lhasa is not Tibet – it is too heavily Chinese-influenced for that. If you want to see a more genuine Tibet, you have to get out into the countryside, where 80% of Tibetans live. This chapter covers areas within an easy drive of Lhasa. You might also consider combination routes involving Gyantse and Shigatse when on a round trip out of Lhasa. See the *Lhasa to Kathmandu* chapter, pages 201–35, for details on Gyantse, Shigatse and sites further west.

While destinations when touring by rental vehicle are commonly monasteries, what's along the way is often more interesting. If you see an opportunity to stop or get off the track, take it. On one trip, we spotted some horseriders in costume. We pulled over and got the driver to ask where they were going. It turned out there was a horse-racing and archery event not far away. We spent several hours watching the races and drinking *chang*. Our Tibetan driver didn't mind – he was enjoying himself, too.

If you string together a lot of temples on a trip, you run the risk of becoming 'templed out'. That is, after visiting the first two or three temples, they all start to look the same. The key to a well-designed trip is variety – visit a temple, a fortress, then take in some countryside, and make impromptu stops along the route. Samye is a good combination of natural sights (eg: crossing of the Yarlung Tsangpo River) and temples. A visit to Lake Namtso places more emphasis on natural beauty.

Some of the sites mentioned here (Tsurphu, Damxung, Samye, Tsedang) can be reached by rental vehicle with driver and guide over a period of two to seven days, depending on how much ground you want to cover, splitting the tariff between four or five passengers. If you are not overnighting, permits should not present problems – you can visit on a day trip. However, be wary of Tsedang and Samye, which have active PSB officers who will check on you – even in the daytime. It's worth keeping in mind that the PSB does not work on Sundays.

NORTH OF LHASA

Popular destinations north of Lhasa are Tsurphu Monastery and Lake Namtso, and the monasteries of Ganden, Drigung, Tidrom and Yerpa. There are several possibilities for touring this northern sector by rental vehicle: you could head straight for Lake Namtso on a two-day sortie; or you could easily spend five days going to Namtso and cutting across overland to Lhundrup, Reting and the monasteries of Drigung, Tidrom and Ganden. Some travellers just target the valley with Drigung, Tidrom, Ganden and Yerpa in two or three days. Locals reach these places by taking pilgrim buses, leaving downtown Lhasa early morning from Barkor Square.

You can also indulge in trekking (which can be rough in Tibet) at various points. With 4x4 pick-ups, hardy trekkers have embarked on longer forays: you could,

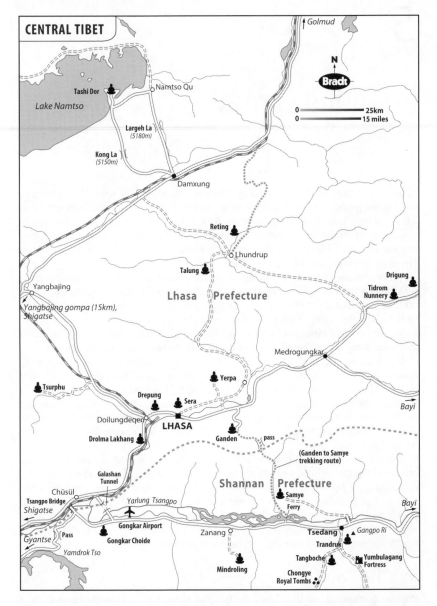

CENTRAL TIBET

↑ Golmud

N

Bradt

0 ————— 25km
0 ————— 15 miles

Lake Namtso

Tashi Dor

Namtso Qu

Largeh La
(5180m)

Kong La
(5150m)

Damxung

Reting

Lhundrup

Talung

Drigung

Tidrom
Nunnery

Yangbajing

Yangbajing gompa (15km),
Shigatse

Lhasa   Prefecture

Medrogungkar

Bayi

Tsurphu

Yerpa

Drepung

Sera

Doilungdeqen

LHASA

Drolma Lakhang

Ganden

pass

(Ganden to Samye
trekking route)

Galashan
Tunnel

Chüsül

Shannan   Prefecture

Samye

Tsangpo Bridge

Ferry

Bayi

Shigatse

Yarlung Tsangpo

Gyantse

Pass

Gongkar Airport

Zanang

Tsedang

Gangpo Ri

Gongkar Choide

Trandruk

Yamdrok Tso

Tangboche

Yumbulagang
Fortress

Mindroling

Chongye
Royal Tombs

for instance, trek from Samye to Ganden, drive from there to Tsurphu, hike on to Yanbajing Gompa, drive on to Tashi Dor, and then trek back to Damxung.

SAMPLE ITINERARIES When planning itineraries, you should keep road conditions in mind: what looks like a short distance on the map might be over atrocious roads, which take a long time to traverse. The run from Lhasa up to Damxung is along a sealed road and thus a fast ride; however, the side road to Tsurphu is abysmal and will chew up a lot of driving time. The sector from Ganden to Damxung cuts through a high rough dirt road and will consume at least 8 hours, probably longer.

top   Nomad woman milking a yak,
         Lake Namtso pages 22–4

centre   Unloading a yak-hair tent —
         from a yak, of course page 23

left   Rock-hard pieces of yak cheese,
         strung together in clusters that
         resemble necklaces page 85

top Dancers parading before a horse-racing event in Gyantse page 210

above left Nomad woman from Yushu

above right Nomad women dressed in their finest, at a horse-race festival in Nagqu page 313

below Archery contestants at a horse-race festival in central Tibet; the riders fire at a target while galloping

opposite page	Novice monk from Labrang Monastery in Amdo. Chinese policy restricts entry of new monks into places like Labrang page 317
top	Three monks on a pilgrimage to Lhamo Latso, the oracle lake, east Tibet pages 270–1
centre	Monks receiving *katas* at Samye Temple Complex, central Tibet pages 194–7
right	Music often serves a ritual or spiritual purpose in Tibet page 37

top   *North face of Mount Kailash, the most revered peak in Asia, and close to the source of four major rivers* pages 259–66

above left   Pilgrims getting off a truck at the start of the Kailash circuit pages 261–6

above right Pack yak unloaded at Darchen, west Tibet page 23

below   Prime trekking territory — views of a valley with village on the route to Everest base camp pages 201–7

top   Horse trekking in Kham to visit
       a nomad encampment page 292

centre Kayaker tackles white water on
       the Parlung Tsangpo, east Tibet
       (CJ) page 181

right   Riders have to deal with the
       elements — here, fresh snow on
       a high pass pages 86–7

above   For more than 1,200 years, the Potala was the winter palace of the Dalai Lama pages 166–70

left   Nomad women on pilgrimage to Lhasa pages 22–4

below left   Lhasan woman with chunks of turquoise braided in her hair; in old Tibet, the wealth and status of aristocratic women was denoted by the quality and amount of jewellery worn page 21

below right   Khampa man from east Tibet with fox-fur cap page 21

Tibet has excellent potential for rafting, with numerous rivers to run. Taking on a handful of rivers with customised tours is high-end company Wind Horse Adventure. They will only set up rafting if presented with a ready-made group of at least four rafters. The company operates one-day trips close to Lhasa as well as customised multiple-day rafting trips in central Tibet, and kayak descents further afield. All equipment for rafting (and kayaking) is supplied, and the company uses professional Nepalese or Tibetan rafters. You must be acclimatised to altitude to handle a rafting trip – meaning that you have spent four or five days at altitude already.

The outfit's most popular sortie is a half-day on the Tolung Chu. Recommended for getting the real feel of rafting in Tibet is a one- or two-day sortie on the Drigung River. On the one-day version, rafters start from Lhasa early morning and are driven several hours to a put-in point. They are provided with wetsuits and thermal clothing, and after brief safety instructions, are dispatched into class III and IV rapids on the Drigung River, experiencing the raw power of the river as no onlooker can. The day trip covers about 25km downriver on the Drigung. Clients are returned to Lhasa the same afternoon, somewhat shaken up. A two-day version of this trip would take in more white water, with overnight camping in a valley near Tidrom Nunnery. Consult the website w windhorsetibet.com and click on 'River Journeys' for more details.

Chris Jones and a Nepalese rafter named Ram made a first kayak descent of the Drigung River in 2003: the knowledge gained from that expedition is what led to the first commercial white-water rafting trips on the river. Chris says there is much to explore on the rivers of Tibet, with stunning rapids up to class V+ in a number of regions. He can organise custom rafting and kayak descents. He has led expeditions for first kayak descents of Rong Chu (Everest region), Yigung Tsangpo (north of Lhasa), Parlung Tsangpo (east Tibet) and the Sutlej (far west Tibet). In remote regions like this, Chris says, villagers often gather at the banks to cheer on the strange riders in their plastic boats. Others may run away, unsure what kind of demon spirits these might be on the water.

Three-day itinerary: Lhasa to Namtso/Tashi Dor
Day 1 Lhasa–Tsurphu–Damxung (overnight Damxung)

Day 2 Damxung over Largeh La to Tashi Dor (overnight Tashi Dor)

Day 3 Hike or horse trek at Namtso for a half-day, and drive back to Lhasa

Three-day itinerary: Lhasa to Ganden, Drigung, Tidrom and Yerpa
Day 1 Visit Ganden for half a day and drive to Drigung (overnight at Drigung)

Day 2 Drive to Tidrom hot springs (overnight at Tidrom)

Day 3 More time in Tidrom, drive to Yerpa (extended hiking time needed), drive back to Lhasa

Five-day itinerary: Lhasa to Drigung, Tidrom and Namtso
Days 1 and 2 Same as above (Lhasa–Ganden–Drigung–Tidrom)

Times have changed dramatically since Heinrich Harrer's account of his amazing escape in *Seven Years in Tibet*, tracing his flight from a British internment camp in India to the safe haven of neutral Tibet in the early 1940s. Since 1959, the escape route has been in the opposite direction, away from Chinese oppression.

That's exactly what the Karmapa miraculously carried out at the dawn of the new millennium. The youth – then 15 years old – was growing increasingly restless about his monastic education. He had been denied access to his spiritual mentors: the Chinese had reneged on promises to allow these lamas to visit Tibet, and refused to allow the Karmapa to visit India. Worse still, he was clearly being groomed as a patriotic alternative to the Dalai Lama. It was simply a matter of time before he would be called upon to denounce the Dalai Lama publicly.

The stakes for the 17th Karmapa to attempt an escape from the Chinese were very high: any mistake would be costly for the highest-profile religious figure living in Tibet. Meticulous planning was essential. In late December 1999, the Karmapa informed his Chinese minders that he was going into solitary retreat in his private quarters for a week, and would not entertain any visitors. Nothing unusual about that, or greatly suspect. But parked outside the monastery was a Mitsubishi SUV, requisitioned by a senior Tsurphu monk for a fundraising trip. And distracting the attention of everyone inside – including Chinese overseers – was a newly acquired television set.

Late on the night of 28 December, with monks and minders engrossed in the new television, the Karmapa changed into civilian dress, slipped out a back window at Tsurphu, jumped into the waiting SUV and stole off into the night. At Tsurphu, meanwhile, his teacher and cook kept up the charade of attending to him while 'on retreat'.

The Karmapa's real retreat was from Tibet: he and his four trusted companions proceeded on a circuitous route across Tibet in the SUV, travelling day and night. They dodged military checkpoints along the way: fortunately, during winter there was little military presence, with several posts unmanned. Approaching a dangerous checkpoint by night, the Karmapa and two others got out of the SUV and skirted the area on foot, scraping their hands and legs on thorn scrub in the darkness. To their immense relief, the SUV driver eventually showed up: he had driven past the checkpoint in darkness.

Day 3 Depart early from Tidrom and drive to Reting and Damxung (a long day over rough dirt roads; overnight in either Lhundrup or Damxung)

Day 4 Drive to Lake Namtso (overnight at Tashi Dor)

Day 5 Hike or horse trek at Namtso half a day and drive back to Lhasa (or continue on the Kathmandu route)

TSURPHU MONASTERY Lying 70km northwest of Lhasa, Tsurphu is the traditional seat of the Karmapa, head of the Karma Kagyu sect. At the beginning of 2000, the Chinese-sanctioned 17th Karmapa made a dramatic escape from Tsurphu, crossing into India just as his predecessor, the 16th Karmapa, had done 40 years earlier. Though the escape was a major embarrassment for the Karmapa's Chinese overseers, the 17th Karmapa has somehow avoided being blacklisted: photographs of him are displayed at the monastery. However, the *gompa* (monastery) does not

And then the SUV simply drove across the unmanned Nepalese border right into the kingdom of Mustang. Here, they abandoned the SUV and switched to travel on foot and by horseback. Hiring fine horses from the Mustang region, they rode hard from Lo Monthang for a few days to reach Kagbeni, and then forged on to a helicopter rendezvous site at Manang, on the Annapurna circuit. From Nepal, they telephoned Tsurphu to find out what was happening: when a stranger answered, they hung up (the fates of the teacher and the cook at Tsurphu are unknown). Flying into the Pokhara vicinity, the Karmapa and his entourage took a taxi to the Indian border, bribing their way past Nepalese border guards.

From here, train and taxis took them through northwest India to Dharamsala. The Karmapa arrived, exhausted, on the morning of 5 January 2000. An hour later, he was greeted in an audience with the Dalai Lama. It was a moment of astonishment and delight – the meeting of two bodhisattvas, and the end of an amazing journey.

The Karmapa's escape echoed the flight of the Dalai Lama from Tibet 40 years earlier. The Dalai Lama is the one person in the world that the Chinese did not want the Karmapa to meet. The Chinese insisted the Karmapa left the motherland on a shopping trip – to get his hands on a black hat, certain musical instruments, and other ceremonial items belonging to his predecessor, the 16th Karmapa, who was based at Rumtek Monastery in Sikkim. You can almost imagine the headlines in China: 'Soul Boy Steps out of Motherland on Black Hat Shopping Expedition'.

The black hat they talk about is sacred. The rightful owner must keep one hand on the hat while wearing it, as it is reputed to have the ability to fly away by itself. That's because, according to legend, the black hat is woven from the hair of countless *dakinis* – celestial female deities, or 'sky walkers'. First mentions of the flying crown date to the 12th century; the present hat dates from a few centuries later and was smuggled out of Tibet to Rumtek. There's a lot more than a hat at stake here: worldwide Kagyu sect assets are estimated to be worth over US$1.2 billion. Will he ever take up residence at Rumtek? Will he wear the sacred black hat? Will it fly off his head? Whatever the case, Ogyen Trinley Dorje is not out on a religious relic shopping spree: he has been granted refugee status by the Indian government.

attract the same volume of pilgrims as it used to – previously, many travelled here to receive the young Karmapa's blessing. There is an air of dereliction at the monastery today; following a witch-hunt for collaborators in the escape, the monastery was turned upside down and many older monks were replaced with novices. Several hundred monks currently live at the monastery.

The monastery was founded in the 12th century by the first Karmapa, Dusum Kyenpa. As the seat of the Karmapa, Tsurphu was the headquarters for instruction of monks from far-flung monasteries of the order, some as distant as Kham. In the 1950s, Tsurphu was home to a thousand monks. In 1959, the 16th Karmapa left for exile in Sikkim, where he founded Rumtek Monastery. Tsurphu Monastery was razed during the Cultural Revolution, but a few parts have been rebuilt, including the impressive assembly hall. The monastery flies its own flag, a blue and yellow ensign. In May 1997, sacred Cham dances were performed at Tsurphu as part of festivities for Saka Dawa (Buddha's birthday) under the watchful eyes of Chinese officials – this dance had been banned for decades. The most curious part of the monastery is a back protector chapel where (dead) animals appear to be the offering: previously whole stuffed yaks, a kangaroo and stuffed birds were suspended from the rafters, but on my last visit these had all been removed, and only stuffed tiger heads remained.

Getting there Tsurphu lies 70km northwest of Lhasa, at the end of a dirt trail off the main road (the turn-off is at the KM3853 marker stone). It takes about 2 hours to reach the monastery from Lhasa: there is an inclined rough road to get to Tsurphu, which sits at 4,420m. Should the need arise, there's a small monastery guesthouse and shops near the gates. Travellers are likely to reach Tsurphu by **4x4**. Locals hop aboard a daily pilgrim bus that departs early in the morning from the west side of Barkor Square, Lhasa, and returns the same day in the afternoon. One other option here: you could **trek** out of Tsurphu by embarking on a four-day foray northward, to Yangbajing Gompa, which lies close to the highway, 15km southwest of Yangbajing town.

The case of the rival Karmapas The lineage of the leaders of the Karma Kagyu sect of Tibetan Buddhism goes back to the 12th century. The 16th Karmapa was born in Tibet in 1924. After fleeing Tibet in 1959, he founded Rumtek Monastery in Sikkim as his principal seat in exile. He died in the USA in 1981, but followers could find no letter or sign from him on how to locate the next incarnate. Four regents of the Kagyu sect in Sikkim were appointed to conduct the search for the 17th Karmapa: Situ Rinpoche, Gyaltsap Rinpoche, Jamgon Kongtrul Rinpoche and Shamar Rinpoche. In 1990, Situ Rinpoche said he found a letter left by the 16th Karmapa, giving clues about his reincarnate. The letter was not shown to the other regents until 1992: its authenticity was disputed. Nevertheless, in April 1992, with Chinese approval, a search party of lamas left Tsurphu Monastery to find the new incarnation. A few weeks later, Jamgon Kongtrul Rinpoche was killed in a car accident – he had previously been designated as the person to find and check the incarnate. A boy from a nomad family in eastern Tibet – appearing to match details given in the letter – was brought to Tsurphu in July 1992. The boy was officially recognised by the Chinese – the first time they recognised a Living Buddha since 1959. On evidence from the search party, the Dalai Lama then recognised the boy also. In September 1992, eight-year-old Ogyen Trinley Dorje was enthroned in an elaborate ceremony at Tsurphu by Situ Rinpoche and Gyaltsap Rinpoche, with Chinese media and government widely represented.

Meanwhile, in Sikkim, violence flared at Rumtek Monastery as rival camps of monks brawled over the Karmapa issue. Indian troops were brought in to hold the peace. The 16th Karmapa's monks were evicted, and Situ Rinpoche's monks forcibly occupied the grounds in late 1993. In 1994, Shamar Rinpoche announced in Delhi that the true Karmapa had been found – a boy from Lhasa by the name of Thaye Dorje. The boy was able to procure travel papers to leave Lhasa by way of Chengdu and Hong Kong to India, where he lived in Kalimpong. In early 2017, Thaye Dorje stunned the Tibetan world with the announcement that he had married a childhood friend from Bhutan and thus had moved there. This opened the way for Ogyen Trinley Dorje to claim the title of 17th Karmapa.

NAMTSO CIRCUIT Namtso is Tibet's largest saltwater lake and, at 4,700m, also one of the highest. You would be unwise to visit Namtso shortly after arriving in Lhasa, as the altitude can be very hard on your system. However, if you have been around Lhasa for a while and are contemplating taking trips at higher elevations, Namtso is a good testing ground: spending a few days here will help you acclimatise to the 4,500m zone. You might want to consider step-by-step acclimatisation strategy: Lhasa lies at 3,650m, Tidrom is 4,300m, Namtso is 4,700m and Everest base camp is around 5,000m. Some arrange 4x4 trips for two days up to Namtso; others hire a vehicle for five days or more to take in the much wider zone of Reting, Tidrom and Drigung monasteries. And others head up for Namtso, and then onwards to Everest and Kathmandu.

Along the Lhasa to Namtso direct (paved) route, you pass by **Yangbajing** (elevation 4,155m), where a small settlement has developed around geothermal power units supplying Lhasa. Yangbajing hot springs, which are 4km off the main highway, are nothing to get excited about – the water is channelled into a large concrete swimming pool with a few deckchairs lying around. It's all a bit derelict and scummy – and expensive to boot. Next stop (about 2 hours from Yangbajing) is **Damxung** (elevation 4,200m), a deadly boring Chinese-built town 170km from Lhasa. Think of this town as an elaborate truck stop – or a glorified railway station – on the Golmud run. There are a number of hotels and guesthouses. Located at a crossroads on the west side of town is **Tienfu Hotel ($)**, a green-tiled building, with beds for Y60 each. Along the main road of Damxung is **Pema Hotel ($$)**, charging Y150 for common room, Y180 for a triple and Y270 for a standard room: this is probably the best choice of a rum lot. Close by is **Jinzhu Hotel ($$)**, with rooms a bit higher in price. There are a number of roadside restaurants in Damxung where truck drivers congregate – you can negotiate rides with them to Lake Namtso.

A further 40km from Damxung brings you to **Lake Namtso**, reached by two routes – in a 4x4 you can enter one way (motoring over Largeh La, 5,180m) and leave by another route (over Kong La, 5,150m). At a tollgate near Damxung, a Y120 per person entry charge is levied to enter Namtso Lake Nature Reserve (this tariff drops to Y60 for the November to April period). Driving on the paved road over Largeh La, it takes an hour to reach Lake Namtso: the road runs through a grassland valley, with the odd nomad encampment visible, and herds of yaks, sheep and goats roaming around. For the nomads, life is dependent on yaks: they live in yak-hair tents and use yak dung as their main fuel source. Some travellers trek into Lake Namtso – a tough hike taking 12 hours (one-way).

Overnighting at Tashi Dor is recommended because bus tours from Lhasa can overwhelm the area during the day: if you stay overnight, it's more tranquil when you take in sunset and sunrise. There are several possibilities for basic lodging at Namtso. The area close to Tashi Dor is crowded with tent guesthouses and metal or thin wooden shacks, each charging about Y50 a bed. Some group tours bring their own tents and camp out. Further back from the lake is a more permanent structure where guests can stay. There are some teahouse-type restaurants operating out of tents, selling soup or noodles. Bring extra food, a flashlight and a good sleeping bag if you can – nights are freezing. There is private generator lighting and electrical supply for a few hours at night.

Namtso is a sacred lake: there are cave-temples, shrines, hermitages and a nunnery for contemplation at **Tashi Dor**. That is, assuming you can get away from the annoying vendors of cheap jewellery and other shoddy wares, and those intent on talking you into posing with various animals for photos (for which you pay, of course). Two large rock towers near the nunnery are considered to be sentinels for the region. It's worth spending a day or more exploring the area, hiking in the hills around Tashi Dor, and poking around the cave-temples. Hermits from the Kagyu and Nyingma sects occasionally occupy the caves in the area. The beautiful turquoise hues of the lake are a source of inspiration, and the vistas will redefine your sense of space. In the distance, to the south, the 7,088m snow cap of Mount Nyenchen Tanglha looms up, along with the range of the same name. A walking circuit of Namtso is a tall order indeed. The lake is roughly 70km long and 30km wide, with a surface area of 1,940km²: it takes nomad pilgrims up to 20 days to circle it. A short walk to the east of Tashi Dor is a site that operates as a bird sanctuary – between April and November there are good chances of sighting migratory flocks, including, if you're lucky, the black-necked crane.

One method of covering more ground in a shorter time is to hire some horses at Tashi Dor. If you hire them, make sure you also hire a mounted Tibetan horseman to come with you. There are a number of reasons for this strategy – mainly that the horses may refuse to go anywhere unless the horseman is present. If you hire the horses for 5 hours, you should be able to get a fair distance along the lake to the west side and, with the help of the horseman, you can visit nomads in their tents in this area. Some wealthier nomad families have jeeps, trucks and motorcycles, but their business is still the same as it ever was – milking yaks, making yak cheese, churning yak-butter tea.

CLASSIC GOMPAS, MOUNTAIN SETTINGS Northeast of Lhasa are a number of ruined or semi-active monasteries, amid spectacular settings. Getting to these places takes you right off the track into small villages. Roads are rough, and the going can be slow.

Ganden Located 40km east of Lhasa, Ganden is a Geluk lamasery founded in the 15th century. Additions in later centuries increased its capacity to support upward of 5,000 monks. Ganden was dynamited to rubble during the Cultural Revolution. Remarkably, a number of its main halls have been rebuilt from scratch. In early 1996, following a ban on Dalai Lama pictures, the 400 monks at Ganden were involved in a riot. PLA troops arrived and fired on the monks – two were believed killed and a number were injured. It is thought a hundred more monks were arrested; an equal number probably fled into the hills. Life has since returned to Ganden. There is a large population of monks (currently estimated at around 400), and reconstruction has continued at a brisk pace. A permanent PSB building up on the hill above the monastery guesthouse keeps a wary eye on everything.

Locals reach Ganden by riding an early morning pilgrim bus from Barkor Square in Lhasa. Ganden Monastery has a Y25 entry fee, and posts a Y20 still camera fee, plus a whopping Y1,500 video camera fee (Y750 for 'inland tourists', meaning Chinese). You can stay at the basic but pleasant **monastery guesthouse ($)**, near the front gates. The tariff is Y15 a bed in six-bed dorms. Trekkers, travellers, pilgrims and visiting monks or nuns all lodge here. Further on is a monastery-run shop, selling the usual dismal selection of packaged noodles, sweets and candles.

The main assembly hall of Ganden is located near a vast square: it is a white structure with gold-capped roofs. If your timing is right, you can hear monks chanting. There are many gilded images of Tsongkhapa in the main chapel. Pilgrims come to be tapped on the head with Tsongkhapa's hat or else the 13th Dalai Lama's shoes. Adjacent to the main assembly hall is a maroon and ochre building which houses a Sakyamuni Buddha statue. A section of this chapel is devoted to the hand-printing of scriptures from woodblocks. In one corner is the *gonkhang* (protector chapel), which is only open to men and which showcases wrathful deities such as 32-armed Yamantaka and six-armed Mahakala, on a horse with a crown of skulls. You can access the rooftop of this building for views.

Ganden is set in a natural, hilly amphitheatre. You can hike around the monastery on a 1-hour *kora* route, with stunning views over the surrounding valleys. Start from the monastery guesthouse and go up the hill to a white building with a red flag and a satellite dish (this is the PSB building); from there head for hilltop prayer flags and follow other prayer flag markers along the route, and other pilgrims. At the far end of the clockwise *kora* is a rock that is said to be able to talk.

Ganden-to-Samye trek For those with stamina and a good food supply, there's an arduous four- to five-day trek from Ganden to Samye, over several 5,000m passes. Groups arrange a guide, cook, yaks and yak handlers to carry gear – all are self-sufficient with food and camping equipment. Even for just two trekkers, the entourage for a tour might encompass seven or so yaks loaded up with food and cooking gear, and tents. Yaks are apparently not permitted to walk right into Samye, so you would have to carry gear for the last stretch, or use a walking-tractor. The trek to Samye starts on the hill above Ganden guesthouse.

Tidrom Nunnery Further to the northeast, about 110km from Lhasa, lies Tidrom Nunnery, which is set in a beautiful valley with numerous hermitages and caves in the surrounding hills. Miraculously, there's hardly a Chinese building in sight, although the nunnery has a huge satellite dish mounted on its traditional rooftop. The nunnery, though small, is home to over a hundred nuns. Pilgrims and visitors come to Tidrom for the **sulphur hot springs**, also frequented by the nuns. The hot springs are said to have magic healing powers – or at the very least, to be good for the treatment of arthritis, gastritis and other ailments. It's a detox for the soul, anyway, to be in such a purely Tibetan atmosphere.

A charming aspect of Tidrom is that it is a walking zone. No vehicles can enter the village: all vehicles stop at a parking lot at the edge of Tidrom, a short walk from the hot springs. The nunnery offers a few rooms (**$**), and a castle-like structure nearby (**$**) offers beds for Y20 apiece in large rooms, with clean toilets outside. There is also **accommodation** in tents. Rooms at the guesthouse (**$**) directly overlooking the hot springs are overpriced and dingy, with rank pit toilets: beds go for Y40 each. Offerings of food in Tidrom are meagre, so best to bring some backup supplies. The nunnery runs a small restaurant serving potato curry soup or *thukpa*, and there are a few teahouses.

At the hot springs, Tibetans bathe either in swimsuit or birthday suit. Piping-hot water at this altitude (4,320m) can be a shock to the system, and can make foreign visitors feel dizzy. Best to take this in small doses until you get accustomed: take a dip for 10 minutes, get out, rest, and go back in again. Those with high blood pressure or a heart condition (or if pregnant) should not partake. That said, these have to be the finest hot springs in central Tibet: the springs are located right near a river, where the water bubbles under a great rock and disappears. There are three hot spring pools with attractive stone-laid enclosures surrounded by wooden fencing (no concrete!). One pool is for men, another for women, and the third pool is mixed: it is extra-hot and lies across a small footbridge. You can get a hot stone treatment, of sorts – there are hot stones below your feet if you step into a pool. Locals rub against smooth hot submerged stone as a kind of massage. No yak-yoghurt scrubs or *tsampa* rubs on the menu, but then again, you're not subjected to flaky New Age music, either. All very low key.

If you stay overnight, you can indulge in a moonlit soak with candles, and – if skies are clear – a magnificent canopy of stars overhead.

Hiking above Tidrom is rewarding, in terms of views and photography. You can hike up to several small *gompas*; there are also nomad tents in the vicinity.

Drigung Monastery Close to Tidrom is Drigung, a monastery impossibly grafted on to a sheer cliff face. Drigung (elevation 4,150m) was originally the base of the Drigung suborder of the Kagyu sect, dating from the 12th century. At one time it housed over 500 monks. Going up switchbacks in a 4x4, you may pass a donkey bearing a body under a blanket: Drigung is reputed to have the best sky burial (*danchag*) ceremony of all. It is said that bodies dispatched here will not fall down into the 'three bad regions'.

The monastery is intriguing due to its location: it offers stupendous views over the entire valley – you can clamber up to the gold-capped roofs for better vistas. You can visit Drigung and move on, or you can stay the night at the **monastery guesthouse ($)**, which has two 12-bed dorms. Although the dorms are basic, the atmosphere is special, as you are staying inside the monastic grounds. Monks supply hot water in vacuum flasks, and there's a small shop selling packaged noodles, candles and drinks. Some group tours camp out in the valley below.

Previously, a large sign was posted near the monastery entrance saying that visitors are not permitted to witness **sky burials** at Drigung. Obviously, photographers sneaking shots with long lenses have upset the monks to the point where they have banished visitors from the sky burial site altogether. Whether this situation will change remains to be seen – ask your guide or driver. In case the monastery policy on visitors does change, here is some information on sky burial (see also page 177). The sky burial site is located about 600m from the *gompa* – a trail to get there starts just below the monastery and then turns uphill. You gain about 200m of elevation on this hike and it takes about 15 minutes to reach the site from the monastery. The site is a large fenced-off area surrounded by prayer flags. It's high on a ridge, with a large rock at centre stage. The ceremony takes place on the rock, with monks present to bless the departed. Sky burial does not take place every day: sometimes there is no body. Other times, there could be four bodies. The timing is also a bit random, but about an hour after sunrise is the probable time. Vultures assemble on the upper slopes waiting for their cue to descend to the rock. This spectacle is not for the faint of heart – it's a grisly ritual where bodies are chopped into pieces and fed to the vultures.

Yerpa, Talung and Reting Three other monastic sites worth looking at lie north of Lhasa: Yerpa, Talung and Reting. **Yerpa**, 45km northeast of Lhasa (well off the main road), used to be a complex of monasteries, with more than 80 meditation caves tucked away in the hills. The area suffered extensive damage during the Cultural Revolution: restoration is ongoing, but in 1998 a major setback occurred when Chinese officials destroyed several temples and caves. There are, however, half a dozen restored temples to reach. Getting to Yerpa is not easy: a 4x4 takes about half an hour from the turn-off to reach the foothills of Yerpa. The driver parks in a village, and then you embark on a strenuous hike. A steep trail ascends to about 4,400m, so you must be acclimatised.

Further north is a rough back route leading to Lake Namtso (see map, page 180). In this direction, the once-great **Talung Gompa** lies in ruins, a victim of the Cultural Revolution. Several temples have been restored and over a hundred monks have taken up residence. The monastery overlooks a village.

If you continue along this route past Lhundrup, you'll reach **Reting**, about 150km from Lhasa. Reting, at an elevation of 4,150m, is the seat of the Reting Rinpoche: this lineage started in the 18th century when the Seventh Dalai Lama appointed his tutor as abbot of Reting. Several of the Reting Rinpoches served as regents during the minorities of the Dalai Lamas. The Fifth Reting Rinpoche ruled from 1933 to

1947 during the minority of the 14th Dalai Lama, and was actually responsible for his discovery. Involved in political intrigue and sexual scandal, the Fifth Reting Rinpoche died in prison in 1947.

There is considerable controversy over the authenticity of the current Reting Rinpoche, a boy essentially chosen by Chinese officials. Born around 1998, the boy lives near the river at Reting in a small monastic compound which has an unusual architectural feature: a police station has been built backing right on to the entrance, effectively blocking it. This means all comings and goings to the compound are closely monitored by Chinese authorities. Any arrangement for a brief audience with the Reting Rinpoche has to go through the police, who will be present to ensure that no unusual messages (or ideas) are passed on. The police will most likely specify a silent audience – no talking and no photographs. Pilgrims can present the Rinpoche with a *kata*, which he will place back over the offerer's head.

Little is left of the splendour of Reting Gompa – it was all destroyed in the 1960s. Sited on a hill, a small assembly hall has been rebuilt, with a few dozen monks in residence. You can visit for a Y30 entry fee. The area is remarkable for its grove of juniper trees, which appear to be twisted and gnarled as an arboreal response to the problems of high altitude and high winds. You can stay in a small **guesthouse** (**$**) at Reting Gompa with teahouse attached, with beds for Y35. That would be the best option as it appears authorities do not welcome travellers in the nearby village of Lhundrup, which has a few poky shops and a gas-refuelling station where vehicles can fill up (remind your driver as this is the only one in this region). Backing Lhundrup is the startling and seemingly unreal vision of a perfectly conical mountain. Driving times: Tidrom to Reting is about 5 hours on rough roads, and Reting to Damxung takes about 3 hours on rough roads.

YARLUNG VALLEY

Southeast of Lhasa lies the cradle of Tibetan culture – the Yarlung Valley. The Adam and Eve of Tibet – from a myth involving a monkey and a demoness – were supposed to have dwelt in Tsedang. The Yarlung dynasty kings had their base in the Yarlung Valley – in the 7th and 8th centuries, they unified the Tibetans and strengthened their identity as a nation. The burial mounds of all the Yarlung dynasty kings are at Chongye. However, these are rather dull to look at: the main attractions southeast of Lhasa are the Samye Temple Complex and Yumbulagang Fortress. With a rented vehicle, you can visit half a dozen sites mentioned here in two or three days. If you're planning to do any hiking, allow more time. You can trek from Samye to Ganden by an arduous route over high passes. You need to be completely self-sufficient for a trip like this. Some group tours tackle the trek with guides, and yaks, donkeys or horses to carry gear.

LHASA TO SAMYE
Drolma Lakhang The exquisite Tara Temple (Drolma Lakhang) is one of the best preserved in central Tibet. This temple lies along the main road, 25km out of Lhasa. It is associated with the Bengali sage Atisha who arrived in Tibet to teach in the 11th century. He died in this area in 1054. The temple is dedicated to the goddess Tara, with whom Atisha had a strong connection. The temple was apparently spared damage in the 1960s because of a request from the government of Bengal, where Atisha is a highly revered figure. The temple is small and active, with 25 monks. The most striking feature is a sutra chanting chapel where 21 life-sized bronze statues of Tara enclose the space. The main image is a Sakyamuni statue; to the left is a small statue of Atisha. On the upper floor is a library, plus some meditation rooms.

Among the statues at Drolma Lakhang is one that has been on a sort of world tour. This is a 1,200-year-old statue of the Buddha that was stolen from Drolma Lakhang in April 1993 by two men with a minivan. It was immediately sold to smugglers in Chengdu for an estimated US$300,000 according to a report in the *People's Daily*. Then it disappeared without trace, until Lhasa customs discovered that it had been shipped to the USA, where a buyer was prepared to pay US$8 million for it, according to the news source. The FBI seized the Buddha statue on arrival, but demanded photographic evidence that it had come from Drolma Lakhang before they would return it. The Tibetans did not have such evidence. Finally, after two years of wrangling, Lhasa customs found a picture taken by a foreign tourist, and the FBI returned the statue to Drolma Lakhang in late 1997.

Interpol estimates that the black market in stolen art and antiquities worldwide results in upward of US$10 billion changing hands annually, making it the world's biggest illegal trade after arms and drugs. The motivation is vast profits with a short turnover time. Original Tibetan art is, of course, highly sought-after, and there is little doubt that Chinese smugglers have been involved in the traffic, dismantling Tibet's heritage piece by piece.

Gongkar The name Gongkar is today associated with Tibet's only commercial airport, but in the days before the first planes arrived in the 1960s, it was known to Tibetans as the location of Gongkar Dzong and Gongkar Choide. The *dzong* (castle) was mostly destroyed, but the Gongkar Choide Monastery remains. The monastery is located 10km west of the airport (turn off at the KM84 marker and go 1km off the road). It was ransacked during the Cultural Revolution: the main hall was used as a barley silo, and murals were defaced with Mao Zedong slogans. Despite the destruction, the surviving mural work at **Gongkar Choide** makes it worth the visit.

Gongkar Airport (elevation 3,700m) lies further east, just off the main road to Tsedang. It was constructed in the late 1970s, with elaborate terminal facilities and a second runway added in 1994. Not far from the airport gates is a crossroads with a cluster of small Chinese hotels and restaurants, and a mini-mart. Several **guesthouses** in this area charge Y30–50 a room; the best is a second-floor guesthouse, running along the top of a string of restaurants. There's also a ramshackle Tibetan guesthouse in the vicinity. Within the airport compound is the **Airport Hotel** (℡ *618 2447*), with 115 rooms ranging from Y140 to Y380. The airport has a post office and a bank with foreign exchange facilities (near the gates).

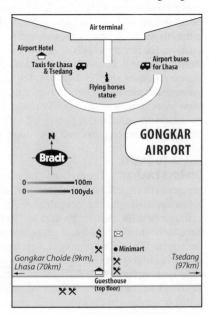

It takes about an hour to drive the 70km from Lhasa to Gongkar, on the route over two bridges connecting to Galashan Tunnel. Gongkar falls in Shannan Prefecture but it is open without permit. That means you can use Gongkar Airport zone as a base to reach out into the Yarlung Valley. You've heard of airports with duty-free zones – this one is a PSB-free zone. Do not confuse Gongkar Airport with Gongkar County (the village 10km east of the airport) or Gongkar Choide.

Mindroling Gompa
Mindroling is the largest Nyingma sect monastery in central Tibet (a second large Nyingma lamasery is Dorje Drak, on the north bank of the Yarlung Tsangpo). Founded in the 17th century, Mindroling was razed by the Mongols in the 18th century, then rebuilt, and again razed during the Cultural Revolution (and rebuilt). Mindroling's imposing façade is constructed in monastic citadel style; the *gompa* impresses with its surprising size and austerity, and skilful construction in stone. The most important chapel lies at the back: it houses a huge Sakyamuni image. To get to Mindroling, turn off the main road near Zanang (aka Zhanang or Dranang) – the monastery is a further 8km away, on a dirt trail.

SAMYE
Samye, an attractive walled temple complex, sits at 3,650m on the north bank of the Yarlung Tsangpo. Samye is fascinating because you get a feel for old Tibet as the buildings are all Tibetan (with rare exceptions). Samye is also unusual because it is fully enclosed by a wall with gates at the compass points. Within the walls, most things are run by the monastery. There's a cluster of small guesthouses, restaurants and shops just outside the east gate, along with China Post. There is some build-up, too, outside the west gate, but nothing at the south gate and very little at the north gate.

Getting there
If you are in a rented vehicle, you have several options. The easiest way to get to Samye is to drive the entire way from Tsedang by crossing the Tsangpo at a bridge just east of Tsedang (see map, page 180) and doubling back on the other side of the river. This means you can be flexible with the itinerary because the driver remains with you. If taking this route, you might want to visit Tsedang (Yumbulagang) first, so you can overnight in Samye.

The second option is to drive to the ferry crossing on the south bank of the Yarlung Tsangpo, opposite Samye: this means leaving your vehicle and driver behind till you return by the same ferry. Some local transport connects with the ferry: a regular **bus** to the Samye ferry crossing (Y35 a head, takes about 4 hours); hiring a taxi from Lhasa (about 3 hours, costs around Y180 for the whole taxi); or taking a **taxi** from Tsedang (taking about 40 minutes, Y80 for the taxi). Transport drops you on the south bank of the Yarlung Tsangpo River at a small compound (KM155 marker stone) with a truck stop inn and a few small shops. Your driver waits with the car for a day or two while the guide takes you along on a ferry ride across the Yarlung Tsangpo. On the other side, a truck picks you up for the 20-minute run into Samye. The 'ferry' is a barge designed for the transport of goods back and forth from Samye. There have been a number of nasty arguments between foreigners and locals over the cost of the barge and the truck. Passage should cost Y10 a person if shared with Tibetan passengers, and a similar amount for a truck on the other side. The ferry will cost more if you and your group are the sole passengers (the whole boat costs Y90 a crossing). Bargaining doesn't work well here as this is a monopoly situation and the operators know it. To avoid ill feelings, leave the matter in the hands of the guide (if you have one), and focus instead on the entrancing Yarlung Tsangpo vistas. Because the barge has to navigate around sandbars, the trip across

Glance at the map of central Tibet and you will spot a lengthy Chinese-engineered concrete bridge that spans the Yarlung Tsangpo to the west of Gongkar Airport. Near that is a site called Chusul. About 5km east of Chusul a massive Tibetan iron-chain bridge once spanned the mighty Tsangpo. It led straight into a temple called Chaksam Gompa – the temple of the iron bridge.

Chaksam Gompa had fallen into disrepair by the late 1930s. A British mission to Lhasa in 1937 describes crossing the Yarlung Tsangpo near this point using a string of yak-hide boats. The dilapidated iron bridge reached as far as an island in the middle of the river. But the temple was intact and active. Both Chaksam temple and bridge were completely destroyed in the Cultural Revolution in the 1960s.

Chaksam is Tibetan for 'iron bridge'. The original footbridge – estimated to be over 135m long – was maintained and repaired by the resident monks, who collected a toll to use it. At the time it was built, around 1430, there were no iron suspension bridges anywhere else in the world. The bridge was the masterpiece of **Tangtong Gyalpo** (1385–1464), the iron-bridge guru. In his younger days, this eccentric yogi was ejected from a yak-hide boat on a river crossing due to his unkempt appearance. His engineering feats were apparently inspired by this incident. He found his true calling in life: building bridges and ferry crossings, intended to link remote villages, promote pilgrimage, and propagate the Buddhist faith. Building bridges was his unique way of accruing merit.

Pilgrimage in old Tibet was an arduous endeavour – seen as a test of resolve, designed to build character. Pilgrims encountered numerous obstacles along the way – from rapacious bandits to unexpected snowfalls – and perilous river crossings. At high altitude, rivers are freezing cold. More to the point, pilgrims could not swim. On the slow-flowing rivers of central Tibet, they would launch across the waters in a yak-hide coracle, made from yak skins stretched over a wooden frame. Pilgrims would crouch down, praying the vessel would not capsize. But if the crossing was via a narrow precipitous gorge with a raging river below, this could only be done by bridging the gap. At some points, pilgrims had to winch themselves upside down across the river on a long yak-hair rope or embark on a kind of early zipline: a terrifying pulley ride via rope across the river. Occasionally, there were primitive rope bridges made from plant fibres, or thick bamboo poles lashed together to make a bridge, but these did not last. Tangtong Gyalpo's iron-chain suspension bridges were built to stand the test of time – and to smooth the pilgrim's passage to sacred sites.

During his long life, the guru is credited with building 58 iron-chain suspension bridges, an equal number of wooden bridges, and establishing more than a hundred ferry crossings using yak-hide boats across the Himalayan region. A

the Yarlung Tsangpo can take up to an hour. The route changes seasonally with the water levels.

🏠 **Where to stay and eat** The best place to stay is **Samye Monastery Guesthouse** (**$$**), which lies just outside the walls at the east gate. This is a large modern building with hot showers available. Rooms go for Y140–280. Inside the walls towards the east gate is the **Monastery Restaurant** (**$**), which has lots of atmosphere, and is crowded with pilgrims. It is part of the monastery compound.

handful of his iron bridges are still in use 500 years later. The iron links miraculously do not corrode: they apparently have a high arsenic content and are in fact more closely matched to steel. That presents a technical challenge as steel-like metals have a very high melting point for forging.

Tangtong Gyalpo was an eccentric anomaly – the sole civil engineer in Tibet, a land of zero engineering. He had to counter extreme taboos against mining (disturbing the spirits of the earth) to get the iron ore to build bridges. He needed an army of blacksmiths to forge the links and set up the spans. This all cost a small fortune. Undaunted, Tangtong Gyalpo came up with his own form of crowdfunding. He devised Tibetan opera as entertainment, and used the proceeds to fund bridges. Ache Lhamo Opera started with a troupe of seven sisters, who also worked on the bridges. This popular form of opera is still performed to this day in Tibetan realms. To keep his blacksmiths and construction workers happy, Tangtong Gyalpo composed rhythmic work-songs. These work-songs are still sung by Tibetans on construction sites today.

The guru's iron-chain suspension bridges were a source of wonder to visiting Chinese and to Europeans, as no such designs existed in their domains. In 1726, a book published in Germany described a Tibetan iron-chain bridge: 'a bridge was built into free air and can be viewed at with astonishment'. Iron-chain suspension bridges started to appear in Europe after descriptions like this were published, some with sketches of the bridge design. But it was not until 1820 that an iron-chain bridge built in England was able to match Tangtong Gyalpo's longest suspension bridge – the 135m-long masterpiece that spanned the Yarlung Tsangpo at Chaksam. Later, when iron links were replaced with wire cables, the spans grew much longer. Odd to think that the engineering marvel of San Francisco's Golden Gate Bridge, with a span of 1,280m, owes much to the visions of Tangtong Gyalpo.

Mad yogi, mystic, scholar, civil engineer, visionary, sculptor, painter, poet, composer of song and dance, architect and physician who devised longevity pills – Tangtong Gyalpo is the Tibetan version of Leonardo da Vinci. His life was long, his achievements many. He travelled widely across the Himalayas, building iron bridges in many sites. In Paro, Bhutan, he set up home with a consort and fathered several sons, who took up his bridge-building mission and continued with his legacy.

Sadly, you will not find any intact iron suspension bridges built by Tangtong Gyalpo and his descendants in Tibet any more. You will only find iron chain-links in museums. However, out of Tibet, some of his bridges can still be found. One is located near Paro in Bhutan; another spans a fast-flowing river near Tawang in Arunachal Pradesh, in India.

There are several small restaurant-guesthouses just outside the walls at the east gate, including **Tashi Guesthouse ($)**, **Mount Hepori Hotel ($)**, and **Friendship Snowland Restaurant** ($). These have dorm-type accommodation with mattresses. Basic rooms and basic food, but adequate.

Nightlife Because of very little ambient light around Samye, there is a fantastic star-show at night – assuming clear skies. Find a rooftop somewhere, lie down, and gaze at the canopy of stars.

If you are in the Gongkar Airport vicinity, or passing by on the way to Samye, make a stop at a Tibetan mastiff breeding facility in the area. The guide or driver should know the location. This breeding facility houses around 300 dogs, mostly Tibetan mastiffs, but there are no Tibetans in sight: the entire operation is run by Chinese entrepreneurs. There's a charge of about Y80 levied on visitors if you want to walk around and take pictures.

Why such a big facility? Here's the short explanation: in March 2011, a red-haired Tibetan mastiff sold for the jaw-dropping sum of US$1.5 million to a coal baron in northern China. The pure-bred male was, he said, 'an investment' – to be loaned out for stud duties (with a price tag probably exceeding US$20,000 per session). Red is a lucky colour: the dog has been christened 'Big Splash'. Prior to that sale, the record price for a Tibetan mastiff was set in 2009, when a wealthy woman bought one for US$586,000 – and sent a convoy of 30 Mercedes-Benz cars to the airport in Xian to pick up her new dog. Those extraordinary sales figures make the Tibetan mastiff the most expensive dog in the world. The dogs at Gongkar are much more affordable – with price tags starting in the region of US$3,000 to US$12,000.

Unfortunately for the breeders, the market for Tibetan mastiffs suddenly crashed around 2015, and the dogs were sent packing – some were even sent to slaughterhouses. The Tibetan mastiff craze went belly-up. Prior to this, the dog was the ultimate status symbol for super-wealthy Chinese. The lion is considered lucky by Chinese, and the Tibetan mastiff has a lion-like mane. Xinhua News Agency reported that among the must-haves for the ultra-rich in north China were these three: a beautiful young wife, a Lamborghini and a Tibetan mastiff – the bigger and more ferocious, the better. That put the Tibetan mastiff into a similar status class as the chihuahuas of socialites in Hollywood. But the Tibetan mastiff is not the sort of dog you carry with one arm. It is about the size of a St Bernard, and just as slobbery. It grows to over 80kg and is known for fiercely defending its master.

Thought to be the oldest guard dog in existence, the Tibetan mastiff has a bloodline going back thousands of years. It evolved as a guard dog for nomads, usually tied up close to the yak-hair tent as a security measure. The dog alerts nomads to intruders, and has been known to take on livestock predators such as wolves and snow leopards. Tibetan nomads, however, are not involved in any way with the breeding operations – these are all Chinese-run except for some centres in Yushu, in northern Tibet. In China, it takes very wealthy patrons to ensure the mastiff is itself guarded. In Beijing, if a dog exceeds a certain height, it can be confiscated and killed on the spot by vigilant authorities. A Tibetan mastiff would exceed those height limits.

What to see and do

Samye Temple Complex Samye is thought to be Tibet's first monastery and its first university. It has been deconstructed and reconstructed a number of times. The monastery is thought to have been founded in the 8th century by King Trisong Detsen, in consultation with Indian sage Padmasambhava. The temple was destroyed during civil war in the 11th century, by fire in the 11th and 17th centuries, by earthquake in the 18th century, and by Mao Zedong's fanatical hordes in the 20th century. Today, only a fraction of its original 108 buildings survive or have been reconstructed.

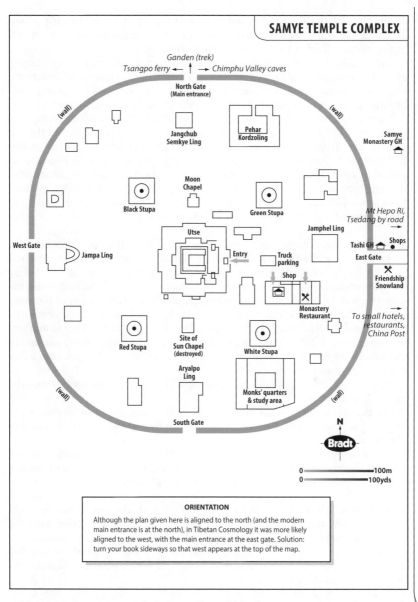

SAMYE TEMPLE COMPLEX

Ganden (trek)

Tsangpo ferry ← ↑ → Chimphu Valley caves

North Gate
(Main entrance)

(wall)

(wall)

Jangchub
Semkye Ling

Pehar
Kordzoling

Samye
Monastery GH

Moon
Chapel

Black Stupa

Green Stupa

Jamphel Ling

Mt Hepo Ri,
Tsedang by road

Utse

West Gate

Jampa Ling

Entry

Truck
parking

Tashi GH   Shops

East Gate

Shop

Friendship
Snowland

Monastery
Restaurant

To small hotels,
restaurants,
China Post

Red Stupa

Site of
Sun Chapel
(destroyed)

White Stupa

Aryalpo
Ling

Monks' quarters
& study area

(wall)

(wall)

South Gate

N

Bradt

0 ━━━━━ 100m
0 ━━━━━ 100yds

ORIENTATION

Although the plan given here is aligned to the north (and the modern
main entrance is at the north), in Tibetan Cosmology it was more likely
aligned to the west, with the main entrance at the east gate. Solution:
turn your book sideways so that west appears at the top of the map.

Adaptations for visitors within the walls include the monastery guesthouse with
restaurant and monastery shop. Most Samye villagers live outside the walls.

Samye's layout is based on Buddhist cosmology: it is a mandalic 3D replica of the
Tibetan Buddhist universe. The temple complex has been constructed according
to the principles of geomancy, a concept derived from India. At the centre of the
Tibetan Buddhist universe lies a mythical palace on top of Mount Meru, which at
Samye is symbolised by the main temple (Utse). Surrounding this is a great 'ocean',
with four great island-continents, and eight subcontinents. If the colour-coded
chortens look a bit out of place in this scheme of things; it's because they were razed

during the Cultural Revolution, and were only reconstructed in the early 1990s, in new brick, with synthetic paints, and without much finesse. Renovation and reconstruction of other parts within the walls is ongoing.

The complex is bounded by an oval wall (the original wall was a zigzag design), pierced by four gates and topped by 1,008 small *chortens* that represent Chakravala, a ring of mountains that surrounds the universe. The wall itself has been hastily restored, using a large amount of concrete – the favourite material of the Chinese.

There are currently about a hundred monks attached to the main temple. The monastery was built long before the rise of the different sects in Tibet. In the late 8th century, Trisong Detsen presided over a debate at Samye between Indian Buddhists and Chinese Zen Buddhists concerning which type of Buddhism should prevail in Tibet. The Indians won. Since that time, the monastery has come under the influence of various sects, such as the Nyingma, Sakya and Geluk traditions. Even today, influences are eclectic. Entry to Samye Monastery is Y40, with Y150 extra charged for interior photos, and Y1,500 for video.

Samye Utse The three-storey temple faces to the east. The upper storeys were removed during the Cultural Revolution, but the gleaming roof was restored in 1989. To the left of the main entrance is a 5m-high stone obelisk; erected by King Songtsen Gampo, it proclaims the Indian school of Buddhism to be the state religion. Inside the main assembly hall of the Utse are statues of the early kings, and images of Padmasambhava and Atisha. The inner sanctum contains a beautiful Sakyamuni image. To the right side of the assembly hall is a Gonkhang or tantric protector chapel with odds and ends such as a stuffed snake and an old musket. To the left of the assembly hall is the Avalokitesvara Chapel, with a fine bas-relief portrait of the bodhisattva.

Upstairs, you can access several chapels and might even be allowed to view the former quarters of the Dalai Lama.

On the second floor is an open gallery with a long string of murals, some depicting the history of Tibet; there is also a damaged mural of the fabled land of Shambhala here.

North of the Utse temple lies the Moon Chapel, and to the south, the Sun Chapel. Four *chortens* (stupas) are positioned respectively to the northeast (green), southeast (white), southwest (red) and northwest (black).

Ling Chapels While Mount Meru is connected with the realms of the gods, humanoids are supposed to live on the four island-continents (*ling*) across a vast ocean, flanked by satellite islands or subcontinents (*ling-tren*). These are all symbolised by one- or two-storey chapels at Samye, some lined with murals, and graced with pleasant courtyards with gardens and potted plants. Others lie in a decayed state, awaiting restoration.

Jamphel Ling, at the east side, is dedicated to Manjughosa. In the 1980s it was a commune office. At the southern end, Aryalpo Ling, dedicated to Hayagriva, was where Indian scholars lived during the great debate of the 8th century. It has undergone some restoration of its murals; on the upper storey are strange murals depicting creatures riding scorpions, dragons and bears. The chapel immediately west of this is worth a visit: it has been renovated with a full set of murals.

Jampa Ling, the chapel near the west gate, is dedicated to Maitreya (Champa or Jampa in Tibetan) and is where the Chinese monks resided during the 8th century. At the entrance hall is a mural showing Samye as it once was. Jangchub Semkye Ling, at the north, was dedicated to Prajnaparamita. Inside is a 3D scale model of Samye. This building is undergoing restoration – it was previously used for wood storage.

Just east of Jangchub Semkye Ling is a north-facing red-walled building – Pehar Kordzoling, a protector chapel. Samye's Sanskrit texts were once stored here in the care of the protector deity Pehar. Pehar's mandate was to watch over the monastery's treasures: among these was a leather mask that was believed to come alive, with the rolling of bulging eyes. After several centuries at Samye, Pehar was removed to Nechung Monastery in Lhasa, and became the protective deity of the state oracle. There was also an oracle at Samye: Pehar's job at Samye was taken over by Tsemar, the red protector, who sat in judgement of the souls of men once a year: evil-doers were chopped to shreds. Pehar Kordzoling is adorned with unusual mural work featuring skulls; though under renovation, the chapel appears to be a site where special rituals are carried out.

Following Chinese occupation, villagers were encouraged to treat the walled sanctuary of Samye as just another part of the village, so pigs, cows, braying donkeys and sheep were herded through the muddy wasteland. Along with a large band of dogs that hung out on the flagstones near the Utse, this gave Samye a somewhat earthy and surreal air – you would round a corner looking for a sacred temple, and instead stray across a pig wallowing in the mud. Although the dogs still lounge around, the other animals have been pushed back outside the walls again.

Hiking at Samye To the east of Samye you can hike to a ridge called **Mount Hepo Ri**, which offers a terrific bird's-eye view of the town. To get there, walk out of the east gate, go to the end of the village, and then veer right to find the trails that lead up the foothills to the ridge-top temple. The hike takes about 30–40 minutes. If there are pilgrims around, you can follow them: they make offerings at the ridge-top temple shrine, festooned with prayer flags. From this vantage point, you can see the elliptical shape of Samye's walled enclosure and something of its cosmic plan. The walls used to be circular (apparently before 1959), but were rebuilt as elliptical. About 500m south of the south gate you can see a grey, three-storey building enclosed by a high wall: this used to be one of the three queens' residences, but there's no access to the place (the other two residences were apparently destroyed).

To the far northeast of Samye is **Chimphu**, which is riddled with hermitage caves (there are said to be 108 of them). Monks and nuns come for retreat here: if visiting, take some *tsampa* and candles as donations. It takes about 40 minutes on a walking-tractor to reach the general area, then a 3-hour hike (round trip), so you'd have to allow 5–6 hours for the visit. If arriving by walking-tractor, make sure the driver waits to take you back to Samye.

There is a five-day trek between Samye and Ganden monasteries. See page 187 for details.

TSEDANG (*Tsetang, Zedang, Nedong; 3,600m; capital of Shannan Prefecture; telephone code 0893*) Tsedang is a Chinese town – or to put it more bluntly, a Chinese eyesore. This is the shape of things to come, as more Chinese settlers move in. With a population over 50,000, the town functions as a Chinese hub in central Tibet. In contrast to traditional Tibetan architecture, which blends into the mountain and desert environment, Chinese structures here look totally jarring, with bland concrete blocks finished in bathroom tiling and blue-tinted glass. And the addition of fake palm trees along some boulevards doesn't help. Behind the concrete curtain, there was an ancient Tibetan town at Tsedang, but it has been marginalised – remnants of an old Tibetan quarter exist to the east of the market area with an active *gompa* and a nunnery. Due to a military presence, there is a surfeit of karaoke bars and bars stocked with young women.

Tsedang is mostly used as a stepping stone to destinations such as Yumbulagang Fortress. There are a few **hikes** on the eastern side of Tsedang that are of middling interest. A 4-hour hike takes you up a mountain trail to **Gangpo Ri monkey cave**. This cave is revered as the mythical site where a monkey (an emanation of Avalokitesvara) consorted with a demoness (an emanation of Tara) to give birth to six children, later leaders of the Tibetan clans. The monkey then instructed them how to cultivate grains in the fertile valley, so Tibet's first cultivated field is supposed to be in the Tsedang area. This tale of the origin of the Tibetan race, involving descent from a monkey, has an oddly Darwinian touch.

Getting there Tsedang is 196km from Lhasa and 97km from Gongkar Airport. Locals use buses running to Tsedang from Lhasa. A **taxi** from Lhasa is possible: the road is smooth, paved and flat, so you can get there in under 3 hours.

Getting around The choice is between regular Volkswagen taxis, motorised three-wheel contraptions (seating two) or bicycle trishaws (also seating two).

Where to stay *Map, below*

A strange cat-and-mouse game goes on with hotels, guesthouses and restaurants in Tsedang, which seems to be a PSB-Mafia-dominated monopoly. Travellers who have tried to stay in non-Chinese-operated guesthouses have been visited by Tsedang PSB officers and told to move along. A number of Chinese hotels refuse to

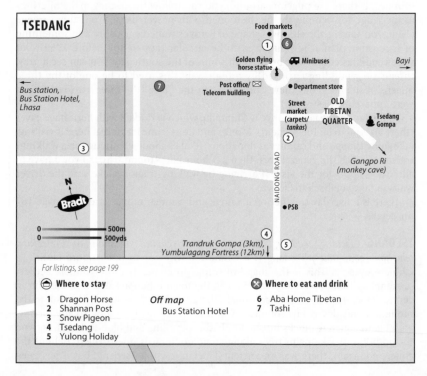

TSEDANG

Food markets
① ⑥
Golden flying horse statue
🚌 Minibuses
Bayi

Bus station,
Bus Station Hotel,
Lhasa

Post office/ ✉
Telecom building

● Department store

⑦

Street market (carpets/ tankas)
OLD TIBETAN QUARTER
🛕 Tsedang Gompa

②

③

Gangpo Ri (monkey cave)

NAIDONG ROAD

N

● PSB

0 ——— 500m
0 ——— 500yds

④
Trandruk Gompa (3km),
Yumbulagang Fortress (12km) ↓
⑤

For listings, see page 199

🛏 **Where to stay**

1 Dragon Horse
2 Shannan Post   *Off map*
3 Snow Pigeon   Bus Station Hotel
4 Tsedang
5 Yulong Holiday

❌ **Where to eat and drink**

6 Aba Home Tibetan
7 Tashi

accept foreigners, including the Golden Crane Hotel. That means, essentially, that you are stuck with overpriced officially approved hotels.

Taking all this into account, the best thing you can do about Tsedang is give the place a miss as an overnight stop. You can aim instead to stay in Samye or Gongkar.

The rough centre of Tsedang is a dusty traffic roundabout with a golden flying horse statue in the middle. Most activity takes place on Naidong Road, the street running south of the roundabout. With a few exceptions, the following hotels are arrayed on or close to Naidong Road.

🏠 **Tsedang Hotel** (190 rooms & suites) Naidong Rd; ☎782 1668. Tsedang's top-rated hotel, used by group tours. **$$$**

🏠 **Snow Pigeon Hotel** (65 rooms & suites) Western side of Tsedang; ☎782 8888. High-rise run by China Telecom. You may be able to bargain prices down. **$$$**

🏠 **Shannan Post Hotel** (60 rooms & suites) 10 Naidong Rd; ☎782 1888. Rooms are in several wings. Posted rates for Chinese guests are much lower than for foreigners, so there might be leverage for bargaining. **$$$**

🏠 **Yulong Holiday Hotel** Located almost directly opposite Tsedang Hotel; ☎783 2888. **$$**

🏠 **Dragon Horse Hotel** 5 Sare Lu, ☎782 3335. Good value, with better rooms in a courtyard off the main street. **$$**

🏠 **Bus Station Hotel** ☎782 6660. Though a bit out of town near the bus station, this Tibetan-run place offers great value for rooms. **$$**

✗ **Where to eat and drink** *Map, opposite*

Even restaurant owners, intimidated by the PSB, may inform Westerners they cannot eat in the restaurant. PSB officers have been seen trailing travellers around the town. Travellers should make efforts to break this stranglehold when it comes to restaurants (try buying drinks only at a Tibetan teahouse to annoy the Beijing Boys).

Two inexpensive places to go are **Tashi Restaurant** ($), which offers Nepali and Western food in a pleasant atmosphere, and **Aba Home Tibetan Restaurant** ($), which, as the name suggests, is a cosy Tibetan place with traditional seating.

Shopping and other practicalities For trip supplies, try the **department store** near the main crossroads, and also the **street markets** nearby. For artefact shopping, the west end of the street markets offers *tankas* and Qinghai carpets. The **post office/ telecom** building is at the main crossroads. One street south is the **Xinhua bookstore** (on the second floor; don't expect much – you might find some posters or maps). There doesn't seem to be a bank that deals in foreign exchange: your best bet is to try Tsedang Hotel.

SOUTH OF TSEDANG The main attraction south of Tsedang is **Yumbulagang Fortress,** 13km from town along a sealed road. A pilgrim bus runs out to the fortress, or you could hire a taxi for a few hours and see several sites *en route,* such as Trandruk. Yumbulagang Fortress crowns a hilltop; it is set in a valley with a village below. Now you see it, now you don't. Yumbulagang is in the RRDCR-CR category (reduced to rubble during the Cultural Revolution and completely rebuilt). Pictures taken in the late 1970s show nothing left of the fortress – it was shorn from the rock. Pictures taken in the 1980s show the entire fortress again. The present building, reconstructed in 1982, is a pretty good copy of the original, though not quite as big. The architecture is rare and distinctive: Yumbulagang Fortress is believed to have been built by the Yarlung dynasty kings in the 7th or 8th century. Later it was converted into a monastery. Now it is a museum of sorts, looked after by some Geluk monks. Waiting at the base of the hill leading to Yambulagang are horsemen seeking lazy tourists for the ride up to the fortress. There may even be the

5

odd camel awaiting your arrival. Hiking or riding up to the hilltop fortress, you can clamber up through several storeys to the two-tiered chapel at the top. From this eyrie, there are fine views of the patchwork of fields in the village below.

On the way out to Yumbulagang, or on the return trip, you can visit **Trandruk Gompa (Falcon-Dragon Temple)**, originally built by King Songtsen Gampo in the 7th century. The monastery is 7km from Tsedang, reached by a good road. The monastery is a warren of chapels: in an upstairs chapel right at the back is the monastery's treasure. Locked in a dusty glass case is a precious *tanka* depicting Avalokitesvara, whose ghostlike image is reputed to be composed of 30,000 pearls sewn into a red tapestry.

A different fork from Tsedang leads 17km south to **Tangboche Monastery**, which, though in a sorry state, is worth checking out for the murals covering the walls of the assembly hall. These murals were commissioned in 1915 by the 13th Dalai Lama (whose image naturally appears among the murals). A further 13km southward brings you to Chongye, where the tombs of all the Yarlung dynasty kings are located. **Chongye Royal Tombs** consist of massive earth mounds, which all look pretty much the same except for their size. This has led to much confusion over who is actually entombed within. The largest tomb is believed to be that of the 7th-century warrior-king, Songtsen Gampo. On top of this tomb is a small chapel, reached by a flight of stairs – it features a statue of Songtsen Gampo, flanked by two of his wives and two important ministers.

6

Lhasa to Kathmandu

THE GREATEST ROAD ROUTE IN HIGH ASIA

The Lhasa to Kathmandu route ranks, in my mind, as the finest in High Asia – because of the ethereal views. You are motoring across the roof of the world, powering over five passes – festooned with prayer flags – all above 4,500m. If you take the Gyantse route, winding up to Khamba La pass, you come to stunning views of the Turquoise Lake (Yamdrok Tso) with snow caps on the Bhutanese border. Three great monasteries – at Gyantse, Shigatse and Sakya – lie along the road route. If you have arranged it with the driver and guide, you can drive all the way to Everest base camp (EBC) – a magical spot that will (literally) blow you away. Even without the base-camp trip, on a clear day you can see some 8,000m peaks right from the roadway, including Cho Oyu (8,153m), near Tingri. And then, if the gods favour you with the right paperwork for an overland crossing, there's a fantastic drop right off the Tibetan plateau – from high-altitude desert, switchbacking down to tropical Nepalese jungle. There is nothing in High Asia that can compare to this roadshow. Lhasa to Kathmandu is an excellent adventure. Nobody said the trip would be easy, though.

LOGISTICS AND TIMING You can take a one-way trip, Lhasa to Kathmandu and cross into Nepal. Or you can take a round trip from Lhasa, going all the way to say, Tingri, and then heading back to Lhasa. Because the road is paved and in decent condition, progress is rapid on this road. Most destinations in this chapter fall under the jurisdiction of Shigatse Prefecture. For that reason, your guide may have to stop at Shigatse PSB to arrange permit stamping and paperwork.

A lot of navigation information is carried in the Lhasa to Kathmandu map (pages 202–3). You can work out turn-offs and where you are by a system of kilometre marker stones by the roadside.

The entire route from Lhasa to Kathmandu is close to a 1,000km via the direct Lhasa–Shigatse route. Add another 100km if you go via Gyantse. If you take side trips to Shegar and Sakya (highly recommended) you add 56km to the journey, since Sakya lies 21km off the main route. There's a major detour of 70km off the main route to reach Everest base camp (EBC; pages 237–66), so that would add another 140km. Adding Gyantse, Shegar, Sakya and EBC means adding about 300km.

Without stops or obstacles, fast drivers can make the run from Lhasa to Kyirong in two days, overnighting at Tingri. With stops, the trip would require a minimum of four days. It's recommended you allow six to seven days, depending on side trips. If you include EBC, build in time for possible delays. Approximate driving times along the route:

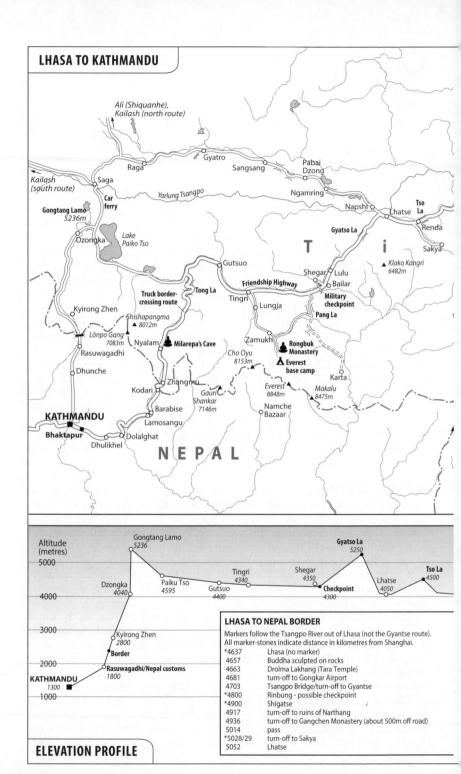

LHASA TO KATHMANDU

Ali (Shiquanhe),
Kailash (north route)

Gyatro
Sangsang
Pabai Dzong
Raga
Kailash (south route)
Saga
Yarlung Tsangpo
Ngamring
Napshi
Lhatse
Tso La
Car ferry
Gongtang Lamo 5236m
Renda
Gyatso La
Dzongka
Lake Paiko Tso
Gutsuo
Shegar
Lulu
Klako Kangri 6482m
Sakya
Friendship Highway
Bailar
Tong La
Truck border-crossing route
Tingri
Lungja
Military checkpoint
Kyirong Zhen
Shishapangma ▲ 8012m
Pang La
Lönpo Gang 7083m
Nyalam
Milarepa's Cave
Zamukh
Rongbuk Monastery
Rasuwagadhi
Cho Oyu 8153m
Everest base camp
Dhunche
Zhangmu
Kodari
Gauri Shankar 7146m
Everest 8848m
Makalu 8475m
Karta
Barabise
Namche Bazaar
KATHMANDU
Lamosangu
Bhaktapur
Dolalghat
Dhulikhel
N E P A L

T i

ELEVATION PROFILE

Altitude (metres)

Gongtang Lamo 5236
Gyatso La 5250
Tso La 4500
5000
Tingri 4340
Shegar 4350
Dzongka 4040
Paiku Tso 4595
Gutsuo 4400
Checkpoint 4300
Lhatse 4050
4000
3000
Kyirong Zhen 2800
Border
2000
Rasuwagadhi/Nepal customs 1800
KATHMANDU 1300
1000

LHASA TO NEPAL BORDER

Markers follow the Tsangpo River out of Lhasa (not the Gyantse route).
All marker-stones indicate distance in kilometres from Shanghai.

*4637	Lhasa (no marker)
4657	Buddha sculpted on rocks
4663	Drolma Lakhang (Tara Temple)
4681	turn-off to Gongkar Airport
4703	Tsangpo Bridge/turn-off to Gyantse
*4800	Rinbung - possible checkpoint
*4900	Shigatse
4917	turn-off to ruins of Narthang
4936	turn-off to Gangchen Monastery (about 500m off road)
5014	pass
*5028/29	turn-off to Sakya
5052	Lhatse

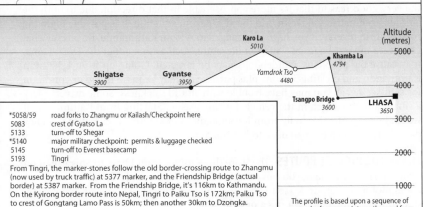

*5058/59	road forks to Zhangmu or Kailash/Checkpoint here
5083	crest of Gyatso La
5133	turn-off to Shegar
*5140	major military checkpoint: permits & luggage checked
5145	turn-off to Everest basecamp
5193	Tingri

From Tingri, the marker-stones follow the old border-crossing route to Zhangmu (now used by truck traffic) at 5377 marker, and the Friendship Bridge (actual border) at 5387 marker. From the Friendship Bridge, it's 116km to Kathmandu. On the Kyirong border route into Nepal, Tingri to Paiku Tso is 172km; Paiku Tso to crest of Gongtang Lamo Pass is 50km; then another 30km to Dzongka. Dzongka to Kyirong Zhen is 66km. From here, it's 32km to the border crossing. From the border crossing to Rasuwagadhi is 20km, and then another 65km to Kathmandu.
* = no exact marker stone

The profile is based upon a sequence of named reference points on the road from Lhasa to Kathmandu shown above on the map. Since the road does not run in a straight line, distances and gradients cannot be measured directly from it.

Lhasa to Shigatse	8 hours (depending on route taken)
Shigatse to Lhatse	3½ hours
Lhatse to Shegar	3 hours
Shegar to EBC	4 hours
EBC to Tingri	5 hours
Rasuwagadhi to Kathmandu	6 hours
Tingri to Kyirong Town	7 hours
Kyirong Town to border *	1 hour

* Where Chinese customs is located. Further ½-hour drive to Rasuwagadhi town, where Nepalese customs is located.

SAMPLE ITINERARY A sample itinerary for a week-long foray from Lhasa to Kathmandu (via southern route through Gyantse with a stop at Everest base camp) might look like this:

Day 1 Drive from Lhasa to Gyantse via Nagartse (Samding), overnight Gyantse

Day 2 See more of Gyantse, short drive to Shigatse, hike *kora*, overnight Shigatse

Day 3 Morning in Shigatse, drive to Sakya, hike around Sakya, overnight in Sakya

Day 4 Drive from Sakya to Shegar, hike at Shegar; overnight at crossroads near Shegar

Day 5 Drive to EBC, overnight there

Day 6 Spend more time at EBC, then drive back to Tingri in the afternoon; overnight in Tingri

Day 7 Drive from Tingri to Kyirong Town, overnight in Kyirong Town

Day 8 Cross the Nepal border and drive on to Kathmandu

Reverse trip The description here follows the Lhasa to Kathmandu route for the very good reason that it's more approachable in that direction due to both the altitude acclimatisation factor and the visa/permit situation. It is possible to do the road route in reverse, if you have an arranged tour from Kathmandu. Be careful what you bring in your baggage – suspect literature, such as that about the Dalai Lama, may cause big problems. Guidebooks may be targeted. Going up from 1,300m in Kathmandu and cresting 5,000m-plus passes, you may be in no mood or condition for sightseeing, as you may have trouble with altitude sickness. Some drivers carry a small tank of oxygen in the vehicle for this reason. Starting from Kathmandu, it would be far preferable to fly from Kathmandu to Lhasa first, acclimatise for a few days there, then go by road back to Kathmandu.

LHASA TO SHIGATSE ROUTES There are three routes from Lhasa to Shigatse. If on a round trip from Lhasa, you can combine routes. For example, for a long loop, you could motor via Yamdrok Tso to Gyantse, and then return to Lhasa via Yangbajing, stopping at various monasteries along the way.

Northern route The northern route via Yangbajing is the least-travelled way of getting from Lhasa to Shigatse, but it makes sense if you've been off to Lake Namtso.

This splendid route is high and rough (not paved), and sometimes used if for some reason the main westward route is blocked. Yangbajing supplies geothermal power to Lhasa; there is a hot spring pool here. Heading southward from Yangbajing you motor across two high passes, Suge La and Dongu La. On the north banks of the Yarlung Tsangpo you can detour along a rough road to Menri Gompa, a small Bon monastery. You cross the Yarlung Tsangpo by car ferry to Dagzhuka, and join the main western route to Shigatse. Approximate driving time (no stops) on this route is Lhasa to Yangbajing, 2 hours; Yangbajing to Suge La, 2½ hours; Suge La to Dagzhuka ferry crossing, 2½ hours; Dagzhuka to Shigatse, 2 hours.

Western route This road follows a canyon running along the Yarlung Tsangpo – it is used by Chinese military and supply trucks to get from Lhasa to Shigatse in the fastest time. It thus sees the heaviest traffic, with convoys of military trucks heading through. The road runs beneath steep canyon walls, and rockfalls may block the road entirely. Slabs of roadway have also been known to disappear into the Yarlung Tsangpo, because engineering skills haven't quite been perfected. The bridge spanning the Yarlung Tsangpo near Rinbung is one-way, meaning that there can be traffic line-ups when the flow is against you. Driving time on this Lhasa to Shigatse route is about 5–6 hours if there are no delays or problems.

Southern route This route via Gyantse to Shigatse is much more dramatic, taking in the beautiful lake of Yamdrok Tso. It is longer, more winding and rougher, so it is not used by supply trucks. This means minimal traffic and far superior views. On the southern route, exiting Lhasa, you cross the Tsangpo Bridge and wind up to Khamba La, with stunning views. Down the other side of Khamba La you reach Nagartse, a village with a small restaurant, plus a guesthouse. If you can, arrange a side trip to Samding Monastery. From Nagartse, the road climbs over Karo La and heads for Gyantse. Approximate driving time on this route is Lhasa to Khamba La, 1½ hours; Khamba La to Karo La, 3 hours; Karo La to Gyantse, 2½ hours; Gyantse to Shigatse, 2 hours.

SOUTHERN ROUTE TO GYANTSE

Drolma Lakhang Exiting Lhasa on either the western route or the southern route (as above), you can visit this well-preserved temple about 25km from Lhasa. See page 189 for details.

Yamdrok Tso From Khamba La, where prayer flags are buffeted by the winds, you get a magnificent view of Yamdrok Tso (the Turquoise Lake), with the large snow cap on the horizon being Kula Kangri (7,554m) on the Bhutanese border. From this vantage point you can see why the Tibetans consider Yamdrok Tso to be a sacred lake. It is Tibet's largest freshwater lake. Your contemplation of the views at the pass may be interrupted by a circus of aggressive vendors – who sell photo-ops with yaks, Tibetan mastiffs or sheep.

Winding down from Khamba La towards the shore of Yamdrok Tso, you can see a hydropower plant, with four Austrian-made turbines. This plant is part of a hare-brained Chinese scheme that drains the lake water to produce electricity for Lhasa during peak demand. The plant is designed as a pumped storage plant with a 90MW capacity. The project has been a total disaster since its inception in 1985. In 1986, due to vigorous objections from Tibetans headed by the Tenth Panchen Lama, work was halted, but was resumed after the Panchen Lama's death in 1989. Overriding international campaigns, the Chinese went ahead with construction, with disastrous results. In 1993, in the village of Dramalung, close to the project, all freshwater wells completely dried up, forcing villagers to rely on the lake for their water supply. In 1996, reports filtered through of the complete collapse of a tunnel leading from the lake to the turbines. The plant started generating power in the late 1990s.

Western environmentalists are concerned that the water level at Yamdrok Tso could drop significantly – or, in a worst-case scenario, that the lake might completely drain away. Authorities in Lhasa insist this is not the case: they say they will pump water back from the Yarlung Tsangpo to replenish the lake water. But even if this were true, it means snow-fed lake water would be replaced with muddy river flow, with uncertain ecological results. One result is certain: the sacred lake is bound to lose its natural deep turquoise colour. Pumping water back up into Yamdrok Tso requires a separate power source: a new dam, under construction on the Nyang River, 30km east of Gyantse, is said to be that source. The building of this dam has spawned an entire town of corrugated roofing, housing Chinese construction workers and engineers.

Nagartse and Samding Monastery Nagartse is the only sizeable village near Yamdrok Tso: rented vehicle drivers headed for Gyantse may break up the long day with a rest stop here. Nagartse has a few restaurants (Lhasa Restaurant, Holy Lake Restaurant) and several guesthouses. Technically a permit is required to stay overnight: Nagartse and Yamdrok Tso are under the jurisdiction of Shannan Prefecture.

Yamdrok Tso is shaped like the pincers of a crab: in the grip of them lies the monastery of Samding, about 8km from Nagartse. You can reach it by 4x4 from Nagartse, or hike in. Nagartse PSB does not seem to like travellers visiting this one, so be discreet when visiting. The monastery is on a hilltop, reached by a set of switchbacks; a few dozen monks are in residence. There are expansive views across the valley from Samding.

Samding Monastery has an odd history. The monastery was probably founded in the 13th century and was associated with the Bodong sect, initiated by Bodong Chokle Namgyel (1306–86). The sect never gained much prominence, although a number of temples within a radius of Samding followed its precepts.

At one time, Samding appears to have had both monks and nuns in residence, and was run by an abbess, one of the only female incarnations in Tibet. The lineage goes back to the 18th century. In 1717, legend has it, the abbess (venerated as Dorje Phagmo or the 'Thunderbolt Sow', believed to be a reincarnation of Tara) transformed herself and her cohorts into pigs to save them from a Dzungar (Mongol) attack. For centuries, the lineage continued uneventfully, until 1937. That year the acting Regent of Tibet announced that the Sixth Dorje Phagmo had been recognised in a young girl, even though the Fifth was still at large. He argued that the transference of souls actually took place in this case before death. The Fifth Dorje Phagmo died the following year, but the Tibetans would not accept the Sixth as the true incarnation and three other candidates were put forward. The matter was hotly disputed by the nominated girl's father, and a costly legal battle drained the funds of Samding and tore its monks and nuns apart with internal strife.

The Sixth Dorje Phagmo (the girl selected in 1937), it appears, hardly took up residence at Samding, since the legal wrangle carried over into the 1950s. In 1959, she fled to India, but the same year decided to return to Tibet by way of China. She then sided with the Chinese and made it clear she did not wish to be a Living Buddha any more. She married and had three children, and held a high government position in Lhasa when last heard of.

If a community of nuns and monks with an abbess at their head sounds like good material for a novel, there is one that draws inspiration from Samding. In his suspense novel *The Rose of Tibet*, author Lionel Davidson combines Yamdrok Tso and Samding to create a place called Yamdring Monastery.

Ralung Gompa Between Yamdrok Tso and Gyantse is a turn-off that leads 5km along a rough dirt road to the tiny *gompa* of Ralung. This monastery used to be much bigger, but its Kumbum and main halls were destroyed. What remains is a single structure, housing a handful of monks, who commute on motorcycles. The place is located in a quiet valley and is little visited.

GYANTSE *(Gyangtse, Gyangze, Jiangzi; 3,950m)*

Gyantse was established as the personal fiefdom of King Pelden Sangpo, in the 14th century. His successor, Rabten Kunsang Phapa (1389–1442), extended the fiefdom's range, and constructed Palkor Choide Lamasery and the mighty Kumbum, both of which are still standing today.

In later centuries, Gyantse developed as an important centre of the wool trade in Tibet, and a bustling caravan stop on the trade route from Lhasa to India. That route – leading to Sikkim and Bhutan – was closed by the Chinese after they took over in 1950. Gyantse has since fallen into obscurity, its role usurped by Lhasa under the Chinese. This situation, however, has left Gyantse intact as a Tibetan architectural entity, which is something quite rare amid all the Chinese destruction and reconstruction. Gyantse has a largely Tibetan population – perhaps around 20,000. There is a huge fort at one end of town, walled-in monastery grounds at the other end, and a ramshackle marketplace with older buildings and alleyways between fort and monastery.

In the late 1940s, Italian photographer Francesco Mele passed through Gyantse. Here's his description of the market:

> Its market is rich, due to the wool trade and the Indian and Chinese imported objects sold there. The shops are near to the main street, and many of them are simply tents. Here women wearing silver and turquoise jewellery sell clothing and household articles … There are even some Nepalese and Bhutanese salesmen, and a few Muslims who have taken the few weeks' journey from Ladak in order to sell their products in Gyantse. Muslims are often employed as butchers of yak and goat here, since the Buddhist religion forbids Tibetans to kill animals. Fresh and dried beef and mutton hang in every part of the market, giving it an oddly surrealist appearance.

Gyantse market appears to have died: there isn't a whole lot happening around the old quarter any more. Instead, various smaller street markets are scattered around the town. Nevertheless, Gyantse is a great place to visit, and will give some idea of what an intact Tibetan town must have looked like.

Buildings in Gyantse date back as far as the 14th century. One of these is the massive *dzong* (fort), occupying a strategic hilltop at the southern end of town. The *dzong* guarded the road to Lhasa, and the invading British expedition of 1903 found it a formidable obstacle. The British eventually stormed the *dzong*, the Tibetan defenders capitulated, and there was no further resistance on the road to Lhasa.

Although the last of the British forces withdrew in 1908, several vestiges of British presence remained in Gyantse, in the form of a British Trade Agent, a British wool-agent station, a British post office (with a telegraph line running to India),

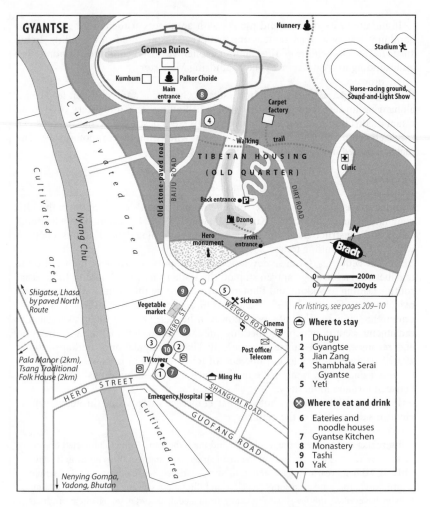

Gompa Ruins

Kumbum Palkor Choide

Main entrance ⑧

Nunnery

Stadium 🏃

Horse-racing ground, Sound-and-Light Show

Carpet factory

④

Walking trail

TIBETAN HOUSING

(OLD QUARTER)

Clinic ✚

Cultivated area

Old stone-paved road

BAIJU ROAD

DIRT ROAD

Back entrance P

🏯 Dzong

Nyang Chu

Cultivated area

Cultivated area

Hero monument

Front entrance

Bradt

0 ━━━ 200m
0 ━━━ 200yds

Shigatse, Lhasa by paved North Route

⑨

⑤ ✖ Sichuan

Vegetable market

HERO ST

WEIGUO ROAD

Cinema 🎬

$

For listings, see pages 209–10

🛏 **Where to stay**

1 Dhugu
2 Gyangtse
3 Jian Zang
4 Shambhala Serai Gyantse
5 Yeti

Pala Manor (2km), Tsang Traditional Folk House (2km)

⑥ ⑥

③ ⑩ ②

TV tower

① ⑦

HERO STREET

Emergency Hospital ✚

🏠 Ming Hu

Post office/ Telecom

SHANGHAI ROAD

GUOFANG ROAD

Cultivated area

Nenying Gompa, Yadong, Bhutan

✖ **Where to eat and drink**

6 Eateries and noodle houses
7 Gyantse Kitchen
8 Monastery
9 Tashi
10 Yak

and later a British-run school for upper-crust Tibetan children. By the 1940s, a great deal of Gyantse's sheep wool production was slated for export to British India. There was little interest in yak wool, which was too harsh in quality, although in the pre-synthetic era the beards worn by Santa Clauses in US department stores were made from yak-tail hair. Gyantse became a funnel for the export of wool due to its location, and wool was brought here from outlying areas of Tibet.

The 1950s saw a period of severe dislocation in Gyantse. In 1954, the town was nearly destroyed by flooding; in 1959 the local industries were virtually dismantled with the exodus of artisans from Tibet and the removal of others to work camps. After putting down the 1959 revolt, the Chinese imprisoned 400 monks and laymen at the monastery of Gyantse. During the Cultural Revolution, the monastery itself was ransacked and dismantled – items of value were either destroyed or shipped back to China. Gyantse Kumbum, however, was spared. Since 1980, the Chinese have attempted to stimulate the handicraft production for which Gyantse was so famous. But if there has been any stimulation, there is little evidence of it in Gyantse's present-day marketplace.

In the late 1990s, Chinese authorities embarked on a propaganda blitz in Gyantse, naming it 'Heroic City' in praise of valiant Tibetan resistance to British troops in 1904. In Chinese terms, the logic runs thus: 'Tibetan patriotic soldiers safeguarded state sovereignty and territorial integrity – defending the Tibet–China Motherland.' These propaganda efforts were most likely tied in with a round of Brit-bashing after the 1997 handover of Hong Kong. First there was the 1997 release of *Red River Valley*, a Shanghai-made epic movie about the British in Tibet, with on-location filming at Gyantse. This was followed by renaming the main street of Gyantse 'Hero Street', and the erection of a huge obelisk as a monument to heroic Tibetan fighters. The monument makes a convenient navigation landmark, right near the town's central roundabout.

GETTING THERE Motoring over several stunning passes on the back route from Lhasa is the best way to get to Gyantse. This trip should take about 6 hours – longer if you stop *en route*. If arriving by **4x4** and overnighting, park the vehicle within your hotel grounds. Locals use buses that run from Lhasa via Shigatse to get to Gyantse. It's a 90km trip.

GETTING AROUND Gyantse cleaves into several distinct zones. To the northern end of town is the old quarter, with Tibetan housing. To the southern end of town, south of the central roundabout, are newer Chinese concrete blocks and Chinese facilities such as the bank, post office, cinema and so on. At all compass points around the town are cultivated fields. There are stupendous views of Gyantse from the uppermost ramparts of the fort.

If you're with a driver and your time is short, drive around to visit sites like Pala Manor, the main monastery, the *dzong* (reached by motor road at the back), and Ani Gompa. Pala Manor can be visited as a stop on the way to Shigatse, or incoming from Shigatse. Gyantse's key destinations would be easy to get to by **bicycle**, if you can lay your hands on one. Gyangtse Hotel has a few bikes, but only for their guests, and they are expensive at Y5 an hour or Y50 a day. An alternative is hiring a **bicycle trishaw** driver in town. If you have more time, Gyantse is a pleasant place to stroll around – you can reach key destinations **on foot**, though it's a long way out to Pala Manor.

🏠 **WHERE TO STAY** *Map, opposite*
Some hotels in Gyantse appear to favour Chinese guests, such as Ming Hu Hotel.

🏠 **Shambhala Serai Gyantse** (10 rooms) This stylish boutique hotel has a terrific advantage over the rest: it is located in an old merchant's house next to Palkor Choide Gompa. **$$$**

🏠 **Gyangtse Hotel** (138 rooms & suites) Shanghai Rd, towards the river; ☎0892 817 2222. This is the place for high-end group tours, with a large dining hall & a souvenir shop. Although cavernous, the hotel has a drab atmosphere. Guests can rent bikes for Y5/hr or Y50/day. Facilities include a business centre, & to one side of the compound is Pala Manor Recreation Centre, offering haircuts & massage. **$$$**

🏠 **Yeti Hotel** 11 Weiguo Lu, ☎0892 817 5555. This hotel is the best deal in town, offering 24hr hot water, clean rooms, comfortable mattresses, & Wi-Fi. A good buffet b/fast is provided, along with a great lobby restaurant for other meals. **$$**

🏠 **Jian Zang Hotel** Hero St, southwest of roundabout; ☎0892 817 3720; e jianzanghotel@ yahoo.com.cn. Good mid-range hotel. **$$**

🏠 **Dhugu Hotel** (30 rooms) Guofang Rd; ☎0892 817 3165. Adequate standard hotel – functional but lacking character. **$**

✗ **WHERE TO EAT AND DRINK** *Map, opposite*
Scattered around town are small eateries, some with only two or three tables. For real Tibetan atmosphere try the **Monastery Restaurant**, in the courtyard of Palkor

6

Choide, which is crowded with pilgrims tucking into their *thukpa* soup or *momos*. **Tashi Restaurant**, near the central roundabout (on the second floor), is a Nepali-run Tibetan-style teahouse serving palatable Indian, Italian and Chinese food. There's a string of small restaurants along Hero Street – Muslim, Tibetan and Chinese styles on offer. The second-floor **Yak Restaurant** is found here, opposite Jian Zang Hotel. Along the same strip (set back off the road) is a small fruit and vegetable market where you can buy peaches and bananas. In the mornings, you may find tiny bakeries serving hot baked goods. Stores in Gyantse are not as well stocked as they are in Shigatse. Worth checking out, and somewhat pricier, is **Gyantse Kitchen**, to the south side of town. This place serves yak pizza, chicken sizzlers and an eclectic range of Western, Tibetan and Indian cuisine.

ENTERTAINMENT
Night Theatre At the horse-racing ground, a nightly light and sound spectacle is staged from April to October, aimed at Chinese tour groups. A cast of 300 Tibetans performs song-and-dance routines, using the entire old town as a lit-up backdrop. That's about as lively as it gets in Gyantse at night. Tickets cost Y280, and performances start at 21.30. As all foreigners must be escorted by a guide and driver when touring Tibet, put your guide to good use and have him/her make all the arrangements for ticketing and driving to the venue.

OTHER PRACTICALITIES Facilities in Gyantse are limited, but include a half-hearted attempt at a department store (shelves bare) and a half-hearted attempt at a bank (staffed by Chinese who appear to have perfected the art of camouflaging themselves as non-bank workers). Further down the street is the **post office**, with long-distance telecom capabilities if you goad the staff. Chances of making long-distance connections are better at the **cybercafés** found at the southwest side of town (see map, page 208). For medical problems, your best bet is likely to be the **Emergency Hospital** on Shanghai Road, past Gyangtse Hotel. Avoid the clinic at the northeast side of town, as it's unsanitary. Gyantse at night is subject to the occasional tuneless wailing from karaoke bars or the sound of kung fu epics emanating from video salons or Tibetan teahouses; there's also a cinema with an antiquated sound system.

WHAT TO SEE AND DO
Horse-racing festival The time when Gyantse really comes to life is during the horse-racing festival, held in the first week of the eighth lunar month (usually sometime in late July or early August). The horse-racing ground is to the northeast side of town. Festivities last for about five days. The jockeys are young boys: the winners (both boy and horse) are festooned with white ceremonial scarves. Large parades, with dancers and singers, and monks in full regalia, accompany the opening and closing ceremonies.

Old quarter Gyantse is a great town to walk around. The Tibetan part of town, towards the gates of Gyantse Gompa, is a fascinating medieval jumble of alleyways, with cows roaming through. Gyantse market used to be located along the stone-paved road close to the main monastery. There's no plumbing in the old quarter (water comes from street taps) and little electrical supply. However, solar cookers have been introduced by the Chinese: these concave-shaped reflectors are found on the flat roofs in the old quarter – they can bring a kettle of water to the boil in a few minutes.

There is a walking trail from the monastery towards the horse-racing ground, which cuts through a cleft in a high ridge (see map, page 208). Along the way is **Gyantse**

After invading in 1903, the British negotiated the right to set up telegraph and post offices in Tibet. This gave the Tibetans access to the international postal system. There were a handful of British post offices, the earliest starting around 1906. The British were not permitted to establish a post office in Lhasa, but three British post offices linked the main trading corridor from Tibet to India: at Gyantse, Phari and Yadong. The mail then went on to Kalimpong, in India.

The postal system for external mail in Tibet was primarily used by Nepalese and Indian traders. Delivery was accomplished by runners: the monasteries, for instance, had their own runners. Ponies were also used, and in the 1930s a Dodge truck operated on part of the route to India. The runners, like most Tibetans, were illiterate and could only identify traders' mail by hand-marked symbols on the envelopes. The mail could be delivered in a fairly short time: officials in Lhasa used to subscribe to newspapers in Calcutta, which might arrive a week or so later. Considering the altitude of the passes along the route, the runners did a remarkable job.

In 1910 the 13th Dalai Lama, who had fled to India, asked the British company of Waterlow to design a Tibetan stamp. Waterlow produced some proofs with a snow lion on them, the symbol of the Dalai Lama. These were rejected by the Tibetans, but they kept the proofs, and the Waterlow design was copied for the first Tibetan stamp issue of 1912. Tibetan stamps were a very haphazard affair. The 1912 issue, done in five different *trangka* values, was printed off woodblocks of 12 stamps. Stamp colour largely depended on what inks were available in the marketplace. Tibetan cancels never bore dates, and the random print runs were never announced – the 1914 issue of stamps was not discovered by the West until 1942.

If you were living in Lhasa in the 1930s and you wanted to get a letter to England, life got complicated. There was no British post office in Lhasa, and Tibet was not a member of the International Postal Union. So you needed two sets of stamps on an envelope – Tibetan and Indian. In Lhasa, they'd cancel the Tibetan postage and forward the item to the Tibetan post office in Gyantse. Somehow the letter would make it across town to Gyantse's British post office, and then go on to Yadong and India, where it entered the international postal system.

Incoming mail was virtually impossible to orchestrate unless sent care of a trader in Gyantse or Phari, who would affix the Tibetan postage and forward the letter. In the process, the actual stamps would be dwarfed by a selection of wax seals, handstamps, chops and registration marks. Red wax seals could only be used by Incarnate Lamas. Few of the Dalai Lama's letters went beyond Sikkim. They were carried by private runners, and enclosed ceremonial silk scarves and perhaps a small bag of gold dust. They could only leave the Potala on auspicious dates.

By the early 1950s, stamp collectors were rushing to buy Tibetan postage. The majority of fake Tibetan stamps and covers started to appear at this time, though the hobby goes back to 1920. Buyers who are offered earlier Tibetan stamps in Kathmandu will probably be shown forgeries nine times out of ten. Covers are now forged so well that only a handful of world experts can tell the difference.

Carpet Factory, where all work is done by hand – carding the wool, spinning, dyeing and weaving. This small operation is a shadow of what Gyantse once was. There's also a clothing factory in Gyantse. A worthy destination to the northeast side of town is **Ani Gompa**, a nunnery with 30 nuns in residence. A tiny chapel here contains a large wooden prayer wheel and some life-sized frescoes, including one that shows the Tenth Panchen Lama (a mural near this used to show the current Dalai Lama, but, under orders, the head was repainted in the likeness of the Fifth Dalai Lama). Behind the nunnery is a cliff face with hermit caves; there's a sky burial site in the vicinity.

The monastery Pictures taken by Leslie Weir on a visit in 1930 show a complex of 16 monasteries within the high walls at the north end of Gyantse (Weir was a British Trade Agent at Gyantse). The monastic town has been razed with the exception of a few of the larger buildings. The monastery goes under different names: Palkor Choide is the older name, but the Chinese refer to it as Palchoi Temple or Baiju Temple, and the road leading up to it as Baiju Road.

The monastery is only accessible by the south gate, where an entry fee of Y45 is charged (additional fees are collected by the monks for photography within the main temple and the Kumbum). The Kumbum appears to be open only in the mornings – in any case, this is the best time to visit. Chapels can be dark, so bring a flashlight.

The Kumbum The main sight of Gyantse is the immense *chorten* or Kumbum in the grounds of the walled monastery at the north end. It was built in the 14th century by Rapten Kunsang Phapa. Kumbum means 'having 100,000 images', and Gyantse Kumbum may well live up to that description. The *chorten* is a deluxe model and quite innovative in its architecture – there is nothing like it elsewhere in Tibet. It has 70 small interlocking chapels that you visit as you spiral your way to the golden plume at the top. Each chapel contains fine statuary, and murals painted in the 15th century by Newari artists.

In aerial perspective, the *chorten* is shaped like a mandala, the embodiment of the Lamaist universe. Pilgrims circumambulate this giant wedding-cake structure: the inner spiralling circuit of the *chorten* is a meditational aid, with the top canopied section representing the highest plane of wisdom. How far you can ascend depends on how adept you are at convincing the caretaker monks to allow you to proceed. The best strategy is to try to follow pilgrims, since entrances to upper regions are hidden behind statues and in dark alcoves (some may be locked). Right near the top you come out below the large all-seeing eyes of Buddha, painted on the upper walls. The chapels here are larger and contain intricate tantric murals and mandalas. Although it may appear you cannot go higher, in fact there are ladders leading above the all-seeing eyes through a trapdoor to an open wooden turret, under the top umbrella-like structure. From here there are panoramic views of Gyantse.

Palkor Choide Lamasery This monastery is believed to have been constructed in 1418–25 by Rapten Kunsang Phapa. Though in the past it served the Sakya and Geluk orders, it is presently looked after by Gelukpa monks. The monastery has miraculously survived with some original statuary intact. More interesting than the ground-floor assembly hall are the chapels on the second floor. On the third or uppermost floor is a shrine to Sakyamuni Buddha, with huge tantric wheel murals of Sakya deities.

Hero monument Facing the central roundabout is a huge three-sided obelisk, with text or characters on each side in Chinese, Tibetan and English. The English side reads: 'Gyangtse Mount Dzong Monument to Heroes'. The monument is set in a large park and was constructed in the late 1990s. The Chinese-style monolith is made of concrete and finished in marble: it sits on a dais similar to one at the Temple of Heaven in Beijing, with Chinese imperial lions – not Tibetan snow lions – standing guard.

Around the base of the obelisk are bas-reliefs which are falling apart, but fascinating. The front section shows the battle of 1904 with Tibetans throwing down rocks, British troops (easily identified by pith helmets and guns) and what appear to be characters with Chinese dress and swords (not historically correct, as there were no Chinese soldiers or advisers at Gyantse in 1904). A side panel shows the British with heavy machinery, and the back panel shows PLA troops waving Chinese flags and people holding portraits of Mao Zedong.

The fort This brooding 500-year-old colossus crowns a hilltop at the southern end of Gyantse. The fort's foundations are of 14th-century vintage, while the thick walls were probably constructed later.

There are two ways to reach the *dzong*: by car or on foot. Hired vehicles can drive up the back of the *dzong* by a switchback road to a parking lot. On foot, access to the *dzong* is by a set of steps at the southeast side, proceeding through the *dzong*'s huge doors to the ticket office. If on foot, consider exiting the *dzong* by walking down the switchback motor road at the back. This will land you in the old town, close to the monastery (see map, page 208). The *dzong* is in theory open 08.00–20.00 in summer and 10.00–18.00 in winter and spring; the entry fee is Y30.

View from the top You can climb right to the top battlements, which offer a superb view of Gyantse town and make a great photo perch. Within the *dzong*, there's actually little to see. Various buildings and battlements were blown to smithereens by Nepalese invaders, then British invaders, and again by the favourite cohorts of Mao Zedong (the Red Guards), leaving a lot of rubble lying around. Even so, it is one of the best-preserved forts in Tibet. A restored section includes a chapel with some dark murals and newish Buddhist statuary.

Toiling on upwards, you come to a viewable room labelled 'Dungeon', which contains a tableau with life-sized figures, one a Tibetan aristocrat (as judge) and four others involved in flogging a prisoner. This is meant to show the harsher side of the feudal serf system in old Tibet. Other descriptions of these nasty feudal times include binding a prisoner in cowhide and throwing him in the river, and scooping out eyeballs or intestines. The Chinese may have overlooked the fact that similar penalties (if not worse) were meted out in imperial China during this era.

A set of Chinese-built concrete steps leads straight up from here to the top of the fort. Mounting these steps can be strenuous – a bit like Stairmaster at altitude. The top turret is about 4m^2 in size and offers breathtaking views (in all senses of the word – you are actually over 200m higher than the town). This eyrie makes an excellent vantage point for orientation and photography.

Pala Manor (⊕ *10.00–18.30 daily; admission Y30*) Over a bridge, on the west side of Nyang River, is a junction with several turn-offs. To the west you can drive or walk 2.5km to Pala Manor, which is an old noble's house in the middle of a small village. The manor belongs to the 'feudal' days when an aristocrat ruled the village and surrounding lands. The walled three-storey manor – mostly constructed of wood – features the former tearoom and stables.

Pala fled Tibet in 1959 and lived out his days in exile. A tableau upstairs shows Pala and his cronies (one the abbot of Palkor Choide Monastery) indulging in the game of mah-jong, drinking tea and taking the occasional shot of whisky. This is meant to show decadence but in today's China, half the population is addicted to mah-jong. You are shepherded around and shown three or four rooms on the uppermost floor. One of these reveals Pala's personal larder – stocks of Kraft cheese, Britannia biscuits and Diamond Jubilee confectionery. Next is a lounge room of sorts, with an ancient gramophone and snow leopard or monkey-fur covers on the cushions. A meditation room features stained glass imported from India.

Downstairs is a room that looks like a shop, with glass cases showing imported wines and goods from France, the USA, the UK, Australia and India. There's a wardrobe crammed with boots, ceremonial wear and fur hats, while another case shows roller skates, football boots and a football (very progressive for Tibet – football, introduced by the British, was banned by the monastic authorities in the 1940s). On the wall is a picture of Pala in the late 1940s and another picture taken in 1956 in India – also in the line-up is the young Dalai Lama, Ling Rinpoche (his tutor) and Ngawang Jigme (who was later to betray the Tibetans).

The extensively restored manor is a showpiece on how the people of Gyantse were exploited by Tibetan nobles – that's before all the major buildings of Gyantse were blown up by the Chinese. To drive this point home, the captions all tell the same narrative: life is far better under Chinese rule. One caption describes a carpet maker who used to live in a 10m² hovel with dirt floors at Pala Manor, but after Chinese liberation was able to shift to a 400m², two-storey home with three cows, a horse, 23 sheep and a colour television.

Tsang Traditional Folk House (*Admission Y30*) Across the road from Pala Manor is a private folk museum with mock-ups of a traditional kitchen, *chang* distillery and mustard-seed oil press. You can taste some home-brewed *chang* while you examine yak-skin bags used for transporting salt.

SIDE TRIPS FROM GYANTSE A turn-off on the west side of Gyantse leads directly south to **Nenying Gompa**, about 20km from Gyantse. This is an active monastery set in a small village. The monastery was nearly destroyed by the invading British in 1903, and later rebuilt, only to be destroyed again during the Cultural Revolution (and then rebuilt). The road here leads southward all the way to Yadong, at the border of Sikkim. There's a military checkpoint at Gala. After that, there are views of Mount Chomolhari from the road. Further south, with the opening of the Tibet–Sikkim border to trade in 2006, there is a border crossing but only for the Chinese it seems.

HEADING NORTHWEST FROM GYANTSE It's a fast, flat run from Gyantse to Shigatse – the ground can be covered in a matter of several hours. There are two monastery stops you can make. The first is at **Drongtse Monastery**, a small place famed for its slate bas-relief carvings. Drongtse is about 9km from the junction in Gyantse. A second possibility is **Shalu Gompa**, which is reached by a turn-off 18km short of Shigatse. The *gompa* is 4km off the main route (you can also visit Shalu on a day trip from Shigatse – see pages 224–5).

SHIGATSE (*Zhigatse, Xigaze, Rigaze, Sangdrutse, Samdrutse, Samzhubze; 3,900m; capital of Shigatse Prefecture*)

Shigatse, the second-largest town in Tibet, has a population of around 60,000. In 2014, Shigatse city was upgraded to a prefecture-level city by the central government, and the county-level city name of Shigatse changed to 'Sangdrutse', 'Samdrutse' or this

SHIGATSE

N

Bradt

0 ___ 300m
0 ___ 300yds

For listings, see pages 217–18

Where to stay

1 Ganggyen Shigatse
2 Holyland
3 Hotel Manasarovar
4 Shigatse
5 Tashi Choetar
6 Tenzin
7 Tsampa
8 Sakya Lundup
9 Shandong

Off map

Gesar
Young House

Where to eat and drink

10 Songtsen Tibetan Restaurant
11 Sumptuous Tibetan Restaurant
12 Third Eye
13 Tibetan Family
14 Wordo Kitchen and museum

Airport, Lhasa

QINGDAO ROAD

Telecom

Wutse

Agricultural
Hospital of
Tibetan Medicine
Shigatse People's
Hospital

Bowling alley

Department
store

Transport Company:
(buses to Gyantse & Lhasa)

Ying Yue

Bank of China

CITS Shigatse

SHANGHAI ROAD

Post

Gesar Hotel, Young House Hotel,
Shalu Gompa, railway station (7km), Gyantse

Transportation

SHANDONG ROAD

ZHUFENG ROAD

Xinhua
bookstore
(2nd floor)

Handicraft
stores

Market
(hardware/
clothing)

Carpets

Dry goods
market

Photo
shops

Tibetan
Quarter

Dzong Museum
(under construction)

Free market
(souvenirs/meat)

Old
Quarter

Hiking trail

Supermarket

TV station

Yarlong Tibetan

Post office/Telecom

China Telecom
Internet Bar

PSB

Tashi

Pedestrian

Bank of
China

Red Cross
office

Ganggyen
Carpet Factory

Pilgrim circuit

Tashilhunpo
Monastery

Lhatse,
Sakya

PLAZA

Qomolangma
Friendship

Park

New
Panchen
Palace

215

tongue-twister: 'Samzhubze'. But in practice, nobody is calling the place Sangdrutse – travel agents and others stick to Shigatse city, located in Sangdrutse district.

Shigatse is dominated by the massive monastery of Tashilhunpo, which dates from the mid-15th century. Shigatse was the power base of the King of Tsang in the 16th century; he was defeated in battle in 1642 by the Mongol leader, Gushri Khan. In 1652, the Fifth Dalai Lama bestowed the title of Panchen Lama on the abbot of Tashilhunpo Monastery. From that time on, the authority of the Panchen Lama outweighed that of the Lhasa-appointed district governor, who occupied the defeated king's castle (the present-day ruined *dzong*) in town.

Apart from Tashilhunpo Monastery and a small Tibetan quarter, Shigatse is heavily Chinese in character, by which is meant an ugly concrete sprawl. There's a weird wind blowing through Shigatse. It's the wind from Beijing, the dusty wind of the Gobi. Look at a Chinese map of Shigatse and you can get some idea of what has transpired. A Chinese map I picked up barely mentions any Tibetan features. Apart from the usual 'No 1 Bus Team' and 'No 2 Guesthouse' is this curious entry, 'Building for Overseas Tibetans'. Could this be the fabled shop where Tibetans from Nepal come to buy their souvenirs?

Some glaring omissions on the map are the large army bases that ring the town. Shigatse is something of a glorified army base, with huge barracks punctuating the landscape. The arrival of the PLA en masse was not auspicious. In 1960, the PLA surrounded Tashilhunpo Monastery (which had hitherto escaped reforms) and seized all 4,000 monks within. Some were later executed, some committed suicide, and large numbers were taken to labour camps. Only 200 monks remained at the Tashilhunpo.

Because of the status of the Panchen Lama and Chinese attempts to manipulate the High Lama, Tashilhunpo Monastery was largely spared Red Guard destruction. By the 1980s, the number of monks in residence crept back up to around 800. In 1995, another major showdown took place at Tashilhunpo Monastery between the monks and Chinese authorities. The dispute erupted over the unfortunate Chinese choice of 11th Panchen Lama, resulting in tremendous upheaval. Many monks were imprisoned or ousted, to be replaced by pro-Chinese monks or those more timid. The head abbot was later sentenced to six years in jail for his part in the proceedings.

GETTING THERE Most travellers will cover the ground from Lhasa to Shigatse by rented vehicle. For locals, there are frequent buses and minibuses that ply the route, with departures from the southeast side of Shigatse. **Taxi** commuting from Lhasa is also possible. Shigatse Peace Airport, located 45km east of town, hosts direct **flights** from Chengdu several times a week. Another possibility is taking the train from Lhasa.

GETTING AROUND To get around Shigatse, you can **walk** to most places. It may also be possible to rent a **bicycle**. Prowling the streets are **bicycle trishaws**, **motorised trishaws** and regular **Volkswagen taxis** – negotiate before setting out. You can also flag down a **walking-tractor** for a ride across town – just jump on the back and pay when you arrive.

Permits Shigatse PSB is open 09.00–13.00 and 16.00–19.00: this is where your guide must go to secure ATPs for all destinations on the way to Nepal, including Everest base camp.

 WHERE TO STAY *Map, page 215*
There's a lot of accommodation in Shigatse, but not much in the budget range. Some hotels are for Chinese guests only. Not described here but possible for lodging are the Qomolangma Friendship Hotel (budget), Wutse Hotel, Shigatse Post Hotel

and Shigatse Telecom Hotel (the last three mid-range). Prices appearing on hotel reception boards are often inflated: some travellers have been able to negotiate reductions of up to 50% off posted rates.

🏠 **Shigatse Hotel** (125 rooms) Shanghai Middle Rd, southeast side of town; 📞0892 882 2525. Group tour hotel. Supposed to be the top-rated hotel in town, but has an oddly derelict atmosphere, with staff that give you glazed-eyeball stares & go back to looking at their cell phones. Facilities include an exchange counter, small business centre, gift shop, bar & several restaurants. **$$$**

🏠 **Holyland Hotel** (90 rooms) 5 Shandong Rd; 📞0892 882 2922. Fancier hotel with lifts. Seems to be mainly Chinese clientele. **$$$**

🏠 **Tashi Choetar** Good central location; 📞0892 883 0111. Comfortable place with Tibetan décor & Wi-Fi. Rooms go for Y350–450. **$$**

🏠 **Gesar Hotel** Located on Longjiang Middle Rd, out of town to the southeast of Shigatse; 📞0892 880 0888. Standard rooms cost around Y300–350, depending on the season. Each room is decorated with a *tanka* of the legendary Gesar of Ling. Target clientele is Chinese tourists, which means you lose in the b/fast buffet sweepstakes. **$$**

🏠 **Hotel Manasarovar** (80+ rooms) 20 Qingdao East Rd; 📞0892 883 9999; e mnsrvr@ public.ls.xz.cn. Run by the Yak Hotel in Lhasa, this hotel is a good mid-range choice for travellers. The hotel has an architectural presence: a grand lobby & a 1st-floor coffee lounge with a pleasant design. There are several restaurants within the hotel. **$$**

🏠 **Tsampa Hotel** Qingdao Rd; 📞0892 966 7888. Modern rooms & bathrooms with Tibetan décor. There is a good Tibetan restaurant on the premises. **$$**

🏠 **Shandong Hotel** (110 rooms) 5 Shandong Rd; 📞0892 882 6138. Ugly white-tiled building

with green windows. Towering 9 storeys, this hotel laid claim to being the tallest in town – but has since been eclipsed by the cheeky Agricultural Bank, a block north. The hotel boasts in-house movies; some rooms have oxygen machines. A number of restaurants lurk within the hotel. The lobby bookstore selection is good. **$$**

🏠 **Ganggyen Shigatse Hotel** (60 rooms) Located close to the gates of Tashilhunpo Monastery; 📞0892 882 0777. Also known as Ganggyen Orchard Hotel, this large Chinese-run concrete block is functional but boring & overpriced. Because of its large number of rooms, proximity to the monastery, & easy drive-in parking access, this hotel is popular with drivers & guides, but that's a matter of convenience for them. You can do much better. **$$**

🏠 **Tenzin Hotel** (30 rooms & suites) Overlooking the market; 📞0892 882 2018. The best choice for a lower-priced hotel in Shigatse, run by a friendly Tibetan family. This place has lots of character. It's several storeys high, with rooftop views & a Tibetan teahouse. Ground-floor hot showers are powered by rooftop solar panels (attempt a shower in the afternoon, not the morning). The shared bathrooms located on each floor are very clean. Some rooms have TV. **$$**

🏠 **Sakya Lundup Palace Hotel** 📞0892 853 0558. Located near the entrance to the New Panchen Palace, this place is run by Sakya Monastery. Rooms are spacious, & there's a sunny atrium bar & restaurant. **$$**

🏠 **Young House Hotel** 262 Shanghai Nanlu; 📞0892 882 7786. A budget option, with rooms for Y120 to Y200. Rooms are small, however. **$**

✖ WHERE TO EAT AND DRINK *Map, page 215*

One positive thing the Chinese brought to Shigatse is stir-fried food. If you are a vegetarian, or simply fancy a vegetable top-up, a good tactic is to shop for fresh vegetables at a small market and take these to the restaurant, where, for a fee, they will cook it all up.

✖ **Tibetan Family Restaurant** You could use some hearty food after doing a circuit of Tashilhunpo Gompa, right? Well, this place could be just the ticket. It is located in the old Tibetan quarter, right near the end of the *kora*.

With its outdoor eating, this is the perfect people-watcher location, as you can see all the pilgrims exiting the *kora*. Serves excellent simple food – from vegetable dishes to yak-meat dishes. **$$**

✗ **Songtsen Tibetan Restaurant** 883 2469. Located along the market street leading to Tashilhunpo Monastery, this place offers Nepali sets, yak sizzlers, yak *momos*, tandoori & *lassis*. Because of its popularity with group tours, it can take a long time to get served here if you hit peak hour in the evening. The same is true of Tashi Restaurant nearby. $$

✗ **Third Eye Restaurant** Located next door to Ganggyen Shigatse Hotel, this place appeals to both Tibetans & tourists, with its great Indian curries & tasty *thukpa* soups. $$

✗ **Sumptuous Tibetan Restaurant** Also located next door to the Ganggyen Shigatse Hotel & run by the same folks as Tibetan Family Restaurant, it has a pleasant back terrace. $$

✗ **Wordo Kitchen** Located to the southeast side of town, this place offers great Tibetan style & food. There's also a private museum upstairs to roam around (page 220). $$

SHOPPING AND SUPPLIES Shigatse is one of the best places in Tibet to replenish your stocks or add to them. It is second only to Lhasa. For trip supplies, check out the department stores first, as these carry canned and packaged goods. Shopping for Tibetan artefacts is best in the Tenzin Hotel area – at the free market, and further east for carpets and handcrafted items. There are also several handicraft shops in town, and a gift shop at Shigatse Hotel. Chocolate and biscuits can be purchased at several well-stocked supermarkets on Shandong Road, in the vicinity of the Holyland Hotel. Shigatse is so big it even has its own bowling alley (the only other place like this in Tibet is in Lhasa).

OTHER PRACTICALITIES Shigatse Hotel and Shandong Hotel have gift shops with a good supply of maps and books. The Xinhua bookstore up the street is fairly useless, though you might stray across a map or poster here.

Banking The Bank of China is near Shigatse Hotel – this is the main branch where you can change travellers' cheques. Smaller branch offices of the BOC downtown may only deal in cash. Some ATMs around town dispense cash to foreign cards: a few are open 24 hours.

Medical There are two hospitals in town, and you would do well to steer clear of both of them.

Email and internet Hotels should offer Wi-Fi access and a business centre with their own computer set-up. China Telecom Internet Bar is a large cybercafé run by China Post – it is located next door to the main post office and is supposed to be open 24 hours. Further south along the same street is a cybercafé. Several smaller places are found opposite the Xinhua bookstore and vicinity.

WHAT TO SEE AND DO

Pilgrim circuit Just as interesting as Tashilhunpo Monastery (pages 220–1) is the cross section of pilgrims who come from far and wide to pay homage. Pilgrims follow a circuit that starts at the gates and circles clockwise around the monastery. Off to the northwest side of the circuit is a sky burial site. Instead of completely looping around Tashilhunpo, most pilgrims continue on a path eastward that finishes at the market in Shigatse's old quarter. There are lots of prayer flags and *mani* stones that mark the route – just follow the pilgrims, and keep an eye out for dogs. The entire circuit takes about 1½ hours. This hike is good orientation for surveying Shigatse from an aerial-type perspective. A good touring plan would be to spend the morning at Tashilhunpo Monastery, visit the carpet factory and new Panchen Palace in this vicinity, and then hike the *kora* to the *dzong* at the east side of Shigatse in the afternoon.

It was close to midnight and Jane (not her real name) was cocooned in her sleeping bag. A loud banging on the door shattered her dreams. Her midnight visitors were six men from the Shigatse constabulary – they burst in, shouting: 'We know who you are!' and 'Where is your Swiss friend?'

Jane could not determine what she had done to incur their wrath, but she was quite shaken by the experience. The men demanded her passport and papers – which she handed over – and interrogated her for several hours. Meanwhile, soundly snoring away on the other side of town, in a deluxe hotel, were the real targets of the raid: Andy (from the USA) and Marie (from Switzerland). After staying in a string of spartan hotels, they'd decided to splurge and clean up.

Shigatse police had been looking in the wrong place. They should have been looking for an American male, not a female. Andy's crime was that he had slipped through and made it to Kailash. This was shortly after 11 September 2001, and everything in west Tibet had closed down due to massive military movements in the west by Chinese troops racing to seal off the Afghan corridor and crack down on the Muslim population in Xinjiang. Andy and Marie, determined to see the mountain of their dreams, hitched rides, hid under blankets in the back of trucks and made it through to Ali after an epic trip on dusty back roads, dodging police and walking around checkpoints at night.

In Ali, they were arrested, fined, and told if they wanted to go to Kailash, it was possible, but only on a high-paying chaperoned 4x4 tour. The tour would be one-way Ali to Kailash, and then on to the Nepal border, where they would have to leave Tibet. The problem was, Andy and Marie both had air tickets from Lhasa to Chengdu, and luggage in Lhasa, with precious film in it. However, seeing no way out of the situation, they paid up for the exorbitant 4x4 deal, got to Kailash and walked the *kora* of their dreams.

But a funny thing happened on the way to the Nepal border: at 04.00, Andy and Marie slipped out of the hotel in Nyalam, and started hitching towards Lhasa. They got as far as Shigatse that day, and took an expensive hotel room. The furious chaperones phoned Shigatse police, but somewhere along the line the genders got mixed up, and Shigatse police thought they were looking for an American female in a low-end guesthouse. Andy and Marie made it back to Lhasa, where they were briefly interrogated and then promptly put on a flight to Chengdu.

Old quarter, free market and *dzong* The Tibetan quarter, near the *dzong*, is quite lively, with a skein of alleys to wander around. There's an extensive free market selling all kinds of souvenirs, such as Tibetan boots, stirrups, hats, bolts of cloth and dried legs of lamb. The target audience is Tibetans (legs of lamb) and tourists (souvenirs). Nearby are several Tibetan teahouses and *chang*-drinking hang-outs.

Photographs from the 1930s show Shigatse Dzong looking like a mini-Potala, with the same classic lines. The fort continued to function as the offices of the *dzongpon* (district governor) until 1950. It was dynamited to rubble during the Cultural Revolution, and remained in ruins for many years. And then, miraculously, from 2005 to 2007, the structure was completely rebuilt in concrete, but otherwise faithful to the original. There are plans to open the *dzong* as a museum of Tibetan culture. All in the interests of generating revenue from tourism, it seems. You can climb up (or drive up) and clamber around the area for good views overlooking the old quarter rooftops.

Wordo Private Museum Located to the southeast side of town in Wordo Kitchen restaurant, this private museum is owned by Kelsang, a former monk at Tashilhunpo, who will guide you around. The fascinating exhibits include Tibetan coins cut in half to provide change, beauty implements used by nomad women, and an old English pressure cooker portered in from Calcutta. The prize exhibit has to be iron chain-links from the great 15th-century bridge-builder Tangtong Gyalpo. Digesting all this, you can get tucked into braised yak ribs or curried potatoes in the restaurant downstairs at Wordo Kitchen.

Carpet factory A short walk from the front gate of Tashilhunpo Monastery is Ganggyen Carpet Factory, which first started operations in 1987 as a project initiated by the Tenth Panchen Lama. To get the project off the ground, he invited the same Tibetan businessman who started up the highly successful Tibetan carpet-weaving venture in Kathmandu to get involved. The factory is part-owned by Tashilhunpo Monastery, and a slice of the profits is donated each year to the monastery. Ganggyen Carpet Factory employs several hundred Tibetans, most of them women. If work is in progress, you can drop in and walk around, and see hand-looming at work. Women weavers often sing as they work – most of the weaving is done from memory, which is quite a feat considering the intricate designs. In addition to carpets, the factory sells wool jackets, sweaters, belts, scarves, bags and blankets. Tibetan horsemen use carpeting as a saddle base: these horse carpets are made here. For carpet purchases, shipping can be arranged right at the factory.

New Panchen Palace South of Tashilhunpo Monastery is a compound with a high wall where the Panchen Lama supposedly stays when in Shigatse. On the rare occasions that he actually is in Shigatse, the palace will therefore be closed to the public. The compound hosts Tibetan-style palatial buildings enclosing a garden courtyard. The original palace at this location dates to the 19th century. In 1955, the Tenth Panchen Lama reconstructed and expanded the palace. The main three-storey structure is larger than the Dalai Lama's summer palace in Lhasa. As you enter the main building, there are magnificent contemporary murals depicting scenes of the King of Shambhala riding forth to do battle with the forces of evil. The kingdom of Shambhala is depicted in a circular mandalic shape, surrounded by snow-capped peaks. Continuing on into the Panchen Palace, rooms are bare of furniture, but you will see chandeliers and stained glass imported from India. You may be shown a room on the second floor with some personal effects of the Tenth Panchen Lama – his writing desk and so on. The most startling exhibit is his stuffed dog, which looks like a large Alsatian. The dog apparently survived its owner by ten years, which raises the question: if the Panchen Lama was reincarnated, did the dog recognise its former owner as the 11th Panchen Lama, or reject him as a fake? (Speaking, in this case, of the enforced Chinese choice of 11th Panchen Lama.)

Tashilhunpo Monastery The Tashilhunpo is the seat of the Panchen Lama, a topic that raises blood pressures on all sides. The monastery is highly sensitive because of the controversy surrounding the 11th Panchen Lama. Pictures of the Chinese-appointed 11th Panchen Lama abound as icons at the monastery, but that's about all you'll see of him – he is sequestered in Beijing, supposedly for reasons of education. However, in 2016, he was conscripted to conduct a Kalachakra Empowerment in Shigatse – a ritual that is more often associated with the Dalai Lama. Obviously, Beijing is trying to boost the profile of China's chosen Panchen Lama. The Dalai Lama's choice of Panchen Lama has been missing in action since 1995, along with his entire family.

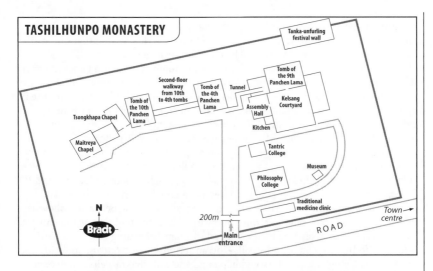

TASHILHUNPO MONASTERY

There are monk-stooges hanging about: take care what you do or say here. Tashilhunpo is immense, a monastic city with temples, assembly halls, living quarters and administrative offices. At its height, it housed up to 5,000 monks. Today, the figure is probably closer to 700.

Tashilhunpo Plaza Near the gates of the monastery is a plaza where you can find caricatures of yourself. There are life-sized statues of foreigners – one with a camcorder, another on a mountain bike, and a backpacker with a diary of some sort. Pilgrims and locals pose with these statues for pictures, or else attempt to get on to the mountain bike handlebars, or fondle the woman with the camcorder. These frozen foreigners are very popular.

Access The grounds of Tashilhunpo Monastery are only fully accessible in the morning. In theory, the monastery is open 09.00–noon and 15.30–18.00. However, in practice, fewer chapels seem to be open in the afternoon. Although there are a number of gates (including one at the northeast wall), only one is sanctioned for entry and exit – you pay a foreigner's entry fee of Y55. Certain halls charge Y150 for photographs or Y1,800 for video. Pilgrims follow an internal temple circuit which is described here, and also an external circuit around the monastery walls.

Main structures As you look northward from the front gates of Tashilhunpo Monastery (see plan, above), you will see several buildings that stand out as taller than the rest. You can roughly identify these off the plan. At the back, right wall is an enormous *tanka*-unfurling the height of a nine-storey building. This is where massive *tankas* of Buddha are unfurled during summer festivities. To the left of the grounds, the largest building is the Maitreya Chapel: it is here that pilgrims begin their tour of the monastery.

The **Maitreya Chapel** houses a 26m-high statue of Maitreya, the Buddha of the Future (Champa in Tibetan), seated on a lotus throne with the right hand in a symbolic teaching pose (which looks like an 'OK' gesture, in which forefinger and thumb are pressed together in a circle). The statue is gold plated: the structure is made of tons of copper and brass, moulded on a wooden frame. Tibetans believe that Champa will return to preside over the world when all human beings have earned deliverance from

6

suffering. Pilgrims crowd in to make offerings and murmur mantras as they make an inner circuit around the statue itself. The fortress-style building that houses the Maitreya was built from 1914 to 1918 by the Ninth Panchen Lama.

The newest building at the Tashilhunpo is the **Tomb of the Tenth Panchen Lama**. It was completed in 1993 and is similar in design to that of the Ninth Panchen Lama. The Chinese government is reported to have donated 500kg of gold for use in constructing the Tenth Panchen Lama's tomb, which may explain the Chinese-style roof. A gilded, jewel-encrusted stupa encloses the embalmed body of the Tenth Panchen Lama, who died in 1989. A life-sized statue of the Panchen Lama is shown at the front of the tomb. Surrounding the stupa are intricate murals. Above the tomb are other sections. You can reach the top floor by a staircase to the left (west side) of the building. Up a few flights of stairs, you reach a room with a gigantic 3D Kalachakra mandalic sculpture and impressive mandala murals on the walls.

Finding the following corridor is a bit tricky: your best bet is to follow the pilgrims. On the second floor, at the southwest side of the building, is the entry to a dim corridor-walkway lined with small, dark chapels heading east. This corridor is lined with Buddhas large and small, Tibetan scriptures, and *tankas*, and with side chapels displaying statues of Tsongkhapa and the Kalachakra deity. The corridor leads from the Tomb of the Tenth to the **Tomb of the Fourth Panchen Lama**. This tall,

THE RENEGADE LAMA

The Panchen Lama, Tibet's second-highest incarnate, traditionally has a seat at Tashilhunpo Monastery in Shigatse. The Panchen Lama (literally 'Precious Scholar') was also known as the Tashi Lama. There is considerable confusion over the number of Panchen Lamas in the lineage. This is because, in the 16th century, the Fifth Dalai Lama declared Losang Chokyi Gyeltsen (then the abbot of Tashilhunpo Monastery) to be the fourth reincarnate in a line that retroactively dated to the 14th century. He also declared him to be a manifestation of the Buddha Amitabha. From this time on, the elder of either the Panchen Lama or the Dalai Lama served as tutor for the other.

Tibetans have never recognised the Panchen Lama's authority to rule over Tibet: his jurisdiction was always restricted to the Shigatse area. However, the Chinese have seen fit to promote rivalry between the Panchen Lamas and the Dalai Lamas.

The Tenth Panchen Lama was born in 1938 in the Koko Nor region (Amdo). He fell into communist hands and was certified in Xining in 1949; his qualifications as an incarnate were accepted under duress by Lhasa. He was then brought to Shigatse in 1952 by the PLA as the Chinese were determined to belittle the Dalai Lama's authority. After the Dalai Lama fled Tibet in 1959, the Tenth Panchen Lama developed, by early accounts, into a mouthpiece for the Chinese. However, after the PLA raided Tashilhunpo Monastery in 1960 and disbanded the monks, the Panchen Lama changed tack and started to openly support the Dalai Lama. In 1961, when asked to move to the Potala to replace the Dalai Lama, the Panchen Lama flatly refused to do so, and dropped out of public view. In May 1962, he delivered a blistering 70,000-character report on conditions in Tibet to Mao Zedong, and demanded that mass arrests be halted and religious freedom restored. This document was kept secret for three decades until an anonymous source turned it over to Tibet Information Network (TIN) in London. TIN had it translated and issued in book form in London in 1998 under the title *A Poisoned Arrow*, which is what Mao Zedong called the report.

russet gold-roofed building houses a large silver stupa, enclosing the embalmed body of Losang Chokyi Gyeltsen, the Fourth Panchen Lama.

Moving along, through a tunnel, you come to the gold-roofed **Tomb of the Ninth Panchen Lama**. It was completed in 1988 and was consecrated by the Tenth Panchen Lama only a week before his own death. During the Cultural Revolution, the bodies of the Fifth through to the Ninth Panchen Lamas were hidden and their identities were confused, so eventually all the remains were placed in a single tomb.

This tomb is attached to an elaborate complex that is the oldest part of Tashilhunpo Monastery, **Kelsang Courtyard**. The courtyard is enclosed by multistorey galleries. Strolling around the different galleries gives you an idea of what the place looked like in centuries past. On the east side of the complex is a printing studio where scriptures are made from woodblocks. To the west side at the mid-levels is a large assembly hall where monks congregate for sutra chanting. Leading off this is a medieval kitchen with mammoth copper cauldrons, giant implements, and fires burning away on a scale that would have had *Macbeth's* witches cackling. This is where food for all the monks is prepared. Debating between monks may take place in Kelsang Courtyard.

Heading back southward, you come to the **Tantric College** where, if your timing is right, prayer ceremonies may be in progress in the assembly hall. In the courtyard

In 1964, the Panchen Lama was asked to denounce the Dalai Lama at the height of the Monlam prayer festival in Lhasa. A crowd of 40,000 gathered outside the Jokhang, and the Panchen Lama delivered a stunning speech of solidarity with the Dalai Lama, and in favour of Tibetan independence. He was promptly placed under house arrest, denounced as a reactionary and brought to trial. After being beaten to induce confessions, the Panchen Lama disappeared, along with his parents and entourage.

The Panchen Lama was taken to Beijing and sentenced to ten years in prison in 1967, much of it spent in solitary confinement. From time to time he was taken out for 'struggle sessions' in a Beijing sports stadium, where he was humiliated in front of thousands of people. In 1978, he was set free again, supposedly a fully reformed man. He lived in Beijing, where he held an important government post. He was married to a Chinese woman and had a daughter: while he was alive, his wife pretended to be his personal secretary to preserve the Panchen Lama's spiritual standing among Tibetans, since none of the Panchen Lama lineage holders had married.

Eventually the Tenth Panchen Lama returned to Lhasa and Shigatse for extended visits, during which he again became increasingly critical of Chinese policy in Tibet. In 1989, he was found dead of a heart attack in Shigatse, at the age of 50. Although he was seriously overweight and a prime candidate for a heart attack, many Tibetans believe he was either given drugs that induced a heart attack, or he was poisoned. When he died, the Chinese infuriated his wife by trying to bar her from memorial ceremonies at Tashilhunpo Monastery. She obstinately continued to live in Panchen Lama's Palace in Beihai Park, Beijing, in a building that is destined for the Chinese-sanctioned incarnate, the 11th Panchen. The 11th Panchen Lama is one of the most hotly disputed reincarnates in the history of Tibet. To read more about him, refer to the *Tibetan Buddhism* section in *Chapter 1*, pages 26–36.

of the **Philosophy College**, monks gather in the mornings to debate the finer points of Buddhist philosophy, vigorously emphasising points with their unique, overarm slapping technique.

Right near the gates is a small monk-run **clinic** that offers Tibetan traditional medicine services. There are over 20 monk-doctors doing diagnosis and dispensing herbal medicines to Tibetan patients.

Side trip to Shalu Gompa To the south of Shigatse (18km away, then an extra 4km off the road) is Shalu Gompa. Shalu is most associated with 14th-century scholar Buton, a prolific translator and writer of sacred texts. During the Cultural Revolution, these precious texts were destroyed. The upper part of the monastery was also destroyed – donations from Chinese patrons account for the present-day green-glazed tiling on the Mongolian-style roof. Parts of the monastery lie derelict, with faded murals, due to lack of funds to renovate. The murals are faded and sooty, making artwork difficult to discern.

There are about 60 monks living here. Shalu's claim to fame is that it is thought to be the place where *lung-gom* runners trained. In the absence of motorised vehicles, the delivery system in ancient Tibet used relays of runners. The monasteries had their own runners – called *lung-gom* (trance-runners). The monks bounding along in a trance were reputed to build up their leg muscles by running on a pile of grain – while meditation masters provided rigorous mental training. During important religious festivals, the monk with the greatest physical and mental abilities would be selected to run to Lhasa – without food, rest or drink. That's a distance of over 200km. If really true, imagine the impact this esoteric training could have on endurance sports at the Olympics. There's no sign of any murals showing the *lung-gom* runners at Shalu, however.

THE *SVAS-TIKA*

At Tashilhunpo and many other monasteries in Tibet you will see what appears to be familiar iconography. Inlaid with turquoise are large emblems called *svas-tikas*. *Svas-tika* is the Sanskrit; the Tibetan word is *yungtrung*. There are two Tibetan designs used – one pointing clockwise (Tibetan Buddhist), the other with an anticlockwise orientation (ancient Bon religion).

No, this has not been taken from the Nazis. Very much the other way around. The Nazis stole this ancient Tibetan symbol for peace and longevity. Then they put it on a white background and tilted it at an angle – and it turned into a symbol of war and destruction. The ancient Buddhist symbol of peace and prosperity (linking of opposites) has been forever tainted by the Third Reich's iconography.

Before the 1930s, the *svas-tika* was used in the West for peaceful applications. It was used as a publishing logo by the Theosophists, and also as a logo in books by Rudyard Kipling. On the Everest expedition of 1924 to Tibet, it was used at the four corners of commemorative stamps for Everest postcards. Probably the most spectacular misunderstanding for the *svas-tika* was in December 1943 when a plane flying the Hump (over the eastern Himalaya from India to China) ran out of fuel. Five American airmen parachuted from the plane into the night – and landed in the vicinity of Tsedang. Seeing what he thought were swastika shapes painted on some houses, the pilot went ballistic: he thought he had somehow stumbled into German-controlled territory. The ancient Indian *svas-tika* symbols are actually painted on Tibetan houses to bring good luck.

Technically, you need a permit to visit Shalu Gompa (obtainable from Shigatse PSB). In practice, if you just take a day trip to Shalu Gompa, the chances are nobody will check for permits.

SHIGATSE TO TINGRI

About 15km west of Shigatse you pass the ruins of **Narthang Monastery**, formerly one of Tibet's three great woodblock printing lamaseries. The other two were at Kumbum (Amdo) and Derge (Kham). Now only Derge Monastery survives as a large-scale printing works for sacred texts. The high crumbling walls of Narthang are visible behind a roadside village: a few monks have returned to the lamasery and several minor buildings have been restored. Further westward, you cross Tso La; shortly after this, at a place between KM5028 and KM5029 marker stones is a turn-off to Sakya, a highly recommended detour of 21km.

LHATSE Further west, you can motor on to **Lhatse** (aka Lhaze or Lhartse), elevation 4,050m. Lhatse could be renamed 'Karaoke-ville'. Everything in Lhatse is strung out along the highway – karaoke bars, eateries, a few truck-stop hotels, a theatre and a fuel station.

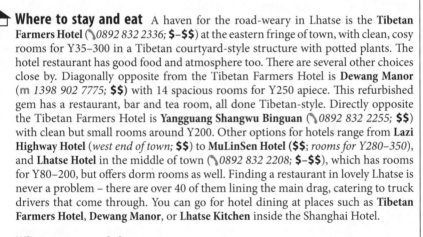 **Where to stay and eat** A haven for the road-weary in Lhatse is the **Tibetan Farmers Hotel** (↘*0892 832 2336; $–$$*) at the eastern fringe of town, with clean, cosy rooms for Y35–300 in a Tibetan courtyard-style structure with potted plants. The hotel restaurant has good food and atmosphere too. There are several other choices close by. Diagonally opposite from the Tibetan Farmers Hotel is **Dewang Manor** (**m** *1398 902 7775; $$*) with 14 spacious rooms for Y250 apiece. This refurbished gem has a restaurant, bar and tea room, all done Tibetan-style. Directly opposite the Tibetan Farmers Hotel is **Yangguang Shangwu Binguan** (↘*0892 832 2255; $$*) with clean but small rooms around Y200. Other options for hotels range from **Lazi Highway Hotel** (*west end of town; $$*) to **MuLinSen Hotel** (**$$**; *rooms for Y280–350*), and **Lhatse Hotel** in the middle of town (↘*0892 832 2208; $–$$*), which has rooms for Y80–200, but offers dorm rooms as well. Finding a restaurant in lovely Lhatse is never a problem – there are over 40 of them lining the main drag, catering to truck drivers that come through. You can go for hotel dining at places such as **Tibetan Farmers Hotel**, **Dewang Manor**, or **Lhatse Kitchen** inside the Shanghai Hotel.

What to see and do There are some hot springs located 11km from Lhatse; they're a bit derelict, with springs channelled into concrete pools, and an entry fee of Y25. At the western edge of Lhatse is a Tibetan *gompa*. The road forks just west of Lhatse, with a branch heading northwest to Kailash, and southwest to Kathmandu. There may be a checkpoint near the junction. After crossing Gyatso La – at 5,250m the highest pass on this route – you reach the Shegar area (pages 229–30).

SAKYA (*Sagya, Sag'ya; 4,000m*) Sakya (Grey Earth) was once the base of the Sakyapa sect that rose to power in the 13th century. The founder of the Sakyapa was Drokmi, who set up a monastery in Sakya in the 11th century. The Sakyapa were strong on magic and sorcery, and permitted their abbots to marry and to drink liquor. This led to hereditary rank (the post alternates between two families), and to a rather unsavoury reputation for worldliness among the monks. Although rank is hereditary, it is believed that seven incarnations of the Buddha of Wisdom (Manjushri) have appeared in the lineage of the Sakyapa.

The rise of the Sakyapa was largely due to 'the Mongol connection'. In the mid-13th century, Mongol warlord Godan Khan invited the leader of the Sakya sect, Sakya Pandita, to educate his people spiritually. Sakya Pandita accepted the task and, under Mongol overlordship, the Sakya school gained great political influence. The Mongol link continued with the succession of Phagpa (nephew of Sakya Pandita) and Kublai Khan. The power of the Sakyapa declined in the late 14th century as the fortunes of the Geluk tradition rose, but Sakya retained its links with Mongolia over the centuries.

In 1959, at the age of 14, Sakya Dagtri Rinpoche was enthroned at Sakya Gompa, becoming the 41st Patriarch (his title is also the Sakya Trizin, or throne-holder). Almost immediately after the event, he and his entourage of teachers and personal staff fled to India. It took Chinese soldiers several months to get to Sakya after the 1959 uprising in Lhasa. The Chinese told the 500 monks at Sakya Gompa that they had supported the Khampa rebels, so the monastery was seized, grain stocks confiscated, and monks and nuns were submitted to *thamzing* ('struggle sessions' – self-criticism and public-criticism sessions where those accused are humiliated and beaten up in front of a crowd of locals).

After getting used to such strange phenomena as trains, cars, buses and aeroplanes, the Sakya Trizin set up a base in exile at Dehra Dun, in Uttar Pradesh, with a Sakya centre and college established in the 1960s. Today there are Sakya centres all over the world, and the throne-holder has toured extensively, teaching in Europe, America and Asia.

Meanwhile, back in Sakya, the bathroom-tiling school of architecture is homing in on the south bank. A huge boulevard with street lighting was constructed at the east side, leading right into the village. Video bars screening noisy Chinese kung fu movies are sprouting up. When the dust settles, this transformation will mean a largely Chinese urban style on the south bank except for the monastery and a cluster of nearby buildings, but the north bank is still Tibetan in character.

Sakya is reached by a side road: it is 21km from the main Lhasa–Kathmandu highway. Locals use pilgrim buses to reach Sakya.

 Where to stay and eat *Map, opposite*

Top of the line for lodging is **Manasarovar Sakya Hotel** (✆ *0892 824 2222*). A standard double goes for Y280 but dorm accommodation may be available for much lower pricing. This place is brought to you by the same folks who run the Yak Hotel in Lhasa and Hotel Manasarovar in Shigatse. The hotel is outstanding (for Sakya, anyway) because it has showers in the rooms – solar-generated hot water should be available in the afternoon and evening. The hotel runs its own restaurant with palatable Indian, Nepali and Western food. Down the street to the east is **Sakya Lowa Family Hotel** (✆ *0892 824 2156;* **$$**) with a cosy teahouse, clean dorms and traditional-style rooms for Y180, but no hot water. At the lower end of the scale, Sakya has some Tibetan truck-stop hotels with – I almost choke on the word – 'beds'. For these, it's a case of BYOB (bring your own sleeping bag). Among these is **Sakya Tibetan Guesthouse ($)**, located close to the *gompa*, with dorm-type beds going for around Y20.

There are hole-in-the-wall eating houses around Sakya: in some places, you can pick out what you want from the kitchen and have it stir-fried. The **monastery teahouse** ($) is a good place to hang out, rubbing shoulders with Tibetan pilgrims, but the menu is limited to soup and *momos*. For more substantial fare, try some Chinese-style restaurants close by on the main street. In this area is **Sakya Farmer's Taste Restaurant** ($), serving Tibetan dishes in a place with Tibetan décor.

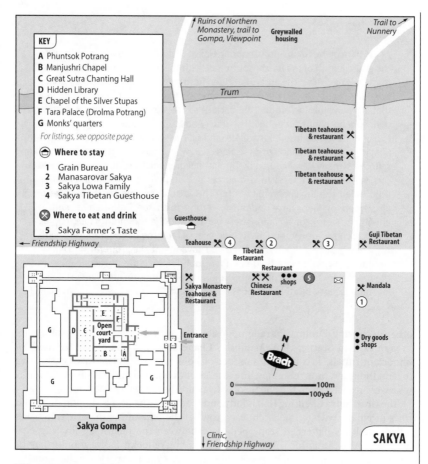

KEY

A Phuntsok Potrang
B Manjushri Chapel
C Great Sutra Chanting Hall
D Hidden Library
E Chapel of the Silver Stupas
F Tara Palace (Drolma Potrang)
G Monks' quarters

For listings, see opposite page

⊖ **Where to stay**

1 Grain Bureau
2 Manasarovar Sakya
3 Sakya Lowa Family
4 Sakya Tibetan Guesthouse

✖ **Where to eat and drink**

5 Sakya Farmer's Taste

Ruins of Northern Monastery, trail to Gompa, Viewpoint
Greywalled housing
Trail to Nunnery

Trum

Tibetan teahouse & restaurant ✖
Tibetan teahouse & restaurant ✖
Tibetan teahouse & restaurant ✖

Guesthouse

← Friendship Highway

Teahouse ✖ ④   ✖ ②   ✖ ③   Guji Tibetan Restaurant ✖
Tibetan Restaurant
Restaurant
✖ ✖   ●●● shops   ⑤   ✉   ✖ Mandala
Sakya Monastery Teahouse & Restaurant   Chinese Restaurant   ①

G   D   C   E   F   Open court-yard   Entrance   ●● Dry goods shops
B   A
G   G

N

Bradt

0 ————————100m
0 ————————100yds

Sakya Gompa

Clinic, ↓ Friendship Highway

SAKYA

What to see and do

Sakya Gompa The immense Mongolian-style outer walls of Sakya Gompa dwarf any other structure in the town. At the corners of the *gompa* walls are corner turrets and watchtowers. The monastery is thought to date to the 13th century, at which time the Sakyapa were powerful enough to employ not only large numbers of Tibetan workers and artisans, but also artisans from India, Nepal and central China to decorate the monastery.

Access is only by the east gate, where an entry fee is charged. You cross a courtyard to gain entry to the inner temple, which surrounds another open courtyard. From this courtyard, try to find a staircase that leads to the upper deck of the monastery, overlooking the central courtyard. You can also walk along the outer parapets for good town views.

Getting into the monastery chapels often requires finding the right monk with the right key. You can tour the main structures here in a clockwise circuit, keyed to the map above.

At the **Phuntsok Potrang** (palace), only an upstairs chapel may be accessible, containing fine murals and statues. Phuntsok Potrang is the former residence of one of the principal lamas of Sakya. The post of leadership in the Sakya sect alternates between two families, one formerly occupying Phuntsok Potrang, the

At the back of the Great Sutra Chanting Hall at Sayka Gompa is a library that runs the entire length of the north–south wall, with shelves of sacred texts reaching from floor to ceiling. The library is hidden from view and access to it may not be possible – to get in, you need to find someone to unlock a small wooden door that allows you to go around the back of all the statues on display. It's pretty dark so a flashlight is needed. The musty atmosphere is positively medieval, evoking the fabled lost library of Alexandria. The library shelving here is about 60m long, 10m high and 1m deep, and filled with thousands of dusty Buddhist scriptures, many hand-copied by Tibetan calligraphers and illuminated in gold or silver ink. Near the northwest corner is a huge manuscript illuminated in gold called the Prajnaparamita Sutra. This is an 8,000-line basic scripture of all schools of Mahayana Buddhism, setting forth the Bodhisattva path to enlightenment in conversations between the Buddha and three of his disciples. The book is so large it requires its own special rack: the pages are 1.75m wide. Apparently Sakya's library survived the ravages of the Cultural Revolution because the books were hidden underground. Above the portico leading to the monastery's central courtyard is another room housing rare Sanskrit palm-leaf manuscripts, but this section is out of bounds.

other occupying Drolma Potrang opposite. The next in line for Phuntsok Palace lives in exile in Seattle, USA. **Manjushri Chapel** is a large chamber once used for important rituals. It contains a number of bookcases, and glass cases enshrining several thousand bronze statues. The statues of Manjushri and Sakyamuni Buddha here were rescued from the rubble of Sakya's northern monasteries.

The **Great Sutra Chanting Hall** is lofty and spacious – the roof is supported by four rows of pillars, with ten pillars in each row. At the base of the massive tree-trunk pillars are lotus-patterned stone pedestals; between the pillars are low carpeted benches with seating for some 400 monks. If you're lucky, Sakya monks may be conducting a sutra-chanting session, in which case you'll experience the acoustics of the hall. The main visual focus of the hall is the row of massive gilded Buddha statuary at the west wall. These statues are surrounded by thousands of artefacts, seals, ceremonial props, ritual vessels and books amassed from all over Tibet. A small doorway leads to a large **hidden library** behind the statues.

Continuing the clockwise circuit, you come to the **Chapel of the Silver Stupas**, which contains 11 silver stupas enclosing the remains of the past throne-holders of the Sakya lineage. Six more stupas (enclosing the remains of important past abbots of Sakya) are found in a small chapel just to the north. In the **Tara Palace** are five stupas of important throne-holders from this family branch. The Tara Palace or **Drolma Potrang** is the former residence of the current Sakya throne-holder, now living in Dehra Dun, India. Only the upstairs chapel is open, displaying superb murals; the altar has images depicting the longevity triad of Amitayus, Vijaya and White Tara.

Hiking at Sakya North On the north side of the river there used to be a monastic complex of 108 chapels. Most were destroyed during the 1960s, but some were converted into houses. Today, the north side is mostly composed of grim, grey-walled Tibetan housing, with brushwood and yak dung lining the ramparts of dwellings, and livestock living in the courtyards. You can hike on the northwest slope up to a small restored *gompa* and viewpoint (you need to find a monk to open the doors here). A precipitous path leads from the monastery along the northeast ridge to **Rinchen Gang Labrang**, an active nunnery rebuilt in 1988, and currently home to about 30 nuns. You can also do the reverse route – go directly from Sakya town up to the nunnery and find the route back to the monastery. Sakya is right off the main road, so it lies in a completely rural area, and there are other directions you can walk into the countryside. Or the countryside may come to you, as herders and traders propel yaks, donkeys or sheep right through Sakya town.

SHEGAR (*Shekar, Shelkar, Xegar, Xin Tingri, New Tingri; 4,350m*) Shegar, set back 7km off the main road, is a small Tibetan settlement with an active monastery at the northern end, at the base of a peak. Right up the rock peak are the imposing ruins of **Shining Crystal Dzong**. The castle was formerly the residence of the governor of Shegar. In 1924, a member of the British Everest expedition marvelled at the fantastic castle, perched on the 5,000m mountaintop, appearing to be fused to the rock. Today barely a single piece stands upright; it was destroyed during the Cultural Revolution.

At around the same time, the extensive **monastery** of Shegar was also destroyed. It once housed 300 Geluk monks, but today there are only a few reconstructed buildings, with a handful of monks in residence. It's worth visiting the monastery building at the base of the mountain, and then hiking up through the ruins towards the peak (watch out for the nettles). There is a path to the summit, but it's difficult to find; take along a local kid as a guide. The path starts about halfway up, to the left

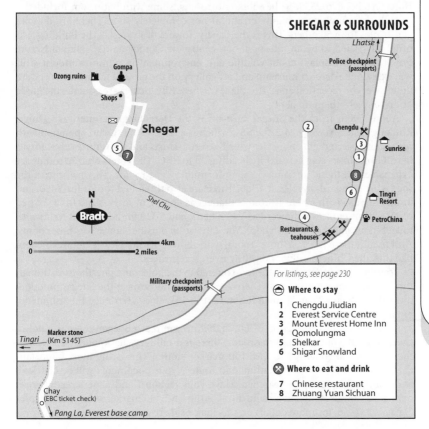

of the ruined fort, and winds around the back of the mountain to the prayer flags at the very top, where, on a clear day, you are rewarded with views of Everest. The old quarter of Shegar is the village clustered closer to the *gompa*. The Chinese section is further southwest, in the vicinity of the post office.

 Where to stay and eat *Map, page 229*
The Shelkar Hotel ($$) is a Chinese concrete compound with a lack of plumbing, overpriced rooms and surly staff. Most travellers skip Shegar itself and stay at the hotels near the main highway and the higher-priced **Qomolungma Hotel** (below). For food in Shegar, there's a Chinese restaurant opposite Shelkar Hotel, and there are several shops with small, low-quality selections of consumer goods.

SHEGAR TO TINGRI (*Major military checkpoint 7km west of Shegar junction*) At the turn-off to Shegar is a busy junction with a handful of hotels and restaurants. Travellers usually opt to stay here and visit Shegar on a day trip. The junction is also the launching point for the ride to Everest base camp (EBC).

There are over a dozen **truck-stop inns** at the junction: the cosiest is **Shigar Snowland Hotel** (aka Kangjong; **$**), with a Tibetan teahouse serving food. Rooms are Y50 each, with no showers. Other truck stops include **Mount Everest Home Inn** (**$**) and **Chengdu Jiudian Hotel** (**$**) – both for around Y40 a room.

Set back from the crossroads are two higher-priced hotels. **Everest Service Centre Hotel** (✆ *0892 826 2833;* **$**) has about 15 rooms, some with bathroom included – though the plumbing is highly erratic, if not completely shot. There are doubles and triples for Y50 a bed. This is the Fawlty Towers of Everest – the building was originally slated to be an interpretation centre for Qomolangma National Nature Preserve, with displays about wildlife and environment in a mini-museum. This will explain the derelict museum and art gallery on the ground floor, and the grand dome over the reception area. This place is where EBC tickets are issued – the guide or driver picks them up here.

About 600m from the Shegar turn-off is the **Qomolungma Hotel** (aka Dingri Zhufeng Hotel; ✆ *0892 826 2775;* **$$**), which is a large Chinese-run operation with restaurant, bar and gift shop. Get your Everest T-shirts and souvenir Everest fossils here. Group tours stay here before heading off to EBC. The hotel's 60-odd rooms are expensive, but there are some cheaper dormitory-type rooms. The majority of the rooms are standard doubles at Y360. There are also three-bed rooms for Y460, and a suite for Y865. There are 12 rooms that act as dorms, of sorts: Y240 for a six-bed room with no toilet or shower (so Y40 a bed), and Y320 for a four-bed room with toilet but no shower (so Y80 a bed). You can use an outside shower for these rooms. And finally, there is a Y50 'hour' room, with shower. It's not clear who uses a room like this, the Chinese military or filthy Everest returnees.

Travellers tend to settle for the food offered in the hotels and guesthouses, though this is pricey for what you get. There are some **restaurants** at the Shegar junction: one called **Zhuang Yuan Sichuan Restaurant** (**$$$**) offers a ten-page English menu, but again it's pricey.

Coming from the direction of Lhasa, before you reach Shegar, there is a **police checkpoint**. Beyond Shegar crossroads, there is a **military checkpoint** 7km west of the junction (at roughly the KM5140 marker stone). This is the most important checkpoint on the Lhasa to Kathmandu route – your documents will be checked, and your luggage may be searched. Have your passport and papers ready. From here, it's 5km west to the Everest turn-off at the KM5145 marker stone. See *Chapter 7*, pages 237–66, for more details on this major side trip.

TINGRI *(Tinggri, Dingri, Dengre, Gangkar, Old Tingri, Lao Tingri, Tingri West; 4,340m)*

Tingri is a Tibetan village arrayed over a hillside. It was once a Tibetan–Nepali trading centre for grain, goods, wool and livestock. This trade largely died out after 1959 but you can still see the odd Nepali trader in Tingri – they occasionally saunter in with a few yaks over Nangpa La pass.

Tingri is essentially one big army base disguised as a village. Tibetan housing hugs the hillside, but at the north end are walled army compounds and telecommunications centre; at the south end are more army compounds. The compounds at the south end are curious – at first sight they appear to be Tibetan buildings. Closer inspection reveals they are Chinese. Could this be a new form of camouflage?

Tingri lies at the edge of a vast plain. There are great views of the Himalayan giants to the south, assuming there's no cloud cover. Everest, or the uppermost part of it, is visible to the far left, but from this distance it doesn't look like a mammoth. However, Cho Oyu, straight ahead, looks stunning. It's worth taking a short hike to the south of Tingri for better views; another viewpoint is from the top of the hill above the village, where there are some old fort ruins. To the west side of Tingri town is a turn-off south where your vehicle can go a short distance to a viewpoint overlooking peaks such as Cho Oyu. There's a checkpoint bar here, but this should not be a problem.

Something to think about as you gaze across the plains: the area was once full of gazelles, blue sheep, antelope and wild asses, who were remarked upon by Everest expedition members in the 1920s and 1930s. This fabulous wildlife sanctuary has completely disappeared – it was decimated by Chinese PLA troops with machine guns, hunting animals for food or for sport. Now all you can see are the odd herds of domesticated sheep, goats or yaks.

🏠 WHERE TO STAY AND EAT *Map, right*

Facilities in Tingri are strung out along the highway. There are half a dozen **Tibetan inns**, including Amdo Guesthouse (**$**), Dingri Sunshine Hotel (**$**), Lao Dengre Hotel (**$**), Everest Guesthouse (**$**), Rong Sha Hotel (**$**) and Hehu Binguan (**$$**). The best of the bunch (Amdo Guesthouse and Lao Dengre Hotel) have cosy Tibetan teahouses with carpeted seating low on

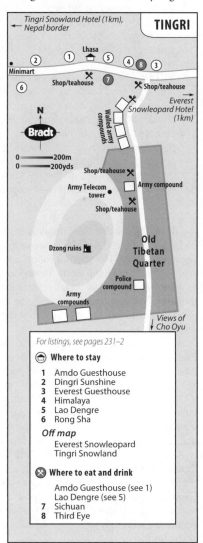

TINGRI

For listings, see pages 231–2

🛏 **Where to stay**

1 Amdo Guesthouse
2 Dingri Sunshine
3 Everest Guesthouse
4 Himalaya
5 Lao Dengre
6 Rong Sha

Off map
    Everest Snowleopard
    Tingri Snowland

🍴 **Where to eat and drink**

    Amdo Guesthouse (see 1)
    Lao Dengre (see 5)
7 Sichuan
8 Third Eye

On 25th April 2015, a mega-earthquake decimated Kathmandu Valley and regions beyond – the area north of Kathmandu and across into Zhangmu and Nyalam in Tibet. Within a few weeks, the massive scale of the disaster became apparent in Nepal: over 9,000 people killed, more than 22,000 injured, and 3.5 million left homeless. Following this were aftershocks, causing more devastation and more deaths in Nepal. It is less clear what happened on the Tibetan side, but it is certain that there was wide-scale destruction around the towns of Nyalam and Zhangmu.

Zhangmu, which used to be the main border crossing from Tibet into Nepal, was closed after the quake. It has reopened to some truck traffic but appears to have assumed a new function as a quasi-military base. Meanwhile, in August 2017, the border crossing at Kyirong, to the west, opened to foreigners.

All this turned Nyalam and Zhangmu, once thriving trading and tourist towns, into forgotten backwaters. However, if you have time on your hands and are looking for a side trip, Nyalam might just be the ticket.

NYALAM There is really only one reason to visit Nyalam: to get closer to Shishapangma south base camp, (although the north base camp can also be approached by another detour on the Kyirong border crossing route). Reaching Nyalam from the main Friendship Highway is about 80km, so a round trip would be a 160km detour. The route from Tingri towards Nyalam goes over a double pass, Tong La, with a north crest at 4,950m and south crest at 5,200m. You may be able to glimpse the 8,000m hulk of elusive Mount Shishapangma from this vicinity.

Nearing Nyalam, at the KM5333 marker stone, is **Milarepa's gompa and cave**. The cave is hidden from view from the main road, which is why you need

the floor. Others like the Himalaya Hotel are more for truck drivers who are not picky about plumbing. You can order *momos* (meat dumplings) and potatoes at the guesthouses. The spartan rooms are around Y25–30 a bed, but can rise to Y80 at the Himalaya Hotel. Both Amdo Guesthouse and Dingri Sunshine Hotel claim to offer hot showers at certain hours for Y10 if you're a guest, or Y15 if you're an outsider. Out of town, about 800m to the west, is **Tingri Snowland Hotel ($)**, with good views of Himalayan peaks from the courtyard. Rooms cost around Y120, with dorms also available.

A kilometre east of Tingri along the main road (KM3193 marker stone) is **Everest Snowleopard Hotel ($$)**, a huge compound used by group tours. Everest base camp permits can be obtained here. The hotel contains over 50 rooms, priced at Y260 a double, but try bargaining – you might be able to cut that price in half, so Y120 for a four-bed room would be more reasonable. The hotel is clean and has a large central courtyard with secure parking for vehicles. There are generator lights for a few hours a night, and televisions in the rooms. There is a small teahouse to one side, and even an 'Everest View' room (on the second floor, in the centre).

Apart from hotel eateries, there are several restaurants along the road – notably the **Sichuan Restaurant ($)**, offering stir-fried dishes. Next to the Himalaya Hotel is the Nepali-run **Third Eye Restaurant ($)**. Attached to Hehu Binguan is **Base Camp Restaurant ($)**, serving good Tibetan and Chinese dishes. A few mini-marts and small shops complete the 'strip' here. Further into Tingri village, there's very little, although you can stray across some tiny shops with a Tibetan teahouse at the back.

the marker stone to locate it. Milarepa's cave is set inside a tiny *gompa*, which was destroyed during the Cultural Revolution but rebuilt in the early 1980s with the help of the Nepalese. In the cave, you can see handprints made by Milarepa, using his mystical powers to hold a huge overhanging rock. Although the cave first belonged to the Kagyu sect, it was taken over by the Geluk order centuries ago. This is probably not reason enough to visit Nyalam, since there is another Milarepa cave near Dzongka on the Kyirong border crossing route.

Nyalam, sitting at 3,750m, is a truck-stop town catering to Nepali and Chinese drivers. To the west of town, you can find the old Tibetan quarter with traditional-style stone buildings and yaks lounging in the doorways.

Further afield, Nyalam is the base for trekking to **Shishapangma south base camp** (pages 249–50). Even if you have no intention of trekking to the base camp, the initial part of this route – accessed from the northwest end of town near a *gompa* – is well worth a day hike, or an overnight hike if you have a tent and sleeping gear.

Due to its former importance as a tourist lay-over spot, Nyalam has guesthouses and restaurants, but these days perhaps more catering to mountaineers.

From Nyalam, the road switchbacks for some 40km in a huge drop off the Tibetan plateau, down through lush jungle terrain with waterfalls spilling over the road – and landslides in monsoon season likely to block the road entirely. The road parallels the fast-flowing Bhote Kosi River (Shishapangma Chu) all the way to the border trading town of **Zhangmu** (Dram, Khasa, 2,300m). Here, goods trucks then cross over the Bhote Kosi River at the Friendship Bridge, and proceed to Nepali customs at Kodari.

TINGRI OVERLAND TO KATHMANDU

Due to the big drop in altitude, this is a spectacular exit route, and you should take it slowly, stopping for a picnic or two. The drive goes west of Tingri for 172km to Lake Paiku Tso, with road surfaces of varying conditions. After skirting around beautiful **Lake Paiku Tso** (4,595m), you climb over **Gongtang Lamo pass** (5,236m) – the highest pass along the route – and then dip down into Kyirong Valley to the town of Dzongka. From Paiku Tso Lake to the crest of Gongtang Lamo pass is around 50km, then it is another 30km from the pass to Dzongka.

The town of **Dzongka** (4,040m) is home to a *gompa* ruined by invading Nepalese in the 18th century. Further along the road is Milarepa's cave hermitage of **Drakar Taso**. Milarepa was an 11th-century sage who enlightened his students through music and poetry, but never founded any monasteries. He lived a mostly itinerant existence in remote areas, living in caves and dining on nettle soup. The mystic is easily recognised in pictures and statuary due to his greenish skin (possibly resulting from eating too much nettle soup) and his pose with his right hand cocked to his ear (to better hear the music of the spheres).

Proceeding further south, the valley opens with rich forest – the first such phenomenon you will encounter if coming from Lhasa. The subtropical vegetation is a clear indication that you have dropped in altitude. Closer to the border is the county town of **Kyirong Zhen** (2,800m), dotted with agricultural patches.

For timing, it will take about 5–6 hours to cover the route from Tingri to the Kyirong border crossing. Tingri to Dzongka is around 245km; Dzongka to Kyirong

6

Zhen (Kyirong Town) is 66km; Kyirong Town via the town of Raso to the actual border crossing is a further 32km. Proceeding at a leisurely pace to take in all the dramatic scenery, you should consider stopping the night in Kyirong Zhen.

KYIRONG ZHEN Kyirong Town (*Kyirong Gou, Gyirong, Kerung; 2,800m*) has morphed from a sleepy backwater into a major stepping stone on the overland route to Nepal. Following this meteoric rise of fortune, Kyirong Zhen has witnessed a bloom of grey concrete – as in the hasty construction of new high-rise buildings. Places to stay include the following: **Geelong Hotel** (✆ *0892 828 2822;* **\$\$**), which has good hot showers and free Wi-Fi, and **Shengdi Langsai** (✆ *0892 828 6828;* **\$\$**), which has clean rooms and hot water, but is a cheaper standard. For eating out, try the Tibetan-owned **Norling Restaurant**, serving mainly Nepalese food. Also good is **Namaseti Restaurant**, which serves Western and Nepalese food.

BORDER LOGISTICS Nepal is 2¼ hours behind Tibet, which operates on Beijing time. Thus, when it's noon in Kyirong (Chinese immigration post), it's 09.45 in Rasuwagadhi (Nepalese immigration post). Bear this in mind when considering banking hours and immigration post hours of opening.

Banking If exiting Tibet, you can change residual Chinese yuan back into US dollars (with original bank receipts). A much better deal is to change Chinese yuan into Nepalese rupees. Change either at a branch of the Bank of China (BOC) or with money changers. When dealing with the latter, it's preferable to do these transactions inside a shop rather than on the street: always carefully count the money offered before presenting your part of the deal. At border crossing towns, you can pay for goods in either Chinese yuan or Nepalese rupees.

Chinese customs and immigration On exit, Chinese customs may search baggage looking for 'antiques', which means anything older than 1959. Immigration checks are simple – you are stamped out.

ON TO KATHMANDU After exiting Tibet, the road continues 20km to the Nepal customs and immigration at **Rasuwagadhi** (elevation 1,800m). If you do not have a Nepal visa issued in Lhasa, you will be stamped in on arrival at the border post. Just provide US\$25 (cash only) for a 15-day visa, US\$40 for a 30-day visa or US\$100 for

FUTURE RAILWAY TO KATHMANDU

Eventually, the Lhasa–Kathmandu railway is slated to travel on the Kyirong route – but road infrastructure comes first. The US\$8 billion Chinese-built railway could take eight or ten years to finish, with the earliest projection for completion being 2022. Projected Chinese engineering plans reveal that up to 85% of the rail route from Kyirong to Kathmandu may be constructed underground, via a series of lengthy tunnels. This is likely due to the fact that the transition from 4,000m at Kyirong down to 1,300m in Kathmandu traverses terrain that is landslide-prone, particularly during the annual monsoon. If and when it gets going, the ride from Kyirong to Kathmandu is projected to take less than an hour, with the train clipping along at 120km/h. Currently, the railway line runs from Lhasa as far west as Shigatse. The Kyirong border crossing lies about 920km from Lhasa via Shigatse, and around 85km from Kathmandu, making that an even 1,000km.

a three-month visa. A passport photo is required. The road then enters the Rasuwa district in Nepal's Langtang National Park, and heads south past Dunche and Trisuli to **Kathmandu**. It is about 85km from the Kyirong border to Kathmandu, taking about 6 hours to cover the route. Rasuwagadhi is 65km from Kathmandu. For more on Kathmandu, see below.

KATHMANDU Once you've crossed the border at Kyirong/Rasuwagadhi, the Nepalese capital is only half a day away by jeep. This brings you into the bazaars of Asan Tole, in old Kathmandu – in former times the trading crossroads of the empires of India, China and Tibet. You'll find more apple pie, ice cream, shampoo and English-language newspapers in a 200m stretch of a street in the Thamel area of Kathmandu than you will in all of Tibet. The trick is not to go berserk when faced with such myriad choices. The sudden change of diet can wreak havoc on your system: switching to apple pie and ice cream after months of living off biscuits in Tibet can be traumatic. Still, clean white sheets, Swedish massage and doses of the BBC won't hurt. They may even be therapeutic.

Kathmandu has great resources for things Tibetan: there are Tibetan monasteries scattered around the valley, and there are Tibetan-run hotels, shops and travel agents in Kathmandu's Thamel district. If you are incoming from Tibet, Kathmandu has all the forbidden and seditious material on Tibet that Chinese officials so diligently search baggage for. Kathmandu has one of the highest concentrations of English-language bookstores of any place in the Indian subcontinent. Lots of secondhand books are available as well. The result is that you can find just about any book on Tibet ever printed. You can find T-shirts emblazoned with prayer flags or Tibetan flags, plus many handcrafted Tibetan items that are superior in quality to those found in Tibet – carpets, for instance. All this is something of an anomaly (or a money-spinner?) because the Nepalese government is heavy-handed in preventing or squashing pro-Tibet demonstrations – or even simple gatherings of Tibetans in Kathmandu. There is a strong presence of Chinese military advisers in Nepal, and Chinese embassy staff in Kathmandu have been observed directing operations by Nepalese police beating and arresting Tibetan demonstrators. Civil unrest in various parts of Nepal has led to violent demonstrations as when fuel shortages occur, for instance. Keep in mind that Nepalese news sources are heavily censored: they tend to paint a rosy picture of the place. More reliable would be keeping an eye on international media on the internet for current news.

Where to stay There are many hotels in Kathmandu to choose from, particularly in the Thamel district. A reliable one with good security, peaceful ambience and central location is **Kathmandu Guesthouse**, in Thamel (\\+977 1 470 0632; e info@ ktmgh.com; w ktmgh.com). Here you can get US$30 rooms, or you can splurge on rooms with garden views for US$60 a night.

ONWARD TRAVEL In the Thamel district of Kathmandu are many adventure **tour operators** who can fix you up with everything from mountain-bike tours to white-water rafting to heli-touring up to Everest or Annapurna. The adventure sports mecca of Nepal is Pokhara, about 8 hours away by bus. For more details about travel in Nepal, see pages 59–60.

6

7

Star Treks

HIGH-ALTITUDE FORAYS TO EVEREST, KAILASH AND BEYOND

This section describes some treks in western Tibet that individuals have successfully tackled, but which are highly challenging, both in terms of physical effort and dodging demands for permits. The rewards? We're talking about a backdrop of the highest peaks on earth here – moonscapes, star treks and stellar vistas! Trekking in Tibet is expeditionary in nature, even if you are part of an organised group. Yaks and porters will ferry supplies. This is one of the few places in the world where trekking is assisted by behemoths, in the form of sturdy yaks. If you plan to trek on your own, you should be looking at the regions of Kham and Amdo in far-eastern Tibet, as you can get past permit restrictions there (see *Chapter 8*).

The more remote the location, the longer the list of permits you will need. Permits to Everest base camp take a minimum 15 days to process; permits for western Tibet, including Kailash, take three to four weeks to process. So you need to work well in advance if venturing out this way, and the process may be ongoing, as other permits may be required *en route*. In other words, start early on the paperwork.

Trekking should entail minimal impact on the local people, and respect for the environment. You can start with your travel agency, by insisting that your driver and crew do not throw garbage out the window of the vehicle – and that any tips given will be contingent on their respect for the environment.

When trekking in an arranged group, ask in advance about conditions for porters. It is the responsibility of the operator to ensure adequate equipment and safety for porters, so by all means press the operator on these concerns. Are the porters properly clothed and equipped for the rigours of mountain travel? In Nepal, there have been a number of accidents – and deaths – involving porters, due to lack of adequate footwear, clothing and gear, poor medical care, and neglect and mistreatment by trek leaders. A porter should not be setting out with a 50kg load to tackle a high snowbound pass in tattered running shoes, but this has happened. Such neglect can result in frostbite. The International Porter Protection Group is lobbying trekking companies to ensure that porters have adequate equipment and that they are provided with the same standard of medical care as trekkers and leaders would themselves enjoy. This means that in the event of illness, a porter is not simply paid off and sent back down a mountain alone – which has resulted in deaths from altitude sickness in Nepal in the past. In Tibet, altitude sickness should not be an issue for porters as Tibetans are well acclimatised. However, some Nepalese trekking outfits bring in their own porters from Nepal who could be from lowland areas, rather than Sherpa porters, who are from highland areas. In Tibet, porters are more commonly used on large expeditions. Organised trekking trips in Tibet are more likely to be yak-supported, or with combinations of porters and yak caravans.

Two excellent guidebooks cover trekking routes in Tibet in detail. Kotan Publishing's *Mapping the Tibetan World* provides details on trekking not only in Tibet but also across the Himalayan range. Gary McCue's *Trekking Tibet* would make a great companion volume to this book if you are keen on trekking. McCue covers treks in the Kham and Amdo regions in his book as well.

A handful of classic Tibet treks – enough to keep you busy for quite some time – are described in the following section. The approaches and trail heads are all reachable by rental vehicle, and in most cases on paved roads. The road to Kailash is paved all the way, except on the back route via Saga, where there is a 50km dirt section. The road to Everest base camp is paved up to Rongbuk (and even further, to the tent camp).

Some trekkers get greedy: you can bag several of the following base camps in a single trip. The route might run from Lhasa to Everest base camp, then on to Kailash, you can complete the *kora* there, and head back to Lhasa, or exit to Nepal via the Kyirong border crossing. This can all be accomplished in 14 days.

TREKKING IN THE EVEREST REGION

There are three main targets in the Everest area: Rongbuk (Everest North Face base camp), Karta (Everest East Face base camp) and Cho Oyu base camp. You can reach Rongbuk by 4x4. Two staging-points to bear in mind are Shegar to the east and Tingri to the west. Refer to the Lhasa to Kathmandu route map, pages 240–1, for locations.

Everest is not in the same class as Kailash when it comes to being a sacred peak. For one thing, the monastery at Everest was only established early in the 20th century (the shrines at Kailash go back to the 13th century). More importantly, Kailash has always been off-limits for climbers, and there are no throngs of Tibetan pilgrims headed for Everest because you can't circumambulate the mountain. Nevertheless, Everest is known to the Tibetans as Chomolungma, which transliterates as Queen (*jhomo*) on an Ox (*glangma*), otherwise more prosaically rendered as 'Mother Goddess of the World'. Tibetans believe that the goddess Miyo Langsangma resides atop Mount Everest: her mount is an ox, although other images show her astride a tiger. She is one of the five Tsering sisters; according to legend, each of these five goddesses inhabits a high peak in the Himalayan region. The goddess is not one to tangle with lightly. Witness what happened to the first expeditions. In 1921, Tibet opened expedition attempts on Everest to British climbers. The monks at Rongbuk were none too keen on the idea of climbers wending their way up a sacred peak: they predicted dire things would come to pass – which, in the case of Mallory and Irvine, they did. The monastery practice of blessing climbers rather than cursing them appears to have started in the late 1920s or 1930s when Nepali Sherpas were employed by the British as porters and cooks. Because Sherpas are Tibetan Buddhist, monasteries started dispensing blessings for safe passage on the mountain. Sherpas climbing from both sides visit monasteries before going to base camp, where they light butter lamps in supplication of various deities. At base camp itself, Sherpas make offerings of *tsampa* and *chang* to the goddess Chomolungma in the belief that the wrathful goddess will turn a blind eye and allow them passage. *Tsampa* is thrown skyward; ice axes and other gear also get a ritual blessing before climbers go higher.

DRIVING TO RONGBUK Everest base camp is remarkable in that it's a drive-in approach. A rough road to the base camp at the north side of Everest was engineered in 1960 for Chinese mountaineering attempts on the summit. It is now completely paved.

If you start from Shegar crossroads in the morning, you should be able to reach Rongbuk Monastery by mid-afternoon, all going well. The distance is around 100km, and driving time is around 3 hours for the whole stretch. Tickets to enter Qomolangma National Nature Preserve are issued at the Everest Service Centre near the Shegar crossroads. You will need a Y180 entry ticket for each person (including the guide), plus a Y400 vehicle entry ticket (this bill should already have been included with your touring itinerary). Your passport is checked at a military checkpoint west of Shegar, and the EBC tickets are checked at Chay (there is no check on the way out, only on the way in). Take your time along this part: the views are stupendous. At **Pang La**, there are views of the entire Himalayan range. You can stop in Tashidzom for noodles at **Benba Guesthouse**, which has a cosy teahouse out the back. From here, a half-hour drive brings you to the village of **Pasum**. Should you require it, Pasum has accommodation in hotels (Snowman Hotel, Y40 a room) and in teahouse tents (around Y15 a bed). Or you can just carry on to Rongbuk and sleep there.

TREKKING TO RONGBUK There are two routes into Rongbuk on foot – from the Shegar end, or from the Tingri end. Trekkers tend to favour the walk in from the Tingri end because there's no checkpoint to contend with and it's easier to hire pack animals in Tingri. However, if your equipment is not that good, or your intention is to get a ride in and trek back, then you should stick to the Shegar route, which has more in the way of lodging and teahouse support. You can combine the routes by taking one route in and the other route out (and consider a side trip to Cho Oyu base camp on the Tingri route). You might want to think about hiring a mule (or yak) and handler to carry supplies and food. Animals are scarce when harvesting is in progress; if you're only going one way with a pack animal, the handler may want compensation for the return journey.

From Tingri The walk into Rongbuk takes about four days. If you are on foot, it seems you dodge permit fees, since you do not go past any checkpoint on this route. The first day's target is not particularly strenuous: the village of **Lungjhang** (4,500m), with beds available. The next day *is* strenuous – it's best to work your way towards the base of **Lanma La** and camp out near a herder's camp. The next day, you can trek over Lanma La (5,150m) and make it to the village of **Zhommug**, where basic lodging awaits. Zhommug is not far from the jeep road that winds in from Shegar: you should be able to reach Rongbuk by the end of the fourth day of trekking.

From Shegar You essentially walk along the jeep road to Rongbuk. The trek takes three to four days; there are enough lodges along the way to qualify this as Tibet's first 'teahouse trekking' route. Starting out from the Tibetan truck stop at the KM5133 marker stone, you can walk to the Everest turn-off at the KM5145 marker stone. There is a checkpoint at **Chay** for EBC tickets. You can hire a mule at Chay for the trip as far as **Tashidzom** (Peruche, 4,075m), where there are some Tibetan-run lodges and a few shops. On the next leg of the journey, between Tashidzom and Chosang, you can stay in **Pasum** (4,100m), which has teahouse-lodges with cheap beds. The last place with beds is Chosang, but trekkers have found the folk here particularly light-fingered and cold-hearted, so you may want to skip this place. From here it is a steady climb to Rongbuk.

Trek alert Tibetan villagers in the Everest region are notoriously prone to thievery. You have to consider that there are not a lot of shops out this way: taking

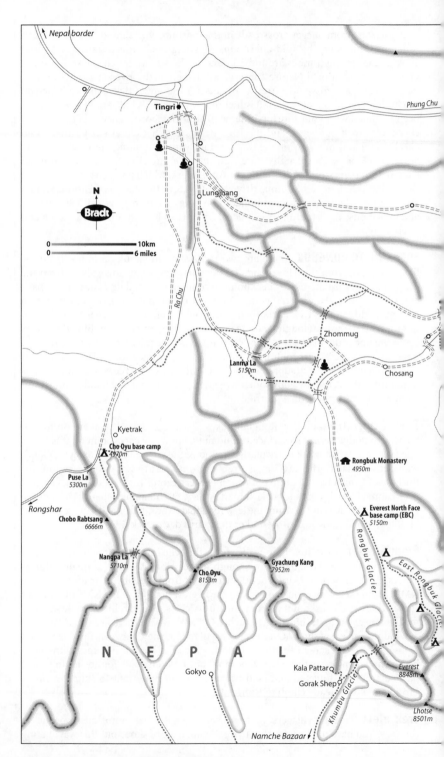

Nepal border

Phung Chu

Tingri

N

Bradt

0 _____ 10km
0 _____ 6 miles

Ra Chu

Lungjhang

Zhommug

Lanma La
5150m

Chosang

Kyetrak

Cho Oyu base camp
4970m

Rongbuk Monastery
4950m

Puse La
5300m

Rongshar

Chobo Rabtsang
6666m

Everest North Face
base camp (EBC)
5150m

Rongbuk Glacier

East Rongbuk Glacier

Nangpa La
5710m

Gyachung Kang
7952m

Cho Oyu
8153m

N   E   P   A   L

Gokyo

Kala Pattar

Gorak Shep

Khumbu Glacier

Everest
8848m

Namche Bazaar

Lhotse
8501m

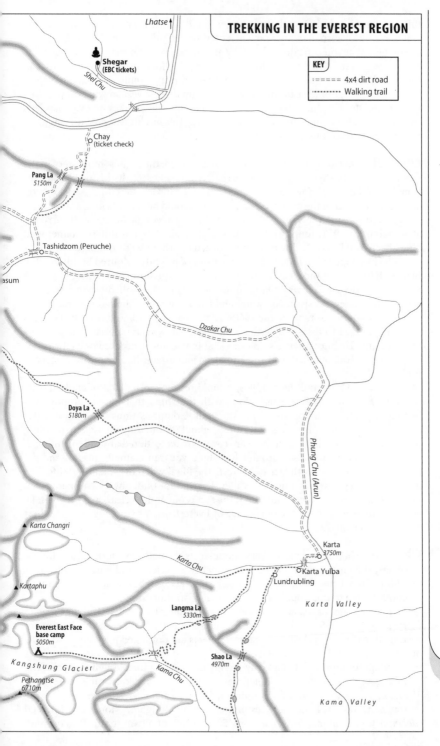

KEY
======= 4x4 dirt road
·············· Walking trail

Lhatse

Shegar
(EBC tickets)

Shel Chu

Chay
(ticket check)

Pang La
5150m

Tashidzom (Peruche)

asum

Dzakar Chu

Doya La
5180m

Phung Chu (Arun)

Karta Changri

Karta
3750m

Karta Chu

Karta Yulba
Lundrubling

Kartaphu

Karta Valley

Langma La
5330m

Everest East Face
base camp
5050m

Shao La
4970m

Kangshung Glacier

Kama Chu

Pethangtse
6710m

Kama Valley

things from visitors is somehow considered fair game. Even hosts at village inns will brazenly take small items, and when confronted, think it is no big deal. Keep an eye on gear that you can't do without – watch those water bottles. Always negotiate carefully and establish prices before consuming any food or drink at teahouses in the area, as there have been problems. Another alarming problem is that innkeepers in the Everest region have been known to beat up their wives. So what do you do – ignore this late at night, or try to step in? It's a tough call. Donkey and yak handlers can be hard to get along with and argumentative. This has little to do with language, and more to do with temperament.

RONGBUK (*Dza Rongphu; 4,950m*) Rongbuk Gompa, the highest monastery in the world, was established in 1902, under the Nyingmapa sect. Its history is sketchy. Rongbuk Valley was known as the 'sanctuary of the birds'. There was a strict ban on killing any animal in the area. Domestic animals could be eaten as long as they were slaughtered outside the valley. The British Everest reconnaissance party, arriving at Rongbuk in 1921, found the animals of the valley extraordinarily tame: wild blue sheep would come down to the monastery. There were hundreds of lamas and pilgrims engaged in meditation in a cluster of brightly coloured buildings. The British did not meet the Head Lama on their first expedition as he was off doing a year's 'time' in a cave. It was common for hermits to go on meditation retreats in caves in the valley, subsisting on water and barley passed to them once a day.

The monastery was razed in the 1960s. At the instigation of Red Guards, Tibetans were encouraged to disassemble the buildings for raw materials, such as precious wood beams. The monastery's stupa was split in two and ransacked of its treasures. The abbot of Rongbuk fled over the Himalaya and established a new monastery at Junbesi in Nepal.

In the late 1980s and early 1990s, rebuilding took place at Rongbuk and its monastery has been resurrected, along with the stupa that figures prominently in tourist photography of the scene. Rongbuk Gompa is unusual because it has a mixed community of monks and nuns – about 20 or so live here. Surrounding the monastery is a village, and there are cave retreats scattered around the hilltops.

There are great day hikes around Rongbuk: you can clamber around and get fantastic views of the north face of Everest. The Big E will blow you away – literally, if a wind comes howling down the valley. Everest does not always co-operate – it might be obscured by low cloud. But if the sun is out and it's clear, Everest will take your breath away, too. At the north face of Everest, you are looking at the highest mountain face on earth.

 Where to stay Rongbuk is very popular with both Western and Chinese travellers, the latter group loaded with expensive cameras and barking into their mobile phones (there is a telecom tower right at Rongbuk that enables mobile reception). Due to this popularity, rooms can be in short supply.

At the steep end for accommodation is the ritzy 'Pink Palace', aka **Drufung Binguan** (\0892 858 4535; **$$**), with 12 rooms going for a hefty Y300 each. At the time of writing, this place was closed. Chinese architects are not noted for their good taste, or for trying to fit designs into the environment, and this one hits a new high under the heading 'abominable'. Doors may be missing, leading to cold temperatures. The plumbing works periodically – sometimes down to one squat loo for the entire hotel. The hotel has a large second-floor dining hall with partial Everest views.

You can stay at a simple **guesthouse** run by Rongbuk Monastery for Y60 (*dormitory, three or four beds in a room;* **$**), or Y200 for a twin room. The common toilet is the pits. Hot water in vacuum flasks can be obtained, but don't expect luxuries here – nights can be very cold, and electricity is in short supply. A teahouse attached to Rongbuk Monastery ($) guesthouse serves noodles and other fare. The **nunnery** uphill has a few rooms for guests ($).

Beyond Rongbuk, a few kilometres further towards Everest base camp, are **tent camps ($)**, which can be reached in your vehicle on a paved road. Each tent can accommodate up to five tourists; that maximum has been set so that a single tent does not corner the business, thus larger groups are divided into different tents. The tents routinely charge Y60 a bed and offer simple meals cooked on a central stove. Watch your stuff – there are no doors that lock. Might be better to leave gear locked

A HAIRY TALE

Sightings of the Yeti, or Abominable Snowman, date back centuries: encounters with these shaggy-haired creatures of snowy realms are woven into the mythology of Tibet, Nepal and Bhutan. But it was the mountaineers tackling Everest and other Himalayan peaks who shone a spotlight on the legendary apeman in the West. In 1951, British mountaineer Eric Shipton, looking for a way up Everest, stumbled across a large footprint in the snow. He put his ice axe next to the footprint to give an idea of scale when he photographed it. However, Shipton was renowned for being a prankster – and therein lies a clue in how the Yeti myth got off the ground.

The 1960 publication of *Tintin in Tibet* by Belgian cartoonist Hergé sealed the legend of the Yeti – and practically sent it into orbit. Never out of print, the comic offers a close-up look at the genial beast and its cave high in the snowbound Himalayas. The Yeti is revealed as a highly sensitive and lonely creature – more adorable than abominable. The Tintin comic certainly stimulated a real quest: explorers and television crews set off to find a live Yeti. This included expeditions by famed mountaineers Edmund Hillary and Reinhold Messner. They all came back empty-handed or else with tales about shadows moving around at night and odd howling noises at high elevations (consistent with mating calls of the snow leopard).

In 2017, an American researcher tackled the legend with DNA analysis. Charlotte Lunqvist, an evolutionary biologist at the State University of New York in Buffalo, tested nine samples that purported to be from the Yeti. These included hair samples collected by nomadic herders in Nepal, a tooth collected from the Tibetan plateau in the 1930s, a leg bone found by a spiritual healer in a cave in Tibet, and a scat sample from Reinhold Messner's Tyrolean museum. Lunqvist's team also analysed samples from bears native to the plateau: the Himalayan brown bear (*Ursus thibetanus laniger*), Himalayan black bear (*Ursus arctos isabellinus*), and the Tibetan brown bear (*Ursus arctos pruinosus*). The latter bear stands as tall as a man on its hind legs, with a heavy neck ruff and hairy ears.

The results of Lunqvist's research? Eight out of nine 'Yeti' samples turned out to be DNA matches with Himalayan bear species. And the ninth sample matched the DNA of a dog. A bit of a dog's breakfast, in other words. Such is the un-bear-able truth about the Yeti. But there is an upside. Very little is known about the bear species of the Tibetan plateau and their behaviour. Lunqvist's detailed analysis of bear DNA lays the groundwork for figuring out how genetically different these rare subspecies are from their common ancestors.

7

in the vehicle. A few problems with the tent camps: there's no privacy (your tent host shares the space with you), the central stove can make the interior quite smoky, and you can freeze your butt off at night. A good sleeping bag comes in handy here.

North Face base camp From Rongbuk (or from your tent camp) you can walk or take the 'eco-friendly' bus for the final stretch on the dirt track out to the North Face base camp (aka EBC), at an elevation of 5,150m. The 'eco-friendly bus' is operated by tourism authorities for the April–October season and costs Y25 a person. Then it closes down, so you can take your own 4x4 for the final leg in the late October to early April low season. The base camp is 8km from Rongbuk and 4km from the tent camps. This might better be termed 'Everest Tourist base camp', as the real base camp for mountaineers lies further on. The tourist base camp is a motley collection of tent teahouses and other temporary structures. You can stay in a teahouse for under a dollar a night. Tibetan vendors pursue visitors and try to sell them fossils and cheap jewellery. The area is a glacial moraine – a bleak and desolate place – but awe-inspiring because it is so close to the Big E. It is also home to the highest post office in the world, a kiosk run by China Post, where for an extra fee you can drop a postcard or two that will be franked with an Everest postmark.

At the edge of the tented area is a sign that says you are not allowed to proceed further, on risk of paying a fine of US$200. Trekking beyond EBC to Advance Base Camp is possible but must be arranged well in advance, like all travel in Tibet. The four-day trek would take you out to the real mountaineering base camp and back.

Beyond base camp lies a trek described by Gary McCue (*Trekking Tibet*) as 'the Highest Trek in the World … an incredible journey to Camp III (6,340m) and to the base of the North Col via the East Rongphu Glacier'. McCue says that the ascent is possible without climbing gear, though it would be advisable to have items such as crampons when traversing the glacier. You need excellent trekking and sleeping gear, and you need to tackle considerable logistics to undertake such a strenuous – and potentially hazardous – journey.

THE BIG E At higher elevations, Everest is scoured by 100km/h winds: the constant threat of avalanche, being crushed by an ice serac (a pinnacle of ice on the surface of a glacier), falling down a crevasse, or succumbing to altitude make it a deadly peak to climb.

In 1921, the Tibetan government opened the Himalaya to the British. The first nine expedition attempts on Everest were made from the Tibetan side in the 1920s and 1930s, because Nepal was inaccessible to Europeans at the time. None of these teams succeeded. Early expedition climbers wore woollens, thick tweeds, Norfolk jackets and studded leather boots. The only hardware was ice axes and primitive crampons, but oxygen tanks were also lugged along. On the third expedition attempt, in 1924, George Mallory and Andrew Irvine were making good time for the summit when they were enveloped in cloud and never seen again (but see pages 246–7). Whether they succeeded in gaining the summit remains one of mountaineering's great mysteries. Another mystery concerns Eric Shipton, who, connected with these British attempts, photographed footprints left by the Yeti (known as *migyu* in Tibetan). Given to practical jokes, it seems likely that Shipton faked the footprints. Failing to summit Everest, Shipton and his climbing cronies set about bagging a host of first ascents on lesser peaks around Everest.

Since the 19th century, Tibet has attracted more than its fair share of visionaries and eccentric travellers; with Everest, spectacularly so. In 1934, British ex-army officer Maurice Wilson announced that he was going to crash-land a Tiger Moth on the slopes of the mountain and climb from there to plant the Union Jack on the summit. Incredibly, Wilson got financial backing, learned how to fly and flew all the way to India, where officials promptly seized his plane. Spurred on by his megalomaniacal brand of divine faith, Wilson found his way through Tibet disguised as a deaf and dumb monk. At Rongbuk, he got on famously with the head lama. Wilson apparently believed that earlier British expeditions had cut an ice stairway straight up the mountain – he thought he would simply climb this staircase and pray his way to the top. He had little equipment, no warm clothing and no mountaineering experience. Another British expedition of 1935 (under Eric Shipton) found his frozen body at around 6,700m.

In 1947, Canadian climber Earl Denman sneaked into Rongbuk to assault the mountain: he got above Camp 3, but turned back. This was the last attempt from the Tibetan side for some time, as the Tibetans banned the issue of travel permits to Tibet. In 1950, after the Chinese invasion, no foreign climbers were allowed in. Western attention had already shifted to Nepal, which had become accessible after 1949. In May 1953, New Zealander Edmund Hillary and Sherpa Tenzing Norgay 'knocked the bastard off' (as Hillary put it), summitting from Nepal as part of a British expedition.

Meanwhile, from the Tibetan side, the Chinese would not allow climbers to attempt the route until they had succeeded in putting Chinese mountaineers on top first. In 1959, the Chinese and the Russians undertook a joint reconnaissance. With the rift between China and Russia in 1960, China carried on the work alone, and then stepped into the Everest spotlight in a big way. In March 1960, the Chinese claimed that all of Everest, as well as an 8km stretch south to Namche Bazaar, belonged to China. At the time, China was busy testing the limits of Indian and Nepalese patience in border disputes. The Everest claim did not sit well with the Nepalese prime minister, who made a counterclaim that all of Everest belonged to Nepal, including parts of Rongbuk Glacier. The same month, a 214-man Chinese expedition arrived at Rongbuk base camp for a summit attempt. A Chinese and Tibetan climbing team reached the summit, but there were no photographs as the summit attempt took place at night. In 1975 (by which time the border between Tibet and Nepal had been firmly delineated as running across the summit) the Chinese mounted another huge expedition. One Chinese and eight Tibetans gained the summit and left a tripod there as definite proof of their ascent. The potential for Tibetan climbers on the slopes of Everest, as opposed to Sherpa climbers, has been little realised, largely because of Tibetans fearing the wrath of the peak's resident goddess. But Tibetan climbers are superbly adapted to altitude and certainly up to the challenge if taboos can be overcome. Of the eight Tibetan climbers who summitted in 1975 from the Tibetan side, one was a woman, simply identified as Phantog. Phantog (also known as Pan Duo) was not only the first woman to summit from the north side of Everest, she narrowly missed being the first woman ever to summit Everest (Junko Tabei, a Japanese woman, summitted from Nepal ten days earlier). To put this in perspective: the first Sherpa woman would not reach the summit of Everest until 1993 – almost 20 years later.

In 1980, the Chinese, satisfied that their claim had been accepted, opened the north side again to foreigners. In August 1980, in contrast to the huge Chinese teams, came a team of two – Italian climber Reinhold Messner and his girlfriend. In one of mountaineering's most extraordinary feats, he made it to the top of Everest, solo and without oxygen, on a variation of the route pioneered by Mallory and Irvine. Two years earlier, climbing from the South Col, Messner and fellow-climber Peter Habeler had been the first to climb the mountain without oxygen.

Until they attempted this feat, it was unknown if a climber would survive reaching the top without oxygen, as past 7,000m is known as the Death Zone (no further acclimatisation is possible). At Everest's peak, a climber without oxygen could suffer debilitating physical and mental problems. Messner did not go in entirely blind – he was a passenger on an unpressurised plane flying at high altitudes, and tested himself without oxygen for short periods. Other climbers have since reached the top of Everest without oxygen, including a female climber, Lydia Bradey from New Zealand, who summitted in 1988.

In 1986 Messner claimed another record – the ascent of all 14 peaks over 8,000m, including ascents of Everest and Shishapangma in Tibet. To date, only a handful of climbers have repeated the feat. Messner also narrowly missed being the first in the race to bag the highest peak on all seven continents. This record fell to Canadian climber Patrick Morrow, who added Carstensz Pyramid (in West Irian/Papua New Guinea) to the equation. More than a hundred climbers have since bagged the Seven Summits. New Zealander Rob Hall raised the bar by conquering the Seven Summits in seven months. Others have gone on to bag the Seven Summits plus the two poles.

Where will it end? Well, there's still the snowboarding record up for grabs: climb the Seven Summits and snowboard down. In 2001, Marco Siffredi snowboarded from the summit of Everest to Advance Base Camp, while a year earlier, Davo Karnicar made the first true ski descent from the summit via the South Col. Marco Siffredi made another snowboard attempt on the Hornbein Couloir in 2002 – and was never seen again. Another Everest descent record: in September 1988, French climber Jean Marc Boivin paraglided from the summit, landing at Camp 2 (Nepalese side) in 11 minutes. The youngest Everest summiteer is a toss-up between two 13-year-olds: Jordan Romero from the USA, who summitted in 2010, and Malavath Poorna from India, who summitted in 2014. The first octogenarian summit was achieved in 2013 by 80-year-old Japanese climber, Yuichiro Miura, who is famed as the daredevil skier in the documentary *The Man Who Skied Down Everest* (accomplished in 1970). But the most incredible feat of all is by the man who did – quite literally – go in blind: Erik Weihenmayer, a blind climber from the USA, reached the summit in May 2001. Weihenmayer went on to bag the Seven Summits.

Almost 90% of Everest climbers fail to reach the summit. Nevertheless, at the last count, over 4,500 ascents of Everest have been successfully made: the figure goes much higher if you count the repeat summiteers. In 2016 alone, there were 641 successful summit bids. Meanwhile, more than 280 deaths have been recorded in climbing attempts on Everest and, grisly but true, most of the bodies still lie where they fell, frozen or decomposing, because it is too difficult and dangerous to bring the bodies down. Roughly a third of the deaths recorded are of Sherpas. Many of the Sherpas act as porters, but others have developed reputations as fine climbers – Apa Sherpa has summitted Everest 20 times, and Ang Rita Sherpa has summitted the peak ten times without oxygen. In May 2005, Nepalese couple Pem Dorjee and Moni Mulepati were the first to marry on the summit.

Politics at the top: Everest is the only place in Tibet where the Tibetan flag can be flown without interference. Sherpa climbers tackling Everest from the Nepalese side are prone to leaving small Tibetan flags fluttering from the summit; they also leave an image of the Dalai Lama in the snow at the summit. When he summitted in 1996, Jamling Norgay (son of Tenzing Norgay, who summitted in 1953) left an ice axe with the flags of Tibet, Nepal, India, the USA and the UN flying from it – which appears much larger than life in an IMAX movie about Everest.

In May 1999, a remarkable discovery was made by climber Conrad Anker at around 8,100m on the upper slopes of Everest. He found George. After going missing for close on 75 years, George Mallory turned up on the internet, of all places: a photograph of his bleached torso was posted by expedition members to their website (w *mountainzone.com*). This did not sit well with descendants of the Mallory family (including Mallory's grandson, George, who summitted Everest in 1995), and nor did other media exposure of the body, including a cover photo for *Outside Magazine*. Those selling the pictures claimed that the photographs were proof that Mallory had been found. Edmund Hillary said it was disgusting to expose the body in such a fashion; the dead should be given some respect.

For Edmund Hillary, there were some tense moments: in Mallory's pockets were notes that showed he was toting more oxygen canisters than previously thought, which means he and Irvine might have been able to make the summit. But no camera was found on Mallory's body. So who got to the top first? Edmund Hillary let slip in his autobiography that he could lay claim to being first, a few steps ahead of Tenzing Norgay. Meanwhile, it was discovered that Tenzing Norgay was not Nepalese at all, but of Tibetan blood, so one of the premier summiteers, fittingly, is Tibetan. He grew up in the village of Moyun, in the Karta Valley, in the shadow of Everest. Seeking a better life, his parents left Tibet and walked over to the Nepalese side: Norgay grew up in Sherpa country. He later eloped with a Sherpa woman named Dawa: looking for work, they trekked to Darjeeling, the base of all the early

MOUNTAIN BURIAL

One of Everest's less salubrious records is being the highest rubbish dump in the world. Some expeditions have been undertaken solely to clear out the hundreds of oxygen bottles and canisters strewn at the highest camp, about 900m below the summit. Something that cannot be as easily removed, however, are the bodies of dead climbers. Because of the weight, carrying back dead alpinists from this zone – at these high altitudes – is exceedingly difficult. Instead, if possible, bodies of climbers are simply pushed into crevasses, a method of dispatch known as 'mountain burial'.

That's indeed if there's still a body left. Macabre sightings at high elevations include partial cadavers. These act as grim landmarks, and reminders of how thin the line is between life and death up here. The area above 7,000m is called the Death Zone because the body cannot acclimatise here. Climbers have to move quickly in this zone before their strength is sapped by dehydration, cold and high altitude.

It is said there is no morality above 8,000m. If climbers stop to help another climber at this elevation, they will most likely have to abandon their own summit attempt. In a 1996 summit attempt, two Japanese climbers on the Tibetan side were heading for the top when they came across three Ladakhi climbers from an Indian expedition. The Ladakhis had summitted but had been forced to spend the night out – though horribly frostbitten they were still alive, and moaning unintelligibly. Not wanting to jeopardise their ascent, the Japanese climbers simply sidestepped the Ladakhis – not offering food, water or oxygen – and carried on to the summit. On the way down from the summit they again passed two of the Ladakhis, who were left to die where they had fallen. Interviewed soon after their descent, one Japanese climber explained that the Ladakhis looked 'dangerous'; the other Japanese climber said: 'We were too tired to help. Above 8,000m is not a place where people can afford morality.'

Everest expeditions. Tenzing Norgay kept his real origins obscure, and finally took out Indian citizenship under the patronage of Prime Minister Nehru. Tenzing Norgay never lied about his origins, but he didn't quite tell the truth, either: it was not until after his death in 1986 that the full story emerged. Here's an intriguing link: Norgay and Mallory may have actually met. Mallory's 1921 expedition passed through Moyun, the village where young Tenzing Norgay lived, and spent the day there. Tenzing Norgay was seven years old at the time.

And here's another conundrum: is climbing in the genes? Edmund Hillary's son Peter summitted Everest, Mallory's grandson George did too, and both the son of Tenzing Norgay (Jamling) and his grandson (Tashi Tenzing) have summitted, making that a three-generation affair.

On 14 May 2005, one man made it to the top of Everest without the hard slog. French test pilot Didier Delsalle made aviation history when he touched down on the summit in his turbo-engine AS350-B3 helicopter for a few minutes. This broke the record for the highest helicopter landing – a record that actually cannot be bettered. By doing this, Didier Delsalle improved the possibility of rescues in future. In fact, he mounted a helicopter rescue of two Japanese climbers on the way out.

KARTA (*Everest East Face base camp; 5,050m*) After driving by 4x4 from either Shegar or Tingri (see map, pages 240–1) a rough road lands you in the village of Karta, at 3,750m. The road to Karta, veering off from the village of Tashidzom, remains dirt and can be dangerous after heavy rain. There are some very narrow spots along this road with deep drop-offs on one side.

From Karta, an arduous ten-day loop takes you through the Kama and Karta valleys with views of Everest's Kangshung Face. Of the three faces of Everest, this is the one rated the most daunting to climb, and the one rarely viewed by Westerners. The 1921 British expedition, exploring the Karta Valley on its reconnaissance of Everest, decided the approach was out of the question. It was not until 1981 that an American team tried to summit the Kangshung Face. They failed, but another expedition with some of the same members succeeded in 1983.

Of the treks described so far, the Karta loop is the most taxing, requiring considerable logistical support. Several outfits can arrange trips, starting from Lhasa.

Caveat Porters and yak handlers in the Karta area have a notorious reputation for being unreliable and reluctant companions. On group tours, histrionic scenes have included porters getting drunk on *chang* at breakfast and not getting under way with the yaks until noon, thus throwing out the daily trekking targets. Furious arguments can erupt over what loads are to be carried on the yaks, porters can be rough in handling duffle bags, and yak handlers may stop and demand extra money before continuing. So it goes on. They are also known to be fond of pilfering loose items.

Kangshung trek To save time and conserve energy, it would be advisable to get a ride to the trail head village of Karta. The approach by road is initially the same as for Rongbuk, with a turn-off at Peruche. From Peruche to Karta is about six bone-jarring hours by 4x4, with repeated river fords. You could trek in – the scenic 90km from Peruche to Karta would take three or four days (a donkey and guide can be hired in Peruche to assist).

Everest East Face base camp can be reached by several routes: a ten-day loop takes in several of these. There are two high passes *en route*: trekkers pick the lower one (Shao La, 4,970m) to go over first as this allows more chance to acclimatise. At the base of Shao La are two glacial lakes, where good campsites are found. If the weather is clear, there are good views of Everest, Makalu and Lhotse from the top of Shao La. Shao La leads into the beautiful Kama Valley which is surprisingly coated with meadows full of rhododendrons and, further on, forests of pine and fir. Westward along the Kama Valley there are many streams to cross, and meadows with wildflowers. From this vantage point, there may be views of Chomo Lonzo. The trek continues to Everest East Face base camp, at a site called Pethang Ringmo by British climber George Mallory. If the weather is co-operative, there are unparalleled views of the Kangshung Face and Kangshung Glacier.

The return trek is made via Langma La, at 5,330m, with steep rocky sections giving way to more gentle pastures. At the Kama River is the medieval village of Lundrubling, with solid houses of stone and timber. With a few hours' trekking to the east, you return to Karta Yulba, which is close to the jeep road at Karta.

CHO OYU BASE CAMP Lesser known than Everest – but no less spectacular – is Cho Oyu, an 8,153m behemoth. You can see the peak quite clearly from Tingri. The walk out (or drive) to its base camp crosses the plains of Tingri in the same direction as the Rongbuk trail. Cho Oyu base camp is nestled at 4,970m, and there is a paved road for most of the route in. You can take a day hike from here towards Puse La for good views. Near Cho Oyu base camp is Kyetrak, with the ruins of a salt depot on the old trading route from Nepal, crossing Nangpa La. The glaciated route is still used by the odd Nepalese trader, and as an escape route by Tibetan refugees, which might explain Chinese military manoeuvres in the area.

SHISHAPANGMA BASE CAMP TREKS

Shishapangma [map, pages 202–3] is the only 8,000m peak totally within Tibet (the others – Everest, Lhotse, Cho Oyu and Makalu – lie on the Tibet–Nepal border). For a long time it was not a question of climbing Shishapangma, but getting to see it. It was not until 1951 that Peter Aufschnaiter (the Austrian who escaped with Heinrich Harrer to Tibet, see page 164) was able to get within 10km of Shishapangma to photograph it. This was only the second photograph taken of the mountain, the first being an aerial one taken in 1950. Shishapangma was the last of the 8,000m giants to fall to climbers.

The first ascent of Shishapangma (Xixabangma) was achieved in 1964. In March of that year, an army of over 200 Chinese support personnel and climbers gathered at the north base camp. Climbers swore to plant the five-starred red flag on the summit 'for the honour of the party and the socialist construction of the Motherland' (as described in the magazine *China's Sports*). The climbers not only put the red flag on the summit, they also deposited a bust of Chairman Mao. The summit was reached by four Tibetan and six Chinese climbers, one of whom, Wang Fuchou, had climbed Everest four years earlier. In 1980, a German climbing team summitted the peak; in 1982, British climbers Doug Scott and Alex MacIntyre reached the top via the southwest face. French climber Didier Givois and two companions not only summitted Shishapangma, they telemark-skied back down it.

Ironically, since the Lhasa–Kathmandu land route is open, Shishapangma is the most accessible of the 8,000m peaks. Entry fee to the region is Y180 per person. There are two approaches to Shishapangma. You can drive to **Shishapangma north base camp** by heading north from the Kyirong border crossing and on to Lake Paiku Tso. Heading along this road is another fork southward, leading to the village of Serlung. Here you can hire yaks and handlers if you want to trek in, or just motor on for the last 15km from Serlung to the north base camp at 4,900m.

7

Shishapangma south base camp, at 4,980m, can be reached by an in-and-out trail from the town of Nyalam, taking about four or five days for the round trip. You head out northwest of Nyalam, following a river through alpine valleys. Because Shishapangma is a conglomerate peak (with several possible summits), it's difficult to determine where the real summit lies.

WEST TIBET

There are two main targets in west Tibet, both taking about a week to reach from Lhasa. The main focus of interest – for both pilgrim and trekker – is Mount Kailash. A second spectacular site is the ruins of the Guge Kingdom near Zanda. You can visit both if you have lots of time and money, and luck on the road. And perseverance, and patience. There are more than 20 checkpoints on the road from Lhasa to Kailash.

Another variable here is that you may not want to return to Lhasa, or even start from Lhasa. Kailash can also be approached, or left, from the road going via the Kyirong border crossing to Kathmandu. There is a shortcut that skirts past Saga and Lake Paiku Tso down to the Kyirong border crossing.

Group tent-trekking tours approach Kailash driving from Lhasa, from Kathmandu (crossing at Kyirong), or by a five-day walk-in route from Simikot (far western Nepal) to Burang. Indian pilgrims arrive as part of a lottery system: they come over the Lipu Lek pass to Burang, then on to Kailash. Some Western group tours have been allowed to follow this same route, trekking in through the Garhwal Himalaya and over Lipu Lek pass.

ROUTES FROM LHASA Travel to Kailash is like one of those epic Marco Polo diary entries: 'Five or six days' hard journey to the west, you come to a great snow-covered mountain which is considered very holy by the Tibetans, who leave articles of clothing as proof of their pilgrimage to it.' The pilgrimage to Kailash has long been considered the most difficult in Asia, due to the sheer distance, harsh weather conditions, the high altitude and lack of any supply points. No matter which way you go, the trip is arduous and you need good planning. Timing is everything at Kailash. It's snowed-in for much of the year, but June and July are generally good months to go. August is not good – monsoon rains can wash away roads and bridges leading in. September is possible. Treks at Kailash start and finish at Darchen, an encampment on the south side of the peak. There are half a dozen routes to Kailash, all of them arduous and time-consuming. Consult the Tibet Autonomous Region map, page xii, for an overview of routing.

HIRING VEHICLES Your travel agent will be making all the arrangements for Kailash touring, most likely, so you have to play along with that agent. Here are some of the variables for transport logistics. These notes were written for the days when individual travel was possible to Kailash – now a very remote possibility. However, you can glean some insight into how the system works by reading through this. A 4x4 driver would be most reluctant to travel alone on any of the Kailash routes. If he gets stuck in mud or trapped while fording a river, there's no way out. If he breaks down, he's stranded in the middle of nowhere, with no chance to get help. You have some options: arrange to hire two 4x4s, or consider hiring a 4x4 and a truck. The cost for a single vehicle in high season including driver, guide and permits is around Y18,000 for a simple 12- to 15-day tour, though you can bargain as low as Y14,000 with some agencies. For a 16- to 20-day tour, the cost might rise to Y25,000. With three vehicles, say with 11 people, you can bargain substantial discounts. The 4x4–truck combination works this way:

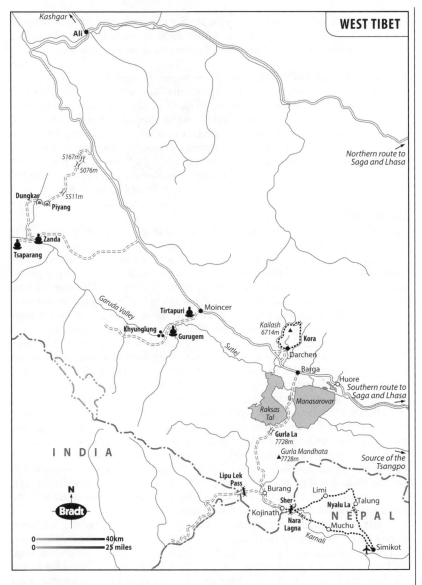

Kashgar

Ali

5167m
5076m
5511m
Dungkar
Piyang
Zanda
Tsaparang

Northern route to
Saga and Lhasa

Garuda Valley
Tirtapuri   Moincer
Khyunglung
Gurugem

Kailash
6714m
Kora
Darchen
Barga
Huore
Southern route to
Saga and Lhasa

Sutlej

Raksas
Tal
Manasarovar

Gurla La
7728m
Gurla Mandhata
7728m
Source of the
Tsangpo

I N D I A

N

Bradt

0   40km
0   25 miles

Lipu Lek
Pass
Burang   Limi
Sher   Limi
Kojinath   Nyalu La   Talung
              Muchu
Nara   N E P A L
Lagna
Karnali   Simikot

a 4x4 can seat three (preferable) or four paying passengers plus guide and driver. A Chinese Dongfeng truck seats two paying passengers in the front cabin, plus driver. The truck acts as a tow vehicle if the going gets rough – it can haul the 4x4 to the next town for repairs. In the back of the truck are all the supplies for the trip: food, fuel, camping gear and so on. You can rotate passengers through the two vehicles. Take as much food and water with you as you can manage from Lhasa: potatoes, vegetables, dried fruit, roasted walnuts, anything that will last the distance. Some folk take along lots of liquid supplies, too. Another good transport configuration is one truck and two 4x4s, if you can find enough people for the journey. This makes more efficient use of the truck by sharing it between two 4x4s. The full circuit of Lhasa via the north route to Kailash and back to Lhasa on the south route is just over 3,000km, a major road trip. Tibetan pilgrims get to Kailash sitting in the open back of a Dongfeng truck, getting thrown around like a sack of potatoes and showered in dust.

PERMITS AND CHECKPOINTS Visiting the region of west Tibet may require a modest stack of permits – TTB, Foreign Affairs Bureau, military and PSB ATP. The paperwork starts in Lhasa, continues in Ali or Darchen, and may require more work in places such as Zanda. For visits to Guge and Kailash, permits seem to work better on the north route via Ali rather than the south route via Paryang. Of course, on group tours, the agent takes care of permits, so most groups go in via the south route. On the south route, there are checkpoints at Saga, Paryang and Barga (close to Kailash); further checkpoints are located near Moincer and before Zanda; but there are no checkpoints on the north route, except possibly close to Ali.

SOUTH ROUTE *See map, page 64*

The south route to Kailash from Lhasa, via Lhatse and Paryang, is more direct (a total of 1,200km), so it is the first choice of tour agencies in Lhasa as well as organised group tours from Kathmandu. There are some high passes on the south route: Paryang and Huore both sit at 4,500m, and between them is a pass of 5,180m. Most travellers take the south route up to Darchen, but if heading back for Kathmandu you would take the road via Paiku Tso to the Kyirong border crossing.

Although the south route has been substantially upgraded, with new bridges and improved surfacing, it is still a long, bleak journey with minimum altitudes of 4,500m and few settlements with only basic facilities. With the exception of Saga, which has a newish hotel, all accommodation along the south route to Kailash is in basic guesthouses with concrete or dirt floors, bedding of dubious cleanliness, electricity (solar or generator) limited to a single dim bulb, and filthy squat toilets, often in a corner of the compound, open to the elements. They cost around Y60 per night (Y120 at Darchen), but bargain if there are not many visitors. Food is expensive and may be limited to dull variations on noodles – it pays to visit the Lhasa vegetable market and fill a sack with produce that lasts well in the dry atmosphere and can be given to the restaurants to cook. Make sure you have plenty of warm clothes, even in summer: a sleeping bag is highly advisable if not strictly essential. Hot water in vacuum flasks is readily available so take drinks, soups and so on, as well as snacks. Try to have a water container that can be filled up from the vacuum flasks as the quantity of discarded mineral water bottles is quite large enough.

Leaving the highway at Lhatse, the road continues 115km to **Sangsang**: it is better to stay here if you cannot reach Saga as the 4,800m altitude at Raga (113km on) and the biting cold wind should only be experienced if there is no choice. **Saga**, 181km from Sangsang, is the usual first day stop for those leaving from Lhatse, and assuming the highway is in good order and you have a good vehicle it should even be possible to complete the 450km from Shigatse in a very long day. Saga is a larger town with a checkpoint (located just before town) and a strong military presence. If stopping in Saga, the Tibetan-owned MuLinSen Hotel (\0892 891 3999), has good rooms, hot water and free Wi-Fi. The ferry over the Tsangpo for the road to Tingri lies just to the west, but the main road heads north over a small pass and follows a feeder stream down to the Dargye River. This is an excellent **camping site** with clear steams flowing from a snow mountain to the east. Crossing various tributaries of the Yarlung Tsangpo, the road passes some ruined watchtowers before old Dzongba where there is a reasonable truck stop 157km from Saga. From here until Paryang there are no reliable camping spots, but there are dramatic sand dunes and some stunning views of the Himalaya. You may also see herds of wild ass (*kyang*) or gazelle (*gowa*) in the region and even the occasional black-necked crane (*trung trung*). Unfortunately, the elegant Tibetan antelope (*chiru*) is no longer found in this region due to severe hunting for its *shahtoosh* wool. The scattered nomad houses use well water either in their compounds or in shared locked huts. Only in the wet season do thin streams flow from the hills into the brackish pools that dot the plain leading south to the Tsangpo.

Paryang, 232km from Saga, is the usual stop after Saga, and has several truck stops and restaurants. There are good camping spots about 20km further on; in some seasons sand midges can be a problem. The final checkpoint with adjacent tea shops is just before the approach to the Marium La pass, which at 5,180m is the highest point on the road, some 126km after Paryang. From here it is a simple but 90km descent to Lake Manasarovar, past another lake and a large flagpole shrine that marks the first view of Kailash. If you fork left here you come to an excellent campground beside a river leading into Manasarovar, although this has become popular in recent years, particularly during the spring Saga Dawa full-moon period when many Indian groups camp at this site. It is an ideal place to spend a rest day and perhaps hike a few hours to visit the attractive Seralung Gompa. Alternatively, you may decide to move on to Chiu Gompa on the northwest corner of the lake, or on to Darchen at Kailash, both around 50km away. The ugly town of Hor is poorly appointed and there is little reason to stop here or at Barga, where the roads to Burang and Ali divide. However, both have checkpoints where permits may be examined.

NEPAL ROUTES *See map, page xii*

High-end group tours are able to trek across a pass from western Nepal via Limi. They fly first from Kathmandu to Nepalgunj and Simikot in the far northwest of Nepal, then embark on a five-day trek over a pass to Kojinath and Burang, where 4x4s take them on to Kailash.

By road, a border crossing at Kyirong opens the way to overlanding to Kathmandu. See *Chapter 6, Lhasa to Kathmandu*, for map profiles and fine detail on this overland route. Exiting Kailash and heading for Kathmandu, you drive from Saga (4,500m) around the south side of beautiful (lake) Paiku Tso, crest a 5,236m pass, and drop down into Kyirong Valley to Kyirong Zhen (2,800m), before heading for the border crossing for Nepal. This is recommended as an **exit route**, because of the altitudes involved, and because there is nowhere to rest and acclimatise. The cheaper Nepalese travel agents favour this route as an incoming way to reach Kailash because it avoids the expense of a flight to Lhasa and the cost of touring in central Tibet. Larger Indian groups use the Paiku Tso route in long convoys of 4x4s. However, a sudden rise to 5,200m followed by a long, rough journey over 4,500m has resulted in several passengers dying each year: they are cremated at a hill near Kailash.

NORTH ROUTE *See map, page xii*

The longest way to Kailash is from Lhasa via Lhatse and Gertse to Ali, then south to Darchen. *En route*, you could make a side trip to Zanda and Tsaparang. Lhasa to Kailash by this route is around 1,900km (the Ali to Darchen stretch is 330km). A return to Lhasa can be made on the south route via Huore and Zongba to Saga. From here, you either continue onwards to Lhasa, or cross the Yarlung Tsangpo by ferry at Saga, detour around the south side of Paiku Tso, and head via the Kyirong border crossing to Kathmandu. Roads are in reasonable shape on the north route because this is the truck supply route to Ali and its army garrisons. Some parts need no roads at all – the trucks forge their own route across grassland.

There are some horrible, polluted, soul-destroying truck-stop towns *en route*. No-name hotels have rough and tumble facilities, if any at all – hot water supply comes in vacuum flasks. Some towns like Tsochen and Gertse have a few small restaurants hidden away. This is the main Lhasa–Ali–Kashgar truck and military supply route, so truck stops cater to the driving crews. Among the truck stops are Sangsang (4,520m), Raga (4,800m), Tsochen (4,650m), Dongco (4,400m), Gertse (4,400m), Tsaka (Yanhu) and Gakyi (4,450m). There are some high passes of 5,000m and 5,200m north of Tsochen. Distances on this route: the main road leaves the southern route 6km after Raga and heads north past some hot springs to Tsochen, 275km away. A further drive of 260km brings you to Gertse, where herds of sheep laden with backpacks of salt are a common sight in the autumn. From here it is a further 385km to Gakyi on the upper Indus, and a final 110km from Gakyi into Ali. The wild terrain in between truck stops makes the journey more than worthwhile: you might see wild asses, antelope and even black-necked cranes. There are a few hot springs along the way, too.

KASHGAR ROUTE *See map, page xii*

Connecting Ali through Yecheng to Kashgar is the wildest route of all. In the past, when Tibet was more accessible to backpackers, some travellers stocked up on food supplies and managed to hitch from Kashgar to Ali, paying the driver. A trip like that would require sitting in the cab: due to a sudden rise in altitude, this route can be fiercely cold, even in summer. For travellers, the stumbling block is **Yecheng**, 250km south of Kashgar, where passage depends on the mood of the PSB men. Sometimes they let travellers through with a friendly wave and no hassles; other times they may intercept travellers and send them back to where they came from. You can rent a vehicle in Yecheng to cover the stretch from there to Ali for around Y3,200 – split among several passengers, that's not too damaging. There are occasional sleeper buses taking 48 hours to cover the Yecheng–Ali route for Y800 a seat. The route traverses one of the highest, bleakest roads in the world, with no supply points along it. Apart from the stunning views, there's little of interest along this route except near Rutok, where some ancient **rock carvings** are found on a cliff near the road. Kashgar is in a remote corner of the PRC, but the Karakoram Highway (KKH) to Islamabad provides a convenient exit or entry (open May to November, with a valid Pakistan visa). The KKH is one of the greatest road routes in High Asia, with dramatic spires of the Karakoram range jutting sharply up in the background, contrasting with the more rounded peaks of the Pamirs from Central Asia.

ALI AND THE GUGE KINGDOM

If you're headed into Kailash by the south route, you may never get to Ali, which would be no loss at all. Well worth a foray north of Kailash, however, are the sites of Toling and Tsaparang (the ancient Guge Kingdom; pronounced *Goo-gay*), and Tirtapuri. The following section describes the approach to the Guge Kingdom from Ali. If you are coming up the road from Kailash, make adjustments and skip sections to suit. If approaching from the south, permits have to be secured in Darchen.

ALI (*Shiquanhe; 4,220m; capital of Ngari Prefecture; telephone code 0897*) Ali is a Chinese concrete monstrosity of a town, with some of the ugliest post-Mao proletarian-monolithic socialist-realist architecture in Tibet. It's composed of concrete cubicles and wooden kiosks, with garbage all over the place. Still, at least there's a lion statue in the middle, not a Mao statue. The town is Chinese to its rotten core – no Tibetan towns existed out this way except for the old capital of

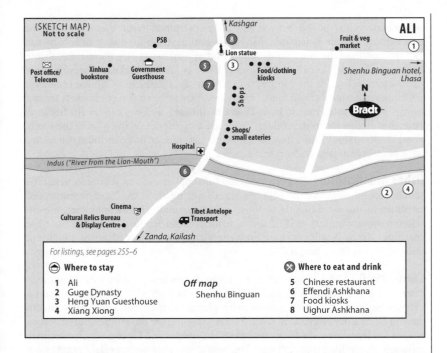

For listings, see pages 255–6

Where to stay

1 Ali
2 Guge Dynasty
3 Heng Yuan Guesthouse
4 Xiang Xiong

Off map
Shenhu Binguan

Where to eat and drink

5 Chinese restaurant
6 Effendi Ashkhana
7 Food kiosks
8 Uighur Ashkhana

Gartok (a nomad tent encampment that has disappeared without trace). Although it is commonly called Ali, the town is also referred to by the name of the river it is located along, the Indus, which the Chinese refer to as Shiquanhe and the Tibetans call Sengghe Tsangpo ('River issuing from the Lion's Mouth'; hence Sengghe Drong or 'Lion Village' is the Tibetan name for Ali).

Ali is easily the biggest town in western Tibet, with the largest military garrison of the region. Army platoons jog around the streets in formation at six in the morning, and again around sunset. After sunset, the top brass head for the karaoke bars and help themselves to the women. Otherwise, there's not a whole lot to see in Ali, apart from a place called the **Cultural Relics Bureau**, which has a display centre. The main reason for visiting Ali is shopping – for food and for permits.

Getting there There's an airfield called Ngari Gunsa, 30km from Ali, with **flights** from Lhasa several times a week. Air China flights from Chengdu land in Lhasa for refuelling and then continue to Ngari Gunsa, elevation 4,274m. The Lhasa to Ngari leg takes around 1½ hours. A glance at the map will show Ali is strategically sited at the junction of the north route from Lhasa, the south route from Kashgar, and onward routes to Zanda and Kailash. Locals may arrive by sleeper bus, covering the distance from Lhasa to Ali in two days.

Where to stay and eat *See map, above*

There are over a dozen hotels in town, of which half are tourist class, meaning rooms with attached bath. Among the better ones are **Xiang Xiong Hotel** (☏ *283 0888;* **$$**) with rooms for Y400, and **Guge Dynasty Hotel** (☏ *266 6111;* **$$**) with rooms for Y350. In the mid-range price category are **Shenhu Binguan** (**$$**) and **Ali Hotel** (☏ *280 0004;* **$$**) with rooms going for around Y250 for a double, while **Heng Yuan Guesthouse** (☏ *282 8288;* **$$**) has rooms for Y180. Near the bus station are some cheaper hotels where beds go for Y30–40, but you may not be permitted to stay there. For food, the best bets are **Uighur restaurants** dishing up central Asian food such as kebabs and nan. Just north of the lion roundabout is **Uighur Ashkhana** ($), a popular kebab and barbecue place, while close to the Indus River is **Effendi Ashkhana**, serving more extravagant dishes. To the southwest side of the lion statue is a Chinese restaurant with quite palatable Sichuan food. Otherwise, there are several supermarkets around town – one is located next to **Heng Yuan Guesthouse** – and you can try the fruit and vegetable market for fresh produce. There are also eateries on the road to the south. Food kiosks in this vicinity may have little nuggets hidden away, including chocolate bars, pineapple in jars, crackers and candles.

Other practicalities You can stock up on **supplies** such as shampoo here. The kiosks around town are the best bet; there's not much in the 'department stores'. Facilities to the western side of town include a small **Xinhua bookstore**, a **post/telecom office** and, just west of this, a **bank**. The Agricultural Bank has an ATM machine. The bank will not change travellers' cheques – only cash euros, pounds or dollars. There's also a **hospital** in Ali.

CANYONS TO ZANDA From Ali, the road to Zanda traverses an entire mountain range – a breathtaking trip, with snowy passes as high as 5,200m and 5,500m – before dropping down to a canyon with ghostly shapes. You drive through this canyon along a dry riverbed to reach Zanda. As you enter the multicoloured gorges, a side road leads to newly discovered caves at **Dungkar** and **Piyang**, which are said to have murals rivalling those at Guge. You would probably need special permits from the Cultural Relics Bureau in Ali to visit. With such a spectacular route, allow an entire day to motor from Ali to Zanda, with frequent stops *en route*. The canyons, with hues of yellow, red and copper, are extraordinary for their phantasmagoric sculpted forms, which appear at times to be like the outlines of dream castles or cathedrals, at other times like gigantic guardian statues or mythical animals. And then there are the near-mythical animals: the extinct ones. The Zanda basin is rich in fossils – in 2007, the skull of a woolly rhinoceros was unearthed, thought to be over three million years old. This woolly rhino is believed to have used its shovel-like horn to clear away snow and find vegetation. Research suggests that Tibet may have acted as an evolutionary cradle for mega-herbivores, allowing for adaptation to extreme cold – essential for the survival of Ice Age giants such as the woolly mammoth and the woolly rhino.

ZANDA (*Tsanda, Tsamda, Tsada, Zada, Zhada, Thöling, Toling; 3,660m*) Zanda is the Chinese name for the ancient Tibetan town of Toling, once the capital of Ngari (west Tibet). Remnants of this capital are scattered around town and the surrounding hills; there are dozens of *chorten*-like structures towards the Sutlej River.

Zanda has a spectacular setting, but it is little more than a glorified army garrison – facilities are for the military, not for the stray tourist. There's a big army base at the southern end of town, and an old Tibetan quarter at the northwest end. In between is a main drag with several **guesthouses**, one of which belongs to the military. **Chongqing Hotel ($$)**, with rooms at Y350, is the best choice, followed by the **Transportation Hotel ($$)**, with rooms going for Y250. Several small Chinese restaurants line the main strip (try **Sichuan Shifang**), and there are some tent-shops (selling supplies out of tents). There's also a **post office** (with telephone), and the **Agricultural Bank** has ATM access though it's not certain this will work. Zanda even has **internet** access.

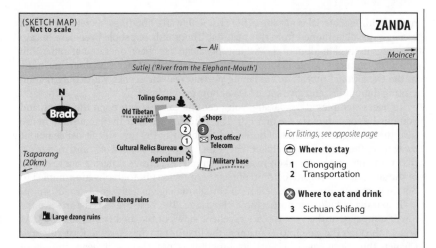

(SKETCH MAP) Not to scale

ZANDA

← Ali
Moincer →

Sutlej ('River from the Elephant-Mouth')

N

Bradt

Toling Gompa
Old Tibetan quarter

Shops

Cultural Relics Bureau

Tsaparang (20km)

Agricultural

Post office/ Telecom

Military base

Small dzong ruins

Large dzong ruins

For listings, see opposite page

🛏 **Where to stay**
1 Chongqing
2 Transportation

❌ **Where to eat and drink**
3 Sichuan Shifang

Permits If you want to visit Toling Gompa in Zanda or the ruins of the Guge Kingdom in Tsaparang, you may need permits from the Cultural Relics Bureau, located near the bank. Tsaparang requires separate permits from Lhasa, Ali and Zanda – put them all together and you are allowed to visit.

Toling Gompa The main sight in town is the largely abandoned Toling Gompa. Toling dates back to the 11th century when a structure was built by Yeshe O, the king of Guge. Assisted by scholar Rinchen Zangpo, he led a revival of Buddhism in western Tibet. Buddhism was snuffed out in a few short years in central Tibet by King Langdarma (who ruled AD838–42), a staunch supporter of the Bon faith. Upon the assassination of Langdarma, Tibet was broken up into lay and monastic pockets of influence. The Guge Kingdom became an enclave that was vital for the survival of Buddhism. King Yeshe O and Rinchen Zangpo promoted cultural exchanges with Indian Buddhists. Although over a hundred monasteries were built in the western region (which at that time encompassed Ladakh), Toling became the most important centre of Buddhist study, and its reputation grew with the arrival of 11th-century scholar Atisha from India. Eventually the kingdom was sacked in the 17th century. In the mid-1960s, Red Guards trashed Toling Gompa.

The main draw at Toling today is the fine **murals** in the few chapels remaining. In addition to destruction by Red Guards, murals in the White Temple have suffered water damage. Similar to those at Tsaparang, the murals are in early Newari and Kashmiri styles, both rarely seen in Tibet. You need a powerful flashlight to view them. The entry fee for Toling Gompa is Y80. From 2016 to 2018, Toling underwent extensive reconstruction and renovation.

Out of town On ridge-tops to the southwest of Zanda are the ruins of two *dzongs* (citadels) made of clay. This is the most peculiar hiking you'll ever do: scrambling over sand and dealing with crevasses of clay. Access to the larger *dzong* (the one to the west) is via a steep trail, and then through a sloping tunnel carved out of clay. Above the tunnel are former cave dwellings and dangerous crevasses. From here you continue climbing, and reach a vantage point with a magnificent view of the Sutlej Valley.

TSAPARANG Located 26km west of Zanda (a 1-hour drive) are the extensive ruins of Tsaparang, the once-powerful capital of the 10th-century Guge Kingdom. The

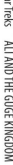

Star Treks   ALI AND THE GUGE KINGDOM

7

main building material is not stone, but clay, with walls, buildings, secret tunnels and escape exits all fashioned from this material. Thousands of people lived here in cave dwellings in this kingdom of clay, which appears to have been operational in the 10th and 11th centuries. Little is known of the history of the **Guge Kingdom**, but some of the exceptional murals at Tsaparang portray realistic scenes with courtiers and visiting dignitaries, and give some idea of how people lived.

To access temples at Tsaparang, you need the caretaker to open the doors, and you need to pay an entry fee of Y110. The Tibetan caretaker lives in a small house near the main gate: if he's not at home, he's probably in the tiny village visible not far away from the ruins. The caretaker may want to see your paperwork, and may insist that no photographs be taken inside the temple structures. Interior photography of the site is a very sensitive point; official permits for photography are complex to obtain (from Beijing), and expensive if you do manage to get them.

Tsaparang is built tier on tier up a clay ridge. The best-preserved parts are the lower ramparts; at the very top are excellent views of the area from the *dzong*. As you go through the gate into Tsaparang, the first thing you see is the **Rust-coloured Chapel**, thus designated because its function is not clear – it bears murals of Tsongkhapa, Sakyamuni and Atisha. The **White Temple** suffered extensive damage to its statuary, but its murals remain intact. Some murals portray Avalokitesvara, the 11-headed, thousand-armed bodhisattva of compassion. The mural style is Kashmiri. The **Red Temple** was destroyed and left open to water damage, but even so, its murals are striking, with beautiful large Tara frescoes. There are engrossing murals here, apparently depicting scenes from daily life at Guge – in one section envoys are arriving by donkey at the court; another part shows a high lama giving teachings. The **Yamantaka Chapel** is dedicated to its resident tantric deity Dorje Jigje: the walls bear murals of deities locked in tantric *yabyum* embraces (see *Glossary*, page 359) with their consorts.

From here, wend your way up clay steps, passing through a fantastic winding tunnel to the uppermost ruins. There's an entire **ruined citadel** at the top. Once past the tunnel, there is a complex of chambers and passageways: the citadel had its own water supply in times of siege, and the king had an escape route tunnel that led off the rear of the ridge.

At the top, the most impressive structure is **Tsaparang Dzong** – the king's simple summer palace – with expansive views over the valley. There are several temple

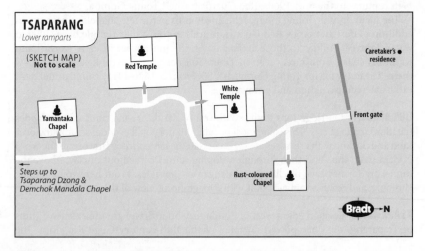

complexes at the top: the most important is the tiny **Demchok Mandala Chapel.** This chapel is usually locked – if you manage to get in, you can view the remains of a large 3D mandala, which was smashed in the Cultural Revolution. The chapel is a *gonkhang* (protector temple), and the site of initiation rites. It is thought that in times of crisis, the king and ministers would come to this chapel to ask for protection or direction. The chapel is dedicated to the protector deity Demchok, who is depicted in murals with his consort Dorje Phagmo. Fascinating tantric murals cover the walls: a flashlight is needed to view them. Depicted are rows of dancing *dakinis*, the female deities who personify the wisdom of enlightenment; below these are gory scenes of disembodiment from hell realms.

TIRTAPURI While Kailash is the main sacred site of western Tibet, there are a number of others on the pilgrim's wish list. After Lake Manasarovar, the most revered site is Tirtapuri, a yellow-streaked rocky landscape with hot springs. After encircling Kailash and Manasarovar, Tibetan pilgrims come to Tirtapuri for a relaxing circuit – the *kora* is only an hour, and there are grassy meadows for picnicking as well as hot water for soothing tired limbs. Tirtapuri lies 10km southwest of Moincer (which has a basic guesthouse), approachable by rented vehicle or truck. There is a short circuit in the Tirtapuri region – you can follow the pilgrims as they walk past elaborate *mani* walls, and sacred caves set in red and white clay cliffs, and pay their respects at a small monastery to a shrine of Guru Rinpoche. Though the entire Tirtapuri circuit takes just an hour, you could allow several hours to stop and drink in the atmosphere and the landscape. At the site, pilgrims bathe – or dip their feet – in several sulphurous **hot spring pools**, which can accommodate three or four people. The hot springs are reputed to have healing powers, and Tibetans search the waters for pellets of lime, for medicinal purposes. Just being able to feel hot water is therapeutic enough for Western visitors. There are plans for a bathhouse, supplied by the milky-white steaming pools, along with a small guesthouse at the *gompa*.

KHYUNGLUNG Beyond Tirtapuri, the side road bends west down the Sutlej, past the important Bonpo *gompa* of Gurugem. After passing through a small gorge, it reaches the village of Khyunglung, about 30km from Moincer. A further 3km onwards, reached by a footbridge, is a remarkable **cave complex** associated with the ancient kingdom of Shangshung. A short visit of 3–4 hours would allow you to poke around in several of the caves and climb up to the silver castle, although much longer would be needed to visit the whole site.

Khyunglung has been described as a cave city, but it has few of the features associated with a permanent settlement. The caves are all of similar size and simple construction, with a raised shrine for fires at the rear without a chimney. Instead of broken pottery and other artefacts found in abandoned caves elsewhere, there are bones, feathers and furs, some quite recent. It would appear that rather than a city, this place acted more as a gathering place for Bonpo shamans on auspicious days, with their retinue perhaps camping near the modern village. Whatever its origins, it is a unique and mysterious site. Since the recent building of a road to Khyunglung (which lies less than 100km from Darchen), it is possible to visit Khyunglung, Gurugem and Tirtapuri on a day trip from Kailash, but remember to get permits in Darchen if you do not already have them.

THE KAILASH REGION

Kailash is the centre of the universe – or at least the Tibetan Buddhist universe. In the Tibetan world-view, at the cosmic axis of the universe lies Mount Meru, the

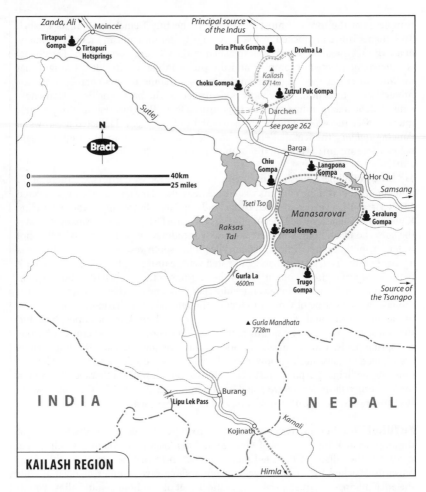

Map labels:

Zanda, Ali
Moincer
Tirtapuri Gompa
Tirtapuri Hotsprings
Principal source of the Indus
Drira Phuk Gompa
Drolma La
Kailash 6714m
Choku Gompa
Zutrul Puk Gompa
Darchen
Sutlej
N
Bradt
see page 262
Barga
0 — 40km
0 — 25 miles
Chiu Gompa
Langpona Gompa
Hor Qu
Samsang
Tseti Tso
Manasarovar
Raksas Tal
Seralung Gompa
Gosul Gompa
Gurla La 4600m
Trugo Gompa
Source of the Tsangpo
▲ Gurla Mandhata 7728m
INDIA
Burang
Lipu Lek Pass
NEPAL
Karnali
Kojinath
Himla
KAILASH REGION

abode of the gods. Mount Kailash is thought to be an earthly manifestation of the mythical Meru. Things are not as simple as this, however, as the Tibetan world-view incorporates existence in multiple dimensions. The Tibetan name for Kailash is Kang Rinpoche (Precious Jewel of Snows); the dome-shaped peak is symmetrical like an uncut diamond, with a permanent cap of ice and snow. At 6,714m, the mountain is modest by Himalayan standards, but nevertheless impressive to view. The peak is sacred to Tibetan Buddhist and Bon adherents, and to the Hindus and Jains of India.

In the late 19th century and early 20th, Kailash assumed mythical dimensions among Western geographers and explorers. For a long time, there was reputed to be a high mountain that was the source of the great rivers of India. But Tibet was inaccessible, so geographers were unsure if this was myth or fact. Finding the source of India's great rivers was a prime geographer's puzzle, on a par with finding the source of the Nile. The British employed Indian pundits, who, disguised as pilgrims, measured distances with prayer beads, and tossed marked logs into rivers to find out where they would pop up further down the line in India.

Eventually, it was discovered that the headwaters of four of Asia's mightiest rivers lay within 100km of Kailash – the Indus, the Yarlung Tsangpo (which later emerges in India as the Brahmaputra), the Karnali (a major tributary of the Ganges) and the Sutlej. Remarkably, the mouths of the same rivers end up as far as 3,000km apart. The Tibetans know the rivers by more prosaic names, identified with the four cardinal directions and four legendary animals. Thus, the Indus becomes the 'River issuing from the Lion's Mouth' (Sengghe Tsangpo or Sengghe Khambab, at the north), the Yarlung Tsangpo becomes the 'River from the Horse-Mouth' (Tamchok Khambab, to the east), the Karnali becomes the 'River from the Peacock-Mouth' (Mabchu Khambab, to the south), and the Sutlej is the 'River from the Elephant-Mouth' (Langchan Khambab, situated in the west).

DARCHEN Also known as Tarchen or Dharchen (4,620m), **Darchen town** is still under construction: a mongrel cross between a Tibetan tent encampment, a Chinese truck-stop, and an attempt at tourist deluxe hotels. As it grows, the adobe hutches dispensing noodles and tea have been replaced by more sophisticated restaurants (including, regrettably, Karaoke television salons). There is even a vegetable market; you can find shops by the river on the eastern side of Darchen. **Lhasa Namgyal Restaurant** opens early and offers Tibetan noodles, bread and sweet tea.

Top of the line for accommodation is the **Himalaya Hotel ($$$–$$$$)**, with rooms going for Y1,000 a night during high season, and probably half that astronomical rate in low season. In the same price range is **Himalayan Kailash Hotel ($$$–$$$$)**, with good rooms but poor breakfast offerings. **Gangchen Hotel ($$)** is smaller, but has good hot showers and cosy rooms, going for Y300 in high season and Y200 in low season. Otherwise, there's not a lot of choice when it comes to places to stay – rooms are little more than a bed for Y60–80 in four-bed rooms, with communal toilets. Among these are **Pilgrim Hotel ($)** with cosy dining room, **Lhasa Holyland Hotel ($)** with nice Tibetan teahouse, and **Sun and Moon Guesthouse ($)**. Competition for rooms is heavy during the peak pilgrimage months of June, July and August, with hotels such as Gangdishi guesthouse being fully booked by Indian pilgrims. Prices tend to be high for what you get (which is little more than a rock-hard bed), so you may have to bargain. Also useful to know is that you can leave your gear here when trekking, in a locked storeroom. There's similar-priced lodging at another compound run by the PSB. It's a good idea to hang around Darchen for a day or two to acclimatise, perhaps taking a day hike up to Serlung Gompa.

There is a small **clinic** in Darchen with oxygen supply, where altitude sickness can be treated. Group tours are also known to use the military hospital in Burang, and may also race clients (patients) over the pass into Nepal to Himla, where helicopter evacuation can possibly be arranged.

KAILASH *KORA* The circuit around the sacred mountain is known as the Kailash *kora*. Tibetans complete the circuit in one long day, starting before dawn and finishing after nightfall. Unless you are super-humanoid, don't attempt this at altitude. The minimum time for most Westerners to complete the circuit would be two days. Most allow three to four days. If you have a tent and want to dawdle, taking in the landscape at a leisurely pace, plan on five days or more. An annoying Y180 fee is levied for the Kailash *kora* for each trekker. There is a checkpoint about 250m past Darchen to check your ticket – if you don't have a ticket, you can buy one there. Porters for the trek can be arranged through a government office for about Y260 a day, or Y780 for the three-day trek. Trekkers should tip the porter at least Y100 at the conclusion of the trek.

What price for accumulating merit? There are rumours of a fast track for doing this: there is ominous talk of the Chinese building a motor road around Kailash, presumably with a toll gate.

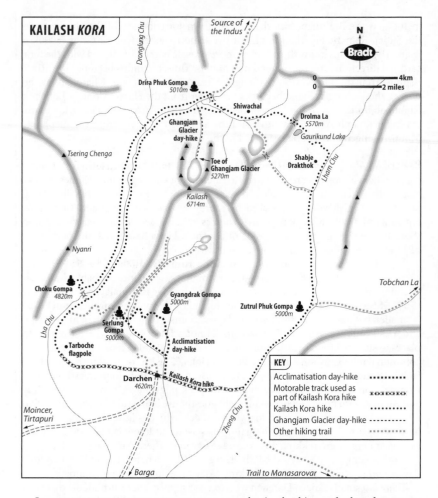

KAILASH KORA

Source of the Indus

Dronglung Chu

N

Bradt

0 — 4km
0 — 2 miles

Drira Phuk Gompa
5010m

Shiwachal

Drolma La
5570m

Gaurikund Lake

Ghangjam
Glacier
day-hike

Tsering Chenga

Toe of
Ghangjam Glacier
5270m

Shabje
Drakthok

Lham Chu

Kailash
6714m

Nyanri

Tobchan La

Choku Gompa
4820m

Gyangdrak Gompa
5000m

Zutrul Phuk Gompa
5000m

Lha Chu

Serlung
Gompa
5000m

Acclimatisation
day-hike

Tarboche
flagpole

Darchen
4620m

Kailash Kora hike

KEY

Acclimatisation day-hike ··········

Motorable track used as
part of Kailash Kora hike ꞁ0ꞁ0ꞁ0

Kailash Kora hike ··········

Ghangjam Glacier day-hike ----------

Other hiking trail ··········

Moincer,
Tirtapuri

Zhong Chu

Barga

Trail to Manasarovar

In group-tour arrangements, porters or yaks (or both) are deployed to carry camping gear and guest duffle bags. The group tours sleep in tents close to monastery guesthouses. Previously, individuals could stay in the monastery guesthouses on the *kora*, but that option seems to have closed down. Don't expect much in the way of food on the circuit, although there may be some teahouse tents along the way. Sometimes the *gompa* guesthouses sell noodles. A clean water supply is essential, so take water bottles and filtering devices (water can also be boiled).

Fellow hikers at Kailash are mainly Indian and Tibetan pilgrims. The Tibetans come from as far away as Kham, usually arriving by 'pilgrim truck'. Tibetan pilgrims comprise many different nomad groups with a fascinating array of costumes, particularly the women. Women coat their faces in *tocha* – a cosmetic made of concentrated buttermilk or roots – to protect the skin from dryness and UV rays. Indian pilgrims come as part of a lottery system run by the Delhi government, in operation since the early 1980s. Each year, up to 10,000 Hindus from all parts of India apply. Finalists are chosen and, after fitness tests, this number is whittled down to about a thousand. Hindu pilgrims are allowed ten days in Tibet. Travelling in groups of around 35, the lucky lottery winners walk across Lipu Lek pass where they are met by Chinese guides and the sacred circuit of their dreams gets under way. However, these lottery pilgrims are dwarfed in number by those wealthier Indian pilgrims who reach Kailash as part of 4x4 convoys.

Acclimatisation hike Strongly recommended is a day trip up to Gyangdrak and Serlung *gompas*, due north of Darchen. These *gompas* are situated at 5,000m: you can complete a triangular loop in about 6–7 hours, returning to Darchen by nightfall. One snag: the uppermost part of the trek requires a permit. However, you can avoid the permit situation by stopping short of Gyangdrak Gompa. This hike serves several functions: you can adapt to the altitude somewhat (by hiking high but sleeping low) and you can find out how to pace yourself at altitude. If intending to trek around Kailash with your own backpack, you might want to take the full load with you on the day hike to find out just how heavy it is.

The Kailash circuit
Day 1 The target of the first day's walk is usually Drira Phuk Gompa, about 8–10 hours from Darchen, including stops. That's because there is accommodation at the *gompa*. If you have your own camping gear, that opens up a lot more options in the schedule, since you can pretty well stop where you want.

POWERING UP AT KAILASH

In Darchen, you can stock up on last-minute supplies, and get your pilgrim supplies, too. At tents and shops at the northeast side of Darchen, pilgrims purchase prayer flags (to drape at the passes), small squares of paper with windhorses embossed on them (to fling around at the main pass) and, for good measure, prayer beads (to mumble mantras with, to get over the high passes). The windhorse (*lungta*) is a beautiful steed who brings good fortune (symbolised by the jewel on its back) wherever it goes. It is also painted on prayer flags – the wind sets the horse in motion, carrying good fortune in all directions.

In their lifetime, all Tibetans aspire to make the sacred pilgrimage to Kailash – some travel enormous distances in the backs of open trucks to get there. Pilgrimage is considered healthy and holy – the most popular time to attempt Kailash is after the annual harvest. When it comes to the Kailash *kora*, there's a kind of merit point system involved: the more you suffer, the greater the merit earned. Some pilgrims attempt not one circuit, but three (often on consecutive days in one season) or 13 circuits, or 108 circuits (spread over a number of years), which assures entry into nirvana. Prostrators, who proceed with inchworm-like motions, flinging themselves to the ground, take 15–25 days to complete the Kailash circuit, and must prostrate through anything in their path, be it snow, mud, slush or whatever. If you see a prostrator going in an anticlockwise direction, it must be a Bon adherent. For Bon believers, Kailash is the spiritual centre of the Shangshung ancient empire of western Tibet.

Punctuating the Kailash circuit are sacred markers in stone – carved *chortens*, carved *mani* stones and cairns with prayer flags. Offerings made by pilgrims at these sites might include pins (said to sharpen mental faculties), discarded clothing (as proof the pilgrim has been there) or *tsampa* (thrown in the air as protection against evil).

Leaving Darchen, head west: you'll know you're on the right trail when you come across a cairn adorned with prayer flags, and with discarded clothing left by pilgrims – tattered shirts, sweaters, worn-out trainers and old socks, as well as yak heads and goat horns. Further on is **Tarboche**, a large flagpole from which flutter long lines of prayer flags. Every year, at Saka Dawa (full-moon day in May or June), thousands of Tibetans gather to celebrate. The flagpole is taken down, and new prayer flags are placed on it, replacing the tattered ones from the previous year. If the pole tilts after it is raised again, it is considered a very bad omen. Pilgrim trucks can reach this site by dirt track, so this is often where Tibetans start the *kora*.

Beyond Tarboche, high on a ridge – a 20-minute climb up from the trail – is **Choku Gompa**, which was originally set up in the 13th century as a shrine. The current building was reconstructed after the Cultural Revolution, and is looked after by monks from the Drukpa Kagyu sect (as are the other two monasteries on the *kora* route). Shiny-eyed pilgrims crowd in to see the monastery's famed treasures: a white stone statue of the Buddha Opame and a sacred silver-embossed conch shell, said to have been Milarepa's.

From Choku, there's a choice of hiking up either side of Lha Chu (River of the Gods), through a canyon with impressive rock peaks, such as Nyanri. At Drira Phuk Gompa, there is a simple concrete building with a few rooms where you can stay – or you can camp out in the grassy fields nearby.

Day 2 You can build in an optional rest day, with a possible half-day hike up to **Ghangjam Glacier** and back. Building in a rest day at **Drira Phuk** gives your body a chance to recover, and will help you acclimatise for the arduous walk over Drolma La. Drira Phuk offers the chance to get quite close to Kailash, on a half-day hike to the toe of Ghangjam Glacier at 5,270m. Assuming clear conditions, there are awesome views of the glistening icy walls of Kailash's north face from this vantage point. You begin to understand why the Tibetans call the peak Kang Rinpoche (Precious Jewel of Snows), and why it is said that a wish made in front of the north face will definitely come true – one day.

Day 3 Heading out of Drira Phuk, you begin the tough ascent to Drolma La. This is the longest haul on the circuit – it takes about 10–12 hours to walk to Zutrul Phuk. Out of Drira Phuk is a bizarre sight: a field littered with discarded clothing. The place is **Shiwachal**, named after a cremation ground in Bodhgaya, India (Shiva-tsal). In this symbolic field of death, pilgrims must leave behind a personal item – clothing, a lock of hair, or even a few drops of blood – as proof of being here. A rock pillar in the middle of Siwachal is covered with scraps of cloth and bracelets.

Toiling upward, you reach **Drolma La**, which is the focus of the entire *kora*. Drolma La means 'Pass of Tara'; a large boulder depicting Tara is festooned with prayer flags. Tibetans attach their own prayer flag, and leave coins, locks of hair or other mementoes of their passage; they fling windhorse squares into the air and shout '*Tso tso tso! Lha Gyalo!*' ('Victory to the gods!'). Down the other side of the pass is a beautiful greenish tarn called **Gaurikund Lake**. Hindus are supposed to take a dip here, but ice skating might be more appropriate. You continue down, down, down – on a descent that is taxing on the knees – to meadows where Tibetans picnic. Eventually, you reach Zutrul Phuk Gompa, which has a basic concrete guesthouse attached.

Day 4 Around the Kailash *kora* are relics left by the great cave-dwelling ascetic Milarepa, who engaged in a competition with sorcerer Naro Bon Chun. At **Zutrul Phuk Gompa**, the reconstructed monastery encloses a cave that Milarepa fashioned with his bare hands – there's a statue of him within. The caretaker monk will show you around, although you may need a flashlight. The final showdown between Milarepa and Naro Bon Chun is said to have taken place on the peak of Kailash: in the ensuing duel, Naro Bon Chun fell, and in so doing, is said to have carved a long vertical cleft in the mountain's south face.

And so, totally knackered, you head back to Darchen to complete the Kailash circuit. Fortunately, it's a level or downhill walk to Darchen, and it doesn't take that long to dribble back into town.

CHIU GOMPA South of Darchen is a scene that frequently appears in photographs of Kailash: a monastery crowning a hill in the foreground and Kailash poking up in the background. The monastery is Chiu Gompa, the most impressive of the *gompas* encircling Lake Manasarovar. It's an easy drive from Darchen.

The ancient monastery is thought to have been the last resting place of the sage Padmasambhava, where he and his consort achieved 'rainbow body'. You can work your way up to the top chapel, with views of the entire area. The **guesthouses** close to Chiu Gompa are cheaper than those of Darchen, and have much better views. They have the added advantage of a bathhouse where sulphurous **hot springs** are channelled, offering the great luxury of washing your hair in hot water. If you are moving on to Manasarovar, this is the place to stay the night rather than Darchen.

MANASAROVAR Tibetans undertake several *koras* in the Kailash region: the first of Kailash itself, the second of Lake Manasarovar, and then a visit to Tirtapuri (some pilgrims tackle Lake Manasarovar first). Lake Manasarovar draws Hindu pilgrims who come for ritual bathing in the icy waters: full submersion in the waters is claimed to ensure enlightenment (Tibetan Buddhists, by contrast, settle for a sip and a splash over the head). Indian pilgrims pick up pebbles from the lakeside and fill containers with holy water when returning home. An entry fee of Y150 is levied to visit **Lake Manasarovar**. A complete circuit of the lake is around 90km: the route is perfectly flat and lies at 4,560m in altitude. A walking circuit takes about four to five days. An option is horse-trekking: you hire horses to ride around the lake, with packhorses carrying gear. If you do this, be sure to take a Tibetan wrangler along.

Eight monasteries encircling the shores of the lake were once so sited to represent the Dharma wheel with its eightfold path. They were destroyed during the Cultural Revolution, but some have been partially restored and remain active. Even if you don't attempt a circuit of Manasarovar, it's well worth driving past Chiu Gompa as far as Gurla La for a glimpse of magnificent **Gurla Mandhata** (7,728m). If you can, try to continue as far as Burang.

If you are contemplating the Manasarovar circuit bring sunscreen and insect repellent. You can start and end the circuit at Chiu Gompa, where there are places to stay. An alternative starting point is the town of Huore, where horses can be hired for an almost complete circuit of Manasarovar, which will cut down on walking time. Foreigners are usually drained of energy after completing the Kailash trek, so taking on the Manasarovar circuit is unusual. But the lake offers pristine hiking, with birdlife visible at certain parts, and a slew of monasteries or ruins along the way. The route usually proceeds from Chiu Gompa past Langpona and Seralung *gompas* to Trugo and Gosul *gompas*, passing by the small lake of Tseti Tso, and continuing north back to Chiu Gompa.

Raksas Tal While Manasarovar is identified with the positive forces of light (the sun), the lake next door, Raksas Tal, is aligned with the forces of darkness (the moon).

For this reason, Raksas Tal is shunned by pilgrims – its waters are rumoured to be poisonous (actually, they're not), as opposed to the healing waters of Manasarovar.

THE ROAD TO BURANG Right down south, close to the Nepal–India border, is the old trading town of Burang, also known as Purang or Taklakot. Burang lies at 3,900m in elevation. The distance from Darchen to Burang is around 110km, a 3-hour drive, if you have a permit to go there. Indian pilgrims enter via Lipu Lek pass and Burang to get to Darchen. Groups of well-heeled Western trekkers are permitted to take a five-day hike from Simikot (in Nepal) to Burang (or over the Lipu Lek pass), and take a rented vehicle to Kailash. The road southward from Kailash to Burang is very scenic, passing between Lake Manasarovar and Lake Raksas Tal, and driving right by Mount Gurla Mandhata.

Gurla Mandhata, though 7,728m high, appears to be quite low from this perspective, and the summit appears so close you almost imagine you could get out and start walking up it. Which is exactly what a couple of American climbers once did (unofficially), telling their startled driver to come and fetch them in a few weeks, after they'd bagged the peak! Gurla La, a pass of 4,600m, offers spectacular vistas, as does Ara La (4,200m). Southward are the pretty villages of Garu and Topa, with handsome, handcrafted houses.

BURANG Also known as Purang (elevation 3,900m), Burang is an old caravan stop on the banks of the Karnali River. Today it functions as a military outpost, with lots of men in green running around. It is aligned along a north–south road: at the north end is a military checkpoint (your documents will be scrutinised); towards the south end are some small **restaurants** and shops, the **post office**, **bank** and **PSB office**. Staying in Burang is a problem as the only sanctioned guesthouse for foreigners is overpriced and run-down. This is the **Peacock Hotel**, with rooms around Y300. The Peacock has two blocks: if staying here, head for the new block, which at least has clean bathrooms and hot water. The **Peacock Guesthouse** has a functional Chinese restaurant. While restaurants in Burang are mediocre, you may be able to buy fresh vegetables at a street market and take them to a restaurant to be stir-fried. Stocks of canned fruit and other items are quite good.

There's good **hiking** and a few things to see in Burang – you can combine several options by taking a western fork out of town. Head towards a bridge that spans the Karnali at the northern end of Burang. There's a small bazaar selling clothing, and some food (a small eatery here) with a few snooker tables. Continue west on a trail that leads up a steep hillside. Set into the cliff face is a remarkable cave-temple, **Gokung Gompa**. The caretaker monk will show you around for a token fee. The monastery ranges over three storeys, set within caves. Cave-dwellings are used as houses in this area. If you carry on over the top of a crest, you'll come to the **Nepalese Bazaar**, where Nepalese goods are sold in exchange for Tibetan wool, which is rolled into huge balls. Concrete shopfronts offer Nepalese and Indian goods, portered in from the Nepalese town of Darchula.

To the northwest of Burang, on a hilltop, you can make out the ruins of Shembaling Gompa. Once the largest monastery in the region, it housed several hundred monks, but was completely destroyed in the Cultural Revolution. Today the biggest active monastery in the region is at the pretty village of **Kojinath** (Korja or Kojarnath), situated 15km southeast of Burang, on the Karnali River right near the Nepalese border.

8

East Tibet, Kham and Amdo

This chapter cleaves into two distinct zones – east Tibet (lying within the Tibet Autonomous Region, TAR), and the parts of Kham and Amdo that are located outside the TAR. These two zones are as different as chalk and cheese when it comes to permits and freedom of movement. In east Tibet, within the TAR, you are hamstrung by permits at every turn, and restricted to rented vehicles with driver and expensive hotels. Outside the TAR, in Kham and Amdo, you can travel by public transport and make your own hotel choices – which will be a lot cheaper. However, because of the logistical obstacles involved, some travellers opt to rent a vehicle and driver for their trip outside the TAR. You can combine the two Tibets in a single trip if you can orchestrate the logistics and paperwork.

The distinction between east Tibet and the Kham region is a murky one. In old Tibet, large swathes of eastern Tibet and Kham were the same entity. The division is an artificial one that was concocted by Chinese officialdom – no doubt to divide and conquer the troublesome Khampas. 'Kham' has thus become an abstract concept – one that is referred to by Tibetans but not mentioned on Chinese maps. The former region of Kham now straddles four Chinese provinces, comprising over 47 Tibetan Autonomous prefectures and counties (there is some confusion over the exact number of prefectures and counties with Tibetan populations). Of the estimated 47 prefectures and counties quoted, roughly half lie within the TAR in east Tibet, and half lie outside the TAR – with six counties in Qinghai, three counties in Yunnan, and 16 counties in Sichuan.

In these regions, you are falling off the map. Even if you can find a decent map of these areas, some locations described are so remote that you'll still need a local guide to find them. This guidebook cannot provide topographic maps of the scale required to pinpoint such locations, but the book can get you to square one – the start of a trek, or the start of a *kora* of a sacred peak. For more detailed mapping and directions, bring along Gary McCue's *Trekking Tibet*, which covers trek and pilgrimage routes at Kawakarpo, Minya Konka, Labrang, Derge and more.

ACCESS TO CHAMDO PREFECTURE

At the time of research, Chamdo Prefecture in the northeast TAR was closed to foreigners. It has been closed since 2008. However, there are indications that the road from Kunming via Deqin to Lhasa may once again be open to foreigners, as it was in the past. If Chamdo Province continues to be closed, that means none of the overland routes from Lhasa to Chengdu or Kunming will work.

Why are regions closed? It could be because these are sensitive zones where self-immolations have taken place, or where Chinese authorities are busy demolishing monastic residences – as at Larung Gar and Yarchen Gar in Serthar

County, Sichuan (for more about this, see the *Religious freedom* round-up on page 41). Areas in the eastern TAR that were closed at the time of writing included Lhamo Latso, Yarlung Tsangpo Grand Canyon, Mount Bonri and all of Chamdo Prefecture. Many permits are required for the eastern section of the TAR. For now, all areas east of Rawok Lake may be closed, including the stretch of road from Baxoi to the Yunnan border.

Some good news from Kham: at the time of research, all counties within Aba/Ngawa Prefecture were open to foreign travellers, including Aba County and Kirti Monastery. Aba County was closed for several years but is now open. All counties in Ganzi Prefecture in western Sichuan are open, except Serthar (Seda) County. All areas of Serthar, including the Larung Gar Buddhist Institute were closed at the time of research. In Amdo, some counties in Golok Prefecture in Qinghai seem to be permanently closed, including Dari/Darlag, Gande/Gabde and Banma/Padme. Foreigners can drive through these counties but cannot stay the night. The birthplace of the Dalai Lama in the village of Taktser was closed to foreign travellers at the time of research. It periodically reopens. Such is the complex state of revolving doors and gates in the eastern region of Tibet.

TRANSPORT AND LOGISTICS A better picture of transport logistics can be gleaned from perusing the maps in this chapter and also looking at the airfares map in *Chapter 2*, page 68. Better yet, get hold of *East Tibet*, a detailed road map made by Gecko Maps from Switzerland.

Flights Nyingtri (Mainling) Airport has grown into a major hub, just east of Lhasa, with more links coming up to other parts of the Middle Kingdom. To leapfrog over road restrictions, there are several useful flights; the main one is Zhongdian–Lhasa, while another is Yushu–Lhasa. Apart from the more obvious Chengdu–Lhasa, Kunming–Lhasa and Xining–Lhasa flights, air travel within the region tends to be angled for Chinese tourist hot spots, such as regular flights (in the April–October season) from Chengdu to Kangding, Daocheng and Jiuzhaigou. Another airport is slated to open in Ganzi, with flights to both Chengdu and Kunming.

Future train A new rail line is currently under construction, connecting Chengdu in Sichuan province with Lhasa, via western Sichuan and the eastern TAR, though it will not be in place until at least 2025.

Road warrior The main transport in these regions will be by road, either in a hired vehicle or public bus. The standard hardy tourist vehicle now used in the TAR is a seven- or eight-seat Hyundai or Buick van; 4x4s are now only used for itineraries that are going off main roads. Outside the TAR, you are free to use public buses, but not if they go into restricted regions. Bus travel is cheap and probably uncomfortable – especially when entering higher-altitude regions. You need to have the mindset of a road warrior to handle longer trips by bus on precipitous mountain routes.

EAST TIBET, WITHIN THE TAR

Few travellers venture into east Tibet because of its lack of key attractions, because transport is difficult, and because it is hard to get permits (parts of east Tibet remain closed, probably due to military presence). As a foreigner, you are restricted by the Public Security Bureau (PSB) to higher-end hotels in most towns, which means you end up paying over Y200 for a double room. But if you want to get right off the track, east Tibet is the place to go.

Loop or linear? That is the route decision to make in advance if using Lhasa as a launching pad. You could make a large loop from Lhasa through east Tibet to Bayi, within the TAR, and come back to Lhasa. Or you can go from Lhasa all the way through east Tibet via Bayi to Derge or Deqin. Once you reach Derge or Deqin, you are in Kham, where you can drop your vehicle and official driver and carry on by yourself. The permit brouhaha stops here.

At the time of writing, all of Chamdo prefecture 🔒 is closed, meaning that overland routes from Sichuan and Yunnan provinces into the TAR are not possible. There are constant rumours about the imminent opening (actually reopening) of the Yunnan route from Zhongdian via Deqin to Lhasa, so enquire about the latest news (see box, opposite).

There are few major monasteries along these routes through east Tibet, but excellent scenic spots abound. And the most scenic of all is tough to access: the Yarlung Tsangpo Grand Canyon – the deepest in the world. This is without a doubt a world-class wonder, but the problem is how to get to see it. The Yarlung Tsangpo Grand Canyon 🔒 is closed to foreign travellers. There are permit hurdles to overcome.

Lhasa to Derge or Deqin takes about 12 days, allowing time for sightseeing, though you could do the trip in eight days. The tariff is likely to be over US$2,500 to cover the cost of vehicle, driver and guide. And the price could rise to US$3,500 for the package.

Lhasa to Chengdu is 2,400km via Chamdo (north route), and 2,080km via Litang (south route). On the first part of the route, you could undertake a tour to Samye and Yumbulagang, and then kick off from Tsedang (pages 197–9). Here you enter Nyingchi Prefecture. Highlights of this region include the sacred lake of Basum Tso; the sacred peak of Mount Bonri (🔒 *closed at time of research*); Mount Namche Barwa; and visits to Monpa, Lhoba and Tengpa villages. However, with the exception of Basum Tso, permits for these places are hard to come by. Permits for eastern TAR are not hard to get, but do take time. Travellers should contact a travel agency at least six weeks in advance to have time to get the required permits.

ROAD CONDITIONS There has been a massive road construction project going on in both Lhoka and Nyingtri prefectures for the past several years. The government has been spending hundreds of millions of dollars to pave roads in the region as well as build numerous new tunnels. As of the summer of 2017, the road going east from Lhasa to Rawok Lake is 95% paved. However, summer monsoon rains still bring flooding and debris to sections, particularly between Bayi and Rawok Lake. Currently, it takes tourist vehicles 2½ hours to go from Lhasa to Tsedang, but around 9 hours to make the 425km drive from Tsedang to Bayi. The main reason for the long driving time is the strict speed limit that is enforced along the way. It takes a further 3 hours to drive the 150km connecting Bayi with Rawok Lake.

THE ROUTE TO BAYI A rail line is under construction from Lhasa to Bayi but is not expected to be completed until at least 2022. Vehicles headed from Lhasa to either Derge or Deqin save considerable driving time by travelling along the north route to Bayi, which is mostly paved. The southern route from Lhasa to Bayi is much rougher and thus takes a lot longer, but winds through spectacular scenery. Some travellers combine both routes as a way of exploring east Tibet: they complete a one-week round-trip loop from Lhasa. The following paragraphs briefly describe that loop, so extract the parts you need to suit your journey. Be aware that the permit situation in east Tibet is difficult: some places require four permits (see pages 133–4).

Basum Tso About 280km east from Lhasa and 48km east of Kongpo Gyamda is a turn-off northward, leading another 47km on a paved road to **Basum Tso** (*Basong Tso, Draksum Tso; 3,470m*). The lake can be reached in 5–6 hours' drive from Lhasa. From the other direction, the lake is 125km from Bayi.

Basum Tso has been granted top-level tourism status by the PRC, meaning it will invariably be flooded with Chinese tourists. This ethereal lake is associated with the legend of King Gesar of Ling, Tibet's epic poem. You can visit enchanting **Tsodzong Gompa**, on a tiny island reached by a pontoon walkway (*Y120 entry fee*). This small *gompa* was rebuilt by Dudjom Rinpoche, the highest-ranking Nyingmapa lama from the Kongpo area. Dudjom Rinpoche died in exile in 1987. Several nuns look after Tsodzong Gompa. The entrance to the lake is located 4km before the actual lake. From here, you can walk or take a Y45 shuttle bus to the lake visitor centre, just before the bridge leading to Tsodzong Gompa.

There is a two-day pilgrim circuit around the lake, but modern pilgrims don't bother – they just take a speedboat for an hour to reach the sacred spots up one end of the lake. There is a landing spot up the far end where you disembark and walk inland to a waterfall site where pilgrims rub themselves against revered stones and squeeze into impossible cave crevices. Join a group on a boat and you can get there for maybe Y40 a person (hiring an entire small boat will cost around Y400 an hour). You can stay in bungalows at **Basum Tso Holiday Resort Hotel ($$)**, complete with a large dining hall. There are 30 double rooms for around Y140 each.

Kongpo route On the southern leg of this route, south of Bayi lies the region of Kongpo, with a distinct ethnic group identified by their traditional dress. You will see Kongpo people coming to visit the nunnery of **Lamaling**, which lies 26km south of Bayi and a further 4km off the road (an easy day trip from Bayi). Lamaling is a tower-like structure with an internal octagonal wooden frame. It is set in grounds with lush gardens and fir trees, and operates its own restaurant. Overseeing Lamaling is Dechen Yudron, who is the eldest daughter of Dudjom Rinpoche, the supreme head of the Nyingma sect who passed away in 1987. Dudjom Rinpoche married twice, and had nine children, some of whom still live in Tibet while others live in exile.

Along the south route to Lhasa from Bayi lies another great draw for pilgrims: the sacred lake of **Lhamo Latso** (🔒 *closed to foreigners*). This place hits the jackpot in the permit sweepstakes: you need four permits (TTB, Foreign Affairs, military, and ATP from PSB). That normally takes three days of wrangling in Lhasa. Assuming your paperwork is in order, after a rough haul from Bayi via Miling and Namshan, you reach Gyatsa. There are decent hotels in all these places. From Gyatsa, a turn-off to the north heads for about 2 hours' drive on a rough road to reach Chongkogye Gompa (4,500m), where rude lodging can be had. The *gompa* was largely destroyed in 1959. From Chongkogye, another drive of 40 minutes – and payment of Y50 per foreigner entry fee – brings you close to a viewpoint for Lhamo Latso. You need to be very well acclimatised to march up the final hill to the viewpoint, as it rests at prayer flags at 5,250m. From the viewpoint you can see Lhamo Latso, the oracle lake, at some distance. The lake sits at 5,080m. In former times, high lamas would venture out to Lhamo Latso to induce visions used in divinations. In the early 1930s, visions conjured up here helped direct Reting Rinpoche's search for the 14th Dalai Lama.

In the spring, this area is busy, with tent teahouses acting as lodging for those who've come in search of Chinese caterpillar fungus and high-altitude herbs. The spring is peak time for pilgrims to engage in a *kora* of Lhamo Latso, which could be accomplished on a long day trip, entering from this point. It's also possible to camp out and undertake treks of several days in this beautiful region. Further west of Gyatsa and Lhamo Latso, the road continues to Tsedang and Samye (pages 191–9).

THE MAGICAL BLUE POPPY

The fabled blue poppy of Tibet was first brought to the attention of the West by British officer and spy Eric Bailey, who spotted some when riding a pony near the Tsangpo in east Tibet in 1913. He pointed out the location to plant hunter Frank Kingdon-Ward, who collected the seeds at the same location in 1924. And sparked near pandemonium when the Royal Horticultural Society displayed the flower in 1926.

Poppy expert Bill Terry says: 'Among plants, none display such a palette of primary colours as the Asiatic poppies. There is no red redder than the red of punicea, no yellow more buttery than integrifolia. The white of superba is whiter than white. The imperial purples of lancifolia and delavayi are unmatched. No blue can compare with the blue of a perfect grandis or betonicifolia.'

There are dozens of poppies of different colour that grow in the Himalayan range, but the most striking is the tall *Meconopsis grandis*, a flower with incredibly blue petals flowering a metre in height at around 4,000m in alpine scree or woodland. The flower is very hardy: it has been observed with the hairs on its stem encased in ice. But the flower is not magical. It has no known medicinal properties.

Because Tibet has long been off the map, unscrupulous marketers have traded on general ignorance in things Tibet-related. Lancôme makes a perfume that says it captures the essence of the Himalayan blue poppy – which is actually not possible, because the blue poppy has zero fragrance. Yves Saint-Laurent created a line of cosmetic cleansing products based on 'health-giving Himalayan Blue Poppy water'. This, he claims, leaves the skin 'relaxed, purified and delightfully replenished'. And a healing spa in Alaska, where blue poppies grow well, advertised a Himalayan Blue Poppy Treatment, where the blue poppy is touted as having health-giving properties.

What will work as a health tonic (a tonic for the senses, at least) is to see for yourself the tall blue poppy growing, in the highlands of Tibet. In the vicinity of Lhamo Latso, if your timing is right, you will see clusters of tiny blue poppies – a different variety. To see the tall Himalayan variety, you need to go on an arduous quest – maybe into the Tsangpo Gorges like Frank Kingdon-Ward. Or go to Bhutan where the blue poppy flowers in the early monsoon – *Meconopsis grandis* is the national flower of Bhutan.

8

BAYI (*Bayi Zhen, 2,950m; capital of Nyingchi Prefecture; telephone code 0894*) In Chinese, Bayi means '8–1', referring to the founding of the People's Liberation Army on 1 August 1927. There's a heavy PLA presence around Bayi – the place is riddled with army garrisons. Tibetans joke that 8–1 stands for eight Chinese for every one Tibetan, which is about the ratio you'll see on the streets of Bayi. The population is around 60,000. Bayi is a totally Chinese town, built in the 1950s and much expanded since – there was originally nothing in the way of Tibetan structures here. So what you see around town are white-tiled structures, China Telecom advertisements, fake palm trees and army garrisons. And mini-brothels. There is a strong relationship between the last two. It is more than a coincidence that Bayi, the second biggest town in eastern Tibet (after Chamdo), with the biggest army garrisons, also hosts the largest array of brothels in eastern Tibet. Mini-brothels line whole boulevards in Bayi, with prostitutes openly plying their trade.

Where to stay and eat For aliens visiting Bayi, accommodation is restricted to a handful of high-end hotels, an arrangement monitored by PSB; other (cheaper) Chinese hotels are not permitted to deal with foreigners. The sanctioned bastions for foreigners include the following options: **Mingzhu** (*Cnr Guangfu & Binhe rds;* ☏*0894 588 2999;* **$$$**) has double rooms from Y525 *and* **Zhongzheng Zangji Xima** (*4 Yingbin Av;* ☏*0894 573 7777;* **$$$**) has double rooms from Y470. There are three cheaper options: **Longdu** (*89 Guangfu Av;* ☏*0894 582 8881;* **$$**), which has double rooms from Y325; **Azalea Hotel** (*408 Guangdong Rd;* ☏*0894 582 3222;* **$$**, *with dbls from Y425*); and **Hongtian Hotel** (*Bai Ma Gang Rd;* ☏*0894 573 9999;* **$$**), which has doubles from Y325.

The main street of Guangdong Lu has numerous small Sichuan restaurants (**$**), as well as Muslim noodle shops with dishes ranging Y25–50. Most restaurants in town are located in this area.

Other practicalities There is limited **internet** access in Bayi, and an **ATM** machine at the Agricultural Bank that accepts foreign cards.

What to see and do Located about 4km south of Bayi town, **Cypress Park** (⊕ *09.00–17.00 daily; Y30*) is home to many old trees along a hillside. The oldest tree is 52m high, 5.8m in diameter and thought to be more than 2,600 years old.

NYINGTRI AIRPORT VICINITY About 50km south from Bayi lies the much-expanded civilian airport of Nyingtri. The positioning of the vast new airport at Nyingtri is no accident: it gives China a great military advantage when facing off with India, where China claims the whole of the nearby Indian state of Arunachal Pradesh as 'South Tibet'.

In high season (May to mid-October), there are several flights daily direct from both Chengdu and Chongqing to Nyingtri Mainling Airport. Future links are expected to Beijing, Xian, Guangzhou, Kunming, Chongqing and Shenzhen. The airport is projected to handle 750,000 passengers and 3,000 tonnes of cargo annually by 2020. Carriers include Air China, Tibet Airlines, Sichuan Airlines and Shenzhen Airlines. It takes about 50 minutes from Nyingtri by taxi to reach Bayi. Landing at Nyingtri is quite challenging as the plane must fly along a winding valley. At 2,950m in elevation, the airstrip is quite low (for Tibet, that is). That lower elevation is attracting more tourism – being 700m lower than Lhasa, it is easier to acclimatise in Nyingtri.

Where to stay

Hilton Linzhi Resort Riga Village, near Nyingtri Airport ✆0894 588 8666; w hilton.com. Prices start at Y900 in this vast hotel located 7km from the airport & about 50km from downtown Bayi. The self-contained maze of 220 rooms features a range of amenities including a pool, gym, spa, private cinema & Tibet's first highland golf course. The location is isolated, with views of the Yarlung Tsangpo from the front terrace, & mountain views at the back. Hilton has more than a hundred hotels in mainland China, including branches in Chengdu, Chongqing & Golmud. Opened in 2017, Hilton Linzhi Resort is its first 5-star foray into Tibet, with more luxury hotels slated to follow in Lhasa & Shigatse. **$$$$**

BAYI TO BAXOI ENIGMAS Along the Bayi–Baxoi stretch lies some fascinating terrain which is extremely difficult to access. This is due to several factors, such as lack of both infrastructure and decent roads. But it also has to do with Chinese military presence, as the region is highly sensitive as it lies close to the Indian border. In the past there have been clashes between Chinese and Indian troops in the region over the borders of Arunachal Pradesh (occupied by India but claimed by China).

The small town of **Linzhi**, lying about 18km east of Bayi, is the gateway to this region but, due to geopolitical conflict, this area is liable to be closed to big-nosed foreigners. About 10km south of Linzhi town is sacred **Mount Bonri**, which, as the name suggests, is an important pilgrimage spot for Bonpos (followers of the ancient Tibetan Bon faith). Bonpos circle the mountain anticlockwise, taking two days, but if you are attempting this you should allow three days (🔒 *closed to foreign travellers*).

Linzhi is the gateway to the Yarlung Tsangpo gorges. Treks into the gorge area are possible but this would have to be arranged well in advance – you won't be able to organise anything from Bayi or Linzhi because of a complicated permit situation. There are even speedboat cruises from Linzhi along the Yarlung Tsangpo River, but at the time of writing only Chinese tourists were allowed on these high-powered vessels.

An unusual feature of Nyingchi Prefecture is that the altitude can dip quite low, with lush forest and monsoonal weather, and that means that Namche Barwa may be obscured by cloud. At 7,756m, **Namche Barwa** is the highest peak in eastern Tibet. The Yarlung Tsangpo stages a dramatic U-turn around Namche Barwa, cutting through the world's deepest gorges (for more on the Tsangpo gorges, see box, pages 6–7).

A highly scenic part of the Bayi–Baxoi stretch that is accessible lies at **Pomi**, where the town is bleak, but the surrounding valleys are stunning, plus you can visit Dodung Monastery. This is a worthy stop for picnicking, photography and hiking. Or stay overnight at **Wangshi Hotel** (*Zha Mu Bridge Rd;* ✆ *0894 566 5666; dbls from Y350;* **$$**) or **Shenying Hotel** (*Bu Xing Jie aka Pedestrian St;* ✆*0894 542 4888; dbls from Y280;* **$$**). The majority of restaurants in town are located on Pingan Road. These are mostly Sichuan restaurants (**$–$$**) along with a few Tibetan-style teahouses (**$–$$**). Dishes cost between Y30 and Y50.

Rawu
Also known as Rawok, the town of Rawu hosts a beautiful pine-forest area with lakes and sandy inland beaches. The town itself is nothing special, with the military given the run of the place, so it's the lakes nearby you should try to reach.

Close to Rawu lie the twin lakes of **Rawok and Ngan Tso**. Located 125km east of Pomi, these lakes may be as far east as foreign travellers can go in the TAR. The stunning alpine lakes lie at an elevation of 3,900m, surrounded by evergreen forest. Both lakes are narrow but 7–8km in length. Ngan Tso is the more westerly lake, with Rawok Lake lying about 4km to the east. The two lakes are connected by a stream. The small village of Ranwu is located on the northeastern shore of Rawok Lake and offers a few small restaurants and basic guesthouses.

In 1924, two British expeditions crossed paths in Lhasa. One was the ill-fated Everest expedition, heading west with the objective of summitting the mighty peak. The second expedition was heading in the opposite direction, east to the Yarlung Tsangpo Gorge, as it was then known. The expedition was led by botanist Frank Kingdon-Ward, with the eccentric Lord Cawdor in tow to provide financial backing. The object was to collect new plant species, and to hunt for a colossal waterfall, rumoured to be 30m tall.

Kingdon-Ward's expedition found waterfalls, but not a colossal one. He collected a staggering amount of flora – some 250 species, including the fabled blue poppy. And he overlooked a terrific discovery right under his nose. He was exploring in a canyon more than double the depth of Arizona's Grand Canyon, deeper than the Rio Colca in the Peruvian Andes, deeper than the Kali Gandaki in Nepal. The definitive discovery that the Yarlung Tsangpo Grand Canyon is the deepest in the world was not announced until the mid-1990s. The colossal 30m waterfall that Kingdon-Ward was hunting was not definitively identified until 1998.

Only now is the canyon starting to be launched as a world-class attraction – surely the eighth wonder of the natural world. The problem, as in Kingdon-Ward's day, is remote and inaccessible terrain. The canyon contains many rare species of flora and fauna, but trails through its wooded slopes are few and overgrown. The weather can be wet (very wet), foggy and unpredictable – the canyon hosts its own unique microclimates. And for foreigners, there's another great obstacle: Chinese officialdom. The main access point is close to Linzhi, which lies near to a heavy military traffic zone.

Hopefully, this situation will change and this remarkable canyon will be easier to access for foreign hikers and even foreign rafters (🔒 *closed to non-Chinese*

Located 35km west of Rawok/Ranwu Lake and 6km off Highway 318 lies **Midui Glacier**. The most accessible glacier in the eastern TAR, Midui cascades off a 6,800m-high mountain located in the Nyenchen Tanglha Range. Tourist vehicles can go to the main parking lot, from where it is a 2km walk to the boardwalk viewing platform. The entrance fee is Y50. 🔒 Lhegu Glacier, located 32km south of Rawok Lake, is likely to be closed to foreign travellers.

BAXOI VIA CHAMDO TO DERGE From the area close to Baxoi, the road splits – northeast to Derge or southeast to Deqin. The longer route is via Chamdo to Derge. 🔒 At the time of writing, all of Chamdo Prefecture was closed to foreign travellers.

Chamdo (*Qamdo; 3,240m*) Chamdo is the major town in east Tibet and the capital of Chamdo Prefecture. It also runs under the name Changdu. It's an administrative town of 80,000 people, with a fair sprinkling of high-rises and the usual Chinese concrete-and-karaoke mayhem layered on top of dilapidated Tibetan structures. Foreigners who make it through the permit hoops are expected to stay at **Chamdo Hotel** (prices unavailable at the time of going to press), which is right next door to the PSB office. Overlooking Chamdo is the Geluk monastery of Jampaling, with close on a thousand monks in residence. The *gompa* dates to the 15th century. About 100km south of Chamdo is Bangda (aka Qamdo Bangda, Bamda, Pomda, Changdu) Airport, a military airport which functions as a civil airport as well. Commercial **flights** from Lhasa to Bangda were tested out in 1999 on Boeing 757s, and there are chartered flights from Chengdu to Bangda. Bangda Airport, *travellers*). Chinese tourists are able to reach the area. They start out on a day's drive from Nyingtri Airport, followed by an arduous two-day hike to Zhacu village. Close to this spot, there's a vantage point with stunning views over a bend in the river, where the mighty Yarlung Tsangpo wraps around the base of Mount Namche Barwa.

An addition at this site is the Namche Barwa Visitor Centre, designed by avant-garde Beijing architect Zhang Ke. The centre houses an exhibition on the history of the canyon, a contemplation space and hiker facilities (including a medical clinic for those struggling with altitude). Down by the river is another facility, a small boat terminal where trips can be taken in direction of Namche Barwa.

You would think that a major attraction like the Yarlung Tsangpo Grand Canyon should be preserved in pristine shape, with revenue derived from tourism. Sadly, that is not the case. Chinese officials have chosen a path of exploitation of resources, in a way that will be highly destructive. The Yarlung Tsangpo is slated to be extensively dammed in the coming years. It is not only the world's highest river with the world's deepest gorge; it has far and away the world's greatest hydro potential, at the Great Bend of the Tsangpo. A proposal made by Chinese engineering consortiums calls for construction of Motuo Dam at the Great Bend, with a staggering output of 38,000MW. That would be far greater than the output of the Three Gorges Dam – currently the world's largest. In 2013, a 3km tunnel was blasted through to the remote village of Motuo, with a sealed road. Motuo, also known as Metok and Medog, is a site sacred to Tibetans as one of the 'hidden valleys'. But now hidden no more. The road boring through mountains to reach Motuo can only mean one thing: a mega-dam is on the drawing board.

at elevation 4,334m, is the highest commercial airport in the world. It's about 2½ hours by road from Bangda to the city of Chamdo.

About 280km east of Chamdo, reached by a long mountainous drive, is **Derge Monastery**, the star attraction on the long-haul Lhasa to Chengdu northern route. Once you get to Derge, permit problems vanish. The dividing line for the TAR is the Yangtse River, and Derge lies 26km north of the Yangtse bridges. There are even privately run guesthouses to choose from in Derge. See the *Derge* entry in the *Routes through Kham* section, page 300, for details.

BAXOI TO DEQIN The road runs from Baxoi via Markham (turn-off to Litang and Chengdu possible) and dips down to the Mekong River past the TAR border, climbs high above the river, then swings into Deqin, set in a high valley in Yunnan's northwestern corner. Once out of the TAR, the chaperoned ride may end – unless you have negotiated further driving. Permit hokum ceases in Deqin, so you can do what you like once in Yunnan. Onwards from Deqin, you can proceed by regular bus or hired vehicle to Zhongdian, and then either loop via Daocheng and Litang to Chengdu, or make a run via Lijiang and Dali to Kunming. See the following sections for details on these destinations.

KHAM AND AMDO: TIBET OUTSIDE THE TAR

These regions offer thrilling experiences of Tibetan culture, grand Himalayan mountains and expansive high-altitude grasslands of the Tibetan plateau. This is the

Tibet that spells adventure, as in trekking, visiting nomads, horseback treks, bicycle expeditions – all the things that would be prohibitively expensive in the permit-ridden TAR. A journey here could take from a few weeks to many months; you'll probably want to visit again. Kham includes much of the eastern third of the Tibetan plateau; Amdo the plateau's northeastern corner. Each region has its distinct dialects, customs and architecture. You'll not only find fewer restrictions on your travels here compared with official Tibet (TAR), but also that the Tibetans tend to be more relaxed and friendly. In fact, according to Chinese statistics, there are more Tibetans in the Chinese provinces adjoining the TAR than there are within the TAR itself.

Religious life and the artistic splendour of the great temples of these regions compare well with those in Lhasa and central Tibet. In fact, there is more religious 'freedom' in regions of Kham. In parts of Yunnan and Sichuan, photos of the Dalai Lama are openly displayed in monasteries, and revered rinpoches in both Kham and Amdo attract a number of followers when giving teachings.

Trekking and cycling opportunities abound. Summer (May–September) is the best time to come, when wildflowers flourish and hillsides turn green with lush grass. Tibetans will be out camping on the grasslands with their herds of yaks, sheep and horses. The last stronghold of the beleaguered nomad culture rests in Kham. Summer is festival time: you might catch one with Tibetan-style singing, dancing, competitions and the grand finale – the horse race. Spring and autumn can be good travelling as well, though snowstorms can upset your plans and the grasslands won't have their flowers and greenery. Winter can be brutally cold with the prospect of stalled transport. Even in summer, the air is cool on account of the 2,000–4,000m elevations. Rain showers often pass through during the summer months, yet soon yield to the intense light of the sun. For maximum enjoyment, allow time to meet people along the way and soak in the wonderful views. Also, by gaining elevation slowly in the early stages, you'll greatly reduce the chance of acute mountain sickness. Banks and ATMs quickly thin out in the high country, so carry a load of Chinese cash to get you through. Towns with ATMs include Xining, Labrang, Yushu, Kangding and Zhongdian (Shangri-La).

The following route ideas are just a few of the many possibilities. We begin with the vast expanses of Kham – Tibetan lands to the east of the TAR and now in northwestern Yunnan, western Sichuan and southeastern Qinghai provinces. Farther north, Amdo spreads across most of Qinghai Province to the northeast of the TAR and includes a bit of northern Sichuan and southwestern Gansu provinces. Qinghai Province has

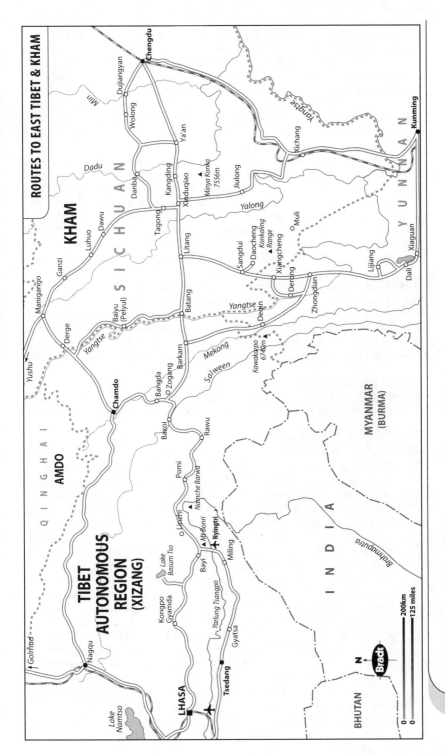

a rather unsavoury reputation as the gulag of China, due to its prison camps in the middle of nowhere. Dissidents and political prisoners are dispatched here. Due to their desert locations, it's hard to escape these camps, which is the whole idea.

Key destinations in Kham and Amdo include huge monasteries, the objective of pilgrims who travel great distances to see them: Zhongdian, Litang, Tagong, Derge, Dzogchen, Sershul, Yushu (Jyekundo), Kumbum, Tongren and Labrang. Trekkers will find remote monasteries, picturesque villages and great snow mountains. Cyclists will be challenged by spectacular high passes in the back country (see box, pages 302–3). There is much to explore in Kham and Amdo.

The descriptions here are route-based for the simple reason that Kham and Amdo cover vast areas. You can easily incorporate the routes with your TAR travels. In the grand scheme of your trip, these routes also fit well with travels in other parts of China and in southeast Asia. Travellers tend to start in the south and work their way north, so descriptions here start in Yunnan Province and wend their way north to Qinghai Province. Routes are equally good in either direction, though northbound may be more attractive in early spring and southbound a good idea in late autumn. Information about the large gateway cities of Kunming, Chengdu and Xining is included with the routes.

ROAD CONDITIONS The governments of Qinghai, Sichuan and Yunnan have spent tens of millions of dollars to upgrade roads through the region in recent years. Most roads are paved, with extensive new tunnels making driving times much shorter than a decade ago. New roads include Xining–Yushu, Xining–Machen, Maduo–Jiuzhi/Nyangpo Yurtse, Lanzhou–Xiahe and Langmusi, Zoige–Chengdu, Chengdu–Kangding and most of Kangding–Zhongdian (Shangri-La) in Yunnan.

ROUTES THROUGH KHAM

Gateway: Kunming You'll likely pass through Yunnan's capital on your way to or from southern Kham. Set beside Lake Dian at 1,890m, Kunming has a very pleasant

CARVING UP TIBET

Vast tracts of what were formerly the Tibetan territories of Kham (east of Lhasa) and Amdo (northeast of Lhasa) were carved up by the Chinese into four neighbouring provinces of the TAR. Tibetans referred to this area as 'Four Rivers, Six Ranges', later used as the name of a Khampa guerrilla resistance movement. The Chinese christened the new slabs of territory 'Tibetan Autonomous Prefectures' (TAPs). The process started under the Chinese Kuomintang regime before 1949, and continued under the communist government from 1950 into the 1980s. Some of the TAPs are enormous: Ganzi TAP in Sichuan, for instance, covers about one-third of Sichuan's land area. On the fringes of the plateau are smaller areas called Tibetan Autonomous Counties (TACs), where Tibetans and other nationalities live in mixed communities. Some TAPs are also occupied by Tibetan-related minority groups, such as the Qiang people of northern Sichuan. The ethnic Tibetan area can be roughly correlated with the Tibetan plateau. On the plateau, the Tibetan nomad culture is still present; where the plateau drops off, the descent is made to Chinese towns. However, there has been lots of Chinese infiltration since the 1950s.

To find out more about these regions, the International Campaign for Tibet (w *savetibet.org*) has a range of publications, including a printed map, *The Eastern Regions of Tibet*.

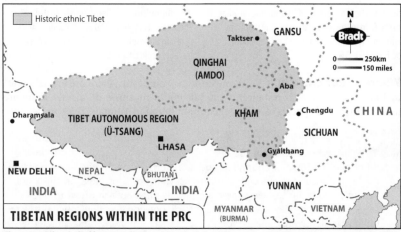

☐ Historic ethnic Tibet		

GANSU

Taktser ●

QINGHAI
(AMDO)

Aba ●

Dharamsala ●

TIBET AUTONOMOUS REGION
(Ü-TSANG)

KHAM

● Chengdu

CHINA

SICHUAN

LHASA ■

● Gyalthang

NEW DELHI ■   NEPAL   BHUTAN

INDIA   **INDIA**   **YUNNAN**

TIBETAN REGIONS WITHIN THE PRC   MYANMAR   VIETNAM
(BURMA)

N

Bradt

0 ——— 250km
0 ——— 150 miles

Chopping Tibet in half In 1965, China redrew Tibet's borders, creating the Tibet Autonomous Region (TAR), reducing ethnic Tibet's area by half. The vast Tibetan region of Amdo was absorbed into the Chinese provinces of Qinghai and Gansu, while huge slabs of Kham were donated to neighbouring provinces of Sichuan and Yunnan. A 2010 census reveals that out of a total 6.2 million Tibetans, an estimated 2.7 million live inside the TAR, while 3.5 million live outside the TAR. So there are more Tibetans living outside the TAR than in it.

climate nearly year-round. You can enjoy the fine **temples**, **parks** and **museums** while getting ready for onward travels. The city offers excellent air, rail and road connections within the province, many other cities in China, and nearby countries. You can **fly** to Lhasa, though this requires the usual permits and 'tour', which can be arranged by a local agent. Kunming is very close to border crossings with Laos and Vietnam, easily reached by **bus** on expressways. Your only option for the Vietnam connection at present is by bus. A new rail link is in the works to Vietnam and will replace the historic French-built line. You can pick up a visa for Vietnam in Kunming; or from the other direction China visas can be obtained in Hanoi. Most nationalities can get their Lao visa at the border, or you can visit the consulate in Kunming. If you're coming from Laos, Chinese visas are available in Vientiane (longer Chinese visas may be possible to obtain here).

 *Where to stay*

☐ **Green Lake** 6 Cuihu South Rd; ☎0871 651 58888. This nice but older hotel remains the most famous one in the Green Lake District of Kunming. Located just a short walk from the lake, it offers Chinese & Western restaurants. Standard rooms from Y900. **$$$$**

☐ **Sofitel Kunming** 777 Huancheng South Rd, Xishan District; ☎0871 686 39888; w sofitel. com. Located 3km from the centre of Kunming, this is an excellent 5-star international hotel offering all amenities including swimming pool, workout room, multiple restaurants & airport pick-up services. Rooms start around Y850. **$$$$**

☐ **Grand Park Kunming** 20 Hong Hua Qiao, Cuihu (Green Lake District); ☎0871 653 86688.

This 4-star hotel is located near Green Lake & offers excellent rooms & service. Standard rooms from Y450. **$$$**

☐ **Hump Hostel** Jinma Biji Sq, Jinbi Rd; ☎0871 636 40359; w thehumphostel.com. The friendliest & cosiest hostel in Kunming that is also close to restaurants & bars. It offers dorms as well as private rooms with en-suite bathrooms. Prices range from Y185 for a private room down to Y45 for a dorm bed. **$$**

☐ **Lost Garden Guesthouse** 7 Huanggong Dong St, Wuhua District; ☎0871 651 11127; w lostgardenguesthouse.com. An excellent guesthouse located a few hundred metres from Green Lake. It serves excellent meals, has staff fluent in English & plenty of information on what to see & do in the region. It offers private rooms with en-suite bathrooms from Y170, and dorm beds for Y60. **$$**

🏠 **Kunming Cloudland Youth Hostel** 23 Zhuantang Lu; ☎ 0871 410 3777. Popular for its pleasant atmosphere & just about any service a traveller could desire. **$**

✗ *Where to eat and drink* If it's mushrooms you desire, there are entire streets in Kunming lined with **restaurants** specialising in mushroom cuisine. There are thought to be 850 species of edible mushroom found in Yunnan. Deep in the hills,

THE HOLY GRAIL OF FUNGUS

When the Old Town of Zhongdian suddenly surfaced, with brand-new buildings made to appear ancient with the clever laying down of moss on the roofs, it instantly laid claim to being the main nightlife area, playing host to dozens of small bars. But by day, a very different trade goes on – selling souvenirs to the Chinese tourists who traipse through.

And what, you wonder, could you possibly take home from Shangri-La? Well, the souvenir shops are packed with imported items that run the gamut from pashmina scarves to cowboy hats, from Tibetan trinkets to expensive jade pieces. But the ultimate souvenir from Shangri-La may be the gift of long life and good health. Fungus would be a good start. Traditional-medicine fungus products are in abundance in the souvenir shops of Shangri-La, with a number processed at local factories.

According to German mushroom expert Daniel Winkler, collecting mushrooms at the eastern side of the Tibetan plateau is of great importance to rural folk, as they can make more in a few weeks of foraging for fungi than they do in an entire year of farming or herding. While varieties such as the cuckoo mushroom are exported to Europe and the matsutake mushroom is flown fresh to Japan, by far the biggest market is domestic – with huge demand from east-coast China.

The trade is dominated by a fungal variety endemic to the Tibetan plateau called *yartsa gunbu* (*Cordyceps sinensis*, also known as Chinese caterpillar fungus). Cordyceps accounts for over 95% of the fungi market value, and in the Tibet Autonomous Region contributes to some 40% of rural cash income. According to Winkler, collection across the Tibetan plateau rakes in around 100–150 tonnes of this bizarre fungus each year. When you consider than a tonne is equivalent to roughly three million cordyceps specimens, that's an awful lot of fungal worms being traded.

The Zhongdian region lies at the crossroads of this intense fungal economy, a paradise for fungophiles – or a nightmare for fungophobes. The caterpillar fungus is the Holy Grail for Chinese tourists. Like something out of *The X-Files*, cordyceps is a parasitic fungus that grows on the larva (caterpillar) of the ghost moth over the winter season, and takes it over, killing it in the process. Thus cordyceps lies somewhere between insect and plant. The Tibetan *yartsa gunbu* means 'summer grass, winter worm', summing up the parasitic process. This thin worm-like 'plant' is hard to find – it must be dug up from surface soil in alpine grasslands above 4,000m in the spring. Cordyceps harvesters head off in large numbers in the spring not only in Tibet, but in Himalayan regions of Nepal and Bhutan. Can this fungus be the source of the fountain of youth? Are dead caterpillars the answer?

Tibetans (often former nomads) make their livelihood from collecting varieties such as chanterelle, morel and matsutake, which are exported to Japan and Europe. The Tibetans also look for a variety of black truffle, and for the highly prized *yartsa gunbu* (Chinese caterpillar fungus), valued for its supposed anti-ageing and aphrodisiac properties. Hotpots are the traditional Yunnan way to savour mushrooms – steeped in a broth flavoured with local ham, for instance. Other dishes include stir-fries with porcini and green pepper, and fungus salad with wild herbs and black vinegar. Bon appetit!

Little is known about this fungus or how it originates, but Tibetan medicinal texts list its remarkable properties as far back as the 15th century, claiming it to be highly efficacious against kidney, lung and heart problems. Chinese caterpillar fungus is reputed to possess not only anti-ageing properties but is also an aphrodisiac, prized as an energy booster that stimulates the circulation and the immune system. It has been fed to racehorses in China to enhance speed and stamina – and used for the same reasons by Chinese athletes. The fungus was much sought-after in China during SARS epidemics. Modern Chinese takes on cordyceps claim it contains anti-cancer, anti-tumour, anti-oxidation, and antiviral properties. Like a lot of traditional Chinese medicine (TCM) cures, there is little evidence that they actually work. Clinical trials in scientific journals have reported some examples of effective TCM treatments, for example against migraines and obesity. They have found some cases where TCM works well in combination with Western medicine, but overall, the record is poor.

Whatever the case, the caterpillar fungus certainly has remarkable inflationary properties: the cost of cordyceps has risen more than 200% over the last two decades in Lhasa, where top-grade specimens are worth close to their weight in gold. The miraculous fungus ranks high on the gift list, and is used for bribery (no money changed hands, just lots of caterpillar fungus). Packets of cordyceps are on sale in Zhongdian, and the worms are added to special dishes in restaurants. None of this is cheap: a rare fungal aphrodisiac with a long list of magical properties is going to cost. Probably more than another famous fungus – the black truffle, prized in France and Italy. However, it is debatable which one costs more per kilo: top-grade cordyceps specimens from the Tibetan plateau, or rare white truffles from Europe. Like cordyceps, the truffle is a fungus imbued with myth, mystery and superstition. In common with cordyceps, the truffle has an aphrodisiac link: the pulling power of truffles could come down to a chemical in their aroma similar to a sex hormone.

With such a large price tag on it, and much profit to be made, there is also a trade in fake caterpillar fungus specimens, with clever copies made from other materials. On offer in Zhongdian are somewhat more affordable fungi for discerning consumers. Yunnan Shangri-La Tibetan Dragon Bioengineering Development Company of Zhongdian produces Jizong Fungus – described as a wild edible fungus from the snowline, best enjoyed in soup or fried or steamed. Or you might like to indulge in Wild Edible Black Fungus (fry it up with pig stomach), or perhaps Gastrodia Elata, said to nourish the kidneys and brain, calm the liver and stop wind. This is best served with chicken, duck or pigeon, or soaked in wine. A good choice would be Herbal Wine, made in Zhongdian from fresh ginseng, centipede, whole worms, lotus flower – the list goes on. This one claims to be excellent for curing impotence, rheumatism and a number of other dodgy ailments.

Popular restaurants in Kunming include:

✖ **Yingjiang Dai** 66 Cuihu Rd; 📞0871 653 37889. Serving popular Yunnan & Dai dishes, including grilled fish & sour pork. Located close to the shore of Green Lake. Dishes Y25–80. $$

✖ **Brooklyn Pizzeria** 11 Hongshan East Rd, 12 Banzhu Cuiyuan, Bldg 6-8; 📞0871 653 33243. One of the best pizza places in the city, also serving sandwiches & imported beer. Pizzas start at Y55. $$

✖ **Park Bar and Grill** Shicui Cultural Centre, Green Lake Area; m 1536 817 1162. Situated in the centre of the famous Green Lake Park, this place serves great American & Mexican dishes.

Prices range from Y50 to Y90. $$

✖ **Salvador's** 76 Wenhua Alley; 📞0871 653 63525. Foreign run, this place has been serving quality Western food for nearly two decades. Main dishes range from Y35 to Y60. $$

☕ **French Cafe** 70 Wenlin Rd; 📞0871 653 82391. Serving excellent pastries & fresh bread along with amazing coffee, the French Cafe is popular among Kunming expats. Prices from Y20 to Y50. $$

✖ **Hongdou Yuan** 142 Wenlin Rd; 📞0871 539 2020. Picture menu showing popular Yunnan fare including cold pork, roasted duck, steamed buns & more. Dishes Y15–20. $

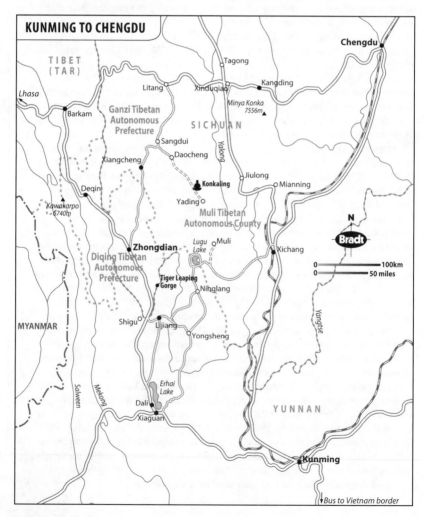

KUNMING TO CHENGDU

Kunming via Zhongdian to Tagong

Dali Old Dali makes an enjoyable stop between Kunming and Lijiang. City walls encircle the restored buildings of the centre. It's very touristy, yet makes a good base for side trips to villages around nearby Erhai Lake. A fantastic mountain hike contours high on the slopes of Cang Shan above; a chairlift hoists you to the heights, where you follow a wide well-made trail southward to a cable car that brings you back to earth and a bus back to Dali.

Lijiang (*2,600m*) Lijiang was used by explorer Joseph Rock as his base in northern Yunnan Province to begin his journeys into Tibetan lands – and you can launch from here, too. The city has much to see, especially in the large and atmospheric old town, and good transport connections. The shining 5,596m Jade Dragon Snow Mountain (Yulong Xueshan) to the north will likely entice you onwards towards Tibet. Lijiang is well worth a visit to meet the Naxi, a minority descended from Tibetan Qiang people. Most likely you will prefer to stay in old Lijiang (Naxi part of town, closed to motor traffic) rather than the new Chinese Lijiang that surrounds it.

Lijiang's wonderful **old quarter** is a UNESCO World Heritage Site, but is unfortunately overrun by legions of Chinese tourists who ramble through in unruly groups, ransacking the shops. There are lots of Naxi-style courtyard inns in the old quarter to suit all budgets, and the food is a brilliant selection of European, Chinese, Naxi and Tibetan – quite an eye-opener if you've spent time in the back country. You can while away time in pleasant cafés and bistros in Lijiang's bustling old town, and sample the local Naxi homemade wine, which tastes similar to port. The old quarter is actually the safest place to be: in 1996, an earthquake levelled the modern part of Lijiang, but left the old wood and stone Naxi buildings mostly intact, which speaks volumes about modern Chinese construction techniques.

 ### Where to stay and eat

Intercontinental Lijiang 276 Xianghe Rd; `0888 558 8888`; **w** ihg.com. For those wanting 5-star luxury, the Intercontinental Lijiang is the perfect place. Located in the southern section of the Old Town, it has a pool, excellent buffet b/fast, numerous restaurants, day spa & tour services. Prices begin at Y1,000. **$$$$**

Zen Garden Hotel 36 Xingren La, Wuxi Rd; `0888 518 9799`; **w** zengardenhotel.com. The Zen Garden is a 3-star hotel located in the heart of the Old Town. It offers 16 standard rooms starting at Y300. **$$**

Garden Inn 7 Wenmiao Alley, Beimen Rd; **m** 1510 887 3494; **w** lijianggardeninn.com. One

NAXI OLD-TIMERS

The Naxi are an intriguing group. Their ancient pictograph script is thought to derive from shamans. Naxi shamans used to conduct rituals similar to Tibetan oracles (the last shamans in Lijiang have long departed). The Naxi not only lay claim to the world's oldest dance score, they lay claim to the oldest orchestra, the oldest musical instruments and the oldest musicians. Naxi orchestra performers average around 80 years old in Lijiang. That's because they're the only ones who remembered the music when it was banned during the Cultural Revolution. The elderly musicians revived the music in the 1990s and are now passing on their skills to a new generation of performers. You can listen to a Naxi orchestra performance every evening at a venue near the centre of old Lijiang. Above the orchestra are photographs of those who have departed from the orchestra and passed on to the heavens above.

of Lijiang's longest-established hostels recently moved to a new location & now offers great bird's-eye views of the Old Town. Dorm rooms start at Y40 & standard rooms start at Y240. **$$**

🏠 **Lijiang Family and Hostel Inn** 20 Guangxi Alley, Guangbi Rd; ✆0888 950 5062. This great family-friendly boutique-style inn is located just a few hundred metres from the Mu Family Mansion. Standard rooms start at Y200. **$$**

What to see and do The old village of **Baisha** just north of town is a fine day trip, as are several Tibetan monasteries. Farther north, an Italian-built cable car runs almost 3km up the flank of **Jade Dragon Snow Mountain**, reaching 4,500m at the top of the lift. The rapid ascent can easily cause altitude sickness: Chinese tourists not only rent parkas, they purchase oxygen canisters. Be warned that you'll have to pay very high entry and cable car fees on the mountain.

Lugu Lake At an altitude of 2,688m, Lugu Lake, northeast of Lijiang, is the centre of the fascinating Mosuo ethnic group. Mosuo women do not marry: they instead take lovers for the length of time that suits them. Children belong to the household of the woman. Getting to Lugu Lake is an all-day affair of 7–8 hours that crosses the deep gorge of the Yangtse, then climbs high into hills. Alternatively, you could overnight at Ninglang, which is itself of interest as a market town with minority groups; it's 3–4 hours from Lijiang. Small towns and villages around Lugu Lake offer hostels and hotels.

🏠 **Where to say and eat**

🏠 **Lugu Lake Yonsamity Resort Hotel** 4 Sanjia Cun; ✆0888 950 5062. This oddly named hotel is located about 1km from the lakeshore & offers lake-view rooms with private bathrooms starting at Y600 & mountain-view rooms starting at Y460. The restaurant serves decent Chinese & Mosuo meals. **$$$**

🏠 **Lao Shay Youth Hostel** Located in the middle of Lige Village; ✆0888 588 1555. This hostel offers lake views as well as bicycle rentals. Dorms start at Y40 & private rooms start at Y160. **$$**

Upward to Zhongdian On the way, you have the option of branching northwest off the main highway to the **First Bend of the Yangtse** at Shigu, where the great river makes a nearly 180° bend to change not only its course, but the course of Chinese history. Back on the main highway, you'll cross the Yangtse and reach the main turn-off for **Tiger Leaping Gorge**, one of the top sights of Yunnan. A road goes all the way through the gorge, but a trail high above provides the best way to experience the scenic splendour. The trail is doable in one long day – or you can take your time and overnight at village guesthouses. Several trails also drop from the road to raging rapids, hemmed in by one of the deepest gorges in the world.

You have a choice of two routes onwards to Zhongdian: the main highway takes a direct route north, or you can go through Tiger Leaping Gorge and continue on a winding mountain road past icy 5,396m Haba Snow Mountain, the travertine terraces at Baishuitai, and up into Tibetan country.

Gateway: Zhongdian Set at a lofty 3,275m, Zhongdian has been christened 'Shangri-La' by the Chinese. The old Tibetan name is Gyalthang. It's the largest town in Diqing Tibetan Autonomous Prefecture and the one with the most facilities.

At the centre of Zhongdian is an entirely new old town – a convincing reconstruction of Zhongdian's old Tibetan quarter, done after Zhongdian was awarded the Shangri-La name by Beijing. With the name of Shangri-La comes

SHANGRI-LA SHENANIGANS

Nobody with their marbles intact would mistake Zhongdian for Shangri-La: it's a bland Chinese city full of concrete and karaoke, which doesn't fit the bill. But Zhongdian is being marketed as the gateway to Shangri-La, in rivalry with other candidates such as Yading and Lijiang. This time, all of Diqing Tibetan Autonomous Prefecture is being pushed as a composite (large monastery in one part, classic pyramidal mountain in another) which helps explain the 2002 official name change from Zhongdian County to Shangri-La County. And this will also explain Diqing Shangri-La Airport, the official name of Zhongdian's airport, on the outskirts of town, with flights to Chengdu, Kunming and Lhasa. The Kunming–Zhongdian–Lhasa flights are likely to be staggered in winter (December–May), but the Kunming–Zhongdian flights should be more regular. Many businesses in Zhongdian blithely use the Shangri-La logo without rhyme or reason: Shangri-La Bus Station, Xianggerila Mini-mart, and so on. It's just another day in Shangri-La.

According to Yunnan spin doctors, Zhongdian is the only possible site for Shangri-La. According to the Sichuan spin doctors, however, the real Shangri-La is located in Yading. Shangri-La County (formerly Zhongdian County) is one of three counties that make up Diqing Tibetan Autonomous Prefecture (the other two counties are Weixi Lisu and Deqin). Diqing TAP covers a grand 23,870km² and is sparsely populated, with around 400,000 people, of whom perhaps 30% are Khampa, or ethnic Tibetan. The percentage rises in Deqin County (population 60,000, of whom perhaps 75% belong to Tibetan or Tibetan-related minority groups).

Due to all the regional dogfights in these parts over which place is the real Shangri-La, Chinese authorities came up with a novel solution. In 2002, they announced the creation of a huge zone to be developed for tourism in western Yunnan and Sichuan, to be called the 'China Shangri-La Ecological Tourist Zone', with development investment projected to run to billions of dollars. This drew howls of protest from exiled Tibetans, who say this is yet another marketing ploy to exploit the Tibetans, and that there can be nothing remotely resembling the utopia of Shangri-La if it falls under Chinese domination. In any case, the Shangri-La Ecological Tourist Zone idea has since vanished into thin air – just like Shangri-La.

tourist expectations, so the old town was built to match those expectations, making it rather like a carbon copy of Lijiang's old town. To add authentic touches, even the new roofs were carpeted in moss. Actually, Shangri-La has been rebuilt from scratch twice. The hundreds of wooden structures here – guesthouses, bars and shops – had little in the way of fire safety measures, and the narrow alleys were perfect for a firestorm. On the night of 10 January 2014, a large fire roared through – possibly due to a careless cigarette or faulty electrical wiring shorting out. Thousands of firefighters, soldiers and police were mobilised to fight the blaze, but Shangri-La burned to the ground. Soon the carpenters were back at it, and Shangri-La has been faithfully resurrected from the ashes – back to its rampant souvenir-selling ways.

Every night there is ethnic dancing at the main square of the old town to complete the picture of happy, smiling minorities. The main sight of Zhongdian is **Sungtseling Monastery** (*Y115 entry fee*), a citadel founded in the 17th century by the

8

Fifth Dalai Lama. Sungtseling has a spectacular setting and is worth half a day of roaming around. It's an easy 5km bus ride north of town.

Tour operators Agencies around town can organise onward travel by air or road to Lhasa. The plane originates in Kunming, stops in Zhongdian and continues to Lhasa. However, planes can be overbooked because there are only flights several times a week from Zhongdian, as opposed to the numerous daily flights from Chengdu to Lhasa. Best to book your Zhongdian–Lhasa flight well in advance, via an agent in Chengdu. The air ticket to Lhasa is around Y1,600 one-way.

An overland trip from Zhongdian to Lhasa is ultra-expensive, costing in the region of US$4,000 for 12 days. The reasons for this exorbitant pricing are hard to fathom, but there seems to be little way around it by bargaining with agencies. There are two agencies close to the old town that deal with foreign individual travellers.

Khampa Caravan, at the centre of Zhongdian (✆ *0887 828 8648*; e *info@ khampacaravan.com*; w *khampacaravan.com*), offers package tours and overland tours to Lhasa for a hefty tariff. Agencies seem to go through the TTB Yunnan office.

Where to stay In addition to the hotels listed below, there are also two hotels outside of town. Right near the gates of Sungtseling Monastery is the mid-range **Songtsam Hotel ($$$$)**, a finely designed place with lots of atmosphere. A high-end hotel with character, located on the outskirts of Zhongdian, is **Banyan Tree Ringha** (✆ *0887 828 8822*; w *banyantree.com/en/ringha/overview*; **$$$$**) with beautiful Tibetan touches in the décor, and fireplaces in the rooms – and a huge price tag to boot.

Arro Khampa Hotel 15 Jinlong St, Dong Lang Rd; ✆0887 888 1006; w arrokhampa.com. Fantastic boutique hotel located in the recently rebuilt Old Town. Excellent staff & all-round great hotel. Standard rooms start at Y950. **$$$$**

Hylandia by Shangri-La 1 Chi Ci Ka St; ✆0887 899 8998; w shangri-la.com/yunnan/ shangrila. The Hylandia is part of the Shangri-La International Hotel chain & is located about 1km north of the Old Town. The hotel has a pool, several restaurants serving Chinese & Western dishes, a travel company & a great b/fast buffet. Standard rooms start at Y950. **$$$$**

Dragon Cloud International Hostel 23 Yi Ruo Mu Lang; m 1890 887 1600. One of the better hostels in the Old Town, the Dragon Cloud offers vehicle hire, bicycle rentals, currency exchange,

ticketing service & a restaurant serving Chinese & Western dishes. Dorm rooms start at Y60; private rooms with bath go for Y200. **$$**

Tavern 47 47 Cuolang Rd; ✆0887 888 1147. Owned by a Korean & Naxi couple, this comfortable hostel is a clean, traditional-style Tibetan house located close to the Old Town. It serves great Korean, Western & Naxi food. Standard rooms with bathroom go for Y150; dorm rooms start at Y45. **$$**

N's Kitchen and Lodge 24 Beimen Rd; ✆0887 823 3870. N's is a basic but friendly lodge-style guesthouse with a good restaurant, bicycle rentals, laundry facilities, currency exchange & local tours. It is located at the north section of the Old Town. Standard rooms Y160; dorms Y40. **$$**

Where to eat and drink Restaurants are great meeting points and also function as nightlife venues, with some places being a bar-restaurant combination. At the south side of the old town, near the big white *chorten*, is an upstairs club and dance-bar where Tibetans hold open-mike nights for singers. In the same vicinity are some Tibetan restaurants that sell yak burgers and yak-steak sizzlers.

Raven Tancheng Wangjiao, Bldg D8; ✆0887 881 1663. Shangri-La's best

bar also has great pizza. Beers start at Y20. **$$**

✗ Compass 50 Shangye St; ☎0887 822 3638. By far the best b/fast in town with fresh-baked goods & muesli . . . & not a bad place for lunch or dinner either. This popular foreign-owned café serves huge burgers, pizza, salads & pasta. Prices between Y30 & Y90. **$$**
✗ Rebgong Shangye St; m 1828 882 0252. Serving excellent Tibetan meals including mom's

Tibetan noodles, yak stew & more. Prices between Y20 & Y50. **$$**
▭ Noah's Cafe Changzheng Rd; m 1398 875 7634. This Shangri-La mainstay has been serving good Western & Chinese food for a long time. Dishes start at Y15. **$**

Side trip to Deqin and Minyong Glacier For most travellers this will be an out-and-back trip, but if you're one of the lucky people to have arranged it, this is also a route to Lhasa, entering the TAR near Yanjing. From Zhongdian, the highway heads northwest over a minor pass, then plunges into the deep gorge of the Yangtse. Near the river you'll come to a crossroads; turn left across the bridge for Deqin and follow the river to Benzilan, a town with hotels. From here the going gets tough with a long climb up and over a triple pass (4,000–4,300m) to Deqin. Nearing Deqin, you'll see a long row of *chortens* at a viewpoint where you can enjoy a splendid panorama (weather permitting) of Mount Kawakarpo, an icy peak on the Yunnan–Tibet border and its female counterpart, 6,054m Miacimu to the south. Mount Kawakarpo is also known as Mount Kawagebo or Mount Meili Xueshan.

The frontier town of **Deqin** is the capital of the county of the same name and sits at 3,290m in a side valley high above the Mekong. The spectacular 5- to 7-hour bus ride from Zhongdian covers close on 200km.

THE TEA-HORSE ROAD

If you are attempting the long overland haul from Lhasa via Deqin to Lijiang (or the reverse route), you are actually following stages of the ancient Tea-Horse Road. In the 7th century Tang Dynasty, Tibetan traders discovered tea on the eastern borders of Tibet, in Yunnan. Tea quickly became a Tibetan staple. In exchange for tea, they traded horses. The Chinese cavalry needed war horses, and the Tibetans had developed a special bloodline of horses – a stocky breed, renowned for endurance and stamina at high altitude.

And so the Tea-Horse Road developed – Chinese tea going west, Tibetan horses going east. The route stretched several thousand kilometres, traversing numerous high passes and taking three months or more to complete. There were over 60 relay stations along the maze of routes. Litang and Lijiang were among these relay stations – market towns trading in musk, furs, herbal medicines, salt, cloth, tea and horses.

Although the Chinese sold them the worst-grade tea-leaves, the Tibetan could never get enough of the stuff. At times, caravans of up to 500 yaks would converge in a town at the frontier of Tibet, waiting for tea to be loaded. This low-grade tea became such an addiction for the Tibetans that tea bricks – stamped with Chinese characters for the weight – were used as actual currency in the Land of Snows. You can find these huge tea bricks on display (and for sale) in shops in Zhongdian and Lijiang.

The lucrative ancient trade in horses has long gone. The Chinese military are no longer interested in horses. But the Tibetan addiction to tea remains – and so does the nomad passion for horses. In the back-country, a fast horse is a status symbol, providing transport over rugged terrain. And Tibetan nomads love horse-racing festivals.

8

The Three Parallel Rivers region in Yunnan was declared a UNESCO World Heritage Site in 2003. It consists of eight geographical clusters divided into protected nature zone areas and scenic areas. No sooner was this region declared a World Heritage Site than mega-dam building started up on the same river stretches, thus endangering the riverine ecosystem that supports the incredible biodiversity of this region. The mighty rivers and canyons that give the site its name are not part of the World Heritage Site, it seems.

There have been calls to change the status of Three Parallel Rivers to a World Heritage in Danger site. Within the site lies Mount Kawakarpo, a highly revered mountain with a pilgrim path around it. In February 2011, a Chinese gold-mining operation started up close to the pilgrim circuit. Infuriated Tibetans pushed equipment worth hundreds of thousands of dollars into a river far below. The mining operation was shut down. But protests against dam construction on the rivers running close to this nature reserve have not been successful.

In December 2013, it was announced that Sanjiangyuan National Nature Reserve's area in Qinghai Province would double in size for the purpose of 'rehabilitation of the land'. By more than coincidence, at the same time that expansion of Sanjiangyuan was announced, another official site said that 90% of nomads in Qinghai Province would be resettled by 2016. The real target of the creation of these national parks and nature reserves appears to be Tibetan nomads, forcing them off their traditional grasslands habitat. The meteoric rise in the number of nature reserves in Qinghai, the TAR, Sichuan and Yunnan coincides with large-scale removal of nomads, with the goal of removing two million nomads from the grasslands in the period 1995–2020.

These are nature reserves on paper only, lacking staff, management and funding. In fact, staff at these parks often do not have any guaranteed source of funding, which has led to a situation where their primary goal has become revenue generation rather than biodiversity conservation.

In 2013, Tibetans from Dzatoe County staged a protest against an illegal mining operator within Sanjiangyuan. The protest was broken up by over 400 military and paramilitary troops, firing machine guns into the air. At least one protester was killed, 14 were hospitalised, and a large number were arrested. Against all odds, the Tibetans of Dzatoe later achieved a rare victory: they took their case to Beijing, where the credentials of the miners were found to have been forged, and the mining operation was shut down.

There is absolutely no reason why Tibetan nomads need to be thrown out of nature reserves. In Bhutan, ethnic Tibetan yak herders live inside wildlife sanctuaries without problems. A better solution within Tibetan regions in the PRC is to create sacred natural sites, managed by Tibetan nomads, which allows for community access to the zone. That was the proposal made for Hoh Xil Nature Reserve, in northwest Qinghai, adjoining Sanjiangyuan. This reserve, also known as Kekixili, was instead inscribed as a UN World Heritage Site in July 2017, which means that China virtually has the UN's full blessing to kick out the nomads from this region.

Three Parallel Rivers of Yunnan was inscribed to the UN World Heritage list in 2003. The 1.7 million ha site consists of eight geographical clusters with nature reserves and scenic areas. The dominant features are the superlative gorges of the Yangtse, Mekong and Salween rivers which run together, coursing through gorges more than 3,000m deep in places, bordered by glaciated peaks over 6,000m high. The site is a biodiversity hot spot, one of the richest temperate regions in the world.

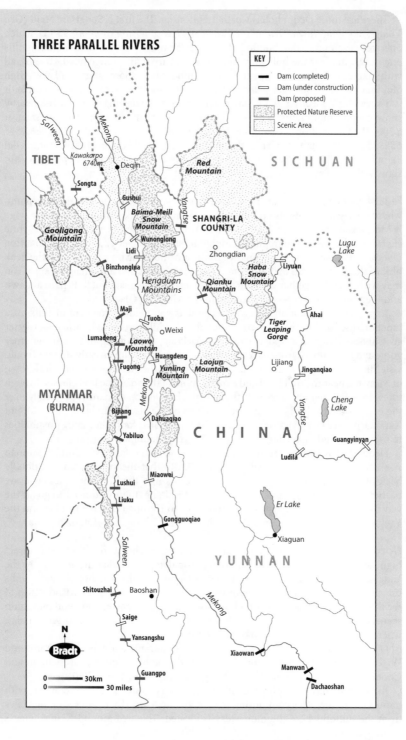

There are three Deqin hotels worth mentioning. The first is **Songtsam Meili** (*Geji Village, Shenping Town, Deqin;* \0887 828 8889; w *songtsam.com/en/;* **$$$$**), which operates seven upmarket boutique lodges in far-northwest Yunnan, including this one in Deqin, near the holy mountain of Kawakarpo. This lodge has 17 rooms, all with magnificent views of the surrounding mountains; rooms start at Y1,950. **High Mountain Resort** (*Gaoshan village;* **$$$**) is just a short walk from Feilai Temple. It is a very clean, locally rated 5-star hotel that offers sweeping views of the nearby snow-capped mountains. Staff speak basic English and standard rooms start at Y500. The final option is **Guangjing Tiantang** (*Near Feilai Temple, Deqin;* \0887 841 6388; **$$**). This clean, conveniently located 3-star hotel is a short walk from Feilai Temple and offers good views of the mountains. Restaurants and shops are within short walking distance. Standard rooms start at Y300.

Feilaisi viewpoint For scenery, head 10km beyond Deqin to **Feilaisi viewpoint**, where the rising sun lights up a string of 6,000m peaks like candles. At centre stage is Mount Kawakarpo, which at 6,740m is Yunnan's highest peak. At Feilaisi's white *chortens*, Chinese photographers indulge in strange Tibet chic rituals – chanting *Om Mani Padme Hum*, throwing rice in the air, and tying on prayer flags. The peak of Kawakarpo is sacred to the Tibetans and has temples and a challenging *kora*. You may wish to club together with other travellers and rent a taxi out to Feilaisi at dawn and then motor on across the Mekong to the Minyong Glacier.

Impressive vistas continue beyond Feilaisi as you follow a road cut in cliffs. At a junction, the road to the TAR continues ahead, while the route to **Minyong Glacier** switchbacks down to a bridge across the Mekong, fast flowing in its narrow inner gorge and far removed from its setting in southeast Asia. With an early start you could visit Minyong Glacier on a day trip. Or stay at one of the guesthouses in the little town of Minyong near the trail head and explore more of the area. The trail climbs through forest to the glacier and a temple, then keeps climbing on a boardwalk directly over the edge of the ice for better and better views of the glacier tumbling down Mount Kawakarpo. See Gary McCue's *Trekking Tibet* (page 364) for other hiking possibilities in the area, including the inner and outer *koras* of Mount Kawakarpo.

Deqin and Minyong are the end of the road – the farthest point in Yunnan you can access without crossing into the TAR. That means you have to double back unless you have arranged permits to cross into the TAR, or unless you are particularly sneaky. If you're heading north to Litang, there's no need to go all the way back to Zhongdian; instead, get transport to Derong (turn left just beyond the Yangtse River bridge) and on to Xiangcheng at the Zhongdian–Litang highway.

North to Litang From Zhongdian, you have a choice of taking the direct highway or a longer and more varied and populated route that drops down to the Yangtse River and winds up a tributary to Derong (which has hotels) and climbs up valleys with prosperous Tibetan villages. On the way you may wish to stop to see the colourful **Redaqupiling Temple**. Both routes have passes and good mountain scenery. Finally, you reach **Xiangcheng** (also known as Xambala or Xiangbala), where the best spot to stay is **Zhaxi Grand Hotel** (*88 Xiangbala North Rd;* \0836 582 6111), which is close to the town centre and restaurants and has clean rooms and Wi-Fi, with standard rooms for Y300. Outside the hotel, numerous Sichuan and Chongqing restaurants line the street. Dishes range from Y15 to Y50 apiece.

Xiangcheng has an impressive hilltop monastery, which is large and active, with monks on motorcycles commuting from here into town. There are sweeping views from the hilltop where the monastery is located. The area around Xiangcheng is dotted with prosperous villages and two- or three-storey farmhouses. It's worth stopping in Xiangcheng to explore.

From Xiangcheng, the highway twists over a 4,870m pass and drops to the tiny settlement of Sangdui and the turn-off for Yading Nature Reserve. You could visit Bangpu Monastery, about 1km north of Sangdui. The highway to Litang climbs on to a vast treeless plateau and a few more passes before the descent to Litang.

Side trip to Yading Nature Reserve On the way, you'll pass through Daocheng (Dabpa), a small, bland town 28km in from Sangdui with a handful of guesthouses. It's the main transport centre for bus connections.

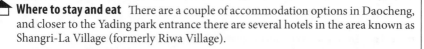 **Where to stay and eat** There are a couple of accommodation options in Daocheng, and closer to the Yading park entrance there are several hotels in the area known as Shangri-La Village (formerly Riwa Village).

Heaven Holiday Hotel 131 Dexi St, Daocheng; 0836 572 1333. Good mid-range option in the centre of Daocheng, with 24hr hot water, Western toilets & Wi-Fi. Standard rooms start at Y300. **$$**

Daocheng International Youth Hostel Across a small bridge at the end of Dexi Rd, Daocheng; 0836 572 7772. Hostel with a small café. Standard rooms start at Y120; dorm rooms for Y35. **$**

Ramada Encore Daocheng Hotel Shangri-La Village; 0836 572 1999. Located just before the Yading park entrance, this modern hotel is perfect for those wanting to stay as close to Yading as possible. Standard rooms start at Y600. **$$$**

Wizard Aden Hotel 1 Chituhe Rd, Shangri-La Village; 0836 572 3111. Located about 2km from the Yading park entrance. In-room Wi-Fi, restaurant & convenient location. Standard rooms start at Y380. **$$**

What to see and do There's a big Tibetan monastery 10km northeast of Daocheng called **Yangteng Gompa** (Xiongdeng Si in Chinese), which houses tens of thousands of Buddhist scriptures as well as many Buddha figures; it's located at the top of a winding switchback route, about 30 minutes by car from Daocheng.

Yading Nature Reserve embraces a realm of crystal-clear gurgling streams, and luxuriant forests of larch, pine, cypress, fir and oak, and majestic snow caps with cascading glaciers and odd-coloured glacial lakes.

To the Tibetans, this region is sacred ground: it is thought to be among the two dozen legendary hidden valleys scattered through the Himalaya, as described in Buddhist scriptures. Each hidden valley is said to have been consecrated by a great Tibetan guru. Clues are contained in Tibetan guidebooks on how to find them, but these places can be very dangerous and difficult to reach. There are three important mountains here: Chenresig (Avalokitesvara; 6,032m), Jambeyang (Manjusri; 5,958m) and Chanadorje (Vajrapani; 5,958m); these have never been climbed and are sacred to Tibetan Buddhists for representing the compassion, wisdom and energy essential to reach enlightenment and the end of suffering. Tibetans believe that it would be sacrilege to climb them, and dream of making a *kora* or pilgrimage around one or all of the mountains. Fifteen *koras* are said to be equal to the accumulated virtues of 100 million murmurings of the sacred mantra *Om Mani Padme Hum*, so some very strenuous hiking could save considerable wear and tear on the voice box.

Human habitation is minimal: there are no permanent residents inside the reserve apart from roving Tibetan shepherds. The nature reserve, first designated in the late 1990s, is pristine and pollution-free; the superb mountain vistas are a tonic for the senses. Shielded by the mountain range, the region has its own microclimate, with an ever-changing show of clouds dispersing over the snow peaks, and a great interplay of lighting conditions revealing new colours.

8

If all that doesn't take your breath away, the altitude will: it's over 4,000m up here. Chinese tourists come armed with oxygen pillows, oxygen canisters and traditional herbal remedies to counter the debilitating effects of high-alpine air. Touted by Sichuan spin doctors as the 'Last Shangri-La', the region attracts lots of well-heeled Chinese tourists, but remains largely unknown to Westerners.

Tourists can either hike into the area or opt, as most do, for a horseback ride. Tourists are led by Khampa wranglers, and seated on woven Tibetan carpeted saddles. The first photo-op stop is near tiny **Tsengu Gompa**, the only temple in the area. Within a few hours by horse, you reach a viewpoint known as **Luorong Pasture**, 14km from the trail head, where overnight camping is provided in tents. From this spot, it's possible to hike up towards a 4,700m pass to see pristine tarns, including one magical lake where, it is said, the future can be divined. If you have more time and camping gear, attempt a *kora*: the small *kora* encircles Chenresig and takes about three days. The big *kora* circumambulates all three sacred peaks in about six days.

Sichuan's Konkaling range has never been easy to get to, or trek around. Yading Nature Reserve is only accessible about six months of the year. You can rule out the winter – when the area is snowed in – and write off the monsoon period, when heavy rains reduce the trails to mud. The best times to tackle the route are April–June and September–November. The access route to Yading snakes in over high passes from the town of Daocheng. It's about 90km from Daocheng to Yading village at the trail head.

The only accommodation in the Yading area is in **tented camps**. The nearest hotel is in the town of Riwa (the nearest large village to Yading). On the way into or out of Yading, make a point of stopping at **Konkaling Monastery** (Gongaling), located west of Riwa. This Gelukpa monastery is the largest in southern Sichuan, housing over 500 monks. In the morning, they're all seated in the lofty main prayer hall, which reverberates with the sound of chanting.

Litang (*Lithang; 4,010m*) Litang is a town with a dusty high street lined with bland Chinese shops and small businesses. It is best used as a launching pad to visit the nearby grasslands and see nomad herders. Club together with other travellers and rent a minivan for the day for Y500 or so.

Litang's claim to fame is the annual **horse-racing festival**, which takes place on nearby grasslands in the first week of August. It was started up by Chinese officials to boost tourism, with fixed dates from 1 to 7 August. On 1 August 2007, a nomad called Rungye Adak snatched the microphone at centre stage and delivered a short speech about nomad grazing problems, about freedom of religion, and about the return of the Dalai Lama. He was promptly arrested and sentenced to eight years in jail. The festival was suspended for ten years but resumed in August 2017. This is the biggest horse-racing festival in the region; there may be other smaller festivals in nearby grasslands.

Around the town, **Litang Gompa** is worth the visit. Litang was a hotbed of resistance to Chinese rule, and the monastery was bombed and strafed by Chinese planes in 1956. It has since been rebuilt and is fairly active. On the outskirts of town at a hilly spot is a **sky burial site**. Some hotels drive guests over to witness the ceremony (assuming there is a body that day), charging Y100 for each tourist. This macabre form of profit-making needs to be discouraged out of respect for the Tibetans. You can hike to the spot yourself, or can arrange to have your driver get there in the morning before going out on a day trip to the grasslands. Do not attempt to take photographs at the sky burial site.

Practicalities The ATMs at the Agricultural Bank will dispense cash. There are several places to stay not far from the bus station.

Where to stay and eat

🏠 **Chongcao Hotel** 168 Xinqu Development Zone; 📞0836 532 6666. This hotel in the centre of town offers large Western-style rooms, Wi-Fi & a Chinese restaurant. The best hotel in town, with standard rooms starting at Y330. **$$**

🏠 **Litang Summer International Youth Hostel** 47 Pingan Rd; m 1801 579 1574. Great value hostel right in town with great customer service. Seem eager to serve! Standard rooms start at Y140; dorm beds go for Y35. **$$**

✗ **Tian Tian Restaurant** 126 Xingfu East Rd; m 1354 146 7941. A great restaurant operated by English-speaking Mr Zheng for well over a decade. It serves great Sichuan food. Popular place for foreign travellers to meet. Dishes between Y15 & Y50. **$$**

Litang to Tagong You're on Highway G318, the southern and most-used overland route between Chengdu and Lhasa. Numerous high passes and steep drops into valley bottoms make this a very challenging highway no matter which direction you head from Litang. Some 18km east out of Litang you have the option of a shortcut north via Xinlong to Ganzi in the northwest corner of Sichuan. The main highway east twists up into high country, culminating in a 4,487m pass before a wild descent into a forested valley and the city of Yajiang on the Yalong River, a major tributary of the Yangtse. A climb over a 4,475m pass brings you to a highway junction in a wide valley just before Xinduqiao, a trading town. The northern branch of the Sichuan–Tibet Highway branches off here; turn on to it for Tagong, just a short 33km jaunt north up the valley, which narrows to a little gorge before opening on to the Tagong Grasslands

Tagong The gorgeous setting at 3,750m and a handful of Westerner-friendly guesthouses and restaurants have made Tagong a traveller's centre, though it's small-scale. The **temple** is well worth a visit with three main chapels full of Tibetan artwork, a *chorten* field behind, and a *kora* lined with prayer wheels. The Tagong area has many good walks among the high, grassy hills to temples, a stupa and viewpoints. If your timing is right (end of summer on lunar calendar) you might catch the annual horse-racing festival of Tagong, which is staged on grasslands about 40 minutes' drive away. And that could be also the time that the annual Cham dancing is staged in the courtyard of the beautiful temple at the centre of Tagong.

🏠 *Where to stay and eat* **Jya Drolma and Gayla's Guesthouse** (📞0836 286 6056; **$**) is located at Tagong Square near Lhagang Monastery. This basic guesthouse is like a homestay with a Tibetan family. Owners Jya Drolma and Gayla are super-friendly and can speak basic English. Bathrooms are clean with 24-hour hot water. Dorms start at Y30. Another option is **Tashi's Guesthouse** (**$$**), a homestay near the main square. Also located near Lhagang Gompa at Tagong Square is **Khampa Café** (m *1830 287 9858;* **$$**), a foreign-owned restaurant serving decent Western and Chinese dishes. You have a choice of brightly painted Tibetan-style indoor seating or an outdoor patio overlooking the temple. A small gallery sells Tibetan arts and crafts.

Located on the grasslands about 30 minutes' drive from Tagong is **Khampa Nomad Ecolodge** (m *1368 449 3301;* w *definitelynomadic.com/dlodge.html;* **$$**). This Tibetan-style ecolodge is owned by an American woman, Angela, and her Tibetan husband, Djarga. The four rooms here offer spectacular views and the lodge has great Tibetan and Western meals – enjoy a yak steak with craft beer. Angela and Djarga offer high-quality treks, horseriding tours and cultural journeys in the area. Rooms start at Y420, including breakfast.

Onwards from Tagong From Tagong, there are route choices. You can carry on eastward to reach the major gateway city of Chengdu, or you can continue north from Tagong,

8

on a spectacular overland route to Yushu. In case you are starting from Chengdu, the following paragraphs give the connecting route from Chengdu to Tagong.

Gateway: Chengdu Chengdu sits at just 500m, giving it a warm climate where even bananas can grow, despite the proximity to the Tibetan plateau just to the west. Surprisingly relaxed for such a big city, Chengdu is a pleasant place to hang out before or after a journey through Tibetan lands. You can enjoy fine temples, museums, parks, varied cuisines and nightlife. Probably the most popular sight is the **Giant Panda Breeding Research Base** just northeast of the city, where you can watch pandas feeding and frolicking in late morning before they begin their epic naps: the easiest way to visit is with a tour arranged by one of the hostels.

Chengdu has the best transport connections in the region with an extensive network of air and rail links to Lhasa and many Chinese cities; international **flights** connect with Europe and many Asian cities. **Bus** routes fan out to the far corners of Sichuan and to Chongqing.

Tourist information Travel agents can be located in hotel lobbies or courtyards. A recommended agent is **Kham Voyage** (m *1838 218 6668*; w *www.khamvoyage. com/en*). Based in Chengdu (Sichuan), this Tibetan-owned company is headed by Nyima Tashi from the Kham region. He arranges unique photography and cultural journeys that usually involve homestays or monastery stays.

 Where to stay and eat Hostels provide great-value accommodation, cafés, Tibet tours and many traveller services.

Chengdu Shangri-La 9 East Binjiang Rd; ☏028 8888 9999. This 5-star international hotel has everything you need, including multiple restaurants, swimming pool, travel agency & gym. Standard rooms start at Y1,050. **$$$$**

Buddha Zen Hotel B6-6 Wenshufang, Wenshu Temple Area; ☏028 8692 9898; w buddhazen-hotel.com. Fantastic boutique hotel located near Wenshu Temple, just a short walk from the metro station. Standard rooms start at Y480. **$$$**

Dorsett Grand Chengdu 168 West Yulong St; ☏028 8332 8666; w dorsett-grand-chengdu.hotel-rn.com. The Dorsett Grand is a well-priced 4-star hotel near the Luomashi metro station & a 15min walk from Tianfu Sq. It offers a gym, restaurant & excellent b/fast buffet, with standard rooms from Y450. **$$$**

Lazybones Backpacker Boutique Hostel 16 Yangshi Jie; ☏028 8669 5778. Another great hostel, located just 25m from the Luomashi metro station (Exit A). The English-speaking staff here are friendly & the hostel offers panda tours, budget Tibet tours, restaurant, bike rentals & laundry service. Standard rooms start at Y185 & dorm rooms go for Y50. **$$**

Loft Design Hostel 4 Xiaotong Alley, Zhongtongren Rd; ☏028 8626 5770. The best hostel in Chengdu is very hip & cool, catering to young backpackers as well as more mature travellers. They have a restaurant & offer tours of the city, laundry service & ticketing services. Standard rooms with bathroom start at Y180 & dorm rooms go for Y50. **$$**

Chengdu to Tagong routes The quick and easy way goes **via Kangding**, 8 hours by bus thanks to good highways and the 4km Erlanshan pass tunnel. Flights to a new airport nearby may be available. Kangding (Dartsedo) has Tibetan temples and travellers' guesthouses and restaurants, though it's mainly a Chinese city.

Kangding

Where to stay

Lamze Linka Hotel 90 Qingge Av; ☏0836 281 6888. Located just 3mins' walk from the

Kangding bus station & less than 10mins' walk from the centre of town, this modern hotel is close

Few Westerners know this alternative route into Tibetan lands that leads through deep river gorges, pretty Tibetan villages and alpine meadows. Side roads branch off to viewpoints and trekking routes on the western side of a range crowned by 7,556m Minya Konka (Minyak Gangkar to Tibetans and Gongga Shan to Chinese). You could also exit by this route, travelling from Tagong via Jiulong to Xichang, and then hopping on a train from Xichang to either Chengdu or Kunming.

XICHANG Xichang is a large, sprawling city about 375km north of Kunming on the main rail line and highway to Chengdu; there's an airport here, too. It's best known for the Xichang Satellite Launch Centre (XSLC) about 64km to the northwest and used for launching geostationary communications and weather satellites. More accessible, the Buddhist and Taoist temple complex of Lu Shan spreads up the forested slope above the west shore of the large lake, Qionghai Hu, 7km south of town. A good museum near the start of the trail illustrates the history of the local Yi minority. On the way to Lu Shan you'll pass a park with sculpture and an architecturally interesting theatre complex. Hotels are widely scattered around town.

XICHANG TO JIULONG An expressway gets you most of the 75km north to Mianning, where the scenery begins. The route to Jiulong climbs past village fields, meadows and dense forest to a pass, then drops precipitously down to the Yalong River. The route follows the river upstream through some narrow gorges, then turns up the Jiulong River to Jiulong, nestled in a valley at 2,960m. Nearing town, you'll see more and more signs of Tibetan culture – architecture, prayer flags and traditional dress.

JIULONG The town has a main street, Tuanjie Dajie, with most of the hotels, restaurants and services; at the end you come to the town square and the **Longhai Hotel** (*12 Wandiao St;* \ *0836 332 3888; $$*). This is one of the few hotels that can officially accept foreign guests. It's clean and in the centre of town, with standard rooms from Y280. Wuxuhai, an alpine lake 25km to the northwest and 800m higher on a paved road, has idyllic scenery amid craggy mountains; lodging, food and horseback rides may be available.

JIULONG TO TAGONG Now you're in Tibetan country as the road leaves the last villages and follows wide valleys through conifer forests and meadows past summer camps of herders to a lofty pass, then down a narrow valley to the first village, Kunkashi, at the KM99 marker stone; here you can detour east to trail heads for Minya Konka (Gongga Shan). The main road follows valleys past very attractive Tibetan villages and joins Highway G318 just 8km east of Xinduqiao. You'll pass some hostels and hotels on the way into town, though Tagong is a more appealing place to stay, about 37km to the north.

East Tibet, Kham and Amdo   KHAM AND AMDO: TIBET OUTSIDE THE TAR

8

to shops & restaurants. Standard rooms start at Y400. **$$**

🏠 **Zhilam Hostel** 72 Baitukan Alley; \0836 283 1100; w zhilamhostel.com. This American-

owned hostel is one of the best in the entire region. It is located 10mins above town in a quiet village & offers a Western restaurant, camping equipment rentals & free travel info on western

Sichuan. Standard rooms start at Y260 & dorms go for Y45. **$$**

🏠 **Konka Youth Hostel** 59 Dongguan Yinle Guangchang St, 3rd floor; ☎ 0836 281 7788. This decent hostel is only 50m left from the bus station & has some English-speaking staff. Private rooms start at Y170, and dorms for Y35. **$**

✕ *Where to eat and drink*

✕ **Malaya Tibetan Restaurant** Yanhe East Rd; ☎ 0836 287 7111. The best Tibetan restaurant in town is located upstairs from the Dico's fast-food joint in the centre of town. It serves yak ribs, cheese *momos*, fresh noodles & other Tibetan food. Dishes cost Y30–100. **$$**

✕ **Zhilam Hostel** (pages 295–6) Serves great soups, burgers & pizzas, along with fresh-baked goods. **$$**

🍵 **Himalayan Coffee and Trading Company** 54 Liuliu Cheng, near the big yak sculpture. Serving easily the best coffee in the eastern Tibetan plateau. American-owned & Tibetan-staffed, this place will meet your coffee & baked goods needs. It also has pizza, wraps & sandwiches. **$$**

Tagong Another 2 hours by bus from Kangding will get you to Tagong. For more of an adventure, consider one of the three routes **via Danba**, a small city hemmed in by the valley of the Dadu River. It's a good base to visit nearby Tibetan villages. The middle route goes **via Wolong**, once famed for its giant panda sanctuary. The 2008 Sichuan earthquake changed all that and left massive devastation behind (even the pandas departed). The road through Wolong has reopened but will probably remain under construction forever. You'll see how dramatically the mountains have been transformed by huge landslides and how people's lives have changed. From Chengdu's Chadianzi bus station, you'll most likely take a bus to Dujiangyan in less than an hour, then look for onward transport to Wolong, probably a minibus. You may have to overnight at a basic hotel in Wolong, then enquire about transport over 4,523m Balangshan pass and down to Rilong, a possible base to explore the three valleys of Four Girls Mountain (Mount Siguniangshan); accommodation is easy to find. The road is good on this side of the pass and continues down the valley to **Danba**. A southern variation avoids Wolong by going via **Ya'an** and a pass over the Xiling Snowy Mountain, then descends to the Danba road west of Rilong; you would probably need your own transport for this. A northern alternative route loops via Wenchuan, Miyaluo, Barkam and Jinchuan. Parts of this road were badly damaged in the 2008 earthquake.

In Danba, most people prefer to stay in the outlying villages. **Tashi Tso Tibetan Homestay** (m *1828 364 5886;* **$$**) is in a large, stone, Tibetan-style home in the village of Zhonglu, 13km from Danba. Rooms start at Y160 and include dinner. The village is located on a mountainside with excellent day-hiking opportunities. Back in Danba town, there's the **Zhaxi Zhuokang Backpackers Hostel** (*35 Sanchahe South Rd;* ☎ *0836 352 1806;* **$**), where staff speak English and can arrange transportation to local villages and local treks. Standard rooms go for Y80, while dorms are Y40.

Suopo Village is famed for its stone towers, picturesque houses and views. It's close enough from Danba you could walk it: from the Rilong–Danba highway junction, head south 3km and turn left on a dirt track just past a blue and white building, follow the dirt track 1.8km across a suspension bridge and downriver to the main part of the village; eventually this will be upgraded to a motorable road. It's worth hiring a guide to take you inside some of the old buildings and one of the towers. **Jiaju Tibetan Village** has a stunning setting in a bowl high above the valley, about 7km north of Danba. **Zhonglu Village** has towers and homestays about 11km northeast on the road to Rilong.

From Danba, a road heads southwest up a craggy gorge that could have come out of a Chinese painting. The road leaves the gorge for a climb to a 3,907m pass, then runs across a plateau past Garthar Choide Monastery to Bamei, where you may need to change transport for the 27km to Tagong.

NORTHERN KHAM SPLENDOURS
Tagong via Ganzi to Yushu and Nangchen
This journey through northwestern Sichuan takes in some of the very best Tibetan landscapes and culture, including many large monasteries and temples. If time limits you to just one excursion in Kham and Amdo, this is the one to do. Derge, famed for its printing monastery, is a worthwhile side trip: it's also a gateway to the TAR on the northern Sichuan–Tibet highway. Yushu, just across the border in Qinghai, was hit by a massive earthquake in 2010 that killed more than a thousand people and destroyed most of the town and surrounding monasteries. It is undergoing reconstruction, and continues to be a major transit centre of the region.

The ride from Tagong goes through beautiful grasslands to a minor pass at 10km. Trees appear along the road as you drop into the valley on the other side. Look for the grey barren ridges of Bamei Stone Forest on your right at about 22km. In another 5km, a group of Sichuan restaurants mark a turn-off on the right for Danba, a worthwhile side trip (see opposite) via high grasslands and a forested gorge. Continue straight 300m into **Bamei** and you'll see a large *chorten* and many small ones on the right.

The 3-star **Bamei Shanzhuang Hotel** (☎ *0836 715 5666*; **$$**) is located at the intersection of Provincial Highways S303 and S215 and accepts foreign travellers, offering standard rooms from Y280.

The friendly **Bamei Art Hotel** (☎ *0836 715 5777*; **$$**) is a great option on Jiaojin Avenue in the centre of town, with Wi-Fi, 24-hour hot water and standard rooms from Y250.

Hillsides on the 79km drive to Dawu have a mix of grasslands and conifer forests – very lush and green in summer with lots of wildflowers. At 37km you enter the Long Deng Grass Land and continue climbing to a pass at 46km, then corkscrew steeply down into a narrow, forested valley with very attractive village houses of log and stone construction. You'll pass lots of *chortens*, too. **Dawu** (Daofu) is a large town on the Jianshui River at 2,980m; the golden-roofed Nyitso Monastery is visible on the hillside to the right just past the centre of town.

None of the hotels has a sign in English, but it's easy to spot the large Tibetan-styled **Ling Que Shi Hotel** (**$**) on the right just before the centre; rooms with bath may go as low as Y100 after bargaining; cheaper rooms without private bath are available as well. Chinese restaurants, including a vegetarian one, are nearby.

The gently rolling highway heads 72km northwest up the Xianshui He Valley, a major tributary of the Yalong River. You'll see pretty village houses and note how the architecture changes as you travel through the Tibetan lands of Kham. The vast spread of Drango Monastery and its Tibetan village come into sight well before the town of Luhuo itself. A large silver sculpture on a roundabout marks the entry to **Luhuo**, set at 3,200m. The big **Golden Yak Hotel** across from the roundabout may be the only place that accepts foreigners; a slightly run-down and noisy room with bath might go for Y100 after a discount. Lots of Chinese and Tibetan restaurants are nearby and across the street. From Luhuo it's possible to take another road north over a pass, then east to **Barkam** (aka Barkham, Maerkang or Markang) and beyond with several options for north Sichuan or Chengdu. You could even loop back to Bamei via Danba. **Drango** ('Head of the Rock') **Monastery** perches high on the hillside north of Luhuo and has a huge, well-decorated assembly hall. A series of *tankas*, said to have been done by a renowned artist, are easy to miss – step back from the altar and look up to see them. Monks are friendly, but watch out for aggressive dogs.

8

Inhabitants of the Tibetan Autonomous Prefectures in Sichuan and Yunnan have a lot more freedom than in Tibet; people appear much more prosperous, with Tibetan entrepreneurs often living in castellated structures (complete with satellite dish on the roof) and driving SUVs. And you will see large Dalai Lama pictures in monasteries in Kham, something that would not be tolerated by Chinese authorities in the TAR.

Historically, the Kham region was beyond the reach of the central Lhasa government and was dominated by heads of powerful clans prior to Chinese invasion. The tall brawny Khampas have a reputation as the fierce warriors of Tibet: in the 1950s, Khampa guerrillas engaged in stubborn resistance to Chinese incursions, and protected the Dalai Lama on his 1959 flight into exile. Though considerably subdued under Chinese rule, the Khampas are nonetheless not intimidated by the Chinese, and are aggressive traders who can be encountered as far off as Nepal and India.

Ganzi (*Garzê, Kardze, Kandze; 3,394m*) The grassland and mountain scenery on this 97km stretch is spectacular. Once past Luhuo, you continue up a valley of grasslands and bits of forest to Zhuwo at 52km, the last village before the highway begins a 19km climb to a pass with a splendid panorama of the glacier-clad Chola Mountains, crowned by 6,168m Chola Mountain. Tents of yak herders lie scattered across the grasslands near the pass. The descent through intensely green valleys leads to the Yalong River and Ganzi, set beside a small swift-flowing river dividing Ganzi into east and west halves. The highway follows the main street, Chuanzang Lu.

Hidden away near the centre, the old and atmospheric **Ganzi Den Gompa** has two halls with fine paintings and sculptures: devoted worshippers prostrate and make *koras*. Look for a gateway with little white *chortens* over a small lane on the north side of Chuanzang Lu between Dongda Jie and Qinghe Lu; or, from the Himalaya Hotel, go up Dongda Jie a bit and turn left up a narrow footpath. **Garzê Monastery** sits prominently on a steep hillside on the north side of Ganzi above the tightly packed Tibetan quarter. You can reach it by walking up the street on the west side of the small river, then curve left a bit on tiny lanes to a staircase that leads to the assembly hall. You'll probably need to ask directions, though getting lost among the twisting walkways can be fun. Or grab a taxi most of the way. Monks debate in the afternoons in a tree-shaded courtyard to the left of the stairs below the assembly hall. Inside, there's a pantheon of Buddhist deity statues, a central Sakyamuni Buddha and lots of very small statues of Sakyamuni Buddha and Tsongkapa. Walls have large paintings, mainly of fierce protectors. Look up near the centre of the hall to see a row of large *tankas*. The highest seat is reserved for the Dalai Lama or Panchen Lama, and is piled with *katas*.

Hotels in Ganzi include **Hotel Himalaya** (*Dong Da St;* ✆ *0836 752 1878;* **\$\$**), which is centrally located and the best hotel in town, with clean rooms, Western-style toilets, and standard rooms starting at Y180. The foreign-owned **Dzachusama Hostel and Café** (*133 Qingke Pudi;* ✆ *0836 752 3882;* w *dzachusama.com;* **\$**) is a clean Tibetan-style home with dorms starting at Y50. **The hotel café** (**\$**) serves good Western food and coffee. Prices range Y20–50. West on Chuanzang Lu across the small river, you'll see a large covered market to the left, a good place to stock up on fruit. Beyond the market area is the major cross-street Dajin Jie; turn left for the popular **Golden Yak Hotel** and another hotel across the street. Minibuses park on this street and there are Tibetan restaurants.

Ganzi vicinity Head out into the countryside to see other **monasteries**. Dongtong (Dongtok) Monastery and the new Dingkhor Chorten are about a 20-minute walk south across the Yalong River, then take the right fork. Pongo Monastery is across the Yalong River, then about 1 hour on the left fork. Beri Monastery is 15km west of town on the north side of the Yalong River. Dargye (Dagei Si) Monastery, nearby hot springs, and **Dargye Monastery Deshi Hotspring Guesthouse** are farther west near Rongbatsa, about 30km from Ganzi. Hadhi Nunnery, a 2-hour walk from here, is home to about 56 nuns. If you're headed south towards Litang, there's a shortcut via Xinlong: the turn-off is 10km east of Ganzi.

Derge via Yaqing (Yarchen) and Baiyu Instead of taking the main highway to Derge via Manigango, take this back road across superb scenery and past many monasteries. Nearly all transport heads to Yaqing, a very popular religious centre near the halfway point; here you can get onward transport to Baiyu. From Ganzi, the route follows the main highway across the Yalong River towards Manigango, then turns south up past villages, then summer camps to a 4,800m pass at 37km with fine scenery all the way. A few mud bogs on the steep 14km descent to the Ah Shi Chu may slow your vehicle. A little shop on the right before the river bridge is a popular stop for instant noodles and maybe other food. A gentle climb through a granite boulder-strewn landscape leads to a broad pass at about 23km. You might like to try a developed hot spring with private bathing pools 21km beyond the pass: look for a walled compound on the left. You'll then pass a couple of villages with *gompas*, set in a grassy valley with a few forests. At 114km from Ganzi you arrive at the signed junction for Yaqing, 7km to the south: there's a checkpoint at the turn-off and police may register you.

Yaqing Yaqing is a religious centre that attracts huge numbers of monks, nuns and laypeople. There are at least two guesthouses/restaurants here; ask people for directions. Expect to pay an overpriced Y50 per bed and don't count on a toilet. Shops are scattered around and are fairly well stocked. Yaqing has two large temples, great piles of *mani* stones, prayer wheels and *kora* routes. It's an amazing place to see.

Continuing 120km farther west via a 4,613m pass (25km from the Yaqing junction) and Ronggai checkpoint (106km from the junction), you will reach **Baiyu** (Pelyul). Pelyul Monastery, towering above the town, dates from 1665. It was built by the king of Derge. Set in a valley at 3,261m, Baiyu is a large town with accommodation and restaurants. The modern **Kunrui Hotel** (*55 Hedong Upper St;* **$$**) is the best option in town as it accepts foreigners. Standard rooms start at Y300.

For much of the 115km north to Derge, you'll follow the Yangtse River; two bridges cross to the TAR 26km before Derge. Even without permits, you could probably get away with going to the other side to inspect abandoned stone watchtowers. The mountains on the Sichuan side harbour many remote monasteries and trekking possibilities that you may wish to seek out. Gary McCue's *Trekking Tibet* has an entire chapter on this region.

Derge via Manigango and Tro La The 92km stretch to Manigango follows the wide valleys of the Yalong River and tributaries, with the minor 4,045m Mukri La about halfway. Many *gompas* line the way and you can make detours to others, such as Beri and Dargye, but you'll have to ask for directions as these are not signed in English on the highway. The icy peaks of the Chola Mountains rise to the south. Manigango, at elevation 3,886m, is a scruffy little crossroads town.

On Highway 317 near the town square is **Manigange Pani Hotel** (☏ *0836 822 2788;* **$**), which is a decent option for both a room and a meal. Standard rooms start at

Y130, while dorms go for Y30. Across the street on the second floor is **Travellers' Teahouse ($)**, a basic hotel that offers clean private rooms from Y60 with shared toilet.

If you arrive early, consider stocking up on food in Manigango, then heading another 12km on the highway towards Derge to camp at the very pretty alpine lake Yihun Lhatso (4,025m), at the foot of the towering Chola Mountains and their glaciers. You can admire the scenery and go hiking; horserides may be available.

You get a view of the lake from the highway on the 42km climb to Tro La (Chola pass), probably the most dramatic motorable pass in Sichuan. A sign at the top gives the elevation as 5,050m, but most maps place this closer to 4,900m. Pavement gives way to bumpy dirt on switchbacks up steep slopes on both sides of the pass: the views keep getting better and better as you near the top. Conifers and meadows fill the valleys on the other side all the way down to Derge. A sign on the left, 30km beyond the pass, marks the turn for Mondrak Monastery in a very pretty and remote setting less than a kilometre off the highway. Small villages line the valley farther down and you'll reach **Keluodong** (Khorlomdo) with a hilltop *gompa* and simple restaurants 86km from Manigango. Below here the Zhil Chu Valley narrows into a gorge that runs for 9.5km, then opens up at a large *chorten* and a group of rock paintings that you may want to visit. At 114km from Manigango, you pull into the large town of Derge. Two bridges lead across the river to the main part of town, which is predominantly Chinese. But if you head up the side valley, you'll reach the far more atmospheric Tibetan quarters and the Bakong Scripture Printing Lamasery, which attracts Tibetan pilgrims and the few Western tourists that venture this way.

Derge (*Dêgê*) Tucked in a deep valley at 3,220m, this former kingdom holds **Bakong Scripture Printing Lamasery**, the largest woodblock printing temple left in the Tibetan world (two others were destroyed, in Narthang and Shol). There are two kinds of ink used here – black for religious texts and red for medical ones. Some 300 laymen under the direction of the abbot assemble texts by hand for shipment to temples in Qinghai, Gansu and Sichuan provinces, as well as to the TAR itself. The lamasery possesses several hundred thousand woodblock plates and a library with rare Sanskrit editions. It's very atmospheric, with two large and well-decorated halls downstairs and the printing operation upstairs. Be sure to climb up the ladder to the roof for fine panoramas and a tiny hall. This is a good vantage point from which to snap photographs of the two-man teams who rapidly turn out hand-printed pages.

From the centre of town, walk 5 minutes up Bagong Jie; admission is Y50. From the lamasery, continue up the valley on the road past a row of *chortens* and prayer wheels to see recently restored **Derge Gonchen**, a large monastery with a splendid assembly hall. You might enjoy a stroll along the narrow lanes of the Tibetan houses and a small temple on the hillsides nearby.

There are several hotel options. **Dege Que Er Shan Hotel** (*Zheng Rd;* \ *0836 822 2167;* **$$**) has a number of wings, and it's best to stay in the newer wing, where standard rooms start at Y280. **Fenglingdu International Youth Hostel** (*243 Chamashang Rd;* m *1500 248 8791;* **$$**) is a great well-run hostel located at the east end of town along the road from Manigango. As you enter town, the hostel is on the left side. Standard rooms cost Y150, and dorms start at Y40.

Beyond Derge The highway continues on to Chamdo in the TAR, where you have the choice of continuing west to Lhasa on the northern route via Nagqu or turning south and catching the southern route via Bayi. If you're thinking of trying to slip through without permits, be aware that the PSB in Chamdo has been extremely vigilant about nabbing permit-less foreigners even during times when the PSB in other parts of the TAR have been relaxed. Whether or not the TAR is in your plans, the short trip to the Yangtse River is a pretty one. The highway continues down the Zhil Chu Valley, meeting the Yangtse in 24km and following the great river 1km to a turn-off for the bridges. You could probably get away with slipping across to the TAR side for a close look at two abandoned stone towers; smaller towers poke out of the hillsides on both sides of this long strategic spot. A rougher road continues south 89km on the Sichuan side to Baiyu, passing tracks and trails to a great many remote monasteries. You could also loop back to Ganzi via Baiyu (page 299).

Dzogchen Gompa Many of the temples in this vast monastery complex glitter with gold. The setting at 3,960m in a meadow, hidden from the main road, is superb – it's worth a side trip from Manigango even if you're not headed all the way to Shiqu. From Manigango, you'll travel the road northwest towards Shiqu and Yushu across grasslands, past a lake then up a long climb to 4,571m Muri La. There are expansive views of grasslands and mountains all the way up. In contrast, the descent is steep and enters a valley. A *mani* wall and *chortens* stand just beyond the turn-off on the left, 50km from Manigango, though the monastery complex is almost completely out of sight, hidden by a glacial moraine beyond the little market town of Zhuqing (Ganda).

There's a **hotel** signed in English on the right 1km from the turn-off and this is probably the best place to stay unless you are undertaking studies at the monastery. The hotel is more of a homestay, with the family living downstairs and four-bed rooms decorated in Tibetan style upstairs (just Y30 per bed). The hotel sign advertises a restaurant/café, but serves only simple Tibetan fare. The town stretches about 1km beyond the hotel with many shops and a few restaurants; try the little Chinese restaurant in a police building on the right. A little farther on the left across a bridge is a bathhouse and a restaurant, both signed in English.

Allow a full day to explore Dzogchen Gompa. If you have an interest in Tibetan Buddhism, you are likely to find people studying here who speak English (also see w www.dzogchenmonastery.cn). The monastery comes into view just a short walk beyond Zhuqing and past several *chortens*. Wooded hills and glacier-clad peaks above the monastery also invite exploration. The first group of buildings includes a large assembly hall with fine wall paintings, *tankas*, and a row of giant statues, mostly of the Buddha. A new assembly hall sits next to it. A nearby temple has a highly ornate golden roof. Shira Sing Buddhist University, the large red building topped with gold, is about 20 minutes farther up the valley. Zangdok Palri Institute has a beautiful new temple with a golden roof about halfway up the valley. The English-speaking Patrul Rinpoche is in charge and has a following of European disciples (he also has a centre in Belgium). Far up the valley you'll reach another golden-roofed building, the Temple of Great Perfection and Dzogchen Pema Tung Great Perfection Retreat Centre, or 'Pema Tung' for short. An ornate Buddha statue is inside. Nearby buildings provide housing for guests and retreatants; you might be able to stay here. If you cross the river before Pema Tung, a trail leads up a glacial moraine for views of an upper valley, rapids and mountains. You can mount day hikes here – or a trek of several days over a high pass to Keluodong (Khorlomdo). Wildflowers grow in great profusion during summer.

Dzogchen to Shiqu This 173km drive curves through immense grasslands and a few minor passes. Many Tibetans set up herder camps in summer. At 6.5km from

All of the Kham and Amdo routes in this chapter make fantastic bicycle rides – if they are accessible to foreigners. Cyclists enjoy meeting people along the way, unobstructed views, fresh air and the freedom of the open road. You don't need to be athletic or undergo training to ride the routes, rather just be in good shape and pace yourself. Taking it easy at the beginning of the ride helps greatly in acclimatisation.

A reliable bicycle and the ability to maintain it will be essential as you cannot count on finding a bicycle shop if something goes wrong. Take a folding spare tyre, a couple of tubes, spare cables, brake pads, chain lube and basic tools. A tent, warm sleeping bag and pad should be carried for the odd long section between accommodations, if you get caught out late or in an unexpected storm. Chinese and Tibetan cuisines are widely available, so there's no need to carry a stove. A down jacket worn under a waterproof shell will keep you from freezing on long descents in rain or snow; mittens will be appreciated on the descents as well.

Most of the time you can find a hotel or guesthouse, and Tibetan families will often invite you inside their house or tent if you ask. Highways and some side roads have paving, but be prepared for sections of dirt and the inevitable construction areas. If dogs come after you, the best thing to do is to stop and pick up some stones, then wait for the dog owners to come out and restrain them. If nobody's home, then flag down a passing vehicle. Tibetans are major-league throwers when it comes to pelting dogs with stones, and you'll be able to make your escape. The worst thing to do is to try to outrun the dogs – the dogs will love the chase, but might nip at you.

KUNMING TO TAGONG A ride the length of Yunnan Province crosses an astonishing variety of landscapes with many minority cultures. You could start from northern Laos or Vietnam as well as the provincial capital Kunming. You'll likely come through the atmospheric old towns of Dali and Lijiang on your way to Tiger Leaping Gorge. Instead of taking the main highway to Zhongdian from here, try the smaller road through Tiger Leaping Gorge and past Baishuitai (travertine terraces) for the best scenery and light traffic. The terrain just keeps getting grander on the side trip to Deqin and Minyong Glacier. More river gorges, high valleys and half a dozen passes will get you north to Litang. Yajiang is the next town east, but too far for one day on account of the passes to be climbed; you'll probably need to camp or seek shelter somewhere, though villages are very sparse. Just one big pass, doable in a day, and a short climb up a valley brings you to Tagong.

XICHANG TO TAGONG VIA JIULONG Like the ride from southern Yunnan, this route provides gradual acclimatisation as you climb into Tibetan lands. The scenery begins just outside Mianning on a climb past fields and forest to a pass, then a steep descent to the Yalong River, where you turn up this great river and its tributaries to Jiulong. Wuxuhai makes an idyllic day trip from here. Continuing north, you're looking at a long day for the 48km climb past forest and meadows

the Dzogchen turn-off, there's a rudimentary hot springs pool on the right and a restaurant on the left. The shallow pool isn't much, and there's no privacy, but you can get a pleasant soak (no charge). Monks come here at night to bathe under the cover of darkness, so it's a strictly male scene then. At 11.3km, you reach a bridge and junction; a road goes right 10km to Shechen (Zhechen) Monastery, to a high pass, then a drop through an alpine gorge and lush picturesque valleys with Tibetan villages. Continue upriver to Tagong.

TAGONG TO XIEWU Bamei, Dawu and Luhuo make convenient overnight stops on the way to Ganzi with a few passes to tackle and superb scenery. Ganzi to Manigango is just a day on the main highway, or you can take the adventurous back road via Baiyu and Derge. The 114km between Derge and Manigango over 5,050m Tro La will be your highest and toughest in the region, best done over two days. Dzogchen Gompa is the highlight on the three-day ride from Manigango to Shiqu. Sershul Monastery, an easy ride beyond Shiqu, is another great monastic complex worth a visit. A pass marks the border with Qinghai Province and a great descent into Xiewu.

XIEWU TO XINING This long haul across grasslands and a bit of semi-desert has no major monasteries or snow mountains unless you leave the main road. Tibetans are as friendly as elsewhere and foreign visitors still a novelty. The highway is nearly all paved and tends to have a smoother surface than roads in northwestern Sichuan; traffic is mostly light.

XINING TO LHASA Highway G109 will take you all the way. Most of this long ride runs across Qinghai Province, and you don't need any permits for this part. If permits are required for the TAR, costs will be relatively low because the TAR part of the ride is so short. The spectacular high-altitude Namtso Lake is a recommended side trip. Only on the last day into Lhasa do you leave the high grasslands for a fun ride down a gorge and valley.

XINING TO CHENGDU You can put together a route connecting Amdo's great monasteries and a great variety of valley, plateau and mountain country. For example, you could head to Tongren's monasteries and temples, perhaps stopping in Xunhua for a side trip east down the Yellow River Gorge and up to the alpine lake in Mengda Nature Reserve. Next, cross into Gansu Province to experience Labrang Monastery, then continue south into Sichuan Province via Hezuo (Heitso), Luchu, Langmusi and Zoige to see monasteries and temples along the way. Down at Chuanzhusi, you have choices of turning north to Jiuzhaigou National Park, east to Huanglong National Park or south to Songpan; from any of these you could continue through deep valleys to Chengdu.

Have a look at travelogues on the internet for route ideas; cyclists have mapped out other challenging trips that you may wish to try. I have cycling travelogues online of all the main routes: a Bangkok–Chengdu ride via Litang at w arizonahandbook.com/Thai_China.htm, and lots more from Kham and Amdo regions on w crazyguyonabike.com (enter 'Bill Weir' in the top search bar to locate entries).

said to be welcoming to Westerners. In another 36km on the main highway, you'll see Juo Gompa on the left and a little restaurant on the right. There's a 4,570m pass 65km from the Dzogchen turn-off, then a descent into a broad grassy valley. Xiazha (Tsatcha), about 23km along the valley, has several restaurants and a bunch of shops, then it's 11km to a gentle pass of 4,365m. The descent takes you into the broad valley of the Yalong River, though the river isn't visible until farther up the valley. In another 40km, Junyung Monastery appears on the left, and then you'll see a dam on the Yalong River several kilometres farther. The highway leaves the main valley for the final stretch to Shiqu, passing Bunyming Monastery on the right along the way.

Shiqu (*Sêrxu, Sershul*) This town set on open grasslands at 4,305m will seem like a big city after days of travelling through villages and tent camps. One of the few hotels that can host alien guests (foreigners) is **Grand Hotel of Sun Tribes ($$)**, located in the middle of town on Deji Upper Street and offering standard rooms for Y320, but it would be preferable to stay at Sershul Monastery Guesthouse (read on).

Sershul Monastery A drive of just 31km along the highway and over a minor 4,570m pass takes you to this large complex spread up a hillside at 4,255m. In contrast to all the golden roofs and fancy halls at Dzogchen, here everything is more earthy and plain, though very atmospheric. Lots of dogs are around, so be on guard for the rare aggressive one. The best way to see Sershul is to walk the *kora* route that encircles it. Start at the long row of prayer wheels lining the front, then follow pilgrims clockwise and hike up high on the hillside with fine views of the monastery and the expansive valley beyond. You can make side trips into the halls along the way. For a place to stay, try the simple **guesthouse** (*Y25/bed*) upstairs in the last large building on the left before the highway crosses a river to the monastery. Conveniently, there's a Tibetan restaurant at one end of the guesthouse and a Chinese one at the other. A **public bathhouse** (*Y10*) is downstairs. The only trick with the guesthouse is finding the woman with the keys who runs it. Other restaurants are nearby, along with shops where you can get groceries and fruit, or outfit yourself in Tibetan clothing. Farther along the highway on the right, you could try the **monastery guesthouse**.

From Sershul, you'll see the kilometre posts count down to zero on the gradual 45km climb to 4,700m Anba La. On the way, look for new settlements at 13km and 33km for people made homeless in the Yushu earthquake. The pass marks the boundary between Sichuan and Qinghai provinces. From the top, the highway switchbacks down a steep slope to a valley, then cruises into the junction town of **Xiewu** (Xiwu; 3,905m) in another 22km. Here you'll reach Highway G214, one of China's most remarkable highways. It runs from near Laos in the far south of Yunnan Province through the entire length of Yunnan, continues through the TAR, then goes north through most of Qinghai Province.

From Xiewu, Yushu is 47km south, while Xining is 764km north. Drogon Gompa has a spectacular setting on a steep hillside above Xiewu. It's worth a visit to see a few of the halls and valley views; the uppermost hall is a protector chapel (women not allowed inside). There's a *kora* route around the *gompa*, also connecting with a row of *chortens* and an enclosed large prayer wheel just above town. Morning is the best time for finding halls open and for photography. Xiewu has at least two **guesthouses**, but they're not signed, so you might have to ask. Chinese and Tibetan **restaurants** are easy to find. There's a **public bathhouse**: head south from the junction towards Yushu and it's on your left. This may be your last chance for a bath for a long time if you are headed north towards Xining. The 47km drive south to Yushu is very pretty and crosses the Yangtse River about halfway.

Yushu (*Gyegu, Jyekundo; 3,769m*) This town has seen major upheavals. It was almost totally destroyed by a severe earthquake in 2010 that killed several thousand people. The entire town was rebuilt from the ground up: the official reopening ceremony of the town took place in November 2013. As part of this reconstruction, the annual July horse-racing festival was shifted from its grasslands location to a big new stadium downtown, where the event is heavily controlled and policed. The other thing of note about Yushu is that it was formerly a major centre for the breeding of Tibetan mastiffs. With the collapse of the market for these dogs among wealthy Chinese, the dogs have been abandoned and have become a hazard around Yushu as they forage on the streets.

Despite its misfortunes, the town acts as a major transport hub, with **buses** headed north to Xining and southwest (via Xiewu) into Sichuan. The road south from town provides a gateway into the TAR and Riwoche Monastery, then comes to the Chamdo–Nagqu highway, the northern route to Lhasa. Yushu Batang airport operates daily flights to Xining and Chengdu and seasonal flights to Lhasa. This makes it a viable gateway town, though located at the far end of Qinghai. But consider this: you can fly from Chengdu to Yushu without too much permit brouhaha, and since Yushu is outside the TAR, you can then make your way eastward through Amdo and Kham.

Tour operator
Gesar Tour m 1390 976 9192; w gesartour. com. The only international travel agency based in Yushu. It organises wildlife tours, photography journeys & cultural tours all over Yushu & Ganzi prefectures.

 Where to stay and eat Several hotels in Yushu cater for foreigners.

 Gesar Palace Minzhu Rd; 0976 882 1999. The best hotel in town is located 100m west from the town square & includes a Chinese-style b/fast. Rooms start at Y300. Outside, there are numerous Sichuan-style restaurants with dishes priced from Y15 to Y50 ($$). **$$**

Pearl Business Hotel 33 Qionglong Rd; 0976 881 1177. Offers surprisingly good value in this remote part of the Tibetan plateau. The clean rooms have Wi-Fi, & the hotel is located near many shops & restaurants. Standard rooms are Y260. **$$**

Yushu Hotel Minzhu Rd; 0976 882 7666. Across the road from the Gesar Palace, about 150m west of the town square. Rooms are dated but spacious. Standard rooms start at Y250. **$$**

Nangchen From Yushu, driving south towards the border with the TAR lies Nangchen County, with its seat at the town of Nangchen.

 Where to stay

Yazhuo Business Hotel Xiangda Dong ad, 100m east of the bus station; 0976 887 5555. In this remote part of Qinghai, the Yazhuo is the best there is. Chinese-Tibetan-style b/fast is included. Rooms have spotty Wi-Fi. Standard rooms are Y300. **$$**

GETTING TO THE SOURCE

The Yellow, Mekong and Yangtse – three of Asia's longest rivers – have their sources in the southern part of Qinghai province. All three headwaters are extremely remote but have incredible beauty, with towering snow-capped peaks, high-altitude grasslands and wildlife such as snow leopards, brown bears, *kyang*, antelope and more. No public transportation will take you to these extreme locations. Contact Gesar Tour in Jyekundo (see above) for details on 4x4 journeys to the river sources.

⌂ **Nangchen Ake** 24 South Xiangda St; ☎0976 887 2228. Located on the main road in Nangchen. Staff do not speak English, but rooms are decent & have 24hr hot water. Standard rooms from Y300. **$$**

What to see and do Several great excursions can be mounted from Nangchen town, including to **Gaden (Gading) Monastery**. Approximately 55km east of town, this 300-year-old monastery is located along a horseshoe bend in the Dzi River, a tributary of the Mekong. A hike above the monastery on the far side of the river provides a fantastic panoramic view of the area. Around 40 monks live at Gaden. To reach it, take a minivan taxi here from Nangchen. The cost will be between Y400 and Y500 for the return journey.

Gar Monastery is located 70km south of the Gaden Monastery and is one of the true secrets of the Kham area. Surrounded by evergreen forests, mountain vistas and wildlife, this monastery is home to around a hundred monks. The monastery is divided into lower and upper sections, with the lower one having a small village next to it. This is a fantastic place to go on a day trip. A taxi ride from Nangchen will cost Y600 for the return journey.

WILD AMDO ROUTE

Yushu to Xining This 811km drive crosses a vast expanse of high grasslands and a bit of desert, providing an opportunity to see and meet friendly Tibetans – many out in summer at camps with their yaks, horses and sheep. The highway is nearly all paved, and tiny towns provide places to stay. Unlike the drive through northwestern Sichuan, you won't see any great monasteries or glacier-clad peaks, though adventurous travellers can detour off the highway to see these. You are likely to see wildlife such as graceful Tibetan gazelles, wolves, birds of many kinds, marmots and thousands of pikas. Eagles, hawks and owls hang out, and you might even see a seagull, far from home.

From Yushu, the highway returns back across the Yangtse on the 47km to Xiewu, then begins a 17km climb to Yan pass (Yingkuoshan) at 4,458m. Summer camps dot the grasslands around the pass, down the other side and out on to a vast valley beyond. At 102km from Xiewu you'll arrive in the spread-out **Qingshuihe**, which has two adjoining **guesthouses** at the far end (north) of town on the right, both with rooms upstairs. The second one is recommended because the Tibetan family welcomes foreigners: beds in four-bed rooms are Y30. You can find good food at Chinese, Hui Chinese and Tibetan **restaurants**. Although it's a large town, don't expect any exotica such as flush toilets, showers or internet. Farther north you cross gentle 4,824m Bapengke (Bayanhar) pass 64km from Qingshuihe. Beyond, you'll roll over minor passes, where the countryside turns arid – with sparse grass and sand dunes, though many valleys have lakes. Shallow lakes of the Yellow River headwaters come into view 180km from Qingshuihe. Then you'll reach the turn-off for **Madoi** (Maduo; 4,205m), one of the larger towns in these parts with several hotels, including **Lingguo Business Hotel** (☎ *0975 834 8888;* **$$**), which is located across from Wenhua Square and is the best option in this high-altitude remote town. It has 24-hour hot water, heating and occasional Wi-Fi, with standard rooms from Y200.

Another 80km onwards, and over a 4,485m pass, and you reach Huashixia. A turn on the right leads past 6,282m **Amnye Machen**, a snow-capped peak sacred to Tibetans. Another turn-off for the area is 12km north of town. You can join Tibetan pilgrims on a week-long *kora* of Amnye Machen if you're self-sufficient, or you can arrange a trek through an agency. This is one of the top sacred sites of Amdo.

Unfortunately, the peak isn't visible from the main highway. Huashixia has one **hotel**, on the right just past a police station at the far end of town: beds in four-bed rooms cost from Y30 and a single is Y60. Lots of restaurants and shops are nearby.

As you near Wenquan, 78km farther north, you'll see hot springs at the edge of town, but sadly the site is trashed and lacks bathing pools. A Tibetan **sacred spot** of hillside prayer flags and *chortens* is just beyond Wenquan and worth a look. On the 109km to Heka, you'll roll over 4,499m Deng pass at 16km and tunnel through Heka Mountain at 94.5km, then descend to **Heka**, surrounded by bright yellow-green fields of rapeseed at a balmy 3,290m. Try the **hotel** on the right just past a hospital near the beginning of town. Rooms start at Y50 for a single and have the luxuries of an indoor toilet and a solar shower down the hall; many restaurants are nearby. The highway rolls over ridges, some of which are sand dunes covered by vegetation on the 75km to **Gonghe**, way down in a valley at 2,855m.

Buses will take the main highway direct to Daotanghe (3,355m) in 42km but, if you arrange your own transport, you can take a very scenic tourist road up the valley (go straight through Gonghe without making any turns), then into grassland hills – culminating at 3,740m Luo He Ya Kou Shan pass and the first view of Qinghai Lake. A swift descent with good views of the lake twists down to Highway G109 on the west edge of a tourist town, known as '151' after an army camp once located here. You can find restaurants and hotels, but prices will likely be high and bargaining worthwhile. Boat tours go out on the lake from the shore.

Where to stay and eat

Huang He Hotel Qinghai Hu South St, Gonghe; \0974 852 2888. An older but decent hotel. Rooms have spotty Wi-Fi; b/fast is offered. Standard rooms start at Y200. **$$**

Huanghe Yiyuan International Hotel Yingbin West Rd, Gonghe; \0974 856 1999. A good 3-star hotel that offers in-room Wi-Fi & is close to restaurants & shops. Standard rooms start at Y230. **$$**

Qinghai Guide Hot Spring Hotel 355 Yingbin Rd, Gonghe; \0974 855 3534. An older hotel, popular for its pool, which is heated from water piped in from a nearby hot spring. Located 1km west of the bus station. Standard rooms start at Y220. **$$**

Qinghai Lake (*Kokonor* or *Blue Lake*) The lake that gives Qinghai Province its name is a huge saline lake with excellent pastureland in the surrounding hills. The rail link goes north of the lake but the road continues for over 100km on the south side through fields of yellow rapeseed and wheat. Many of the farmers are recent Muslim immigrants, and there are some tensions with the Tibetan herdsmen, whose winter pasture they have taken over.

On the western side of the lake is a birders' hot spot (season is March to early June) called **Niao Dao** (Bird Island – but actually it is a peninsula). Lying about 50km from the cheap guesthouses at Heimahe, Niao Dao bird sanctuary is inhabited by cormorants and, in spring, by bar-headed geese, gulls, terns and even an occasional black-necked crane. You can also reach Niao Dao by bus direct from Xining Bus Station – a journey that takes about 5 hours. At Qinghai Lake, you can lodge at **Tian Houyuan Hotel** (m *1534 649 6678;* **$$**) located at the KM2109 marker stone; a pleasant 3-star with a Chinese restaurant and rooms starting at Y300.

Back on the main route: turn right on busy Highway G109 for the 50km to Daotanghe and another 101km to Xining: a left turn would take you on the long haul to Golmud and Lhasa. At 8km past Daotanghe you have a choice of continuing on the expressway or turning left on a paved loop road to Riyueting – a pass famed as the route taken long

8

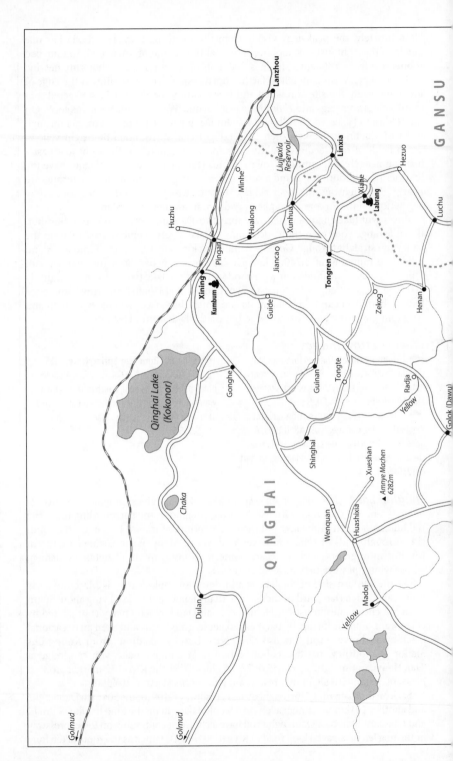

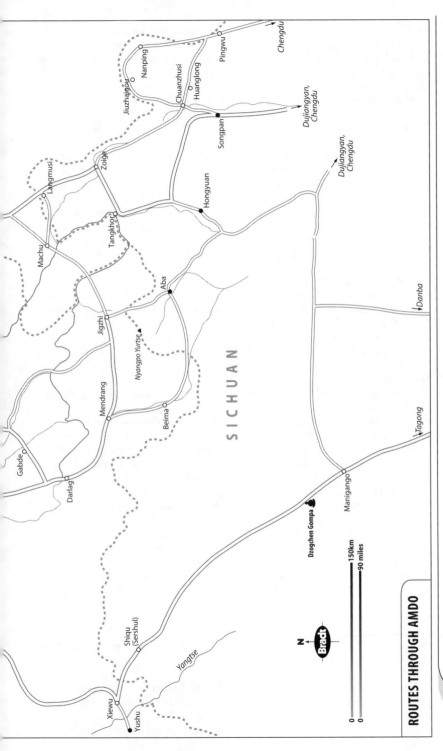

ROUTES THROUGH AMDO

S I C H U A N

Chengdu

Pingwu

Huanglong

Chuanzhusi

Nanping

Jiuzhaigou

Songpan

Dujiangyan, Chengdu

Zoige

Langmusi

Hongyuan

Dujiangyan, Chengdu

Tangkhor

Machu

Aba

Danba

Jigzhi

Nyangpo Yurtse

Mendrang

Beima

Tagong

Gabde

Darlag

Manigango

Dzogchen Gompa

150km

90 miles

0

0

N

Brad

Shiqu
(Sershul)

Yangtse

Xiewu

Yushu

ago by Princess Wencheng on her journey to Tibet and now marked by a pair of small pavilions and lots of prayer flags. It's very popular with Chinese tourists to take in the grassland scenery and snap photographs. The small city of Huangyuan, 49km beyond Daotanghe, is worth a stop to see **Zanpulinka Palace**, a four-story temple-like building on the left as you enter town. The six-floor **Huangyuan Xinshui Hotel** has good rooms nearby on the right just beyond the river bridge.

Xining The capital and largest city of Qinghai Province has a population of 2.1 million and spreads out at the junction of three valleys at 2,275m. It's a pleasant city with many parks and Westerner-friendly hostels and restaurants. You may want to stay a few days to see the sights, whether you need to acclimatise before heading on to the Tibetan plateau, or just want to take in city life after a spell in the back country. Most of the city is on the south slope of a valley, so you'll likely be heading uphill when going south, downhill when going north. A river flowing from the south bisects the centre and has parks along it; most places to stay and eat are east of this river. The cool dry air will come as a welcome change if you are travelling from lower elevations to the east. The Bank of China has ATMs at many locations around the city.

Tour operators
Mystic Tibet Tours m 1820 971 5464; w mystictibettours.com. Tibetan owner Gonkho serves as the lead guide for this company, which specialises in treks & cultural journeys in the more remote mountains of Amdo & Kham.

Snow Lion Tours Located at Suite 408, Xiadu Daji St; 0971 816 3350; e info@snowliontours. com; w snowliontours.com. They also have an office in Lhasa.

 ## Where to stay

Sofitel Hotel 63 Wusi West Rd; 0971 766 6666; w accorhotels.com. The Sofitel is Xining's only 5-star hotel. It is located in the western business district at the far end of the city. The hotel boasts an indoor pool, gym, Chinese & Japanese restaurants & an international b/fast buffet. Standard rooms start at Y650. **$$$**

Qinghai Hotel 158 Huanghe Rd; 0971 614 8999; w qinghaihotel.com. This upgraded high-rise hotel is located on the south side of downtown, about 4km from the railway station & 30km from the airport, & includes a buffet b/fast in the room price. Standard rooms start at Y550. **$$$**

Sanwant Hotel 79 Changjiang Rd; 0971 820 1111; w www.sanwant.com.cn/en. The Sanwant is located in the centre of the city within walking distance of Dongguan Mosque, Shuijing

Market & plenty of restaurants. Standard rooms start at Y450. **$$**

Enraton International Hotel 59 Dongguan St; 0971 816 0999. Located in the heart of Xining's large Muslim quarter in the east part of the city, near many restaurants & shops, & it's just a short walk to the Dongguan Mosque. Standard rooms start at Y280. **$$**

Lete Youth Hostel 5 Bldg, International Village Apt, 16th Fl; 0971 820 2080/90. Has wonderful views atop a high-rise just south of the centre. Prices range from Y25 per bed in a dorm to Y120 for a dbl room. The hostel features English-speaking staff, regional maps for sale, internet computers, free Wi-Fi, Western b/fasts & a coffee bar. **$**

Where to eat and drink
For views atop a revolving restaurant, you might try the 28th-floor **Rotary Western Restaurant** at 55 Xi Dajie.

Elites Bar and Grill Qiyi Rd; m 1389 747 2199. American owner Jesse keeps this place stocked with great steaks, burgers & pizzas. Prices start at Y30. **$**

Yixin Mutton Baiyu Alley; 0971 817 9336. In a city with hundreds of mutton restaurants, this one stands above them all. In addition to amazing roast mutton, they serve

Muslim noodles, roasted potatoes & fresh bread. Dishes start at Y20. **$**

⌨ Green House Coffee 222 Xiadu Av; ✆0971 820 9376. Easily the best coffee place in town, this establishment also serves great pastries, made-to-order sandwiches & pizza, muesli & smoothies. There's Wi-Fi & it's popular with foreigners. **$**

⌨ Amdo Café 19 Ledu Lu; ✆0971 821 3127; w amdocraft.com. Has good pastries, coffees & teas along with Tibetan crafts & postcards in a non-smoking setting. Located on the east side of the street, halfway between Xiadu Dajie & Kunlun Zhonglu, one block east of Nan Xiaojie. **$**

What to see and do The **Qinghai Provincial Museum** at 58 Xiguan Daji and West Wusi Lu is worth a visit for exhibits on Qinghai's history, Tibetan arts and the July bicycle race around Qinghai Lake. **Jinta Si**, the small Tibetan temple on the south side of the centre at 19 Hongjuesi Jie (just east of Nan Dajie), has three large standing Buddhas and many smaller statues. **Beishan Si**, a Taoist temple complex just north of town on the lower slopes of Beishan (best to take a taxi), has a huge two-storey hall near the entrance, many small halls and a flower garden to the left, and several more halls high up on the steep hillside, reached by steep steps or a winding trail. **Ding Xiang Yuan** is a large Chinese Buddhist temple complex below Nan Shan: the entrance is just east of the Kunlun Bridge roundabout. Visit the **landscaped park** atop Nan Shan for greenery and views. If you're into classical Greek and Roman sculpture, a park high atop Beishan north of town is full of them (take a taxi). A large Chinese Hui (Muslim) community lives just east of the centre near the large Dongguan Mosque; colourful lights play on the mosque exterior after dark.

Kumbum Monastery This large monastic complex is located 26km southwest of Xining. To get here, look for a bus or taxi on the west side of the road just south of the Kunlun Bridge roundabout. Admission is a steep Y80.

Kumbum (Taersi in Chinese) is the most famous monastery in Amdo and one of the six great Geluk monasteries of the Tibetan plateau. In its prime, Kumbum once housed 3,000 monks, but under Chinese rule it was closed down for a period. Since it reopened in 1979 the monastery has housed about 400 monks, with half the buildings functioning in museum mode. The former abbot, Ajia Rinpoche, fled in 1998 to seek asylum in the USA: he was the highest-ranking monk in the Chinese Communist Party.

Situated in the largely Muslim county of Huangzhong, the temples here were protected during the Cultural Revolution and contain some of the greatest artworks of Amdo. However, Kumbum is a major Chinese destination, and the monks are tightly controlled, which affects the atmosphere. There is a guesthouse here with rooms from Y80, with cheaper hotels on the market streets, though you can base yourself in Xining and visit for the day by public bus or minibus taxi.

Kumbum is the birthplace of Tsongkhapa, founder of the Gelukpa sect in the early 15th century. Inside a spectacular green-tiled building is a silver pagoda containing the earthly belongings of Tsongkhapa. The monastery is thought to have been built (in the 16th century) around a legendary pipal tree, said to bear a Buddha-like image on every leaf. The tree is accredited with magical powers. The temple is famed, too, for its elaborate yak-butter sculptures – in the shape of animals, landscapes and religious figures – which can reach 15m in length. Festivals at Kumbum attract large numbers of Tibetan pilgrims. Because Kumbum is easily accessed (being so close to Xining) it unfortunately also attracts large numbers of Chinese tourists, who stand next to cardboard cut-outs to have pictures taken. The monastery has a disturbingly commercialised air about it. The best time to visit is during a festival: tour agents in the Xining hotels can tell you of any upcoming festivals.

Taktser The birthplace of the present Dalai Lama is about 27km eastward from Kumbum, and about 7km from the small attractive monastery of Shadzong. It is likely to be closed to foreigners, but enquire as to current status. Tsongkhapa spent some years at the mountain-top *gompa* of Shadzong, and the 13th Dalai Lama also visited and meditated there. Today, this small forested zone is popular with picnickers at weekends. Taktser itself is situated on a ridge above the valley; the Dalai Lama's humble house was reconstructed in 1986. The easiest way to visit these sites is to hire transport for a day in Xining or try your luck hitching at the turn-off. Tour agent **Tibetan Connections** (page 71) occasionally puts together a group tour for Taktser and other off-the-beaten-track sights near Xining. A little-used side road leads through the hills from Taktser to Kumbum.

NORTHERN ROUTE TO LHASA
Xining–Golmud–Lhasa Once notorious for having one of the world's most miserable bus rides, this route has become a breeze now that the rails go all the way. The road journey is much slower and will appeal to those who enjoy expansive views across desert landscapes and lofty grasslands. Highway G109 runs all the way and is nearly all paved, though parts will be under construction. Most of this journey lies within Qinghai Province, so you won't need permits until the last section across the TAR, and this part of the TAR tends to be relatively relaxed, so independent travel *might* be possible. Check with other travellers and online forums for the latest word. Cyclists looking for an adventure will enjoy this route: there's less up and down than a ride across eastern Tibet or the run from Lhasa to Nepal.

Xining to Golmud This 780km section of highway skirts the south shore of Qinghai Lake, then the southern edge of the Qaidam Basin – a vast area of salt marsh, saline lakes and desert *playas*. For notes on visiting Qinghai Lake and Bird Island, see pages 307–10. The train skirts the north shore of Qinghai Lake, then across the Qaidam Basin.

Golmud Commonly pronounced and spelled Geermu, this city of about 200,000 lies at an elevation of 2,800m. It has a leafy centre with parks. Seemingly in the middle of nowhere, Golmud exists to serve oil, gas and other mineral-extraction industries in the Qaidam Basin.

 Where to stay and eat The PSB has prohibited small hotels from accepting foreigners, so your options may be limited to those listed below.

For food, Golmud has a variety of Chinese **restaurants** including many Muslim noodle restaurants, which are very popular throughout Qinghai. Supermarkets provide your last chance to stock up on exotic fruit and other goodies for hundreds of kilometres in any direction.

DoubleTree by Hilton 15-02 South Kunlun Rd; 0979 896 9999. In the middle-of-nowhere Qinghai is this excellent 4-star hotel, complete with pool, gym, restaurants & spa. Standard rooms start at Y650. **$$$**

Yellow River International Hotel 62 Middle Kunlun Rd; 0979 725 7888. This large hotel is 3km from the train station & within walking distance of downtown. It offers in-room Wi-Fi, a restaurant & gym. Standard rooms start at Y400. **$$**

Xinglong Mansions 46 Bayi East Rd; 0979 725 5555. This is 3km from the train station, clean and has friendly staff. Outside are numerous restaurant choices. Standard rooms start at Y240. **$$**

Golmud to Lhasa You're looking at 1,260km by road, 1,142km by rail, on routes that roughly parallel each other. Because nearly all passengers now go by train, roadside businesses have suffered from fewer customers, and some settlements have faded away. You can count on finding something at least every 100km, with the accommodations tending to be very basic and cheap while restaurants are good and cheap. Larger communities have internet cafés, but you're unlikely to find bathhouses or hotels with showers until the towns of Amdo, Nagqu and Damshung in the TAR. There's a checkpoint 33km south of Golmud staffed by a few bored soldiers who probably won't be interested in you.

The route enters a valley and begins a long gentle climb with constantly changing panoramas of arid mountains. Farther along, the valley widens with striking views of sand dunes and the glacier-clad Kunlun Mountains The climb peaks at the 4,767m Kunlun Shankou pass, 160km south of Golmud. From here until the final descent into Lhasa Valley you'll be rolling across high grasslands above 4,000m. Just before Tuotuohe, 422km south of Golmud, you cross the broad Yangtse River at a site famed among the Chinese as the First Bridge over the Yangtse. At 615km south of Golmud you'll top out at the highest pass on the route, 5,231m Tanggu La on the Qinghai–TAR border – with great panoramas of mountains, glaciers and valleys. A Tibetan tent restaurant at the pass may serve noodle soup and *tsampa*. There's no checkpoint. Another 90km and a minor pass brings you to **Amdo**, a rough-and-tumble-looking town, but people are friendly. **Hotels** tend to be basic with the usual pit toilet out back. There's said to be one hotel with a shower, or you can use the public shower (Y8) just east on the left from the central junction. An **internet café** is located just north on the right from the central junction. Amdo has lots of Chinese and Tibetan **restaurants**. You'll find many Tibetan posters and other souvenirs for sale. A pleasant stroll leads west from the central junction, then left past Tibetan houses up the grassy hillside to prayer-flag-festooned towers and a good view of the Amdo area.

Back on the highway, another 138km gets you over a 4,880m pass and down to **Nagqu**, the first city since Golmud. Drop by **Shabten Monastery** to meet the friendly monks and see colourful artwork. Nagqu has a **horse-racing festival** every August, but instead of being held on grasslands close to the city, the venue has shifted to a concrete stadium where the audience is a long distance from the racers and performers. **Nakqu Hotel** and others in the centre have expensive rooms. Or try the basic **Keyan Hotel** (no English sign) on the right side of the highway most of the way through town and across from a giant army building. Basic single rooms cost Y40, 'deluxe' rooms with sink and toilet go for Y80, but you'll have to visit a public bathhouse for a shower. Nagqu has **restaurants**, **supermarkets** and **internet cafés**. The highway continues through grasslands past views of snow peaks 166km to Damshung. Although the town has plenty of Chinese and Tibetan hotels, restaurants, supermarket and internet, it's best known as the turn-off for Namtso, one of Tibet's largest and most beautiful lakes. For more on Namtso, see *Chapter 5*, pages 184–6.

The 75km from Damshung to Yangbajing (Yangpachen) provides more views of the icy Tanggula Range, crowned by 7,162m Mount Nyenchen Tanglha. The Tibetan village of Yangbajing is 2km off the highway to the right and has basic hotels and good restaurants. Clouds of steam rising in the distance mark geothermal activity where there's a hot springs resort, but it costs a hefty Y100 for a dip or Y300 for the hotel. From Yangbajing, the highway follows a roaring river down to the Lhasa Valley. You'll see trees for the first time in many days. Getting through the Chinese outskirts of **Lhasa** takes a long time. When you sight the lofty Potala Palace, you've finally arrived.

8

EXPLORING CENTRAL AMDO
Xining via Aba to Chengdu This route could be very tough going, with a complete lack of buses (try trucks instead). It goes through the heartlands of the Golok nomads, who are known for their stubbornness and, previously, fierce banditry. Many Golok nomads are now being settled in concrete housing developments under official Chinese policy to remove the nomads from the grasslands.

Xining to Guide and Golok Close to Kumbum, the main road heads south over the mountains and down to the Yellow River at Guide, 75km from Xining. This is a more attractive route than the road that heads off the Yushu highway before the Sun Moon pass. Guide is a poor, largely Muslim county town, and there is little reason to stop here, apart perhaps for the hot springs fed into bathhouses some 15km southwest of town. There are several monasteries in the nearby side valleys, but all are poorly appointed and there are very few monks. The main road south is the principal route to Golok. It bypasses the small counties of Guinan and Tongte. Roads west from the main road lead to bridges over the Yellow River from either of these two towns to link up with the Xining–Yushu route. Guinan and Tongte are hardly ever visited, but worth a day or two if you have the time. All monasteries are outside Guide town; the most important is Serlag, but the muddy track that leads to it may be impassable.

After Tongte, the road leads down again to the Yellow River at Radja Gompa, 220km from Guide, which is an enclave of Golok and has long been important in Amdo's history. Truck stops and basic restaurants are available on the south side of the bridge and the monastery is at the foot of the holy mountain Khyunggon, which takes half a day to circumambulate.

Golok Situated 2 hours (70km) further south on the grasslands is the prefectural capital of Golok (aka Dawu or Machen), 210km from Huashixia on the Yushu road. This is an entirely new town with a single very long high street, although all facilities are concentrated near the crossroads. The **county guesthouse**, which you may be forced to stay in, is a little more expensive than the others, but offers occasional hot showers.

From here, it is possible to arrange for guided tours of the seven-day **Amnye Machen circuit**, though this can be very expensive. Roads west lead to Xueshan, the traditional starting point of the seven-day circuit. In trekking terms, this is a fairly easy walk, with two gradual passes of 4,500–4,900m, and is best done in May–October, when pilgrims abound and nomads will have their flocks in the area. Although the trek can be completed in seven days at normal walking pace (around 5 hours a day), complications could arise with the weather, making it longer. Camping gear is essential. Winter is extremely cold in Golok, with temperatures often below −30°C, but summer rainfall is relatively light and bearable.

From here, a road leads southwest 80km towards the small county town of **Gabde**. The side valleys down to the Yellow River from Gabde shelter several important monasteries of the Geluk, Nyingma and Jonang sects. A small monastery 12km along the main road to Darlag holds frequent festivals attended by thousands of Golok. **Darlag** (aka Dari or Jumi) can be reached in under 2 hours (50km) from Gabde or directly from Huashixia (195km) on the main Xining to Yushu road. It is beside the Yellow River and the most important nearby monastery is 15km west of town – a large Nyingma monastery called Traling (Chalangsi in Chinese).

From Darlag, the road goes 105km southeast to **Mendrang** (Manzhang in Chinese) village on an upper tributary of the Yangtse. A rough road leads from Mendrang for a distance of 65km to the Nyingma monastery of Tartang, one of the largest in Golok (a number of festivals are held here each year, particularly a winter festival). Sixty kilometres south of Mendrang is Beima county, one of the most attractive areas of Golok, lying between the rolling grasslands of the Yellow River and the forested gorges of southern Amdo. It is similar in landscape to Serthar, Zamthang and Aba counties in Sichuan and, like these, it possesses many monasteries. There are numerous large monasteries in these four counties.

Before reaching town is a nine-storey tower and a road west that leads to one of the wildest valleys in Tibet. But it is just south of town that the most remarkable *gompas* are found, in unique style with many *mani*-stone walls. This is a back road to Aba and although there is no bus, it is well worth hiring a vehicle to go this way, taking two days if possible and stopping at the *gompas en route*.

From Mendrang the road heads east past the Golok's other holy mountain, **Nyangpo Yurtse** (Nyenpo Yurtse, Nyenbo Yurtse; 5,369m), set in a remarkably pristine environment of craggy peaks and lakes, an area not used for grazing. The road continues to the tiny county town of **Jigzhi** (260km from Darlag), a truly remote nomad town.

Jigzhi is the gateway to the prime **trekking area** of Nyangpo Yurtse, a stunning mountain range. The region offers treks ranging from four to seven days in length. An experienced guide is highly recommended. You can arrange a guide from Xining (see Mystic Tibet Tours in Xining for details, page 310); reaching Jigzhi (Jigdril) town can be arranged by taking an early morning bus from Xining bus station. From Jigzhi, a local taxi to Nyangpo Yurtse will cost Y150–200 each way. Entrance is Y120 per person.

There is an infrequent bus service on a rough sandy road which crosses the Yellow River twice to reach the county town of **Machu** (Maqu) in Gansu, from where roads lead to Lamosi (Langmusi) and Gahe near Luchu on the main Linxia–Zoige road. If you travel this roundabout route from Xining to Machu, be sure to allow extra days for bus problems or sightseeing. For a place to stay, **Himalaya Hotel** (*Gesar West St;* ✆*0941 612 8888;* **$$**) is a good choice in Machu, offering Wi-Fi and friendly staff and a short walking distance to many Chinese restaurants. Standard rooms start at Y300.

This route then joins the Labrang–Songpan route as far as Zoige. Then it heads east back to the elbow of the Yellow River and south 135km to the grasslands county town of Hongyuan (which can also be reached from Songpan in 180km). Hongyuan is a small, modern county town set in a broad grassy valley. The large monastery of Mewa lies in a side valley nearby, and houses over a thousand monks.

Fifty kilometres south is a turn-off to the county town of **Aba**, one of the richest regions in Amdo. Traders from this region, including monks working for the many large monasteries, can be found all over Tibet. Aba and Zamthang contain huge monasteries: within walking distance of Aba are vast *gompas* from the Geluk, Bonpo and Jonang sects, as well as smaller Sakya and Nyingma centres. Zamthang has two valleys, the easternmost of which also has a huge Jonang presence and several small Nyingma *gompas*. Since 2008, there has been considerable trouble at **Kirti Gompa** in Aba, with the monastery locked down a number of times by the PLA and Chinese police. Kirti is an epicentre for self-immolations: a number of monks have committed suicide by immolating themselves as a form of protest. Kirti Gompa houses over a thousand monks – or used to (many have been arrested). Access to the area may be blocked by military checkpoints.

Leaving the grasslands over a pass, the road enters Gyarong, a series of forested gorges where small kingdoms of the Qiang survived until early last century. The dialect and costumes here are distinct from other areas of Amdo. At Sonmalu, the main road heads southeast through the county of Lixian to Wenchuan and thence Chengdu (328km from Sonmalu). Around 60km west of Sonmalu lies the prefectural capital of Barkam, a large administrative centre of little interest to travellers (Barkam is 200km from Hongyuan). Villages nearby, however, both on the valley floor and on small plateaus set on steep slopes, are worth a visit. At a junction 25km west of town, a road goes south to Danba, with onward connections to Tagong, Litang and Kangding. Further west from the junction, the road joins the Do Chu River, which can be followed west towards the remote counties of Serthar and Zamthang.

AMDO MOUNTAIN TWISTER

Xining via Labrang to Chengdu
Highways twist across rugged mountains, linking prominent temples amid spectacular scenery on the route from Xining to Chengdu. You can also approach this region from Lanzhou, the capital of Gansu Province and home to an excellent provincial museum. Tongren has several monasteries and temples worth a visit, if you are heading southeast from Xining or southwest from Lanzhou. From Xining, it's a quick trip east down the Huang Shui Valley to Pingan, then south over the Laji Shan. You may wish to go via Xunhua and make a side trip east through Jishi Gorge of the Yellow River (Huang He) and up a side valley to Tian Chi (Heaven Lake) in an alpine setting at Mengda Nature Reserve before continuing on to Tongren.

If you start from Lanzhou, you can stop at Yongjing, 80km to the southwest, for the boat ride to **Bingling Si** (1,000 Buddha Caves). Like other grottos on the silk routes, you can see many Buddhist scenes sculpted and painted in alcoves hewn from cliffs. The remote setting on a tributary of the Yellow River protected them during the Cultural Revolution. A Y5 taxi ride from Yongjing will take you to the boat ticket office at the reservoir, just above the dam. Covered speedboats are the most popular option and take just an hour to reach the site and cost about Y110 a person. Slow boats also do the trip, but would take most of a day. At Bingling Si, you pay the Y50 entry fee, then walk a paved loop past the grottos and a 27m-high Maitreya Buddha. You must stay with your guide and group and return on the same boat. From Yongjing, get transport to Xunhua – via the Jishi Gorge if you can – then continue to Tongren.

Tongren (*Repkong*) Tongren is a town famed for its traditional fresco painters. Mazelike lanes lead through the 700-year-old Rongwo Gongchen Monastery here. You'll also find hotels and restaurants in town, including **Rebgong Norbang Travel Inn** (*Xuelian East Rd;* ✆*0973 872 6999;* **$$**), which is the best choice for comfortable lodging in Tongren, with friendly staff and a nice Tibetan-feel to it. Standard rooms start at Y200. **Heping Hotel** (*Maixiu Rd;* ✆*0973 872 4188;* **$**) is a clean budget hotel located near the town centre with standard rooms starting at Y130.

Wutun Xiazhuang Monastery, famed for the high-quality paintings of resident artists, has upper and lower sections 6km north of town. Large paintings on the walls show the Buddha and his supporting cast: these have been recently painted with great skill by local artists. The oldest chapel houses a great statue of Maitreya (Future Buddha).

The main attractions of the area are the two small **art schools**, Yangoo and Mangoo (known as Wutun to the Chinese), which have provided mural and *tanka* painters for all of Amdo's monasteries. You'll likely see artists at work and have the opportunity to purchase a painting.

Several other monasteries are found in the hills and 25km south of town is a hot spring where you can bathe. Shortly before the hot spring, a side valley west leads past an important Bonpo *gompa* towards the holy mountain of Amnye Shachung (Jakhyung).

Head west across the Longwu He to see the colourfully decorated **Gomar Great Chorten**. Brightly painted bas-reliefs depict bodhisattvas, guardians and decorative designs. After walking the *kora* and spinning the prayer wheels, you can climb up to the higher levels, finally reaching a shrine room filled with Buddhist statues, paintings, books and a photo of the Dalai Lama. You could walk the 6km back to Tongren on a small road.

The 100km journey southeast to Xiahe has a lot of variety. It starts with 14km north along the Longwu He Valley, passing many Buddhist *chortens*, temples, villages and fields, then turns up a canyon reminiscent of the American southwest. Mud-walled Buddhist villages blend perfectly into the arid landscape. Guashizeshi village has a large *gompa*. A couple of passes later, you arrive in Ganjia Grasslands in Gansu Province, and a third pass brings you to Xiahe, a town next to the impressively large and active Labrang Monastery. Xiahe and Labrang lie along the Daxia He (Sang-chu) Valley at 2,920m. Hotels, restaurants and other travellers' needs are in the Chinese section east of Labrang and the Tibetan quarter is to the west. The town cleaves into distinct populations: Tibetan, Hui Muslim and Chinese. Strangely enough, Tibetan devotional items such as prayer wheels and *katas* are mostly sold by Hui Muslims (who are Chinese except for their religion).

Labrang Monastery Labrang Monastery was founded in 1709 and rapidly grew to become one of the six great Gelukpa monasteries. The main assembly hall was rebuilt after being destroyed by fire in 1985, but most of the other halls survived the Cultural Revolution relatively intact, and contain beautiful works of art. You will most likely see elaborate yak-butter sculptures. The monks' quarters have been rebuilt in recent years and some are spacious and comfortable. A 3km *kora* lined with prayer wheels surrounds the complex and is well worth the walk. The temples and colleges of Labrang can only be visited on a morning or afternoon official tour. Labrang acts as a major teaching centre and monks come from not only the 108 satellite *gompas* scattered throughout nearby counties, but also from central Tibet and Mongolia. Thus the number of monks is somewhat fluid, although there are likely to be around 2,000 here. There is also a small nunnery and Nyingma temple on the far side of the complex. You can be sure that with such a large contingent of monks, the Chinese keep a close eye on proceedings. Surveillance was stepped up upon the arrival of the Chinese-appointed Panchen Lama to take up residence in 2011 – in an attempt to legitimise his religious role.

At a cool 2,900m, **Xiahe** makes an excellent base for hiking. Foreigners tend to stay longer than intended at Labrang, not only because of the monastery and Western food, but also because of the opportunity to see the surrounding hills and grasslands. Bikes can be hired to reach the Sangke grasslands region, where picnics are available in Tibetan-style tents, and where horses can be hired. The nearby hills offer good opportunities for day walks, and you may be offered butter tea and yoghurt if you reach the nomad camps higher up, but beware of dogs! The most vicious dogs are chained up, but some of the others do present a serious danger if you enter their territory unbidden. Carry a walking stick, some stones or a *gokor* (a lump of lead on a string) if you plan to visit these areas. The dogs around the monastery are generally very docile, but still should not be approached.

Where to stay

Nirvana Hotel 247 Yagetang; `0941 718 1702`; w nirvana-hotel.net. Owned by a Dutch-Tibetan couple, this is easily the best place in town. The restaurant serves great Western & Chinese dishes, the stocked bar is great, & the interior Tibetan design is perfect. Standard rooms start at Y300. **$$**

Labrang Baoma Hotel Zhaxiqi Rd; ☎0941 712 1078. Offers both modern rooms & Tibetan-themed rooms. Staff speak basic English. Standard rooms from Y300; dorms for Y40. **$$**

Overseas Tibetan Hotel 77 Renmin Rd; ☎0941 712 2642. Tibetan owner Losang, fluent in English, has been serving guests here for around 20 years. Services include tours of the area, bike rentals, laundry & a great restaurant. Standard rooms for Y200 & dorms for Y50. **$$**

Labrang Red Rock International Youth Hostel 253 Yagetang; ☎0941 712 3698. The best youth hostel in Xiahe has nice rooms, friendly staff, solar-powered hot water & a restaurant. Standard rooms for Y160 & dorms from Y50. **$$**

✕ Where to eat and drink

✕ Nirvana Restaurant and Bar (see Nirvana Hotel, page 317) Serves delicious Tibetan, Western & Chinese dishes along with great espresso. It also has a long list of alcoholic drinks. **$$**

✕ Nomad Restaurant Cnr Zhaxiqi & Tengzhi rds on the 3rd floor; ☎0941 712 1897. This Tibetan-owned hotel has an English menu with Tibetan, Chinese & a few Western dishes. Restaurant overlooks Labrang Monastery. Price range is Y15–50. **$$**

✕ Tara Restaurant 268 Yagetang, on ground floor of the Tara Guesthouse. This Tibetan restaurant is popular with monks from nearby Labrang Monastery. Serves Tibetan style *momos* & noodles. Dishes Y15–40. **$$**

Langmusi On the north side of Hezuo (Heitso), just an hour southeast of Xiahe, you'll see the unusual **Milarepa Buddhist Palace**, a temple tower with eight storeys. Each floor has a gallery of statues from the Tibetan Buddhist pantheon, along with large paintings and *tankas*, many of which tell the story of Milarepa, a great yogi who overcame enormous difficulties to attain enlightenment. Travelling 3 hours south of Hezuo brings you to the turn-off for **Langmusi**, a Chinese–Tibetan town that straddles the White Dragon River on the Gansu–Sichuan border. A walk north across the river leads up to Sertri Gompa. A sky burial site is higher up, and visitors may be allowed to watch from a respectful distance. On the Sichuan side, you can walk south to Kerti Gompa, then continue up a gorge past a few sacred caves for some good hiking. Many travellers enjoy riding a horse across the countryside with Langmusi Tibetan Horse Trekking. Guided walking trips are also available.

🏠 Where to stay

Langmusi Hotel Opposite the entrance of Kiri Monastery; ☎0941 667 1555. The nicest hotel in town has large rooms & a convenient location. Standard rooms for Y450. **$$**

Boke Youth Hostel Inside a courtyard near the China Post Office; m 1880 666 1900. This hostel has both dorms & private rooms, along with a small restaurant. Call the manager for him to meet you on the main road to lead you here. Dorms from Y40 to Y60. **$**

Nomad's Youth Hostel On main street in Langmusi; ☎0941 667 1460. Small, somewhat cramped hostel on the main road in town. Can assist with arranging tours & treks of the area. Dorms for Y35. **$**

✕ Where to eat and drink

✕ Leisha's On the main road in Langmusi; m 1891 941 7143. This friendly Muslim-owned restaurant serves fresh apple pie, huge yak burgers along with noodles, & Chinese dishes. Dishes between Y20 & Y50. **$$**

🍽 Black Tent Café Directly across from the Langmusi Horse Trekking Company. This Tibetan-style restaurant serves Western & Tibetan dishes along with fresh coffee. **$$**

Zoige and Tangkhor From the Langmusi turn-off, the highway heads southeast over a small pass, then across swampy grasslands to **Zoige**, a town at 3,470m with a fine monastery. Hotels and restaurants are near the centre. About 65km southwest from Zoige is the town of **Tangkhor**. A shared taxi from Zoige to Tangkhor will cost Y35 a person and takes a bit over an hour. Tangkhor is a great off-the-beaten-track place to experience real Tibetan nomad culture (summer months are best). At 3,450m in elevation, Tangkhor sits atop some of the best grasslands in eastern Tibet and is located near a scenic stretch of the Yellow River. During the summer months from June to the end of September, the nearby grasslands are filled with Tibetan nomads living in their tents while herding their yaks and sheep. The grasslands can be reached by local taxi for Y100–200 return from Tangkhor. In town, you can stay at the **Tangkhor Palace Hotel** (☏*0837 228 2888;* **$$**), which is located across from the police station in the centre of town.

Chuanzhusi Continuing southeast, you'll experience vast grasslands, then drop steeply into a valley to the junction town of Chuanzhusi. This place relies almost entirely on the tourist trade and has lots of hotels and restaurants, but many businesses will try to overcharge, so be prepared for a little negotiating.You have three options for continuing to Chengdu: north to Jiuzhaigou, east to Huanglong, or south to Songpan. Small taxis, minibuses or jeeps can be hired for journeys to the national parks of Huanglong or Jiuzhaigou. Expect a hefty tariff for the 105km journey to Jiuzhaigou. You could try sharing a taxi with others or joining an existing group in a minibus.

Jiuzhaigou Famed for its alpine landscapes, Jiuzhaigou lies to the north over a 3,200m pass. It is billed as China's 'first five-star resort'. What that means is that this scenic area can cause serious damage to your wallet: be prepared for very high entry fee and bus fees to see the park. The park entry fee alone is Y80–220, depending on the season. *En route* to Jiuzhaigou is a large Bonpo monastery, Gamal Gonchen, with over 400 monks and a nearby nunnery. Once over the pass out of the Min Valley, there are numerous guesthouses near the park entrance but, along with park fees, guide fees, food and accommodation, this is an expensive circus – and one packed with Chinese tourists to boot. At the five-star-rated **InterContinental Resort Jiuzhai Paradise**, there's no need to worry about bad weather: this place has several huge wings entirely enclosed with Perspex domes – including artificial hot springs and a whole Tibetan village (that's artificial, too).

🏠 **Where to stay and eat**

🏠 **Sheraton Jiuzhaigou Resort** 301 Provincial Rd;☏0837 773 9988. Five-star luxury located 1.5km from the park entrance. Hotel offers a spa, indoor pool, multiple restaurants & travel services. Standard rooms start at Y900. **$$$$**

🏠 **Tibetan Barley Inn** 7 Arangka Upper St;☏0837 777 4282; **w** tibetanbarley.com. An elegant boutique Tibetan home, this is a comfortable & fun choice at Jiuzhaigou. The restaurant serves Western & Tibetan food &

desserts. Staff can arrange horse treks & transport in the area. Standard rooms start at Y280. **$$**

🏠 **Friendship Hostel** Located at Pengfeng Village, 1.5km west from the main park entrance; **m** 1582 820 1354. English-speaking staff at this nice hostel offer a free van service to the park entrance each morning. Restaurant serves good Western & Chinese food. Standard rooms for Y190 & dorms for Y50. **$$**

What to see and do See the park website (**w** *jiuzhai.com*) to check on current entry and transport fees (switch website to English version). Around Jiuzhaigou, horses can be arranged to ride up the two main valleys, which contain numerous vibrantly coloured pools connected by small waterfalls on the valley bottom, while the forest

8

extends to the snow peaks above. The scenery is stunning but, although it is a panda park, you are unlikely to see any black-and-white furries – or indeed any wildlife – most probably because the animal populations have been decimated by poachers.

Huanglong Park Huanglong Park is closer to Songpan, lying on the eastern side of Shar Dungri, a Bon holy mountain, and is cheaper and less visited than Jiuzhaigou. Huanglong is famed for its terraced travertine pools of many colours. On the downside, admission is a steep Y200. Many tourists, however, simply negotiate horses and guide for other treks in the mountains around. The most popular currently is a one- to three-day journey into the Niao Me (Nyenyul) Valley. In this valley lie several Bonpo monasteries, including the important Gyagar Mandi (which is built on an Indian model) and the Sakya monastery of Jara, as well as a famous waterfall called Zaga Pubu and a set of hot springs. It is also possible to reach this valley by road from a turn-off 30km to the south of Songpan. Be sure to check out the guide and precisely what services you are paying for before parting with any money. Most horse trekking is arranged from Songpan.

Songpan This has long been an important trading town for tea, musk, furs and gold. Songpan is an ancient Chinese garrison town with drum towers and walls. Qiang and Tibetan women visiting the market wear elaborate headdresses of amber and coral. It has become a major tourist destination due to the impressive nearby national parks. New guesthouses and budget hotels are built every year, so check around. The best deal is likely to be **Emma's Guesthouse** (\ *0837 723 1088;* **$$**) on Shunjiang Cun, at the north end of Songpan. English-speaking Emma has been running this top-notch guesthouse and restaurant for over a decade. She offers nice rooms, good food and excellent advice on horse trekking in the area, with standard rooms for Y180, or a dorm for Y50. **Emma's Kitchen** (**$**), in the same place, serves good-value Chinese and Western dishes, ranging between Y20 and Y40. Another option is **Guyun Guesthouse** (\ *0837 723 1368;* **$$**) located directly opposite Songpan bus station. This simple guesthouse is comfortable and has 24-hour hot water, with standard rooms for Y160 and dorm beds for Y40.

There is an airport at Songpan, used by tourists who fly from Chengdu *en route* to Jiuzhaigou. The bus ride from Chengdu to Songpan takes at least a full day, and delays are frequent after summer rains due to landslides and heavy traffic.

The Min Valley is a well-forested gorge (where it hasn't been deforested) and many of the villages are set high above the road. The area is the home of the Qiang people, who are believed to be descendants of the ancient Ch'iang tribe that ranged widely across the north of the plateau before the period of the Tibetan kings. Nowadays they are principally agriculturalists, with wheat and maize as their main crops, although many keep a few domestic animals stabled in large courtyards or on the ground floor of their three-storey stone and timber houses.

From Songpan, you have about 330km to go south through the Min River Valley to Wenchuan and Dujiangyan, then out on to the Sichuan Basin to Chengdu. On this route, you witness severe destruction in the Min River Valley caused by the 2008 Sichuan earthquake. If you're taking one of the routes to Chengdu via Pingwu, you may wish to stop at the excellent **Sanxingdui Museum** of prehistoric bronze works located outside Guanghan, 40km north of Chengdu. Another 22km farther south, the **Buddhist Monastery of Divine Light** (Baoguang Si) near Xindu is also worth a stop. For information on the large yet appealing city of Chengdu, see *Gateway: Chengdu* in this chapter, page 294, and also the entry on Chengdu in *Chapter 2*, page 69.

9

The Tibetan World

A prophecy is attributed to the great sage Padmasambhava (8th century AD): 'When the iron bird flies and horses run on wheels, the Tibetan people will be scattered like ants across the face of the earth, and the Dharma will come to the land of the redskins.' Whether this is what he actually said, or whether somebody made it up later to suit the situation, the Tibetans are certainly widely scattered, but not across the face of the earth. They are mostly scattered across the Himalaya. In the old Tibetan flat-earth world-view, however, they would be at the edges of the earth as the Tibetans knew it (which did not much extend beyond the Asian/Indian continent). Of the following destinations, the most rewarding trips are those to the high Himalayan regions inhabited by Tibetans.

Journeys to these places can be stymied by formidable obstacles, both physical and bureaucratic, but if you make it you are rewarded with glimpses of the traditional way of life and festivals no longer seen in Tibet itself. You will also be rewarded in other ways. There is a great chance to view the Tibetan plateau's rare wildlife, for instance: in Gangtok, Sikkim, there is a superb open zoo that allows you to get up close with rare Himalayan species. Sightings of these species in Tibet itself is only possible in extremely remote regions. Adventure sports are eminently more accessible in the Himalayan regions of Nepal and northern India, with skiing, white-water rafting, paragliding, heli-touring and mountaineering on offer. The only ski resort across the entire Himalayan region is at Gulmarg in Jammu and Kashmir, India. If you have deep pockets, heli-skiing is possible to arrange from Pokhara – the adventure sports centre of Nepal. While you can organise rafting in Tibet, you must have a prearranged group and the cost will be well above the cost of similar sorties in Nepal. Since travel in Nepal has few restrictions, it's easy to meet others to share white-water rafting and other adventures. That is simply not possible in Tibet where all people entering the region must have their itinerary mapped out in advance.

Probably the most surprising thing you learn as you visit different parts of the Tibetan world is that the Tibetans are not really unified, except in their common beliefs. Tibetans are a very tribal people. Historically, while different groups recognised the power of the Dalai Lama (centred in Lhasa), they were never obligated to the central Tibetan government, and were beyond its control. Centuries ago, rivalry between sects of Tibetan Buddhism openly took place, sometimes leading to battles. Tension between 'clans' and rival sects is ongoing, even in exile.

China has its beady eyes on these lands. Mao Zedong is credited with this handy claim: 'Tibet is the palm of China, and Ladakh, Nepal, Sikkim, Bhutan and NEFA are its fingers.' By NEFA, he meant North-East Frontier Agency, the older name for the present Indian state of Arunachal Pradesh. Chinese troops have made incursions into border regions, particularly in Ladakh and Bhutan. On Chinese maps, the whole of Arunachal Pradesh is shown as 'South Tibet', meaning China wants to claim it – no doubt because of its huge hydropower potential.

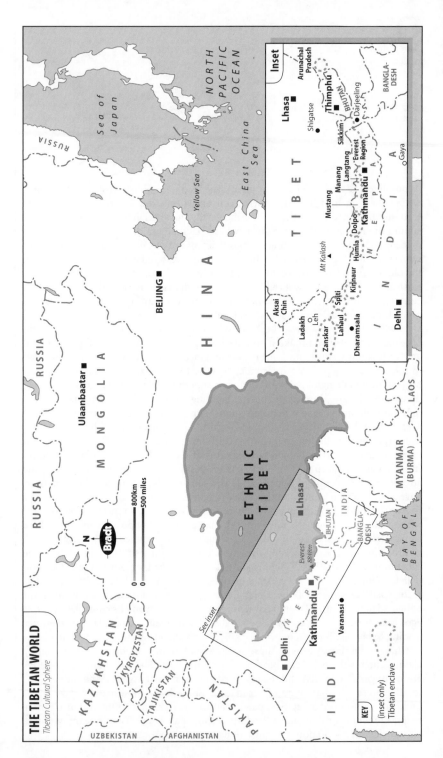

THE TIBETAN WORLD
Tibetan Cultural Sphere

Inset

Arunachal Pradesh

Lhasa ■
Shigatse ●

Thimphu ■
Darjeeling ●
BHUTAN
Sikkim

BANGLA-DESH

T I B E T

Everest Region
Langtang
Manang
Mustang Kathmandu ■
Dolpo N E P A L
Humla
Mt Kailash ▲
Kinnaur
Spiti
Lahaul Dharamsala ● Delhi ■
Zanskar
Leh ○
Ladakh
Aksai Chin

Gaya ○

I N D I A

RUSSIA

Sea of Japan

NORTH PACIFIC OCEAN

East China Sea

Yellow Sea

BEIJING ■

C H I N A

Ulaanbaatar ■

M O N G O L I A

RUSSIA

N
Bradt

800km
500 miles
0
0

KAZAKHSTAN

KYRGYZSTAN

TAJIKISTAN

PAKISTAN

UZBEKISTAN   AFGHANISTAN

I N D I A

Delhi ■

Kathmandu ■
Varanasi ●

N E P A L

Everest 8848m ▲

See inset

ETHNIC TIBET

Lhasa ■

BHUTAN

BANGLA-DESH

INDIA

MYANMAR (BURMA)

LAOS

BAY OF BENGAL

KEY
(inset only)
Tibetan enclave

322

For a great overview of these diverse Tibetan regions, a remarkable guidebook is *Mapping the Tibetan World* (Kotan Publishing, 2000). This book is a very ambitious project, covering the entire Tibetosphere in 420 pages, with over 280 maps.

TIBET IN EXILE

Until the mid-20th century, there was little motivation for Tibetans to leave the sanctuary of Tibet: some Buddhist masters travelled back and forth to India, and certain groups such as the Sherpas migrated southward over the Himalaya. The exodus of Tibetans from their homeland really began in earnest with the escape of the Dalai Lama in 1959, who was soon followed by some 60,000 of his people. Today, Tibetan refugees continue to escape, dodging Chinese bullets and biting snowstorms to negotiate high passes when crossing from Tibet into Nepal.

In exile, the Dalai Lama has established nearly 200 monasteries, with over 15,000 monks. There are estimated to be about 145,000 Tibetan refugees living in exile, mostly in India (101,000) and Nepal (perhaps 16,000), with 26,000 in the rest of the world. The West has been very reluctant to accept Tibetan refugees, although occasionally the doors have opened a crack, allowing 2,000 to settle in Switzerland, 3,500 in the USA and 1,700 in Canada. In pockets of the Himalaya in India and Nepal, you can see Tibetan culture in a more pristine environment, without Chinese troops and police. Traditions disrupted in Tibet, or festivals that are no longer permitted in the TAR, can be seen in places like Dharamsala. The main Tibetan exile location is India. A rough breakdown of where they live is as follows: in northwest India, there are about 21,000 in Himachal Pradesh, 6,500 in Uttar Pradesh, and 5,000 in Ladakh; in central India, about 8,000; in south India, approximately 30,000; in northeast India, an estimated 8,000; while 14,300 live in West Bengal and Sikkim.

India's relations with China are cool, perhaps even cold – as in Cold War. Although India was quick to recognise the PRC when it came to power in 1949, tempers flared over border disputes, with a major showdown in 1962. China considers parts of Sikkim and Arunachal Pradesh to be its territory, as it has never recognised the India–China border drawn up by the colonial British in 1914. China lays claim to 90,000km² of territory in Arunachal Pradesh. In late 1962, the PLA invaded, humiliating the Indian defenders: their artillery and trucks failed to work in the high-altitude conditions and many Indian soldiers fled. Thousands of Indian soldiers were killed. The PLA were within a few days' march of Calcutta when the USA airlifted military supplies to India, at which point the PLA abruptly turned around and left, withdrawing to the old borderline. A few months later, Pakistan ceded 25,000km² of disputed Kashmiri territory under its control to China, which enabled the Chinese to build a strategic mountain road connecting Xinjiang to Tibet through the zone of ceded territory (known as Aksai Chin).

In the late 1960s and 1970s China openly armed and trained separatist militants in northeastern India. Since the 1970s, China has given military support to Pakistan, and is believed to be the source of Pakistan's supply of Silkworm missiles – capable of striking Indian cities – and there are strong suspicions that China provided critical expertise and components to enable Pakistan's nuclear testing in 1998. China has given military support and training to three nations surrounding India: to Pakistan, Burma and Bangladesh.

India sees both Pakistan and China as border threats. In 1998, India's Defence Minister, George Fernandes, accused Beijing of stockpiling nuclear weapons and extending military airfields in Tibet. In May 1998, India went nuclear: it shocked the world by conducting a series of nuclear tests in Rajasthan. This resulted in economic sanctions by the USA, which was hypocritical considering America's nuclear arsenal. Beijing got the message loud and clear: China is not the only nuclear power in the region. A few weeks later, Pakistan exploded a series of nuclear devices, raising the stakes of destabilisation dramatically. The spectre of three nuclear-capable nations facing off in the Himalaya is all too real, with India and Pakistan becoming very confrontational.

DHARAMSALA Arriving in India in 1959, exiled Tibetans did not fare well in the hot and humid conditions, and were susceptible to diseases and viruses not found on the Tibetan plateau. Where they could, Tibetans gravitated to mountain zones with cooler climates – to places like Manali, Mussoorie, Bir and Dehra Dun – which are all located in the mountain regions north of Delhi. There is a cluster of Tibetan settlements scattered throughout this area.

The base of the Tibetan government-in-exile is Dharamsala, a former British hill station in Himachal Pradesh, 520km north of Delhi. India tolerates this government-in-exile, but does not officially recognise it: India does not allow Tibetans to engage in political work, but as one exile put it, 'everything we do here is political'. Tibetans do not belong to India either. Most Tibetans are barred from taking out Indian citizenship, so they remain stateless – most just have Indian resident certificates. Even Tibetans born in India – who have never been to Tibet – may choose to remain stateless, although they have the option to take out Indian citizenship. This is due to their determination to one day see their homeland independent as it once was.

Dharamsala is the lifeline for Tibetan culture. The Dalai Lama resides here, along with the ministers and cabinet of the government-in-exile, and the oracle of Tibet. At Gangchen Kyishong are the offices of the Central Tibetan Administration, with various ministries and information centres, as well as the Tibetan Computer Resource Centre and the Library of Tibetan Works and Archives (LTWA). The LTWA acts as a repository for ancient books and manuscripts from Tibet; a team of Tibetan scholars is engaged in translation, research and publication of books. Among other educational centres around Dharamsala is the Amnye Machen Institute, a small centre for advanced Tibetan studies; the institute also endeavours to expose Tibetans to Western literature and culture through translations. Among their publications is a fine map of Lhasa City.

Knowledge of Tibetan medicine is continued through the Tibetan Medical and Astro Institute, the only one of its kind in the world. It dispenses herbal medicines and trains students in Tibetan medical practices; research on new herbal medicines is also carried out here. The Tibetan arts have been revived through the Norbulingka Institute (for Tibetan artisans) and TIPA (Tibetan Institute of Performing Arts). The Tibetan Children's Village, mainly looking after orphans, is operated by the Dalai Lama's sister Jetsun Pema. In Dharamsala you can see festivals celebrated in full fashion, and Tibetan Buddhist ceremonies that carry real meaning (since they're not restricted, as they are in Tibet itself). Among the bigger celebrations are Losar (new year) and Monlam.

The Tibetan community in exile is not as cohesive as you might think. There are various points of view on Tibetan independence – some believe in full independence, others in limited autonomy. Some favour the use of force, by fighting a guerrilla war. When it comes to the government-in-exile, the Dalai Lama has tried to establish a quasi-democratic set-up, but this doesn't always work, as few would like to oppose him in public. This is where people get confused: opposing a point of view of the Dalai Lama is taken as a mark of disrespect.

Educated Tibetans say not enough steps have been taken for ushering the Tibetan community into the modern world – for example, translating modern literature into the Tibetan language. Nor is the faith of Tibetan Buddhism unified. Apart from the four main schools of Tibetan Buddhism, there are a number of offshoots or subsects. A major rift in the community developed in 1997 over a wrathful spirit with three bloodshot eyes, wreathed in the smoke of burning human flesh. Known as Dorje Shugden (Powerful Thunderbolt), this spirit seems to have originated in the 17th century: he is regarded by some as a protector deity, and by others as a murderous demon. The Dalai Lama, beginning in 1976, discouraged the propitiation of Shugden worship on the advice of the state oracle. In 1996, the Dalai Lama prohibited Shugden services in state offices and in government-in-exile-run monasteries, on the grounds that it is damaging to Buddhism. The subject is arcane and complex: several Dalai Lamas – the Fifth and 13th in particular – tried to stop the practice and teaching of Dorje Shugden worship. The controversy is ongoing: the Chinese, happy at any exile strife, have seized upon the rift to restore Shugden temples in occupied Tibet.

High points Dharamsala is divided into two very different parts: Kotwali Bazaar and lower Dharamsala, and McLeod Ganj in upper Dharamsala. The centre of activity for the Tibetan exile community is McLeod Ganj, set in forested mountain slopes. This laid-back town of perhaps 7,000 has lots of small restaurants and cafés where travellers hang out. There are numerous attractions related to Tibetan culture. As well as seeing the temples, you can visit the Tibet Museum – near the Dalai Lama's residence – offering two floors of displays. Apart from these attractions and the opportunity to take meditation classes, there is excellent trekking in the Dharamsala region, with camping trips of up to a week possible. Other activities include paragliding.

Low points During peak tourist seasons (June and November), the tiny town of McLeod Ganj gets so crowded that it's difficult to find a room in a hotel or guesthouse. People find the place so relaxing they just stay on: there's a very real danger of lingering over apple pie or chocolate cake in the cafés of McLeod Ganj and completely losing track of time.

Bizarre notes Nechung Monastery – the former Lhasa seat of the state oracle – was rebuilt in Dharamsala, with 70 monks studying the sacred rituals surrounding the oracle. The oracle is a man who acts as a medium to convey messages to the Dalai Lama from Dorje Drakten, a protector deity. The messages are used in important decision-making. Ceremonies where the oracle goes into a trance are secret: the oracle is dressed in a traditional brocade costume and a heavy headdress of precious metals. The ceremonial headdress is thought to weigh 20kg: normally it is too heavy to be worn without support. However, when in a trance, the oracle's strength increases considerably, and attendants quickly strap on the headdress. During the trance, the oracle is said to dance around as if the headdress weighs nothing.

Best time to go March to June, plus October to November. Watch out for the monsoon (July to mid-September). Winters can be very cold in Dharamsala, but February is when Losar (new year) is usually celebrated.

Red tape Indian visas are valid for three to six months (and longer is possible); multiple-entry visas are also available. Obtaining an Indian visa within Asia is difficult. The best place to get one is Bangkok, Thailand – requiring six working days to process.

9

Getting there You can reach McLeod Ganj by day or overnight **bus** from Delhi, taking about 12–15 hours for the 520km drive. The closest **railway** station is Pathankot. There's an airfield at Gaggal, connecting to Delhi, Kulu and Simla, but it does not appear to be much used, and **flight** schedules are erratic.

Following up A slew of mini-guides to Dharamsala appear on the site w dharamsalanet.com (click on 'Travel').

BODHGAYA, SARNATH AND SOUTH INDIA Bodhgaya, in Bihar state (in north-central India, due south of Kathmandu, and 15km from the town of Gaya), is the place where the Buddha attained enlightenment under a Bodhi tree. The original Bodhi tree was destroyed, but a sapling taken from it was introduced back from Sri Lanka and this exercise was then repeated half a dozen times. The present tree is part of the grounds of Mahabodhi Temple. Bodhgaya is today a site of special significance because the Dalai Lama has conducted Kalachakra initiations here. These esoteric initiations were once highly secret and exclusive, and were only conducted in Tibet. In the ceremony, the initiator would harmonise inner elements of the body and mind to bring about harmony and peace in the outer world. In an attempt to counter humankind's destructive forces, the Dalai Lama has dispensed with exclusivity, conducting Kalachakra initiations around the world: more than 200,000 devotees attended initiations in Bodhgaya in 2017, travelling from all over the Tibetan world.

Another Kalachakra empowerment site and Indian pilgrimage site visited by the Dalai Lama is Sarnath, 10km from Varanasi. Sarnath is the site of the Buddha's first sermon at Deer Park, 'Setting in Motion the Wheel of the Law'. Symbolising this sermon is the golden sculpture of the wheel with two deer that sits over the entrance of most temples in Tibet and is the national emblem of Tibet.

Like neighbouring countries, the Indians are not keen on large groups of Tibetans amassing, which explains scattered settlements in central India (8,000 Tibetans) and south India (30,000 Tibetans) where frontier-type settlements were hacked out of humid jungle. The temples of Sera, Ganden, Drepung and Tashilhunpo were built anew at Mundgod, Mysore and Bylakuppe.

TIBETAN KINGDOMS AND FIEFDOMS

Apart from the Tibetan realms already mentioned in this book (Tibet proper, Tibet outside the TAR, Tibet in exile), there is another realm: a fourth Tibet. It is largely composed of kingdoms and fiefdoms that broke away from Tibet centuries ago, when Tibet itself still had ruling kings. The people in these places speak and read Tibetan, and follow Tibetan cultural practices, but otherwise have developed their own worlds. They do not identify with Tibetan exiles, nor do they particularly want to attract them.

INDIA Bordering the Himalayas in the north of India are a host of ethnic Tibetan areas. These make a great escape from the chaos of India as they are sparsely populated and have fresh air, blue skies and intact ecosystems. Across the range, from Ladakh to Sikkim and Arunachal Pradesh, there is a movement to preserve ecosystems, with a focus on small-scale organic farming.

Ladakh and Zanskar The kingdoms of Ladakh and Zanskar (northwest India) originally splintered from west Tibet. Tibetans settled in Ladakh between AD500 and 600. Upon the death of the king of Ngari (western Tibet) around AD930, his kingdom was split between his three sons, one taking Guge and Burang, another Ladakh, and the third Zanskar and Spiti. The kingdoms of Ladakh and Zanskar changed hands numerous times. The most famous king of Ladakh, Senge Namgyal (1616–42), overran the kingdom of Guge in west Tibet, and even threatened central Tibet. By the end of the 17th century, Ladakh's power was in decline, leaving it vulnerable to Muslim incursions.

Due to its strategic location, Leh (the capital of Ladakh) once hosted a busy trading bazaar, attracting caravans from Kashgar, Khotan, Yarkand, Lhasa and Rawalpindi. With India's independence in 1947, Ladakh was absorbed into the Indian state of Jammu and Kashmir. Pakistan contested the borders and seized Baltistan, plus a part of Ladakh and a part of Kashmir. In 1962, the Chinese attacked Ladakh and took over the region east of Nubra, effectively ending any trade. There's now a heavy Indian military presence in Ladakh, to counter potential threats from Pakistan and China.

High points Dominating Leh is a derelict palace, built in the same monumental style as the Potala. Accommodation in Leh ranges from homey family-run guesthouses to more Spartan rooms in monasteries – to luxury hotels. A hybrid experience for the 'adventurous luxury traveller' is provided by high-end touring company Shakti Himalaya: you can check their website to glean ideas: w shaktihimalaya.com.

There are many monasteries within easy driving range of Leh; some, such as Hemis Gompa, host traditional festivals and monastic dances. Most imposing of the lamaseries is Tikse Gompa, a fantastic complex that occupies a whole hillside 17km upstream along the Indus River from Leh; the main hall houses a 15m-high seated gold image of Maitreya. Another real high point is Khardung La, a pass 40km north of Leh that sits at 5,606m and lays claim to being the world's highest motorable roadway. There are excellent trekking and mountaineering opportunities in Ladakh and Zanskar – you can put your own small group together and head out with a guide and donkey to carry gear. In winter, around February, you can indulge in one of the strangest hikes in the Himalaya – trekking along the frozen Zanskar River. It's not certain how much longer this trek will last. The icy voyage is becoming more dangerous as climate change leads to unstable conditions, meaning you might well be standing on thin ice. During the July/August summer months, the exact same river turns into a whirling torrent of white water, with excellent rafting.

Low points In snow-blocked months, the only way in is to fly to Leh from Delhi, and flights are often overbooked or cancelled, or both. Travellers have also experienced the opposite – they've made it into remote Zanskar but then have been unable to get out due to heavy snowfall. Faced with the prospect of being trapped in Shangri-La for six months till summer, there are two ways out: radio for an Indian helicopter airlift (expensive), or hike out along the ice on the frozen Zanskar River (slippery).

Bizarre notes Although royalty has largely disappeared from Ladakh, Zanskar still has two kings. The King of Zanskar lives in Padam, and the King of Zangla controls one castle and four villages. Ladakh has its own ice hockey team, with equipment donated by Canadian and American teams.

In September 2017, the inaugural Expedition India adventure race was run – starting in Leh, and incorporating white-water rafting, mountain biking and trekking along a 450km route, all over 4,000m. The extreme altitude took its toll on the international teams: the race was won by Team Jabberwok, from South Africa.

9

Red tape No special permits are required to visit – an Indian visa suffices. However, certain areas are out of bounds to tourists.

Getting there Due to sporadic fighting between the Indian Army and Kashmiri militants, the Srinagar to Leh route is not recommended (although you can travel from Leh to Lamayuru and back to Leh). Travellers use the Manali to Leh route to enter or exit Ladakh and Zanskar (you should also be aware that foreigners have gone missing in the Kulu Valley near Manali under mysterious circumstances – *do not trek alone in this region*). Although **buses** have been known to wheeze over the high passes on the 475km Manali–Leh route, it is best negotiated by a **4x4** vehicle such as a jeep. Along the route lies Tanglang La – at 5,330m, one of the highest road crossings in the world. The Manali–Leh road is generally open from July to October.

Following up Andrew Harvey's *A Journey in Ladakh* (1983) is the classic travelogue about the region, based on his 1981 trip.

Lahaul, Spiti and Kinnaur

The little-visited valleys of Lahaul and Spiti, accessed from Manali, are very Tibetan in character. No special permits are needed to enter Lahaul, but permits are required for parts of Spiti. Lahaul is reached over the 3,980m Rohtang pass, while access to Spiti is via the 4,550m Kunzum La pass. Long ago, both Lahaul and Spiti were ruled by the kingdom of Guge in far west Tibet. This is reflected in the now-rare Kashmiri style of artwork found at Tabo Gompa in Spiti, which is similar to that of Tsaparang (Guge Kingdom) in west Tibet. Tabo Gompa houses one of the Tibetan world's finest collections of Buddhist art, with seven chapels bearing frescoes and a number of Guge-style *chortens*. May to June is the best time to visit these areas. Getting around is possible by bus, hired taxi or trekking. You might consider hiring a vehicle for the journey, splitting the cost with several others. Inner Line Permits for Spiti are obtained in Rekong Peo, and will be scrutinised at the military checkpoint of Sumdo.

Southeast of Spiti is the Kinnaur region, where local people wear green felt hats. Like Lahaul and Spiti, Kinnaur was once part of the Guge Kingdom. The main focus of pilgrims to Kinnaur is the sacred mountain of Kinnaur Kailash (6,050m), which Hindus set out to circle clockwise. It is thought that Shiva comes from Mount Kailash in west Tibet to winter at Kinnaur Kailash – and to smoke hashish. Kinnaur can be accessed from Shimla; there is also a route leading from Kinnaur to Spiti.

Darjeeling, Kalimpong and Sikkim

Darjeeling and Kalimpong in northeast India were once controlled by Sikkim, but in the 18th century Kalimpong was lost to the Bhutanese while Darjeeling fell to the Nepalese. Eventually, the lands fell into the hands of the British East India Company, which developed the region as a tea-growing centre. Darjeeling is a former British hill station – a cool place at 2,100m, and the base for trekking in the area. From Darjeeling there are ethereal views of Kangchenjunga, at 8,595m the third-highest peak in the world. There are several Tibetan monasteries around Darjeeling; great places to visit are the zoo – featuring rare Himalayan animals such as the red panda and the snow leopard – and the Himalayan Mountaineering Institute (HMA) which was run by Tenzing Norgay until his death in 1986, and now houses a climbing museum and climbers' training centre. Apart from being a resort, Darjeeling is a major educational centre, attracting the children of wealthy Sikkimese and Bhutanese.

From Darjeeling you can take a bus, jeep or taxi to Kalimpong. In the days of the British Raj, the main wool-trade route to Lhasa was via Kalimpong and Sikkim through Yadong to Gyantse. This trading route closed in 1962 as a result of border clashes between China and India, and was reopened in mid-2006. Kalimpong is a small trading town – famed for its cheese – with several Tibetan monasteries. The town attracts Indian tourism.

From Darjeeling or Kalimpong you can take a shared ride into Sikkim. Sikkim used to be a Tibetan kingdom – a kind of vassal state. Later, it was run by the Rajas of Sikkim; in 1975, it was annexed by India (China also claims the whole of Sikkim). The story of the demise of Sikkim has all the elements of a fairy tale – with a bad ending. In Darjeeling in 1959, the crown prince of Sikkim, Palden Thondup Namgyal, met Hope Cooke, an American on a study trip in India. He married her in 1963 at a ceremony at Gangtok Monastery; two years later he became king and she was given the title of queen. But the match did not sit well with the people of Sikkim. Hope Cooke remained distant: she never converted to Buddhism and she made frequent trips to Europe and America with the couple's two children. In 1973, there was a wave of unrest in Sikkim, and Indian troops took advantage of the situation to place the royal family under house arrest. Hope Cooke eventually left the king, returned to New York with her children, and filed for divorce. In 1975, the Sikkim National Congress voted to incorporate Sikkim into India. The monarchy was abolished, and Sikkim was annexed as the 22nd federal state of India. The deposed king died in 1982 in a New York cancer clinic.

Sikkim is a mellow escape from the chaos of India – the state is small, with a low population and lots of forested areas. Due to its hilly terrain, it is a nation of small farmers, and in 2015 declared itself the first all-organic state in India. In 2016, Kangchenjunga National Park was inscribed to the World Heritage list. This park offers majestic trekking opportunities if you can organise the guide and permits.

Gangtok, elevation 1,500m, is the capital of Sikkim. It is a pleasant place and remarkably clean for India. In fact, it has been voted the cleanest city in India several times. A spacious walking mall, MG Marg, marks the centre of town. In Gangtok you can find the former royal palace and royal chapel, which aren't open to the public, but go around to the back entrance and you can see part of the complex. In another section of town is the Institute of Tibetology, with a fine collection of artefacts and Buddhist literature.

Some of the most impressive sights of Gangtok are its views of magnificent Mount Kangchenjunga. If you get a hotel high uphill, you can have that view right out your window – and this need not cost the earth, either. There are long sets of stairs leading uphill above MG Marg to reach these viewpoint hotels.

A short 6km taxi ride from town brings you to a remarkable zoological park, set in a forested area of 230ha. The zoo has only a dozen or so Himalayan species, each given spacious enclosures that mimic natural conditions. The species include the red panda, snow leopard, Himalayan tahr, Tibetan wolves and blue sheep. I am not a fan of zoos, but this one is unique for India and well worth the visit. There is a 2.5km pathway through the park, so allow lots of time to visit, and keep your driver on hold at the gates for the return trip to Gangtok.

About 25km from Gangtok is Rumtek Monastery, built as a replica of Tsurphu Monastery (near Lhasa; see pages 182–4 for more about Tsurphu) by the exiled head of the Kagyu sect, who fled Tibet in 1959. The spiritual heart of Sikkim is the Nyingma monastery at Tashiding.

There are excellent treks north of Gangtok, usually arranged in small groups with permits, porters and horses. The prize trek is up towards the base camp of mighty

Kangchenjunga. Most roads in Sikkim are in excellent shape, though somewhat precipitous at times. A few trekkers have managed to walk along the old British roads between monasteries. There's a small network of relatively unknown and unused old British service roads that can be used as alternatives to the main roads or steeper walking tracks. However, you will need your own maps as some roads are overgrown, and there are few (if any) guesthouses so you will need camping equipment, too.

Another scenic highlight is the drive towards 4,350m Nathu La on the Sikkim–Tibet border to wave Tibetan flags at PLA border guards. Currently, only Indian tourists are allowed to go to the actual border. Foreigners are only permitted to go as far as Changu Lake, which is short of the border. Indian tourists come to the lake to take selfies with yaks, which can be rented out to ride to a small temple on the other side of the lake. A cable car takes tourists higher up to a viewpoint.

There are rumours that group tours may one day be allowed access to cross into Tibet at Nathu La. The border crossing is open to traders from Tibet and Sikkim for seven months a year, from May to November. Then it is closed because of freezing weather conditions. By road from Gangtok to Lhasa is around 480km, and the direct drive can be completed on the same day. Far preferable would be to break the journey at Gyantse and rest there.

When to go The best months are April–May (spring flowers in bloom) and October–November (post-monsoon). Winters are cold, with occasional snowfalls.

Red tape Darjeeling is open without permit. You can easily obtain a two-week permit for Sikkim in either Darjeeling or Siliguri, and an extension of two more weeks should be possible (longer permits for Sikkim may require booking a trek with an agency in advance). If just planning to go to Gangtok, you can pick up an Inner Line Permit for ten days or so right at the Sikkim border post.

Getting there Half of the thrill is getting there: the '**toy train**' – a narrow-gauge railway completed in 1881 – winds up from Siliguri for the 80km to Darjeeling, passing tea plantations and misty mountains. The closest **airport** to Darjeeling and Kalimpong is Bagdogra. You can **overland** from Darjeeling via the border town of Kakarbhitta to Kathmandu.

Following up A mixed photographic work and travel narrative is *Footsteps in the Clouds: Kangchenjunga a Century Later*, by Pat and Baiba Morrow (Raincoast, 2000).

Arunachal Pradesh
Tucked into northeast India, sandwiched between Sikkim and Bhutan, lies the state of Arunachal Pradesh. Home to ethnic Tibetans, the region has strong links to Tibet, being the birthplace of the Sixth Dalai Lama; citing those strong historical links as justification, China claims all of Arunachal Pradesh as 'South Tibet'. Since Arunachal Pradesh holds by far the greatest hydropower potential in India, this interest from China is more than casual.

Due to the extreme sensitivity of this border region, bristling with Indian army posts, it is one of the few places in India where an advance permit is needed. Costing around US$70, the permit can be obtained through an agent in India, who will email it to you after payment. Places you intend to visit must be stated on the permit – usually focused on the road to Bomdila and Tawang.

Tawang is home to several large monasteries, plus a small one dedicated to the Sixth Dalai Lama. About 25km from Tawang is a beautiful waterfall site; just upstream on the same river is a bridge built by Tangtong Gyalpo (see box, pages

192–3), who built many such bridges in Tibet, Bhutan and beyond in the 15th century. Very few of them remain, and you won't find any in Tibet itself, but the one near Tawang is still functioning more than 500 years later.

Arunachal has a pristine environment, with intact forest and high-altitude terrain. Hunting is prohibited, and logging is not allowed unless with a permit. Lhaghyal Monastery has preserved 35km² of forest around the *gompa* to conserve as a habitat for red pandas.

NEPAL Nepal is a small country sitting on a border shared with an up-and-coming superpower. The Nepalese have no desire to confront the PLA, so the Nepalese government has worked closely with the Chinese since their invasion of Tibet, and fully supports the Chinese position in Tibet. In the late 1960s, the Chinese requested help in snuffing out Khampa resistance operating from Nepalese territory, in the region of Mustang. After Henry Kissinger blocked arms drops and American support to the Khampas, and the Dalai Lama appealed to the Khampas to lay down their arms, the Nepalese Army surrounded the last guerrillas in Mustang and ambushed them. Most were killed; the rest were thrown in jail for lengthy periods.

Since the entire royal family was gunned down in mid-2001, Nepal has experienced great instability. Civil war erupted, with fierce battles between the Nepalese Army and Maoist insurgents. Thousands of civilians and military were killed, particularly in remote border regions. In November 2006, a peace accord was signed between the government and the rebels, with a new constitution and new national anthem. In 2008, Nepal became a republic, albeit one where the constitution is still under debate, and there is an air of unrest, with frequent strikes and protests against corrupt government practices.

After a mega-earthquake hit central Nepal in April 2015, killing 9,000 people and causing hundreds of thousands of homes to collapse, some US$3 billion was donated by countries eager to assist. Two years later, not even a third of that funding had been distributed – it simply disappeared into some deep pockets. The government at one point announced the sale of rotting rice – the rice had been donated by Nepal's neighbours, but kept in storage. An air of uncertainty and unease prevails in Nepal, so it's best to keep updated on the situation in Nepal through news websites.

Nepal is the main conduit for refugees escaping Tibet, intent on reaching Tibetan settlements in India. They hike over high passes to the south of Tingri and Sakya to reach Nepal. Refugees run a gauntlet through Nepal – Nepalese police routinely rob Tibetans and there have been cases of them raping Tibetan women. Tibetan refugees entering Nepal used to be taken care of by the UNHCR, and allowed to travel on to the safe haven of India. However, this policy changed around 2004: some refugees have been handed back to Chinese authorities (in contravention of UN guidelines) and others have been jailed in Nepal.

About 20,000 Tibetan exiles live in Nepal, but they are not recognised as Nepali citizens – they cannot get a Nepali passport, and a number of them are still living in Tibetan refugee camps. No politicking is allowed – Nepalese officials have sworn to co-operate with the Chinese and swear they will not allow any demonstrations by Tibetans in Nepal. Nepalese police regularly crack down on 10 March gatherings, and have even broken up indoor gatherings of Tibetans when sensing a political undercurrent. The office of the representative of the Dalai Lama in Kathmandu was closed down in 2005, along with a Tibetan refugee organisation. That same year, after India suspended supplies of arms to the Nepalese Army, the Nepalese turned to the Chinese for help. The Chinese immediately pledged US$1 million in military aid and dispatched truckloads of weapons overland from Tibet into Nepal.

The Nepalese press is blatantly pro-Chinese, muzzling voices that support the Tibetan cause. Nepalese police and authorities will go to ridiculous lengths to silence Tibetans living in Nepal. In July 2011, Nepalese authorities even shut down gatherings by Tibetans celebrating the birthday of the Dalai Lama. Oddly, however, Kathmandu is the best place in Asia or the Indian subcontinent to buy materials on Tibet, such as Free Tibet stickers, Free Tibet T-shirts, Tibetan flags, HHDL pictures, books, magazines and DVDs. However, display of such items around Bodnath Stupa is not tolerated by the authorities.

Two of Nepal's major foreign exchange earners centre around Tibetans: carpets and tourism. The Tibetan carpet industry – centred in Kathmandu – was initially set up by exiled Tibetans in the early 1960s as part of a Swiss aid project to benefit Tibetan refugees in Nepal. The venture became wildly successful, but sales have dwindled in recent years, putting Tibetan refugees out of work. Tourism in Nepal is prominently connected with Tibetans: several of Kathmandu's popular temples are Tibetan, and the commonest trekking routes are through Sherpa or ethnic Tibetan regions.

Sherpas, a group that migrated from Tibet centuries ago, are directly involved in the tourist, trekking and mountaineering industries. They are often wealthy businesspeople who run lodges, guide groups and so on. Sherpas speak a language similar to Tibetan – they can converse with Tibetans, but have no written language. They are followers of Tibetan Buddhism. Sherpas have been sympathetic to the Tibetan cause, and have formed a kind of 'underground' to help refugees arriving in Nepal. There are probably around 20,000 Sherpas living in Nepal, with the strongest base around the Khumbu area. Sherpas are identified by their last name 'Sherpa' as in Jangbu Sherpa or Tashi Sherpa. Other Tibetan-related groups in Nepal are the Lhobas from Mustang and the Dolpopas from Dolpo.

High points In Kathmandu, Bodnath Stupa is the main Tibetan temple area, surrounded by Tibetan-run shops and businesses; further out from Kathmandu is the Monkey Temple in Swayambunath. Nepal is the most 'developed' of any of the .trekking destinations in the Himalaya. In a hurry? If you have deep pockets, you can arrange for a small group to helicopter into Everest base camp for lunch from Pokhara. You probably wouldn't want to stay there much longer as you might chunder your entire lunch due to altitude sickness bearing down. Or you could helicopter into Annapurna base camp for a few hours to catch some high-altitude rays.

Teahouse trekking is the easiest way to visit regions with Sherpa or Tibetan-related populations – places such as Solo Khumbu, Langtang and Annapurna. The easiest place to start a trek is the second-biggest town, Pokhara, an 8-hour bus ride from Kathmandu. Lakeside Pokhara is a great place to hang out and is teeming with adventure sports companies, hosting trekking, rafting, canyoning and paragliding. You can also find yoga and retreat centres.

A day's bus ride from Pokhara is Lumbini, the birthplace of the Buddha. This is a low-key town with many temples from different nations, including some Tibetan-style temples. China is investing US$3 billion in Lumbini, although the nation is atheist. Go figure. The idea is to transform the small town into the premier place of pilgrimage for Buddhists from around the world, with an airport, highway, hotels, convention centre, temples and a Buddhist university.

A visit to the restricted Mustang, Dolpo or Limi trekking regions requires self-sufficient camping trips, usually only in groups, with a liaison officer and special permits worth US$550 per trekker. Both Dolpo and Mustang used to lie on old salt-trading routes from Tibet: Tibetans took salt and wool south to exchange for grains from India.

Low points Kathmandu has become one of the most polluted cities in Asia – with loads of dust in the air.

In peak seasons – October especially – popular trails can be jammed with trekkers, and lodges can be full. Near Namche Bazaar, Lukla airstrip waiting room can get pretty wild as trekkers and mountaineers duke it out to get on the overbooked light aircraft back to Kathmandu. Failure to make it on to a flight may mean a meaningless ten-day walk back.

Bizarre notes Mustang is a Himalayan kingdom that was governed by King Jigme Parbal Bista, the 25th monarch in a line stretching back to the 14th century. He lost the title when Nepal became a republic in 2008; the ex-king died in 2016. The former royal family still wields influence in Mustang, breeding the finest horses of the region.

The seat of the former royal family is Lo Manthang, one of the rare Tibetan-style citadels with walls still intact. Trekkers take a week to reach the town, hiking in from Jomosom. There is, however, a road all the way to Lo Monthang, so privately hired vehicles can make the journey in a much shorter time. Not having the time nor the stamina to trek for a week, Nepalese dignitaries (and foreigners) have been known to drop in for tea by helicopter, landing in a wheat field next door to the former monarch's humble palace.

Best time to go Go in the October–early December or March–April trekking seasons. Avoid the mid-June to late-September monsoon season, when trails are slippery and roads can be washed out, with frequent landslides and mudslides.

Red tape Fifteen-day or one-month visas are available on arrival at Kathmandu airport. Two-month visas are easy to get and extendable. If you go trekking, you may need a permit for each region to be visited. These are best obtained in Kathmandu or Pokhara.

Getting there Most trips have a start or end point (or both) in Kathmandu, although a good alternative is Pokhara. Good trekking equipment can be bought in Kathmandu and Pokhara – a lot is left behind by expeditions.

Inspiration *House of Snow* (Head of Zeus, 2016) is a comprehensive anthology of great writing about Nepal, particularly strong on adventure. *The Snow Leopard* by Peter Matthiessen (1978; repr. Penguin, 1996) is a finely wrought account of a journey to Dolpo. Matthiessen also wrote the text for *East of Lo Monthang* (Shambhala Publications, 1995), a photobook featuring pictures of Mustang by Thomas Laird. In the fiction line, *Escape from Kathmandu* by Kim Stanley Robinson (1989; repr. St Martin's Press, 2000) takes the reader on a wild ride, with some hilarious excursions to the Tibetan side. A walk on the mystical side is *Surfing the Himalayas* by Frederick Lenz (St Martin's Press, 1997), claiming to discover mystical insights via snowboarding. Lenz created his own cult in the USA, bilking his followers of large amounts of cash before he passed on to another realm. Online, you can access the *Kathmandu Post* at w kathmandupost.ekantipur.com. Be aware that newspapers in Nepal are subject to heavy-handed censorship.

BHUTAN In the Himalaya, of the vast area that was once the spirited domain of the Tibetan religion and culture – stretching from Ladakh to Yunnan – only the tiny enclave of Bhutan survives as a self-governing entity, with Tibetan Buddhism

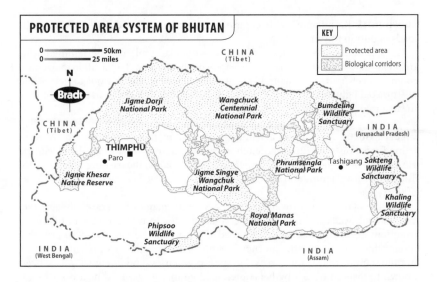

as its state religion (Outer Mongolia, far to the north, is also independent and follows Tibetan Buddhism, but its people and language are Mongolian). With an area of 47,000km², Bhutan is roughly the size of Switzerland, and seeks to be as neutral. It allows India to control its foreign policy in exchange for military protection from China. To protect itself from a takeover by India, Bhutan has held a seat at the UN since 1971.

Although Bhutan was self-governing since the 17th century in a kind of theocracy, the Bhutanese monarchy is a hereditary dynasty begun in the early 20th century. Ugyen Wangchuck, previously the governor of Bhutan, was crowned hereditary monarch of Bhutan in 1907 with British support, after his role as intermediary between the British and the Tibetans during the Younghusband expedition of 1903.

King Jigme Singye Wangchuck, who came to power in 1972, fostered the entry of Bhutan into the international community, establishing diplomatic relations with many countries. King Jigme Wangchuck also fostered the traditional culture of Bhutan to the point of strong-arming other ethnic cultures. Officially, the population of Bhutan is only 780,000 people. The predominant ethnic groups in Bhutan – the Drukpas and Monbas – migrated from Tibet centuries ago. Bhutan, however, is not a safe haven for refugee Tibetans, whom the Bhutanese fear will build up in greater numbers and power (there are several thousand currently living in Bhutan). Due to a falling-out over Tibetan refugees, Bhutan has few contacts with the Tibetan government-in-exile. Nor are the Bhutanese keen on a large Nepalese presence. The southern lowlands are mostly occupied by people of Nepalese origin. The government has banned the speaking of Nepalese, and it has an ongoing programme to boot as many ethnic Nepalis as possible back to Nepal, citing their failure to assimilate to Bhutanese culture and learn the language as the reason for their marching orders. More than 100,000 of these people languished in refugee camps in southeast Nepal, though at least a third of those have since managed to emigrate to the USA to start their lives anew.

In November 2008, the king stepped down and handed the crown to his son, Jigme Khesar Namgyal Wangchuck, the fifth king in the lineage.

The official faith of Bhutan is Drukpa Kagyu, a tantric form of Tibetan Buddhism (and a subsect of the Kagyu order); also practised is Buddhism of the Nyingma school; in Nepalese areas, the faith is Indian- and Nepali-influenced Hinduism. Bhutan's national language, called Dzongkha, is related to Tibetan but is quite different from the Lhasa dialect. Dzongkha is a compulsory subject at school, although the medium of instruction is English.

High points American biologist Edward Wilson claims that the only way to preserve biodiversity and prevent species extinction is to set aside 50% of the earth's land area to be turned over to nature. Sounds like a tall order, but Bhutan has actually accomplished this goal. More than 50% of Bhutan's land area is devoted to national parks, wildlife reserves and wildlife corridors (see map, opposite). Bhutan is aiming to become the greenest nation on the planet, with vast swathes of forest, all-organic farming and no GM crops.

Bhutan has a pristine environment, untouched by industrial development, except that it is allowing the construction of mega-dams on its rivers by Indian consortiums, with most of the power slated to be exported to India. The best way to see this beautiful land is by trekking or 4x4 safari; more recently, white-water rafting and mountain biking have been introduced. Top treks include the one north through Jigme Dorji National Park towards 7,236m Mount Chomolhari on the Tibetan border.

A major extension of this same trek is to continue on through Laya, negotiating multiple high passes and crossing into Wangchuck Centennial National Park. The route continues east to Thangze, then heads south to Daralo. Along the way, there are spectacular views of Gangkar Puensum – the world's highest unclimbed peak at 7,520m at the summit, and slated to stay that way (the sacred peak is off-limits to climbers). Christened 'the Snowman Trek', this is one of the longest and toughest in the Himalaya, taking 28 days or so to complete. The trek is yak-assisted for carrying gear in some sections, because horses and mules cannot handle the snow and ice coating the high passes.

Bhutan is famed for its traditional festivals – elaborate affairs with parades, Cham sacred dances and archery contests. For a temple festival, spectators turn up in their finest national robes (*kho* for men and *kira* for women). In addition to the national dress, men or women wear a ceremonial scarf, and men often wear argyle woollen socks and Western sneakers. Bhutan is the best place in the Tibetan world to see traditional-style architecture still proudly showcased – such as the parliament buildings of Thimphu and the numerous *dzongs* and *gompas* across the country. Even petrol stations are built in traditional style. Along with the architecture go the fine arts of fresco painting and the making of Buddhist statuary. On a hill overlooking Thimphu Valley is a gigantic seated Shakyamuni Buddha that towers 51.5m – one of the tallest in the world. The gilded bronze statue was completed in 2015.

Low points The crippling cost of getting into Bhutan may prove hazardous to your wallet, but it's also the factor that keeps the tourist masses at bay.

Bizarre notes To the far east of Bhutan lies Sakteng Wildlife Sanctuary which is said to be a place where the yaks and the yetis can roam in peace. Don't know about the yetis, but you will certainly see yaks there. The region is inhabited by the Brokpa, who moved from Tibet centuries ago. They are semi-nomad yak herders. You can trek between Merak and Sakteng towns, going over a 4,100m pass. This place proves that Tibetan nomads can coexist with wildlife, which the Chinese say is not possible.

9

Best time to go The best seasons are autumn (November) or spring (April/May). Avoid the June–October monsoon. However, if you are looking for flora, May and June are when glorious rhododendrons and blue poppies are in bloom.

Red tape Access is restricted – visitors are allowed only in a group tour or by personal invitation from a party in Bhutan. This policy keeps the numbers down to around 200,000 visitors a year. They fly into Paro (west of the capital of Thimphu) or come overland through Phuntsoling or Samdrup Jongkar. There are three domestic airports: at Tashigang and Bumthang (in the east) and Gelepgu (in the south). With advance clearance, visas are issued at the place of arrival. On group tours a set fee of US$210–280 a day is levied on each visitor, depending on the kind of trip and the season. This may sound very high, but it includes all the bills (accommodation, food, trekking equipment and transport). The tariff must be paid up front by wiring money to the Bhutan tourism authorities. Paperwork can take several months to complete if going through an agent outside Asia; in Kathmandu, the red tape can be completed in a week.

Following up Barbara Crossette's book *So Close to Heaven* (Vintage Books, 1996) explores the vanishing Buddhist kingdoms of the Himalaya. Jamie Zeppa's travel narrative, *Beyond the Sky and the Earth* (Riverhead Books, 1999) is an excellent personal take on the kingdom. For up-to-date information and news snippets on Bhutan, check these websites: **w** kuenselonline.com (national daily English-language newspaper), **w** bootan.com and **w** bhutan.com.

MONGOLIA Apart from a few monastic visitors, there is no Tibetan presence in the independent nation of (Outer) Mongolia. It is not a Tibetan kingdom or fiefdom, but the country is mentioned here because it preserves Tibetan Buddhist practices: the national faith of Mongolia is Tibetan Buddhism. Tibet has strong historical connections with Outer Mongolia. The Sakya sect established relations with the court of Godan Khan in the 1240s – an ongoing link. At the court of Kublai Khan in the 13th century, a great contest took place to see which philosophy had the greatest power – Islam, Nestorian Christianity, Confucianism, Taoism or Tibetan Buddhism. The last prevailed, but it was not until the 16th century, under Altan Khan, that Tibetan Buddhism really took hold in Mongolia. Altan Khan conferred the Mongolian title Dalai Lama (meaning 'Ocean of Wisdom') on Sonam Gyatso (the Third Dalai Lama). Despite Chinese protests, the current Dalai Lama has visited Mongolia a number of times since 1990, drawing huge crowds. He has established teachings there through his own monks. With the revival of Tibetan Buddhism in Mongolia, the Dalai Lama has a new ally. Buddhism is also rejuvenating in the Mongolian-populated areas of Russia – Buryatia and Tuva – on China's sensitive border zones.

Mongolia makes an interesting case study: it was a Tibetan Buddhist nation under communist (Russian) domination and then regained its independence soon after the collapse of the Soviet Union in 1991. In the 1996 election, the Mongolian Democratic Coalition garnered most of the seats, ending 75 years of communist rule. This is the scenario that intrigues Tibetans most – a similar fall of the Chinese Empire (with breakaway slabs being Tibet, Xinjiang and Inner Mongolia).

In the Stalin era, 700 larger and 1,000 smaller monasteries were destroyed in Mongolia, and thousands of monks were executed by the Russians in an attempt to wipe out Tibetan Buddhism, the predominant faith in Mongolia. A handful of larger monasteries survived (such as the one at Karakorum) and now, out on the grasslands, felt tents (*gers*) are converted for use as temples as Tibetan Buddhism enjoys a comeback. Also staging a comeback is Mongolian military hero Genghis Khan. After the last Russian troops left in 1992, Genghis rode back in, appearing larger than life, on the screen in a 4-hour epic movie playing at cinemas in Ulaanbaatar. His fat bearded face also popped up on banknotes, and on the label of Chinggis Khan Vodka, a twist on the national Russian beverage.

All of which makes the Chinese very nervous – they're not keen on Genghis nationalism spilling over the border into their zone of Inner Mongolia (Genghis Khan's tomb is located in Inner Mongolia). Genghis brings back bad ancestral memories for the Chinese – in the early 13th century his hordes of horsemen surged with ease over the Great Wall, which was designed to keep them out. The Mongols weren't in any hurry to leave, either – the sons and grandsons of Genghis (particularly Kublai Khan) hung around China for the rest of the 13th century. Thus relations with Chinese-controlled Inner Mongolia are testy. There are hardly any Mongolians left in Inner Mongolia anyhow – out of a population of 20 million, perhaps only two million are reckoned to be Mongolians (the rest are Han Chinese settlers). This is what the Dalai Lama points his finger at: Inner Mongolia has been swamped by Han Chinese and has totally lost its identity.

A funny thing happened to Inner Mongolia – its grasslands were decimated by cashmere goats. Exploiting production in Mongolia and Tibet, China managed to monopolise the global cashmere market. But it came with a hefty price – the strategy was to vastly increase the number of goats that bear this wool, highly prized by buyers in Europe. Unfortunately, cashmere goats are not grasslands friendly – they do not nibble grass like yaks. They pull it out by the roots. The grasslands of Inner Mongolia were turned into desert: the dust was then picked up by the wind and started raining down on Beijing. At this point, Beijing put the brakes on the goat breeding, and the cashmere industry turned its attention to buying the precious wool from the grasslands of Outer Mongolia.

This region, both Inner and Outer, is sometimes referred to as 'Minegolia' because it is intensively exploited for coal. There is also heavy mining of copper and rare earths to feed China's voracious appetite for minerals.

High points Ulaanbaatar is a bleak place, with Soviet-style apartment blocks blotting the skyline, but it has an incredible fine arts museum, with intricate bronze statuary and stunning woven or painted *tankas*, some showing scenes of Lhasa and the Potala. The beautiful statuary in this museum is largely the work of 17th-century master sculptor Zanabazar, who studied in Tibet and returned to Mongolia to spread Tibetan Buddhism.

There are more animals in Mongolia than people – many more – with animal husbandry the mainstay of the economy. With a population of 2.3 million spread over an area of 1.56 million km², Mongolia is very sparsely inhabited, with herds of gazelles, wild camels, wild asses and bighorn sheep roaming the wilderness. An easier wilderness site to reach is Terelj National Park, 80km from Ulaanbaatar (2 hours by road). This offers adventure activities such as rafting, riding, skiing and mountain biking. The Gobi Desert is home to an unexpected amount of wildlife. To see this kind of pure environment, go to the mountainous Lake Hovsgol region in the northwest, or to the Gobi in the southwest.

Low points Food in Mongolia – at least supplementary food, aside from the main course – is hard to find, and revolves around meat. Bring your own in the form of freeze-dried soups or meals to supplement the Mongolian meat-based staples.

Bizarre notes Large, whimsical postage stamps feature subjects such as a Mongolian cosmonaut (sent into space on a Russian craft), Mickey Mouse, and Fred Flintstone riding a dinosaur past some *gers*. Also featured on stamps are Taras (Tara is the goddess of compassion), and tantric deities locked in *yabyum* (page 359) embraces. On the 1-tugrig banknote, the snow lion appears, as it used to on pre-1950 Tibetan money (the watermark on this bill is an image of Genghis Khan).

Best time to go Winter is severe with possible heavy snowfall and sub-zero temperatures, made even more sub-zero by howling winds. In other words, go in the summer, from June to September. The Nadam Fair – featuring horse racing, wrestling and archery – takes place in July.

Red tape Individual travel restrictions have eased up since the 1990s. The easiest way to get into Mongolia is to extend your stay off the TransMongolian Express. Some long-term visas are available direct from embassies from places such as London or Vientiane (Laos). It's hit and miss: some embassies issue them, others don't. Monkey Business (aka Monkey Star), a Belgian travel agent with offices in Hong Kong and Beijing, seems adept at getting these visas at short notice – it runs tours to (Outer) Mongolia. You can also get (Outer) Mongolian visas in Ulan Ude (on the TransMongolian, near Lake Baikal), and in Hohhot, the capital of Inner Mongolia. Ulaanbaatar is a very good place to pick up a long Chinese visa.

Getting there Journeys to Mongolia invariably start and end in Ulaanbaatar. A single passenger **rail** line traverses the country from north to south, linking Moscow to Beijing via Ulaanbaatar. There are few roads in Mongolia, but a **4x4** can go almost anywhere on the grasslands in the summer, so no road is required. As an individual, you'll most likely have to get together with other travellers to rent a vehicle. The trick is to find a vehicle that has gasoline/petrol, as there's a severe shortage of the precious stuff. Mongolia is one of the few countries left where ancient Russian turboprop jets are still in use, on domestic runs. And you may even stray across an old AN-2 biplane parked at an airfield – it may be on display as a vintage **aircraft**, or it might actually still be in service.

Following up Tim Severin's book *In Search of Genghis Khan* (Atheneum, 1991). On the net, w ubpost.mongolnews.mn carries snippets of news and other data.

Appendix 1

FAUNA EXTRAORDINARY

Adapting to the harsh high-altitude conditions of the Tibetan plateau is some remarkable wildlife. Some animals, such as the wild yak, are so well adapted to the altitude that they cannot survive at lower elevations.

This is a brief introduction to some of the unusual mammals and birds of Tibet, and their links to mythology. Sadly, rather than a listing of fauna you might be able to spot, it is more a listing of endangered species – these species may soon end up being mythical. In the 1940s, American adventurer Leonard Clark reported about Tibet: 'Every few minutes we would spot a bear, a hunting wolf, herds of musk deer, kiang, gazelles, big horned sheep, or foxes. This must be one of the last unspoiled big game paradises.' Tibetans only took what wildlife they needed, so impact was minimal. The coming of the Chinese in the 1950s changed all that: Chinese soldiers machine-gunned wildlife not only for food but for export to China – and for sport. Tibet's once-plentiful wildlife now faces extinction: in the last 50 years, large mammals have gone the way of the bison in North America.

Due to poaching for its valuable undercoat, the Tibetan antelope's days are numbered. The fleet-footed Tibetan antelope can easily outrun any predator (except a wolf), but it cannot evade poachers equipped with 4x4 vehicles and high-powered guns. The Tibetan antelope's undercoat is the finest wool in the world, gossamer in weight and texture, soft yet incredibly warm. Poachers feed an underground network that supplies Kashmiri weavers, who spin shawls for wealthy buyers. The trade is outlawed, but poaching continues. The snow leopard is hunted for its pelt and for parts used in Chinese traditional medicine.

If you want to view Himalayan wildlife and birds, the best bet is Bhutan, which has a network of national parks and strong conservation policies in place. American biologist George Schaller has worked for the last two decades to get reserves established in parts of Tibet and Pakistan. He has been instrumental in the creation of a huge Changtang Nature Reserve in northern Tibet (page 11).

The species at the start of the following list are 'flagship species' and have been given longer text. The names in parentheses are Latin (scientific name), followed by the Tibetan name(s).

MAMMALS

Tibetan antelope (*Pantholops hodgsoni*) Tibetan: *chiru, tso*. The Tibetan antelope inhabits high desert plateau. The females are hornless, but the males sport a pair of long slender upright horns, which could make them the source of unicorn myths in Tibet that date back several centuries (viewed in profile, the chiru would appear to have one long horn). The chiru's fine wool is a special adaptation that traps layers of warm air close to its body so it can survive snow blizzards where the thermometer plummets to –40°C. The chiru's underwool, known as *shahtoosh*, is the finest animal fibre in the world. The chiru has never been tamed or reared in captivity: the only way to get *shahtoosh* is through killing the animals and skinning them. Although the trade in *shahtoosh* is illegal, it has pushed the chiru to the brink of extinction, with fewer than 100,000 remaining. Their last hope is the creation of a Changtang nature reserve with adjoining ones in Xinjiang and Qinghai.

Snow leopard (*Panthera uncia*) Tibetan: *ganzig, saa*. Unique in its camouflage – a greyish spotted coat, blending in with its terrain – the snow leopard is a nocturnal hunter, mostly active at dusk and dawn, and particularly fond of stalking blue sheep, ibex and marmots. By day it sleeps in caves or on rocky ledges. It inhabits remote high-altitude terrain from 3,000m to 5,500m, with the largest numbers left in northwest India – in Ladakh, Spiti and Lahaul. The snow leopard is about the size of a large dog. It has adapted ingeniously to life in extreme snowy terrain: its large paws act like snowshoes, and its enormous tail is used to stabilise acrobatic leaps – and at night is wrapped around body and face like a scarf to withstand freezing temperatures. Because of its throat-bone structure, the snow leopard is a non-roaring cat, but is known to make strange howling cries during the January–March mating season. So elusive and stealthy is the snow leopard that the first movie film to capture it in action was not taken until the dawn of the 21st century. The snow leopard is highly endangered, with numbers remaining estimated at under 7,000; it may soon become as mythical as the snow lion. Seeing one: captive animals are held at the Darjeeling snow leopard breeding programme in northeast India.

Takin (*Budorcas taxicolor*) Tibetan: *bamen, dong gyemtsey*. The takin is a hairy hoofed herbivore with a bulbous nose and backward-facing horns. It is a strange mix of moose, musk-ox and wildebeest, and can weight up to 400kg, with a body 2m long. The takin favours the forested slopes of the eastern Tibetan plateau, particularly in southeast Tibet and in Bhutan, where it inhabits dense forest. There are four subspecies: the Bhutan takin, Mishmi takin (Tibet), Shensi takin and Sichuan takin (China). There are probably fewer than 5,000 remaining. Seeing one: the takin is the national animal of Bhutan; a handful of captive takins are kept at a reserve overlooking Thimphu.

Wild yak (*Bos mutus*) Tibetan: *drong*. An enormous creature: an adult male can weigh up to 1,000kg (equivalent to double the weight of a domestic yak), and can stand almost 2m high at the shoulder. *Bos mutus* is the Latin name given to distinguish the wild yak from the domestic one (designated as *Bos grunniens*, which means 'grunting ox' – a nod to the yaks' habit of grunting when agitated or when calling their young). Interbreeding between the two species occurs when wild yak males enter domestic herds and abscond with females. Wild yaks graze mostly on grass and herbs. They are superbly adapted to altitude and are sure-footed over rough terrain. Herds travel on snow in single file, carefully stepping on footprints left by the lead yak. The wild yak's long shaggy coat enables it to withstand violent winds and snowstorms. A sighting of wild yaks is rare today, although possible in remote parts of Qinghai.

Tibetan wild ass (*Equus kiang*) Tibetan: *kyang*. The largest of the Asiatic asses, this animal actually shares a lot in common genetically with the zebra, minus the stripes. But it follows a very different social system. The kyang is now mostly found in the Changtang in Tibet. The British Army attempted to domesticate them in 1904 for use as pack animals, but failed. Huge herds of kyang used to graze the highlands of Tibet, but today sightings are rarer. They may be spotted in groups of 20–200 in remote regions of Tibet.

Alpine musk deer (*Moschus sifanicus*) Tibetan: *lawa, larna*. The musk deer does not have antlers. Instead, both males and females have two large fang-like extruding upper canines for defence purposes. The musk deer has been hunted for centuries for the male's musk pod, located in front of the genitals. The musk obtained fetches a high price, used for its medicinal qualities and in the preparation of perfume, although most modern perfumiers use synthetic musk. Hunting has severely depleted numbers of the musk deer.

Blue sheep (*Pseudois nayaur*) Tibetan: *naya*. Blue sheep combine features of both goat and sheep. They have a slate-grey coat that appears more bluish in winter but turns brownish in summer, to blend in with its surroundings. Adult rams have large horns that curve up, outward and downward. The females have smaller horns. Blue sheep can congregate in herds of up to 200.

Marco Polo sheep

(*Ovis ammon hodgsoni*)
Tibetan: *nyen*. Huge males have massive curling horns, and thus are prized in hunting as trophy animals. The sheep is found in the Pamir region, at the intersection of China, Afghanistan, Tajikistan and Pakistan. The sheep is named after Marco Polo: in his day, nobody in Italy believed his story about the preposterous horns of this wild sheep. An estimated 11,000 remain. There is a close Tibetan cousin, the Tibetan argali sheep.

Tibetan brown bear (*Ursus arctos pruinosus*) Tibetan: *dremo, tremong*. The Tibetan brown bear can stand up to 1.8m, as tall as a man, which is probably why the species (and its footprint) are likely to be mistaken for a yeti. The highly endangered Tibetan brown bear ranges into higher altitude zones. Lower down in forests is the smaller Himalayan black bear (*Ursus thibetanus laniger*).

Red panda (*Ailurus fulgens*) Tibetan: *og dong kar*. This mammal has long been thought to be a distant relative of the giant panda because it shares the peculiar habit of feeding largely on bamboo, and because it has similar teeth and paws. But the red panda is actually more closely related to raccoons; this chestnut-coloured 'cat-bear' is small, with a ringed bushy tail half its length. It is a tree dweller, inhabiting dense bamboo forests to the eastern side of the Tibetan plateau, including parts of China, Nepal, India, Bhutan and Burma. The red panda is hunted for its pelt, used to make traditional hats in Yunnan. Seeing a live one: Gangktok Open Zoo in Sikkim is the best place: it has a panda breeding centre.

Tibetan sand fox (*Vulpes ferrilata*) Tibetan: *wa, wamo*. This species is endemic to the Tibetan plateau, and inhabits open steppe such as the vast desert of the Changtang. Its sandy colouring allows it to blend in easily with the desert. The Tibetan sand fox has a peculiar chunky head and is bigger than the common fox, which is also present in Tibet (mostly found in forested zones). The Tibetan sand fox keeps the rodent population in check, especially pikas (mouse-hares). The sand fox is hunted for its pelt, which is made into hats.

Himalayan marmot (*Marmota himalayana*) Tibetan: *kunpo, sho, jibi*. Also known as the 'Tibetan snow pig', this species is commonly seen throughout the plateau on the plains and in grassy mountain valleys. This large rodent is related to the north American marmot. Himalayan marmots live in large colonies in networks consisting of deep burrows. Their shrill whistling call alerts all animals in the vicinity to danger from predators. The marmot is hunted for its thick golden-brown fur.

BIRDS There are over 500 species of birds recorded in Tibet, 660 recorded in Pakistan and 800 in Nepal. Bhutan is the best place for birdwatching in the Himalaya, with over 700 species, including magnificent pheasants such as the satyr tragopan. For many years, it was believed that no birds flew over the high peaks of the Himalaya. Now, it appears that half a dozen species do fly over the world's highest peaks, the ultimate high-fliers of the avian world. Yellow-billed choughs have been sighted at altitudes of 7,000m by climbers attempting Everest, and snow pigeons have been spotted flying over peaks at 8,300m.

Himalayan griffon vulture (*Gyps himalayensis*) Tibetan: *mkha, khor*. The Himalayan griffon vulture has been sighted riding 'blue thermals' over Everest, at altitudes of 9,000m. As with other vultures, the bird feeds mainly from carcasses of animals, with one peculiar twist in Tibet: this bird gathers in clusters at sky burial ceremonies to consume human corpses. It is thus an iconic bird in Tibetan lore. In Tibetan, *jhator* (sky burial) means 'offering to the birds'. The bearded vulture also shows up at sky burial ceremonies.

Lammergeier (*Gypaetus barbatus*) Tibetan: *gobo*. Also known as the bearded vulture, this bird soars across the length of the Himalaya. It has a wingspan of up to 2.8m, making it Eurasia's largest raptor. The lammergeier has an unusual feeding routine: soaring to a great height, this vulture drops bones from its talons on to rocks far below, and then swoops down to feed on the exposed bone marrow.

Bar-headed goose (*Anser indicus*) Tibetan: *kalaha, gangpa*. Astronauts on the wing: bar-headed geese can fly at altitudes up to 9,000m, clearing the Himalaya twice each year to complete an epic migration. When winter is over, the geese leave their feeding-grounds in the lowlands of Nepal and India, going from near sea level straight up to 8,000m, heading over Himalayan peaks to breeding grounds in Amdo (Qinghai Lake), Outer Mongolia and Kyrgyzstan. An inner layer of down feathers helps stop the bird from freezing to death, while an outer layer of tightly woven feathers apparently waterproofs the goose and prevents build-up of body ice that would cause the bird to plunge to its doom. The bar-headed goose has been clocked flying at 80km/h, but with a tailwind it can rocket along at up to 160km/h. The honking of the bar-headed goose in the mountains is a sure sign you are in Tibet. Seeing one: some have been sighted in parks in Lhasa, mixed in with other geese. Look for geese with several black bars visible at the back of the head – that's where the name comes from.

Black-necked crane (*Grus nigricollis*) Tibetan: *trung trung*. This is the tallest of the birds in Tibet, up to 1.5m high; much of its height is in the neck, which is black with a red cap. There are estimated to be fewer than 9,000 black-necked cranes remaining in the wild.

In mating rituals, pairs of cranes leap into the air and utter loud bugling sounds. Most cranes migrate every year from Tibet to Bhutan. Gangtey Gompa (central Bhutan) hosts an annual festival to welcome flocks of cranes that arrive in late October, and depart again for Tibet in mid-February. In Buddhist lore, black-necked cranes are regarded as highly auspicious, and are depicted in temple frescoes.

Appendix 2

LANGUAGE AND USEFUL GESTURES

TIBETAN LANGUAGE Any attempt you make at speaking Tibetan, however awkward, will be greatly appreciated in a place where the language has such a low profile compared with the use of Chinese. It's worthwhile carrying two phrasebooks to handle situations: one Tibetan, the other Mandarin Chinese. Many Tibetans – particularly in the towns – understand some Mandarin, but will most likely not appreciate attempts to communicate with them in Chinese. Phrasebooks become doubly useful if they have Tibetan script: you can point to phrases if the pronunciation is not getting through (this is limited by a literacy factor, however). Good non-verbal communication can be achieved through use of pictures. Examination of pictorial subjects can lead to long dialogue – carry a book with pictures of Tibet, or brochures about Tibet, and carry photos of your family and your city. You can derive a lot of dialogue from learning numbers in Tibetan, and not just for pricing. Numbers can be used in other creative ways: how many children do you have? How many yaks?

Tibetan is a difficult language to speak, with a number of different dialects. Lhasa dialect (the standard dialect) employs a series of rising and falling tones – up to eight of them. Tonal usage increases with talking in a polite manner. There are also letters that are retroflex, glottal, aspirated or non-aspirated. Unfortunately, there is no accurate way to render these complexities in English phonetics, so what follows is a rough attempt, and one that you should polish by reviewing with a Tibetan speaker.

Tibetan is an ancient language that borrows modern words such as 'post office', 'fax machine' or 'airport' from the nearest language. Within Tibet, these terms may be taken from Chinese, while in India the word might come from English or Hindi, which all leads to a standardisation headache. But consider this: it's sometimes possible to use an English word (with a twisted accent) and be understood – the Tibetan for 'jeep' is *jip*, and the Tibetan for 'Landcruiser' is *landkrusa*. It's difficult to find Tibetans to practise with in the West. You can attune your ear by listening to Tibetan-language radio broadcasts (see *Internet resources*, see opposite).

Tibetan terms used in this book can be put to good use as speaking vocabulary. A yak is a yak, and *tsampa* is *tsampa* (nobody else in the world eats the stuff). Also usable are words such as *dzong* (castle), *gompa* (monastery) and *tsangpo* (river). For more vocabulary, check the *Glossary* (pages 358–9; some terms are Sanskrit, not Tibetan).

Useful phrases Here are a few useful phrases for pidgin Tibetan speakers: *tashi delek!* is an all-purpose opener, meaning: 'greetings!', 'how are you?', 'congratulations!' or 'best wishes!' *Yapodu* or *yabadoo* means 'good' (thumb up) while *yapo mindu!* means 'bad!' (little finger down). Vital to your survival is the phrase *kale kale*, which means 'slow down', when spoken to a maniacal driver. Etiquette when you reach the prayer flags on the top of passes in Tibet requires you to shout, at the top of your lungs, '*Tso-so-so-so-so! Lha Gyalo!*', which means 'Victory to the gods!'

Phrasebooks and recordings There are several Tibetan phrasebooks available for English speakers, but phrases are only as good as the sounds you can elicit from them. If you don't have an audio recording, go over the sounds with a Tibetan speaker, or have a native speaker help you record your own English–Tibetan version. Try downloading an app for language learning to your phone or tablet.

Giving access to a much wider range of spoken Tibetan are DVD packages which cost around US$50 each, such as *Learning Tibetan* (EuroTalk Interactive) with innovative games and quizzes. The EuroTalk version can be purchased online as an app through iTunes, with several caveats. EuroTalk uses a stock list for all its language products. Questions such as 'Where is the beach?' have limited currency in Tibet. And a lot of entries are vocabulary, not phrases. Watch out also for the cover art! More serious language learners should look into comprehensive Tibetan language packages from Shambhala Publications (**w** shambhala. com), such as *Fluent Tibetan*, with 26 hours of audio on CD or DVD.

Internet resources More advanced tuning of the ear can be achieved by listening to radio broadcasts in Tibetan on the web, at three sites: **w** vot.org (with MP3 downloads), **w** rfa.org and **w** voanews.com (video news). These sites are blocked in China: Radio Free Asia and Voice of America are both Washington-based, with part of the broadcast in Tibetan. Voice of Tibet, established in Norway in 1996, is the one of the oldest dedicated radio stations broadcasting in the Tibetan language. To try your writing skills in Tibetan script, go for a spin on a Mac. Most Mac computers come with a Tibetan keyboard installed. Go to the flags at the upper right of the screen.

Openers

greetings (good fortune)	*tashi delek*	བཀྲ་ཤིས་བདེ་ལེགས།
goodbye (spoken to the person staying)	*kaleshu*	ག་ལེར་བཞུགས།
goodbye (spoken to the person leaving)	*kalepay*	ག་ལེར་ཕེབས།
pleased to meet you	*kerang tukpa gapo chung*	ཁྱེད་རང་ཐུག་པར་དགའ་པོ་བྱུང་།
how are you?	*kerang debo yinbe?*	ཁྱེད་རང་བདེ་པོ་ཡིན་པས།
I'm fine	*nga debo yoe*	ང་བདེ་པོ་ཡིན།
where are you going?	*kerang kawa droga?*	ཁྱེད་རང་ག་པར་འགྲོ་ག
what's your name?	*kerangi mingla karey re?*	ཁྱེད་རང་གི་མིང་ལ་ག་རེ་རེད།
my name is ...	*nge mingla ... yin*	ངའི་མིང་... ཡིན།
I only speak a little Tibetan	*nga perkay teets teets shingi yur*	ངས་བོད་སྐད་ཏོག་ཙམ་ཏོག་ཙམ་ཤེས་ཀྱི་ཡོད།
I don't understand	*ngay hako masong*	ངས་ཧ་གོ་མ་སོང་།
Do you understand?	*kerang hakosong ngay?*	ཁྱེད་རང་གིས་ཧ་གོ་སོང་ངས།

Getting personal

where are you from?	*kerang lungpa kane yin?*	ཁྱེད་རང་ལུང་པ་ག་ནས་ཡིན།
I am from X	*nga X ne yin*	ང་ X ནས་ཡིན།
UK/Canada/Australia	*injilungpa /kanada / ostrelia*	ཨིན་ཇིའི་ལུང་པ་ / ཁེ་ན་ཌ་ / ཨོ་སེ་ཊེ་ལི་ཡ།

America/France	*ahri/farenci*	ཨ་རི། / ཕ་རན་སི།
Tibetan/Chinese/Nepalese	*perpa/gyami/pelpo*	བོད་པ། / རྒྱ་མི། / བལ་པོ་
How old are you?	*kerang lo katsay yin?*	ཁྱེད་རང་ལོ་ག་ཚོད་ཡིན།
nomad/farmer	*drokpa/shingpa*	འབྲོག་པ། / ཞིང་པ།
monk/pilgrim	*trapa/nekorpa*	གྲྭ་པ། / གནས་སྐོར་པ།
married/single	*changsa/migyang*	ཆང་ས། / མི་རྒྱང་། (མི་ཉེང་)
husband/wife	*kyoka/gyemen*	ཁྱོ་ག / སྐྱེ་སྨན།
mother/father	*ama/apa*	ཨ་མ། / ཨ་པ།
children/son/daughter	*puku/pu/pumo*	ཕུ་གུ་ (ཕྲུ་གུ) / བུ། / བུ་མོ།
younger brother	*chungpo*	གཅུང་པོ་
younger sister	*chungmo*	གཅུང་མོ།
older brother	*jojo*	ཇོ་ཇོ་ (ཅོ་ཅོག)
older sister	*aja*	ཨ་ཇེ།

Flattery

good/very good	*yapo du/yapo shedra re*	ཡག་པོ་འདུག / ཡག་པོ་ཞེ་དྲགས་འདུག
The food is great!	*kala shimpo du!*	ཁ་ལག་ཞིམ་པོ་འདུག
I love this place!	*nga sacha dila gapo yur!*	ང་ས་ཆ་འདི་ལ་དགའ་བོ་ཡོད།
beautiful	*nying jepo du*	སྙིང་རྗེ་པོ་འདུག
very interesting	*nangwa dropo shedra re*	སྣང་བ་འགྲོ་པོ་ཞེ་དྲགས་རེད།
I feel happy	*gyipo du*	སྐྱིད་པོ་འདུག
we had a good time!	*ngantso gyipo chung!*	ང་ཚོ་སྐྱིད་པོ་བྱུང་།
good luck	*lamdro yongbar shok*	ལམ་འགྲོ་ཡོང་བར་ཤོག

Negatives, questions, requests

yes, that's it	*re, de rang re*	རེད། དེ་རང་རེད།
yes, okay	*digi re*	འགྲིག་གི་རེད།
no problem	*kay chegi mare*	གང་ཡང་(གས)་བྱེད་ཀྱི་མ་རེད།
no	*mare (mindu)*	མ་རེད་ (མིན་འདུག)
not okay, no good	*yapo mindu*	ཡག་པོ་མི་འདུག
thank you	*tujeche*	ཐུགས་རྗེ་ཆེ།
that's enough	*dik song*	འགྲིག་སོང་།
need	*gerh*	དགོས།
don't want (don't like)	*mo gerh*	མི་དགོས།
I don't know	*nga shingi meh*	ངས་ཤེས་ཀྱི་མེད།
sorry, excuse me	*gohnda*	དགོངས་དག
can I take a photo?	*nga par gyapna digi rebay?*	ངས་པར་བརྒྱབ་ན་འགྲིག་གི་རེད་པས།

what's this called in Tibetan?	perke nangla di kandres lab gire?	བོད་སྐད་ནང་ལ་འདི་ལ་ག་འདྲེ་ས་ལབ་ཀྱི་རེད།
what does this mean?	di thondak karey re?	འདིའི་དོན་དག་ག་རེ་རེད།
where/where is?	kapa/kaba du?	ག་པར་ / ག་པར་འདུག
what?	karey?	ག་རེ།
when?	kadu?	ག་དུས།
who?/why?/how?	su?/karey jeni?/kandres?	སུ་ / ག་རེ་བྱས་ནས་ / གང་འདྲ་སེ།
how much (how many)?	katsey?	ག་ཚོད།
how far?	ta ringpo rebay?	ཐག་རིང་པོ་རེད་པས།

Red tape

passport	chikyur lakteb	ཕྱི་སྐྱོད་ལག་དེབ།
permit	chokchen	ཆོག་མཆན།
PSB office	gonganju (Chinese word)	གུང་ཨན་ཇུད། (རྒྱ་སྐད།)
	sangwe nyen tokbe lekung! (Tibetan)	གསང་བའི་ཉེན་རྟོགས་ལས་ཁུངས། (བོད་སྐད།)
tourist	takorwa	ལྟ་སྐོར་བ། (ཡུལ་སྐོར་བ།)
I need a translator	nga la gegyur cheken chik gerh	ང་ལ་སྐད་སྒྱུར་བྱེད་མཁན་གཅིག་དགོས།
what's the problem?	gang ngel karey tresong?	དཀའ་ལས་ག་རེ་འཕྲད་སོང་།

Medical

sick/very sick	nagi du/shedra nagi du	ན་གི་འདུག / ཞེ་དྲགས་ན་གི་འདུག
altitude sickness	zatuki natsa	ཛ་དྲུག་གི་ན་ཚ། (ལ་དུག)
headache/fever	gonagi du/tsawa pargi du	མགོ་ན་གི་འདུག/ ཚ་བ་འཕར་གྱི་འདུག
diarrhoea/stomach ache	troko shegi du/troko nagi du	གྲོད་ཁོག་བཤལ་གྱི་འདུག/ གྲོད་ཁོག་ན་གི་འདུག
cold/cough	champa nagi du/lo gyabgi du	ཆམ་པ་ན་གི་འདུག / གློ་བརྒྱབ་ཀྱི་འདུག
feel dizzy	goyu korgi du	མགོ་ཡོམ་འཁོར་གྱི་འདུག
I was bitten by a dog	khi chik gi sogyab song	ཁྱི་གཅིག་གིས་སོ་བརྒྱབ་སོང་།
I need a doctor right away	nga la gyokpo amchi laten gerh	ང་ལ་མགྱོགས་པོ་ཨེམ་ཆི་ (སྨན་པ་) དགོས།
oxygen	sog lung	སྲོག་རླུང་། (འཚོ་རླུང་།)
emergency	zatrak	ཛ་དྲག
hospital	menkhang	སྨན་ཁང་།
pharmacy	men tsongkhang	སྨན་ཚོང་ཁང་།
medicine	men	སྨན།

Transport

ticket	*pasey* (Indian-Tibetan word)	པ་སེ། (དབྱིན་སྐད།)
	zinyik (Tibetan)	འཛིན་ཡིག (བོད་སྐད།)
plane	*namdru*	གནམ་གྲུ།
motor vehicle	*mota* (Indian-Tibetan)	མོ་ཊ།
	noomkor (Tibetan)	སྣུམ་འཁོར། (བོད་སྐད།)
bicycle	*gangkor*	རྐང་འཁོར།
horse	*ta*	རྟ།
I'd like to hire a jeep	*nga jip chik lander yur*	ང་འཇི་བ་ཅིག་གླ་འདོད་ཡོད།
I'd like to hire a Landcruiser	*nga landkrusa chik lander yur*	ང་ལནྜ་ཀི་ཀུ་རུ་ས་(སྣུམ་འཁོར་ཏོ་ཡོ་ཏ་) གཅིག་གླ་འདོད་ཡོད།
Do you rent bicycles?	*gangkor laya yurbe?*	རྐང་འཁོར་གཡར་ཡལ་ལ་(རྒྱུ་)ཡོད་པས།
how much for an hour?	*chutsu chik la katsey re?*	ཆུ་ཚོད་གཅིག་ལ་ག་ཚད་རེད།
how much for a day?	*nyima chik la katsey re?*	ཉི་མ་གཅིག་ལ་ག་ཚད་རེད།
what time is the bus?	*jijger lun korte chutsu katserla drogi re?*	སྤྱི་སྤྱོད་རླངས་འཁོར་དེ་ཆུ་ཚོད་ག་ཚད་ལ་འགྲོ་གི་རེད།
guide	*lamtriken*	ལམ་འཁྲིད་མཁན།
driver	*siji* (Chinese word)	སི་ཧྲི། (རྒྱ་སྐད།)
	kalowa (Tibetan)	ཁ་ལོ་བ། (བོད་སྐད།)
go slowly please	*kale kale drorok nang*	ག་ལེ་ག་ལེར་འགྲོ་རོགས་གནང་།
please stop here	*dila kag rok nang*	འདི་ལ་བཀག་རོགས་གནང་།

Trekking

tent	*kur*	གུར།
sleeping bag	*nyeche*	ཉལ་ཆས།
stove	*tapga*	ཐབ། (ཐབ་ཀ)
I want to hire a yak	*nga yak chik ladoe yur*	ང་གཡག་ཅིག་གླ་འདོད་ཡོད།
porter	*jalak kyerken*	ཅ་ལག་འཁྱེར་མཁན།
is this the trail to X?	*di X la dro sai lamka rebay?*	འདི་ X ལ་འགྲོ་སའི་ལམ་ཁ་རེད་པས།
how many hours will it take to reach X?	*X pardu chutsu katsey gorgi re?*	X བར་དུ་ཆུ་ཚོད་ག་ཚད་འགོར་གྱི་རེད།

Places

I want to go to X	*X la drondoe yur*	X ལ་འགྲོ་འདོད་ཡོད།
airport	*namtang*	གནམ་ཐང་།
post office	*drakhang*	སྦྲག་ཁང་། (ཡིག་ཟམ)
bank	*ngukhang*	དངུལ་ཁང་།

PSB office	*gonganju*	གུང་འན་ཅུད།
temple	*lakhang*	ལྷ་ཁང་།
market	*trom*	ཁྲོམ།
photo shop	*barkhang*	པར་ཁང་།
bookshop	*teb tsongkhang*	དེབ་ཚོང་ཁང་།
museum	*dem tonkhang*	འགྲེམས་སྟོན་ཁང་།

Lodging

hotel	*drukhang*	འགྲུལ་ཁང་།
guesthouse	*dronkhang*	མགྲོན་ཁང་།
room	*khangpa*	ཁང་པ། (ཁང་མིག)
bed	*nyetri*	ཉལ་ཁྲི།
can I see the room?	*khangpa la migtana digi rebay?*	ཁང་པ་ལ་མིག་བལྟས་ན་འགྲིག་གི་རེད་པས།
do you have a room with private toilet?	*khang panang lola sangcher yur rebay?*	ཁང་པའི་ནང་ལོགས་ལ་གསང་སྤྱོད་ཡོད་རེད་པས།
where can I leave luggage?	*nge jalak dintso kawar shakka?*	ངའི་ཅ་ལག་འདི་ཚོ་ག་པར་བཞག་ག (འཇོག་གས)
telephone	*kapa*	ཁ་པར།
key	*deymi*	ལྡེ་མིག
blanket	*nyejay*	ཉལ་ཆས། (གམ་པ་ལེ)
candle	*yangla*	ཡང་ལ།
toilet/paper	*sangcher/sangcher shuku*	གསང་སྤྱོད་ / གསང་སྤྱོད་ཤོག་ཀུ
shower/hot shower	*trukhang/chu Tsapoe tru*	ཁྲུས་ཁང་ / ཆུ་ཚ་པོའི་ཁྲུས།
towel	*ajo*	ཨ་ཆོར།
Thermos of hot water	*chu tsapo chadam gan*	ཆུ་ཚ་པོ་ཇ་དམ་གང་།

Food

hungry	*trokok toki du*	གྲོད་ཁོག་ལྟོགས་གི་འདུག
thirsty	*kha komgi du*	ཁ་སྐོམ་གྱི་འདུག
restaurant	*sakhang*	ཟ་ཁང་།
tearoom	*jakhang*	ཇ་ཁང་།
can you bring me . . . ?	*. . . chig kyer yongrok nang?*	· · · ཅིག་འཁྱེར་ཡོང་རོགས་གནང་།
bowl of noodles	*tuk pa porpa chig*	ཐུག་པ་ཕོར་པ་གཅིག
meat dumplings	*sha momo*	ཤ་མོག་མོག
stir-fried vegetables	*tsoma ngowa*	ཚོད་མ་རྔོས་པ།
meat	*sha*	ཤ
yoghurt	*sho*	ཞོ།
water	*chu*	ཆུ།

boiled water	*chu kolma*	ཆུ་འཁོལ་མ།
sweet Indian tea	*cha ngarmo*	ཇ་མངར་མོ།
yak-butter tea	*cha suma*	ཇ་སྲུབ་མ། (པོད་ཇ)
homebrewed beer	*chang*	ཆང་།
salt	*tsa*	ཚྭ།
sugar	*che makara*	བྱེ་མ་ཀ་ར། (ཅི་ནི)

Bargaining

how much is this?	*gong katsey re?*	གོང་ག་ཚད་རེད།
do you have any . . . ?	*kerang-la . . . yurbe?*	ཁྱེད་རང་ལ་ · · · ཡོད་པས།
big/small	*chenpo/chung chung*	ཆེན་པོ་ / ཆུང་ཆུང་།
old/new	*nyingpa/saba*	རྙིང་པ། / གསར་པ།
too expensive	*di gong chenpo shedra du !*	འདི་གོང་ཆེན་པོ་ཞེ་དྲགས་འདུག
can you give me a better price?	*gong jak tupki rebe?*	གོང་གཅོག་ཐུབ་ཀྱི་རེད་པས།
discount	*gong jakya yurbe*	གོང་གཅོག་ཡས་ཡོད་པས།

Time

today	*tering*	དེ་རིང་།
now	*tanda*	ད་ལྟ།
tonight	*togong*	དོ་དགོང་།
yesterday/tomorrow	*kesa/sangyin*	ཁ་ས། / སང་ཉིན།
morning/afternoon/evening	*shoke/chitro/gongtak*	ཞོགས་ཀ། / ཕྱི་དྲོ། / དགོང་དག་(དགོང་དྲོ།)
year/month/week/ day/hour	*lo/dawa/zankor/ nyima/chutsu*	ལོ། / ཟླ་བ། / གཟའ་འཁོར། / ཉི་མ། / ཆུ་ཚོད།
Monday	*sa dawa*	གཟའ་ཟླ་བ།
Tuesday	*sa migma*	གཟའ་མིག་དམར།
Wednesday	*sa lhakba*	གཟའ་ལྷག་པ།
Thursday	*sa pubu*	གཟའ་ཕུར་བུ།
Friday	*sa pasang*	གཟའ་པ་སངས།
Saturday	*sa pemba*	གཟའ་སྤེན་པ།
Sunday	*sa nyima*	གཟའ་ཉི་མ།

Numbers

0	*lekor*	ཀླད་སྐོར།	1	*chik*	གཅིག
2	*nyi*	གཉིས།	3	*sum*	གསུམ།
4	*shi*	བཞི།	5	*nga*	ལྔ།
6	*druk*	དྲུག	7	*dun*	བདུན།
8	*gye*	བརྒྱད།	9	*gu*	དགུ།

10	ju	བཅུ།	11	ju chik	བཅུ་གཅིག
12	ju nyi	བཅུ་གཉིས།	13	jok sum	བཅུ་གསུམ།
14	jub shi	བཅུ་བཞི།	15	jo nga	བཅོ་ལྔ།
20	nyi shu	ཉི་ཤུ།	30	sum ju	སུམ་ཅུ།
40	shib ju	བཞི་བཅུ།	50	ngab ju	ལྔ་བཅུ།
60	druk chu	དྲུག་ཅུ།	70	dun ju	བདུན་ཅུ།
80	gyeb ju	བརྒྱད་ཅུ།	90	gub ju	དགུ་བཅུ།
100	gya tamba	བརྒྱ་ཐམ་པ།	500	nyab gya	ལྔ་བརྒྱ།
1,000	chik tong	གཅིག་སྟོང་།	2,000	tong-trak nyi	སྟོང་ཕྲག་གཉིས། (ཉིས་སྟོང་།)

1 million   sayachik (or: bumju)   ས་ཡ་གཅིག (འབུམ་ འབུམ་བཅུ།)

Geographical terms, map features

river	gyuk chu (also: tsangpo)	རྒྱུག་ཆུ། (དེ་བཞིན་ གཙང་པོ)
spring	chumi	ཆུ་མིག
hot spring	chutsen	ཆུ་ཚན།
village	trongsep	གྲོང་གསེབ།
town	trongte	གྲོང་སྡེ།
fort	dzong	རྫོང་།
monastery	gompa	དགོན་པ།
ice/snow	kyakpa/kang	འཁྱགས་པ། / གངས།
rain	charpa	ཆར་པ།
pass	la	ལ།
hill, mountain	ri	རི།
plain, plateau	tang	ཐང་།
lake	tso (also: yumco, caka, nor)	མཚོ།
map	sabtra	ས་བྲ།
compass points:	chang (N), lho (S), shar (E), nub (W)	བྱང་། ལྷོ། ཤར། ནུབ།

TIBET ONLINE

For additional online content, articles, photos and more on Tibet, why not visit **w** bradtguides.com/tibet.

USEFUL GESTURES Tibetans respond to some gestures common in the West, but others can throw you for a loop. In old Tibet, a respectful form of humble greeting was to extrude the tongue (which had better be pink, because the tongue of an evil person was reckoned to be brown or black). The gesture is still used in remote parts of Tibet. Belgian cartoonist Hergé has some fun with this: when confronted by cheeky Tibetans poking out their tongues at him, Captain Haddock in the comic Tintin in Tibet responds with rude hand gestures. Once you get started on gestures, it's easy to build a repertoire for repeat situations: pointing vigorously to your watch or a camera, for instance, to get a certain message across.

Approval, or not

Good *yagodu!*
Fist with thumb up, indicating positive approval, also signals 'okay' *yapodu!*
gucci gucci! Two thumbs up (jiggled up and down) is a begging gesture, demanding money or otherwise

Bad *yapo mindu!*
Fist with little finger down – applied to things or people or concepts ('what you are doing is bad'). The little finger held to edge of eye indicates 'evil eye'.

Commands

Come here *del-phi*
Similar to Western gesture, but hand down (not up) and use whole hand, not finger

Go away *pa-phi*
Flick hand out, using whole palm, not finger

Slow down *kale kale*
Hand parallel to ground and move up and down, slowly, to tell your Landcruiser driver; also used as hitchhiking signal.

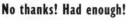

No thanks! Had enough!

Up to here *yasong!*
Bring open palm up under the chin.
Used to indicate enough food or drink.

Placing open palm on chest can convey similar idea – when you don't want something offered, like cigarettes.

Requests

Need a place to sleep *nyi nyayri*
Place palm to side of head and tilt head

Need a telephone *kaba*
Mimic phone with hand to ear

Signalling confusion

Don't know *nga hako masong*
Twist hand with fingers apart in a screw-in-the-lightbulb gesture. Can also use head-shaking and head-scratching to indicate doubt.

Crazy *nyon-pa*
Twist fingers at temple

Stupid *koog-ta-chen*
Slap forehead with open palm

Hello

Greeting hello *tashi delek*
Bring single hand up to the forehead, with edge of palm outward

High-level greeting
Palms together in prayer,
head slightly bowed – religious gesture of humility, used by prostrators, and frequently used by the Dalai Lama.

Goodbye

Goodbye *kaleshu* (spoken to the person staying)
kalepay (spoken to the person leaving)
Wave, like Western gesture

High-level goodbye
Palms up, facing inward, and bow slightly. Used when saying goodbye to monk or important person. Another gesture is touching foreheads.

CHINESE LANGUAGE Such is the dominance of Mandarin Chinese in Tibet that, in order to get hotel rooms, obtain food in restaurants, talk to truck drivers or deal with officialdom, you need some knowledge of Chinese. However, if you are talking to a Tibetan, it's far preferable to stay with Tibetan language.

Though there are eight major dialects in China, the standard version is Mandarin, or Beijing dialect. Mandarin is a tonal language – it takes a musical ear to get the hang of the tones. Without mastery of the tones, your efforts at Chinese will be unintelligible, reducing you to a gibbering curiosity. Written Mandarin Chinese is no easier: it draws on a fund of about 50,000 characters (originally pictographs), although literate Chinese need only knowledge of about 5,000 characters.

Pinyin is the romanisation system used for rendering Chinese sounds into approximate English. There are several quirks in Pinyin pronunciation. The vowels are rather tricky, and some consonants are pronounced differently: Pinyin 'c' is pronounced 'ts', Pinyin 'q' sounds like 'ch', Pinyin 'x' comes out as 'sh', and Pinyin 'zh' is pronounced 'j'. Thus on Chinese maps you may see the place names 'Xigaze' (Shigatse), 'Qamdo' (Chamdo) and 'Zhangmu' (Jangmu). Pinyin romanisation, in addition, uses accents over the letters to indicate tones (these are not employed in this book). The word *ma* for example, can have four different meanings depending on whether the tone is flat, rising, fall-rising or falling ('mother', 'hemp', 'horse' or 'swear'). Thus you could be trying to rent a horse and end up with a bag of hemp. For tones, accented Pinyin is of limited help: the best thing is to go over phrases with a Chinese native speaker to get the sounds right.

Useful phrases Good all-purpose words are *keyi* (OK, yes, agreed), *mei wenti* (no problem) and *hen hao* (thumbs up, very good). Another form of 'yes' in agreement is *dui*, which is often used in a rapid-fire sequence, as in *dui-dui-dui-dui-dui*. A catchy idiomatic phrase for 'so-so' is *mama-huhu*, which literally means 'horse-horse-tiger-tiger'.

Phrasebooks and recordings Phrasebooks become doubly useful if they have Chinese characters next to them: you can point to the characters if the pronunciation is not getting through. Another feature to look for is a mini-dictionary at the back of the phrasebook. There are a number of pocket-sized phrasebooks on the market, including those in the Rough Guides, Berlitz, BBC and Eyewitness series. Because Mandarin Chinese derives its meaning from tones, it's well worth chasing audio-enabled language-learning versions to get the sounds right. Rosetta Stone Language Group puts out DVDs with full audio. Easier to get at are apps under iTunes or Google Play where free Chinese phrases with script and audio can be accessed – or you can purchase more extensive versions which are self-driven once downloaded.

Internet resources Attune your ear to Mandarin by listening to radio and video broadcasts in Chinese at **w** rfa.org (Radio Free Asia) and **w** voa.gov (Voice of America).

Openers

hello	*ni hao*
goodbye	*zaijian*
pleased to meet you	*hen gaoxing renshi ni*
how are you?	*ni hao ma?*
very well, thank you	*wo hen hao, xiexie*
where are you going?	*ni dao nali?*
what's your name?	*ni jiao shenme?*
my name is …	*wo jiao …*
I only speak a little Chinese	*wo ju dongde idiendien hanyu*
I don't understand	*wo budong*
do you understand?	*dong ma?*

Getting personal

where are you from?	*ni cong nali lai?*
I am from Britain/Canada/Australia	*wo cong yingguo/jianada/oadaliya … lai*
America/France	*meiguo/faguo*
Tibet/China/Nepal	*xizang/zhongguo/niboer*
how old are you?	*ni ji sui?*
my job is …	*wode gong zhuo shi …*
I'm married/single	*wo jiehunle/wo shi danshen*
husband/wife	*zhangfu/qizi*
mother/father	*mama/baba*
children/son/daughter	*haizi/erzi/nuer*
brother/sister	*xiongdi/jiemei*

Flattery

good/very good	*hao/hen hao*	beautiful	*piaoliang*
terrific food!	*hen hao chi!*	that's great!	*haojile!*
cheers! (toasting)	*ganbei!*	I had a great time!	*wo hen kaixin!*
I love this place!	*wo hen xihuan zhege difang!*	good luck!	*zhu ni hao yun!*

Negatives, questions, requests

yes	*shi*	I want to take a photo	*wo yao zhao ge xiang*
OK/no problem	*hao*	what's this called in Chinese?	*zhege zhongwen jiao shenme?*
no	*bu*		
no (don't have)	*mei you*	please write it down for me	*qing ni bang wo xiexialai*
not OK/no good	*bu hao*		
please/thank you	*qing/xiexie*	what does that mean?	*shenme yisi?*
enough, thank you	*goule, xiexie*	where/where is ... ?	*nali?/... zai nali?*
I want/need	*wo yao*	when?/who?/why?/how?	*shenme shihou?/shui?/weishenme?/zenme?*
don't want/don't like	*bu yao*		
sorry, excuse me	*duibuqi*	how much/many?	*duoshao?*
I don't know	*wo bu zhidao*	how many kilometres?	*duoshao gongli?*

Red tape

passport	*huzhao*	tourist	*lu-ke*
visa	*qianzheng*	I need a translator	*wo xuyao fangyuan*
travel permit	*tong xing zheng*	what's the problem?	*yo shenme wenti?*
PSB office	*gonganju*		

Medical

sick/very sick	*sheng bingle/bingde hen zhong*	doctor	*yisheng*
		need a doctor	*jao ge yisheng*
altitude sickness	*gao shan bing*	please help	*qing bang mang*
I feel dizzy	*wo touyun*	emergency	*jinji qingkuang*
headache/fever	*touteng/fashao*	hospital	*yiyuan*
diarrhoea	*laduzi*	oxygen	*yangqi*
stomach ache	*xiaohua bu liang*	pharmacy	*yaodian*
cold/sore throat	*ganmao/hou-long teng*	medicine	*yao*

Transport

ticket	*piao*	let's go!	*zouba!*
plane	*feiji*	for a whole day?	*yitian duoshao qian?*
taxi	*chuzuche*	we want to hire a	*women yao yiliang jipu*
jeep	*jipu*	jeep	
truck	*kache*	where is the bus	*qichezhan zai nar?*
bus	*gonggong qiche*	station?	
bicycle	*zixingche*	what time is the bus	*dao ... de gongche*
driver	*siji*	to ... ?	*shenme shihou kai?*
I want to hire a	*wo yao zu yiliang*	guide	*daoyou*
bicycle	*zixingche*	slow down please	*qing ni man idien*
how much for an	*yige xiao shi duoshao*	stop here!	*qing zai zheli ting!*
hour?	*qian?*		

Trekking

tent	*zhangpeng*	where can I hire	*wo sheme difang keyi*
sleeping bag	*shuidai*	yaks?	*gu yitou mao niu?*
how much a day?	*yitian duoshao qian?*		

Places

I want to go to ...	*wo yao qu ...*	PSB office/foreign	*gonganju/waishi ke*
airport	*feijichang*	affairs branch	
bus station	*qichezhan*	Buddhist temple	*fo si*
railway station	*huochezhan*	market	*shichang*
post office	*youji*	bookshop	*shudian*
cybercafé	*wang ka*	museum	*bowuguan*
Bank of China	*zhongguo yinhang*		
(foreign exchange)			

Lodging

main tourist hotel	*binguan*	dormitory	*duorenfang*
smaller hotel	*fandian*	single room	*danrenfang*
guesthouse	*zhaodaisuo*	double room	*shuangrenfang*
can I see the room?	*wo keyi kan fangjian a?*	room with bath	*dai yushi de fangjian*
where can I leave	*wo xingli fang narli?*	toilet/paper	*cesuo/shouzhi*
luggage?		shower/hot shower	*linyu/re linyu*
telephone	*dianhua*	towel	*maojin*
key	*yaoshi*	vacuum flask of hot	*yo re kaishui de*
room	*fangjian*	water	*shuiping*

Food

hungry	*duzi e*	meat	*rou*
thirsty	*kouke*	water	*shui*
restaurant/café	*fandian/kafeiguan*	boiled water	*kaishui*
let's eat!	*chi fanba!*	mineral water	*kuangquan shui*
do you have ...?	*ni you ... ma?*	tea	*cha*
noodles	*miantiao*	black tea	*hong cha*
rice	*mifan*	green tea	*lu cha*
biscuits	*binggan*	coffee	*kafei*
soup	*tang*	beer	*pijiu*
stir-fried vegetables	*chao shucai*		

Bargaining

how much is this?	*duoshao qian?*	too expensive	*taigui*
do you have …?	*ni you … ma?*	do you have	*yo pianyi yidian de*
big/small	*da/xiao*	anything cheaper?	*ma?*
old/new	*jiu/xin*		

Time

today	*jintian*	Monday	*xingqi-yi*
now	*xianzai*	Tuesday	*xingqi-er*
tonight	*jinwan*	Wednesday	*xingqi-san*
yesterday/tomorrow	*zuotian/mingtian*	Thursday	*xingqi-si*
morning/afternoon/	*zaoshang/xiawu/*	Friday	*xingqi-wu*
evening	*wanshang*	Saturday	*xingqi-liu*
year/month/day/hour	*nian/yue/zhi/xiaoshi*	Sunday	*xingqi-tian*

Numbers

0	*ling*	15	*shiwu*
1	*yi*	20	*ershi*
2	*er*	30	*sanshi*
3	*san*	40	*sishi*
4	*si*	50	*wushi*
5	*wu*	60	*liushi*
6	*liu*	70	*qishi*
7	*qi*	80	*bashi*
8	*ba*	90	*jiushi*
9	*jiu*	100	*yi-bai*
10	*shi*	500	*wu-bai*
11	*shiyi*	1,000	*yiqian*
12	*shier*	2,000	*liangqian*
13	*shisan*	1,000,000	*yi baiwan*
14	*shisi*		

Geographical terms, map features

river	*he* (also *jiang*)	province	*sheng*
lake	*hu*	snow	*xue*
mountain	*shan*	map	*ditu*
summit, peak	*feng*	compass points:	*bei* (N), *nan* (S),
pass	*shankou*		*dong* (E), *xi* (W)
valley	*shangu*		

A2

Appendix 3

GLOSSARY

For details of popular icons, refer to the *Jokhang* section of the *Lhasa* chapter, pages 154–8.

ani	nun
Bon	pre-Buddhist religion of Tibet
chang	fermented barley beer, a potent milky liquid
chorten	inverted bell-shaped shrine containing relics, or the ashes or embalmed body of a high lama (*stupa* in Sanskrit)
dharma	the word of the Buddha and his teachings
dorje	'thunderbolt', a sceptre-like ritual object, made of brass and used against the powers of darkness
dzong	castle or fort, usually grafted on to a high ridge
gompa	active monastery
gonkhang	protector chapel at a monastery
Kalachakra	the 'Wheel of Time', a complex supreme tantra associated with the mystical land of Shambhala
kata	white greeting scarf, made of cotton or silk, presented on ceremonial occasions or offered at monasteries
kora	clockwise circuit of a sacred temple, lake or mountain
lakhang	chapel or inner sanctuary
lama	master spiritual teacher or guru
Losar	Tibetan New Year, usually celebrated around February
mandala	mystical circle (often enclosing a square) representing the Buddhist cosmos and used as a meditational aid (*chilkor* in Tibetan)
mani stone	stone tablet inscribed with a mantra, often included as part of a *mani* wall, composed of many such stones
mantra	sacred syllables repeated many times as part of spiritual practice, such as *Om Mani Padme Hum* ('hail to the jewel in the lotus heart', a phrase addressed to the Buddha)
momo	Tibetan meat dumpling
Monlam	the Great Prayer Festival, around the time of Losar
nirvana	release from the cycle of mortal existence and rebirths
potrang	palace
prayer flag	small flag printed with sacred prayers, activated by the power of the wind
prayer wheel	large fixed wheel or small hand-held wheel containing mantras and activated by the spinning of the wheel
prostrator	pilgrim who measures the distance to a sacred destination with the length of his or her body, flung prone along the ground

rinpoche	'precious one', a reincarnate lama, also known when young as a *tulku*
Saka Dawa	day of Buddha's enlightenment, celebrated around June
Shambhala	Buddhist 'Pure Land', a Tibetan utopia where disease and ageing are unknown, said to be located deep in the mountains to the north of the Himalaya
sutra	sacred text, the written or spoken teachings of the Buddha
tanka	painted portable scroll, usually depicting a deity, on fine cotton or silk; can be used as a teaching aid. May be used as a wall hanging
tantra	the 'web of life', or *vajrayana*, is the form of Buddhism most often associated with Tibet; it employs radical steps to seek enlightenment within a single lifetime
torma	ritual 'cake' sculpted from *tsampa* and yak butter
tsampa	ground barley flour, a Tibetan staple food
tulku	reincarnate lama
yak	hairy high-altitude cattle, or 'cow with a skirt'
yabyum	tantric sexual pose of deity and consort, symbolising fusion of opposites, and often misconstrued by Westerners as sexual activity without any tantric significance

CHINASPEAK
Chinese rhetoric on Tibet is an odd mix of the irrational and the predictable. This quotation is taken from the magazine *Beijing Review*, 1983, describing the Lhasa uprising of 1959:

> The imperialists and a small number of reactionary elements in Tibet's upper ruling clique could not reconcile themselves to the peaceful liberation of Tibet and its return to the embrace of the Motherland. The reactionary elements were intent upon launching an armed rebellion, negating the agreement and detaching Tibet from China. Abetted by the imperialists, they continued to sabotage and create disturbances. Despite the central government's consistent persuasion and education, they finally launched an armed rebellion on March 10, 1959. But, contrary to their desires, this rebellion accelerated the destruction of Tibet's reactionary forces and brought Tibet onto the bright, democratic, socialist road sooner than expected.

This puts forward the standard Beijing position on Tibet, unchanged for the last 60 years. For maximum effect, try to listen to this stuff spoken out loud, with a shrill Chinese accent and lots of static.

China's Tibet
To reinforce the idea that Tibet is not a separate country, attach the word 'China' to it. Chinese-produced tourist brochures and maps all specify 'Tibet, China', or 'China–Tibet'. China branding is found all over: China Post, Chinapolice, China Mobile. There's even a book titled *Chinese Tibetan Opera*.

Chinese characteristics
This phrase is trotted out to justify major Chinese modifications. The phrase 'democracy with Chinese characteristics' means a one-party system. In 2005, when pressed by President Bush about greater freedom for the Chinese people, President Hu Jintao reassured him that China would pursue 'democratic politics with Chinese characteristics'.

Counter-revolutionary
Anyone who opposes official policy, an enemy of the state, or someone 'committed with the goal of overthrowing the political power of the dictatorship of the proletariat and the socialist system'. Despite an official Beijing repeal of this crime to placate international critics, those previously convicted of it still languish in prison. Now,

prisoners continue to be convicted and are either held without charge or trial, or charged with being either a spy or a terrorist (the latter term more in vogue since 9/11: 11 September 2001). Another term is 'reactionary'.

The Dalai In June 1998, when President Clinton went on national Chinese television to say he thought the Dalai Lama was 'an honest man', this must have been news to a billion Chinese, who are more used to hearing him cursed as a treasonous demon. In rhetoric, the Chinese often employ the abbreviated form 'the Dalai', which is considered insulting by the Tibetans. Followers of the Dalai Lama are called 'the Dalai clique'. Chinese news sources call the exiled leader a 'splittist' and even 'a major hindrance to the development of Tibetan Buddhism'.

Democratic reform Chinaspeak for the period immediately after the 1959 Lhasa uprising and the flight of the Dalai Lama, when authorities set about dismantling the Tibetan culture in earnest – wading in there with machine guns where necessary.

Demonising the people This term surfaced during the 2008 Beijing Olympics, when protests staged by foreigners in support of human rights in Tibet were decried by the Chinese press as 'hurting the feelings of the Chinese people', or even worse, deeply hurting their feelings. Which could actually mean hurting the feelings of the People's Republic of China.

Foreign imperialists General all-purpose scapegoats. It is never specified which country they're from, but the popular candidates are 'bad elements' from Taiwan, the USA, the UK and Germany. After the Dalai Lama received the Nobel Peace Prize, Norway was added to the blacklist.

Harmony and unity The cornerstones of Chinese national policy. And if it takes machine guns and mass arrests and torture to maintain the cornerstones, so be it. Unity means one party only.

Hot topic This denotes anything like taxes or price increases that dissidents (reactionaries) supposedly capitalise on to foment unrest and demonstrations. Tibetan independence is, of course, very hot. So is the Dalai Lama; when asked what they think of him, most Chinese squirm and try to drop the subject like a hot potato.

Internal affairs Chinese shorthand for 'back off, it's a domestic dispute, it's no concern of yours what we do behind closed doors, so don't meddle in our affairs'.

Minority nationality The minorities, or non-Hans, are viewed as being part of the big happy Han family, even if they don't speak the same language. A minority theme park outside Beijing presents them spending their time dancing and singing, rather like happy children. Within Tibet, however, the Tibetans are less politely referred to as 'barbarians'.

The Motherland As well as referring to mainland China, this term embraces any parts of Asia that China wants to occupy. A number of China's neighbours have had trouble with this concept, including Russia, India, Taiwan, Vietnam and the Philippines. 'Love the Motherland' was the name of a campaign for Chinese schoolchildren in 1998. Splitting the Motherland is an all-embracing, heinous crime in Chinese eyes.

Peaceful liberation A reference to the entry of the People's Liberation Army into Tibet in 1950. Some Chinese sources admit that the invasion was in fact not entirely peaceful – some Tibetans resisted, so the PLA was reluctantly forced to machine-gun the hapless

Tibetans to clear them out of the way. Mostly, however, the people loved the PLA, according to official sources.

Princess Wencheng The tale of the Chinese bride of 7th-century King Songtsen Gampo is often trotted out by the Chinese propaganda machine in efforts to stake an early Chinese claim to Tibet, saying that she had great influence over the king. In fact, he had a Nepalese wife and three Tibetan queens as well. A multimillion-dollar 'opera' about Princess Wencheng is staged in Lhasa (see box, pages 146–7).

Re-education Mainly for monks, teaching them to see that black is white, and white is black, to say the Dalai Lama is bad, and to say the Chinese-chosen Panchen Lama is good. Sometimes monasteries are closed to tourism while this is in progress. The authorities might as well hang out a sign: 'Closed For Revision'.

Serfdom The pre-1950 state of the ordinary Tibetan, locked into exploitation by Tibetan nobility and monastic overseers. The Chinese broke down this class system by replacing the Tibetan masters with harsher Chinese ones.

Soul Boy The 11th Panchen Lama, a child into whose soul the Tenth Panchen was reincarnated. The boy is the most hotly disputed reincarnate in Tibetan history. The Tibetan choice for this incarnate has been missing for over 20 years. 'Soul Boy' is a translation of the Chinese term applied to reincarnations, *Lingtong* (*ling* = soul, *tong* = boy/child). Tibetans find the translation annoying and misleading.

Spiritual pollution An odd term for an atheist nation to develop but this refers to interference from outside sources, such as Westerners, in the form of books, tapes, videos and so on. Some of these are 'black' (political pollution), others 'yellow' (pornographic pollution).

Splittists Favourite Chinese term for those advocating independence for Tibet, or separatists. The idea here is that the Motherland must stay whole; anybody who splits off a piece will ruin the symmetry. Other chunks where splittists seem to be hard at work include Xinjiang, Mongolia and Taiwan.

State secrets Though there is no clear definition of what they are, revealing state secrets is an act punishable by years in jail. This charge has been applied to Tibetans who email abroad about demonstrations. The secrets are whatever the authorities deem to be sensitive matters at the time. People can also be jailed for 'spreading rumours'.

Appendix 4

FURTHER INFORMATION

BOOKS Some of the following books, multimedia materials and websites are frowned upon, restricted or simply outlawed in China. Do not attempt to bring in risqué material if travelling to Tibet. Books with straight printed material should not be a problem, but visual material is different – customs and soldiers will flip through a book looking for artwork such as the Tibetan flag or pictures of the Dalai Lama.

Kathmandu is the best place in the subcontinent to find materials on Tibet, especially maps and books (in or out of print). Just about everything published on Tibet can be found at Tibet Book Store in Thamel, Kathmandu. Mention of Tibetan or Taiwanese independence or criticism of Beijing's policies is in theory forbidden in Hong Kong SAR. In practice, however, books continue to circulate, and protests not possible in China itself (such as marking the anniversary of the Tiananmen Square Massacre) are still tolerated in the colony.

For such a little-visited place, Tibet has generated an extraordinary amount of literature. What's listed here is just the tip of the iceberg. You can glean lots more information from the websites of specialist publishers. These include:

W **shambhala.com** Shambhala Publications, USA
W **wisdompubs.org** Wisdom Publications, USA and UK
W **tricycle.com** Tricycle Books and quarterly magazine
W **paljorpublications.com** Paljor Publications, India.

History, political intrigue

Avedon, Richard, *In Exile from the Land of Snows*, HarperCollins, 1998. A classic that first appeared in 1984.

Brown, Mick, *The Dance of 17 Lives*, Bloomsbury, 2005. About the intrigue and controversy surrounding the 17th Karmapa.

Hilton, Isabel, *The Search for the Panchen Lama*, Penguin, 2000.

Lustgarten, Abrahm, *Tibet's Great Train*, Times Books, 2008. Ace reporting, mixing political history and the building of the railway to Lhasa.

Shakya, Tsering, *The Dragon in the Land of Snows*, Columbia University Press, 1999. Definitive history of Tibet since 1947, from a Tibetan scholar.

Human rights, testimonials, activism

Amnesty International, *Persistent Human Rights Violations in Tibet*, London, 1996.

Choedrak, Tenzin, *The Rainbow Palace*, Bantam, 2000.

Gyatso, Palden, *Fire Under the Snow*, Harvill Press, 1997 (published in the USA as *The Autobiography of a Tibetan Monk*).

Marshall, Steven, *Tibet Since 1950: Silence, Prison or Exile*, Aperture, 2000. This collaboration between Human Rights Watch and Aperture Books draws on a wide range of sources and photographers.

Pistono, Matteo, *In the Shadow of the Buddha*, Dutton, 2011.

Buddhism

Batchelor, Stephen, *Confessions of a Buddhist Atheist*, Random House, 2010.
Dzongsar Jamyang Khyentse, *What Makes you not a Buddhist*, Shambhala, 2008.
Thurman, Robert, *Inside Tibetan Buddhism*, Collins, 1995.

The Dalai Lama (as author)

My Land and My People, Warner Books, 1997. A reprint of the 1962 edition of the autobiography of the Dalai Lama.
Freedom in Exile, Harper, 1991. Part two of the Dalai Lama's autobiography.
Ethics for the New Millennium, Riverhead, 2001. The Dalai Lama delivers his timely message to a world sadly lacking in moral values.

The Dalai Lama (as co-author)

Chan, Victor, *The Wisdom of Forgiveness*, Hodder Mobius, 2005.
Cutler, Howard, *The Art of Happiness: A Handbook for Living*, Hodder & Stoughton, 1999.

Tibetan culture

Baker, Ian, and Shrestha, Romio, *The Healing Arts of Tibet*, Thames & Hudson, 1997.
Goldstein, Melvyn, and Beall, Cynthia, *Nomads of Western Tibet: The Survival of a Way of Life*, UC Press, 1990.
Larsen, Knud, and Sinding-Larsen, Amund, *The Lhasa Atlas: Traditional Tibetan Architecture and Townscape*, Serindia, 2001.

Environment

Buckley, Michael, *Meltdown in Tibet*, Macmillan, NY, 2014. A photo companion to this is *Tibet, Disrupted*, a 330-page multimedia work published in 2016, and available on the Apple iBooks platform.

Exploration, mountaineering, adventure

Anker, Conrad, and Roberts, David, *The Lost Explorer: Finding Mallory on Mount Everest*, Simon & Schuster, 1999.
Baker, Ian, *The Heart of the World*, Penguin, 2004. Exploring the remote Tsangpo Gorge.
Berry, Scott, *A Stranger in Tibet*, Kodansha, 1989.
Buckley, Michael, *Eccentric Explorers*, Canada, 2009.
Hammleb, Jochen, *et al.*, *Ghosts of Everest: The Search for Mallory and Irvine*, The Mountaineers, 1999.
Harrer, Heinrich, *Seven Years in Tibet*, Harper Perennial, 2005 (originally published in 1953).
Hopkirk, Peter, *Trespassers on the Roof of the World*, Oxford University Press, 1982.
Norgay, Jamling Tenzing, *Finding My Father's Soul*, Harper, 2001 (written by the son of Everest's premier summiteer).
Peissel, Michel, *Barbarians at the Gate*, Henry Holt, 1997.
Thubron, Colin, *To a Mountain in Tibet*, Chatto & Windus, 2010. At the age of 70, veteran British travel writer Colin Thubron heads off to tackle the Kailash *kora*.
Venables, Stephen, *Everest: Kangshung Face*, General Publishing, 1989.

Travel narratives

Deutschle, Phil, *The Two Year Mountain*, Bradt Travel Guides, 2012.
French, Patrick, *Tibet, Tibet: A Personal History of a Lost Land*, HarperCollins, 2003.
Kerr, Blake, *Sky Burial*, Snowlion Publications, 1997.

Le Sueur, Alec, *Running a Hotel on the Roof of the World*, Summersdale, 1998.

Guidebooks

Akester, Matthew, *Jamyang Khyentse Wangpo's Guide to Central Tibet*, Serindia, 2017. Revisits over 200 pilgrimage sites covered by a 19th-century Tibetan master.

Ibbotson, Sophie and Lovell-Hoare, Max, *Kashmir* Bradt Travel Guides, 2014

McCue, Gary, *Trekking Tibet*, The Mountaineers, 2010.

Osada, Yukiyasu, and Kanamaru, Atsushi, *Mapping the Tibetan World*, Kotan Publishing, 2000. A very ambitious project, now becoming dated.

Walters, Martin, *Chinese Wildlife* Bradt Travel Guides, 2008

Photobooks

Borges, Phil, *Tibetan Portrait*, Rizzoli, 1996.

Harris, Brian, *Tibetan Voices*, Pomegranate, 1996.

Nomachi, Kazoyoshi, *Tibet*, Shambhala, 1997.

Rowell, Galen (photographer, with text by the Dalai Lama), *My Tibet*, University of California Press, 1990.

Young readers

McGinnis, Mark, *When the Buddha was an Elephant*, Shambhala, 2015. Comprises 32 illustrated animal wisdom tales selected from the 550 tales of *The Jataka*, intended to be read by novice monks.

Rose, Naomi, *Tibetan Tales for Little Buddhas*, Clear Light Publishing, 2004. Three traditional tales that exemplify Tibetan Buddhist beliefs are superbly illustrated by artist Naomi Rose.

Fiction

Davidson, Lionel, *The Rose of Tibet*, Gollancz, 1962. A terrific read.

Dickie, Tenzin (ed), *Old Demons, New Deities*, OR Books, 2018. A collection of 21 short stories from contemporary Tibetan writers.

Hilton, James, *Lost Horizon*, William Morrow, 1933 (reprinted many times since). The book that gave the world Shangri-La.

Koonchung, Chan, *The Unbearable Dreamworld of Champa the Driver*, Penguin Books, 2014. Translated into English, this is a hilarious account of a Tibetan driver exploring the China–Tibet dynamic. The author is Chinese, but banned in China.

Mitchell, Ken, *Stones of the Dalai Lama*, Douglas & McIntyre, 1993.

Norbu, Jamyang, *Sherlock Holmes: The Missing Years*, Bloomsbury, 2001. Written by a Tibetan iconoclast and scholar.

Pemba, Tsewang Yishey, *White Crane, Lend me Your Wings*, Niyogi Books, 2017. A novel written by a Tibetan is a rarity.

Rampa, Lobsang T, *The Third Eye*, Corgi, 1956 (reprinted many times since). Masterful New Age hokum.

Tshe Ring Dbang Rgyal, *The Tale of the Incomparable Prince*, HarperCollins, 1996. An 18th-century classic revived in translation from the earliest novel in the Tibetan language.

OTHER MEDIA
CD

Freedom Chants, Gyuto Monks. Cerebral sacred music from India.

Heartstrings. Album by Tenzin Choegyal.

In a Distant Place and *Quiet Mind.* Two albums of the many performed by Nawang Khechog.

Tibet Tibet and *Coming Home.* Two albums by exiled female singer, Yungchen Lhamo.

DVD, film and video

Here are some major movies related to Tibet, in order of release date.

Lost Horizon, directed by Frank Capra, Columbia TriStar, 1937. The movie that spread the legend of James Hilton's Shangri-La far and wide.

Kundun, directed by Martin Scorsese, Touchstone Pictures, 1997. Superb biopic about the early years of the Dalai Lama.

Red Corner, directed by Jon Avnet, MGM, 1997. Set in Beijing, but concerned with the judicial system and human rights. Stars Richard Gere.

Seven Years in Tibet, directed by Jean-Jacques Annaud, Columbia TriStar, 1997. Stars Brad Pitt and David Thewlis, and introduces Tibetan actress Lhakpa Tsamchoe (later to star in *Himalaya*, see below). Based on the adventures of German POWs Heinrich Harrer and Peter Aufschnaiter in the early 1940s.

The Cup, directed by Khyentse Norbu, 1998. The first major movie directed by a Tibetan, a Rinpoche resident in Bhutan. It's about football-crazed monks at a monastery in northern India. In Tibetan and Hindi. Norbu followed this up with *Travellers & Magicians*, filmed in Bhutan.

Saltmen of Tibet, directed by Ulrike Koch, Switzerland, 1998. About the salt-route caravans from Tibet to Nepal, a trade now mostly extinct. Filmed in Tibetan and in the secret salt language (with cryptic salt-language subtitles).

Windhorse, directed by Paul Wagner, Paul Wagner Productions, 1998. Based partly on a true story about a singer who must flee Tibet. At great risk, the director took video of actors on location in Lhasa. This 'docudrama' was filmed in Tibetan and Chinese and stars Dadon, a famous Tibetan singer who escaped into exile in 1992 and now lives in the USA.

Himalaya, directed by Eric Valli, 1999. A stunning French–Nepalese co-production with an all-Tibetan cast, filmed in Dolpo, Nepal, in Tibetan. Stars Lhakpa Tsamchoe. The movie offers great insight into the nomadic way of life.

The Touch, directed by Hong Kong cinematographer Peter Pau, 2002. A family of acrobats are called upon by a Buddhist monk sect to retrieve a valuable artefact. Corny plot, but superb cinematography, some scenes shot on location in Lhasa and central Tibet. Stars Michelle Yeoh.

Tibet: Cry of the Snow Lion, directed by Tom Peosay, 2003. A vivid documentary about the situation in Tibet, with a wealth of interview material and unusual archival footage.

We're No Monks, directed by Tibetan cinematographer Pema Dhondup, 2004. Shot on a shoestring budget with unknown actors, this movie tells the fictional story of four disaffected young Tibetan exiles in Dharamsala who are catapulted into a violent mission of protest.

Dreaming Lhasa, directed by Tenzing Sonam and Ritu Sarin, 2005. A terrific dramatic feature involving unknown Tibetan actors, about an ex-monk who has escaped from Tibet into India to deliver a charm-box to a missing resistance fighter.

10 Questions for the Dalai Lama, directed by Rick Ray, 2007. An intimate look at the Dalai Lama – the man and the philosophy – through the lens of film-maker Rick Ray, who tends to oversimplify key issues.

Murder in the Snow, directed by Mark Gould, 2009. A gripping documentary that recounts how Chinese troops opened fire on Tibetan escapees on a high pass in September 2006, in full view of Western climbers attempting a nearby peak – and the moral morass that resulted.

The Sun Behind the Clouds, directed by Tenzing Sonam and Ritu Sarin, 2010. Filmed mostly in 2008, this documentary focuses on the Tibetan struggle for freedom and where it is heading.

When the Dragon Swallowed the Sun, directed by Dirk Simon, 2010. This documentary examines the Free Tibet movement from different angles over a seven-year period, with a wealth of interview material.

The Silent Holy Stones, directed by Pema Tseden, 2013. Pema Tseden is the first Tibetan graduate of The Beijing Film Academy. This is his groundbreaking debut: filmed in Tibetan language with an all-Tibetan cast, on location in Amdo. The film narrates the story of a young monk's obsession with television.

Drokpa, directed by Yan Chun Su, 2016. This documentary is a moving portrait of the last nomads in eastern Tibet.

WEBSITE DIRECTORY

Accessing the 'wrong' sites has landed Chinese surfers in jail. That does not happen to foreign surfers, but it gives an idea of just how sensitive the internet is in the Middle Kingdom. Periodic purges of cybercafés in China have resulted in a number of them being shut down; those that stay in business are required to install monitoring software (called 'Internet Police 110') that shields banned sites and alerts local authorities when such sites are being accessed. There are thought to be over 40,000 internet police at work in China – real people whose job is to entice and catch cyber-dissidents. Networks in China are required to use domestically produced software.

A number of the following sites are banned in China and are most likely firewalled. Some, such as those listed in the section on human rights, are extremely sensitive. At the same time, it is surprising what is still accessible from within Tibet and China. Strangely enough, sites that were firewalled in Lhasa did not appear to be so in Chengdu (and vice versa for other sites). Maybe it's a case of different sensitivities in different places? To check if a website is blocked, go to this handy site and enter the URL: w **greatfirewallofchina.org.**

A few tests here will show that YouTube is blocked all over China. Sometimes sites become unblocked. Other times, sites are blocked in some parts of China but not other parts. Go figure.

The net is your news lifeline in a place like Lhasa, where no foreign print news sources can be found. Staying up to date on current politics and travel conditions is very important. The following sites can assist with trip preparation, and give you the latest information.

SEARCHING FOR IT
w **google.com**
w **metacrawler.com**
w **amazon.co.uk or** w **amazon.com**   To use Amazon, go to travel and browse by subject.

CURRENCY CONVERSION
w **xe.com/ucc**   Universal currency converter, one among many such sites.

WEATHER
w **cnn.com/weather**   Extended forecasts for Lhasa, Shigatse and more.
w **weather.yahoo.com**   Go to 'Asia' for five-day forecasts for Lhasa and other Asian cities.

TRAVEL WARNINGS
w **fco.gov.uk/travel**
w **travel.state.gov**
w **smartraveller.gov.au**
w **voyage.gc.ca**   UK, US, Australian and Canadian official travel warning bulletins.

GENERAL NEWS
w **worldnews.com**
w **iht.com**
w **guardian.co.uk**
w **bbc.co.uk**
w **globeandmail.ca**

ASIA/INDIA NEWS
w edition.cnn.com/asia

AIRPORT INFORMATION
w **airportcitycodes.com** Ever wondered where your bags are being routed to? This site can bring up many Chinese airport codings.

AIRLINES
Websites of Air China and China Southern Airlines, the main domestic carriers flying into Lhasa.
w **airchina.com.cn/en**
w **global.csair.com**

BANKING
w **visa.com** Use the ATM locator at the foot of the homepage to find Agricultural Bank branches in Lhasa and beyond.
w **mastercard.com** Use the ATM locator to find a machine in Kathmandu or Chengdu.

HEALTH
w **high-altitude-medicine.com** Delves into the high-altitude health strategy.
w **drwisetravel.com**
w **cdc.gov/travel**
w **travelhealth.co.uk**

SURFING TIBET Some websites appear in other relevant parts of this book. For links on the Tibetan World (Bhutan, Nepal, northwest India, Outer Mongolia) see *Chapter 9*, pages 321–38. For tips on Tibetan language, see pages 344–51.

w **himmies.com** In support of the book you now hold is a website with travellers' tales, dodgy advice, warped insights and provocative discussion related to travel in the Tibetan world. Log on to find out more.

GATEWAY SITE
w **tibet.net** Official site of the CTA (Central Tibetan Administration or government-in-exile) offering loads of links.

CURRENT TRAVEL CONDITIONS IN TIBET
w **thelandofsnows.com** and w **kekexili.typepad.com** Two good sites from a contributor to this guidebook, Jamin York, who has been touring Tibet for some time. Also has information for touring Nepal, Ladakh and Bhutan.
w **cafespinn.com/en** Café in Lhasa that dispenses some good travel advice on getting itineraries together.
w **savetibet.org/wp-content/uploads/2013/05/TibetanChinaTravelGuide.pdf** This downloadable PDF is a political guide to Tibet, originally published in 2008.
w **yowangdu.com** Some non-political Tibet advice, with 108 travel tips.

VIRTUAL/INTERACTIVE TIBET
w **atlasofemotions.org** HH Dalai Lama requested that Dr Paul Ekman, an expert on emotions and gestures, create this amazing online atlas. Interactive, and well worth the visit.
Verne Available as a free Android app, this game uses 3D Google Earth mapping, and centres on the Everest region – taking in base camps on both Tibetan and Nepalese sides. You can navigate around the slopes, summit Everest, and even encounter yaks and blue sheep.

A4

Google Earth Pro Use a search function to download the app for this fantastic free web resource that allows you to zoom over the Himalaya and fly low over Lhasa, though it's sketchy on Tibet, and the place names seem to be Pinyin, thus not matching the names in this guidebook. These 'moving maps' offer a quasi-3D simulated view, similar to virtual maps that pilots use in the cockpits of modern jets.

W **panoramas.dk/fullscreen2/full22.html** If you want to know what the panoramic view looks like from the summit of Everest, go to this site and search keyword 'Everest'.

EVEREST HOMEPAGE

W **everestnews.com** Every 8,000m peak should have one: this site has everything you need to know about the Big E and all the climbing trivia.

W **everest1953.co.uk** Another web page devoted to Everest, with a British slant.

TIBET'S ENVIRONMENT

W **meltdownintibet.com** Website by the author focusing on China's mega-dam building plans for Tibet.

W **freetibet.org/resources** UK-based Free Tibet Campaign outlines environmental issues.

W **tew.org** Click on 'Geography' for satellite maps and theme maps from Tibet Environmental Watch.

W **savetibetanrivers.org**

CHINESE VIEWPOINTS

W **www.china-embassy.org/eng/** From Washington: click on 'Topics' in the sidebar and go to 'China's Tibet' for Chinese rhetoric.

W **en.tibet.cn** China–Tibet Information Centre: official source with some news and touring.

W **tibet-tour.com** Slick site from Tibet Tourism Bureau, Shanghai branch (TTBS).

W **chinasite.com** A gateway site with many links, many in the Chinese language and a number banned in China.

TIBET NEWS SOURCES

W **thetibetpost.com** Online newspaper from Dharamsala, available for viewing in three languages: Tibetan, Chinese and English.

W **phayul.com** News source for the Tibetan community in exile, based in India.

W **tibet.net** Government-in-exile site. *Tibetan Bulletin*, from Dharamsala, can be accessed from this site.

W **tibet.ca** World Tibet Network News is archived here, via CTC, Canada. The archives go back several decades.

TIBETAN BLOGGERS Inside Tibet, brave bloggers have been shut down and are unable to reach an international audience. Or they have been jailed for trying to do so. An exception is Tibet's most famous blogger, Woeser, who lives in Beijing.

W **highpeakspureearth.com** Has English translations of Woeser's blog, *Invisible Tibet*.

W **jamyangnorbu.com** Tibetan pundit and controversial essayist Jamyang Norbu runs his blog, *Shadow Tibet*, at this site.

ACTIVISM

W **tibetnetwork.org** Acts for co-ordination of 180 Tibet support groups, and gives information on how to locate groups around the world.

W **tibet.org/Resources/TSG** Worldwide listing of support groups. Site is case-sensitive, so needs capitals.

W tibetsociety.com Website of the oldest Tibet support group, founded in the UK in 1959 by Hugh Richardson.

W savetibet.org Site for ICT Washington and branches in Europe. Tibet Press Watch newsletter can be accessed from the website.

W freetibet.org UK organisation, Free Tibet Campaign.

W studentsforafreetibet.org Students for a Free Tibet.

W tibetjustice.org Tibet Justice Centre, based in California.

HUMAN RIGHTS

W un.org/en/universal-declaration-human-rights/index.html Full text of the Universal Declaration of Human Rights, also available as a PDF

W hrw.org

W hrichina.org Human rights in China are under scrutiny on this site.

W tchrd.org Dharamsala-based centre for human rights.

W amnesty.org An organisation banned in China.

TIBETAN BUDDHIST LEADERS

W dalailama.com The Dalai Lama's homepage, which includes webcasts.

W kagyuoffice.org/karmapa Homepage for Ogyen Trinley Dorje, the 17th Gyalwang Karmapa.

Index

Page numbers in **bold** refer to main entries; those in *italics* refer to maps

INDEX OF ADVERTISERS